AN ECONOMIC SURVEY OF ANCIENT ROME

ROME AND ITALY OF THE REPUBLIC

VOLUME I

AN ECONOMIC SURVEY OF ANCIENT ROME

EDITED BY

TENNEY FRANK

IN COLLABORATION WITH

T. R. S. BROUGHTON	R. G. COLLINGWOOD	A. GRENIER
R. M. HAYWOOD	A. C. JOHNSON	J. A. O. LARSEN
R. S. ROGERS	V. M. SCRAMUZZA	J. J. VAN NOSTRAND

OCTAGON BOOKS

A DIVISION OF FARRAR, STRAUS AND GIROUX

New York   1975

AN ECONOMIC SURVEY OF ANCIENT ROME

VOLUME I

ROME AND ITALY OF THE REPUBLIC

BY

TENNEY FRANK

OCTAGON BOOKS

A DIVISION OF FARRAR, STRAUS AND GIROUX

New York   1975

Reprinted 1975
by special arrangement with The Johns Hopkins Press

OCTAGON BOOKS

A DIVISION OF FARRAR, STRAUS & GIROUX, INC.
19 Union Square West
New York, N. Y. 10003

This book has been reproduced from an original in the
Brown University Library

Library of Congress Cataloging in Publication Data

Frank, Tenney, 1876-1939, ed.
    An economic survey of ancient Rome.

    Reprint of the ed. published by the Johns Hopkins Press, Baltimore.
    CONTENTS: v. 1. Frank, T. Rome and Italy of the republic.—v. 2.
Johnson, A. C. Roman Egypt to the reign of Diocletian.—v. 3. Collingwood,
R. G. Roman Britain. Van Nostrand, J. J. Roman Spain. Scramuzza, V. M.
Roman Sicily. Grenier, A. La Gaule Romaine.—v. 4. Haywood, R. M.
Roman Afric. Heichelheim, F. M. Roman Syria. Larsen, J. A. O. Roman
Greece. Broughton, T. R. S. Roman Asia.—v. 5. Frank, T. Rome and Italy
of the empire—[v. 6] General index to v. 1-5.
    Includes bibliographies and indexes.

    1. Rome—Economic conditions—Collected works. 2. Rome—Provinces
—Collected works. I. Title.
HC39.F72   1975   330.9'37   75-1062
ISBN 0-374-92848-7

Manufactured by Braun-Brumfield, Inc.
Ann Arbor, Michigan

Printed in the United States of America

PREFACE

This is the first volume of an economic survey of the ancient Roman world. The larger sections are being written by T. R. S. Broughton (Asia), R. G. Collingwood (Roman Britain), A. Grenier (Gaul), R. M. Haywood (Africa), A. C. Johnson (Egypt), J. A. O. Larsen (Greece), R. S. Rogers (Syria), V. M. Scramuzza (Sicily), J. J. Van Nostrand (Spain), and the general editor (Italy). The survey will require four volumes and is to be completed by the end of 1935.

Our first aim is to present the sources (literary, epigraphical, papyrological) and to give due attention to the economic meaning of the archaeological evidence. It is not our intention to carry the survey beyond the middle of the fourth century A. D. We have yielded to the request of several modern economists in providing English translations of all the significant passages quoted. In order to avoid the possible enticement of reading our own prejudices into the sources, we have decided to employ good translations made by others whenever they are available. If we find it necessary to depart from such translations or from the text used in them, we give explicit warning. In the first volume, for instance, the editor has ventured to offer only four emendations of the text. We wish at the very beginning to thank the publishers (G. P. Putnam's Sons) and the editors of the Loeb Classical Series for their very generous permission to use their volumes freely in this work. We have taken many pages from their versions of Appian, Cicero, Dio, Livy, Plutarch, Polybius, Suetonius, and others. The Oxford Press has kindly permitted us to use some paragraph's of Hardy's translations appearing in their *Roman Laws and Charters*, and G. Bell and Sons have generously placed at our disposal the translation of Varro by Lloyd Storr-Best.

It was our desire to follow a uniform scheme in all the monographs of this survey, but this attempt had to some extent to be abandoned. For instance, what is especially needed for Egypt is a good source book of documents, whereas in treating some of the western provinces a connected thread of narrative on which to string the numerous scattered facts seemed preferable. The present volume on Republican Rome and Italy had of course to contend with difficulties regarding the reliability of early sources, to include masses of material that refer to the public finances of the ruling state, and to deal in some measure with conditions that extended beyond Italy into the provinces. The plan used in this volume will not serve as a model for the rest.

It is not our purpose here to theorize. The early work in Roman economic history was produced largely in the day when Hegelian methods had popularized aprioristic habits of thought in historical interpretation, and we believe that it is now wise to return to the sources. Furthermore we have tried to keep in mind the specialist's propensity to interpret history in the light of his own interests. We hope here to avoid the allurements of economic determinism. For such reasons we have preferred to assemble the sources and let others draw the facile anthropogeographical inferences. But we shall not shun the essential tasks of explaining obscure passages if we can, and of bringing related facts into proximity.

In this first volume a full quotation of all pertinent passages was not possible without exceeding the limits of our resources and a reasonable respect for just proportions. However all that is most significant has been included, and the references to minor facts have been given. All the sources have been culled at first hand, and laboriously sifted. Some omissions are due to the decision that the passages were unreliable or a mere repetition of something better stated in a previous source. In this matter the editor's judgment is to be blamed if errors have been made. As for the bibliography at the end a middle course had to be chosen. A full list of pertinent books and articles would have required a second volume. Much of the early synthetic work is hopelessly out of date, thanks to archaeological researches, and many recent titles could be omitted because their substance appeared elsewhere in more adequate form. It is with regret that many important archaeological articles had to be slighted, and the decision to omit was made only because the excellent Catalogue of the German Institute at Rome is generally available.

In citing Polybius we use the numbering of the Büttner-Wobst and Loeb editions. The Verrine orations of the Actio Secunda are numbered 1 to 5 respectively, without a repetition in each case of the numeral II. In several instances, when sums and prices were given, it seemed desirable to add a modern approximation reckoned in the gold content of the dollar, but while the book was in press the dollar suffered from thrombosis, and recovery seems rather uncertain. All we can do now is to warn the reader that the references are all to the dollar of 1932.

The editor wishes to thank Dr. R. M. Haywood, Dr. Gertrude Malz, and Miss Elsa Graser for very generous aid in the arduous work of reading for data and revising the manuscript of this volume. A deep sense of gratitude also compels him to add that without the financial aid given by the Rockefeller Foundation this survey could not have been undertaken.

THE EDITOR.

April, 1933.

TABLE OF CONTENTS

INTRODUCTION

BEFORE THE GALLIC FIRE, 387 B. C.

CHAPTER I

FROM THE GALLIC FIRE TO THE FIRST PUNIC WAR, 387–264 B. C.

CHAPTER II

DURING THE FIRST AND SECOND PUNIC WARS, 264–200 B. C.

CHAPTER III

DURING THE EASTERN WARS, 200–150 B. C.

CHAPTER IV

THE GRACCHAN PERIOD, 150–80 B. C.

CHAPTER V

FROM SULLA TO AUGUSTUS, 80–30 B. C.

INTRODUCTION

BEFORE THE GALLIC FIRE 387 B. C.

I. THE EARLY REPUBLIC

The student of Greek economic and social history finds in the works of Homer, Hesiod, and Solon very important reflections of actual conditions for the centuries before historians began to write. In studying early Roman history we have no such sources. Roman literature began about 240 B. C., when Rome was already master of the whole of Italy, and that early literature—the epics of Naevius and Ennius—is lost. Historical writing began with Fabius Pictor, about 200 B. C., but even his work has disappeared, as has that of all the many annalists who wrote before Livy. The accounts of Fabius Pictor were fairly sound and they were taken over by his successors, so that their contents are not wholly lost to us. But it was only what he saw and what he could gather from older observers still living that can be called reliable history.

For his century there were also Greek and Sicilian writers, who reported the Pyrrhic and the First Punic Wars with reasonable accuracy and whose accounts have survived in writers like Polybius, Diodorus, and Plutarch. All this gives us rather full history from about 280 B. C. Before that time we are seldom on sure ground. From the beginnings till the revolution that inaugurated the Republic (about 509 B. C.) we have in the legends that Livy and Dionysius recorded no certain foundation for work. But modern excavations, in the cemeteries in and about Rome and about the early walls and temples of Rome, have at least afforded us a usable picture of what Rome was like at the end of the Regal period and during the early Republic.

After the founding of the Republic, the rather legal-minded magistrates and priests began to keep meager but accurate records. The lists of the consuls were kept, since the years were counted by them, and they are on the whole dependable. The pontifex maximus set down brief notes on the occasion of public sacrifices (for eclipses, bad harvests, victories, defeats, pestilences, etc.) and it seems that most of these notes survived. Treaties were inscribed and, as most of them were kept in

1

Jupiter's temple on the Capitoline, many of them escaped destruction. Laws and decrees of the Senate (very few at most) seem to have survived even from the fifth century. Some of this material perished in the capture of Rome by the Gauls in 390, but a serious effort was made to restore what was important. The bare outline of the history of the fifth century seems to be fairly dependable, even though it was lavishly dressed out at a later day by the addition of legends that had been treasured by noble families. It is not till the fourth century B. C. that we find that skeleton of records full enough to make it worthwhile to attempt a consistent quotation of sources.

Here we shall briefly review the archaeological remains that tell something of the conditions in Rome and Latium before the Gallic fire. There are no traces of human habitations in the vicinity of Rome during the bronze age. Perhaps the activity of the Latian volcanoes kept settlers away. During the early centuries of the iron age (1000-700 B. C.) the ancestors of the Latins came in from the north and gradually planted villages over an area of about 2,000 square miles west of the Apennines, between modern Civita Castellana and Anzio. The tribes lived on agriculture and pasturage; for a long time they imported very little foreign ware, but made simple pottery, some bronze implements and a few iron utensils, and in general they lived in peace (no iron weapons are found in their tombs). They belonged to a race that burned their dead. The first Roman village—on the Palatine hill, comprising about 40 acres—was settled about 800 B. C.

During the eighth and seventh centuries the Latins were crowded into narrower confines. The lands that lay north of the Tiber were over-run by inhuming peoples, apparently at first by Umbrians and Sabines and presently by Etruscans.[1] Inhuming peoples (Sabines and Volsci) also pressed in on the east and south, some settling on the outer hills of Rome and some taking possession of Antium and southern Latium. After these invasions the Latins were confined to an area of about 1,200 square miles, but were probably more closely packed because of the arrival of refugees from the villages lost to the enemy. About 650 B. C. the villages of several hills of Rome were united in one city, as appears from the fact that the extended cemetery that lay between

---

[1] Von Duhn, *Italische Gräberkunde*, pp. 437-608, and art. "Italien," in *Reallex. d. Vorgesch.*, VI; Randall-MacIver, *Villanovans and Early Etruscans*; Della Seta, *Italia Antica*.

them—near the Forum—ceased to be used about that time.[2] If persistent tradition is to be accepted, the villagers of Rome had already,
before that time, given up the customary government under town-meet-
ings and annual praetors in favor of elective kings.   External pressure
of invading peoples may well account for this.   Certain it is that during the last century of monarchy, at least, Etruscan princes from north
of the Tiber somehow secured control of Rome and made it the capital
of a principality that in time extended over most of the Latin villages
and beyond, as far south, in fact, as Anxur (Tarracina), some sixty
miles south of Rome.

Archaeology reveals the fact that under the Etruscan régime of the
sixth century Rome became for a while a powerful city.[3]   The kings
organized an army with which they were able to subject, and apparently
destroy, several towns like Alba Longa and Antemnae.   Like the rulers
of other Etruscan cities they invited Greek and Punic commerce to their
harbor.   To be sure Roman excavations have not revealed tombs with
rich jewelry and plate from the early period such as have been found in
nearby cities like Palestrina, Cervetri, or Conca.   That, however, was
not to expected, since the subsoil of Rome and its suburbs has been
turned over and over for more than two thousand years.   Again, the
scarcity of Attic ware in Latium, abundant in many Etruscan cities,
does not necessarily mean the absence of Greek contacts in Latium at
the end of the sixth century.   The Greek vases were brought to other
cities for use in tombs.   The Romans, preferring incineration and—as
the Twelve Tables show—avoiding the luxurious burials of the Etruscans, simply did not develop a market for these vases.   The finds under
the shrine of Vesta show that some Attic ware was used in the cults.[4]

---

[2] Bryan, "Italic Hut Urns," *Mon. Am. Acad. Rome*, IV, 1925, 151.   For early
Roman cemeteries see Boni, in *Notizie degli Scavi*, 1903, 1906, and 1911; Pinza,
Monumenti Antichi, XV, and *Storia delle civiltà antiche*, 1923; Von Duhn, *Ital.
Gräberk.*, 458 ff.; Antonielli, in *Bull. Paletnologia It.*, 1924, 154 ff.; Platner and
Ashby, *Topogr. Dictionary, sub voc.* "Sepulcretum."

[3] Frank, *Economic History of Rome*, 1920, 13 ff. (2nd ed., 16 ff.) ; *Roman Buildings
of the Republic*; Scott, "Early Roman Traditions," in *Memoirs Am. Acad. Rome*,
1929; Gelzer, "Latium," in Pauly-Wissowa, *Realenc.*, XII, 951; L. A. Stella, *Italia
antica sul mare*, 1930, ch. V.

[4] *Notizie d. Scav.*, 1900, 175.   Tradition held that Roman labor gilds had existed
since the time of the kings.   Gilds of some kind are referred to in the Twelve Tables
(8, 27) ; see Gummerus in Pauly-Wiss., *Realenc.*, VII, 1442; Pais, *Storia Critica*, I,
778; De Sanctis, *Storia dei Romani*, II, 471; Tamborini, in *Athenaeum*, 1930, 291
and 452.

Despite the wholesale destruction of early Roman relics, there are traces in the beautiful terra-cotta ornaments found in many places at Rome of a large number of public buildings and temples that belong to the period in question.[5] The destruction has gone so far that frequently only one fragment of a slab is left to tell the tale of a whole building. It is not the quantity but the quality and the wide provenience of these fragments that speak so unmistakably of a prosperous city. The list provided by Mrs. Van Buren's *Figurative Terra-Cotta Revetments in Etruria and Latium* proves that many public and private buildings at Rome were decorated as beautifully as those of Caere, Veii, Velitrae, and Satricum. We have scanty fragments from both ends of the Capitoline, from at least three buildings above the *scalae Caci* on the Palatine, and one from the region of the Palatine *Lararium*. Two fragments come from the early Regia of the Forum. Several bits are derived from various buildings at the *comitium*. From the Esquiline we have an excellent fragment of a wounded Amazon more than life-size, a fine fragment of a frieze representing a chariot procession, probably from a luxurious tomb, and a good satyr's head from some temple-tiles near Santa Maria Maggiore. Nothing of the kind has as yet been turned up from the early Diana temple on the Aventine or the Quirinus temple on the Quirinal, but these also were of the sixth century. We have evidence, therefore, of some fourteen or fifteen buildings of Rome of about Tarquin's day on which artists were employed who would have been welcome in Athens itself. The city of Rome did not again produce in one generation so many buildings of high artistic merit till several centuries later.

In amount these fragments are less impressive than those of the cities nearby that have lain less disturbed. But the quality and the large number of sites prove that Rome was well in the center of the artistic or industrial current. The architectural adornments of Velitrae and Satricum [6] south of Rome prove the presence of excellent Greek workmen in Latium. Veii, the Etruscan neighbor thirteen miles north of Rome, has recently yielded an Apollo statue [7] that compares favorably with any work of this period known in Greek lands. At Rome itself we have the foundations of the Capitoline temple built

[5] E. D. Van Buren, *Figurative Terra-cotta Revetments in Etruria and Latium*; Mrs. Strong, in *Jour. Rom. Stud.*, 1914, 157; Ducati, *Storia dell'arte etrusca*, 245 ff.
[6] Della Seta, *Museo di Villa Giulia*.

by the last Tarquin.[8] Its dimensions are 197 by 180 feet, being in fact more extensive than those of any temple found in the wealthiest cities of Etruria proper. And the walls of regal Rome enclosed an area of about 700 acres. Though it would be incorrect to hold that the whole area was inhabited, since the walls seem to have been extended to make use of natural escarpments, the city was far larger than Caere and Praeneste, which have yielded very rich treasures of gold jewelry and silver ware from the East.[9]

We have a right, then, to assume that Rome was one of the strongest and wealthiest cities of Italy in the last decades of the monarchy, that it was in touch with the commerce of the Mediterranean world, that it supported a strong army and a large population employed in the building trades and in the industries that made ware for soldiers, farmers, urban dwellers, and the court.

Upon the ejection of the Etruscan régime (Varronian date, 509) the city began to lose power and importance. The Latin cities that had been subject to Tarquin seem to have asserted their independence,[10] thereby decreasing the revenues that had flowed toward Rome. The Sabellic mountaineers took advantage of the political confusion, making inroads into southern Latium. Building operations continued for a while, but on a more moderate scale. Two modest temples (dedicated to Saturn and to Castor) were completed within the next two decades, and thereafter little was done. There are no evidences of any contacts with transmarine commerce for a long period after the expulsion of the kings. It would seem that the artisans and merchants who had been supported by the vigorous activities of a luxurious court must have found themselves stranded. The population,[11] which is given as

[7] Ducati, *Storia dell'arte etrusca*, loc. cit. Compare the terracotta statues (provenience not given) that are briefly reported in *Bull. Metropolitan Museum*, 1933, 30, by Miss Richter.

[8] **Paribeni**, in *Not. Scav.*, 1921, 38; Scott, " Early Roman Traditions," in *Memoirs Am. Acad. Rome*, 1929.

[9] Curtis in *Memoirs Am. Acad. Rome*, III (Bernardini Tomb), V (Barberini Tomb). L. Adams, *A Study in the Commerce of Latium*, 1921. See arts. " Caere," " Praeneste," " Satricum," " Veii," in *Reallex. d. Vorgesch.*, for references to the excavations. For the early wall of Rome, see Lugli, in *Historia*, 1933, 1.

[10] Frank, *Roman Economic History*, ch. iii.

[11] These early statistics are usually rejected partly because the Roman area was small, partly because early nations generally enumerate only warriors. The first objection is invalid because Rome's population under Tarquin lived not only on the produce of the Ager Romanus but also on the profits of a large principality and on

130,000 in 508, dwindled to 103,000 in 30 years, if the statistics are dependable. Rome receded into the position of a lethargic agricultural community.

There are a few documents of some importance that seem to be assignable to the half century following the revolution and that give some insight into the economic conditions. The first is the famous treaty—political and commercial—between Rome and Carthage, which Polybius quotes and places in the year after the revolution. It reads as follows:

Polybius 3, 22, 1-13:

Γίνονται τοιγαροῦν συνθῆκαι Ῥωμαίοις καὶ Καρχηδονίοις πρῶται κατὰ Λεύκιον Ἰούνιον Βροῦτον καὶ Μάρκον Ὡράτιον, τοὺς πρώτους κατασταθέντας ὑπάτους μετὰ τὴν τῶν Βασιλέων κατάλυσιν, ὑφ' ὧν συνέβη καθιερωθῆναι καὶ τὸ τοῦ Διὸς ἱερὸν τοῦ Καπετωλίου. ταῦτα δ' ἔστι πρότερα τῆς Ξέρξου διαβάσεως εἰς τὴν Ἑλλάδα τριάκοντ' ἔτεσι λείπουσι δυεῖν. ἃς καθ' ὅσον ἦν δυνατὸν ἀκριβέστατα διερμηνεύσαντες ἡμεῖς ὑπογεγράφαμεν. τηλικαύτη γὰρ ἡ διαφορὰ γέγονε τῆς διαλέκτου καὶ παρὰ Ῥωμαίοις τῆς νῦν πρὸς τὴν ἀρχαίαν ὥστε τοὺς συνετωτάτους ἔνια μόλις ἐξ ἐπιστάσεως διευκρινεῖν. εἰσὶ δ' αἱ συνθῆκαι τοιαίδε τινές· ἐπὶ τοῖσδε φιλίαν εἶναι Ῥωμαίοις καὶ τοῖς Ῥωμαίων συμμάχοις καὶ Καρχηδονίοις καὶ τοῖς Καρχηδονίων συμμάχοις· μὴ πλεῖν Ῥωμαίους μηδὲ τοὺς Ῥωμαίων συμμάχους ἐπέκεινα τοῦ Καλοῦ ἀκρωτηρίου, ἐὰν μὴ ὑπὸ χειμῶνος ἢ πολεμίων ἀναγκασθῶσιν· ἐὰν δέ τις βίᾳ κατενεχθῇ, μὴ ἐξέστω αὐτῷ μηδὲν ἀγοράζειν μηδὲ λαμβάνειν πλὴν ὅσα πρὸς πλοίου ἐπισκευὴν ἢ πρὸς ἱερά, . . .

τοῖς δὲ κατ' ἐμπορίαν παραγινομένοις μηδὲν ἔστω τέλος πλὴν ἐπὶ κήρυκι ἢ γραμματεῖ. ὅσα δ' ἂν τούτων παρόντων πραθῇ, δημοσίᾳ πίστει ὀφειλέσθω τῷ ἀποδομένῳ, ὅσα ἂν ἢ ἐν Λιβύῃ ἢ ἐν Σαρδόνι πραθῇ.

ἐὰν Ῥωμαίων τις εἰς Σικελίαν παραγίνηται, ἧς Καρχηδόνιοι ἐπάρχουσιν, ἴσα ἔστω τὰ Ῥωμαίων πάντα.

Καρχηδόνιοι δὲ μὴ ἀδικείτωσαν δῆμον Ἀρδεατῶν, Ἀντιατῶν, Λαρεντίνων, Κιρκαιτῶν, Ταρρακινιτῶν, μηδ' ἄλλον μηδένα Λατίνων, ὅσοι ἂν ὑπήκοοι· ἐὰν δέ τινες μὴ ὦσιν ὑπήκοοι, τῶν πόλεων ἀπεχέσθωσαν· ἂν δὲ λάβωσι, Ῥωμαίοις ἀποδιδότωσαν ἀκέραιον. φρούριον μὴ ἐνοικοδομείτωσαν ἐν τῇ Λατίνῃ. ἐὰν ὡς πολέμιοι εἰς τὴν χώραν εἰσέλθωσιν, ἐν τῇ χώρᾳ μὴ ἐννυκτερευέτωσαν.

" The first treaty between Rome and Carthage dates from the consulship of Lucius Junius Brutus and Marcus Horatius,[12] the first consuls

the industry and commerce of an important trading center. The second objection fails because migrating nations must number all souls, as did the Helvetians (Caes., B. G., 1, 29), and because the Romans took account of children in assigning lands. In this case the figures correspond with archaeological facts (see Am. Jour. Philol., 1930, 313 ff.).

[12] Reasons for accepting this date (509-8 B. C.) are given in Frank, Economic History of Rome, ch. ii, note 29; Last, in Camb. Anc. Hist., VII, 859. For a vigorous

after the expulsion of the kings, and the founders of the Temple of Jupiter Capitolinus. This is twenty-eight years before the crossing of Xerxes to Greece. I give below as accurate a rendering as I can of this treaty, but the ancient Roman language differs so much from the modern that it can only be partially made out, and that after much application, by the most intelligent men. The treaty is more or less as follows: 'There is to be friendship between the Romans and their allies and the Carthaginians and their allies on these terms: The Romans and their allies are not to sail beyond [13] the Fair Promontory unless forced by storm or by enemies: it is forbidden to anyone carried beyond it by force to buy or carry away anything except what is required for the repair of his ship or for sacrifice.

Men coming to trade [14] may conclude no business except in the presence of a herald of town-folk, and the price of whatever is sold in the presence of such shall be secured to the vendor by the state, if the sale take place in Libya or Sardinia.

If any Roman come to the Carthaginian province in Sicily, he shall enjoy equal rights with others.

The Carthaginians shall do no wrong to the peoples of Ardea, Antium, Laurentium, Circeii, Terracina, or any other city of the Latins who are subject to Rome.[15] Touching those Latins who are not subjects, they shall keep their hands off their cities, and if they take any city shall deliver it up to the Romans undamaged. They shall build no fort in the Latin territory. If they enter the land in arms, they shall not pass a night therein'."

Since this Punic treaty was presumably offered to the new Republic to take the place of the one that had been signed by the defunct royal government, the clauses were probably adapted to some extent from the earlier agreement. The treaty therefore assumes that the Romans would continue sailing the seas as they had under the Etruscan régime. They probably did not engage in commerce after the explusion of the Etruscans. The document, at least, is not to be used as evidence that

attack upon this date see Täubler, *Imperium Romanum*, 354-376, with bibliography. For early commerce see Adams, *A Study in the Commerce of Latium.*

[13] That is, *west of.* The treaty leaves Libya open to trade under conditions.

[14] That is, at Carthage, as the end of the paragraph states.

[15] These cities had apparently been subject to Rome during the Etruscan régime. They had not yet broken from Rome, but did so very soon after 509.

they did. It is, however, a revelation of Punic policy on the seas. Carthage allowed free trade only in western Sicily, which had a hinterland not readily closed. In Libya (from Utica southward) and Sardinia trade could be carried on only under the eye and with the permission of a Punic state official. West of the cape near Utica all was *mare clausum*. (In the next treaty Sardinia and southern Spain were included in the same category.) In contrast to this monopolistic policy, Rome was—and always remained—an open port without restrictions, and we are probably justified in assuming that it had been so under the preceding régime. The treaty is one of the most important of ancient documents relating to commerce.

Another document, the Cassian treaty with the Latins, is political in its scope, but it assumes the existence of *commercium* between Rome and the Latins in its reference to the settlement of contracts, and thereby gives a new clue to Roman commercial policy. The treaty (perhaps a summary) as reported by Dionysius 6, 95, reads as follows:

Dionysius 6, 95, 2:

Ῥωμαίοις καὶ ταῖς Λατίνων πόλεσιν ἁπάσαις εἰρήνη πρὸς ἀλλήλους ἔστω, μέχρις ἂν οὐρανός τε καὶ γῆ τὴν αὐτὴν στάσιν ἔχωσι· καὶ μήτ' αὐτοὶ πολεμείτωσαν πρὸς ἀλλήλους μήτ' ἄλλοθεν πολέμους ἐπαγέτωσαν, μήτε τοῖς ἐπιφέρουσι πόλεμον ὁδοὺς παρεχέτωσαν ἀσφαλεῖς βοηθείτωσάν τε τοῖς πολεμουμένοις ἁπάσῃ δυνάμει, λαφύρων τε καὶ λείας τῆς ἐκ πολέμων κοινῶν τὸ ἴσον λαγχανέτωσαν μέρος ἑκάτεροι· τῶν τ' ἰδιωτικῶν συμβολαίων αἱ κρίσεις ἐν ἡμέραις γιγνέσθωσαν δέκα, παρ' οἷς ἂν γένηται τὸ συμβόλαιον.

" Between the Romans and the cities of the Latins there shall be peace so long as heaven and earth shall last. Neither shall carry on war or invite enemies from any source, or permit an enemy a safe passage through its territory against the other. When either is at war, the other shall give aid with all its forces. Both shall share equally in all booty and plunder taken in a common war. In the case of private sales and contracts,[16] judgments shall be rendered within ten days in the courts of that city in which the sale was made."

Since this treaty was seen by Cicero,[17] it is probably authentic and

---

[16] This clause seems to assume liberal forms of sale outside of such barter as required an immediate exchange of goods and price.

[17] Cicero, *pro Balbo*, 53. Cf. Livy, 2, 33, 4 and 9; Festus, 166 L, 276 L; Cato in Peter, *Hist. Rom. Frag.*, 58; also Rosenberg, in *Hermes*, 54, 145, and Gelzer, "Latium," in Pauly-Wissowa, *Realenc.*, XII, 953; Last, in *Camb. Anc. Hist.*, VII, 487 ff.

the traditional date (about 493 B. C.) is wholly plausible, though it has not always been accepted without question.

The close union between Rome and the Latins had important material consequences. The Etruscan régime at Rome had, of course, shattered the old union of the Latin cities and had subjected the rest of Latium to the king at Rome. The Punic treaty of 508 reveals the fact that Rome hoped to perpetuate her hegemony, but it also shows that some of the southern towns were apparently claiming autonomy so that Rome did not feel compelled to defend them if attacked except on condition that they be given back to her. The disagreement soon went so far that the Latins formed a league of their own without Rome, the boundaries of which may be inferred from a fragment of Cato (Peter, 58):

Lucum Dianium in nemore Aricino Egerius Laeuius Tusculanus dedicauit dictator Latinus. hi populi communiter: Tusculanus, Aricinus, Lanuuinus, Laurens, Coranus, Tiburtis, Pometinus, Ardeatis Rutulus.

" The Latin dictator, Egerius Laevius of Tusculum, dedicated the grove of Diana in the woods of Aricia. The peoples of the following towns participated: Tusculum, Aricia, Lanuvium, Laurentes, Cora, Tiber, Pometia, Rutulian Ardea."

It is likely, therefore, that the Cassian treaty at the same time recognized the independence of this group of cities and cemented an alliance of the group with Rome. This league was apparently not very effective so long as the direction of the troops rested in alternate years with Rome and with the Latins, but it was at least a beginning of unification and provided a wedge for Rome's hegemony. The members of the league suffered few losses of territory after it was formed and, before the century was over, the power of the league extended as far as Tarquin's sway had reached. However, that very fact reveals how much Rome had been weakened politically (and, of course, economically) by the expulsion of the Tarquins. It required a whole century for the league to regain what Rome had lost.

The document cited by Cato, apparently from an inscription erected by the league at Diana's shrine at Nemi, gives us an idea of the extent of Rome's own territory a few years after the revolution. Her boundaries were the sea on the west, the cities of Lavinia, Ardea, Lanuvium,

Aricia, and Tusculum on the south, Tibur on the west (perhaps Gabii
is to be excluded as an ally), and there was certainly only a small strip
of land north of the Tiber river.   All told, Rome now had arable territory of about 300 square miles and, since a farmer with the tools of that
day could hardly care for more than five acres of land, it could employ
nearly 40,000 able-bodied work folk (men and women).   We may also
assume that during that period of frequent hostilities at least half of
these would live with their families inside the walls of Rome.

II. THE CLASS STRUGGLE

During the fifth century there was, according to all the Roman writers, a vigorous class struggle between the patricians and plebeians.
Livy and Dionysius [18] teem with long speeches and arguments, which
are, of course, only attempts on the part of late writers to present as
vividly as possible the situation and the facts as they understood them.
Since no complete minutes were kept of senatorial debates at that time,
these historians could not have had reliable sources on which to build
their hypotheses, which we must therefore omit.

We know very little about the classes of early Rome except that intermarriage between them was prohibited at the time of the Twelve Tables
(Cic. de Rep., 2, 63) and that plebeians could not at first hold magistracies and priesthoods.   The plebeians are therefore accurately represented as striving strenuously for the right to hold office.   But that is
not all.   They are also represented as fighting for economic relief,
relief from debts and from arrest, imprisonment, and slavery because
of debts.   Since we know that Rome suffered economically after the
expulsion of Tarquin, that the population dwindled because industry
and building decayed, and that the debtor laws of the Twelve Tables
were very harsh, we are inclined to think that the fight for economic
relief may have been basic and that the demand for political equality
was raised largely in order to win the power by which to gain economic
relief.

The explanation of how these class distinctions had arisen is lost
to us.   Tradition assumes [19]—there could hardly have been any docu-
mentary evidence—that the patricians were the descendants of those

[18] Livy, 3, 9-57; Dionysius, 10, 1-60.
[19] Livy, 1, 8, 7; Festus, 6 L; Cicero, de Rep., 2, 23.

foremost citizens who had been selected by Romulus to serve as senators. The modern historians [20] who assume a racial origin for the distinction have based their guess upon parallels that prove nothing. It is now usual to assume that the distinction arose chiefly by the operation of common economic and social laws.[21] But proof for any theory is simply not available. We must remember that at Rome the people had passed through many vicissitudes that gave opportunities for the intervention of many kinds of political, economic, and personal forces. They had settled on fairly fertile lands which were apt to be raided from all sides, they had been driven into narrower quarters by Sabines and Etruscans, they had under stress of invasions adopted a monarchy instead of annual magistrates, and they had then had to submit to one or more Etruscan kings who temporarily industrialized the community, brought in sea-borne trade, organized a strong army, and who may well have begun to introduce the kind of serfdom that was usual in Etruria.

There are certain archaeological facts that bear on the question, but the facts are not yet fully recorded nor is the interpretation of them certain. The water tunnels (emissaria) that keep the levels of the lakes of Nemi and Albano at a constant and safe level seem to date from the regal period or from the early republic. Likewise certain extensive drainage tunnels [22] below Velitrae and elsewhere are of early date. All of these must have been very costly and designed to improve farm lands over large areas. They seem to indicate the presence of great landlords who could command large resources of labor, *perhaps of serfs*. The problem can only be indicated here and left to new and extended investigation. There is a lost history of economic and social changes underlying all this that would read as interestingly as that of early Greece. But without contemporaneous descriptions we dare not attempt to enucleate the precise sources of the decisive distinctions between patricians and plebeians that had somehow emerged.

It would be equally futile to attempt to explain the Roman tradition

---

[20] E. g., Zöller, Binder, Ridgeway, Conway, Rose, and many others.

[21] E. Meyer, *Geschichte d. Alt.*, II, 80; Botsford, *Roman Assemblies*, 38 ff.

[22] The cuniculi are discussed by De la Blanchère, in " Mél. d'arch." 1882, and art. " Cuniculus," in *Daremberg-Saglio*. Cf. *Röm. Mitt.*, 1915, 185; Frank, *Econ. Hist.*, 2nd ed., 8; and Fraccaro, *Di alcuni lavori idraulici*, 1919 (with extensive bibliography). Fraccaro has examined chiefly domestic villa-drains of a later day. Neumann, *Die Grundherrschaft*, 1900, believes that the Etruscans brought serfdom into Latium but does not mention these works that might support his theory. Dionysius, 9, 5, 14, mentions serfs in Etruria.

concerning early land-holding and the origins of private property.[23]
Just because Homeric society knew family ownership of land is no
reason for assuming it in early Rome. Homeric society had borrowed
much from the Mycenean, whereas the ancestors of the Romans settled
an almost vacant plain. Personal ownership of land probably dated
from the first settlement of the soil. Tradition mentions original allotments of ground into two acres by Romulus, which indicates a Roman
belief that private property had existed from the beginning of Rome.
Furthermore the "Servian" organization (probably fifth century)
seems to imply a rather wide-spread holding of small plots. But we
have no authentic history to rely upon in the matter. Agriculture and
trade had advanced so far in the terramara times that one is prone to
assume private ownership of land even for that period.

There are a few facts connected with the class struggle of the fifth
century that may be relied upon, since they produced the peculiar
institution of the tribunate, the codification of custom known as the
Twelve Tables, the Valerio-Horatian and Canuleian laws, and the
admission of plebeians to the consular tribunate. These items we may
trust, even if we reject the stories in Livy and Dionysius of how they
came into being. Tradition holds that the plebeians objected to serving
in the army while having no standing in the government [24] whereby to
protect their property and themselves from imprisonment for debt.
Getting no relief, they withdrew outside the walls (the "Secession"),
threatening to found a separate city. A compromise was reached
whereby the plebeians were to have the right to meet annually to elect
officers (*tribuni*, at first two or four, later ten) who were to be *sacro-
sanct*,[25] and who would have the right to give *auxilium* to any plebeian

[23] Mommsen, who believed in family ownership in early Rome, drew his conclusions chiefly from late recorded legends that mention land division by Romulus,
Numa, and others (Dionys., 2, 7, 4; 3, 1, 4; Cic., *de Rep.*, 2, 16; 2, 26; Varro,
R. R., 1, 10, 2; Plut., *Publ.*, 21, 10; Festus, 476 L; Pliny, *N. H.*, 18, 7). It is
difficult to see how any reliable record of such events could have survived. The
trend in recent discussions based upon a study of Roman archaeology and comparative sociology seems to favor the assumption of private property in early Latium
before the founding of Rome. The Terramara people, for instance, were agriculturists a thousand years before "Romulus," raising wheat, beans, flax, and
probably some wine. They also kept cattle, sheep, goats, pigs, and asses, and, at
least in the later period, horses. Such advanced economy cannot long resist the
intrusion of individual ownership among self-governing peoples.

[24] Livy, 3, *passim.*

[25] Rosenberg, in *Hermes*, 1913, 371 (with bibliography).

arrested on any charge. The existence of this peculiar tribunate in historical times is proof that the story of its origin is plausible.

III. THE TWELVE TABLES

Somewhat later, according to a plausible tradition, the plebeians complained that the legal customs—especially those regarding debts— were being administered in the courts at the whim of the patrician consuls, and that the laws should be written down and posted so that all citizens might receive equal treatment. Their contention finally bore fruit in the substitution for the consuls of an executive board of ten men (*Decemviri*) who drew up a code of Twelve Tables that were posted in the Forum in 450 B. C. (corrected date: about 443). Only chance quotations of these laws have survived. I shall here give those that are in any way of importance for economic history, accepting the text and numbering as given by Bruns-Gradenwitz, *Fontes Juris Romani Antiqui,* 7th ed. (see also Girard, *Textes de droit romain*).

A Selection from the Fragments of the Twelve Tables

Tabula I

1. Si in ius vocat, ito.[26] Ni it, antestamino: igitur em capito.

" If the complainant summon the defendant before the magistrate, he shall go; if he do not go, the plaintiff may call a bystander, and take him by force."

2. Si calvitur pedemve struit, manum endo jacito.

" If the defendant attempt evasion or flight, the complainant may lay hands upon him."

3. Si morbus aevitasve vitium escit, iumentum, dato. Si nolet, arceram ne sternito.

" If the defendant be prevented by sickness or old age, the complainant shall provide a conveyance; but he need not provide a covered carriage unless he choose."

4. Assiduo vindex assiduus esto; proletario iam civi quis volet vindex esto.

"A freeholder shall find a freeholder as *vindex* or surety; a proletary shall find such surety as he can."

---

[26] The fragments of Tabula I show that the state provided a court, but no police or prosecuting machinery.

Tabula III

1.   Aeris confessi rebusque iure iudicatis xxx dies iusti sunto.[27]

" In the case of an admitted debt or of awards made by judgment, 30 days shall be allowed for payment."

2.   Post deinde manus iniectio esto.   In ius ducito.

" In default of payment, after these 30 days of grace have elapsed, the debter may be arrested and brought before the magistrate."

3.   Ni iudicatum facit aut quis endo eo in iure vindicit, secum ducito, vincito aut nervo aut compedibus xv pondo, ne maiore, aut si volet minore vincito.

" Unless the debtor discharge the debt, or some one come forward in court to guarantee payment, the creditor may take the debtor away with him, and bind him with thongs or with fetters, the weight of which shall not be more (but, if the creditor choose, may be less) than 15 pounds."

4.   Si volet suo vivito.   Ni suo vivit, qui eum vinctum habebit, libras farris endo dies dato.   Si volet, plus dato.

" The debtor may, if he choose, live on his own means.   Otherwise the creditor that has him in bonds shall give him a pound of spelt a day, or, if he choose, more."

6.   Tertiis nundinis partis secanto.   Si plus minusve secuerunt, se fraude esto.

"After the third market day the creditors may take their several portions; and any one that obtains more or less than his just share shall be held guiltless."

Tabula IV

1.   Cito necatus insignis ad deformitatem puer.

" Monstrous or deformed offspring may be put to death."

2.   Si pater filium ter venum duuit, filius a patre liber esto.[28]

" But if the father sell the son a third time, the son shall be free from his father."

---

[27] Imprisonment and enslavement for debt is plausibly represented in all the tradition as the chief cause of the plebeian effort to win political equality with the patricians (Livy, 2, 23, 1; 2, 24, 6-8; 2, 27).   On *nexum* see de Zulueta, in *Law Quarterly Review*, 1913, 137; Radin, " Secare partis," in *Am. Jour. Philol.*, 1922, 32; and Girard, *Manuel de droit romain.*   See also Westermann, *Upon Slavery in Ptolemaic Egypt*, 48.   The old interpretation of *secare partis* as referring to the debtor's body is hardly acceptable.

[28] This line is cited chiefly as a legal device (by use of fictitious sales) for liberat-

3. Illam suam suas res sibi habere iussit claves ademit, exegit.

"The husband may divorce such a woman, take her keys, and drive her forth."

Tabula V

3. Uti legassit super pecunia tutelave suae rei, ita ius esto.[29]

"The provisions of the will of a paterfamilias concerning his property and the tutelage of his family, shall be law."

4. Si intestato moritur, cui suus heres nec escit, adgnatus proximus familiam habeto.

"If the paterfamilias dies intestate and without *suus heres,* his nearest agnate shall succeed."

5. Si adgnatus nec escit, gentiles familiam habento.

"Failing an agnate, the *gentiles* shall succeed."

8. Civis Romani liberti hereditatem lex XII tab. patrono defert, si intestato sine suo herede libertus decesserit.

"If a freedman die intestate, and without *suus heres,* the Law of the Twelve Tables gives succession to the patron."

10. Haec actio (familiae erciscundae) proficiscitur e lege XII tabularum.

"The action *familiae erciscundae* proceeds from the Law of the Twelve Tables."

Tabula VI

1. Cum nexum faciet mancipiumque, uti lingua nuncupassit,[30] ita ius esto.

"The legal effect of every nexum, and of every conveyance made

ing the son from the *patria potestas,* but it probably harks back to a practice of placing sons in *peonage.*

[29] Till recently historians have been prone to doubt this clause because later laws circumscribed the absolute right of disinheriting sons. But the line is clear; see "Familia," in *Realenc.,* and in *Thes. L. L. (familia = res* in early Latin). Cf. Frank, *Social Behavior in Ancient Rome,* 130. Lines 4 and 5 are not necessarily survivals of family or clan ownership, as Mommsen supposed. Line 8 recognizes the existence of *liberti* (and consequently of slaves) and their right to make testaments. Line 10 provides for the handling of an estate of a deceased as a unit, doubtless in order to facilitate its preservation from dismemberment in an aristocratic society.

[30] Again historians have been averse to assuming liberal forms of sale and contracts in all cases, cf. Karlowa, *Röm. Rechtsgeschichte,* II, 612; but in view of the large amount of foreign trade that passed through the Forum in the days of the kings, it is not strange that the witnessed spoken word should constitute a contract. See notes 31 and 43, and Frank, *Soc. Behavior,* 125 ff.

with the money and the scales shall rest upon the declarations made in the transaction."

3.   Usus auctoritas fundi biennium est, . . . ceterarum rerum omnium . . . annuus est usus.

"A prescriptive title is acquired after two years' possession in the case of realty; after one year's possession in the case of other property."

Tabula VII

11.   Venditae—et traditae (res) non aliter emptori adquiruntur, quam si is venditori pretium solverit vel alio modo satisfecerit, veluti expromissore aut pignore dato;[31] quod cavetur—lege XII tab.

" Things sold and delivered shall not become the property of the vendee until he has paid or otherwise satisfied the vendor, as, for instance, by guarantee or pledge."

12.   Sub hac condicione liber [32] esse iussus si decem milia heredi dederit, etsi ab herede abalienatus sit, emptori dando pecuniam ad libertatem perveniet: idque lex XII tab. iubet.

"A slave freed by will, upon condition of giving ten thousand (i. e. a certain sum) to the heir, may, in the event of being alienated by the heir, obtain his freedom by payment of this sum to the alienee."

Tabula VIII

2.   Si membrum rup[s]it, ni cum eo pacit, talio [33] esto.

" If a man break another's limb, and do not compromise the injury, he shall be liable to retaliation."

3.   Manu fustive si os fregit libero, CCC, si servo, CL poenam [34] subito.

" For breaking a bone of a freeman, the penalty shall be 300 *asses* (pounds of copper); of a slave, 150 *asses*.

---

[31] The phrase *vel alio modo satisfecerit*, etc., lends strong support to the interpretation adopted in the preceding note. See also note 43.

[32] In the early days when slaves and *nexi* were all of Latin or neighboring stock and spoke Latin, when also slaves were relatively few, emancipation with immediate enrollment as citizens was made easy. The custom continued later, though slaves were then of foreign stock.

[33] The restricted right of *talio* was continued for a long time in order to compel the culprit to submit to judicial arbitration.

[34] These sums are probably those of the original document, when the *as*, or pound of copper, was rated at one per cent of the price of an ox. Hence the penalty for breaking a limb would be three oxen. See Livy, 4, 30, 3, and Festus, 268 L, on the value of bronze (1 sheep = 10 pounds; 1 ox = 100).

4. Si iniuriam faxsit, viginti quinque poenae sunto.

"For personal injury, 25 *asses.*"

8. a. Qui fruges excantassit.[35]— b. . . . neve alienam segetem pellexeris . . .

"A man who shall remove his neighbor's crops to another field by incantations, or conjure away his corn . . ."

9. Frugem — aratro quaesitam noctu pavisse ac secuisse puberi (XII tabulis) capital erat, suspensumque Cereri [36] necari iubebant,— inpubem praetoris arbitratu verberari noxiamve duplionemve decerni.

"For a person of the age of puberty to depasture or cut down a neighbour's crop by stealth in the night, shall be a capital crime, the culprit to be devoted to Ceres and hanged; but if the culprit be under the age of puberty, he shall be scourged at the discretion of the magistrate, or be condemned to pay double the value of the damage done."

18. a. XII tabulis sanctum, ne quis unciario fenore amplius exerceret.[37]— b. Furem dupli condemnari, feneratorem quadrupli.

"A usurer exacting higher interest than the legal rate of one ounce per pound per annum is liable to fourfold damages, a thief is liable to twofold restitution.

21. Patronus si clienti fraudem fecerit, sacer esto.[38]

"A patron that wrongs his client shall be devoted to the infernal gods."

27. His (sodalibus) potestatem facit lex [39] (XII tab.), pactionem quam velint sibi ferre, dum ne quid ex publica lege corrumpant.

---

[35] Saint Augustine (*de Civ. Dei*, 2, 9) quotes Cicero, *de Rep.*, as including *sive carmen condidisset quod infamiam faceret*, but he often inserts his own explicative phrases in quotations. Furthermore it would seem that the jurists of the Republic stretched these clauses to cover libel, as though *carmen* could here refer to libellous poetry. It is now generally believed that these clauses referred originally only to instances of magic incantation. Cf. *Am. Jour. Phil.*, 1927, 108; Huvelin, *La notion de l'injuria*; Beckmann, *Zauberei und Recht*, 1923.

[36] An instance where religious penalties had not yet been displaced by civil penalties.

[37] The first reference to interest rates at Rome. Since the copper pound was divided into twelve ounces, the annual rate of one ounce for the use of a pound (8⅓%) seems natural. In Cicero's day the normal rate was 6%.

[38] The institution of clientage is here recognized in law, but the relationship was still left to the protection of the deities.

[39] This interesting clause reveals the early existence of gilds, (of laborers?) It is barely possible, therefore, that Plutarch (*Numa*, 17) and Florus (1, 6, 3) had access to some authentic document, older than these tables, from which they

3

"Associations (or clubs) may adopt whatever rules they please, provided such rules be not inconsistent with public law."

Tabula IX

1. 2. Privilegia ne inroganto; de capite civis [40] nisi per maximum comitiatum—ne ferunto.

1. " No laws shall be proposed affecting individuals only."

2. " The assembly of the centuries alone may pass laws affecting the *caput* of a citizen."

Tabula X [41]

2. . . . hoc plus ne facito: rogum ascea ne polito.

" More than this shall not be done. The wood of the funeral pile shall not be smoothed with the axe."

3. Extenuato igitur sumptu tribus reciniis et tunicula purpurae et decem tibicinibus tollit etiam lamentationem.

" Not more than three mourners wearing *ricinia,* one wearing a small tunic of purple, and ten flute-players may attend the funeral."

8. . . . neve aurum addito. At cui auro dentes iuncti escunt.

" Gold shall not be burned or buried with the dead, except such gold as the teeth have been fastened with."

Tabula XI

1. Conubia ut ne plebi cum patribus essent.[42]

" Patricians shall not intermarry with plebeians."

drew their list of eight labor-gilds existing in the regal period. The clause gives autonomy to such gilds in so far as their decisions do not infringe the laws of the state. Of course, it is not likely that the full import of such a grant of autonomy was realized or that any theory of a corporate " person " had as yet been thought out.

[40] These clauses prove for the early day a clear conception of the equality of status before the law in respect to all citizens.

[41] These clauses (2, 3, 8) of the tenth table reveal a strong effort of the republican community to break away from the expensive burial customs that had arisen during the period of Etruscan domination. The Etruscans buried their dead with elaborate ceremonies, apparently assuming some kind of " survival." The Latins generally followed the custom of cremation.

[42] This law, added in the second year of the decemvirate, reveals a desire of the board, now aristocratic, to legalize a class distinction that was becoming customary. The effects of this clause were annulled by the lex Canuleia five years later.

Tabula XII

1. Lege autem introducta est pignoris capio, veluti lege XII tab. adversus eum, qui hostiam emisset [43] nec pretium redderet; . . .

" The seizure of a pledge shall be allowed, on default of payment, against the purchaser of a sacrificial victim."

These tables are a summary of confused customs. The religious penalties are survivals of primitive Latin practices; the large powers of the *pater* in making a will (later circumscribed by law) reveal the influence of an old landed aristocracy; the liberal clauses regarding forms of sale and contract preserve the consequences of much trading that went on during the Etruscan régime sixty years before. Probably the forms became more strict during the next fifty years of isolation. The burial restrictions show a conservative attempt to abolish Etruscan custom and revert to old native usage. Table IX is proof that the plebeian struggle for equality had made some progress, but the eleventh shows that where religious objections could be raised, it was temporarily checked. The whole constitutes our best body of evidence regarding social and economic conditions of the fifth century B. C.

In 449 the Decemviral board was abolished, the consulate restored, and tribunes were again recognized as inviolable and again given the right to summon the plebeian assembly.[44] Four years later the lex Canuleia voided the prohibition of intermarriage between patricians and plebeians.

IV. THE " SERVIAN " CONSTITUTION

In 444 a significant change in the constitution was made. In the place of consuls, it was decided to elect as chief magistrates military tribunes with consular power (Livy, 4, 6, 8). To this office the plebeians were to be eligible, and six might be elected when wars demanded it, though at times only two or three are found in the list. (Perhaps in these cases our sources fail to give the full list). The plausible suggestion has been made that this institution was not only a compromise

[43] The clause reveals the practice of making sales and purchases on credit. The purpose of the clause is to provide security in such sales in the case of goods that are bought for offerings and therefore will obviously not be recoverable.

[44] Very few plebiscites having the force of law were passed before 287 B. C. Cf. Botsford, *Roman Assemblies*, 275.

to satisfy the plebeian demand for office, but that it also marked a reorganization of the army so as to introduce the hoplite system of the Greeks, and to classify the citizens definitely according to their ability to provide hoplite arms and armor.[45]   The change took place at a time when there was much warfare with the Volsci and Aequi, and it seems to be significant that it was about this time that the censorship [46] was first instituted at Rome.   We shall therefore give at this place the Roman tradition regarding the so-called " Servian " classification of the citizen body of the army.

Tradition attributes the standard classification of the centuriate assembly to Servius, but this ascription is universally rejected.   We are not sure that the statistics given actually belong to the year 443, but the numbers are not unreasonable for the period, and the introduction of censors and the change to six executives mark a logical point for a new classification of the populace or a remodelling of an old system.   The traditional [47] figures given for the " Servian " classification of troops (men of seventeen years and over, both active soldiers and seniors) are as follows:

```
 18 centuries, 1,800 knights . . . . . . . . . . . (census of first class)
 80 centuries, 8,000 men of 1st  class . . (census of 100,000 asses)
 20 centuries, 2,000 men of 2nd class . . (census of   75,000 asses)
 20 centuries, 2,000 men of 3rd  class . . (census of   50,000 asses)
 20 centuries, 2,000 men of 4th  class . . (census of   25,000 asses)
 30 centuries, 3,000 men of 5th  class . . (census of   12,500 ( ?) asses)
  2 centuries,   200 engineers and artisans . . (ranked with first class)
  3 centuries,   300 musicians, supernumeraries, and proletarians
 ───          ──────
 193          19,300
```

This would make four legions (two active, and two for defence) of about 4,200 men each, plus artisans, etc., and cavalry for the four legions.   When voting in the centuriate assembly (at elections for consuls, and at legislation) the citizens not actually enrolled in the army would take their appropriate place (according to property) with their

---

[45] Nilsson, in *Jour. Rom. Studies*, 1929, 1.

[46] Livy, 4, 8; 9, 34, 7; Dionys., 11, 63; Cic., *ad Fam.*, 9, 21; Zon., 7, 19. Soldiers were paid a stipendium after 406 (Livy, 4, 59, 11; 4, 60, 5-8).

[47] Livy, 1, 43; Dionys., 4, 16, differs only in minor details; Cic., *de Rep.*, 2, 39, differs more but seems to be quoting from memory.   The minimum property qualification was probably lowered several times.   See Botsford, *Roman Assemblies*, 84; Rosenberg, *Unters. zur röm. Centurienverfassung*, 1911; Stuart Jones, in *Camb. Anc. Hist.*, VII, 432 ff.

proper centuries. The knights would then have eighteen votes, the citizens of the first class eighty, etc., while all the poor citizens beneath the fifth class would be crowded together with the one century of proletarians and count altogether for only one vote. In fact, if the knights and the citizens of the first class voted with one accord, they, though probably a minority of the citizen body, would carry the elections. The theory seems to have been that the citizens who had most at stake and who bore the brunt of the military service (being placed in the front ranks because they could afford to provide full armor) were the men who should decide the elections, who should make the decisions about war and peace, and pass the laws.

The one hundred and ninety-three centuries are generally assumed to be too large a number for the Servian city and also for the city of 443 B. C. However, the classification may be reasonable, both for the size of the city and its territory and for the census figures given us for the latter period. As we have seen, Rome had an arable territory in the early Republic (and it remained stationary for a century) of about 300 square miles. If two-thirds of the acreage was farmed by labor (men and women) that could care for only about five acres each, we may assume 25,000 at work on farms, that is, a farm population (besides shepherd folk) of about 50,000. Many of these would live in the city. The city, however, had an area of over a square mile, which, with the low, small adobe houses of the day, counting an average of four persons to each, would readily hold over a hundred thousand.[48] Even assuming that half the rural labor dwelt inside the walls, we have ample room for a complete free population of some 125,000 souls within the state. Now the census statistics,[49] which in the early census (according to Pliny, *N. H.*, 33, 16) reckoned all capita libera, are as follows:

508 B. C.....130,000....(Dion. 5, 20)
503 B. C.....120,000....(Hieron. Ol. 69, 1)
498 B. C.....150,700....(Dion. 5, 75, probably incorrect)

[48] The city of the "four regions" had about 30,000,000 square feet of habitable land. Houses of this period did not average over 500 square feet so that, if we allow generously for streets and public buildings, we may still assume room for twenty-five to thirty thousand dwellings and a population of well over 100,000.

[49] See *Am. Jour. Phil.*, 1930, 317 ff., for a discussion of these statistics. It will of course be objected that early nations usually enumerated only men capable of bearing arms, but since Rome took account of children in allotting public land, the objections need not be valid for Rome.

493 B. C.....110,000....(Dion. 6, 96)
474 B. C.....103,000....(Dion. 9, 36)
465 B. C.....104,714....(Livy, 3, 3, 9)
459 B. C.....117,319....(Livy, 3, 24, 10)

There are no statistics for the next sixty-six years, but for 392, after the capture of Veii, Pliny (*N. H.*, 33, 16) gives 152,573 *capita libera*. These figures diminish from 130,000 to 103,000 in the first three decades of the Republic; and that diminution we expect because of the economic stagnation due to the expulsion of the king. The figures are quite reasonable, and the number for 443 (sixteen years after 459) would doubtless have been about 125,000 *capita libera,* a number that we have above found plausible for the city and its acreage.[50]

The classification by coined *asses* must, of course, belong to the period of coinage (the third century), and we cannot be certain that the recalculation into the new standard of value did not coincide with a remodelling of the whole system, but there is no hint anywhere of such a remodelling except for a lowering of the qualifications of the fifth class. It is a striking fact that the property rating of the first class is so low. 100,000 asses (10,000 denarii) would buy only a little over 3,000 bushes of wheat in Polybius' day. It is only one twenty-fifth of the senatorial census requirement of Cicero's day. However, since half the army was drawn from the first class, the qualification could not be placed high. Any farmer who owned 20 jugera of good land (13 acres) with a simple adobe house, a pair of oxen, a few sheep, and a year's crop of wheat (say 160 bushels) would apparently qualify for the first class. Another striking fact is that there is so little difference between the classes. In gold values of today the first four classes rate as follows: first—$2,000, second—$1,500, third—$1,000, fourth—$500. Today one would hardly suppose that such distinctions were worth making. It would seem that the system was made at a time of

---

[50] Now it is often asserted that in modern European cities one would not get four legions, or nearly 20,000 *propertied* men in a population of 125,000 souls. However, in a primitive Latin community where hoe-culture was the rule, property was more widely distributed than in modern Germany and England. It is far more evenly distributed in western American states than anywhere in Europe. If with Dionysius we multiply the men of the assembly by three, we get about 60,000 *capita libera* belonging to the first five classes, after which we may assign 65,000 *capita libera* to the proletariat and the incapacitated to reach the 125,000 assumed for the census of 443 (sixteen years after the 117,000 of 459 B. C.).

rather primitive conditions, when, furthermore, landed property was fairly evenly divided.

It is not improbable that the fifth class, as Mommsen assumed, was calculated to include those who had only the traditional heredium of two jugera with a hovel and the necessary appurtenances. Such " property holders " doubtless hired out as farm laborers while the women did the gardening and spinning. In speaking of this early rural economy, therefore, it is useless to assume many *latifundia* of extensive acreage. The traditional stories of nobles like Cincinnatus, Curius, and Fabius who farmed their own few acres between magistracies represent normal conditions among the senators of the fifth century.

In 406, according to Diodorus, 14, 16, 5, " war broke out between Rome and Veii, during which the Romans first paid their soldiers for their annual campaigns." This new military expense was the first heavy financial burden assumed by the state. Ten years later (*ibid.* 93, 2) Veii was captured. Diodorus goes on to say that " Rome sold the booty including the captured males," and three years later " divided the Veientane land among the Romans, giving four jugera to each " (*ibid.* 102, 4). Livy, 5, 30, 8, differing but slightly, says that seven jugera were given to each plebeian, mentioning later (6, 4, 4, for 387 B. C.) that some of the land was given to the Veientanes who had been friendly, and presently adding (6, 5, 8) that four tribes (wards) were organized from the *new* citizens. Since in 367 there was a demand for distribution of the public land, we may assume that some of the Veientane land was left unsettled. The probability is that both needy Romans and those of the enemy who had not resisted to the end received allotments, and that a good half of Veii's 300,000 jugera might still remain as public land. The significant fact is that the poor of the city were now settled as voters of good standing, and that the four new wards of small landowners very much strengthened the voting power of the plebeians in the assembly and gave considerable power to the democratic element. The victories of the plebeians after the Gallic fire were in some measure due to this land-distribution.[51] The great accretion of public land which could be rented by ambitious men of capacity and means introduced into politics an economic contention that not even the Gracchi could exorcise 250 years later.

[51] I shall set down here for what they may be worth references in the early books of Livy (up to 390) to items of economic interest.

1. *Buildings* (the first nine items could hardly be based on safe records; buildings like the carcer, circus, pons, tabernae, would hardly bear inscriptions) :

Temple of Jupiter Feretrius, Livy, 1, 10, 7.
Temple of Janus, Livy, 1, 19, 2; Varro, *L. L.*, 5, 165; Plut., *Numa*, 20.
Temple of Jupiter Elicius, Livy, 1, 20, 7.
Curia, Livy, 1, 30, 2; Cic., *de Rep.*, 2, 31.
Pons Sublicius, Livy, 1, 33, 6.
Carcer, Tullianum, Livy, 1, 33, 8; Festus, 490 L.
Circus, Livy, 1, 35, 8; Dionys., 3, 68; Livy, 1, 56.
Tabernae, of Forum, Livy, 1, 35, 10; Dionys., 3, 67.
Stone walls, sewers, Livy, 1, 38, 6-7; walls, Livy, 1, 44, 3; sewers, Livy, 1, 56.
Temple of Diana, Livy, 1, 45, 2; Dionys., 4, 25-6.
Temple of Jupiter, Livy, 1, 38, 6-7; 1, 53, 2-3; 1, 55; 2, 8, 6-8 (509).
Temple of Castor, Livy, 2, 20, 12; 2, 42, 5 (499-484 B. C.).
Temple of Saturn, Livy, 2, 21, 1 (497).
Temple of Mercury, Livy, 2, 21, 7 (495).
Temple of Ceres, Dionys., 6, 17 (493).
Temple of Fortune, Livy, 2, 40, 12 (488).
Temple of Apollo, Livy, 4, 25, 3; 4, 29, 7 (433-1).
Temple of Mater Matuta, Livy, 5, 19, 6; Plut., *Cam.*, 5 (396).
Temple of Juno Regina, Livy, 5, 23, 7; 5, 31, 3 (396-2).

Building operations were vigorous under the Tarquins, and the new republic continued with energy for some ten or fifteen years. Thereafter there was only one small temple built for a century.

2. *References to grain and harvests:*

Envoys sent to buy grain, Livy, 2, 9, 6 (508).
Famine because of secession, grain bought, Livy, 2, 34, 2-7 (492-1).
Lack of grain, Livy, 2, 51, 2 (477).
Grain brought from Campania, Livy, 2, 52 (476).
Scarcity of grain, Livy, 3, 31, 1 (456).
Famine and pestilence, Livy, 3, 32, 2 (453).
Famine, Livy, 4, 12, 6-11 (440).
Minucius sells cheap grain the next year, Livy, 4, 13, 7 and 16, 2 (439).
Grain bought, Livy, 4, 25, 4 (433).
Drought, Livy, 4, 30, 7 (428).
Scarcity due to pestilence, Livy, 4, 52, 4-6 (411).
Scarcity due to pestilence, Livy, 5, 31, 5 (392).
Famine due to Gallic raid, Livy, 5, 48, 2 (390).

The priestly tablets were apt to record famines, but whether they had records of the buying of grain is doubtful. The references to famine are so numerous that we are justified in believing that Latium was overpopulated at this time, and it is probable that the thin soil of Latium was suffering to some extent from over-cropping in cereals.

3. *Booty:*

There are many indefinite references to booty (Livy, 2, 17, 6; 2, 42, 2; 3, 10; 3, 22, 9; 3, 29, 4; 3, 31, 4; 3, 61, 10; 3, 70, 13; 4, 10, 7; 4, 19, 6; 4, 29, 4; 4, 53, 10; 4, 55, 8; 5, 14, 7; 5, 19, 8; 5, 22; 5, 23, 10; 5, 25, 7-10, Veii; 5, 26, 8). The booty, according to Livy, is usually sold and the proceeds deposited in the treasury, but at times the soldiers get a part. Captives are usually sold.

However the references to the proceeds of the capture of Suessa Pometia, employed for the building of the temple of Jupiter in Livy, 1, 53, 2-3, are of dubious value. Livy gives the amount as forty talents of silver, i. e. 3,200 Roman pounds. Pometia may have had much silver plate as, of course, Caere had, but forty pounds would be a more reasonable figure. The booty of Veii may have been considerable and, if it is true that the treasury received a tithe of this (Livy, 5, 25, 7-10), including the value of all the land taken, the treasury probably received much silver and gold. A golden bowl was sent to Delphi (Livy, 5, 28; Diod., 14, 93), and three golden plates deposited in Jupiter's temple (Livy, 6, 4, 2-3).

4. *Agrarian distributions and colonization:*

Lex Cassia agraria of 486, Livy, 2, 41, and Dionys., 5, 75. Tradition speaks of a distribution of public lands in terms that resemble those of the Gracchan laws. It is best, with Mommsen (*Röm. Forsch.*, II, 153), to disregard the details as unworthy of faith.

Lex Icilia de Aventino publicando, Livy, 3, 31 and 32 (454). Dionys., 10, 32, says the tablet was still in existence. This is not a real agrarian law. The Aventine seems to have been public property (formerly perhaps belonging to some king). Squatters were removed, the land declared public and made available for the extension of the city. The hill became the residence of the very poor (E. Meyer, *Hermes*, XXX, 14).

Colonization: the details are very uncertain for, though the dates of colonies were usually kept, many early colonies fell a prey to wars and were recolonized, so that records were confused.

1. Ostia claimed to be a citizen colony of Ancus Marcius (Livy, 1, 33; Pol., 6, 2, 9; Cic., *de Rep.*, 2, 33). The claim is reasonable (cf. L. R. Taylor, *Cults of Ostia*, 2 ff.) but the oldest remains as yet found are those of the fourth century fortified camp (Calza, in *Not. Scav.*, 1923, 178). *Latin colonies* were founded by the Latin league. Roman citizens who enrolled lost their Roman franchise and accepted Latin status.

1-5. *Signia*, 495, Livy, 2, 21. *Velitrae*, 494, Livy, 2, 30; 492, Livy, 2, 34; 404, Diod., 14, 34. *Norba*, 492, Livy, 2, 34; Dionys., 7, 13. *Ardea*, 442, Livy, 4, 11; Diod., 12, 34. *Circeii*, 393, Diod., 14, 102. These dates seem to be reliable, at least in the cities where excavations have turned up early remains, as at Signia, Norba, Ardea and Velitrae.

CHAPTER I

FROM THE GALLIC FIRE TO THE FIRST PUNIC WAR

A. TO THE LATIN WAR

1. *The Gallic Catastrophe.*

That the Gauls captured Rome was known in Greece (by Aristotle, born 384; cf. Plut., *Cam.,* 22; and by Theopompus, born 376; cf. Pliny, *N. H.,* 3, 57: "For Theopompus only says that the city was taken by the Gauls "). The circumstantial accounts in Livy, 5, 36-55, Diodorus, 14, 114-16, and Plutarch, *Camillus,* must rest largely upon legend; and though Livy seems to be more accurate than Diodorus in placing the battle on the left bank of the Tiber, the descriptions of the destruction are not based upon contemporary sources, for there were none. There can be no doubt that during a long occupation most of the property both of Rome and of Latium suffered severely. The traditional notes in Livy regarding the ensuing poverty and debts are therefore reasonable. It is also apparent that the disaster had serious political effects in that Rome's hegemony was constantly questioned by the Latins during the next half century. However, archaeology has proved that the Gauls did respect the sacred structures of Rome to a large extent (Roberts, "The Gallic Fire and Roman Archives," in *Mem. Am. Acad.,* II, 1918, 55 ff.; Frank, *Roman Buildings of the Republic,* 53, 78, 83).

The ransom price is reported as 1,000 pounds of gold by Livy, 5, 48, and Diodorus, 14, 116; by several later writers as 2,000. It is difficult to believe that any record of the amount existed. The sum is well-nigh incredible, but the sack of Veii had doubtless brought some gold into the Treasury and into the Temple of Jupiter, and Marseilles is said to have contributed to the ransom. For the discussion of the sources see De Sanctis, *Storia dei Romani,* II.

2. *Economic Stress and the Licinio-Sextian Legislation.*

Livy's account of the following years speaks repeatedly of financial difficulties which were somewhat alleviated by the legislation of 367. It has been the custom of historians to consider this an anticipation of the Gracchan conditions (cf. Niese, in *Hermes,* 1888, 410;

De Sanctis, *Storia dei Rom.*, II, 216 ff.; Beloch, *Röm. Geschichte*, 344). But the economic notes in Livy and others may well come from the priestly annals, which were certainly kept with some care after the Gallic fire. And that the Gallic raid caused much distress is certain. Livy, 6, 11, 9 (385 B. C.) speaks of debts incurred in rebuilding, then of debts leading to riots (6, 31, 2; 378 B. C.), then in the same year (6, 32, 1) of still further debts incurred because of taxes levied for the sake of rebuilding the walls of Rome, and again in the same year (6, 34, 2) of imprisonment for debt. Finally in 6, 36, he gives the items of the Licinio-Sextian relief measures which he says were passed in 367 (6, 42, 11). There are three items. Livy, 6, 35, 4-5: creatique tribuni C. Licinius et L. Sextius promulgauere leges omnes aduersus opes patriciorum et pro commodis plebis: unam de aere alieno, ut deducto eo de capite quod usuris pernumeratum esset, id quod superesset, triennio aequis pensionibus persolueretur; alteram de modo agrorum, ne quis plus quingenta iugera agri possideret; tertiam, ne tribunorum militum comitia fierent consulumque utique alter ex plebe crearetur.

"When Licinius and Sextius were elected tribunes, they proposed only such measures as abated the influence of the patricians while forwarding the interests of the plebs. One of these had to do with debts, providing that what had been paid as interest should be deducted from the original sum, and the remainder discharged in three annual installments of equal size. A second set a limit on lands, prohibiting anyone from holding more than five hundred jugera (of public land). A third did away with the election of military tribunes, and prescribed that of the consuls, one, at any rate, should be chosen from the plebs."

That the first item (the scaling down of debts) is reasonable appears from what precedes and from the later legislation devised to alleviate debts. The second item (restriction of acreage in public tenancies) is equally reasonable. Veii with its 300,000 jugera had recently been taken. Rome's plebeians might receive four jugera each and still leave nearly half of the territory unassigned, on which there would be room for several hundred large state tenancies. The item is supported by the information (7, 16, 9, 357 B. C.) that Licinius was fined for breaking his own law, that in 298 several men were fined for exceeding the legal limit of holdings (Livy, 10, 13, 14), and that in 293

(Livy, 10, 47, 4) the aediles procured the conviction of a number of graziers (again in 193; Livy, 35, 10, 11). In the year 167 B. C. Cato, in a speech, mentions the existence of a law prohibiting the holding of more than 500 jugera of public land (*Oratorum Rom. Frag.* Malc., I, 195). Appian, *B. C.*, 1, 8; and Plut., *Ti. Gracc.*, 8, mention such a law as existing before the Gracchi but do not give a date. Varro, *R. R.*, 1, 29, also mentions the law, as do later writers (Vell., 2, 6; Gell., 6, 3, 40; etc.) who may possibly depend on Livy. That the disturbance was very serious is proved by the fact that Camillus dedicated a temple to *Concord* when peace between the classes was re-established (Ovid, *Fasti*, 1, 637; Plut., *Cam.*, 42). And the dates of temples were accurately kept. Historians have generally accepted the third item (the admission of plebeians to the consulship) because the Fasti after 363 contain plebeian names. To accept the record of the political contest and to ignore the record that stresses the economic causes of that contest is not a plausible procedure. It must be remembered that debts involved far more than property since the Decemviral Code permitting enslavement for debt was still valid. Livy's account of the law has recently been accepted by Fraccaro, *Studi*, 1914, 1, 71; Gelzer, *Die Nobilität*, 16; Münzer, *art. Licinius Stolo* in Pauly-Wissowa, Realenc. XIII, 1926; Vançura, *art. Leges agrariae*, Realenc. XII, 1164, and may be considered as authentic.

3. Continued Legislation in Favor of Debtors.

The Licinian-Sextian law did not solve the financial difficulties, for throughout the next thirty years serious new experiments were tried by way of limiting the rate of interest and by bankruptcy legislation. For the year 357, Livy (7, 16, 1) has the statement:

De unciario fenore a M. Duillio, L. Menenio tribunis plebis rogatio est perlata.

" The measure fixed the rate of interest at one twelfth and was carried through by M. Duillius and L. Menenius, tribunes of the people." This was a reenactment of the law of the Twelve Tables (Tac., *Ann.*, 6, 16) which had probably fallen into abeyance during the financial stress following the Gallic catastrophe. One twelfth ($8\frac{1}{3}$ per cent) was a natural rate of interest before money was coined, when the pound of copper, divided into twelve ounces, was the regular medium of exchange. See Billeter, *Geschichte des Zinsfusses*, 116-33. Suggestions that this means 12 per cent (i. e. 1 per cent per month) or 10 per cent, assuming a ten-month year, need not be considered.

But this law provided little relief, and five years later, in 352 (Livy, 7, 21, 5-8), a commission was appointed with extensive powers to lend state funds and to adjust mortgages and bankruptcies. Gaius, *Inst.*, 4, 23: (Lex Marcia) adversus faeneratores, ut si usuras exegissent, de his reddendis per manus injectionem cum eis ageretur, may refer to this measure. Livy's statement (7, 21, 5-8) reads:

. . novi consules fenebrem quoque rem, quae distinere una animos videbatur, levare adgressi solutionem alieni aeris in publicam curam verterunt quinqueviris creatis quos mensarios ab dispensatione pecuniae appellarunt. Meriti aequitate curaque sunt, ut per omnium annalium monumenta celebres nominibus essent; fuere autem C. Duillius, P. Decius Mus, M. Papirius, Q. Publilius, et T. Aemilius. Qui rem difficillimam tractatu et plerumque parti utrique, semper certe alteri gravem cum alia moderatione tum impendio magis publico quam iactura sustinuerunt. Tarda enim nomina et impeditiora inertia debitorum quam facultatibus aut aerarium mensis cum aere in foro positis dissolvit, ut populo prius caveretur, aut aestimatio aequis rerum pretiis liberavit, ut non modo sine iniuria sed etiam sine querimoniis partis utriusque exhausta vis ingens aeris alieni sit.

. . "the new consuls (P. Valerius Publicola, G. Marcius Rutulus) set themselves to obtain relief in the matter of interest-rates also, which appeared to be the sole obstacle to harmony. They made the discharge of debts a concern of the state, appointing five commissioners, whom they called bankers, from their having the disposition of the money. These men by their impartiality and diligence fairly earned the distinction which attaches in all the histories to the names of Gaius Duillius, Publius Decius Mus, Marcus Papirius, Quintus Publilius, and Titus Aemilius. In the discharge of a very difficult duty, involving always a hardship for one of the parties, and in most instances for both, they managed matters wisely in other respects, and, in particular, they expended without throwing away the public funds. For with long-standing accounts, embarrassed more by the debtors' neglect than by their lack of means, they dealt in one of the following ways: either they paid them out of the treasury—taking security for the people first—at the banking tables they had set up in the Forum; or they settled them upon a valuation, at fair prices, of the debtor's effects. And so, not only without injustice, but even without complaint from either side, a vast amount of indebtedness was cleared off."

This is one of the most important economic experiments in Roman history. Since Livy would have no record of how the commission proceeded unless the available copy of the law defined methods of procedure, we cannot be certain that Livy's details are wholly reliable. However Gaius' brief quotation from the law (quoted above) indicates that the text of the law defined methods rather explicitly. Livy's account is therefore probable, namely, that the state treasury, through the commission, took over some mortgages on sufficient security, and in other cases supervised the settlement of mortgages by permitting bankruptcy proceedings or a surrender of a part of the property in satisfaction of the debt. The purpose was apparently not only to reduce the sum of nerve-racking debts, but also to prevent enslavement for debt (cf. Livy, 7, 19, 5), which was still legally recognized. The commission consisted of two patricians and three plebeians, all from among the foremost statesmen of the day.

Five years after this (in 347) the legal rate of interest was reduced to half an ounce per pound (4⅙ per cent) and a moratorium was again arranged. Presumably the treasury itself had to submit to its share of losses on the mortgages that its commission had assumed five years before. When the state treasury assumed the burden of the mortgages it is not surprising that pressure was soon exerted to reduce the interest rate. Public advantage is seldom as well guarded as private. Livy's statement (cf. Tac., *Ann.*, 6, 16) reads (7, 27, 3-4):

Semunciarium tantum ex unciario fenus factum, et in pensiones aequas triennii, ita ut quarta praesens esset, solutio aeris alieni dispensata est; et sic quoque parte plebis adfecta fides tamen publica privatis difficultatibus potior ad curam senatui fuit. Levatae maxime res, quia tributo ac dilectu supersessum.

" But the rate of interest was reduced from one ounce per pound to one half ounce, and debts were made payable, one-fourth down and the remainder in three annual instalments; even so some of the plebeians were distressed, but the public credit was of greater concern to the senate than were the hardships of single persons. What did the most to lighten the burden was the omission of the war-tax and the levy."

Again after five years (in 342) Livy, 7, 42, 1, has the statement:

Praeter haec invenio apud quosdam L. Genucium tribunum plebis tulisse ad plebem ne fenerare liceret; . . .

" In addition to these transactions, I find in certain writers that Lucius Genucius, a tribune of the plebs, proposed to the plebs that it should be unlawful to lend at interest."

Livy seems to be uncertain about this law, but Appian, *B. C.*, 1, 54, mentions an old law forbidding the taking of interest, and Tacitus (*Ann.*, 6, 16), after citing the above-mentioned rates of one ounce and half-ounce respectively, adds *postremo vetita versura* " finally the taking of interest was forbidden." The Genucian law was therefore probably passed, though it soon became a dead letter: Livy, 8, 28, shows that imprisonment for debt was still in vogue fourteen years after this. It may be that the measure was aimed chiefly at the state-mortgages and that when these had finally been disposed of private money-lenders again gained influence enough either to have the Genucian law repealed or to be able to disregard it.

The agitation regarding debts quieted down somewhat because of the colonization that went on during the period in question (see below). In 358 many citizens were settled on the lands of Southern Latium that had belonged to Pometia, and two tribus, the Pomptine and the Publilian, were then instituted (Livy, 7, 15, 12). Furthermore some effective colonization, of which we shall speak presently, followed the Latin war. In 339 the Publilian law gave legal validity to plebiscites (Livy, 8, 12, 14). We are therefore not surprised to find that legislation was soon devised to strike at the very roots of the ancient evil of enslavement for debts which had been permitted by the Twelve Tables. Since these Tables were not directly amenable to nullification the correct procedure was to make the old clause harmless. Hence in 326, according to Livy, 8, 28, 1 and 8-9, a further law was passed:

Eo anno plebei Romanae velut aliud initium libertatis factum est, quod necti desierunt; mutatum autem ius ob unius feneratoris simul libidinem simul crudelitatem insignem. L. Papirius is fuit, cui cum se C. Publilius ob aes alienum paternum nexum dedisset, . . . Victum eo die ob impotentem iniuriam unius ingens vinculum fidei; iussique consules ferre ad populum ne quis, nisi qui noxam meruisset, donec poenam lueret, in compedibus aut in nervo teneretur; pecuniae creditae bona debitoris, non corpus obnoxium esset. Ita nexi soluti, cautumque in posterum ne necterentur.

" In that year the liberty of the Roman plebs had, as it were, a new beginning; for men ceased to be imprisoned for debt. The change in the law was occasioned by the notable lust and cruelty of a single usurer, Lucius Papirius, to whom Gaius Publilius had given himself up for a debt owed by his father. . . . On that day, owing to one man's outrageous injury, was broken a strong bond of credit, and the consuls were ordered to carry a proposal to the people that none should be confined in shackles or in the stocks, save those who, having been guilty of some crime, were waiting to pay the penalty; and that for money lent, the debtor's goods, but not his person, should be distrainable. So those in confinement were released, and it was forbidden that any should be confined thereafter."

This is the famous Lex Poetelia-Papiria which was long considered a partial Magna Charta of plebeian rights. Though it could not repeal the law of the Twelve Tables, it did effectually render its permission of personal seizure for debts unenforceable. There are occasional instances of peonage later, but these are probably lapses due to personal contracts entered into under stress and were probably not enforceable in court at normal times. Cicero, de Rep., 2, 59, refers in general terms to this law: nexa civium liberata, nectierque postea desitum, " the bonds of citizens were released and thereafter binding for debts ceased." Varro, L. L., 7, 105, attributes the law to C. Poetelius, the dictator of 313: Hoc (nexum) C. Poetelio Libone Visolo dictatore sublatum ne fieret, et omnes qui bonam copiam jurarunt, ne essent nexi, dissoluti: " the right to enslave for debt was taken away by the dictator Poetelius and all who declared themselves bankrupt were released from debt slavery." Cf. Botsford, Roman Assemblies, 310; Pais, Ricerche, IV, 44; Cambridge Anc. History, VII, 545.

4. Colonization, 390-340 B. C.

The colonization of this period was vigorous. The Veientane land was not allotted to colonies but to a large extent assigned to individuals in four-jugera (Diod., 14, 102, 4) or seven-jugera lots (Livy, 5, 30, 8, in 393), while some was also given to friendly Veientanes (Livy, 6, 4, 4). Livy implies that all plebeians shared in the allotment whether or not they owned land before. But since four new wards were organized in the new territory (Livy, 6, 5, 8; 387 B. C.), we must assume that a large part of it went to propertyless men. After that distribution there could have been but few landless Romans. In 383 two Latin colonies (Nepete and Sutrium) were planted on the northern border of the Veientane land (Livy, 6, 21, 4, and Velleius, 1, 14), presumably to protect the individual settlers. Thus the Latins, who as members of the Latin league had shared in the dangers of the war with Veii, received a share of the land—where they could be most useful.

The contests with the Volsci also led to settlements. Satricum was settled as a Latin colony in 385 (Livy, 6, 16, 6) but suffered severely in subsequent disasters and was finally destroyed in 346 (Livy, 7, 27), but the Latin colony at Setia planted in 382 (Livy, 6, 21, 4, and 30, 9; Velleius, 1, 14, 2) survived. With Setia to protect the valleys, Rome found it possible in 358 to send out individual Roman settlers into the neighborhood, and from these she organized the two wards Pomptina and Publilia (Livy, 7, 15, 12). In the six new wards we may assume that over twenty thousand poor citizens were settled; the four Latin colonies may well have had about two thousand men each. Rome's available acreage was therefore more than doubled.

5. *Buildings.*

There are but few other items reported that have any economic significance. The city itself apparently grew but little. A few votive temples were built, the remains of none of which have been found, but since they were quickly completed they were probably small. The following are mentioned:

In 392, a temple on the Aventine to Juno Regina, who was exorcised from Veii; Livy, 5, 21-3; 31; 52. See Platner and Ashby, *Top. Dict.*, 290.

In 388, a temple to Mars vowed during the Gallic battle; Livy, 6, 5, 8. Perhaps this was the temple outside the Capena gate. Platner and Ashby, 327-8.

In 375, a temple to Juno Lucina, of which little is known; Pliny, *N. H.,* 16, 235; Platner and Ashby, 288.

In 367, Camillus built the temple to Concordia because of the peace-

4

ful settlement of the class struggle by means of the Licinian-Sextian laws; Ov., *Fasti,* 1, 641; Plut., *Cam.,* 42. Cf. Platner and Ashby, 138. It was rebuilt on a larger scale in 121 and again in 10 A. D. (*Mem. Am. Acad.,* V, 53).

In 345 Camillus vowed a temple to Juno Moneta during his war with the Aurunci. It was dedicated the next year; Livy, 7, 28. This was on the arx and must have been of fair size, since later in the Republic it was used for the mint; Platner and Ashby, 289.

The city walls also had to be rebuilt after the Gallic catastrophe and this required enormous energy and expense for a city of perhaps 100,000 souls. Livy reports these operations first in 6, 32, 1 (377 B. C.) where he says: " there was no prospect of relief from the old debts, since a tax was levied to build a stone wall which the censors had contracted for." Twenty-four years later the wall was still being built (Livy, 7, 20, 9, 353 B. C.), this time apparently by the army, for Livy says: " They led their army home; and the rest of the year was consumed in building the walls and towers." Most of this wall (especially where the position was weak) was built of tufa cut out of the hills near the Tiber some ten miles up the river. The quarry (Grotta Oscura) lies in territory that belonged to Veii before its destruction. The blocks average 2 x 2 x 3-5 feet. The stone wall, about five and a half miles long, varied in thickness according to local needs but averaged about twelve feet thick and twenty high, was backed by a buttressed mound of earth fifty feet thick on the Quirinal, and at the level part—for about a mile—was faced by a ditch which when somewhat enlarged later measured one hundred feet in width and thirty in depth. Some five million cubic feet of cut stone must have been used in the wall. The cutting at the Grotta Oscura quarry was presumably done by Veientane captives, for the quarry marks seem to be in the Etruscan alphabet. But the building—if Livy is accurate—was done partly by contract, partly by army labor. (Frank, *Roman Buildings of the Republic,* 112; Platner and Ashby, 350; G. Säflund, *Le Mura di Roma,* Oxford Press, 1932.) It is hardly necessary to assume with Säflund that Greek architects were called in to build these simple walls.

6. *Commerce—Second Treaty with Carthage.*

Of foreign commerce we know but little during this period, though the second treaty with Carthage may possibly indicate that there was some. Of industry also there are but few indications in the finds of archaeologists. However Rome's soil has been so frequently turned over for 2,000 years that few objects of that period could possibly survive. We shall revert to the subject later.

It is within this period that Rome's second treaty with Carthage falls, a treaty which would seem to indicate that a large trading city like Carthage found it profitable to be on good commercial terms with Rome, small and unprogressive though she was. Polybius gives the treaty as follows (3, 24, 1-13, 348 B. C.) :

Μετὰ δὲ ταύτας ἑτέρας ποιοῦνται συνθήκας, ἐν αἷς προσπεριειλήφασι Καρχηδόνιοι Τυρίους καὶ τὸν Ἰτυκαίων δῆμον. πρόσκειται δὲ καὶ τῷ Καλῷ ἀκρωτηρίῳ Μαστία, Ταρσήιον· ὧν ἐκτὸς οἴονται δεῖν Ῥωμαίους μήτε λῄζεσθαι μήτε πόλιν κτίζειν. εἰσὶ δὲ τοιάδε τινές· " ἐπὶ τοῖσδε φιλίαν εἶναι Ῥωμαίοις καὶ τοῖς Ῥωμαίων συμμάχοις καὶ Καρχηδονίων καὶ Τυρίων καὶ Ἰτυκαίων δήμῳ καὶ τοῖς τούτων συμμάχοις. τοῦ Καλοῦ ἀκρωτηρίου, Μαστίας, Ταρσηίου, μὴ λῄζεσθαι ἐπέκεινα Ῥωμαίους μηδ' ἐμπορεύεσθαι μηδὲ πόλιν κτίζειν. ἐὰν δὲ Καρχηδόνιοι λάβωσιν ἐν τῇ Λατίνῃ πόλιν τινὰ μὴ οὖσαν ὑπήκοον Ῥωμαίοις, τὰ χρήματα καὶ τοὺς ἄνδρας ἐχέτωσαν, τὴν δὲ πόλιν ἀποδιδότωσαν. ἐὰν δέ τινες Καρχηδονίων λάβωσί τινας, πρὸς οὓς εἰρήνη μέν ἐστιν ἔγγραπτος Ῥωμαίοις, μὴ ὑποτάττονται δέ τι αὐτοῖς, μὴ καταγέτωσαν εἰς τοὺς Ῥωμαίων λιμένας· ἐὰν δὲ καταχθέντος ἐπιλάβηται ὁ Ῥωμαῖος, ἀφιέσθω. ὡσαύτως δὲ μηδ' οἱ Ῥωμαῖοι ποιείτωσαν. ἂν ἔκ τινος χώρας, ἧς Καρχηδόνιοι ἐπάρχουσιν, ὕδωρ ἢ ἐφόδια λάβῃ ὁ Ῥωμαῖος, μετὰ τούτων τῶν ἐφοδίων μὴ ἀδικείτω μηδένα πρὸς οὓς εἰρήνη καὶ φιλία ἐστὶ (Καρχηδονίοις). ὡσαύτως δὲ μηδ' ὁ) Καρχηδόνιος ποιείτω. εἰ δέ, μὴ ἰδίᾳ μεταπορευέσθω· ἐὰν δέ τις τοῦτο ποιήσῃ, δημόσιον γινέσθω τὸ ἀδίκημα. ἐν Σαρδόνι καὶ Λιβύῃ μηδεὶς Ῥωμαίων μήτ' ἐμπορευέσθω μήτε πόλιν κτιζέτω, . . . εἰ μὴ ἕως τοῦ ἐφόδια λαβεῖν ἢ πλοῖον ἐπισκευάσαι. ἐὰν δὲ χειμὼν κατενέγκῃ, ἐν πένθ' ἡμέραις ἀποτρεχέτω. ἐν Σικελίᾳ, ἧς Καρχηδόνιοι ἐπάρχουσι, καὶ ἐν Καρχηδόνι πάντα καὶ ποιείτω καὶ πωλείτω ὅσα καὶ τῷ πολίτῃ ἔξεστιν. ὡσαύτως δὲ καὶ ὁ Καρχηδόνιος ποιείτω ἐν Ῥώμῃ."

"At a later date they made another treaty, in which the Carthaginians include Tyre and Utica, and mention, in addition to the Fair Promontory (of Africa), Mastia and Tarseum (of Spain) as points beyond which the Romans may not either make marauding expeditions, or trade, or found cities. This treaty is more or less as follows : ' There is to be friendship on the following conditions between the Romans and their allies and the Carthaginians, Tyrians, and the people of Utica and their respective allies. The Romans shall not maraud or trade or found a city on the farther side of Fair Promontory, Mastia, and Tarseum. If the Carthaginians capture any city in

Latium not subject to Rome, they shall keep the valuables and the men, but give up the city. If any Carthaginians take captive any of a people with whom the Romans have a treaty of peace, but who are not subject to Rome, they shall not bring them into Roman harbours, but if one be brought in and a Roman lay hold of him, he shall be set free. The Romans shall observe the same restriction. If a Roman gets water or provisions from any place over which the Carthaginians rule, he shall not use these provisions to wrong any member of a people with whom the Carthaginians have peace and friendship. The Carthaginians shall observe the same rule. If either infringe this rule, the aggrieved person shall not take private vengeance, and if he do, his wrongdoing shall be public. No Roman shall trade or found a city in Sardinia and Libya nor remain in a Sardinian or Libyan post longer than is required for taking in provisions or repairing his ship. If he be driven there by stress of weather, he shall depart within five days. In the Carthaginian province of Sicily and at Carthage he may do and sell anything that is permitted to a citizen. A Carthaginian in Rome may do likewise '."

Polybius gives no date for this treaty, but Livy, 7, 27, 2, says that in 348 B. C. " a treaty was signed with the Carthaginian envoys who came with a request for a treaty of friendship ", and Diodorus mentions, though only in passing, a treaty for that year (16, 69, 1). See *Cambridge Ancient History*, VIII, 859, for a discussion—with bibliography—of the date, which has been needlessly questioned by several historians (e. g. Schachermeyr, in *Rhein. Mus.*, 1930, 350 ff.). The mention of Spanish places (Tarseum) precludes an earlier date, the reference to Latins not subject to Rome precludes a later date. The treaty seems to assume that Romans are engaged in commerce on the seas, but this is not a necessary assumption. It may only mean that Carthage, now that it is establishing closed seas in Libya, Southern Spain, and Sardinia, has decided to ask all the treaty powers that may presumably enter commerce to recognize her policy. We know that Marseilles—a commercial power—would not recognize it. Since Rome did, she probably took but little interest in her own traders, if there were any. In return for the acquiescence she secured a promise that Carthage would not establish any permanent interests on the coast of Latium. Now, as before and after, Rome permitted foreign traders to enter her harbor. Rome never adopted a policy of *mare clausum*.

The only other item of economic interest for this period is the first
levy of a five per cent tax on the price of slaves at manumission (Livy,
7, 16, 7: 357 B. C.). Strange to say, the law was passed by the army
in the field, temporarily organized into a citizen group voting by
wards. The money was to be set aside as a sacred treasury to be drawn
upon only at times of great stress and apparently was not so used until
during the second Punic war (in 209 B. C., Livy, 27, 10, 11) when
it is said that 4,000 pounds of gold had accumulated. The slaves that
were being manumitted were doubtless Veientane captives in the main.
Manumission of slaves was of very frequent occurrence throughout
Roman history (see the last chapter).

B.   FROM THE LATIN TO THE FIRST PUNIC WAR, 340-264 B. C.

1. *Chronology* (Varronian dates).
   Latin War   340 B. C.
   Publilian Law   339
   Great Samnite War   326-04; Caudine Forks   321
   Appius Claudius Censor   312
   War with Samnites, Etruscans, Gauls   298-90
   Lex Hortensia   287
   Occupation of Ager Gallicus   285
   War with Pyrrhus   281-272
   First Punic War begins   264

2. *The Roman Federation.*
   This period of eighty years is the most amazing in Roman history
because of the sudden development of Rome's political power. In 393
the city (urban and rural) had only 152,000 citizens all told (*capita
libera;* Pliny, *N. H.,* 33, 16). Subsequent growth was slow because
of the Gallic disaster and frequent wars. Thus in 339 the population
had risen only to 165,000 (Euseb., Olymp., 110, 1, Armen. Version).
But there was this difference that now nearly all men were property
owners, thanks to the settlement of the Veientane and Pomptine
regions. Roman acreage of arable land was now, after this doubling,
about 600 square miles (about 1600 sq. km.). That is to say each
square kilometer was called upon to feed one hundred souls, which
even with intensive hoe culture was a rather heavy task. This fact

doubtless accounts for the Roman seizure and distribution of some lands after the Latin war, though the Latins near Rome were generally left undisturbed. Livy, 8, 11, 13-14:

Latium Capuaque agro multati. Latinus ager Privernati addito agro et Falernus, qui populi Campani fuerat, usque ad Volturnum flumen plebi Romanae dividitur. Bina in Latino iugera, ita ut dodrante ex Privernati complerent, data, terna in Falerno . . .

"Latium and Capua were deprived of territory. The Latin territory taken, with the addition of that belonging to Privernum, together with the Falernian—which had belonged to the Campanian people—as far as the river Volturnus, was parcelled out amongst the Roman plebs. The assignment was two *iugera* in Latium supplemented with three-fourths of a *iugerum* from the land of Privernum, or three *iugera* in the Falernian district," . . .

(An early boundary stone in the ager Falernus is published in *C. I. L.*, I², 400.)

This distribution to individuals of small plots in different areas was uneconomical, but not unfair. By trading or selling portions and buying others an individual could doubtless unite enough land to make a usable area of a few jugera in one place. By 318 (Livy, 9, 20, 6) enough citizens had moved to the ager Falernus to justify the formation of the Tribus Falerna. It became a famous region for wine, and later was all owned by a few wine-raisers. Beloch (*Röm. Ges.*, 536 and 620) calculates the ager Falernus as about 200 square kilometers, hence some 25,000 plebs might have received three jugera each there. If 25,000 plebeians likewise received two jugera each in Latium, we may calculate that Rome confiscated some 50 square miles from the Latins or about 8 to 10 per cent of Latium.

The most important results of the war (together with the consequences of the Capuan alliance the year or two before) were political. The Latin league was now broken and in its place Rome built up about herself as leader a federation of cities with varied rights. A number of cities were given the full franchise at Rome, others a restricted franchise, with the hope of future favors. Some cities were given only an alliance with the duty of contributing to the federal army, while several cities were promoted to the " Latin " status. Rome now led a federation which extended from Falerii to Pompeii. Livy's statement of the arrangement is as follows, and is generally accepted as substantially correct:

Livy, 8, 14, 2-12: Lanuvinis civitas data sacraque sua reddita, cum eo ut aedes lucusque Sospitae Iunonis communis Lanuvinis municipibus cum populo Romano esset. Aricini Nomentanique et Pedani eodem iure quo Lanuvini in civitatem accepti. Tusculanis servata civitas quam habebant, . . . Et Antium nova colonia missa, cum eo ut Antiatibus permitteretur, si et ipsi adscribi coloni vellent; . . . Ceteris Latinis populis conubia commerciaque et concilia inter se ademerunt. Campanis . . . Fundanisque et Formianis, quod per fines eorum tuta pacataque semper fuisset via, civitas sine suffragio data. Cumanos Suessulanosque eiusdem iuris condicionisque cuius Capuam esse placuit. Naves Antiatium partim in navalia Romae subductae, partim incensae, . . .

" The Lanuvini were given citizenship, and their worship was restored to them, with the stipulation that the temple and grove of Juno Sospita should be held in common by the citizens of Lanuvium and the Roman people. The Aricini, Nomentani, and Pedani were received into citizenship on the same terms as the Lanuvini. The Tusculans were allowed to retain the civic rights which they enjoyed, . . . To Antium likewise a colony was dispatched, with an understanding that the Antiates might be permitted, if they liked, themselves to enroll as colonists; . . . The rest of the Latin peoples were deprived of the rights of mutual trade and intermarriage and of holding common councils. The Campanians . . . were granted citizenship without the suffrage; so too were the Fundani and Formiani, because they had always afforded a safe and peaceful passage through their territories. It was voted to give the people of Cumae and Suessula the same rights and the same terms as the Capuans. The ships of the Antiates were some of them laid up in the Roman dockyards, and some were burnt . . . "

After citizenship of two different grades had thus been given to most of the Latins, the Aruncans, and the Campanians, the Ager Romanus, which had been about 600 square miles before the war, was now as reckoned by Beloch (loc. cit., 391), about 2400 square miles, that is, the Roman state now had about four times the arable land that it had had before the war and in addition had treaties that permitted the acquisition of land in an added area of considerable size. Since several of these newly acquired portions—Campania, for instance, with its population of at least 200,000—were as thickly settled as the old Ager Romanus, we should expect a trebling or quadrupling of the census. The census figures are not very explicit on this point, since, after the rapid expansion, the censors no longer issued lists of all *capita libera* but only of adult males (see *Am. Jour. Philology,* 1930, 321 ff.). In an undated census, probably of 332 or 329 (Livy, 9, 19) this list is given as 250,000, which would mean a total free population of about 750,000. Rome had become the strongest power in Italy, and her political and military organizations now worked very effectively.

The great war with Samnium began in 326, and complete peace was not established till 290 when Rome had compelled practically all the tribes and cities of Italy from the Arno to Magna Graecia to join her federation and accept her leadership.   Then in 285 the Gauls who had taken possession of the coast lands between Ariminum and Ancona were driven out and the land confiscated.   Finally, as a result of the war with Pyrrhus (281-272) all the Greek states of Southern Italy were attached to Rome as naval allies.   Rome through her federation now dominated the whole of the peninsula.   In fact, the people of an area of about 500 square miles directed the politics of an area of one hundred times that size.

3. *Colonization.*

This rapid expansion resulted in a gradual reorganization of Italy. Many tribes were incorporated in the state outright and given citizenship, as, for instance, the Hernicans, the Sabines, the Vestini, the Aequi, the Picentes, some of the Etruscans, notably Caere, and some cities bordering on Campania.   In addition some lands were confiscated on which to plant colonies: usually Roman citizens were colonized in groups of 300 at seaport towns, while " Latin " colonies of Romans, Latins, and Allies together in groups of 2000–5000 were usually planted inland where protective barriers or centers of Romanization were needed.   The *citizen-colonies* of 300 men each were, for this period:

338   Antium (Livy, 8, 14, 8).
?   Ostia, effectually recolonized at about the same time.
329   Tarracina (Livy, 8, 21, 11; Vell., 1, 14, 4).
296   Minturnae (Livy, 10, 21, 8; Vell., 1, 14, 6).

296   Sinuessa (*ibid.*)

283   Sena Gallica (Livy, *Epit.* 11; Pol., 2, 19, 12).

The Latin colonies of 2–5000 (in which both Roman citizens and Latins shared) are:

334   Cales (Livy, 8, 16; Vell., 1, 14, 3; 2,500 colonists).

328   Fregellae (Livy, 8, 22, 2).

314   Luceria (Livy, 9, 26, 1-5; Vell., 1, 14, 4, and Diod., 19, 72, 8, place it earlier; 2,500 colonists).

313   Saticula (Festus, 458 L; Vell., 1, 14, 4).

313   Suessa Aurunca (Livy, 9, 28, 7; Vell., 1, 14, 4).

312   Interamna on the Liris (Livy, 9, 28, 8; Diod., 19, 105, 5; 4,000 men).

303   Sora (Livy, 10, 1; Vell., 1, 14, 5; 4,000 men).

303   Alba Fucentia (*ibid.*; 6,000 men).

299   Narnia (Livy, 10, 10, 5).

298   Carsioli (Livy, 10, 13, 1; 4,000 men).

291   Venusia (Vell., 1, 14, 6).

c. 290-86   Castrum Novum (on the Adriatic? Livy, *Epit.* 11).

c. 290-86   Hadria (*ibid.*).

273   Cosa (Livy, *Epit.* 14; Vell., 1, 14, 7).

273   Paestum (*ibid.*).

4. *Census*

The available census statistics (of adult male citizens) are:

c. 332   250,000 (Livy, 9, 19, 1).

293   262,321 (Livy, 10, 47, 2).

289   272,000 (Livy, *Epit.* 11).

279   287,222 (Livy, *Epit.* 13).

275   271,224 (Livy, *Epit.* 14).

The increase, despite liberal grants of the franchise to Italians, is very moderate, partly because of the losses in the heavy warfare, partly because citizens who accepted allotments in Latin colonies lost their citizenship and were no longer counted.

The heavy colonization in which some 50,000 shared, must have had some economic effects. It attracted Romans to agriculture in new areas at a time when the poverty of Latium might otherwise have induced citizens to enter industry and commerce on the seas; it probably reduced

intensive cereal farming in Latium by attracting men to colonies, even
if a majority of the allotments in the colonies went to Latins and allies.
(In the next century wine and olive culture and grazing seem to have
made progress over cereal culture near Rome). It probably bound a
large number of Italian cities to Rome commercially and severed them
from each other, and at the same time, because of certain clauses in the
treaties, it opened opportunities for Romans at home to invest in property throughout Italy. Henceforth the Romans were destined to be an
agrarian people. By 275 B. C. there were about 272,000 adult male
citizens, i. e. probably nearly a million persons all told. They probably
constituted a fourth of the population of the peninsula and they possessed about one seventh of the 50,000 square miles of Italian land south
of the Rubicon, but that was to a large extent the better part. We have
no statistics of property values available. (For lists of colonies see
Kornemann, art. *Colonia* in *Realenc.*, IV, and Beloch, *Röm. Geschichte*,
522–621.).

5. *The Beginning of Roman Coinage.*

Rome was very slow to begin the issue of coins. At the time of the
Twelve Tables fines were levied in weights of bronze, for pieces of
bronze weighed out by pounds and ounces had been the customary
medium of exchange and of estimating values for hundreds of years.
For the sake of convenience a law [1] was passed about the same time that
in collecting fines the treasury would equate values as follows:

$$1 \text{ ox} = 10 \text{ sheep} = 100 \text{ pounds bronze}$$

From 406 B. C. the state paid the soldiers' stipends with bronze and
presumably collected the taxes needed for such expenses in the form of
bronze. This unprogressive machinery was continued during most of
the fourth century, two centuries after the Greeks of Southern Italy
had begun to coin silver.[2] We can barely conceive how it was possible
for the treasury to lag in this fashion before the Latin War. That the
delay continued thereafter, when the Campanians—long used to a silver
coinage—became citizens of Rome, is very difficult to believe. And

---

[1] The lex Julia-Papiria of 430, completing the lex Aternia-Tarpeia of 454, Cic.,
de Rep., 2, 60; Festus, 268-70 L.

[2] Tarentum, Metapontum, Lucania, and some of the Sicilian cities were coining
silver about the year 550 B. C.; Cumae began about 500 or soon after, Naples
about 450. Carthage began coining while conducting a war in Sicily, about
410 B. C.

that it continued, as has recently been argued, during the great Samnite War when Roman armies campaigned for some twenty years in the latitude of Naples and Capua goes beyond belief. The treasury then supplied pay not only to the Roman troops but also to the Campanian soldiers, who could hardly have been satisfied with uncoined copper; it had to provide food for several legions year after year, and much of this had to be bought in silver-using cities—for a direct supply from Latium was out of the question with the means of transportation then available. Besides, the engineers and smiths of the army had constantly to procure a supply of iron for swords and lance points and this had to be bought outside of Latium. Quite apart from numismatic arguments based upon coin-types, the economic arguments of this nature must be considered in attempting to date Rome's coinage.[3]

Now the statements about Rome's coinage found in late writers like Pliny and Festus are inconsistent, at times demonstrably wrong, and do not take into account the Romano-Campanian coinage that existed some time before Rome struck silver (the denarius) at home. Historians of coinage have usually followed Mommsen's school in dating various issues of Romano-Campanian silver from about 335, and have

---

[3] In the Samnite Wars Rome took and sold many prisoners besides other booty so that presumably silver was acquired that could be coined. Livy's general statements about booty are not to be accepted as fully reliable for this period but we may set them down as indicating the generals' (somewhat boastful) reports. Livy, 9, 15, 7 (319 B. C.), *praeda ingens* from Luceria; 9, 37, 10 (310), *aurum, argentum* in Etruria; Diod., 20, 80 (307), more than 5,000 captives; Livy, 10, 17 (296), booty sold; Livy, 10, 19, 22 (296), 2,120 Etruscans captured; 10, 20, 15 (296), 2,500 captives; 10, 29, 17 (295), 8,000 captives; 10, 31, 3 (295), 1,740 captives released at a ransom of 310 *asses* each (Perhaps Fabius is the source and he may have reckoned the amounts in two-ounce *asses*); 10, 31, 7, 2,700 captives; 10, 34, 3 (294), 4,700 captives; same year, 10, 37, 3, 2,000 captives; 10, 39, 3 (293), 4,270 captives and rich booty; 10, 42, 5 (293), 3,870 captives; 10, 45, 11 (293), 10,000 captives; 10, 45, 14 (293), less than 3,000 captives. Even if we reduce the sum of 50,000 captives by half, these would bring a very large amount of metal into the treasury. It is difficult to suppose that Rome held to copper coinage under the circumstances. Besides, Papirius Cursor is reported to have brought 1,830 pounds of silver in his triumph in 293, and much silver must have been found in the looting of Etruscan towns. The 2,533,000 *aeris gravis* reported by Livy, 10, 46, 5, for 293 and the 380,000 *aeris gravis* recorded in 10, 46, 14, are probably the two-ounce *asses* that Fabius knew in his youth. The same coin is probably meant when Livy (10, 37, 5) says that in 293 the three cities—Volsinii, Perusia, and Arretium—were fined 500,000 pieces of bronze and that the Faliscans were fined 100,000 (Livy, 10, 46, 12). The sum total of these amounts gathered in three years would then be about 750,000 pounds of bronze. It is likely that the silver taken was calculated in terms of bronze *asses*.

then tried to relate the statements of Roman writers to the denarial system after 269 (see the several works of Haeberlin, and especially *Die Systematik des ältesten röm. Münzwesens,* 1905). More recently, Giesecke, *Italia Numismatica,* 1928, and Mattingly, *Roman Coins,* 1928, have questioned the system, and the latter, in the *Jour. Rom. Studies,* 1929, 19, has insisted that the Romano-Campanian coins were first struck during the Pyrrhic War and held the field till after the Hannibalic War, when the denarius was introduced. Since it will be many years before an agreement can possibly be reached between these two schools, we cannot here discuss the question. The views that were held to be orthodox till recent years may be found in Grueber, *Coins of the Republic* (British Museum), and Hill, *Hist. Rom. Coins.* An attempt to evaluate this older system for economic history may be found in Frank, *Economic History of Rome,* ch. V.

According to this system Rome issued in her own mint bronze in pieces of one pound and fractions thereof from about 330, and drachmas and double drachmas of silver issued by some Campanian mints by contract, and it is assumed that the ratio of silver to bronze stood at about 120:1. The bronze *asses* gradually diminished in size for some sixty years. The reason seemed to lie in the fact that warfare used up much copper and also blocked the source of the Etruscan supply, while at the same time silver as a commodity fell in value for some years because of the larger supply marketed in Greece after Alexander's conquest. After the wars were over the peace prices returned, Rome organized a new system, issuing silver denarii that weighed 4.55 grams, to be worth ten two-ounce coppers; that is, the ratio of 120:1 was reestablished and bimetallism preserved. The lighter denarius of a trifle under 4 grams—the denarius that remained unchanged for nearly three centuries—was then introduced about 217 B. C. together with a reduced copper coin.

For calculations of values I shall adhere to this old system while waiting for more convincing evidence than has as yet appeared that most of the types should be dated fifty years or more later. For the estimates to be made in the following chapters the threatened revision will not matter greatly, if ever it is adopted, since we shall simply have to assume more extended issues of the Romano-Campanian silver in the place of Roman denarii.

Our literary references to early coinage are late, inconsistent, and in part demonstrably incorrect. They are as follows:

Pliny, *N. H.*, 18, 12 (cf. Pliny, *N. H.*, 33, 43): Servius rex ouium boumque effigie primus aes signavit: " King Servius first stamped bronze, using a figure of a sheep or ox." (This statement is certainly incorrect.)

Varro, *L. L.*, 5, 169 (cf. 174 and 182, also Festus, 87 L): *as* erat libra pondo: " The *as* weighed a pound."

Livy, *Epit.* 15: Tunc primum P. R. argento uti coepit (c. 269): " Then first the Roman people began to use silver [4] (coins)."

Pliny, *N. H.*, 33, 44: Librale pondus aeris imminutum est bello Punico primo: " The weight of the one-pound *as* was reduced during the *First Punic War.*"

Festus, 87 L: Bello Punico populus Romanus, pressus aere alieno, ex singulis assibus librariis senos fecit, qui tantundem ut illi valerent: [5] " The Roman people, oppressed by debts, during the Punic War, divided the one-pound *as* into six, each of which was to have the value of the one pound *as.*" Later, 468 L, Festus refers the reduction to the Second Punic War.

Pliny, *N. H.*, 33, 42-44: populus Romanus ne argento quidem signato ante Pyrrhum regem devictum usus est.[6] libralis — unde etiam nunc libella dicitur et dupondius—adpendebatur assis; quare aeris gravis poena dicta, . . . (43) Servius rex primus signavit aes. antea rudi usos Romae Timaeus tradit.[7] signatum est nota pecudum,

---

[4] According to the old view this is taken as referring to the denarial system, disregarding the Romano-Campanian coins. Mattingly, on the other hand, assumes that 269 is the date of the Romano-Campanian silver and that the denarial system is much later.

[5] Since silver was in use at the time, copper could hardly have been the standard metal. The reduction was probably due to increase of value because of scarcity. Few will admit that the reduction was so late.

[6] This, of course, agrees with Livy; see note 4. Probably Livy, Pliny, and Festus all depend upon some mistaken reconstruction of coinage history concocted by Varro. Since the commissioners of the mint acted without the orders of a *lex*, few actual records about coinage were kept, and its history could not be accurately reconstructed later. However the laws passed would probably survive in the archives, so that the statements about a " lex Flaminia " should not be rejected in haste.

[7] The attribution of coinage to Servius is, of course, mistaken; but the fact that Timaeus—who wrote about 275—considered Roman bronze coinage very old, is significant. See *Not. Scav.*, 1928, 83, for some recent finds of coins of about 300 B. C.

unde et pecunia appellata. maximus census $\overline{\text{CXX}}$ assium fuit illo rege, et ideo haec prima classis . . . (44). Argentum signatum anno urbis CCCCLXXXV, Q. Ogulnio C. Fabio cos., quinque annis ante primum Punicum bellum. et placuit denarium pro X libris aeris valere,[8] quinarium pro V, sestertium pro dupondio ac semisse. librale autem pondus aeris inminutum est bello Punico primo, cum inpensis res p. non sufficeret, constitutumque ut asses sextantario pondere ferirentur. ita quinque partes lucri factae, dissolutumque aes alienum:[9]

"The Roman people made no use even of coined silver before the period of the defeat of King Pyrrhus. The *as* of copper weighed one libra; and hence it is that we still use the terms 'libella' and 'dupondius.' Hence it is, too, that fines and penalties are inflicted under the name of 'aes grave,' . . . (43). King Servius was the first to make an impress upon copper. Before his time, according to Timaeus, at Rome the raw metal only was used. The form of a sheep was the first figure impressed upon money, and to this fact it owes its name, 'pecunia.' The highest figure at which one man's property was assessed in the reign of that king was one hundred and twenty thousand asses, and consequently that amount of property was considered the standard of the first class. . . . (44). Silver was not impressed with a mark until the year of the City 485 (269 B. C.), the year of the consulship of Q. Ogulnius and C. Fabius, five years before the First Punic War; at which time it was ordained that the value of the denarius should be ten librae of copper, that of the quinarius five librae, and that of the sestertius two librae and a half. The weight, however, of the libra of copper was diminished during the First Punic War, the republic not having the means to meet its expenditure: in consequence of which, an ordinance was made that the *as* should in the future be struck of two ounces weight. By this contrivance a saving of five-sixths was effected, and the public debt was liquidated."

Pliny, *N. H.*, 33, 47: Aureus [10] nummus post annos LI percussus

---

[8] This statement is absolutely incorrect.

[9] Pliny makes the same error as Festus; see note 6.

[10] This is the restored text of Mommsen. The manuscripts differ in the case of both numerals. Modern authorities differ widely about the date of the first gold coinage. Bahrfeldt, *Röm. Goldmünzen*, 1923, 10, insists on 269 B. C.; Hill, *Hist. Rom. Coins*, 37, prefers 242; Mommsen, *R. Münzwesen*, 300, accepts 217; Willers, in *Corolla Num.*, 312, adopts 209 B. C. We shall discuss the date in the next chapter.

est quam argenteus ita, ut scripulum valeret sestertios vicenos, quod efficit in libram ratione sestertii, qui tunc erat $\overline{V}DCCLX$ (?): " The first golden coin was struck fifty-one years after that of silver, the scruple of gold being valued at twenty sesterces; a computation which gave, according to the value of the sesterce then in use, 5760 (?) sesterces to each libra of gold."

6. *Value of Money, and Prices.*

What is the value of these coins in gold and in commodities? We shall begin with the second century system when something like a stable standard had been adopted. At that time the denarius weighed one-seventh of an ounce (3.9 grams) so that eighty-four were struck to the pound (327.45 grams); and it remained quite constant at that weight till Nero's day. The pound of gold (327.45 grams) was usually (except at times of abundant gold) reckoned at 1,000 denarii, so that the ratio was about 12:1 and, since the Troy ounce of gold today sells at \$20.67, the Roman pound of gold would be worth about \$217.75. Hence the denarius ought to be reckoned at 21.7 cents. However, since in the classical period the ratio often falls slightly below 12:1 and hardly ever rises above, I shall in this volume reckon the *denarius at 20 cents, the sesterce at 5 cents, and the as at $1\frac{1}{4}$ cents* in equating metallic values.

Between 269 and 217 (if we adopt the orthodox dating) the denarius was heavier, weighing 4.55 grams, and ought therefore to reckon at 23-24 cents for that period, if we assume the same gold ratio. What the ratio was we do not know, but gold was then scarce at Rome and seems to have been costly as a commodity. The ratio is usually reckoned about 15:1 or over. What the metal values were in useful commodities it is more difficult to say.

For the convenience of the court the lex Julia Papiria had before the Veian War equated values for fines as follows:

$$1 \text{ ox} = 10 \text{ sheep} = 100 \text{ pounds bronze}$$

In the coinage of 269 the Roman pound weighing one-sixth more was adopted, but the court was not likely to concern itself with this. Since the pound now made 6 *asses* and 10 were worth a denarius, the ratio in silver probably stood:

$$1 \text{ ox} = 10 \text{ sheep} = 60 \text{ denarii}$$

and I assume that this ratio probably remained even when the denarius was reduced an eighth in 217. For purposes of fines, therefore, we would say that, in silver values, the ratio

$$1 \text{ ox} = 10 \text{ sheep} = \$12 \ (1 \text{ sheep} = \$1.20)$$

would represent prices recognized by the court in the primitive agrarian conditions of the fourth and third centuries. But we may be very sure that prices of cattle and of bronze fluctuated very much and that conservative court reckonings did not always represent actual values.

There are some other statements that may be of some little use. When about 406 the state began to provide horses for cavalry, the price for two (*paribus equis*, Festus, 247 L) was 1,000 pounds of bronze (*mille assarium*, Varro, *L. L.*, 8, 71), and is calculated by later writers (Livy, 1, 43, 9; Festus, 71 L) at 10,000 *asses*. This is of course the one-ounce *as* of the second century (1,000 pounds of 273 grams = 10,000 ounces at $\frac{327}{12}$). One horse ought therefore to be worth 5,000 one-ounce *asses* of the second century (each one-sixteenth of a denarius) or 312.5 denarii = \$62.50. But, in the first place, soldiers' allowances reckoned 10 asses to the denarius and perhaps the knights therefore were allowed 500 denarii for each horse, secondly the allowance may have been liberal because the knight seems to have had the obligation of replacement. Perhaps \$62.50 may be considered a fair price for a good cavalry horse, though the knight may have received \$100 for each.

Again the yearly sum for fodder (the *hordearium aes* = the "barley bronze") for two horses was 2,000 *asses* (Livy, 1, 43, 9; Fest., 91 L). Later, according to Polybius, 6, 39, barley was given instead of money and the allowance was 504 modii (126 bushels) per year for the two horses. Assuming the military ratio of 10 *asses* = 1 denarius, this will give 200 denarii for 504 modii, or $\frac{2}{5}$ denarius the modius, or $1\frac{3}{5}$ denarii (32 cents) the bushel. Since barley usually sold at from one-half to two-thirds the price of wheat, we may reckon wheat as worth a little less than 3 denarii the bushel (3 sesterces the modius, which happens to be the normal price in Cicero's day).

We have then the following tentative prices in silver for the third century:

a cavalry horse	\$62–\$100
an ox	\$12–\$20

a sheep	$1.20–$2
a bushel of wheat	about 60 cents
a bushel of barley	about 32 cents

The calculations have too many unknown quantities to be of much value, but the figures prove to be reasonable when compared with later prices. We can hardly make any use of the ransom price of captives given by Livy, 10, 31, 4, for the year 295 (310 *asses* per head), since it is difficult to suppose that he refers either to the old one-pound *as* or to the late one-ounce *as*. If Fabius was Livy's source the coin may have been one of the intermediate ones used in Fabius' youth.

7. *Art and Industry.*

In *Etruria* [11] art was still vigorous and showed some originality though there are numerous signs of decay. The tomb-paintings are numerous and reveal certain new motives, especially in their preoccupation with funerary scenes. Typical are the François tomb of Vulci with its Macstrna scene, the Orchus tomb at Corneto, and much good work at Orvieto and Clusium. Several excellent statues in bronze from Etruria and Umbria show that Tuscan art was closely in touch with Greece in the fourth century, that artists were adequate in their technique, and that the native bronze industry had not deteriorated. Characteristic pieces are the Mars of Todi and a fine head from Cagli and a large number of smaller bronzes.

There is also a new vigor in architectural terracotta work for pediments of temples. After the fall of Veii, both Falerii and Volsinii seem to have prospered. Two old Faliscan temples were redecorated in the Hellenistic style and a new one, handsomely ornamented, was erected, and two temples at Volsinii (Orvieto) have also supplied rich remains from this period.

At the opening of the third century the artistic and industrial activity of Etruria is reflected by the terracotta decoration at Vulci, Orvieto, Falerii, Vetulonia, Telamo, and by the interesting reliefs of the tomb *degli Scudi* at Caere. The artists were still in close touch with Greece and quickly reflected any and every Hellenistic invention.

It is difficult to suppose that *Rome*, the most flourishing state in Italy, was not likewise a center of such art, but of that supposition,

---

[11] See Ducati, *Storia dell'arte etrusca*, 411 ff., for descriptions, bibliography, and, in vol. II, illustrations.

frequently made, we have little proof. A single terracotta head of this period—a very beautiful one—has survived in the suburbs of Rome (Della Seta, *Villa Giulia,* 271). After the great Samnite war there were a number of temples built, chiefly due to vows made by generals on the battlefield. The list, given by Wissowa,[12] is:

302 ⸗ Temple of Salus, on the Quirinal
296 Bellona
295 Juppiter Victor, and Venus Obsequens
294 Victoria, and Juppiter Stator, both on the Palatine
293 Quirinus, and Fors Fortuna
291 Aesculapius on the island
278 Summanus
272 Consus

Of these, the Temple of Salus was decorated with frescoes made by an ancestor of Fabius Pictor, the first native painter mentioned. They were doubtless done in the Etruscan style (cf. Pliny, 35, 19). In the Temple of Bellona Appius Claudius placed shields that bore portraits of his ancestors. The Temple of Aesculapius was decorated with paintings (Varro, *L. L.,* 7, 57) perhaps made at the time of the building. The Temple of Consus had at least a portrait in fresco of its dedicant, Papirius Cursor (Festus, 228 L.), and several temples of the next period were so embellished. We happen to have a fragment of a military scene from a fourth century tomb of the Esquiline. It belongs to the good fresco work of the period, and leaves the impression that at Rome the art was not inferior to that of Capua and Etruria. But it may be, of course, that the artists were imported. Not a fragment has been identified with certainty from any of the temples mentioned above, but since efforts were made to decorate these interiors, and we have one fragment from near Rome, we may assume that some, at least, had the usual terracotta revetments and pediments known from so many Etruscan temples of the period. Of statuary we hear only that the Senate erected statues (probably terracotta or bronze) of Pythagoras and Alcibiades (Pliny, *N. H.,* 34, 26), but where these were made we do not know. Certainly the judgments of South Italian towns deter-

---

[12] Wissowa, *Religion und Kult. der Römer,* Anhang II. Platner and Ashby, *Top. Dict. of Anc. Rome,* give the references.

mined the choice of these two, and perhaps supplied the sculptors. It is fair to assume that these temples were not unlike those of Falerii.

In Praeneste,[13] at the eastern edge of Latium, a vigorous industry in artistic bronze is proved for the period by the numerous finely decorated mirrors and ornamental bronze boxes (cistae) that have been found in the graves. The ornamental handles are usually moulded, but the plane surfaces are charmingly engraved with representations of Greek mythological scenes. This excellent output is usually attributed to the survival of an old Etruscan industry at Praeneste that had partly fallen into the hands of Campanian-Greek workmen, a natural development in a city that lay on the highway between Capua and Etruria. A mirror inscribed *Vifis Pilipus* (Vibius Philippus) *cailavit* would indicate that Campanian-Greeks were to some extent engaged in the work. The inscriptions are in Latin but the names of the mythological personages frequently show the influence of Etruscan pronunciation (Alixentr, Casenter, etc.). The surprising fact is that one of the most charming boxes bears an inscription of a Roman maker:

Novios Plautios med Romai fecid (Dessau, I. L. S., 8562) " Novius Plautius made me at Rome."

The natural inference from this inscription is that Rome also had its industry in these wares. Whether Praeneste or Rome was the center of the industry, we cannot yet say.

Pottery of a good grade was still being made in Southern Etruria on old Greek models (cf. *Boll. d'Arte,* 1916, 367, for Falerii). And the Latin colony of Cales (founded 334) was soon producing a successful, if not beautiful, ware (Pagenstecher, *Calenische Reliefkeramik,* cf. *C. I. L.,* 1², 405-417.). Rome, to judge from the finds in the simple Esquiline graves, was at this time using the cheap black " Campanian " ware (Dressel, *Ann. d'Inst.,* 1880, 328) but, of course, was also making ordinary ware in her own potteries (in figlinis, Varro, *L. L.,* 5, 50). Here simple burial rites did not call for the elaborate urns demanded by the Etruscans, and there was probably no luxury-trade as yet for household demands.

The continued wars must also have supported a steady industry in

[13] Jahn, *Die Ficoronische Cista;* Della Seta, *Villa Giulia,* 339; Matthies, *Die Praen. Spiegel;* Savignone, in *Boll. d'Arte,* 1916, 367; Ernout, in *Mem. Soc. Ling.,* 1905; Gummerus, art. " Industrie und Handel," in *Realenc.,* IX; *C. I. L.,* I², supp., 721-22.

the making of weapons, armor, vehicles of transport, and military
clothing, and there is no reason to suppose that Roman shops did not
supply the household utensils and table ware, the furniture and the
farm implements that were needed in the city and the nearby country.
From the activities of Appius Claudius, the famous liberal censor of
312 B. C., we draw the conclusion that there was a fairly large free
industrial class at Rome which made their needs felt and their political
power evident.   The day of ubiquitous slaves had not yet arrived.

Appius Claudius, as censor, built an underground aqueduct at state
expense for the purpose of bringing pure water into the thickly settled
quarters of the city (the famous Aqua Appia), and then laid out and
graded the Appian Way as far as Capua (for military rather than
economic purposes, presumably).   He admitted the right of sons of
ex-slaves to hold curule office, and permitted urban people who did not
own land to register in whatever tribes they chose.   This last measure
seems to imply that there were enough free laboring-men in the city so
that, if they were allowed to register in the rural wards, they might
control the votes of more than the four city wards.   And the same fact
is implied in the act of the censors of 304, who restricted the registration of the urban landless voters to the four urban wards.   The decree
seems not to have had special reference to freedmen, though Plutarch
(*Popl.*, 7) thought it did.   The passages in Diodorus and Livy bearing
on the subject are discussed by Mommsen,[14] De Sanctis [15] (who emphasizes the military importance of the measure adopted when citizens
were needed for the legions) and E. Meyer,[16] (who calls attention to
the social and economic aspect of the decree).   The passages are as
follows:

Diod., 20, 36, 1-4:

τῷ δήμῳ γὰρ τὸ κεχαρισμένον ποιῶν οὐδένα λόγον ἐποιεῖτο τῆς συγκλήτου. καὶ
πρῶτον μὲν τὸ καλούμενον Ἄππιον ὕδωρ ἀπὸ σταδίων ὀγδοήκοντα κατήγαγεν εἰς
τὴν Ῥώμην, καὶ πολλὰ τῶν δημοσίων χρημάτων εἰς ταύτην τὴν κατασκευὴν ἀνήλωσεν
ἄνευ δόγματος τῆς συγκλήτου· μετὰ δὲ ταῦτα τῆς ἀφ' ἑαυτοῦ κληθείσης Ἀππίας
ὁδοῦ τὸ πλέον μέρος λίθοις στερεοῖς κατέστρωσεν ἀπὸ Ῥώμης μέχρι Καπύης, ὄντος
τοῦ διαστήματος σταδίων πλειόνων ἢ χιλίων, . . . κατέμιξε δὲ καὶ τὴν σύγκλητον,

---

[14] *Staatsrecht*, III, 435.
[15] *Storia dei Romani*, II, 226.
[16] Art. " Plebs," in Conrad, *Handwörterbuch*.   It is interesting to find that the
state would undertake such public works as the draining of the Veline Lake as
early as 290 B. C. in order to provide land for settlement. Cic., *ad Att.*, 4, 15, 5.

οὐ τοὺς εὐγενεῖς καὶ προέχοντας τοῖς ἀξιώμασι προσγράφων μόνον, ὡς ἦν ἔθος, ἀλλὰ
πολλοὺς καὶ τῶν ἀπελευθέρων υἱοὺς ἀνέμιξεν· ἐφ᾿ οἷς βαρέως ἔφερον οἱ καυχώμενοι
ταῖς εὐγενείαις. ἔδωκε δὲ τοῖς πολίταις καὶ τὴν ἐξουσίαν ὅποι προαιροῖντο τιμήσασθαι.

(Appius Claudius as censor) " favoring the populace, disregarded
the senate. First he built for the city through 80 stadia the Appian
aqueduct that bears his name, taking for the work a large amount of
money from the public treasury without the permission of the Senate.
Then he paved with hard stone a large part of the Appian Way that
leads from Rome to Capua, a distance of over 1,000 stadia . . . He
also brought new men into the Senate by choosing not only nobles and
distinguished men as had been the custom, but also sons of liberti, so
that those who boasted patrician birth were offended. In addition he
gave the citizens the privilege of enrolling in whatever tribe they
wished."

Livy, 9, 29, 5:

Et censura clara eo anno Ap. Claudi et C. Plauti fuit; memoriae
tamen felicioris ad posteros nomen Appi, quod viam munivit et aquam
in urbem duxit; . . .

" Noteworthy, too, in that year was the censorship of Appius Claudius
and Gaius Plautius; but the name of Appius was of happier memory
with succeeding generations, because he built a road, and conveyed a
stream of water into the City."

Livy, 9, 46, 10-14:

Ceterum Flavium dixerat aedilem forensis factio, Ap. Claudi censura
vires nacta, qui senatum primus libertinorum filiis lectis inquinaverat,
et posteaquam eam lectionem nemo ratam habuit nec in curia adeptus
erat quas petierat opes, urbanis humilibus per omnes tribus divisis
forum et campum corrupit. . . . donec Q. Fabius et P. Decius censores
facti, et Fabius simul concordiae causa, simul ne humillimorum in
manu comitia essent, omnem forensem turbam excretam in quattuor
tribus coniecit urbanasque eas appellavit.

" Now Flavius had been elected aedile by the faction of the market-
place, which had become powerful in consequence of the censorship of
Appius Claudius. Claudius had been the first to debase the Senate by
the appointment of the sons of freedmen, and afterwards, when no one
allowed the validity of his selection and he had failed to gain the influ-

ence in the senate-house which had been his object, he had distributed
the humble denizens of the city amongst all the tribes, and had thus
corrupted the Forum and the Campus Martius. . . . until Quintus
Fabius and Publius Decius became censors (304 B. C.), and Fabius,
partly for the sake of harmony, partly that the elections might not be
in the hands of the basest of the people, culled out all the market-place
mob and cast them into four tribes, to which he gave the name of
Urban."

If there are but slight indications of industry at Rome, we need also
to recall the heavy colonization that continued during the fifty years
after the censorship of Appius Claudius which tended to drain off the
propertyless citizens with offers of land. This movement suffices to
explain why industrial development ceased at Rome and why there are
seldom any rumors of class disturbances for over a century and a half
after Claudius' censorship.

8. *Commerce.*

Some time during the fourth century Rome built a heavy stone wall
about a small enclosure of 120 by 193 meters at the mouth of the Tiber,
not on but near the river. The site has not been fully excavated, but
the material of the wall indicates that it was built not long after the
middle of the century.[17] This fortification may either indicate that
Rome needed protection against the " pirates " of Antium—a city that
was captured in 340—or that Rome was now interested in commerce
on the sea. The area is exceedingly small, only five and a half acres,
and would hardly hold more than a small garrison, it contained no
store rooms so far as is apparent, and apparently it had no docks.
Furthermore there is no evidence of any increase in the town till the
Gracchan day. It would be daring to conclude from these walls that
the Romans were engaged in seaborne trade. The purport of the
Carthaginian treaty of 348 (renewed in 305, Livy, 9, 43, 26) we have
discussed above. It may, but need not, be an indication that Romans
were trading in Sicily and Libya. In 282 some Roman ships appeared
at the harbour of Tarentum and were attacked on the plea that they
were violating an old treaty by appearing in Tarentine waters. It is
generally supposed that they were on their way to the Adriatic colonies
recently founded. The inference is that Roman traders had not

---

[17] Calza, *Guida di Ostia*, 25; Frank, *Roman Buildings*, 21.

appeared at South Italian towns up to that date. The supposition of Polybius when he wrote about the naval efforts of the Romans in the First Punic War was that they had had no experience at sea.[18] The fair inference from all this seems to be that the heavy inland colonization, necessitated by the warfare in Italy, kept the Romans out of commercial as well as out of industrial development.

There are no reliable facts with which to attempt an estimate of Rome's private or public wealth for this period. See the unsuccessful attempt of Cavaignac, *Population et Capital,* ch. IX.

[18] Rome seems to have had no navy of any importance before 260 B. C. In 338 (Livy, 8, 14, 8) Rome had deprived Antium of her fleet (*naves longae abactae*) and some of the ships seem to have been kept (*ibid.*, 12, *partim in navalia Romae subductae*); the rest were burned and their beaks attached to the speaker's platform (*partim incensae, rostris earum suggestum . . . adornari placuit*). In 311, we are told (Livy, 9, 30, 4), the people elected two naval officers to fit out a fleet (*duumviros navales classis ornandae reficiandaeque. causa*), and in the next year this fleet is reported raiding the coast near Pompeii, but without much effect (Livy, 9, 38, 2). In 282 (Livy, *Epit.* 12; App., *Sam.*, 7, 1) a fleet of some ten Roman ships appeared off Tarentum and was attacked by the Tarentines as violating an old treaty that forbade the Romans to sail beyond the Lacinian cape. Several ships were sunk. Finally in the Punic treaty of 272 (Pol., 3, 25) Carthage pledged herself to provide transportation in case a joint attack were made on Sicily. It would appear, therefore, that Rome had some few ships at various times before the Punic War, but a very inadequate number.

When the First Punic War broke out and Rome had to invade Sicily, it was necessary to ask the " naval allies " of South Italy for transportation, since Rome had no ships (Pol., 1, 20, 14). Then after three years of warfare Rome decided to build a fleet with which, if possible, to drive off the seas the Punic fleet which was bringing troops and supplies to the army in Sicily. The year 260 seems to mark the beginning of a real navy.

CHAPTER II

DURING THE FIRST AND SECOND PUNIC WARS

I. CHRONOLOGY, 264-200 B. C.

264 First Punic War begins. First naval battle, 260; Regulus in Africa, 256.

241 End, cession of Sicily to Rome.

242 Office of praetor peregrinus.

232 Ager Gallicus colonized.

229 First Illyrian War.

227 Sicily organized as province.

225 Gallic invasion.

220 Second Illyrian War.

218 Hannibal invades Italy. Second Punic War, 218-201.

217 Defeat at Trasimene Lake; 216, Cannae, Capua revolts; 207, Metaurus.

201 Treaty of peace.

II. CENSUS STATISTICS (ADULT MALE CITIZENS), AND COLONIES

264 B. C.	292,234	(Livy, *Epit.* 16, cf. *Eutrop.*, II, 18)
251 B. C.	297,797	(Livy, *Epit.* 18)
246 B. C.	241,212	(Livy, *Epit.* 19)
240 B. C.	260,000	(Hieron., Olymp., 134, 1)
233 B. C.	270,713	(Livy, *Epit.* 20)
208 B. C.	137,108	(Livy, 27, 36)
204 B. C.	214,000	(Livy, 29, 37)

The *ager Romanus* comprised about 10,000 square miles, or a fifth of Italy below the Rubicon before the Second Punic War. The losses of the First Punic War are reflected in the decrease of over 50,000 in the census of 246. Since some of this loss should have appeared in the figure for 251, our manuscript of Livy, *Epit.* 18 may be incorrect.

The item for 233 is corroborated by the interesting summary given by Polybius, 2, 24, of the Roman and allied forces mustered on the occasion of the Gallic invasion (see below). The number for 208, which shows a decrease of nearly 50%, is usually altered by editors, but may be the correct census figure. The defection of Capua in 216 would account for a loss of about 50,000, since Capua could contribute 34,000

56

men for active service (Livy, 23, 5, 15); the defeats at the Trebia, Trasimene Lake, Cannae, and in Spain had cost about 50-60,000 legionaries; furthermore, the censors did not always count the troops stationed outside Italy (Livy, 29, 37), and may have disregarded the four legions in Spain, the two in Sardinia, the two in Sicily, and those guarding Gaul. At any rate the number given for 208 does not represent a full census. The figure for 204 (214,000) probably gives the correct number of free adult males for the period just before the close of the war. The two wars had cost Rome nearly a third of her adult male citizens and doubtless the Italian allies suffered fully as much. For the census of the period see Beloch, *Bevölkerung der Griech-Röm. Welt;* E. Meyer, " Bevölkerungswesen," in Conrad, *Handwörterbuch;* Nissen, *Ital. Landeskunde,* II, 99; Ruggiero, *Diz. Epig., s. v.* Censor; De Sanctis, *Storia dei Romani,* III, 327; Frank, in *Classical Philology,* 1924, 329, and *American Journal of Philology,* 1930, 313; Kromayer und Veith, *Heerwesen und Kriegführung,* 306; Liebenam, art. " Dilectus," in *R. E.*

The population of the rest of Italy (comprising 40,000 square miles or about four fifths of the peninsula south of the Rubicon): Polybius, 2, 24, gives a muster of the active allied forces drawn up by Rome before the Gallic invasion of 225. The figures are derived from Fabius Pictor and are probably correct so far as they go:

Polybius, 2, 24, 3-16:

μετὰ μὲν δὴ τῶν ὑπάτων ἐξεληλύθει τέτταρα στρατόπεδα Ῥωμαϊκά, πεντάκις μὲν χιλίους καὶ διακοσίους πεζικούς, ἱππεῖς δὲ τριακοσίους ἔχον ἕκαστον. σύμμαχοι δὲ μεθ᾽ ἑκατέρων ἦσαν οἱ συνάμφω πεζοὶ μὲν τρισμύριοι, δισχίλιοι δ᾽ ἱππεῖς. τῶν δ᾽ ἐκ τοῦ καιροῦ προσβοηθησάντων εἰς τὴν Ῥώμην Σαβίνων καὶ Τυρρηνῶν ἱππεῖς μὲν ἦσαν εἰς τετρακισχιλίους, πεζοὶ δὲ πλείους τῶν πεντακισμυρίων. τούτους μὲν ἀθροίσαντες ὡς ἐπὶ Τυρρηνίας προεκάθισαν, ἐξαπέλεκυν αὐτοῖς ἡγεμόνα συστήσαντες. οἱ δὲ τὸν Ἀπεννῖνον κατοικοῦντες Ὄμβροι καὶ Σαρσινάτοι συνήχθησαν εἰς δισμυρίους, μετὰ δὲ τούτων Ούένετοι καὶ Γονομάνοι δισμύριοι. τούτους δ᾽ ἔταξαν ἐπὶ τῶν ὅρων τῆς Γαλατίας, ἵν᾽ ἐμβαλόντες εἰς τὴν τῶν Βοίων χώραν ἀντιπερισπῶσι τοὺς ἐξεληλυθότας. τὰ μὲν οὖν προκαθημένα στρατόπεδα τῆς χώρας ταῦτ᾽ ἦν. ἐν δὲ τῇ Ῥώμῃ διέτριβον ἡτοιμασμένοι χάριν τῶν συμβαινόντων ἐν τοῖς πολέμοις, ἐφεδρείας ἔχοντες τάξιν, Ῥωμαίων μὲν αὐτῶν πεζοὶ δισμύριοι, μετὰ δὲ τούτων ἱππεῖς χίλιοι καὶ πεντακόσιοι, τῶν δὲ συμμάχων πεζοὶ μὲν τρισμύριοι, δισχίλιοι δ᾽ ἱππεῖς. καταγραφαὶ δ᾽ ἀνηνέχθησαν Λατίνων μὲν ὀκτακισμύριοι πεζοί, πεντακισχίλιοι δ᾽ ἱππεῖς, Σαυνιτῶν δὲ πεζοὶ μὲν ἑπτακισμύριοι, μετὰ δὲ τούτων ἱππεῖς ἑπτακισχίλιοι, καὶ μὴν Ἰαπύγων καὶ Μεσσαπίων συνάμφω πεζῶν μὲν πέντε μυριάδες, ἱππεῖς δὲ μύριοι σὺν ἑξακισχιλίοις, Λευκανῶν δὲ πεζοὶ μὲν τρισμύριοι, τρισχίλιοι δ᾽ ἱππεῖς, Μαρσῶν δὲ καὶ Μαρρουκίνων καὶ Φρεντανῶν, ἔτι δ᾽ Ούεστίνων, πεζοὶ μὲν δισμύριοι, τετρακισχίλιοι δ᾽ ἱππεῖς. ἔτι γε μὴν κἂν Σικελίᾳ καὶ Τάραντι στρατόπεδα δύο παρεφήδρευεν, ὧν ἑκάτερον ἦν ἀνὰ τετρακισχιλίους καὶ διακοσίους πεζούς, ἱππεῖς δὲ διακοσίους. Ῥωμαίων δὲ καὶ Καμπανῶν ἡ πληθὺς πεζῶν μὲν· εἰς εἴκοσι καὶ πέντε κατελέχθησαν μυριάδες, ἱππέων δ᾽ ἐπὶ ταῖς δύο μυριάσιν ἐπῆσαν ἔτι τρεῖς χιλιάδες. ὥστ᾽ εἶναι τὸ [κεφάλαιον τῶν μὲν προκαθημένων τῆς Ῥώμης δυνάμεων πεζοὶ μὲν ὑπὲρ πεντεκαίδεκα μυριάδες, ἱππεῖς δὲ πρὸς ἑξακισχιλίους, τὸ δὲ] σύμπαν πλῆθος τῶν δυναμένων ὅπλα βαστάζειν αὐτῶν τε Ῥωμαίων καὶ τῶν συμμάχων πεζῶν ὑπὲρ τὰς ἑβδομήκοντα μυριάδας, ἱππέων δ᾽ εἰς ἑπτὰ μυριάδας.

" Each of the consuls was in command of four legions of Roman citizens consisting of five thousand two hundred foot and three hundred horse. The allied forces in each consular army numbered thirty thousand foot and two thousand horse. The cavalry of the Sabines and Etruscans, who had come to the temporary assistance of Rome, were four thousand strong, their infantry above fifty thousand. The Romans massed these forces and posted them on the frontier of Etruria under the command of a praetor. The levy of the Umbrians and Sarsinatae inhabiting the Apennines amounted to about twenty thousand, and with these were twenty thousand Veneti and Cenomani. These they stationed on the frontier of Gaul, to invade the territory of the Boii and divert them back from their expedition. These were the armies protecting the Roman territory. In Rome itself there was a reserve force ready for any contingency, consisting of twenty thousand foot and fifteen hundred horse, all Roman citizens, and thirty thousand foot and two thousand horse furnished by the allies. The lists of men able to bear arms that had been returned were as follows. Latins eighty thousand foot and five thousand horse, Samnites seventy thousand foot and seven thousand horse, Iapygians and Messapians fifty thousand foot and sixteen thousand horse, Lucanians thirty thousand foot and three thousand horse, Marsi, Marrucini, Frentani, and Vestini twenty thousand foot and four thousand horse. In Sicily and Tarentum were two reserve legions, each consisting of four thousand two hundred foot and two hundred horse. Of Romans and Campanians there were on the roll two hundred and fifty thousand and about twenty-three thousand horse; so that the total number of Romans and allies able to bear arms was more than seven hundred thousand foot and seventy thousand horse." . . .

The sum of regular allied forces here given is about 375,000 (if we subtract the Cisalpine peoples, and the enfranchised Sabines), but this list is not made on the same basis as the Roman census, for the Roman census recorded all adult male voters, whereas the list of allies gave only males fit for *active* service in the army (i. e. able-bodied citizens of allied tribes and cities between 17 and 46 years of age). Furthermore, this list does not mention the southern Greeks (who were exempt from army service) nor the Bruttians (who were employed in menial service). Hence we should have to .multiply the given list by two (approximately) to make the sum correspond to the Roman census list of about 273,000 adult males. The complete population of Italy, south of the Rubicon, in 225 was therefore about four million souls, one fourth of whom were Romans. Almost one fourth of the allied troops (85,000) were Latins living in cities that had been colonized by Rome, and they were to a large extent Romanized.

The colonization of the period was usually, but not always, determined by military considerations. We hear of only four Roman colonies (maritime colonies of 300 citizens each), and these were planted along the coast during the First Punic War when Carthage was threatening Italy:

264 Castrum Novum in Etruria (Vell., 1, 14)

247 Alsium in Etruria (Vell., 1, 14; cf. Livy, 27, 38)

247 Aesis on the Adriatic coast (Vell., 1, 14)

245 Fregenae in Etruria (Livy, *Epit.* 19; Vell., 1, 14)

The three colonies planted in Etruria are fairly near Rome and doubtless were organized to protect Rome from the raids of the Punic navy.

The *Latin colonies* of the period were fairly large and were all planted at strategic points with reference to the needs of the Federation:

268 Ariminum (Livy, *Epit.* 15; Vell., 1, 14) was founded at the north edge of the Ager Gallicus, recently taken from the Senones. Its military purpose is evident.

264 Firmum (Vell., 1, 14) was planted on the coast a little further south to hold the Picentes in check.

258 Beneventum (Pol., 3, 90; Livy, *Epit.* 15; Vell., 1, 14) was designed to separate the Samnites and Lucanians and to protect the approaches to the Adriatic from Capua.

253 Aesernia (Livy, *Epit.* 16) was to hold the head waters of the Volturnus, which penetrated the heart of northern Samnium.

246 Brundisium (Livy, *Epit.* 19; Vell., 1, 14; Zon., 8, 7) was organized to serve as Rome's port for the East, at a time when the Punic fleet had cut off Rome's maritime approaches to the Adriatic.

241 Spoletium (Livy, *Epit.* 20; Vell., 1, 14) was planted in Umbria on the road that led from Rome to Ariminum. Its strong walls later repelled the assaults of Hannibal.

Being planted to serve military needs at important points, all these colonies were fairly large. Beloch, *Ital. Bund.*, 143, estimates the territory of Ariminum at about 250 square miles, Beneventum (some of it mountainous) at 400, Brundisium at about 150. The number of colonists is not given, but, since the two rather large colonies of 218 received 6,000 landholders each, we may hazard an average of at least 4,000 for each of the six mentioned. Of the 25,000 or more colonists that we have assumed, not more than half need have been Roman citizens. The Romans who settled in the Latin colonies of this period were denied the right, formerly granted, of regaining citizenship by returning to Rome. These new colonies were to be permanent and Rome did not wish the colonists to desert their posts.

The Ager Gallicus. In 232 the popular tribune Flaminius, against the vigorous opposition of the Senate, passed a plebiscite to distribute to citizens the Ager Gallicus, that apparently was being rented out for the benefit of the treasury. Perhaps citizens had been objecting to being assigned to Latin colonies where they had to give up their status and assume responsibilities in surroundings not always friendly. At any rate the war indemnity of 241 relieved the treasury so that the land rents were not needed. Viritane assignments had been made during the previous century at Veii and in the ager Falernus, but in the ager Gallicus the assignment was to be made nearly 200 miles from Rome with no organized city life available nearby. Polybius, in speaking of it, repeats the criticism which he found in Fabius, who of course shared the point of view of the aristocracy which profited from renting the public land. The words of Polybius are as follows:

Polybius 2, 21, 7-8:

κατεκληρούχησαν ἐν Γαλατίᾳ Ῥωμαῖοι τὴν Πικεντίνην προσαγορευομένην χώραν, ἐξ ἧς νικήσαντες ἐξέβαλον τοὺς Σήνωνας προσαγορευομένους Γαλάτας, Γαΐου Φλαμινίου ταύτην τὴν δημαγωγίαν εἰσηγησαμένου καὶ πολιτείαν, ἣν δὴ καὶ Ῥωμαίοις ὡς ἔπος εἰπεῖν φατέον ἀρχηγὸν μὲν γενέσθαι τῆς ἐπὶ τὸ χεῖρον τοῦ δήμου διαστροφῆς, . . .

"the Romans divided among their citizens the territory in Gaul known as Picenum, from which they had ejected the Senones when they conquered them. Gaius Flaminius was the originator of this popular policy, which we must pronounce to have been, one may say, the first step in the demoralization of the populace."

The law was called *de agro Piceno et Gallico viritim dividendo*; Cic., *Cato*, 11, *Brut.*, 57. Cato, quoted by Varro, *R.R.*, 1, 2, 7, defines the Ager Gallicus as being

the land between Ariminum and Picenum (ultra Agrum Picentium) that was
assigned *viritim*.

Presumably the Senones had driven out some Picentes (as well as Umbrians) so
that the region could be called " Picenus et Gallicus " or " Gallicus in Piceno." There
is no evidence that any part of real Picenum was assigned at this time (cf. *Klio*,
1911, 373). There were about 500 square miles of arable public land between Ancona
and Ariminum. With assignments of seven jugera there would be room for 60,000
settlers. Rome, with a census of about 270,000, certainly did not have that number
to spare. Since a Gracchan boundary stone (*C. I. L.*, I², 719, restored in 82 B. C.)
has been found near Pisaurum, there can be no doubt that some land remained
public at this time. The law was famous, and a forerunner of the Gracchan reforms
(cf. Livy, 21, 63, 4; Cic., *de Inv.*, 2, 52, and *Brut.*, 57; Dionys., 2, 26, 5).

Finally, in 218, large Latin colonies of 6,000 settlers each were sent
to

218   *Cremona* (Pol., 3, 40; Livy, *Epit.* 20; Vell., 1, 14);
218   *Placentia* (Pol., 3, 40; Livy, *Epit.* 20; Ascon. in Cic., *Piso,* 2;
         Vell., 1, 14).

These two colonies were designed to hold the Gauls of the Po Valley in
check. They had to be recolonized after the war.

Such was the colonization and, though most of it was military in
purpose and Latin in name, it was so extensive that we may assume that
by 218 every man who desired a plot of land had secured one, that
Roman and Latin " small farmers " were well distributed over Italy
when Hannibal invaded the peninsula, and that agricultural opportunities had once more attracted men away from entering other occupations.
Had Rome developed her industry and commerce instead of her agrarian
colonies, she would not have had the man power to withstand the
brilliant generalship of Hannibal.

III. PUBLIC EXPENSES AND INCOME DURING THE FIRST PUNIC WAR

During the war the losses of ships and men not only in battle but
even more by storm were enormous because of the Roman ignorance of
sea-craft. The figures given by Polybius are as follows:

1, 20, 10, Rome built 100 quinqueremes and 20 triremes.
1, 25, 7 (256 B. C.), a fleet of 330 decked ships was fitted out for the
     invasion of Africa. Every ship bore 300 rowers and 120 soldiers.
1, 36, 10 (255), Rome launched 350 ships.
1, 37, 2, all but 80 vessels of her fleet were destroyed by storm.

1, 38, 6 (255), Rome built 220 ships in three months.

1, 39, 6 (253), lost 150 ships in a storm.

1, 51, 12, and 54, 8, lost most of the fleet.

1, 63, 6, Polybius states that during the war Rome lost some 700 quinqueremes. This number clearly contains some duplications. Tarn, in *Jour. Hell. Stud.*, 1907, pp. 48 ff., estimates the loss at about 500, and we shall accept his estimate here.

We are to assume that Rome distributed the contracts for ships to some extent among the Greek ports of South Italy where the art of shipbuilding was better known then at Rome, and doubtless Greeks and Etruscans were hired to direct the work done at Rome and the Latian coast towns. The funds, however, the Roman treasury had to supply, until the last year of the war, when the treasury was exhausted. The ships were then provided by private subscription, the state mortgaging the proceeds of the anticipated booty and indemnity to the private citizens who provided the ships. This method of financing a war was borrowed from the Greek " liturgy " and is an interesting anticipation of war loans. Polybius' account of the first fleet is as follows:

Pol., 1, 20, 9-10; 13-14:

Θεωροῦντες δὲ τὸν πόλεμον αὐτοῖς τριβὴν λαμβάνοντα, τότε πρῶτον ἐπεβάλοντο ναυπηγεῖσθαι σκάφη, πεντηρικὰ μὲν ἑκατόν, εἴκοσι δὲ τριήρεις. τῶν δὲ ναυπηγῶν εἰς τέλος ἀπείρων ὄντων τῆς περὶ τὰς πεντήρεις ναυπηγίας διὰ τὸ μηδένα τότε τῶν κατὰ τὴν Ἰταλίαν κεχρῆσθαι τοιούτοις σκάφεσι, πολλὴν αὐτοῖς παρεῖχε τοῦτο τὸ μέρος δυσχέρειαν. . . . ὅτε γὰρ τὸ πρῶτον ἐπεχείρησαν διαβιβάζειν εἰς τὴν Μεσσήνην τὰς δυνάμεις, οὐχ οἷον κατάφρακτος αὐτοῖς ὑπῆρχε ναῦς, ἀλλ' οὐδὲ καθόλου μακρὸν πλοῖον οὐδὲ λέμβος οὐδ' εἷς, ἀλλὰ παρὰ Ταραντίνων καὶ Λοκρῶν ἔτι δ' Ἐλεατῶν καὶ Νεαπολιτῶν συγχρησάμενοι πεντηκοντόρους καὶ τριήρεις ἐπὶ τούτων παραβόλως διεκόμισαν τοὺς ἄνδρας.

" When they saw that the war was dragging on, they undertook for the first time to build ships, a hundred quinqueremes and twenty triremes. As their shipwrights were absolutely inexperienced in building quinqueremes, such ships never having been in use in Italy, the matter caused them much difficulty, . . . When they first undertook to send their forces across to Messene not only had they not any decked ships, but no long ships at all, not even a single boat, and borrowing fifty-oared boats and triremes from the Tarentines and Locrians, and also from the people of Elea and Naples, they took their troops across in these at great hazard."

Of the manning of the ships for the African expedition in 256 Polybius writes:

1, 26, 7-9:

καὶ τὸ μὲν σύμπαν ἦν στράτευμα τούτων τῆς ναυτικῆς δυνάμεως περὶ τέτταρας καὶ δέκα μυριάδας, ὡς ἂν ἑκάστης νεὼς λαμβανούσης ἐρέτας μὲν τριακοσίους, ἐπιβάτας δ' ἑκατὸν εἴκοσιν. οἱ δὲ Καρχηδόνιοι τὸ μὲν πλεῖον καὶ τὸ πᾶν ἡρμόζοντο πρὸς τὸν κατὰ θάλατταν κίνδυνον· τό γε μὴν πλῆθος αὐτῶν ἦν ὑπὲρ πεντεκαίδεκα μυριάδας κατὰ τὸν τῶν νεῶν λόγον. ἐφ' οἷς οὐχ οἷον ἄν τις παρὼν καὶ θεώμενος ὑπὸ τὴν ὄψιν, ἀλλὰ κἂν ἀκούων καταπλαγείη τὸ τοῦ κινδύνου μέγεθος καὶ τὴν τῶν πολιτευμάτων ἀμφοτέρων μεγαλομερίαν καὶ δύναμιν, στοχαζόμενος ἔκ τε τοῦ τῶν ἀνδρῶν καὶ τοῦ τῶν νεῶν πλήθους.

" The whole body embarked on the ships numbered about a hundred and forty thousand, each ship holding three hundred rowers and a hundred and twenty soldiers. The Carthaginians were chiefly or solely adapting their preparations to a maritime war, their numbers being, to reckon by the number of ships, actually above one hundred and fifty thousand. These are figures calculated to strike not only one present and with the forces under his eyes but even a hearer with amazement at the magnitude of the struggle and at that lavish outlay and vast power of the two states, which may be estimated from the number of men and ships."

Of the building of a fleet by private means he writes as follows:

Pol., 1, 59, 1-3, & 1, 59, 6-8:

ὁμοίως δὲ Ῥωμαῖοι ψυχομαχοῦντες, καίπερ ἔτη σχεδὸν ἤδη πέντε τῶν κατὰ θάλατταν πραγμάτων ὁλοσχερῶς ἀφεστηκότες διά τε τὰς περιπετείας καὶ διὰ τὸ πεπεῖσθαι δι' αὑτῶν τῶν πεζικῶν δυνάμεων κρινεῖν τὸν πόλεμον, . . . ἔκριναν τὸ τρίτον ἀντιποιήσασθαι τῶν ἐν ταῖς ναυτικαῖς δυνάμεσιν ἐλπίδων, . . . χορηγία μὲν γὰρ οὐχ ὑπῆρχε πρὸς τὴν πρόθεσιν ἐν τοῖς κοινοῖς· οὐ μὴν ἀλλὰ διὰ τὴν τῶν προεστώτων ἀνδρῶν εἰς τὰ κοινὰ φιλοτιμίαν καὶ γενναιότητα προσευρέθη πρὸς τὴν συντέλειαν. κατὰ γὰρ τὰς τῶν βίων εὐκαιρίας καθ' ἕνα καὶ δύο καὶ τρεῖς ὑφίσταντο παρέξειν πεντήρη κατηρτισμένην, ἐφ' ᾧ τὴν δαπάνην κομιοῦνται, κατὰ λόγον τῶν πραγμάτων προχωρησάντων. τῷ δὲ τοιούτῳ τρόπῳ ταχέως ἑτοιμασθέντων διακοσίων πλοίων πεντηρικῶν, . . .

" And yet the Romans did not give in. For the last five years indeed they had entirely abandoned the sea, partly because of the disasters they had sustained there, and partly because they felt confident of deciding the war by means of their land forces; but they now determined for the third time to make trial of their fortune in naval warfare. . . .

The treasury was empty, and would not supply the funds necessary for the undertaking, which were, however, obtained by the patriotism and generosity of the leading citizens. They undertook singly, or by two or three combining, according to their means, to supply a quinquereme fully fitted out, on the understanding that they were to be repaid if the expedition was successful. By these means a fleet of two hundred quinqueremes was quickly prepared " . . .

We may attempt a general estimate of the expenses of the war.

The *army* consisted of two legions and auxiliaries in 264 and 263 (Pol., 1, 11, only one consul). A legion had 4,000 men and 300 horse (Pol., 1, 16) and probably as many auxiliaries. From 262 to 241 the army generally had four legions (Pol., 1, 16). In the early years a part of the army seems to have been dismissed for the rainy season (Pol., 1, 17, 6); and at times some of the soldiers were temporarily placed in naval service (Pol., 1, 49). A conservative estimate would be that 16,000 legionaries and 1,200 horse and fully as many allied troops were employed for about twenty years. In Polybius' day the citizen soldiers received 120 denarii the year and the allies received some 48 modii of grain (Pol., 6, 39); and I shall assume that the stipend was about the same in the First Punic War, whatever the coin may have been in which it was paid. There was not much foraging in Sicily; Rome either bought grain in Sicily (1, 18, 11; 52, 8) or sent it from Rome (Pol., 1, 52, 5). The army costs sum up about as follows:

Stipends to legions =   about 44,000,000 den.
Grain supplies [1] at 2 sest. per modius =   about   8,640,000 den.
Horses,[2] engines, baggage, and grain transport = (?) 10,000,000 den.
                                                         _____
                                                          62,640,000 den.

[1] I assume that the citizens paid for their grain out of their stipend, as in Polybius' time (Pol., 6, 39) but that the allied troops were given 4 modii per month. I also assume a low price for grain for the army, 2 sesterces the modius (instead of 3, which was the price found in the preceding chapter and was the price during the next century; see Ch. III). Much of the grain was doubtless bought in Sicily. The distribution made by Metellus at Rome in 250 for 1 *as* the modius (Pliny, 18, 17) was at the victory games, and the wheat, of course, was taken as booty at the capture of Palermo. The price was therefore very far below normal.

[2] Each cavalryman was given two horses, each costing 1,000 libral *asses* (Ch. I, end). 2,400 were therefore in constant service, and probably at least 10,000 were needed during the twenty-four years. The siege engines were used extensively during the last half of the war and of course the engineers were constantly making new

The *navy* had 100 quinqueremes and 20 triremes in 260 (Pol., 1, 20, 10). It kept in operation in 259-7 (Pol., 1, 24, 9; 25). In 256, for the invasion of Africa, it was raised to 330 decked ships, mostly of large size (1, 25, 7) with a large number of transports (1, 26, 14), each ship bearing 300 rowers and 120 soldiers (1, 26, 7). Most of the fleet was in action through 256 (1, 29, 9). In 255 it was fitted out with 350 vessels (1, 36, 10), but all except 80 were lost. However it was at once brought up to the number of 300 and operated in 254 and 253 till half of these were lost (1, 38, 5-7 and 10; 1, 39, 1-6). In 251 (1, 39, 8) there were only 60 ships and these were needed for bringing supplies to Sicily. In 250 the number had been raised to 200 (1, 41, 3). A part was lost in 249 in battle, a part in storms (1, 51, 11; 1, 53, 5; 1, 54, 8). Thereafter till 242 there was no fleet of any importance. The last fleet was built in 242 by private contributions (1, 59, 8) and this won the great battle that ended the war in 241.

The average number of quinqueremes in service was about as follows:

260-257	probably six months per year, about	100
256	for about two months,	about 300
255-3	probably six months per year, about	300
252-1	probably six months per year, about	60
250-49	probably six months per year, about	200
248-43	probably six months per year, about	50
242-1	probably six months per year, about	210

This amounts to about 2,600 war vessels for one-half year of service. As for transports we have only two statements: that in 249 there were 800 transport vessels (Pol., 1, 52, 6) and that in 241 Lutatius had 700 (Diod., 24, 11). For the navy at its best Polybius once (1, 26, 7) vouches for 300 rowers and 120 soldiers per ship, but here he is referring to the perilous invasion of Africa. To be conservative we may perhaps assume an average of 250 rowers and 100 soldiers. The naval soldiers would probably be citizens and receive the regular stipend, the crew would probably be allies and receive the ration of 4 modii the month. Apparently the full navy did not operate over six months

weapons. The Romans usually needed a baggage mule and driver for about every ten soldiers, and grain for both (Kromayer und Veith, *Heerwesen und Kriegführung*, 394); and, though the armies were often stationary during this war, provisions sometimes had to be hauled the length of Sicily (Pol., 1, 52, 6). 10,000,000 denarii ·is therefore a conservative estimate.

per year. We have no statement about the cost of a ship at Rome, but in fourth century Athens a trireme came to about 9,000-12,000 drachmas;[3] perhaps 15,000 denarii might be accepted as a reasonable amount for a quinquereme at Rome. The transports[4] I shall estimate hypothetically at one-fourth the cost and allow one-fourth the crew. If the number rose to 800 in 249, we may—considering the losses sustained—reckon on at least twice that number as built during the course of the war; and a goodly number must have been in service throughout the war, let us say at a guess, 250. Naval costs would then be somewhat as follows:

Cost of 500 war vessels and 1,600 transports	c. 8,100,000 den.
Stipends for marines for the war, 60 den. the year	15,600,000 den.
Rations of 4 mod. the month at 2 sest. the mod.	7,800,000 den.
Rations for transport crews	3,600,000 den.
	35,100,000 den.

At a conservative estimate the main expenses of the war must have amounted to at least 100,000,000 denarii of 4.55 grams[5] (about $24,000,000; $1,000,000 per year).

Income

Taxes. We have no definite statements about taxes at this time, but Polybius (1, 58, 9) says they were high. The usual *tributum simplex* of peace times was only a one-mill tax, but this was frequently doubled and trebled during later wars. About 200 B. C. the peace tax was nearly 1,000,000 denarii the year[6] and, since the population was larger in 264, we may probably assume from 50-60,000,000 from this source for the period of the war. There was also considerable public land being rented out by the state in the Ager Gallicus, but we cannot estimate the returns. Furthermore, Hiero was forced to pay an indemnity

---

[3] Busolt-Swoboda, *Griech. Staatskunde*, 1220; Robbins, F. E., in *Class. Phil.*, 1918, 363.

[4] We do not know the size of transports, but they had to be large enough to be serviceable in cruises from Rome to Africa. That they cost on the average a fourth as much as a warship is a mere guess. In 43 B. C. Dolabella's 100 transports were all over 2,000 amphoras' burden (Cic., *Fam.*, 12, 15, 2) i. e. about 50 tons.

[5] We may well hesitate, therefore, to follow the recent hypothesis that Rome had no silver coinage of her own till after this war. How could she finance such undertakings with copper and a Campanian coinage?

[6] See the calculations of De Sanctis given in the next chapter under *Income*.

of 100 talents in 263 (nearly 500,000 denarii). These items might well cover about two-thirds the cost of the war.

The rest probably came from the sale of captives and other booty. When Palermo fell, fourteen thousand of its inhabitants bought their freedom at 2 minas each (200 den., Diod., 23, 18, 5) and we may perhaps take this as the average price for the thirteen thousand sold at the same place. Twenty thousand captives were taken in Africa and sent to Rome (Pol., 1, 29, 7). Agrigentum, which fell in 263, yielded " many slaves and much booty of every kind " (Pol., 1, 19, 15), but the Greek citizens could hardly have been sold. Several minor places were also taken by storm in 258 (Pol., 1, 24, 10 ff.), but figures are not given. Finally we must attempt to reckon in the ships' crews captured: at Mylae, thirty (Pol., 1, 23, 7), at Tyndaris, ten (25, 4), at Ecnomus, sixty-four (28, 14), at Hermaeum, one hundred and fourteen (36, 11, probably an exaggeration), at the Aegates islands, seventy ships yielded ten thousand captives (61, 8). After a battle, of course, the crew would be far from full. Using the ratio given for the last battle we may assume about thirty thousand captives from the crews. Counting 200 denarii for each (the ransom price at Palermo), the war captives may have yielded over 15,000,000 denarii. If the rest of the booty yielded 10,000,000 denarii, we have accounted for most of the costs of the war. During the final two years (see passage above) the last navy was built by private funds, the richest citizens being asked to provide a ship each or to combine in groups of two or three in order to provide one. These assessments would presumably come to 5,000-15,000 denarii per man for about 500 citizens, unless " equipment " refers also to the supply of rowers. That, however, would seem unlikely, since slave-rowers are never mentioned in this war. The sale of prisoners and booty from the last victory may well have amounted to enough to repay those contributors, for 70 ships with their crews were captured (Pol., 1, 61, 6).[7]

After the war the treasury received from Carthage by way of war indemnity 320 talents of silver per year for 10 years or nearly 2,000,000 denarii the year—about a fifth of the cost of the war. Since for many years the state had but small expenses, we may assume that the taxpayers were given back a part of their extra heavy war-taxes out of this sum. The treasury at any rate was so far relieved of

[7] Orosius' report of 32,000 prisoners seems to be an exaggeration.

pressure that it was possible within nine years to distribute the rent-paying public lands of the Ager Gallicus to the people. Polybius gives the final terms of peace as follows:

Polybius, 1, 62, 8-9, 63, 3:

" ἐπὶ τοῖσδε φιλίαν εἶναι Καρχηδονίοις καὶ Ῥωμαίοις, ἐὰν καὶ τῷ δήμῳ τῶν Ῥωμαίων συνδοκῇ. ἐκχωρεῖν Σικελίας ἁπάσης Καρχηδονίους καὶ μὴ πολεμεῖν Ἱέρωνι μηδ᾽ ἐπιφέρειν ὅπλα Συρακοσίοις μηδὲ τῶν Συρακοσίων συμμάχοις. ἀποδοῦναι Καρχηδονίους Ῥωμαίοις χωρὶς λύτρων ἅπαντας τοὺς αἰχμαλώτους. ἀργυρίου κατενεγκεῖν Καρχηδονίους Ῥωμαίοις ἐν ἔτεσιν εἴκοσι δισχίλια καὶ διακόσια τάλαντ᾽ Εὐβοϊκά."

(63, 3): τόν τε γὰρ χρόνον τῶν φόρων ἐποίησαν ἥμισυν, χίλια τάλαντα προσθέντες, τῶν τε νήσων ἐκχωρεῖν Καρχηδονίους προσεπέταξαν, ὅσαι μεταξὺ τῆς Ἰταλίας κεῖνται καὶ τῆς Σικελίας.

" There shall be friendship between the Carthaginians and Romans on the following terms, if approved by the Roman people. The Carthaginians to evacuate the whole of Sicily and not to make war on Hiero or bear arms against the Syracusans or the allies of the Syracusans. The Carthaginians to give up to the Romans all prisoners without ransom. The Carthaginians to pay to the Romans by instalments in twenty years two thousand two hundred Euboean talents." (63, 3) . . . " they reduced the term of payment by one half, added a thousand talents to the indemnity, and demanded the evacuation by the Carthaginians of all islands lying between Sicily and Italy."

IV. MINOR ITEMS OF ECONOMIC INTEREST

The Sicilian tithe.[8] Up to 242 B. C. Rome had taken defeated peoples into the federation and had not exacted tribute. But the possession of Sicily would require a standing army there. Hiero and Carthage had collected tithes on cultivated land, and cattle-taxes on pasture land. In the part of Sicily that Rome now took over from Carthage she imposed this system, except in some cities that had aided her in the war. These favored cities were either accepted as allies or as tribute-free subjects. We do not know what the tithe in grain amounted to at this time, but it may have been as much as 2,000,000 modii (500,000 bushels), since it came to 3,000,000 modii in Cicero's day (Cic., *Verr.*, 2, 3, 163), that is, after the Syracusan kingdom had

---

[8] Carcopino, *Le Loi de Hiéron*; Rostovtzeff, *Stud. röm. Kol.*; *Camb. Anc. Hist.*, VII, 793 ff.

been added. Port dues of 5% were also continued from the preceding régime, but probably did not amount to much at first.

The grain was collected in accordance with the excellent system devised by King Hiero whereby the cultivators were very carefully protected against over-exactions. The contracts for each city were let by the quaestors in Sicily, and Roman contracting firms were not permitted to bid. The produce was sent to Rome. The army, when all four legions were in the field, would need about 800,000 modii. The residue was presumably marketed at Rome. Since the city at this time had a population of at least 200,000, requiring over 8,000,000 modii per year, the Sicilian state supply probably took care of a tenth of the need. We do not hear of any complaints from the Roman landlords that the state was interfering with their market. Presumably wine and olive culture was increasing in Latium so that foreign grain was welcome. At any rate the Roman army very soon grew to such a size that it could use all the provincial grain and much more. Then the Latian farmers had no cause to object to the importation of the Sicilian tribute.

The Affair of Volsinii (Zonaras, 8, 7, see text below). Shortly before the First Punic War the aristocracy of Volsinii (Orvieto) appealed to Rome, saying that they had been driven out by their former " slaves " who had taken possession of their property and the whole city government. The passage seems to indicate that there had been *serfdom* at Volsinii, that the landlords had set their serfs free when they needed their services in the army, and that these ex-serfs had then proceeded to seize the lands and the government. Since the Latin language had no word for *serf*, the Roman historians employed the word *servus*, but it is wholly likely that the Etruscan aristocracy not only here but through a large part of Etruria had imposed serfdom upon the Villanovan population. Rome defeated the rebels, took the town, and razed it. A new town (modern Bolsena) was built a few miles to the west. Rome restored the old government and gave back their property to the landlords. We do not know whether serfdom was continued, but there is no definite trace of serfdom in Etruria in Roman days, except that renters (coloni) seem to be a humbler class in Etruria than elsewhere (cf. the *coloni* of Domitius in 49: Caes., B. C., 1, 34; 56). It should be added that Rome carried back much booty from Volsinii, especially in the form of bronze statues and statuettes. At this time bronze was much needed at Rome. A Greek humorist suggested that Rome went into the war because of her passion for art objects in bronze (Pliny, *N. H.*, 34, 34: propter MM statuarum Volsinios expugnatos obiceret [Metrodorus Scepsius]). The text of Zonaras is as follows: [9]

Zonaras, 8, 7:

Ἐπὶ δὲ Κυίντου Φαβίου καὶ Αἰμιλίου ὑπάτων πρὸς Οὐολσινίους ἐστράτευσαν ἐπ᾽ ἐλευθερίᾳ αὐτῶν· ἔνσπονδοι γὰρ ἦσαν αὐτοῖς. οἳ ἀρχαιότατοι Τυρσηνῶν ὄντες ἰσχύν τε περιεποιήσαντο καὶ τεῖχος κατεσκεύασαν ὀχυρώτατον, πολιτείᾳ τε εὐνομουμένῃ ἐκέχρηντο, καὶ δι᾽ αὐτὰ πολεμοῦντές ποτε τοῖς Ῥωμαίοις ἐπὶ πλεῖστον ἀντέσχον. ὡς δ᾽ ἐχειρώθησαν, αὐτοὶ μὲν ἐξώκειλαν εἰς ἁβρότητα, τὴν δὲ διοίκησιν τῆς πόλεως τοῖς οἰκέταις ἐπέτρεψαν, καὶ τὰς στρατείας δι᾽ ἐκείνων ὡς τὸ πολὺ ἐποιοῦντο· καὶ τέλος ἐς τοῦτο προήγαγον σφᾶς ὡς καὶ δύναμιν τοὺς οἰκέτας καὶ φρόνημα ἔχειν καὶ ἐλευθερίας ἑαυτοὺς ἀξιοῦν. . . . οὔτ᾽ οὖν φέρειν σφᾶς οἱ ἀρχαῖοι πολῖται οὔτε καθ᾽ ἑαυτοὺς δεδυνημένοι ἀμύνασθαι, λάθρᾳ πρέσβεις εἰς τὴν Ῥώμην ἀπέστειλαν. . . . δι᾽ οὖν ταῦθ᾽ οἱ Ῥωμαῖοι τὸν Φάβιον ἐπ᾽ αὐτοὺς ἔστειλαν. καὶ ὃς τούς τε ἀπαντήσαντας αὐτῷ ἐξ ἐκείνων ἐτρέψατο καὶ πολλοὺς ἐν τῇ φυγῇ φθείρας κατέκλεισε τοὺς λοιποὺς εἰς τὸ τεῖχος, καὶ προσέβαλε τῇ πόλει. καὶ ὁ μὲν ἐνταῦθα τρωθεὶς ἀπέθανε, θαρσήσαντες δ᾽ ἐπὶ τούτῳ ἐπεξῆλθον. καὶ ἡττηθέντες αὖθις ἀνεχώρησαν καὶ ἐπολιορκοῦντο· καὶ εἰς ἀνάγκην λιμοῦ ἐμπεσόντες παρέδωκαν ἑαυτούς. ὁ δὲ ὕπατος τοὺς μὲν ἀφελομένους τὰς τῶν κυρίων τιμὰς αἰκισάμενος ἔκτεινε καὶ τὴν πόλιν κατέσκαψε, τοὺς δὲ αὐθιγενεῖς, καὶ εἴ τινες τῶν οἰκετῶν χρηστοὶ περὶ τοὺς δεσπότας ἐγένοντο, ἐν ἑτέρῳ κατῴκισε τόπῳ.

" In the consulship of Quintus Fabius and Aemilius the Romans made an expedition to Volsinii to secure the freedom of its citizens; for they were under treaty obligations to them. These people were the most ancient of the Etruscans; they had acquired power and had erected an extremely strong citadel, and they had a well-governed state. Hence, on a certain occasion, when they were involved in war with the Romans, they resisted for a very long time. Upon being subdued, however, they drifted into indolent ease, left the management of the city to their servants, and used those servants also, as a rule, to carry on their campaigns. Finally they encouraged them to such an extent that the servants gained both power and spirit, and felt that they had a right to

---

[9] There are also meager references to the affair in Val. Max., 9, 1, ext. 2; Florus, 1, 21. Since Rome expected her allies to provide troops for the federal forces, it was hardly to her interest to promote serfdom anywhere inside of Italy, and that is probably why the institution disappeared in Etruria after Rome gained control. However, in the case of Volsinii, the rebels were probably reduced to actual slavery by way of punishment. In other places they presumably became tenants (*coloni*, cf. the *coloni* of Domitius Ahenobarbus, mentioned by Caesar, *B. C.*, 1, 56).

freedom. . . . Hence the old-time citizens, not being able to endure them, and yet possessing no power of their own to punish them, despatched envoys by stealth to Rome. . . . This, then, was the occasion which led the Romans to send Fabius against them. He routed those who came to meet him, destroyed many in their flight, shut up the remainder within the wall, and made an assault upon the city. In that action Fabius was wounded and killed, whereupon the enemy gained confidence and made a sortie. Upon being again defeated, they retired and underwent a siege; and when they were reduced to famine, they surrendered. The consul scourged to death the men who had seized upon the honours of the ruling class, and he razed the city to the ground; the native-born citizens, however, and any servants who had been loyal to their masters were settled by him on another site."

An exchange of prisoners with Carthage soon after the Punic War (Pol., 1, 83, 7-11):

τῶν Καρχηδονίων τοὺς πλέοντας ἐξ Ἰταλίας εἰς Λιβύην καὶ χορηγοῦντας τοῖς πολεμίοις καταγόντων ὡς αὑτούς, καὶ σχεδὸν ἀθροισθέντων τούτων εἰς τὴν φυλακὴν εἰς τοὺς πεντακοσίους, ἠγανάκτησαν οἱ Ῥωμαῖοι. μετὰ δὲ ταῦτα διαπρεσβευσάμενοι, καὶ κομισάμενοι διὰ λόγου πάντας, ἐπὶ τοσοῦτον εὐδόκησαν ὥστε παραχρῆμα τοῖς Καρχηδονίοις ἀντιδωρήσασθαι τοὺς ὑπολειπομένους παρ' αὑτοῖς αἰχμαλώτους ἐκ τοῦ περὶ Σικελίαν πολέμου. ἀπὸ δὲ τούτου τοῦ καιροῦ πρὸς ἕκαστα τῶν παρακαλουμένων ἑτοίμως καὶ φιλανθρώπως ὑπήκουον. διὸ καὶ πρὸς μὲν τοὺς Καρχηδονίους ἐπέτρεψαν τοῖς ἐμπόροις ἐξαγαγεῖν αἰεὶ τὸ κατεπεῖγον, πρὸς δὲ τοὺς πολεμίους ἐκώλυσαν. μετὰ δὲ ταῦτα τῶν μὲν ἐν τῇ Σαρδόνι μισθοφόρων, καθ' ὃν καιρὸν ἀπὸ τῶν Καρχηδονίων ἀπέστησαν, ἐπισπωμένων αὐτοὺς ἐπὶ τὴν νῆσον οὐχ ὑπήκουσαν· τῶν δ' Ἰτυκαίων ἐγχειριζόντων σφᾶς, οὐ προσεδέξαντο, τηροῦντες τὰ κατὰ τὰς συνθήκας δίκαια.

" The Carthaginians when they captured traders coming from Italy to Africa with supplies for the enemy, brought them in to Carthage, and there were now in their prisons as many as five hundred such. The Romans were annoyed at this, but when on sending an embassy, they recovered all the prisoners by diplomatic means, they were so much gratified, that in return they gave back to the Carthaginians all the remaining prisoners from the Sicilian war and henceforth gave prompt and friendly attention to all their requests. They gave permission to their merchants to export all requirements for Carthage, but not for the enemy, and shortly afterwards, when the mercenaries in Sardinia on revolting from Carthage invited them to occupy the island, they refused. Again on the citizens of Utica offering to surrender to them they did not accept, but held to their treaty engagements."

A change in the constitution in the direction of equal suffrage.[10] By the Hortensian law of 287 the plebeians had gained so much more than equal rights with the patricians that the tribal assembly now had full legislative power by the side of the centuriate assembly of all the populus. Now that the distinction between patricians and plebeians had broken down, liberalism took a new direction in an effort to aid the poor against the new mixed nobility of large land-holders who were also in general the office-holders. And as the centuriate assembly, based on property qualifications, still elected the chief magistrates, there was a demand that the class qualifications be modified in such a way that the poor would receive a larger representation in this assembly. We know from later conditions that the reform was carried through, whether by legislation or by censorial command, but no historian mentions the date. Since Livy's second decade has been lost, we assume that the event was told of in that portion; probably the date was about 240 B. C. The result of this reform was that, while the division by property classes was still kept, it was modified in effect by superimposing the ward division of 35 tribus over the division by classes, and by equalizing the votes of the classes, so that the small land-holders of the rustic wards hereafter could control elections if they tried (see De Sanctis, *Storia dei Romani,* III, 353 ff.). There resulted, however, no noticeable change in the quality or class of the men elected, because during the period of the great wars the people continued to elect to high office senators of prestige and experience in governmental affairs. In fact the senatorial land-holding nobility increased in power and influence during the period.

There followed in 232 the distribution of the Ager Gallicus by Flaminius, of which we have spoken above, which showed the effectiveness of the poorer classes in legislation. In his censorship Flaminius secured an appropriation for the building of the Via Flaminia up to Ariminum (cf. " Flaminia Via," *Realenc.*), the building of a new Circus (the Flaminian) for the populace (Livy, *Epit.* 20; Varro, *L. L.*, 5, 154), and he also supported the Claudian plebiscite (see below) which was aimed at keeping the nobility out of commercial enterprise. There was also attributed to his influence a *lex Metilia de fullonibus* which

---

[10] De Sanctis, *Storia dei Romani*, III, 355-81, discusses the matter excellently and gives a full bibliography.

seems to have been a sumptuary law proscribing the use of expensive clothing during the war (Pliny, *N. H.,* 35, 197).

During the Second Punic War we hear practically nothing about any class contentions. The nobles who ruled the Senate were felt to be directing the great war wisely, and they in turn needed the adhesion of the populace and refrained from acts of tyranny. It was an era of concord between the classes.

War with Queen Teuta of the Illyrians.[11] In 230 Rome sent envoys to warn the Illyrians not to molest traders operating in the Adriatic Sea. Rome had had a colony on the Adriatic coast for over fifty years and now had four colonies there. It is surprising that piracy had gone on unquestioned. But Rome had had no fleet till recently and apparently showed little interest in Adriatic trade despite the planting of Brundisium in 246. Polybius writes about the origin of the war as follows:

Polybius, 2, 8, 2-4:

καὶ πλείους ἀπὸ τοῦ στόλου χωριζόμενοι πολλοὺς τῶν Ἰταλικῶν ἐμπόρων ἔσθ᾽ οὓς μὲν ἐσύλησαν, οὓς δ᾽ ἀπέσφαξαν, οὐκ ὀλίγους δὲ καὶ ζωγρίᾳ τῶν ἁλισκομένων ἀνῆγον. οἱ δὲ Ῥωμαῖοι, παρακούοντες τὸν πρὸ τοῦ χρόνον τῶν ἐγκαλούντων τοῖς Ἰλλυριοῖς, τότε καὶ πλειόνων ἐπελθόντων ἐπὶ τὴν σύγκλητον, κατέστησαν πρεσβευτὰς εἰς τὴν Ἰλλυρίδα τοὺς ἐπίσκεψιν ποιησομένους περὶ τῶν προειρημένων Γάϊον καὶ Λεύκιον Κορογκανίους.

. . . . " a number of them (the Illyrians) detached themselves from the fleet and robbed or killed many Italian traders, capturing and carrying off no small number of prisoners. The Romans had hitherto turned a deaf ear to the complaints made against the Illyrians, but now when a number of persons approached the Senate on the subject, they appointed two envoys, Caius and Lucius Coruncanius, to proceed to Illyria, and investigate the matter."

App., *Ill.,* 7-8, and Zonaras, 8, 19, add a few items of dubious authenticity. The envoys mentioned here were put to death, whereupon Rome declared war. The passage speaks of the traders as " Italians," that probably means south Italian Greeks in the main. The passage also says that the Romans " had hitherto turned a deaf ear to complaints made against the Illyrians," which would seem to signify

---

[11] See the excellent account by Holleaux, in *Camb. Anc. Hist.,* VII, 822 ff. and especially 829.

that there were few Roman merchants trading even with the Roman and Latin colonies of the Adriatic (see Holleaux, in *Camb. Anc. Hist.*, vii, 822 ff.).

The Claudian Law of 218. Livy (21, 63, 3) gives the substance of this plebiscite as follows: ne quis senator cuive senator pater fuisset maritimam navem quae plus quam trecentarum amphorarum esset haberat—" that no senator or senator's son should have a seagoing vessel of over the capacity of 300 jars " (about 225 bushels). Livy adds, " this size would suffice to transport products from the farms: gainful occupation was unseemly in the case of senators." This apparently gives the most important reason for the enactment, but it was also felt at all times that senators must be near enough to the city to receive summons to attend the Senate at short notice. The passage may imply that some senators had entered maritime trade. But the protracted disregard of piracy in the case of the Illyrians would seem to imply that few senators had any interest in sea-going trade. Julius Caesar enacted a similar law in 59 B. C. (Digest, L, v, 3).

Finally we may mention the fact that Rome kept the Appian Way in repair during this period of wars. The aediles were responsible for the milestone (*C. I. L.*, I², 21) placed 51 miles from Rome about 250 B. C., and a consul (214 or 212?) for one found near Privernum (*C. I. L.*, I², 17).

Silver: the statement has been made that Rome would not have had silver enough for the issuing of the denarius till about 194 B. C. (cf. Sydenham, in *Num. Chron.*, 1932, 93). But more silver came to Rome during the period 264-220 than in the war with Philip. We know, for instance of these items:

Hiero's indemnity (Pol., 1, 16)	about 90	talents paid
Booty of Duilius (*C. I. L.*, I², 25)	about 50	talents
Ransom price at Palermo (Diod., 23, 18)	466	talents
Punic indemnity imposed in 242	3,200	talents
Punic indemnity imposed in 238	1,200	talents
Ransom price at Eryx (Livy, 21, 41) probably about	50	talents
	5,056	talents

If, in addition, a half of the 75,000 or more prisoners mentioned above were sold to Greek traders for silver at the price of 2 minas (price at Palermo), if the cities taken in Sicily (Agrigentum, Palermo, Camarina, etc.) provided a thousand talents in plate and other booty, and if the victories over the Celts in 225-2 and over Illyria in 229 and 219 yielded another thousand, we can conservatively reckon that some 8,000 talents of silver came to Rome during this period, i. e. before the Hannibalic War, and this sum would coin into more than 40,000,-000 denarii of the weight used in the early heavy coins. Hence there certainly is no difficulty in assuming large issues of denarii in addition to Romano-Campanian coins before the Hannibalic War.

According to Giglioli's spacing of the Duilian inscription in *Notizie degli Scavi*, 1930, 346, the booty amounted to about 3,000,000 *asses*, or 300,000 denarii if the two-ounce *as* is meant. We do not know what the gold and silver coins were, but, if the 3600 gold coins were of the usual Hieronic types of 7.61-9.56 grams, the gold would equal about 800,000 *asses*. The rest (2,200,000 *asses*) might consist of 160,000 eight-obol silver pieces = about 220,000 denarii. (The inscription has (((1))) 1 (?), which might be any number between 150,000 and 200,000. I consider the inscription a fairly accurate copy of the original; see *Class. Phil.*, 1919, p. 74.)

V. PROPERTY VALUES AT THE END OF THE THIRD CENTURY

At the beginning of the Second Punic War, the city-state had an area of about 7,000 square miles, with a population of adult male citizens of about 270,000, or a free population of nearly one million souls, a half of whom probably lived in and about Rome and Capua. The taxable property—all citizens owning property worth more than 1,500 asses were liable to the tax—has been estimated at about nine hundred million denarii on the basis of a passage in Livy (39, 7, 5), which says that, since the treasury had a surplus, the proceeds of the booty brought home by Manlius from Asia in 187 were to be used for the repayment of the taxes of past years that had not already been repaid. During the Second Punic War the lowest tax, called *tributum simplex*, had been a direct tax of one-tenth of one per cent, or a " one-mill " tax. This had been doubled or trebled as need required. In 187 there was still unpaid twenty-five and a half times this *tributum simplex*, according to Livy, and this amount was to be covered by the Manlian booty (Livy, 39, 7, 1) which De Sanctis, *Storia dei Romani*, III, 2, 626, estimates as follows:

2,103 lbs. gold =   2,103,000 denarii
220,000 lbs. silver =   18,480,000 denarii

127,000 Attic tetradrachmas =	508,000 denarii
250,000 Cistophori =	750,000 denarii
16,320 Philippi =	432,480 denarii
212 gold crowns (usually of one pound) =	212,000 denarii
	22,485,480 denarii

Now in the passage cited (Livy, 39, 7, 5) we are told that it was decreed: ut ex pecunia quae in triumpho translata esset stipendium conlatum a populo in publicum, quod eius solutum antea non esset, solveretur. " that the taxes which had not yet been repaid should now be paid back out of the money that had been carried in the triumph." Then Livy adds that the urban quaestors repaid twenty-five and one-half asses per thousand (vicenos quinos et semisses in milia aeris), that is to say twenty-five and a half times the tributum simplex. The statement is not absolutely clear, but it seems plausible that the 22 million denarii covered the payment in question. If that is so, an average " one-mill " tax during the Hannibalic War amounted to about 900,000 denarii, and the taxable property (all property over 1,500 asses) would be somewhat less than one thousand million denarii (less than $200,000,000).[12]

VI. THE PUBLIC FINANCES DURING THE SECOND PUNIC WAR

A. EXPENSES.

1. *The army stipend.* The legions varied in number from six to twenty-five during the eighteen years of war, and aggregate 353 legions of one-year's service (De Sanctis, *Storia dei Romani,* III, 2, 317 ff. and 632 ff.; cf. Hallward, *Camb. Anc. Hist.,* VIII, 104). The chief cost per legion was the stipend, which was as follows (Polybius, 6, 39, 12):

Infantry, per legion,	4,140,	at 120 den. =	496,800 den.
Centurions, per legion,	60,	at 240 den. =	14,400 den.
Cavalry, per legion,	300,	at 360 den. =	108,000 den.
			619,200 den.

[12] Cf. Cavaignac, *Population et Capital,* 95. For comparison we may add that New Jersey, which has about the same area as Rome had in 200, has about three times the population and twenty-five times the property evaluation.

If we consider that at times some of the troops were dismissed in winter to save expense, we may estimate the average annual stipend per legion at about 500,000 den. Taking De Sanctis' figures for the legions (353 legions for one year) the stipend for all the legions [13] during the war = ... nearly 180,000,000 den.

2. In addition Rome supplied the *wheat to the allied troops,* who numbered about 5,000 men to each legion. This ration may be reckoned at one bushel (4 modii) of wheat per month (Pol., 6, 39) for an average of about nine months each year; or a total of 16,000,000 bushels during the war. The price of wheat in peace times was about 3 denarii the bushel (see section 6). But I assume that in the South, in Gaul, and in Spain some of the grain was procured by foragers. For this I shall deduct a fourth.[14]

Cost of wheat for the allied troops.... about 36,000,000 den.

3. Kromayer-Veith, *Heerwesen,* 394, reckon on a *baggage train* of at least 400 mules with their drivers for each legion. Probably more than 15,000 mules were purchased for the war, at a cost of, say, 2,000,000 denarii. *Food and fodder* for transport division: about 21 modii of barley and 4 of wheat for beast and driver were required each month [15] (Pol., 6, 39). Since we have to assume 353 legions for a year and we count barley at half the price of wheat, we may reckon the food supply of this service at about 13,000,000 denarii. That is, the land transport service would come to about 15,000,000 denarii.

4. There is no way of reaching a satisfactory estimate of the *cost of the metals and materials* used for the army over and above the individual supply. The soldiers furnished their own first equipment (bronze helmet, leather breastplate, shield of wood, leather, and iron, sword, and lance; Pol., 6, 22), but the corps of 100 smiths and engineers that was attached to each legion was kept very busy supplying new weapons. Iron, bronze, leather, and timber were in great demand during

[13] When Scipio went to Spain in 209 to take charge of two full legions, he was given 400 talents (= 2,400,000 denarii, Pol., 10, 19). Perhaps this was intended to suffice for two years.

[14] Rome exacted a tribute of grain from Sicily and Sardinia which I shall reckon in the items of receipts.

[15] Polybius, 6, 39, reckons 7 medimni of barley for *2 horses* and 2 medimni of wheat for the knight and his man every month. The medimnus = 6 modii.

the war. For such materials I shall hazard a guess of 6 denarii per man per year (including allies), amounting to......about 20,000,000 den.

5. *The navy and shipping.* During the war Rome had about 200 war vessels in regular service,[16] mostly quinqueremes. The losses were not great because Rome soon gained command of the seas. Some of the ships were supplied by the *socii navales,* but not many. We may estimate that the state built some 300 war vessels and some 600 transports during the war. (In the previous war Rome had had at least 800 transports; Pol., 1, 52, 6; Diod., 24, 11). We have no usable data recording the cost of these vessels. But since at Athens in the fourth century a trireme fully equipped was estimated at from 9,000 to 12,000 drachmas, we may, as before, assume 15,000 denarii for these quinquiremes and perhaps about a fourth of this amount for transport vessels. The cost of ships, therefore, would be about:

$$300 \times 15,000 + 600 \times 4,000 \text{ or......about 7,000,000 den.}$$

For 250 rowers for each of 200 war vessels and 60 for each of 500 transports, citizens below the fifth class of the census, as well as freedmen, allies, and even slaves were now being employed; while the legionaries (about 100 to each war vessel) served as marines. We must assume that at least some 80,000 rowers were fed for six months per year during about ten years of the war. The cost would be:

80,000 $\times$ 18 ($=$ 24 modii at $\frac{3}{4}$ den.) $\times$ 10, or about 14,400,000 den.

If in addition some 12,000,000 denarii went into stipends to 20,000 marines for about ten half-years and further expenses into upkeep and repairs, the total naval costs may have come to about 35,000,000 den.

It seems reasonable, therefore, to estimate the whole public outlay during the eighteen years of this war at about 286,000,000 denarii ($57,000,000). The silver denarius at the time weighed about 4 grams and equated normally with gold at a ratio of about 1 : 12. It will be remembered that the indemnity exacted from Carthage at the end of this war was 10,000 talents ($=$ 60,000,000 den.) payable annually in equal instalments over a period of fifty years, or about one-fifth of this amount; but of course the cash value of the 10,000 talents payable in fifty annual instalments was hardly a third as much if the normal interest rate was 6%.

[16] Busolt-Swoboda, *Griech. Staatskunde*, 1220; Robbins, in *Class. Phil.*, 1918, 363. See the data given above for the naval expenses of the First Punic War.

The amounts that we have itemized above seem exceedingly small when one considers that this was the costliest war of ancient times and was fought by the two nations that were generally considered the strongest. During the last year of the World War several nations expended as large a sum in one week as Rome spent all told in eighteen years, and the American costs in bonds and taxes from April, 1917 to November, 1918 mounted to as much every day. Yet Rome's task in financing the war was extremely difficult. The free population of the Roman nation was then about 1,000,000. Her property value has been estimated at about $200,000,000 (see above).

B. INCOME.

1. *Citizen tax.* The regular one-mill tax brought in only about 900,000 denarii the year (see above for property values). In 215 we happen to hear that a double tribute was exacted (Livy, 23, 31: senatus . . . decrevit ut eo anno duplex tributum imperaretur). The tax was probably raised much higher during the war; since even after much treasure had been brought in over twenty-five levies of supertaxes were still unpaid in 187, and the *liturgy* imposed on the wealthy in 214 amounted to from thirty to fifty times the *tributum* (Livy, 24, 11). But, even assuming that the tax rose to five or six mills, the proceeds were far from sufficient. The regular *tributum simplex* for eighteen years and the twenty-five and a half levies of supertaxes that we know of would amount to only about 40,000,000 denarii. It is likely therefore, that taxes had been higher than our few references indicate and that a part had been repaid out of the booty of the last years of the war. Considering the strenuous efforts to borrow and exact moneys, we may well assume an average four-mill tax at least, which would have brought in.................................about 65,000,000 den.

2. The *vectigalia* brought but little. The proceeds of the 5% tax on the value of manumitted slaves, instituted in 357 (Livy, 7, 16, 7), were set aside in a sacred treasury for emergencies. The import and export duties collected at a few harbors (2½-5%) were still insignificant. The salt monopoly could not have been very profitable when the state sold six pounds of salt for a cent (Livy, 29, 37). After the distribution of a large part of the Ager Gallicus the state had but little public land to rent out until after the confiscations carried on in this war. On these items I am not inclined to allow more than..............about 10,000,000 den.

3. *Tithe of Sicily and Sardinia.* At the time of Verres Sicily could supply about 750,000 bushels of wheat (Cic., *Verr.*, 2, 3, 163) and Sardinia probably a third as much. But Syracuse did not become a part of the province till about 210. Sicily was in the war zone for two years, and only a small part of Sardinia was subdued till after the war. I shall count the two as contributing an average of about 500,-000 bushels for sixteen years and estimate the price as above, which would make..............................about 24,000,000 den.

4. *The sacred treasure* obtained from the 5% tax on the price of manumitted slaves was used in 209 (Livy, 27, 10, 11, quoted below): it contained 4,000 pounds of gold issued at the high valuation of about 16 : 1, making...........................about   5,000,000 den.

5. *Booty* (only large amounts are reported but, since the war was fought largely among allies in Italy, plundering was not always permissible, even when towns were taken by force).

a) Capua, Livy, 26, 14, 8 :

2,070 pounds of gold =	about 2,600,000 den.
31,200 pounds of silver =	about 2,600,000 den.

b) New Carthage,[17] Polybius, 10, 19 (proceeds of all) :

600 talents =	about 3,600,000 den.

c) The victory at Metaurus yielded (Polybius, 11, 3) :

300 talents =	about 1,800,000 den.

d) Tarentum,[18] Plut., *Fab.*, 22, brought to the treasury :

3,000 talents =	about 18,000,000 den.

e) Scipio brought home from Spain in 206 (Livy, 28, 38, 5), in addition to coined silver :

14,342 pounds of silver =	about 1,200,000 den.

f) Scipio brought home from Africa [19] after the war (Livy, 30, 45, 3) :

133,000 pounds of silver =	11,172,000 den.

[17] Livy, 26, 47, 7, reports about 276 pounds of gold plate and 18,300 pounds of coined silver besides much other booty.

[18] Livy, 27, 16, 7, reports 30,000 slaves, which would yield about one third of the amount given by Plutarch; Livy's text also reports 83,000 pounds of gold, which is of course an error. Perhaps the figure was $\overline{\mathrm{V}}$xxxiii (5033) instead of $\overline{\mathrm{LXXXIII}}$, since L and V are frequently interchanged. In that case the slaves brought about 6,000,000 denarii, the gold about 5,000,000 denarii, the silver and the rest about 7,000,000 denarii.

[19] This sum includes 25,000 pounds of silver exacted as immediate payment for the

g) If we conjecture 10,000,000 denarii for the possessions of Hiero and for other booty of Syracuse,[20] we have all told:

about 50,000,000 den.

It would not be an overestimate to raise this by 30% for the treasure taken from smaller places, and estimate all the booty gathered at:

about 65,000,000 den.

The items of income 1-5 (tribute, vectigalia, tithes, sacred tax, and booty) sum up to........................about 169,000,000 den.

The final indemnity of 10,000 talents amounts to an added 60,000,000 denarii, but this was not in sight till the very end of the war and then was collected in fifty annual payments. It is of course possible that taxes were higher than we have assumed. However, the items considered above were very far from paying the expenses of the war, and we must now consider the other ways and means devised during the war for raising funds. Here there are eleven items reported which must be reviewed at some length.

6. *Extraordinary items of income.*

1) *A new coinage involving a slight inflation.* When Hannibal approached the city in 217, causing men to hoard their money and cutting off Rome's supply of Etruscan bronze, the state reduced the bronze *as* from two ounces to one, thereby enticing back to the mint quantities of the metal; at the same time it reduced the silver denarius by about one-eighth, issuing 84 pieces instead of 72 to the pound, and equating the denarius with sixteen *asses* instead of ten. This slight inflation was probably intended not only to increase the amount of currency in circulation at a time of much hoarding, but also to readjust the copper and silver to prevailing market ratios and to adjust the metals to rising war prices. Doubtless the larger coins were soon brought to the mint for reissue, and the state made some profit on whatever metals it may have had. (There is no reason to think that there was much silver or bronze in the vaults.) The sources for this account are:

Festus, 470 L: numerum aeris perduct⟨um esse ad XVI asses *lege Fla⟩minia minus solvendi.* (Part of line restored by Müller.)

200 loaded transports seized during the truce (Livy, 30, 38, 1-2), the 20,000 pounds of silver (Eutrop., 3, 23, 2) found at Zama—Hannibal's war chest—booty from raids in Africa, and perhaps the first indemnity payment of 200 talents.

[20] Livy, 25, 31, 8: *pecunia regia* and " much booty " mentioned in 25, 31, 11.

" The number of *asses* (equated with the silver denarius) was extended to sixteen by the ' Flaminian law on reduced payments.' "

Pliny, *N. H.*, 33, 45: Postea, Hannibale urgente, Q. Fabio Maximo dictatore, asses unciales facti placuitque denarium sedecim assibus permutari. . . . Ita res publica dimidium lucrata est, in militari tamen stipendio semper denarius pro decem assibus datus est.

" Afterwards when Hannibal was endangering Rome in the dictatorship of Fabius Maximus one-ounce *asses* were made and it was decided to exchange the denarius for 16 of these. . . . Thus the state profited by a half, but in paying soldiers the denarius was counted as 10 *asses*."

Testimony of the coins (cf. Grueber, *Coins of the Republic;* Hill, *Historical Roman Coins,* 37-51; Giesecke, *Italia Numismatica,* 244-276; Mattingly, *Roman Coins,* 23 ff., and *Journal of Roman Studies,* 1929, 31 ff.). It is difficult to date coins of this period. However, it is generally agreed that the coins themselves do not reveal a sudden reduction, but that from about 242 B. C. to about the middle of the Hannibalic war the bronzes were gradually being reduced from two ounces to one, while the silver denarius was similarly reduced from four scruples (4.55 grams) to about three and a half scruples some time during the early issues. Perhaps the law simply confirmed what the mint-masters had already tried to do.

Both Festus and Pliny make serious errors regarding coinage in other passages; they may be unreliable here. Since Festus seems to cite a document called " lex Flaminia ", we may well believe that after Hannibal entered Northern Etruria, Flaminius asked for a law reducing the bronze *as*, partly because of hoarding, partly because the supply was being cut off by Hannibal's approach. Pliny attributes his law to Fabius a few months later. It may well be that Fabius revised the Flaminian law and also safeguarded bimetallism by equating the new bronze with a reduced denarius. That this was dishonest inflation, as Pliny holds, is improbable. The Roman state had no paper currency, bonds, or debts; hence it would hardly gain much by lightening the coins. Most of its payments were made to soldiers and these we are told explicitly were to continue in denarii (120 per year), as before. Nor would private debtors profit much, since all debts of any considerable amount were, of course, reckoned in silver. The silver coin was reduced only about one eighth, hardly enough, one would suppose, to compensate for the rise of prices during a disastrous war. The laws seem to be intelligent measures designed to draw out hoards, to increase the stock of currency, to save bimetallism, to legalize measures already tried by the mint-masters, and to recognize the rise in the cost of living. The state did obtain some benefit from them in so far as it had bullion in the vaults, but it is not likely that there was a large amount of this in 218, after the Gallic and Illyric wars.

Gold coins were also struck, perhaps for the first time at Rome.

Pliny, 33, 47 (Mommsen's text): Aureus nummus post annos LI percussus est quam argenteus ita ut scripulum valeret sestertios vicenos.

" Gold was coined 51 years after silver (269 or 268 B. C.) so that a scruple was worth 20 sesterces."

This would be about 217 B. C. and would coincide with the reformed coinage of Flaminius-Fabius. The ratio of gold to silver on the new silver standard would be about 17 :1, which is very high, if the normal rate had been 12 or 15 :1. But this would be justified by the financial stress.

There are two series of gold coins that seem to belong to this period (see Bahrfeldt, *Röm. Goldmünzenprägung,* 4-22, for a description). The 3, 2, 1 scruple pieces bearing a Marshead and eagle and marked respectively LX, XXXX, XX (sesterces), and the 6, 4, 3 scruple pieces marked with an " oath-scene." These have been dated by various numismatists between 269 and 200 B. C. on the basis of similarity to other coins, but it is not likely that Rome had much gold at the earlier dates proposed. At the beginning of the war Rome may have had some gold, taken in the Gallic and the Illyric wars. During the Second Punic War Rome took in the royal treasure of Hiero in 212 which certainly contained gold (Livy, 25, 31), found 2,070 pounds of gold at Capua in 211 (Livy, 26, 14, 8), over 270 pounds at New Carthage in 210 (Livy, 26, 47, 7), a large amount at Tarentum in 209—we have conjectured 5,033 pounds—, and Metaurus yielded " much gold " in 207 (Livy, 28, 49). Probably the sum would amount to over 10,000 pounds in addition to the 4,000 pounds in the " sacred treasury " (Livy, 27, 10, 11). Furthermore in 210 the financial commission appointed in 216 gathered in most of the gold available at Rome (Livy, 26, 36), doubtless for coinage. The citizens of Rome must have had far more gold than those of Capua. All told some 20,000 pounds of gold may have been taken into the treasury between 212 and 207, which would yield nearly 6,000,000 one-scruple pieces (each worth 20 sesterces).

For the proposed dating by others see the summary in Bahrfeldt, *op. cit.,* 4-8, and Mattingly, in *Jour. Rom. Stud.,* 1929, 33. Numismatists are prone to over-stress coin-types in dating. When introducing a new coin which would circulate largely outside of Rome (the oath-scene coin does not even bear a denomination) Rome might well call in a southern artist who would be apt to model his type on old southern coins. Rome found much gold between 212 and 207 when suffering from the worst financial stress possible. Hence, despite the arguments based on types, I feel inclined to place several issues during various periods of this war: the

Mars issues for use at Rome and in Italy, and the oath-scene coins probably for use in the South, in the campaigns in Greece 212-205, and in buying grain from Egypt.

If all the gold and silver found during the war was coined, the new issues probably amounted in value to some 75,000,000 denarii.

2) *A loan from Hiero in 216.* After the disaster at Cannae, the praetor of Sicily was authorized to approach King Hiero of Syracuse for money and for food supplies for the army operating in Sicily. From Livy, 23, 38 it appears that this was a loan which the state intended to repay. Apparently Hiero fell before the payment was made. This is the only instance of an external loan recorded for this war, though it may well be that Marseilles aided Rome with loans as well as with ships (cf. *art. Massalia,* in *R-E.,* XIV, 2133).

Livy, 23, 21, 5-6: T. Otacilius ad unicum subsidium populi Romani, Hieronem, legatos cum mississet, in stipendium quanti argenti opus fuit et sex mensum frumentum accepit; Cornelio in Sardinia civitates sociae benigne contulerunt. et Romae quoque propter penuriam argenti triumviri mensarii rogatione M. Minuci tribuni plebis facti, L. Aemilius Papus, qui consul censorque fuerat, et M. Atilius Regulus, qui bis consul fuerat, et L. Scribonius Libo, qui tum tribunus plebis erat.

" Titus Otacilius, having sent ambassadors to Hiero, the only source of assistance the Romans had, received as much money as was wanting to pay the troops, and a supply of corn for six months. In Sardinia, the allied states contributed liberally to Cornelius. The scarcity of money at Rome also was so great that on the proposal of Marcus Minucius, a plebeian tribune, a financial triumvirate was appointed, consisting of Lucius Aemilius Papus, who had been consul and censor, Marcus Atilius Regulus, who had been twice consul, and Lucius Scribonius Libo, who was then plebeian tribune."

Since there were two legions in Sicily, the sum requested must have been over 1,000,000 denarii. The appointment of a banking commission was important. It was still in existence in 210, and probably through the war. It may well have been responsible for some of the issues of gold coin, for in 210 it had charge of the collection of jewelry and precious metals (Livy, 26, 36).

3) *Contracts for supplies on indefinite credit* were also resorted to in 215 when the elder Scipios, who were operating in Spain, begged for supplies, especially for clothing and grain. The corporations of publicans that dealt in state contracts (tax-gathering and building contracts) were urged to supply what was needed and to transport the

goods to Spain with the promise of a first lien on moneys that might accrue to the treasury. Nineteen men belonging to three corporations took the contract on the condition that they would be exempt from active service and that the state would insure the goods against loss from storm or enemy. The amount of this "credit" is not given in the sources, nor are we told when it was paid. It is noteworthy that grain had to be shipped from Rome to Spain. The loan on this occasion could not have been large, but it is possible that the device was used more than once. The pertinent passage in Livy follows.

Livy, 23, 48, 9-49, 3: prodeundum in contionem Fulvio praetori esse, indicandas populo publicas necessitates cohortandosque, qui redempturis auxissent patrimonia, ut rei publicae, ex qua crevissent, tempus commodarent conducerentque ea lege praebenda, quae ad exercitum Hispaniensem opus essent, ut, cum pecunia in aerario esset, iis primis solveretur. haec praetor in contione edixit, quo*que die* vestimenta *ac* frumentum Hispaniensi exercitui praebenda, quaeque alia opus essent navalibus sociis, esset locaturus. ubi ea dies venit, ad conducendum tres societates aderant hominum undeviginti, quorum duo postulata fuere: unum, ut militia vacarent, dum in eo publico essent, alterum, ut, quae in naves inposuissent, ab hostium tempestatisque vi publico periculo essent. utroque impetrato conduxerunt, privataque pecunia res publica administrata est.

"It was resolved, therefore, that Fulvius, the praetor, should present himself to the public assembly of the people, point out the necessities of the state, and exhort those persons who had increased their patrimonies by farming the public revenues, to furnish temporary loans for the service of that state from which they had derived their wealth, and contract to supply what was necessary for the army in Spain, on the condition of being paid the first when there was money in the treasury. These things the praetor laid before the assembly, and fixed a day on which he would let on contract the furnishing of the army in Spain with clothes and corn, and with such other things as were necessary for the crews.

"When the day arrived, three companies, of nineteen persons, came forward to enter into the contract; but they made two requests: one was that they should be exempt from military service while employed in that revenue business; the second was that the state should bear all losses of the goods they shipped, which might arise either from the attacks of the enemy or from storms. Having obtained both their requests, they entered into the contract,[21] and the affairs of the state were conducted by private funds."

4) *Crews supplied by "liturgy."* In 214 when a fleet had to be equipped quickly for the impending war in Sicily the Senate imposed a "liturgy" on the propertied classes of the kind well known from Athenian practice and from the last year of the First Punic War. Rowers were to be supplied by private individuals according to wealth. For instance, men rated from 50,000 to 100,000 *asses* must supply and pay the wage of a rower for six months and supply him with food for a month, while senators had to supply eight men for a year. There is no mention of any proposal to repay these outlays.[22]

Livy, 24, 11, 7-9: Cum increbresceret rumor bellum in Sicilia esse, T. Otacilius eo cum classe proficisci iussus est. cum deessent nautae, consules ex senatus consulto edixerunt, ut, qui L. Aemilio C. Flaminio censoribus milibus aeris quinquaginta ipse aut pater eius census fuisset usque ad centum milia, aut cui postea tanta res esset facta, nautam unum cum sex mensum stipendio daret; qui supra centum milia usque ad trecenta, tris nautas cum stipendio annuo; qui supra trecenta usque

---

[21] Three years later it was discovered that two of the contractors had defrauded the state by using unseaworthy transports and collecting insurance on false bills of lading. Livy, 25, 3, 9-11:

"Postumius was a farmer of the revenue, who, for knavery and rapacity, practised through a course of many years, had no equal except Titus Pomponius Veientanus, ... As the state had taken upon itself the risk of any loss to the commodities conveyed to the armies which might arise from storms, not only had these two men fabricated false accounts of shipwrecks, but even those which had really occurred were occasioned by their own knavery, and not by accident. Their plan was to put a few goods of little value into old and shattered vessels, which they sank in the deep, taking up the sailors in boats prepared for the purpose, and then falsely reporting the cargo as many times more valuable than it was."

Postumius absconded and was banished by a vote of the people; Livy, 25, 4, 4.

[22] Since a slave's wage amounted to about 2 sesterces and food per day (in Cato's times), the cost for each man sent would be over 200 denarii the year (or 3,200 *asses*), that is, from thirty to fifty times the *tributum simplex* of peace times. This would indicate that general taxation must have risen far above a *tributum duplex* or *triplex*. The percentage of the tax was not graduated. We cannot estimate how many citizens were in each bracket nor can we, with Cavaignac, *Pop. et Cap.*, base an estimate of the property of the five classes on this passage. A hundred war vessels had just been ordered (Livy, 24, 11, 5), but we are not told that all of these were manned under this law.

ad deciens aeris, quinque nautas; qui supra deciens, septem; senatores octo nautas cum annuo stipendio darent. ex hoc edicto dati nautae armati instructique ab dominis cum triginta dierum coctis cibariis naves conscenderunt. tum primum est factum, ut classis Romana sociis navalibus privata inpensa paratis conpleretur.

" When rumour prevailed that war had broken out in Sicily, Titus Otacilius was ordered to proceed thither with his fleet; but as there was a deficiency of sailors, the consuls, in conformity with a decree of the senate, published an order that those persons who themselves or whose fathers had been rated in the censorship of Lucius Aemilius and Gaius Flaminius, at from fifty to one hundred thousand asses, or whose property had since reached that amount, should furnish one sailor and six months' pay; from one to three hundred thousand, three sailors with a year's pay; from three hundred thousand to a million, five sailors; above one million, seven sailors; that senators should furnish eight sailors with a year's pay. The sailors furnished according to this proclamation, after being armed and equipped by their masters, embarked with cooked provisions for thirty days. This was the first time that the Roman fleet was manned at the expense of individuals."

5-8) In the same year, 214 B. C., the men who usually took state *building-contracts* promised to continue " business as usual " on undated promises to pay, the owners of *slaves* that had been recruited for the army after Cannae and were now set free also offered to accept notes; *trust funds* of orphans and widows were taken over by the state at the stipulated rates of interest, and many of the knights and centurions in the army contributed their pay to the Treasury.[23]

Livy, 24, 18, 10-15: Cum censores ob inopiam aerarii se iam locationibus abstinerent aedium sacrarum tuendarum curuliumque equorum praebendorum ac similium his rerum, convenere ad eos frequentes, qui hastae huius generis adsueverant, hortatique censores *sunt,* ut omnia perinde agerent locarent, ac si pecunia in aerario esset: neminem nisi bello confecto pecuniam ab aerario petiturum esse. convenere deinde

---

[23] The public building contracts were not large during this war, and we have not attempted to make any estimate of their cost. The slaves that the state requisitioned were 8,000 in number (Livy, 22, 57, 11; Val. Max., 7, 6, 1, says 24,000). Some had of course fallen in battle, but they may have been paid for. The cost to the state may have been about 3,000,000 denarii. The trust funds we cannot estimate but, since women were often large property owners, the funds may have amounted to many million denarii.

domini eorum, quos Ti. Sempronius ad Beneventum manu emiserat, arcessitosque se ab triumviris mensariis esse dixerunt, ut pretia servorum acciperent; ceterum non ante quam bello confecto accepturos esse. cum haec inclinatio animorum plebis ad sustinendam inopiam aerarii fieret, pecuniae quoque pupillares primo, deinde viduarum coeptae conferri, nusquam eas tutius sanctiusque deponere credentibus qui deferebant quam in publica fide. inde si quid emptum paratumque pupillis ac viduis foret, a quaestore perscribebatur. manavit ea privatorum benignitas ex urbe etiam in castra, ut non eques, non centurio stipendium acciperet, mercennariumque increpantes vocarent qui accepisset.

" Since the censors, in consequence of the poverty of the treasury, had abstained from letting contracts for the repairs of the sacred edifices, the furnishing of curule horses, and similar matters, the persons who had been accustomed to attend auctions of this description came to the censors in great numbers and exhorted them to transact all their business and let out the contracts in the same manner as if there were money in the treasury, saying that none of them would ask for money out of the treasury before the war was concluded. Afterwards the owners of those slaves whom Tiberius Sempronius had manumitted at Beneventum came to the censors, stating that they had been sent for by the public banking commission to receive the price of their slaves, but that they would not accept it till the war was concluded. When this disposition on the part of the commons to sustain the impoverished treasury had manifested itself, first the property of minors and then the portions of widows began to be brought in, for the persons who brought them were persuaded that their deposit would nowhere be more secure and inviolable than under a public pledge. If any thing was bought or laid in for the widows and minors, an order upon the quaestor was given for it. This liberality in individuals flowed from the city into the camp also, insomuch that no horseman or centurion would accept his pay, and those who would accept it were reproached with the appellation of mercenary men."

9) *A call for contributions of jewelry, plate, and precious metals.* In 210 there was again great difficulty in finding and paying for rowers. Again it was proposed to resort to a forced " liturgy " as in 214. When many objections were raised at the heavy burdens being imposed,

the consul proposed that the senators should, rather give as much as possible to a voluntary contribution. (It is not called a loan when first mentioned [Livy, 26, 36], but the state repaid the contributions later [Livy, 29, 16], and the consul according to this later passage had promised repayment at some suitable time.) This offering was meant to induce others to follow their example. Even jewelry and plate were accepted. Since the Oppian law had already (Livy, 34, 1) limited very severely the amount of jewelry and plate that could be used by individuals, the amount of gold and silver deposited was probably large. The repayment in 204, 202, and 200 proved difficult. (In the spring of 1917, when Italy was in need of gold, Professor Lanciani called attention to this passage in Livy, and on Rome's birthday a procession of thousands of Italians marched through the forum to deposit in baskets their free-will offerings for the state, in emulation of their ancestors.)

Livy, 26, 36, 5-8, 11-12; Laevinus speaks: aurum, argentum, *aes* signatum omne senatores crastino die in publicum conferamus, ita ut anulos sibi quisque et coniugi et liberis, et filio bullam, et, quibus uxor filiaeve sunt, singulas uncias pondo auri relinquant; argenti, qui curuli sella sederunt, equi ornamenta et libras pondo, ut salinum patellamque deorum causa habere possint, ceteri senatores libram argenti tantum; aeris signati quina milia in singulos patres familiae relinquamus: ceterum omne aurum, argentum, aes signatum ad triumviros mensarios extemplo deferamus nullo ante senatus consulto facto, ut voluntaria conlatio et certamen adiuvandae rei publicae excitet ad aemulandum animos primum equestris ordinis, dein reliquae plebis. . . . senatu inde misso pro se quisque aurum *et* argentum et aes in publicum conferunt tanto certamine iniecto, ut prima aut inter primos nomina sua vellent in publicis tabulis esse, ut nec triumviri accipiundo nec scribae referundo sufficerent. hunc consensum senatus equester ordo est secutus, equestris ordinis plebs. Ita sine edicto, sine coercitione magistratus nec remige in supplementum nec stipendio res publica eguit; paratisque omnibus ad bellum consules in provincias profecti sunt.

" Let us, senators, bring into the treasury to-morrow all our gold, silver, and coined bronze, each reserving rings for himself, his wife, and children, and a bulla for his son; and he who has a wife or daughters, an ounce weight of gold for each. Let those who have sat in a curule chair keep the ornaments of a horse, and a pound weight of silver, that they may have a salt-cellar and a dish for the service of the gods, and let the rest of the senators keep only a pound of silver, let each father of a family reserve five thousand coined *asses*. All the rest of our gold, silver, and coined bronze, let us immediately carry to the triumviri for banking affairs, no decree of the senate having been previously made, so that our voluntary contributions, and our emulation in assisting the state, may excite the minds, first, of the equestrian order to emulate us, and after them of the rest of the community.' . . . The senate was then adjourned, and every member brought his gold, silver, and bronze into the treasury, each vying with the other to have his name appear among the first on the public tables; so that neither the triumviri were sufficient for receiving nor the notaries for entering the names. The unanimity displayed by the senate was imitated by the equestrian order, and that of the equestrian order by the commons. Thus, without any edict, or coercion of the magistrates, the state neither wanted rowers to make up the numbers, nor money to pay them; and after every thing had been got in readiness for the war, the consuls set out for their provinces."

In the year 204, Laevinus proposed that these contributions be returned. One-third was paid back at once (recent victories had brought in booty), a third was to be paid in two years, and the rest in four years.

Livy, 29, 16, 1-3 (cf. 26, 36 and 31, 13): Altera item res, prope aeque longo neglecta silentio, relata a M. Valerio Laevino est, qui privatis conlatas pecunias se ac M. Claudio consulibus reddi tandem aequum esse dixit; nec mirari quemquam debere in publica obligata fide suam praecipuam curam esse; nam praeterquam quod aliquid proprie ad consulem eius anni, quo conlatae pecuniae essent, pertineret, etiam se auctorem ita conferendi fuisse inopi aerario nec plebe ad tributum sufficiente. grata ea patribus admonitio fuit, iussisque referre consulibus decreverunt, ut tribus pensionibus ea pecunia solveretur; primam praesentem ii, qui tum essent, duas tertii et quinti consules numerarent.

" Another affair, likewise, which had been passed over in silence for an almost equally long period, was laid before the Senate by Marcus Valerius Laevinus, who said that equity required that the moneys which had been contributed by private individuals, when he and Marcus Claudius were consuls (210 B. C.), should now at length be repaid. Nor ought any one to feel surprised that a case, where the public faith was pledged, should have engaged his attention in an especial manner; for, besides that the matter appertained, in some degree, peculiarly to the consul of that year in which the money was contributed, he was himself the author of the measure when the treasury was drained and the people were unable to pay the taxes. This suggestion was well received by the Senate, and, bidding the consuls propose the question, they decreed, that this money should be paid in three instalments; that the present consuls should make the first payment immediately, and that the third and fifth consuls from that time should make the two remaining payments."

The third payment fell due in the year 200, when the state needed new resources for its Macedonian war. Hence public land was given to satisfy the claims, with a stipulation, however, that the state could reclaim these lands, if desired. They were never reclaimed.

Livy, 31, 13, 5-9: cum et privati aecum postularent, nec tamen solvendo aere alieno res publica esset, quod medium inter aecum et utile erat decreverunt, ut, quoniam magna pars eorum agros volgo venales esse diceret et sibimet emptis opus esse, agri publici, qui intra quinquagesimum lapidem esset, copia iis fieret: consules agrum aestimaturos et in iugera asses vectigal testandi causa publicum agrum esse imposituros, ut, si quis, cum solvere posset populus, pecuniam habere quam agrum mallet, restitueret agrum populo. laeti eam condicionem privati accepere; trientabulumque is ager, quia pro tertia parte pecuniae datus erat, appellatus.

" The demands of the private creditors being equitable, and the state being unable to discharge the debt, they decreed a middle course between equity and convenience; resolving that ' whereas many of the creditors mentioned that lands were frequently exposed to sale, and that they themselves wished to become purchasers, they should, therefore, have liberty to purchase any lands belonging to the public which lay within fifty miles of the city; that the consuls should make a valuation of these, and impose on each acre one as, as an acknowledgment that the land was the property of the public, in order that, when the state should become able to pay, if any one chose rather to have the money than the land, he might return it.' The private creditors accepted the terms with joy; and that land was called *Trientabulum* because it was given in lieu of the third part of their money."

10) *The sacred treasury used.* In 209 the state used the four thousand pounds of gold that had accrued from the five per cent tax on the value of manumitted slaves, a tax established 148 years before, and set apart for a special emergency treasure. Willers has plausibly suggested (*Corolla Num.,* 310) that the gold coins of 6 and 3 scruples that bear a youthful Janus-head were issued from this gold (Bahrfeldt, *Römische Goldmünzen,* and Giesecke, *Italia Numismatica,* 194, place this series earlier). If the gold was rated with silver at the war price of 16 : 1, the 4,000 pounds would equal about 5,000,000 silver denarii.[24]

Livy, 27, 10, 11-13: Cetera expedientibus, quae ad bellum opus erant, consulibus aurum vicensimarium, quod in sanctiore aerario ad ultimos casus servabatur, promi placuit. prompta ad quattuor milia pondo auri. inde quingena pondo data consulibus et M. Marcello et P. Sulpicio proconsulibus et L. Veturio praetori, qui Galliam provinciam erat sortitus, additumque Fabio consuli centum pondo auri praecipuum, quod in arcem Tarentinam portaretur; cetero auro usi sunt ad vestimenta praesenti pecunia locanda exercitui, qui in Hispania bellum secunda sua fama ducisque gerebat.

" While the consuls were getting in readiness all the other things which were necessary for the war, it was resolved that the vicesimary gold, which was preserved in the most sacred part of the treasury as a resource in cases of extreme exigency, should be drawn out. There were drawn out as many as four thousand pounds of gold, from which five hundred pounds each were given to the consuls, to Marcus Marcellus and Publius Sulpicius, proconsuls, and to Lucius Veturius, the praetor, who had by lot obtained Gaul as his province; and in addition, one hundred pounds of gold were given to the consul Fabius, as an extraordinary grant to be carried into the citadel of Tarentum. The rest they employed in contracts, for ready money, for clothing for the army which was carrying on the war in Spain, to their own and their general's glory."

[24] We have already reckoned this item above as a source of income. Numismatists are prone to choose the date of this withdrawal of gold for one of the gold issues known, but we ought to bear in mind that there were at least six occasions during the war when the treasury received much gold.

11) *A call for volunteers and contributions.* In 205 when Scipio proposed to invade Africa—which would require new levies, more ships, and much new equipment, which the state saw no means of providing—the Senate at the suggestion of Scipio resorted to a general appeal for volunteers and contributions in money and kind. Since Scipio was generally popular and offered a program that appealed to the imagination, this method proved very successful, especially in Etruria.

Livy, 28, 45, 13-21 (also important for the industries of Etruria) : Scipio cum, ut dilectum haberet, neque impetrasset neque magnopere tetendisset, ut voluntarios ducere sibi milites liceret, tenuit et, quia inpensae negaverat rei publicae futuram classem, ut quae ab sociis darentur ad novas fabricandas naves acciperet. Etruriae primum populi pro suis quisque facultatibus consulem adiuturos polliciti : Caerites frumentum sociis navalibus commeatumque omnis generis, Populonienses ferrum, Tarquinienses lintea in vela, Volaterrani interamenta navium et frumentum, Arretini tria milia scutorum, galeas totidem, pila gaesa hastas longas, milium quinquaginta summam pari cuiusque generis numero expleturos, secures rutra falces alveolos molas, quantum in quadraginta longas naves opus esset, tritici centum et viginti milia modium, et in viaticum decurionibus remigibusque conlaturos ; Perusini Clusini Russelani abietem in fabricandas naves et frumenti magnum numerum ; abiete ex publicis silvis est usus. Umbriae populi et praetor hos Nursini et Reatini et Amiternini Sabinusque omnis ager milites polliciti ; Marsi Paeligni Marrucinique multi voluntarii nomina in classem dederunt. Camertes cum aequo foedere cum Romanis essent, cohortem armatam sescentorum hominum miserunt. triginta navium carinae, viginti quinqueremes, decem quadriremes, cum essent positae, ipse ita institit operi, ut die quadragesimo quinto, quam ex silvis detracta materia erat, naves instructae armataeque in aquam deductae sint.

" Scipio, though he could not obtain leave to levy troops, a point which he did not urge with great eagerness, obtained leave to take with him such as volunteered their services ; and also, as he declared that the fleet would not be the occasion of expense to the state, he obtained permission to receive what was furnished by the allies for building fresh ships. First the cities of Etruria engaged to assist the consul

to the utmost of their respective abilities. The people of Caere furnished grain and provisions of every description for the crews; the
people of Populonia furnished iron; those of Tarquinii, cloth for sails;
those of Volaterrae, timber for ships and grain; those of Arretium,
three thousand shields and as many helmets, and of javelins, Gallic
darts, and long spears, they undertook to make up to the amount of
fifty thousand, an equal number of each description, together with as
many axes, mattocks, bills, buckets, and mills, as should be sufficient
for forty men of war, as well as a hundred and twenty thousand pecks
of wheat; and they also offered to contribute to the support of the
foremen and rowers on the voyage. The people of Perusia, Clusium,
and Rusellae furnished firs for building ships, and a great quantity of
grain. Scipio also received firs out of the public woods. The states of
Umbria, and, besides them, the people of Nursia, Reate, and Ami-
ternum, and all those of the Sabine territory, promised soldiers. Many
of the Marsi, Paeligni, and Marrucini volunteered to serve in the fleet.
The Camertes, as they were joined with the Romans in a league on
equal terms, sent an armed cohort of six hundred men. Having laid
the keels of thirty ships, twenty of which were quinqueremes, and ten
quadriremes, Scipio prosecuted the work with such diligence, that, on
the forty-fifth day after the materials were taken from the woods, the
ships, fully equipped and armed, were launched."

12) *The sale of public land.* That same year the Senate sold a
portion of the public land acquired by the capture of Capua a few years
before. This was a very unusual procedure. The land lay near the
Clanius, north of Cumae.

Livy, 28, 46, 4-6: et quia pecunia ad bellum deerat, agri Campani
regionem a fossa Graeca ad mare versam vendere quaestores iussi, indi-
cio quoque permisso, qui ager civis Campani fuisset, uti is publicus
populi Romani esset; indici praemium constitutum quantae pecuniae
ager indicatus esset pars decuma. et Cn. Servilio praetori urbano
negotium datum, ut Campani cives, ubi cuique ex senatus consulto
liceret habitare, ibi habitarent, animadverteretque in eos, qui alibi
habitarent.

" As there was a scarcity of money to carry on the war, the quaestors were ordered to sell a district of the Campanian territory extending from the Grecian trench to the sea, with permission to receive infor-

mation as to what land had belonged to a native Campanian, in order that it might be put into the possession of the Roman people. The reward fixed for the informer was a tenth part of the value of the lands so discovered. Gnaeus Servilius, the city praetor, was also charged with seeing that the Campanians dwelt where they were allowed, according to the decree of the Senate, and to punish such as dwelt anywhere else."

The extraordinary measures recorded above are as follows:

B. C.

217   Recoinage at reduced weight.

216   A loan from Hiero.

215   Contracts for supplies let to knights on credit.

214   Wages of rowers paid by a 3-5 per cent supertax levied upon the wealthy.

214   Building contracts let on credit.

214   Slaves bought on credit.

214   Trust funds of widows and orphans borrowed.

214   Remission of officers' stipends.

210   Voluntary contributions of metals, plate, and jewelry (later repaid).

205   Calls upon municipalities for materials and food for the African expedition.

205   Sale of public lands.

Presumably these items covered the expenses not paid by the more regular income mentioned above. The financing of the war may therefore be summed up somewhat as follows:

Expenses		Receipts	
Army stipends.	180,000,000 den.	Citizen tribute.	65,000,000 den.
Food for allied		Tithes	24,000,000 den.
troops	36,000,000 den.	Port dues, rent-	
Land transport.	15,000,000 den.	als, etc......	10,000,000 den.
Arms, etc., for		Booty	65,000,000 den.
armies	20,000,000 den.	Sacred treasury	5,000,000 den.
Navy and trans-		Loans, contribu-	
port	35,000,000 den.	tions, super-	
	286,000,000 den.	taxes, etc....	117,000,000 den.
			286,000,000 den.

In this summary there is some slight duplication, since some of the "contributions," especially of grain and material, lessened the expenses and since also some of the loans were paid back from booty during the last years of the war. But this is as far as we are able to go with the figures provided by the sources. The estimate must be considered as hypothetical in many respects. However it may provide some idea of the relative scale of the various financial operations. It is fair purely from the side of gold values to equate the denarius with 20 cents (see on *Coinage* above). Since the war lasted seventeen years, we may reckon the expense as averaging about three and a third million dollars the year at a time when all Roman property was worth about $200,000,000 and when the Roman population was somewhat over one million souls.

The terms of the treaty of peace of 201 are summarized by Polybius (15, 18) as follows:

ᾙν δὲ τὰ κεφάλαια τῶν προτεινομένων ταῦτα. πόλεις ἔχειν κατὰ Λιβύην ἃς καὶ πρότερον εἶχον ἢ τὸν τελευταῖον πόλεμον ἐξενεγκεῖν Ῥωμαίοις, καὶ χώραν ἣν καὶ τὸ παλαιὸν εἶχον, κτήνη καὶ σώματα καὶ τὴν ἄλλην ὕπαρξιν, ἀπὸ δὲ τῆς ἡμέρας ἐκείνης ἀσινεῖς Καρχηδονίους ὑπάρχειν, ἔθεσι καὶ νόμοις χρῆσθαι τοῖς ἰδίοις, ἀφρουρήτους ὄντας. ταῦτα μὲν οὖν ἦν τὰ φιλάνθρωπα, τὰ δ' ἐναντία τούτοις πάλιν τὰ κατὰ τὰς ἀνοχὰς ἀδικήματα γενόμενα πάντα Καρχηδονίους ἀποκαταστῆσαι Ῥωμαίοις, τοὺς αἰχμαλώτους καὶ δραπέτας ἐκ παντὸς ἀποδοῦναι τοῦ χρόνου, τὰ μακρὰ πλοῖα παραδοῦναι πάντα πλὴν δέκα τριήρων, ὁμοίως καὶ πάντας τοὺς ἐλέφαντας. πόλεμον μηδενὶ τῶν ἔξω τῆς Λιβύης ἐπιφέρειν καθόλου μηδὲ τῶν ἐν τῇ Λιβύῃ χωρὶς τῆς Ῥωμαίων γνώμης· οἰκίας καὶ χώραν καὶ πόλεις, καὶ εἴ τι ἕτερόν ἐστι Μασαννάσου τοῦ βασιλέως ἢ τῶν προγόνων ἐντὸς τῶν ἀποδειχθησομένων ὅρων αὐτοῖς πάντα ἀποδοῦναι Μασαννάσᾳ· σιτομετρῆσαί τε τὴν δύναμιν τριμήνου καὶ μισθοδοτῆσαι μέχρι ἂν ἐκ Ῥώμης ἀντιφωνηθῇ τι κατὰ τὰς συνθήκας· ἐξενεγκεῖν ἀργυρίου τάλαντα μύρια Καρχηδονίους ἐν ἔτεσι πεντήκοντα, φέροντας καθ' ἕκαστον ἐνιαυτὸν Εὐβοϊκὰ τάλαντα διακόσια· ὁμήρους δοῦναι πίστεως χάριν ἑκατὸν οὓς ἂν προγράψῃ τῶν νέων ὁ στρατηγὸς τῶν Ῥωμαίων, μὴ νεωτέρους τεσσαρεσκαίδεκα ἐτῶν μηδὲ πρεσβυτέρους τριάκοντα.

" The principal points of the conditions proposed were as follows. Carthage was to retain all the cities she formerly possessed in Africa before entering on the last war with Rome, all her former territory, all flocks, herds, slaves, and other property: from that day onward the Carthaginians were to suffer no injury, they were to be governed by their own laws and customs and to receive no garrison. These were the lenient conditions; the others of a contrary kind were as follows: Reparation was to be made to the Romans for all acts of injustice committed by the Carthaginians during the truce: prisoners of war and deserters who had fallen into their hands at any date were to be delivered up: they were to surrender their ships of war with the exception of ten triremes, and all their elephants: they were not to make war at all on any nation outside Africa and on no nation in Africa without consulting Rome: they were to restore to King Massinissa, within the boundaries that should subsequently be assigned, all houses, lands, and cities, and other property which had belonged to him or to his ancestors: they were to furnish the Roman army with sufficient corn for three months and pay the soldiers until a reply arrived from Rome regarding the treaty: they were to contribute ten thousand talents in fifty years, paying two hundred Euboic talents each year: finally they were to give as surety a hundred hostages chosen by the Roman general from among their young men between the age of fourteen and thirty."

VII.   CASUAL REFERENCES TO ECONOMIC ITEMS DURING THE WAR

Grain, supplies and prices. We have no normal grain prices for the period. Rome was at times hard pressed for grain. When, for instance, there were twenty-six legions and two hundred and fifty ships in service, about 3,000,000 bushels (12,000,000 modii) had to be found. This was about six times as much as the tithe provided. In 215 a special requisition for grain was laid on Sardinia (Livy, 23, 41, 6-7). In 216 Hiero was asked to provide grain for the army in Sicily, as we have seen (Livy, 23, 21, 5-6). In 210, after Hannibal had raided Latium, wheat rose to $2\frac{1}{2}$ denarii the modius (probably over three times the normal price); hence the Romans sent envoys to Egypt to buy grain (Pol., 9, 44) and compelled the rural folk to go back to their farms and increase production (Livy, 28, 11). In 205 they received grain from as far north as Arretium (Livy, 28, 45). We also learn indirectly that some of Scipio's supplies of grain came from Spain (Livy, 30, 26, 6). Italy, so far as it was not being devastated by the enemy, must have gone heavily into cereal culture.

It was partly in order to help grain growing—though also partly for the sake of revenue and for political rehabilitation—that the Senate hastened the recuperation of Sicily and Capua. The proconsul of Sicily made especial efforts after the fall of Syracuse to get emigrant Sicilians to return and resume farming (Livy, 27, 5) and the Senate even sent a messenger to the Olympic games in Greece to extend a public invitation to Sicilians to return with a promise that their properties would be restored (Livy, 27, 35, 4). At Capua in the first heat

8

of anger the Senate confiscated all the land and proposed to banish the citizens to north of the Tiber, leaving only merchants, freedmen, shopkeepers, and artisans in the city (Livy, 26, 34, and 27, 3, and 11) and even repeating the order later (Livy, 28, 46, 6). But, though Livy has forgotten to mention the fact, the Senate must have relented, as is usually the case with war exactions, for presently we find that the Capuan farmers were allowed to remain as renters (De Sanctis, *Storia,* III, 2, 342-7) and later to regain their citizenship. Probably the Senate needed the grain and the revenue and discovered that it could find neither citizen renters nor colonists in those days of increasing levies. The rehabilitation of Placentia sacked by the Gauls (Livy, 31, 21) and of Genoa burned by Mago (Livy, 30, 1) were, of course, due to military reasons.

After the war, when supplies stored for the army were thrown on the market at a reduced price in order to please the populace, the price fell exceedingly low, and some grain merchants gave their supplies to the shippers to pay the freight charges (Livy, 30, 38, 5). Twice at this time the price of 1 denarius per bushel (a sesterce the modius) is quoted (Livy, 30, 26, 5-6; 31, 4, 6), and finally the aediles disposed of the African stock at half this price (Livy, 31, 50).

These figures—from 20 cents to $2.00 the bushel—give us the very low and very high prices. In Delos the price of wheat about the middle of the century ranged between 4 and 7 drachmas the medimnos (from $\frac{2}{3}$ to $1\frac{1}{6}$ denarii the modius, Beloch, *Griech. Gesch.,* iv, 313). At Rome the normal price may therefore have been about 3 sesterces the modius (or 3 denarii, $=$ 60 cents, the bushel). Barley would be about half this price. This is the average price we found for the preceding chapter, and it is also the average price for the periods of Cato and of Cicero.

Devastation of South Italy. The sad devastation of almost all of South Italy from Capua to Tarentum between 216 and 204 brought very serious consequences not only to agriculture but to the political future of Rome and Italy. After the defeat at Cannae most of this region gradually accepted the side of Hannibal. Then began the awful series of counter attacks which wiped out some 400 villages (App., *Pun.* 134). Rome began to meet revolts with harsh measures, hoping thus to stop defections, whereas Hannibal's early policy was naturally to protect those who had joined his cause and from whom he now had to find his sustenance. But he, too, had presently to punish defection or to move loyal peoples out of their homes to cities that he could defend.

Polybius 9, 26, 2-8.

ἅμα γὰρ τῷ γενέσθαι τὴν Καπύην τοῖς Ῥωμαίοις ὑποχείριον εὐθέως ἦσαν, ὅπερ εἰκός, αἱ πόλεις μετέωροι, καὶ περιέβλεπον ἀφορμὰς καὶ προφάσεις τῆς πρὸς Ῥωμαίους μεταβολῆς· ὅτε δὴ καὶ δοκεῖ μάλιστα δυσχρηστηθεὶς 'Αννίβας εἰς ἀπορίαν ἐμπεσεῖν ὑπὲρ τῶν ἐνεστώτων. οὔτε γὰρ τηρεῖν τὰς πόλεις πάσας πολὺ διεστώσας ἀλλήλων δυνατὸς ἦν, καθίσας εἰς ἕνα τόπον, τῶν πολεμίων καὶ πλείοσι στρατοπέδοις ἀντιπαραγόντων, οὔτε διαιρεῖν εἰς πολλὰ μέρη τὴν αὑτοῦ δύναμιν οἷός τ' ἦν. εὐχείρωτος γὰρ ἔμελλε τοῖς ἐχθροῖς ὑπάρξειν καὶ διὰ τὸ λείπεσθαι τῷ πλήθει καὶ διὰ τὸ μὴ δύνασθαι πᾶσιν αὐτὸς συμπαρεῖναι. διόπερ ἠναγκάζετο τὰς μὲν προδήλως ἐγκαταλείπειν τῶν πόλεων, ἐξ ὧν δὲ τὰς φρουρὰς ἐξάγειν, ἀγωνιῶν μὴ κατὰ τὰς μεταβολὰς τῶν πραγμάτων συγκαταφθείρῃ τοὺς ἰδίους στρατιώτας. ἐνίας (δὲ) καὶ παρασπονδῆσ' ὑπέμεινε, μετανιστὰς εἰς ἄλλας πόλεις καὶ ποιῶν ἀναρπάστους αὐτῶν τοὺς βίους. ἐξ ὧν προσκόπτοντες οἱ μὲν ἀσέβειαν, οἱ δ' ὠμότητα κατεγίνωσκον.

" For as soon as Capua fell into the hands of the Romans the other cities naturally became restless, and began to look round for opportunities and pretexts for revolting back again to Rome. It was then that Hannibal seems to have been at his lowest point of distress and despair. For neither was he able to keep a watch upon all the cities so widely removed from each other,—while he remained entrenched at one spot, and the enemy were manoeuvering against him with several armies,— nor could he divide his force into many parts; for he would have put an easy victory into the hands of the enemy by becoming inferior to them in numbers, and finding it impossible to be personally present at all points. Wherefore he was obliged to abandon completely some of the cities, and withdraw his garrisons from others: being afraid lest, in the course of the revolutions which might occur, he should lose his own soldiers as well. Some cities again he made up his mind to treat with treacherous violence, removing their inhabitants to other cities, and giving their property up to plunder; in consequence of which many were enraged with him, and accused him of impiety or cruelty."

Some typical instances of Roman and Punic severity are these: Livy, 24, 20, 4-6 (214) Rome storms some nine towns, taking captive or killing 25,000 and apparently razing the towns; Livy, 24, 47, 14, destroys Atrium, taking 7,000 captives; Capua and Syracuse were looted, though the citizens were not enslaved; Tarentum was looted and 30,000 prisoners taken and sold, though these, as Livy (27, 16, 7) says, may have been slaves and not citizens. Croton was looted and largely destroyed by the Bruttian partisans of Hannibal (Livy, 24, 3); Hannibal destroyed Herdonea (Livy, 27, 1). Diodorus, 27, 9, adds, though perhaps on dubious authority, that Hannibal at last slew 20,000 who refused to leave Italy with him.

The result of all this was that at towns razed by the Romans the Senate confiscated most of the land and declared it ager publicus, that at towns deserted because they lay in the path of the countermarching armies or because Hannibal had devasted the country Rome later took possession of all lands no longer claimed. After the war there were few colonists for such land and most of it lay unused until the state rented it to graziers. Certain it is that Roman ranches extended very widely over Lucania and Apulia during the next two centuries and that the extensive public lands which the Gracchi wished to colonize fell to the state at this period. It is also quite apparent that Rome's success at producing olive oil and wine with profit during the next century was due in part to the destruction of the southern gardens during this war.

Captives, slave labor, prices of slaves. The use of slaves increased rapidly during the war. The lack of man-power is stressed repeatedly (cf. Livy, 28, 11). Slaves were much in demand when a large part of the land-owners had to leave their farms for army service (the mortality rate in the armies facing Hannibal was unusually high), and when free labor was extensively drawn upon for rowers in the navy and transport service, and again later when the renters of the public lands needed slaves for their ranches. Enslavement of war captives increased during the war. There were apparently few taken at Syracuse or Capua, but 30,000 were taken at Tarentum in 209.

We do not happen to have any statement about the normal price of slaves for the period for Rome. The prices that occur in Plautus are apparently Greek prices and usually refer to captive women and hetaerae not used for labor. (Various courtesans, *Mercator,* 429 and *Pseud.,* 52: 2,000 drachmas; *Curc.,* 63, *Merc.,* 432, *Most.,* 300: 3,000 drachmas; *Epid.,* 52: 4,000 drachmas; *Mercator,* 440: 5,000; *Curc.,* 64, *Pers.,* 665: 6,000. An able-bodied slave is quoted at 2,000 in *Capt.,* 364; a child at 600, *ibid.,* 974.)

In the First Punic War we noticed that 14,000 captives at Palermo were allowed to go free at a ransom price of 200 denarii. During the Second Punic War the ransom price varied. After exchanging prisoners with Fabius in 217, Hannibal had a surplus of 240 for which he received 250 drachmas (denarii) per man [25] (Livy, 22, 23, 6, says $2\frac{1}{2}$ pounds of silver = about 210 denarii). After Cannae in 216 Hannibal set the following ransom prices on his prisoners: for citizen soldiers, 300 *quadrigati*; for allies, 200; for slaves, 100; for knights, 500 (Livy, 22, 52, 3, and 58, 4. Polybius, 6, 58, gives 3 minas = 300 denarii without specifying differences).[26] He probably did not set the price high, for Rome was then very poor and he had more captives than he could readily dispose of in Italy in war time. Rome refused to ransom these. At Casilinum in 216 the small Praenestine garrison of about 300 men was released on the payment of $\frac{7}{12}$ of a pound of gold per man (Livy, 23, 19, 16). At the ratio of 12 : 1 this would equal 583 denarii per man. Praeneste was prosperous and Hannibal doubtless set a high price for that reason.

Finally, after the war was over and the Romans had invaded Macedonia, the Achaeans permitted the Romans to ransom the Roman prisoners of war that Hannibal had sold in Greece. The price per man was 500 denarii (Livy, 34, 50), which was probably fairly high, since the Romans were then considered prosperous. It is perhaps permissible to infer from these prices that able-bodied slaves brought about 400–500 denarii. This was also the average price in Greece at the turn of the century (Beloch, *Griech. Gesch.*, IV, 322).

Some attempt might be made to estimate the slave population from the statement that the sacred treasury had by the year 209 accumulated 4,000 pounds of gold from the 5% manumission tax on freed slaves (Livy, 27, 10, 12). This tax was instituted 148 years before (Livy, 7, 16, 7). This gold amounted to about 4,000,000 denarii at the prewar ratio and would imply an average of 1,350 slaves set free per year throughout the period, if slave prices averaged 400 denarii. This

[25] Plutarch, *Fabius*, 7, 5, says 250 drachmas. Perhaps he calculated the $2\frac{1}{2}$ pounds of silver into the lighter coins of his own day.

[26] The *quadrigatus* of that period was worth $1\frac{1}{2}$ denarii, but before long it was reduced to the size of the denarius. Probably Polybius had seen some of these lighter coins, for he refers to the citizen soldiers. If Livy took his figures from Fabius Pictor, we should assume the ransom prices to be 450, 300, 150, 750 denarii respectively.

may be compared with 16,000 per year at the end of the Republic (see *Am. Jour. Phil.*, 1932, 360). Since in the early Republic slaves were treated with some liberality, being granted citizenship on liberation, we may perhaps hazard a guess that this number represented at least 5% of the whole body and that the whole number of slaves had been about 10 to 15% of the population during the third century. But there are too many unknown quantities in the reckoning to make it of positive value.

The knights' corporations. We have very little information about the semipublic corporations of knights during this war. Under item 3, of extraordinary financial measures enumerated above, we noticed that nineteen men forming three corporations of knights (Livy, 23, 48 and 49) undertook to supply the Spanish army on credit in 215, on condition that the state exempt them from war service and bear all losses from attack or storm. If this refers only to grain and clothing for two legions, the amount required would hardly be $200,000 (1,000,000 denarii) or an investment of $10,000 each. The knights were apparently of no great importance and, when Livy speaks of " the wealth they had derived from state contracts," one may suspect him of an anachronism. Two of the men, as we have seen, subsequently defrauded the state by charging for rotten hulks that were not seaworthy. It is difficult to believe that the state continued them in service thereafter.

Later, in 214, the knights who took state contracts in public building operations offered to do the necessary " repairs to sacred edifices " on credit and presumably were given the contracts (Livy, 24, 18, 10). But there are very few traces of building operations during this war. Knights were not employed in the collection of the citizen tax or the tithes of the provinces and, after the distribution of the Ager Gallicus, there was but little public land from which to collect rentals. The state did not as yet own mines, and the port-dues, if indeed any were collected at this time, must have been very small. On the whole we must conclude that the semipublic corporations of knights were rather insignificant during the Second Punic War.

Commerce. Before the war there seems to have been but little sea-going commerce in Roman hands. We conclude from Polybius that Rome took little interest in the complaints of the Italian (Southern

Greek) merchantmen who were attacked by Illyrian pirates (Polybius, 2, 8, 1-4: "From time immemorial the Illyrians had oppressed and pillaged vessels sailing from Italy. . . . Though complaints against the Illyrians had reached the Roman government in times past, they had always been neglected; but now (230 B. C.) when more and more persons approached the senate on this subject, they appointed two ambassadors to go to Illyricum and investigate." (See Holleaux' full discussion in *Cambridge Ancient History,* VII, 829 ff.) The same fact seems to be implied by the Claudian plebiscite, passed apparently in 220, which forbade senators to take an active part in commerce; Livy, 21, 63 (a dead letter in Cicero's day; *Verr.,* 5, 45, but revived by Caesar): "Flaminius was also hated by the senators on account of a new law that the tribune Q. Claudius had passed against the senate, a law which Flaminius alone of the senators supported, that no senator or senator's son should have any ship of over 300 amphorae (= about 225 bushels); this would suffice to carry grain from their fields: all gainful occupation on the part of senators appeared unseemly." (The law seems, however, to imply that a merchant class was growing which feared competition from senators.)

There is also the curious fact that Rome did not make a commercial treaty with her new ally Massinissa after the war, so that there was no trade between Italy and Numidia until 146 B. C. (Fenestella in Suet., *de Poetis,* 6, 1).

However, despite this lack of interest in commerce, a vigorous trade in necessities of war and food grew up during the war, carried partly by the navy's transport service, partly by merchantmen, and in part by state contractors. The supplies sent to Spain in 215 (Livy, 23, 48; see above) were procured and carried by state contractors, while praetors and governors of Sicily and Sardinia were constantly sending supplies to Rome and to Scipio in Africa by means of naval transports. But there is also mention in one instance of merchants who lost money on their cargoes of grain when they found the market at Rome already glutted (Livy, 30, 38). The Delian inscriptions (see next chapter) indicate that Romans did not enter trade to any extent till after the Gracchan days. Italian commerce continued largely in the hands of South Italians operating especially from the Greek cities of Campania and southern Italy.

Industry. War industries must have flourished in supplying arms and armor, military clothing, and implements, besides ships and wagons, but of this also we have no information except in the case of some allied Etruscan cities that offered various articles of equipment to Scipio in 205 (Livy, 28, 45, see above):

Caere offered grain and all kinds of provisions for the crews.

Populonia gave iron (probably from the mines of Elba).

Tarquinii, cloth for sails.

Volaterrae, timber and grain.

Arretium, 3,000 shields, 3,000 helmets, 50,000 Gallic spears and as many javelins, and axes, mattocks, bills, buckets, and mills enough for forty ships, besides grain and provisions. (Arretium was apparently an important manufacturing city specializing in iron and bronze ware.)

Perusia, Clusium, and *Rusellae* gave fir and grain.

In general, however, industries must have suffered when every available man was levied for war service.

The flourishing industries of the South must have suffered severely during the war. Capua lost her corporate existence in 211, many of her foremost citizens were executed for treason, and her lands were confiscated and rented out, presumably to the original holders (Livy, 26, 11 and 16; 27, 3 and 11). Since the main part of the urban as well as the rural population remained, industries were not wholly destroyed, and in the next century we hear again of a restoration of the old activity. Presumably Rome had placed some of her war contracts there. Tarentum, another town of diverse production, suffered similarly when captured first by Hannibal and then by the Romans (Livy, 25, 8; 27, 15). The latter plundered the town, took 30,000 prisoners, and confiscated much of the land. Tarentum never again recovered her former prestige in commerce and manufacturing.

There was, of course, no great building activity at Rome during the war. The walls had to be repaired in 212 in view of the fact that Hannibal was not far off (Livy, 25, 7, 5). A few temples were vowed by generals (Livy, 22, 9, 10; 27, 25) and we are told (Livy, 24, 18) that the contractors were willing to carry on ordinary repairs on credit. But in general nothing was done by way of construction that could be postponed.

It is interesting to find the mention of a workman's gild as early as about 200 B. C. *C. I. L.*, I², 364 records a collegium of cooks at Falerii; the officers of it are freeborn folk.

In order to gain some impression of industrial capabilities of Hellenistic engineers of this period it is well to read the fascinating description in Athenaeus (5, 206-9) of the ship of 4000 tons built for king Hiero at Syracuse by a Corinthian ship-architect. The date is about 230 B. C.:

"Hieron, the king of Syracuse, he who was in all respects friendly to Rome, not only interested himself in the building of temples and gymnasia, but was also a zealous shipbuilder, constructing wheat-transports, the construction of one of which I will proceed to describe. For material he caused timber to be brought from Aetna, enough in quantity for the building of sixty quadriremes. In keeping with this, he caused to be prepared dowels, belly-timbers, stanchions, and all the material for general uses, partly from Italy, partly from Sicily; for cables hemp from Iberia, hemp and pitch from the river Rhone, and all other things needful from many places. He also got together ship-wrights and all other kinds of artisans, and from them all he placed in charge the Corinthian Archias as architect, urging him to attack the construction zealously; and he personally applied himself diligently to the work during the days it required. One half, then, of the entire ship he finished in six months (lacuna) and as each part of the ship was completed it was overlaid with tiling made of lead; for there were about three hundred artisans working on the materials, not including their assistants. This part of the ship, then, was ordered to be launched in the sea, that it might receive the finishing touches there. But after considerable discussion in regard to the method of pulling in into the water, Archimedes the mechanician alone was able to launch it with the help of a few persons. For by the construction of a windlass he was able to launch a ship of so great proportions in the water. Archimedes was the first to invent the construction of the windlass. The remaining parts of the ship were completed in another period of six months; it was entirely secured with bronze rivets, most of which weighed ten pounds, while the rest were half as large again; these were fitted in place by means of augers, and held the stanchions together; fixed to the timbers was a sheath of leaden tiles, under which were strips of linen canvas covered with pitch. When, then, he had completed the outside surface, he proceeded to make complete the inner arrangements.

" Now the ship was constructed to hold twenty banks of rowers, with three gangways. The lowest gangway which it contained led to the cargo, the descent to which was afforded by companion-ways of solid construction; the second was designed for the use of those who wished to enter the cabins; after this came the third and last, which was for men posted under arms. Belonging to the middle gangway were cabins for men ranged on each side of the ship, large enough for four couches, and numbering thirty. The officers' cabin could hold fifteen couches and contained three apartments of the size of three couches; that toward the stern was the cooks' galley. All these rooms has a mosaic flooring made of a variety of stones, in the pattern of which was wonderfully wrought the entire story of the *Iliad*; also in the furniture, the ceiling, and the doors all these themes were artfully represented. On the level of the uppermost gangway there were a gymnasium and promenades built on a scale proportionate to the size of the ship; in these were garden-beds of every sort, luxuriant with plants of marvellous growth, and watered by lead tiles hidden from sight; then there were bowers of white ivy and grape-vines, the roots of which got their nourishment in casks filled with earth, and receiving the same irrigation as the garden-beds. These bowers shaded the promenades. Built next to these was a shrine of Aphrodite large enough to contain three couches, with a floor made of agate and other stones, the most beautiful kinds found in the island; it had walls and ceiling of cypress-wood, and doors of ivory and fragrant cedar; it was also most lavishly furnished with paintings and statues and drinking-vessels of every shape.

" Adjoining the Aphrodite room was a library large enough for five couches, the walls and doors of which were made of boxwood; it contained a collection of books, and on the ceiling was a concave dial made in imitation of the sun-dial on Achradina. There was also a bathroom, of three-couch size, with three bronze tubs and a wash-stand of variegated Tauromenian marble, having a capacity of fifty gallons. There were also several rooms built for the marines and those who manned the pumps. But beside these there were ten stalls for horses on each side of the ship; and next them was the storage-place for the horses' food, and the belongings of the riders and their slaves. There was also a water-tank at the bow, which was kept covered and had a capacity of twenty thousand gallons; it was constructed of planks, caulked with pitch and covered with tarpaulins. By its side was built a fish-tank enclosed with lead and planks; this was filled with sea-water, and many fish were kept in it. On both sides of the ship were projecting beams, at proper intervals apart; on these were constructed receptacles for wood, ovens, kitchens, handmills, and several other utensils. Outside, a row of colossi, nine feet high, ran round the ship; these supported the upper weight and the triglyph, all standing at proper intervals apart. And the whole ship was adorned with appropriate paintings. There were also eight turrets on it, of a size proportional to the weight of the ship; two at the stern, an equal number at the bow, and the rest amidships. To each of these two cranes were made fast, and over them portholes were built, through which stones could be hurled at an enemy sailing underneath. Upon each of the turrets were mounted four sturdy men in full armour, and two archers. The whole interior of the turrets was full of stones and missiles. A wall with battlements and decks athwart the ship was built on supports; and on this stood a stone-hurler, which could shoot by its own power a stone weighing one hundred and eighty pounds or a javelin eighteen feet long. This engine was constructed by Archimedes. Either one of these missiles could be hurled six hundred feet. After this came leather curtains joined together, suspended to thick beams by means of bronze chains. The ship carried three masts, from each of which two stone-hurling cranes were suspended; from them grappling hooks and lumps of lead could also be directed against assailants. An iron paling which encircled the ship also protected it against any who attempted to climb aboard; also grappling-cranes of iron were all about the ship, which, operated by machinery, could lay hold of the enemy's hulls and bring them alongside where they would be exposed to blows. Sixty sturdy men in full armour mounted guard on each side of the ship, and a number equal to these manned the masts and stone-hurlers. Also at the masts, on the mast-heads (which were of bronze), men were posted, three on the foremast, two in the maintop and one on the mizzenmast; these were kept supplied by the slaves with stones and missiles carried aloft in wicker baskets to the crow's-nests by means of pulleys. There were four anchors of wood, eight of iron. The trees for the mainmast and mizzenmast were easily found; but that for the foremast was discovered with difficulty by a swineherd in the mountains of the Bruttii; it was hauled down to the coast by the engineer Phileas of Tauromenium. The bilge-water, even when it became very deep, could easily be pumped out by one man with the aid of the screw, an invention of Archimedes. The ship was named ' Syracusia '; but when Hieron sent her forth, he changed the name to ' Alexandris.'   The boats which it had in tow were first a pinnace of three thousand talents burden; this was propelled entirely by oars.   After this came fishing-boats of fifteen hundred talents burden, and several cutters besides.   The numbers composing the crew were not less than (lacuna).   Next to these just mentioned there were six hundred more men at the bow ready to carry out orders.   For any crimes committed on board there was a court composed of the skipper, pilot, and officer at the bow, who gave judgment in accordance with the laws of Syracuse.

" On board were loaded ninety thousand bushels of grain, ten thousand jars of Sicilian salt-fish, six hundred tons of wool, and other freight amounting to six hundred tons.   Quite apart from this was the provisioning of the crew.   But when Hieron began to get reports of all the harbours, either that they could not receive his ship at all, or that great danger to the ship was involved, he determined to send it as a present to King Ptolemy at Alexandria; for there was in fact a scarcity of grain throughout Egypt.   And so he did; and the ship was. brought to Alexandria, where it was pulled up on shore."

CHAPTER III

DURING THE EASTERN WARS: 200–150 B. C.

I. CHRONOLOGY

200–196	Second Macedonian War
197	Philip defeated at Cynoscephalae
195	Cato governor of Spain
194	Evacuation of Greece
193	Citizen colonies sent to South Italy
192–189	War with Aetolians and Antiochus the Great
189	Battle of Magnesia
189–188	War with Galati of Asia
184	Cato's censorship
183	Citizen colonies at Parma and Mutina
181	Latin colony at Aquileia
173	Latins struck off citizen rolls
171	War declared on Perseus
169	Lex Voconia
168	Paullus defeats Perseus at Pydna
167	Epirus plundered. Citizen taxes cease
161	Lex Fannia
154	Lusitanians revolt
149	Third Carthaginian War; Macedonian revolts

II. POPULATION AND LAND

1. Census Statistics (adult male citizens):

204	214,000	Livy, 29, 37
194 [1]	143,704	Livy, 35, 9
189 [2]	258,318	Livy, 38, 36
179 [3]	258,294	Livy, *Epit.* 41
174 [4]	269,015	Livy, 42, 10
169	312,805	Livy, *Epit.* 45
164	337,452	Livy, *Epit.* 46; Plut., *Paul.*, 38
159	328,316	Livy, *Epit.* 47
154	324,000	Livy, *Epit.* 48
147 [5]	322,000	Hieron, Ol., 158, 2

1. The low number of this year is probably explained by the fact that the census-takers sometimes failed to register the soldiers serving abroad. In 194 there were about eight legions (c. 40,000 men) abroad and many marines.

2. The large increase seems to be due, not only to a full registration of soldiers, but in part to the fact that this year the Campanians (c. 40,000) were registered for the first time after their defection (Livy, 38, 36).

3. Livy says the number was affected by the decree of the consuls that socii and Latins must register in their home towns. There was also a pestilence in 187 when the army came back from the East (Livy, 38, 44), and again in 181-180 (Livy, 40, 19 and 36).

4. The pestilence of 174 (Livy, 41, 21) kept the number down somewhat.

5. The list had reached the high point in 164, after which it decreased till 136 when the number is 317,933. That is, the increase for forty years had been at the rate of 3% the year, or, excluding the re-enrolled Campanians, about 2% between 204 and 164. From then on, during the next twenty-eight years, there was a decrease of about 20,000, though only one small colony had been sent out in that period. The decrease was probably due to the growth of slave-worked estates and the consequent migration of poor farmers to the Po Valley.

a. Losses of citizens and allies in war (no record of deaths from disease):

Date

201	Livy, 31, 2	7000 in Gaul
200	31, 22	2000 in Gaul
199	32, 7	6700 in Gaul
196	33, 36	3000 in Gaul
194	34, 47	5000 in Gaul
193	35, 5	5000 in Gaul
190	37, 46	6000 in Spain
186	39, 20	4000 in Liguria
185	39, 30–31	5600 in Spain
181	40, 32	1000 in Spain
180	40, 40	1500 in Spain
173	42, 7	3000 in Liguria
171	42, 60	2200 in Macedonia
170	43, 9–11	10,000 in Illyricum
155–154	App., *Iber.*, 56	6000 + 9000 in Spain
153	App., *Iber.*, 45	6000 in Spain
153	App., *Iber.*, 46	4000 in Spain
151	App., *Iber.*, 58	7000 in Spain

2. Territorial Expansion.

a. Treatment of Public Land.

Appian, *B. C.*, 1, 7: Ῥωμαῖοι τὴν Ἰταλίαν πολέμῳ κατὰ μέρη χειρούμενοι γῆς μέρος ἐλάμβανον καὶ πόλεις ἐνῴκιζον ἢ ἐς τὰς πρότερον οὔσας κληρούχους ἀπὸ σφῶν κατέλεγον. καὶ τάδε μὲν ἀντὶ φρουρίων ἐπενόουν, τῆς δὲ γῆς τῆς δορικτήτου

σφίσιν ἑκάστοτε γιγνομένης τὴν μὲν ἐξειργασμένην αὐτίκα τοῖς οἰκιζομένοις ἐπιδιῄρουν
ἢ ἐπίπρασκον ἢ ἐξεμίσθουν, τὴν δ' ἀργὸν ἐκ τοῦ πολέμου τότε οὖσαν, ἢ δὴ καὶ
μάλιστα ἐπλήθυεν, οὐκ ἄγοντές πω σχολὴν διαλαχεῖν ἐπεκήρυττον ἐν τοσῷδε τοῖς
ἐθέλουσιν ἐκπονεῖν ἐπὶ τέλει τῶν ἐτησίων καρπῶν, δεκάτῃ μὲν τῶν σπειρομένων,
πέμπτῃ δὲ τῶν φυτευομένων. ὥριστο δὲ καὶ τοῖς προβατεύουσι τέλη μειζόνων τε
καὶ ἐλαττόνων ζῴων. καὶ τάδε ἔπραττον ἐς πολυανδρίαν τοῦ Ἰταλικοῦ γένους,
φερεπονωτάτου σφίσιν ὀφθέντος, ἵνα συμμάχους οἰκείους ἔχοιεν. ἐς δὲ τοὐναντίον
αὐτοῖς περιῄει. οἱ γὰρ πλούσιοι τῆσδε τῆς ἀνεμήτου γῆς τὴν πολλὴν καταλαβόντες
καὶ χρόνῳ θαρροῦντες οὔ τινα σφᾶς ἔτι ἀφαιρήσεσθαι τά τε ἀγχοῦ σφίσιν ὅσα τε
ἦν ἄλλα βραχέα πενήτων, τὰ μὲν ὠνούμενοι πειθοῖ, τὰ δὲ βίᾳ λαμβάνοντες, πεδία
μακρὰ ἀντὶ χωρίων ἐγεώργουν, ὠνητοῖς ἐς αὐτὰ γεωργοῖς καὶ ποιμέσι χρώμενοι τοῦ
μὴ τοὺς ἐλευθέρους ἐς τὰς στρατείας ἀπὸ τῆς γεωργίας περισπᾶν, . . .

" The Romans, as they subdued the Italian peoples successively in
war, used to seize a part of their lands and build towns there, or enrol
colonists of their own to occupy those already existing, and their idea
was to use these as outposts; but of the land acquired by war they
assigned the cultivated part forthwith to the colonists, or sold or
leased it. Since they had no leisure as yet to allot the part which
then lay desolated by war (this was generally the greater part), they
made proclamation that in the meantime those who were willing to
work it might do so for a toll of the yearly crops, a tenth of the grain
and a fifth of the fruit. From those who kept flocks was required a
toll of the animals, both oxen and small cattle. They did these things
in order to multiply the Italian race, which they considered the most
laborious of peoples, so that they might have plenty of allies at home.
But the very opposite thing happened; for the rich, getting possession
of the greater part of the undistributed lands, and being emboldened
by the lapse of time to believe that they would never be dispossessed,
absorbing any adjacent strips and their poor neighbours' allotments,
partly by purchase under persuasion and partly by force, came to
cultivate vast tracts instead of single estates, using slaves as labourers
and herdsmen, lest free labourers should be drawn from agriculture
into the army."

This famous passage is a part of the preface to the discussion of the Gracchan
reforms. The seizures mentioned in the first sentence often amounted to a third
if the war had been very costly; but there are numerous instances of peace treaties
that carried no exactions. Ten per cent of Italian land would be a generous estimate of the property taken, and a large part of this is assignable to the areas
devastated during the Second Punic War (see the next section). These areas of
public land the state was willing to rent out at the exceedingly low rental of a
tithe immediately after the Punic war because of the scarcity of colonists or

buyers. This was meant as an interim arrangement, but became permanent in Italy (except in Campania), probably because it was the influential Romans who took a large part of the leases. The social and economic consequences of the system instituted about 200 B. C. are well described in the last sentence of the paragraph. Since most of the Gracchan boundary stones have been found in the south, it is very likely that the public land that had been acquired before 218 B. C. had already been colonized by that time. Hence this passage of Appian applies mainly to the lands taken in consequence of decisions made during and immediately after the Second Punic War.

b. Cities Incorporated and Lands Confiscated.

During the war cities in the south had fallen before the attacks of Hannibal and of Rome (Appian, *Hann.*, 60, 61, *Pun.*, 134). Some of these were restored and left independent as before or incorporated in the Roman state; others lost their lands to the Roman public treasury. We can trace the existence of some of these lands in later colonization, but much of the territory was taken up in the large leaseholds which proved to be a bone of contention in the Gracchan days. After the war P. Sulpicius, as dictator, was sent south to investigate the status of the various cities which had fallen out with Rome (Livy, 30, 24, 3) and it was doubtless his decisions and revisions of previous decisions that were accepted as final.

With the aid of Beloch's researches (*Röm. Gesch.*, 583-96), we can give a partial list of the districts that were incorporated in the Ager Romanus at this time. This list comprises not only the confiscated lands, so far as these are known, but also several towns that were incorporated with full rights in the citizen body of Rome.

Samnium. In 214 (Livy, 24, 20, 4) Fabius was sent into Samnium to punish the towns that had revolted to Hannibal. He harassed the Caudine lands and captured Cubulteria, Telesia, and Compsa and took prisoners (cf. Livy, 23, 39, 6). He probably confiscated the lands of these towns. Some of Scipio's soldiers were given public land in Samnium, two jugera for each year of service (Livy, 31, 49, 5), but we are not told where. Telesia seems later to have received a Gracchan colony (Beloch, *Röm. Gesch.*, 494-5), and Gracchan boundary stones have been found not far from Abellinum (*C. I. L.*, I², nos 643-5).

In *Lucania* we know of public lands from Eburum southward along the Tanagra River, near Forum Popillii, Tegianum, Atina down past Grumentum to the coast; also on the western coast from Buxentum to Blanda. The evidence is as follows: Eburum had duumviri and belonged to the Fabian tribe (*C. I. L.*, X, 451); Forum Popillii was settled on public land in 132 (*C. I. L.,* I², 638); a Gracchan surveyor's mark (*C. I. L.,* I², 642) has been found near Tegianum and another near Atina (*ibid.,* 639); Grumentum had *praetores duumviri* (*C. I. L.,* X, 208), which indicates an early subjection to Rome, due probably to the Roman victory there in 205 (Livy, 23, 37, the territory of the town extended to the sea near Heraclea). Hence the Ager Romanus, partly because of conquest, partly because of friendly incorporation, ran through the center of Lucania from Campania to the southern coast. On the western coast a citizen colony was planted at Buxentum in 194 (Livy, 34, 45), and Blanda seems early to have become Roman, since its magistrates are duumviri. It was taken by the Romans in 214 (Livy, 24, 20, 5). Perhaps a half of Lucania fell to Rome before 200, though enough remained independent to make an effective resistance to Rome in the Social War.

In *Bruttium* the forest of Sila, comprising most of the lower peninsula, became Roman property (Cic., *Brut.,* 85), and so much of the southern coast was taken that colonies were planted at Croton (194, Livy, 34, 45), Thurii (Copia, 193, a Latin colony, Livy, 35, 9) and Scolacium (a Gracchan citizen colony), also Vibo (192), and Tempsa (194) on the western coast. It would seem that half of Bruttium must have been confiscated.

In *Apulia,* Tarentum lost some of its territory because of its defection to Hannibal (Livy, 44, 16) and on this a Gracchan colony was settled. Arpi also suffered for its treason (Pol., 3, 88; Livy, 24, 45-47) by the loss of land, on which the citizen colony of Sipontum was settled in 194 (Livy, 34, 45). Some confiscated lands seem also to have been given to veterans (Livy, 31, 4).

It is impossible to estimate the acreage of these confiscations; the colonies settled during the second century were relatively small, not for lack of land, but rather because after the Hannibalic War there were few colonists to send. The larger part of the land was probably rented out to ranchers and plantation owners. At any rate, when the Gracchan commissions in 132-22 had distributed much public land, there was still enough left so that Livius Drusus could propose some twelve new colonies. We also have evidence in Livy (33, 42, 10, and 35, 10, 12) that ranchers began to run cattle over public lands to such an extent that the fines collected from transgressors were considerable in amount.

9

3. *Colonization.*

Velleius Paterculus, I, 15, 1-3 :

Deinde neque dum Hannibal in Italia moratur, neque proximis post excessum eius annis vacavit Romanis colonias condere, cum esset in bello conquirendus potius miles quam dimittendus et post bellum vires refovendae magis quam spargendae. Cn. autem Manlio Volsone et Fulvio Nobiliore consulibus Bononia deducta colonia abhinc annos ferme ducentos septendecim, et post quadriennium Pisaurum ac Potentia interiectoque triennio Aquileia et Gravisca et post quadriennium Luca. Eodem temporum tractu, quamquam apud quosdam ambigitur, Puteolos Salernumque et Buxentum missi coloni, Auximum autem in Picenum abhinc annos ferme CLXXXV. (Velleius is sometimes careless about dates).

" Thereafter, during Hannibal's stay in Italy, and in the next few years subsequent to his departure, the Romans had no leisure for the founding of colonies, since, while the war lasted, they had to find soldiers, rather than muster them out, and, after it was over, the strength of the city needed to be revived and concentrated rather than to be dispersed. But, about two hundred and seventeen years ago (189 B. C), in the consulship of Manlius Volso and Fulvius Nobilior, a colony was established at Bononia, others four years later at Pisaurum and Potentia, others three years later still at Aquileia and Gravisca, and another four years afterwards at Luca. About the same time (although the date is questioned by some) colonists were sent to Puteoli, Salernum, and Buxentum, and to Auximum in Picenum, one hundred and eighty-five years ago."

Livy, 31, 4, 1-3 (200 B. C.) :

Exitu huius anni cum de agris veterum militum relatum esset, qui ductu atque auspicio P. Scipionis in Africa bellum perfecissent, decreverunt patres, ut M. Iunius praetor urbanus, si ei videretur, decemviros agro Samniti Apuloque, quod eius publicum populi Romani esset, metiendo dividendoque crearet. creati P. Servilius, Q. Caecilius Metellus, C. et M. Servilii—Geminis ambobus cognomen erat—, L. et A. Hostilii Catones, P. Villius Tappulus, M. Fulvius Flaccus, P. Aelius Paetus, T. Quinctius Flamininus.

" At the end of this year (201), when a bill was proposed to give land to the veterans who had completed the war in Africa under the leadership and auspices of P. Scipio, the Senate decreed that M. Junius the urban praetor, if it seemed best to him, should hold an election of a board of ten to survey and assign lands from the Roman public lands in Samnium and Apulia. The men elected were, etc."

Livy, 32, 29, 3-4 (198 B. C.):

C. Atinius tribunus plebis tulit, ut quinque coloniae in oram maritimam deducerentur, duae ad ostia fluminum Vulturni Liternique, una Puteolos, una ad Castrum Salerni: his Buxentum adiectum, trecenae familiae in singulas colonias iubebantur mitti. triumviri deducendis iis, qui per triennium magistratum haberent, creati M. Servilius Geminus, Q. Minucius Thermus, Ti. Sempronius Longus.

" Gaius Atinius, plebeian tribune, caused an order to be passed, that five colonies should be led out to the sea-coast; two to the mouths of the rivers Vulturnus and Liternus; one to Puteoli; and one to the fort of Salernum. To these was added Buxentum. To each colony three hundred families were ordered to be sent. The commissioners appointed to conduct them thither, and who were to hold the office for three years, were Marcus Servilius Geminus, Quintus Minucius Thermus, and Tiberius Sempronius Longus."

Livy, 34, 45, 1-5 (194 B. C):

Coloniae civium Romanorum eo anno deductae sunt Puteolos, Volturnum, Liternum, treceni homines in singulas. item Salernum Buxentumque coloniae civium Romanorum deductae sunt. deduxere triumviri Ti. Sempronius Longus, qui tum consul erat, M. Servilius, Q. Minucius Thermus. ager divisus est, qui Campanorum fuerat. Sipontum item in agrum, qui Arpinorum fuerat, coloniam civium Romanorum alii triumviri, D. Iunius Brutus, M. Baebius Tamphilus, M. Helvius, deduxerunt. Tempsam item et Crotonem coloniae civium Romanorum deductae. Tempsanus ager de Bruttiis captus erat; Bruttii Graecos expulerant; Crotonem Graeci habebant. triumviri Cn. Octavius, L. Aemilius Paulus, C. Laetorius Crotonem, Tempsam L. Cornelius Merula, Q. . . . , C. Salonius deduxerunt.

" In this year colonies of Roman citizens were settled at Puteoli, Vulturnum, and Liternum, three hundred men in each place. Colonies of Roman citizens were likewise established at Salernum and Buxentum. The lands allotted to them had formerly belonged to the Campanians. Tiberius Sempronius Longus, who was then consul, Marcus Servilius, and Quintus Minucius Thermus, were the triumviri who settled the colony. Other commissioners also, Decimus Junius Brutus, Marcus Baebius Tamphilus, and Marcus Helvius, led a colony of Roman citizens to Sipontum, into a district which had belonged to the Arpinians. To Tempsa, likewise, and to Croton, colonies of Roman citizens were led out. The lands of Tempsa and been taken from the Bruttians, who had formerly expelled the Greeks from them. Croton was possessed by Greeks. In ordering these establishments, there were named, for Croton, Gnaius Octavius, Lucius Aemilius Paullus, and Gaius Laetorius; for Tempsa, Lucius Cornelius Merula, Quintus . . . and Gaius Salonius."

Livy, 34, 53, 1-2 (194 B. C.):

Exitu anni huius Q. Aelius Tubero tribunus plebis ex senatus consulto tulit ad plebem, plebesque scivit, uti duae Latinae coloniae una in Bruttios, altera in Thurinum agrum deducerentur. his deducendis triumviri creati, quibus in triennium imperium esset, in Bruttios Q. Naevius, M. Minucius Rufus, M. Furius Crassipes, in Thurinum agrum A. Manlius, Q. Aelius, L. Apustius.

" At the end of that year Q. Aelius Tubero, tribune of the plebs, in accordance with a senatus consultum, proposed to the plebeian assembly, and the plebs voted, that two Latin colonies should be sent, one to the Bruttians, the other to the Thurine land. A board of three was elected with authorization for three years; etc."

These two colonies were duly settled in 193 and 192:

Livy, 35, 9, 7-8 (193 B. C., see preceding):

Eodem anno coloniam Latinam in castrum Frentinum triumviri deduxerunt A. Manlius Volso, L. Apustius Fullo, Q. Aelius Tubero, cuius lege deducebatur. tria milia peditum iere, trecenti equites, numerus exiguus pro copia agri. dari potuere tricena iugera in pedites, sexagena in equites. Apustio auctore tertia pars agri dempta est, quo postea, si vellent, novos colonos adscribere possent. vicena iugera pedites, quadragena equites acceperunt.

" During this year a Latin colony was established in the Frentine camp by commissioners appointed for the purpose, Aulus Manlius Vulso, Lucius Apustius Fullo, and Quintus Aelius Tubero, who had proposed the order for its settlement. There went out three thousand foot and three hundred horsemen, a very small number in proportion to the extent of the land. Thirty iugera might have been given to each footman, and sixty to a horseman, but, by the advice of Apustius, a third part was reserved, that they might afterwards, when they should judge proper, send out thither a new colony. The footmen received twenty iugera each, the horsemen forty."

Livy, 35, 40, 5-6 (192 B. C.) :

Eodem hoc anno Vibonem colonia deducta est ex senatus consulto plebique scito. tria milia et septingenti pedites ierunt, trecenti equites; triumviri deduxerunt eos Q. Naevius, M. Minucius, M. Furius Crassipes; quina dena iugera agri data in singulos pedites sunt, duplex equiti. Bruttiorum proxime fuerat ager; Bruttii ceperant de Graecis.

" In this year a colony was settled at Vibo, in pursuance of a decree of the Senate and an order of the people; three thousand seven hundred footmen, and three hundred horsemen, went out thither, conducted by the commissioners Quintus Naevius, Marcus Minucius, and Marcus Furius Crassipes. Fifteen iugera of ground were assigned to each footman, double that quantity to a horseman. This land had been last in the possession of the Bruttians, who had taken it from the Greeks."

Livy, 37, 46, 9 to 47, 2 (190 B. C.) :

ex Gallia legatos Placentinorum et Cremonensium L. Aurunculeius praetor in senatum introduxit. iis querentibus inopiam colonorum, aliis belli casibus, aliis morbo absumptis, quosdam taedio accolarum Gallorum reliquisse colonias, decrevit senatus, uti C. Laelius consul, si ei videretur, sex milia familiarum conscriberet, quae in eas colonias dividerentur, et ut L. Aurunculeius praetor triumviros crearet ad eos colonos deducendos. creati M. Atilius Serranus, L. Valerius P. F. Flaccus, L. Valerius C. F. Tappo. XLVII. Haud ita multo post, cum iam consularium comitiorum appeteret tempus, C. Laelius consul ex Gallia Romam rediit. is non solum ex facto absente se senatus consulto in supplementum Cremonae et Placentiae colonos scripsit, sed, ut novae coloniae duae in agrum, qui Boiorum fuisset, deducerentur, et rettulit et auctore eo patres censuerunt.

" Lucius Aurunculeius, the praetor, introduced to the Senate the deputies of Placentia and Cremona, in Cisalpine Gaul. When they complained of the want of colonists, some having been carried off by the casualties of war, others by sickness, and many having left the colonies through disgust at the vicinity of the Gauls, the Senate decreed that Gaius Laelius, the consul, if he thought proper, should enroll six thousand families to be distributed among these colonies, and that Lucius Aurunculeius, the praetor, should appoint commissioners to conduct the colonists. Accordingly, Marcus Atilius Serranus, Lucius Valerius Flaccus, son of Publius, and Lucius Valerius Tappo, son of Gaius, were nominated to that office.

Not long after, as the time of the consular elections drew near, the consul, Gaius Laelius, came home to Rome from Gaul. He not only enrolled the colonists, according to a decree of the Senate, passed in his absence, as a supplement to Cremona and Placentia, but proposed— and, on his recommendation, the Senate voted—that two new colonies should be established in the lands which had belonged to the Boians."

Livy, 37, 57, 7-8 (190 B. C.):

Eodem anno ante diem tertium Kal. Ianuarias Bononiam Latinam coloniam ex senatus consulto L. Valerius Flaccus, M. Atilius Serranus, L. Valerius Tappo triumviri deduxerunt. tria milia hominum sunt deducta; equitibus septuagena iugera, ceteris colonis quinquagena sunt data. ager captus de Gallis Bois fuerat; Galli Tuscos expulerant.

" In the same year, on the third day before the calends of January, Lucius Valerius Flaccus, Marcus Atilius Serranus, and Lucius Valerius Tappo, triumvirs, settled a Latin colony at Bononia, according to a decree of the Senate. Three thousand men were led to that place. Seventy iugera were given to each horseman, fifty to each of the other colonists. The land had been taken from the Boian Gauls, who had formerly expelled the Etruscans."

Livy, 39, 23, 3-4 (186 B. C.):

extremo anni, quia Sp. Postumius consul renuntiaverat peragrantem se propter quaestiones utrumque litus Italiae desertas colonias Sipontum supero, Buxentum infero mari invenisse, triumviri ad colonos eo scribendos ex senatus consulto ab T. Maenio praetore urbano creati sunt L. Scribonius Libo, M. Tuccius, Cn. Baebius Tamphilus.

" Towards the close of the year, because the consul Spurius Postumius reported that in travelling along the coast of Italy for the purpose of holding the inquisitions he had found two colonies deserted, Sipontum on the upper sea, and Buxentum on the lower, in pursuance of a decree of the Senate, Lucius Scribonius Libo, Marcus Tuccius, and Gneius Baebius Tamphilus, were appointed commissioners for conducting colonies thither by Titus Maenius, city praetor."

Livy, 39, 44, 10 (184 B. C.) :

Eodem anno coloniae duae, Potentia in Picenum, Pisarum in Gallicum agrum, deductae sunt. sena iugera in singulos data. diviserunt agrum coloniasque deduxerunt iidem tresviri, Q. Fabius Labeo, et M. et Q. Fulvii, Flaccus et Nobilior.

" This year, two colonies were established, Potentia in Picenum, and Pisaurum in the Gallic territory. Six iugera were given to each settler. The same commissioners had the ordering of both colonies and the division of the lands, Quintus Fabius Labeo, Marcus Fulvius Flaccus, and Quintus Fulvius Nobilior."

Livy, 39, 55, 5-9 (183 B. C.) :

illud agitabant, uti colonia Aquileia deduceretur, nec satis constabat, utrum Latinam an civium Romanorum deduci placeret. postremo Latinam potius coloniam deducendam patres censuerunt. triumviri creati sunt P. Scipio Nasica, C. Flaminius, L. Manlius Acidinus.

Eodem anno Mutina et Parma coloniae civium Romanorum sunt deductae. bina milia hominum in agro, qui proxime Boiorum, ante Tuscorum fuerat, octona iugera Parmae, quina Mutinae acceperunt. deduxerunt triumviri M. Aemilius Lepidus, T. Aebutius Parrus, L. Quinctius Crispinus. et Saturnia colonia civium Romanorum in agrum Caletranum est deducta. deduxerunt triumviri Q. Fabius Labeo, C. Afranius Stellio, Ti. Sempronius Gracchus. in singulos iugera data dena.

" They decided to establish a colony at Aquileia, but were not able to decide whether it should consist of Latins or Roman citizens; at last, however, they passed a vote in favour of a Latin settlement. The commissioners appointed for the purpose were Publius Scipio Nasica, Gaius Flaminius, and Lucius Manlius Acidinus. In the same year, colonies of Roman citizens were led out to Mutina and Parma. Two thousand men were settled in each colony, on lands which had lately belonged to the Boians, and formerly to the Etruscans; they received

at Parma eight iugera, at Mutina five each. These colonists were
conducted by Marcus Aemilius Lepidus, Titus Aebutius Parrus, and
Lucius Quinctius Crispinus. The colony of Saturnia, also consisting
of Roman citizens, was settled on the lands of Caletra by Quintus
Fabius Labeo, Gaius Afranius Stellio, and Tiberius Sempronius
Gracchus. Ten iugera were assigned to each man."

Polybius, 2, 35, 4:

περὶ ὧν ἡμεῖς συνθεωρήσαντες μετ᾽ ὀλίγον χρόνον αὐτοὺς ἐκ τῶν περὶ τὸν Πάδον
πεδίων ἐξωσθέντας, πλὴν ὀλίγων τόπων τῶν ὑπ᾽ αὐτὰς τὰς Ἄλπεις κειμένων, . . .

" As I have witnessed them (the Celts) not long afterwards entirely
expelled from the plain of the Po, except a few communities close
under the Alps."

Livy, 40, 29, 1-2 (181 B. C.):

Colonia Graviscae eo anno deducta est in agrum Etruscum, de
Tarquiniensibus quondam captum. quina iugera agri data; tresviri
deduxerunt C. Calpurnius Piso, P. Claudius Pulcher, C. Terentius
Istra.

" The colony of Graviscae was established this year in a district of
Etruria, formerly taken from the Tarquinians, and five iugera of
land were given to each settler. The commissioners who conducted it
were Gaius Calpurnius Piso, Publius Claudius Pulcher, and Gaius
Terentius Istra."

Livy, 40, 34, 2-4 (181 B. C.) and 43, 17, 1 (169 B. C.):

Aquileia colonia Latina eodem anno in agrum Gallorum est deducta.
tria milia peditum quinquagena iugera, centuriones centena, centena
quadragena equites acceperunt. tresviri deduxerunt P. Cornelius
Scipio Nasica, C. Flaminius, L. Manlius Acidinus.

Eo anno (169) postulantibus Aquileiensium legatis, ut numerus
colonorum augeretur, mille et quingentae familiae ex senatus consulto
scriptae,

" In the same year (181) the Latin colony of Aquileia was estab-
lished in the Gallic territory. Three thousand foot soldiers received
each fifty iugera, centurions a hundred, horsemen a hundred and forty.
The three commissioners who conducted the settlement were Publius
Cornelius Scipio Nasica, Gaius Flaminius and Lucius Manlius
Acidinus."

" This year (169), when the ambassadors of the Aquileians demanded that the number of the colonists should be increased, one thousand five hundred families were enrolled by a decree of the Senate; "

Since one man could not work as much as ten acres with hand tools, it is apparent that the colonists of Aquileia were to have leisure for garrison duty and to draw their livelihood from land rents. The same is true of the colony of Luna planted in 177 (see below).

Livy, 40, 43, 1, 180 B. C. (see art. *Luca* in R-E.) :

Pisanis agrum pollicentibus, quo Latina colonia deduceretur, gratiae ab senatu actae; triumviri creati ad eam rem. Q. Fabius Buteo, M. et P. Popilii Laenates.

" To the Pisans, offering ground for the establishment of a Latin colony, thanks were returned by the Senate, and triumvirs were appointed to conduct that business; these were Quintus Fabius Buteo, Marcus Popilius Laenas, and Publius Popilius Laenas."

Livy, 41, 13, 4-5, 177 B. C. (see art. *Luna* in R-E.) :

et Lunam colonia eodem anno duo milia civium Romanorum sunt deducta. triumviri deduxerunt P. Aelius, M. Aemilius Lepidus, Cn. Sicinius; quinquagena et singula iugera et semisses agri in singulos dati sunt. de Liguribus captus ager erat; Etruscorum ante quam Ligurum fuerat.

" The same year a colony of two thousand Roman citizens was settled at Luna. The triumvirs, Publius Aelius, Marcus Aemilius Lepidus, and Gnaius Sicinius, planted it. Fifty-one iugera and a half of land were given to each. This land had been taken from the Ligurians and had been the property of the Etrurians before it fell into their possession."

Livy, 42, 4, 3-4 (173 B. C.) :

Eodem anno, cum agri Ligustini et Gallici, quod bello captum erat, aliquantum vacaret, senatus consultum est factum, ut is ager viritim divideretur. decemviros in eam rem ex senatus consulto creavit A. Atilius praetor urbanus M. Aemilium Lepidum, C. Cassium, T. Aebutium Parrum, C. Tremellium, P. Cornelium Cethegum, Q. et L. Apuleios, M. Caecilium, C. Salonium, C. Munatium. diviserunt dena iugera in singulos, sociis nominis Latini terna.

" During the same year, on its appearing that large tracts of land in

Gaul and Liguria, which had been taken in war, lay unoccupied, the Senate passed a decree that those lands should be distributed in single shares; and Aulus Atilius, city praetor, in pursuance of the said decree, appointed ten commissioners for that purpose, namely Marcus Aemilius Lepidus, Gaius Cassius, Titus Aebutius Parrus, Gaius Tremellius, Publius Cornelius Cethegus, Quintus and Lucius Apuleius, Marcus Caecilius, Gaius Salonius, and Gaius Munatius. They apportioned ten iugera to each Roman, and three to each Latin colonist."

Livy, 43, 3, 1-4 (171 B. C.) a colony in Spain:

Et alia novi generis hominum ex Hispania legatio venit. ex militibus Romanis et ex Hispanis mulieribus cum quibus conubium non esset, natos se memorantes, supra quattuor milia hominum, orabant, ut sibi oppidum, in quo habitarent, daretur. senatus decrevit, uti nomina sua apud L. Canuleium profiterentur eorumque, si quos manumisissent; eos Carteiam ad Oceanum deduci placere; qui Carteiensium domi manere vellent, potestatem fieri uti numero colonorum essent, agro adsignato; Latinam eam coloniam esse libertinorumque appellari.

" There came also from Spain another embassy, from a new race of men. They, representing that they were the offspring of Roman soldiers and Spanish women to whom the Romans had not been united in wedlock, and that their number amounted to more than four thousand, petitioned for a grant of some town to be given them in which they might reside. The Senate decreed that they should put their names and the names of their freedmen on a list before Lucius Canuleius; that it was the Senate's pleasure that they should be settled as a colony at Carteia, on the ocean; that such of the present inhabitants of Carteia as wished to remain there, should have the privilege of being considered as colonists, and should have lands assigned them; that this should be deemed a Latin settlement, and be called a colony of freedmen."

Summary of Colonies:

a. Maritime colonies of citizens	No. of colonists	Jugera to each
194 Volturnum	300 families	?
194 Liternum	300 families	?
194 Puteoli	300 families	?
194 Salernum	300 families	?

194	Buxentum	300 families	?
194 ?	Pyrgi (Livy, 36, 3, 6)	?	?
194	Sipontum	?	?
194	Tempsa	?	?
194	Croton	?	?
184	Potentia in Picenum	?	6 jugera
184	Pisaurum in Picenum	?	6 jugera
184 ?	Auximum (cf. Livy, 41, 27, 10)	?	?
181	Graviscae	?	5 jugera

b. Agrarian citizen colonies

183	Mutina	2,000 men	5 jugera
183	Parma	2,000 men	8 jugera
183	Saturnia	?	10 jugera
177	Luna	2,000	51½ jugera

c. Latin colonies

193	Copia (Thurii)	3,000 pedites	20 jugera
		300 equites	40 jugera
192	Vibo Valentia	3,700 pedites	15 jugera
		300 equites	30 jugera
190	Placentia and Cremona	6,000 families	?
189	Bononia	3,000 families	ped. 50 jugera
			eq. 70 jugera
181	Aquileia	3,000 pedites	50 jugera
		? centurions	100 jugera
		? equites	140 jugera
180	Luca	(3,000 ?)	?

d. Allotments to individuals:

200	Scipio's veterans (Livy, 31, 49, 5)	2 jug. for each year's service
180	Forty thousand Ligurians were taken from their homes by force and settled near Beneventum (Livy, 40, 38, 6)	
173	Viritane gifts in Po Valley (Livy, 42, 4)	10 jugera to citizens 3 to allies

e. Sales of Campanian land to individuals:

205   Along the coast (Livy, 28,
         46)   ?   ?
199   *Sub Tifatis* (Livy, 32, 7)   ?   ?

The nine maritime colonies of the south received " families " and
the allotments were doubtless as large as in the Latin colonies of the
south, i. e. 15-20 jugera.   For the thirteen citizen colonies of this type
we may assume about 4,000 families receiving about 60,000 jugera.
The four agrarian colonies for citizens received about 8,000 men
requiring some 150,000 jugera.   The five Latin colonies were larger
because planted at points of some danger.   To induce Romans to give
up citizenship in order to direct the affairs of a new city, larger lots
had to be given.   The farmers of Bononia and Aquileia were to be men
of means and some leisure.   At this time of shortage of men at Rome,
it is likely that many of the settlers were not citizens.   These five colonies and the supplements to Venusia, Placentia, and Cremona required
about 25,000 men and 550,000 jugera.   The distribution to Scipio's
veterans was apparently not large, since many of them enrolled at
once for the eastern war.   The sale of land along the coast in 205
could hardly have been very extensive.   Two colonies were planted
here later.   We have no way of estimating the viritane settlements
of 173.

At any rate it would be safe to say that from forty to fifty thousand
settlers, mostly citizens, found land during the first 30 years of the
century and that at least a million jugera (c. 1,000 square miles) of
good farm land was used for this purpose.   The rest of the public
land was rented out on tithes.

The area of the Ager Romanus before the Hannibalic War has been
estimated by Beloch (*Röm. Gesch.*, 621) at about 24,000 square kilometers.   The areas confiscated and incorporated during this war can
hardly be determined.   They were, as we have seen, rather extensive
in Samnium, Lucania, Apulia, and Bruttium.   Beloch (in *Bevölkerung*,
320) adds 10,000 square kilometers for this (excluding the Sila forest
and the Taurasian district—about 3,000 square kilometers), which
seems to me a fair estimate.   Then he assumes 18,000 for Cispadane
Gaul, incorporated little by little during the years 200-180.   That is
to say, the Ager Romanus of 200 B. C. was about 34,000 square

kilometers, or about 13,000 square miles, and by the end of the period (150 B. C.) about 55,000 square kilometers, or about 21,000 square miles. However, in estimating property values and taxes, one must bear in mind that the property taken during the Punic War did not begin to be productive till after the war, that much of it was fit only for pasturage, and that considerable portions of the arable land were given away for the settlement of *Latin* colonies at Copia, Vibo, Placentia, Bononia, and Luca, so that they fell away from the category of ager Romanus.

4. *Estimates of the National Wealth about 200 B. C.*

Probably the safest estimate is that made by De Sanctis, *Storia dei Romani*, III, 2, 623 ff. based on the passage in Livy (39, 7) which gives the money and booty brought to the treasury by Manlius Volso in 187 and adds that the (extra) tribute not yet paid back should now be repaid *ex ea pecunia*, and that twenty-five and a half asses per thousand (of property value) were thus repaid; that is to say, since the *tributum simplex* during the Punic War had been a one-mill tax, twenty-five and a half times the *tributum simplex* was distributed. Since the booty in question amounted to about 22,500,000 denarii (see chapter ii), it follows—if all the booty was used for this purpose— that the *tributum simplex* had averaged nearly 900,000 denarii the year, and that the taxable property of the five classes had amounted to a thousand times that sum. We assume then that Roman property near 200 B. C. was worth about one thousand million denarii. (The unknown items in the assumption are: 1) was all the booty and only the booty used for the twenty-five and a half payments? 2) were the unpaid items all from the period of the Punic War?)

If the Ager Romanus (before the inclusion of the gains during the war) amounted to 25,000 square kilometers (two and a half million hectares, i. e. 6,175,000 acres) and two-thirds of the national wealth might be assumed to consist in land, the average price per acre in 200 B. C. would be about 100 denarii. This is a reasonable figure when we consider that about a half (a large part of the areas of Southern Latium and of the Sabine, Umbrian, and Picentine districts) was nearly worthless, and that expensive vineyards and olive groves had made but little advance as yet on Roman lands (In the middle of the century normal grain-land seems to be worth about 250 den. per jugerum: see below, under Agriculture).

Cavaignac, *Pop. et Capit.*, 95 ff., assumes 40,000 square kilometers, but the new accretions during the war were not yet productive. He next assumes that the property classification used in 214 for the assignment of naval "liturgies" (Livy, 24, 11) corresponded to the four upper classes of the census—a very hazardous guess. He then ventures to assign the number of citizens to each class (his conjecture is, for the six classes, 7,000, 20,000, 10,000, 25,000, 70,000, and 130,000) but gives too large a proportion to the proletariat for an agricultural state of relatively few slaves. He also is venturesome when he assumes 100,000 hectares of Roman land planted in vines and olives before 200 B. C. Hence, when he reaches a minimum of property value which is fifty per cent higher than that accepted by De Sanctis, his calculation rather tends to confirm faith in De Sanctis' estimate of a thousand million denarii. With a census of about 220,000 adult males, or nearly a million citizens, our figure rates the average citizen as worth about 1,000 denarii (or $200).

During the fifty years following 200 B. C. property increased rapidly in extent and in value. Much of the land taken during the Punic War was made productive, partly by the settlement of citizen colonies, partly by rental to ranchers, partly by the grant of citizenship to the native holders. (A part was alienated to Latin colonies; see above.) Furthermore citizen colonies were planted north of Rome (e. g. Potentia, Pisaurum, and Auximum, Mutina and Parma, Saturnia and Luna) and Gallic lands were also assigned in ten-jugera lots to individuals. By 150, the productive Ager Romanus had been (apart from alienations to Latin colonies) increased by at least fifty per cent. Furthermore by that time vine and olive-raising had increased extensively and had in many places more than quadrupled the value of the land. There was also a very decided increase in the number and value of slaves, and finally Rome received indemnities and booty that amounted to more than 200,000,000 denarii (see below). It would not be an exaggeration to assume that in 150 B. C. the property value had more than doubled—perhaps trebled—over that of 200, while the population had increased about fifty per cent.

III. NATIONAL INCOME AND EXPENSES, 200-157

Since the treasury was about empty in 200 B. C., since we have a fairly full list of the more important items of income and expense for a large part of the period in Livy, and since, finally, there is a brief treasury statement (Pliny, *N. H.*, 33, 55) for the year 157 B. C., it is worth while to attempt an estimate of Rome's public finances for the years 200-157. The chief items of income were derived from several important war indemnities, booty, the Spanish mines, citizen taxes up to 167 (Pliny, *N. H.*, 33, 56), port dues, rentals of public lands in Italy, and the provincial tithe.   The chief expenses were for the army, the navy, and for public buildings including streets, sewers, and the water supply system.   The magistrates of Rome received no salaries, so that the cost of the civil service was slight.   We must also keep in mind that in 187 the treasury repaid old supertaxes collected during the Punic War (see preceding section, 3, 2) amounting to about 22,500,000 denarii, and that in 157 it had in the vaults coins and ore to the value of 25,500,000 denarii (Pliny, *N. H.*, 33, 55).

In the following we reckon a pound of gold at 1,000 denarii, a pound of silver at 84 denarii, a talent of silver at 6,000 denarii.   The silver coins of Spain—called *oscenses* by Livy—weighed about the same as the Roman denarius.   The Macedonian gold Philippei were reckoned as weighing forty to the pound, the Attic tetradrachma as = 4 denarii, the Asiatic cistophorus as = 3 denarii.   No account is here taken of copper, which is mentioned only a few times.   We shall quote in full the passages that refer to booty and indemnities because they have been neglected in our source books.   These passages apparently derive from fairly accurate copies of treasury accounts.   The items of booty from Spain probably include the proceeds of the Spanish mines up to the year 178.   Thereafter the knights seem to have operated the mines.

A. Income.

1. *Indemnities and booty, 200-157:*

201 B. C.   The indemnity imposed on Carthage in 201: Livy, 30, 37, 5:

decem milia talentum argenti, discripta pensionibus aequis in annos quinquaginta, solverent; . . .

" That they should pay ten thousand talents of silver, in equal annual instalments distributed over fifty years." Polybius, 15, 18, agrees: " 200 Euboic talents of silver the year for fifty years." Pliny, *N. H.*, 33, 51, says 800,000 pounds of silver, no gold; which agrees roughly with Livy. If money rented at 6%, the cash value was less than a third of this amount.

201 B. C.   Scipio's triumph in 201 B. C.: Livy, 30, 45, 3:

argenti tulit in aerarium pondo centum triginta tria milia. militibus ex praeda quadringenos aeris divisit.

" He brought into the treasury one hundred and thirty-three thousand
pounds of silver. He distributed to each of his soldiers four hundred
asses out of the spoils."

This passage is inserted here for the record. The amount, however, was brought
in before 200 and is therefore not included in the summary for the period 200-150.

200. L. Cornelius Lentulus, in ovation over Spain: Livy, 31, 20, 7:
argenti tulit [ex praeda] quadraginta tria milia pondo, auri duo milia
quadringenta quinquaginta. militibus ex praeda centenos vicenos
asses divisit.

" He carried to the treasury forty-three thousand pounds' weight of
silver, and two thousand four hundred and fifty pounds' weight of
gold. To each of the soldiers he distributed, of the spoils, one hundred
and twenty *asses.*"

200. L. Furius, in triumph over Gauls: Livy, 31, 49, 2:

triumphavit de Gallis in magistratu L. Furius praetor et in aerarium
tulit trecenta viginti milia aeris, argenti centum milia mille quingentos.

" He carried into the treasury three hundred and twenty thousand
asses, and one hundred and one thousand and five hundred denarii."

199. L. Manlius Acidinus, from Spain: Livy, 32, 7, 4:

mille ducenta pondo argenti, triginta pondo ferme auri in aerarium
tulit.

" he conveyed to the treasury one thousand two hundred pounds' weight
of silver, and about thirty pounds' weight of gold."

197. C. Cornelius Cethegus in triumph over Gauls, and Q. Minucius
over Ligurians and Gauls: Livy, 33, 23, 7 and 9:

aeris tulit in triumpho ducenta triginta septem milia quingentos,
argenti bigati undeoctoginta milia; septuageni aeris militibus divisi,
duplex centurioni, triplex equiti . . . . . . aeris tralata ducenta
quinquaginta quattuor milia, argenti bigati quinquaginta tria milia et
ducenti; militibus centurionibusque et equitibus idem in singulos datum, quod dederat collega.

" He carried in his triumph two hundred and thirty-seven thousand
five hundred asses, and of silver denarii, stamped with a chariot, sev-
enty-nine thousand. He distributed to each of his soldiers seventy
asses, to a centurion double and a horseman triple that sum. . . . . . .

Two hundred and fifty-four thousand asses were conveyed to the treasury, and of silver denarii, stamped with a chariot, fifty-three thousand two hundred. He likewise gave to the soldiers, horsemen, and centurions, severally, the same sums that his colleague had given."

196. Cn. Cornelius Blasio from Hither Spain, and L. Stertinius from Farther Spain: Livy, 33, 27, 2-4:

tulit prae se auri mille et quingenta quindecim pondo, argenti viginti milia, signati denarium triginta quattuor milia et quingentos. L. Stertinius ex ulteriore Hispania, . . . quinquaginta milia pondo argenti in aerarium intulit et de manubiis duos fornices in foro bovario . . . unum in maximo circo fecit et his fornicibus signa aurata inposuit.

" He carried in the procession one thousand five hundred and fifteen pounds' weight of gold, twenty thousand of silver; and in coin, thirty-four thousand five hundred denarii. Lucius Stertinius, from Farther Spain, . . . carried into the treasury fifty thousand pounds' weight of silver; and out of the spoils taken built two arches in the cattle-market, . . . and one in the great Circus; and on these arches placed gilded statues."

196. Indemnity imposed on Philip V of Macedonia: Livy, 33, 30, 7:
mille talentum daret populo Romano, dimidium praesens, dimidium pensionibus decem annorum.

" That he should pay to the Roman people one thousand talents: one-half at present, the other in instalments within ten years."

This agrees with Polybius, 18, 44: 1,000 talents, half at once and half in instalments spread over ten years. The Romans excused Philip from further payments in 191; Pol., 21, 3. *Loeb ed.*

196. M. Claudius Marcellus in triumph over the Gauls: Livy, 33, 37, 11-12:

aeris lata trecenta viginti milia, argenti bigati ducenta triginta quattuor milia. in pedites singulos dati octogeni aeris, triplex equiti centurionique.

" three hundred and twenty thousand asses of bronze were brought, two hundred and thirty-four thousand silver denarii, stamped with a chariot. Eighty *asses* were bestowed on each foot soldier, and thrice that amount on each horseman and centurion."

10

195. M. Helvius, in ovation over the Celtiberi, and Q. Minucius Thermus in triumph over Hither Spain: Livy, 34, 10, 4 and 7.

argenti infecti tulit in aerarium decem quattuor milia pondo septingenta triginta duo et signati bigatorum septendecim milia viginti tres et Oscenses argenti centum undeviginti milia quadringentos undequadraginta. . . . hic quoque tulit argenti pondo triginta quattuor milia octingenta et bigatorum septuaginta tria milia et Oscensis argenti ducenta septuaginta octo milia.

" He (Helvius) carried into the treasury, of silver bullion, fourteen thousand seven hundred and thirty-two pounds; of coined, seventeen thousand and twenty-three denarii; and Oscan denarii, one hundred and nineteen thousand four hundred and thirty-nine. . . . The latter (Thermus) also brought into the treasury thirty-four thousand eight hundred pounds' weight of silver, seventy-three thousand denarii, and of Oscan denarii two hundred and seventy-eight thousand."

195. Nabis of Sparta agreed to pay 500 talents, 100 at once and the rest in eight annual payments of 50: Livy, 34, 35, 11:

et talenta centum argenti in praesenti et quinquaginta talenta in singulos annos per annos octo.

" at present, one hundred talents of silver; and fifty talents, annually, for eight years."

In 192 Nabis was killed (Livy, 35, 35, 19), so that the full indemnity was not paid; Rome probably received 200 talents in all.

194. M. Porcius Cato in triumph over Hither Spain: Livy, 34, 46, 2-3:

tulit in eo triumpho argenti infecti viginti quinque milia pondo, bigati centum viginti tria milia, Oscensis quingenta quadraginta, auri pondo mille quadringenta. militibus ex praeda divisit in singulos ducenos septuagenos aeris, triplex equiti.

" He carried in the procession twenty-five thousand pounds' weight of unwrought silver, one hundred and twenty-three thousand silver denarii, five hundred and forty thousand pieces of Oscan silver; and one thousand four hundred pounds' weight of gold. Out of the booty, he distributed to each of his soldiers two hundred and seventy *asses,* and three times that amount to each horseman."

194. T. Quinctius Flamininus in triumph over Philip: Livy, 34, 52,

4-11 (This probably included 500 or 600 talents paid in cash by Philip and 100 paid by Nabis.) :

triduum triumphavit. die primo arma, tela signaque aerea et marmorea transtulit, plura Philippo adempta, quam quae ex civitatibus ceperat; secundo aurum argentumque factum infectumque et signatum. infecti argenti fuit decem et octo milia pondo et ducenta septuaginta, facti vasa multa omnis generis, caelata pleraque, quaedam eximiae artis; et ex aere multa fabrefacta; ad hoc clipea argentea decem. signati argenti octoginta quattuor milia fuere Atticorum; tetrachma vocant; trium fere denariorum in singulis argenti est pondus. auri pondo fuit tria milia septingenta quattuordecim et clipeum unum ex auro totum et Philippei nummi aurei quattuordecim milia quingenti quattuordecim. tertio die coronae aureae, dona civitatium, tralatae centum quattuordecim; . . . . . . secuti currum milites frequentes ut exercitu omni ex provincia deportato. his duceni quinquageni aeris in pedites divisi, duplex centurioni, triplex equiti.

" Flamininus' triumph lasted three days. On the first day there were carried in procession armour, weapons, bronze and marble statues, of which he had taken greater numbers from Philip than from the states of Greece. On the second, gold and silver, wrought, unwrought, and coined. Of unwrought silver, there were eighteen thousand two hundred and seventy pounds' weight; and of wrought, . . . many vessels of various sorts, most of them engraved, and several of exquisite workmanship; also a great many others made of bronze; and, besides these, ten shields of silver. The coined silver amounted to eighty-four thousand Attic coins, called tetradrachmas, containing each about the weight of silver of three denarii. Of gold there were three thousand seven hundred and fourteen pounds, and one shield wholly of gold: and of the gold coin called Phillippics, fourteen thousand five hundred and fourteen. On the third day there were carried golden crowns, presented by the several states, to the number of one hundred and fourteen; . . . . . . a numerous body of soldiers followed, as the whole army had been brought home from the province. Among these he distributed two hundred and fifty *asses* to each footman, double to a centurion, triple to a horseman."

Plutarch, *Flam.*, 14, gives 43,270 pounds silver instead of 18,270, citing Tuditanus. Perhaps this is due to a misreading of XVIII as XLIII. The amount probably included 600 talents of indemnity due from Philip and 100 due from Nabis.

191. M. Fulvius Nobilior in ovation over Farther Spain: Livy, 36, 21, 11:

argenti bigati prae se tulit centum triginta milia et extra numeratum duodecim milia pondo argenti, auri pondo centum viginti septem.

" He carried in the procession a hundred and thirty thousand silver denarii, and besides the coin, twelve thousand pounds' weight of silver, and a hundred and twenty-seven pounds' weight of gold."

191. P. Cornelius Nasica in triumph over the Boii: Livy, 36, 40, 12-13:

aureos torques transtulit mille quadringentos septuaginta unum, ad hoc auri pondo ducenta quadraginta septem, argenti infecti factique in Gallicis vasis, non infabre suo more factis, duo milia trecenta quadraginta pondo, bigatorum nummorum ducenta triginta quattuor. militibus, qui currum secuti sunt, centenos vicenos quinos asses divisit, duplex centurioni, triplex equiti.

" He deposited in the treasury a thousand four hundred and seventy-one golden torques; and besides these, two hundred and forty-seven pounds' weight of gold; two thousand three hundred and forty pounds' weight of silver, some unwrought, and some formed into vessels of the Gallic fashion, not without beauty; and two hundred and thirty-four thousand denarii. To the soldiers, who followed his chariot, he distributed one hundred and twenty-five asses each, double to a centurion, triple to a horseman."

190. M. Acilius Glabrio in triumph over Antiochus and the Aetolians: Livy, 37, 46, 3-4:

praelata in eo triumpho sunt signa militaria ducenta triginta, et argenti infecti tria milia pondo, signati tetrachmum Atticum centum decem tria milia, cistophori ducenta undequinquaginta, vasa argentea caelata multa magnique ponderis; tulit et suppellectilem regiam argenteam ac vestem magnificam, coronas aureas, dona sociarum civitatium, quadraginta quinque, spolia omnis generis.

" In the procession there were carried two hundred and thirty military ensigns; of unwrought silver, three thousand pounds' weight; of coin, one hundred and thirteen thousand Attic tetradrachms, and two hundred and forty-nine thousand cistophori; of chased silver vessels, a great number and of great weight. He bore also, the king's silver furniture and the splendid wardrobe; of golden crowns, presents from the allied states, there were forty-five, with spoils of all kinds."

These items contain much silver plate that cannot be estimated.

189. L. Aemilius Paullus carried home a quantity of booty from Spain, according to Polybius, 31, 22 (*Loeb*), an item not mentioned by Livy.

189. L. Aemilius Regillus in a naval triumph over Antiochus: Livy, 37, 58, 4:

in eo triumpho undequinquaginta coronae aureae translatae sunt, pecunia nequaquam [tanta] pro specie regii triumphi, tetrachma Attica triginta quattuor milia ducenta, cistophori centum triginta duo milia trecenti.

" In this procession were carried forty-nine golden crowns; the quantity of money was by no means great considering the appearance of the triumph over the king, being only thirty-four thousand two hundred Attic tetradrachms and one hundred and thirty-two thousand three hundred cistophori."

189. L. Cornelius Asiaticus in triumph over Antiochus: Livy, 37, 59, 3-6:

tulit in triumpho signa militaria ducenta viginti quattuor, oppidorum simulacra centum triginta quattuor, eburneos dentes mille ducentos triginta unum, aureas coronas ducentas triginta quattuor, argenti pondo centum triginta septem milia quadringenta viginti, tetrachmum Atticorum ducenta viginti quattuor milia, cistophori trecenta viginti unum milia septuaginta, nummos aureos Philippeos centum quadraginta milia, vasorum argenteorum—omnis caelata erant—mille pondo et quadringenta viginti tria, aureorum mille pondo viginti tria. . . . . militibus quini viceni denarii dati, duplex centurioni, triplex equiti. et stipendium militare et frumentum duplex post triumphum datum; *iam* proelio in Asia facto duplex dederat.

" He carried in his triumph two hundred and twenty-four military standards; models of towns, one hundred and thirty-four; elephants' tusks, one thousand two hundred and thirty-one; crowns of gold, two hundred and thirty-four; pounds' weight of silver, one hundred and thirty-seven thousand four hundred and twenty; Attic tetradrachms, two hundred and twenty-four thousand; cistophori, three hundred and twenty-one thousand and seventy; gold pieces, called Philippics, one hundred and forty thousand; silver vases, all engraved, to the amount of one thousand four hundred and twenty-three pounds' weight; of gold vases, one thousand and twenty-three pounds' weight; . . . Twenty-five denarii were given to each of his soldiers, double that sum to a centurion, triple to a horseman; and after the triumph, their pay and allowance of corn were doubled. He had already doubled them after the battle in Asia."

This makes nearly 18,000,000 denarii, but it seems to include 500 talents of indemnity, see Livy, 37, 45, 14.

189.   Indemnity imposed on the Aetolians: Livy, 38, 9, 9 (cf. Polybius, 21, 30, Loeb. In this case gold would be received for silver at the ratio of 10 : 1; Livy, 38, 11, 9):

quingenta Euboica ut daret talenta, ex quibus ducenta praesentia, trecenta per annos sex pensionibus aequis; . . .

" they should pay five hundred Euboic talents, two hundred of this sum at present, and three hundred in six equal annual payments;"

189.   Indemnity exacted from Antiochus: Livy, 37, 45, 14:

pro impensis deinde in bellum factis quindecim milia talentum Euboicorum dabitis, quingenta praesentia, duo milia et quingenta, cum senatus populusque Romanus pacem comprobaverint; *milia* deinde talentum per duodecim annos.

·" towards the expenses of the war you shall pay fifteen thousand Euboean talents; five hundred immediately, two thousand five hundred when the Senate and people of Rome shall have ratified the peace, and one thousand annually for twelve years after."

These terms were carried out. (Cf. Livy, 38, 58; Polybius, 21, 42, 19 *Loeb*, and Appian, *Syr*. 38.) Probably Scipio brought home 500 talents of this with his booty and Manlius 2500 with his.

187.   M. Fulvius, in triumph over the Aetolians, Livy, 39, 5, 14-17:

aureae coronae centum duodecim pondo ante currum latae sunt; argenti pondo milia octoginta tria, auri pondo ducenta ʻquadraginta tria, tetrachma Attica centum octodecim milia, Philippei nummi duodecim milia trecenti viginti duo, signa aenea septingenta octoginta quinque, signa marmorea ducenta triginta, arma tela cetera spolia hostium, magnus numerus, ad hoc catapultae, ballistae, tormenta omnis generis; duces aut Aetoli et Cephallanes aut regii ab Antiocho ibi relicti ad viginti septem. multos eo die, priusquam in urbem inveheretur, in circo Flaminio tribunos praefectos equites centuriones, Romanos sociosque, donis militaribus donavit. militibus ex praeda vicenos quinos denarios divisit, duplex centurioni, triplex equiti.

"There were carried before Fulvius' chariot golden crowns to the amount of one hundred and twelve pounds' weight; of silver, eighty-three thousand pounds; of gold, two hundred and forty-three pounds; of Attic tetradrachms, one hundred and eighteen thousand; of the coin called Philippics, twelve thousand three hundred and twenty-two; bronze statues, seven hundred and eighty-five; marble statues, two hundred and thirty; arms, weapons, and other spoils in great quantities: besides these, catapults, ballistas, and engines of every kind; and in the procession were led twenty-seven commanders, either Aetolian and Cephallenian, or belonging to king Antiochus and left with them. Before he rode into the city, in the Flaminian circus, he presented great numbers of tribunes, prefects, horsemen, and centurions, both Romans and allies, with military gifts; to each of the soldiers he distributed out of the booty twenty-five denarii, double to a centurion, triple to a horseman."

187. Cn. Manlius Vulso, in triumph over the Galati in Asia, Livy, 39, 7, 1-2 and 5:

in triumpho tulit Cn. Manlius coronas aureas ducenta duodecim, argenti pondo ducenta viginti milia, auri pondo duo milia centum tria, tetrachmum Atticum centum viginti septem milia, cistophori ducenta quinquaginta, Philippeorum aureorum nummorum sedecim milia trecentos viginti; et arma spoliaque multa Gallica carpentis travecta, . . . militibus quadragenos binos denarios divisit, duplex centurioni, triplex in equites, et stipendium duplex dedit: . . . senatus consultum factum est, ut ex pecunia quae in triumpho translata esset, stipendium collatum a populo in publicum, quod eius solutum antea non esset, solveretur. vicenos quinos et semisses in milia aeris quaestores urbani cum fide et cura solverunt.

"Gnaius Manlius carried in the triumph two hundred and twelve golden crowns; two hundred and twenty thousand pounds' weight of silver; two thousand one hundred and three of gold; one hundred and twenty-seven thousand Attic tetradrachms; two hundred and fifty thousand cistophori; sixteen thousand three hundred and twenty golden Philippics; together with abundance of Gallic arms and spoils in chariots. . . . He distributed to each of his soldiers forty-two denarii, and double that sum to a centurion; to the horsemen triple, and he gave a double stipendium. . . . A decree of the Senate was passed, ordering, that such part of the taxes, contributed to the public funds by the people, as was not yet repaid should be discharged out of that which had been carried in the procession to the treasury. Accordingly the city quaestors, with care and fidelity, paid out twenty-five and a half *asses* per 1,000 *asses* of property-value."

Manlius had lost a part of his booty in Thrace (Livy, 38, 40-41); nevertheless the amount is so large that we may surmise that it includes the 2,500 talents of indemnity paid by Antiochus to Manlius (Livy, 38, 37, 7). The last clause seems to indicate that since the *tributum simplex* was one-tenth of one per cent of property values, this repayment amounted to 25½ times the simple tribute. Since the whole amount brought by Manlius comes to 22,500,000 denarii, the average annual tax remitted would be nearly 900,000 denarii.

185. M. Manlius Acidinus in ovation over Hither Spain:

Livy, 39, 29, 6-7:

tulit coronas aureas quinquaginta duas, auri praeterea pondo centum triginta duo, argenti sedecim milia trecenta, et pronuntiavit in senatu decem milia pondo argenti et octoginta auri Q. Fabium quaestorem advehere: id quoque se in aerarium delaturum.

"He carried in the procession fifty-two golden crowns, one hundred and thirty-two pounds' weight of gold, with sixteen thousand three hundred pounds of silver; and announced in the Senate that his quaestor, Quintus Fabius, was bringing ten thousand pounds' weight of silver, and eighty of gold, and that he also would carry it to the treasury."

During the next ten years the amounts of booty are much smaller: 184. Livy, 39, 42, 4: G. Calpurnius Piso and L. Quinctius Crispinus in a triumph over Farther Spain brought in 24,000 pounds of silver and 166 golden crowns.

183. Livy, 40, 16, 11: A. Terentius Varro deposited 9,320 pounds of silver and 149 pounds of gold from Hither Spain.

180. Livy, 40, 43, 5: Q. Fulvius Flaccus in a triumph over the Celtiberi of Spain, 155 pounds of gold, 173,200 denarii. His footsoldiers received 50 denarii each, centurions double, knights triple.

179. Livy, 40, 59, 2: Q. Fulvius Flaccus in triumph over the Li-

gurians brought no money but gave his footsoldiers 300 *asses,* his centurions 600, his horsemen 900.

178. Livy, 41, 7, 1-3: T. Sempronius Gracchus brought 40,000 pounds of silver from the Celtiberi, and Albinus, 20,000 pounds from the Lusitani. The donative in each case was 25, 50, and 75 denarii respectively.

177. Livy, 41, 13, 6-7: G. Claudius Pulcher in a triumph over the Histri and Liguri brought 307,000 denarii and 85,702 victoriati. The donatives were 15, 30, 45 denarii, but only half as much to the allied troops.

175. Livy gives no details for the triumph of T. Sempronius Gracchus, the ovation of M. Titinius Curvus, or the triumphs of Aemilius Lepidus and Mucius Scaevola of this year. Probably little money was brought, but Gracchus brought home large numbers of Sardinian captives.

174. Livy, 41, 28, 6: Appius Claudius Cento in an ovation over the Celtiberi is reported to have deposited 10,000 pounds of silver and 5,000 ($\overline{\text{V}}$) pounds of gold.

Probably the $\overline{\text{V}}$ is a mistake for L. The Celtiberi had very little gold.

167. At the end of the Third Macedonian War L. Aemilius Paulus, in triumph over Perseus, brought home, according to Livy, 45, 40, 1, the sum of 120 million sesterces = 30,000,000 denarii. Polybius, 18, 35, 4, reports that Perseus had stored up a treasure of 6,000 talents, which would equal about 36,000,000 denarii. Pliny, 33, 56, reports $\lceil$ MMM $\rceil$ sesterces, which probably is a mistake for $\lceil$ MCC $\rceil$, the amount given by Livy. The sum of the items given by Diodorus, 31, 8, 11, and by Plutarch, *Aem. Paul.,* 32, approximates that of Livy. It was after receiving this treasure that Rome ceased to tax citizens; Pliny, 33, 56.

167. Livy, 45, 43, 4: L. Anicius Gallus in triumph over the Illyrians. These people were very poor and the amounts accordingly small: 27 pounds of gold, 19 pounds of silver, 13,000 denarii, and 120,000 victoriati.

The donatives were 45, 90, 135 denarii.

The text is probably in error here: amounts of silver under 1,000 lbs. are seldom reported. MIX has been suggested.

Here the Livian record breaks off.

166-50. The *Fasti Triumphales* record triumphs of Claudius and Sulpicius in 166, of Fulvius in 158, of Claudius in 155, all over petty Ligurian tribes; and according to Appian, *Iber.,* 58, Mummius triumphed over the Lusitanians in 152. The amounts brought in by these five triumphs would be small, probably not over 10,000 pounds of silver.

Summary of the Indemnities and Booty Listed Above

a) Indemnities from Carthage, Philip, Nabis, Aetolia, Antiochus, and Ariarathes from 200 to 150 B. C. amount to 26,760 talents. Paid before 157, about 25,350 talents = ... 152,100,000 den.

b) Booty from the East (tetradrachma = 4 den.; cistophorus = 3 den.; victoriatus = $\frac{1}{2}$ den.; gold Philippei = $\frac{1}{40}$ pound of gold; gold crowns average 1 pound) amounts to 31,735 pounds of gold; 669,113 pounds of silver; 5,787,000 denarii. If we reckon a pound of gold as 1,000 denarii and a pound of silver at 84 denarii, this makes about 94,000,000 denarii in all. From this we must deduct various partial payments of indemnity that the generals deposited with their booty and which are included under (a). The booty from the East then comes to about.......................... 70,000,000 den.

c) Amounts received from Spain (products of mines as well as booty till the year 178, and booty thereafter till 157):

gold, 6,316 pounds; silver, 350,352 lbs.; 1,738,100 den.
The sum of the items from Spain = ... 37,500,000 den.

d) The booty from Gaul and Histria = about...... 2,000,000 den.

2. *Public Mines in Spain after 178.*

The production of the Spanish mines was apparently reported by the Spanish proconsuls as part of their booty till about 178, when the knights' corporations seem to have taken over the mines (see below). In about 140 B. C. these mines were producing for the state some 9,000,000 denarii (Polybius, 34, 9). Judging from the sums brought in before 178 I assume that the production then was not over 1,000,000 denarii the year. The increase per year, if regular, which is not likely, would approximate 200,000 denarii. The returns of these mines at that rate, from 178 to 157 B. C., would therefore approximate. . . . . ·. . .50,000,000 den.

The mines in Macedonia were not reopened till 158.

3. *The tax on citizens.*

The citizen tax was discontinued in 167 (Pliny, *N. H.,* 33, 56: tributum pendere desiit; cf. Cicero, *de Off.,* 2, 76; Plut., *Paul.,* 38). The fact that it " ceased " at this time and that Cato in 184 applied a super-tax would indicate that the *tributum simplex,* a one-mill property-tax, had been collected from 200 to 167. During the Second Punic War this tax amounted to about 900,000 denarii the year according to De Sanctis' reckoning (Ch. III, II, 3, e above). Since property values had increased rapidly after that war, we may safely reckon on twice that amount, that is, for 33 years, about. . . . . .60,000,000 denarii.

4. *Income from Public Lands in Italy.*

a. Campanian lands. The Campanian lands were rented outright by the censors (Livy, 27, 11, 8; *Lex Agr.* of 111 B. C., line 21). At a rental of a third of the produce, since there were 200,000 jugera (Suet., *Jul.,* 20), they should have yielded about 2,000,000 denarii the year, but the rental was so mismanaged that the returns were slight. Squatters took possession of large parts of the land so that the consul was sent to resurvey them in 173 (Livy, 42, 1, 6; 19, 1), and Livy adds that the rentals had not then been collected. Even after 173 the state's equities were neglected, so that in 162 a praetor had to pay heavy sums for the release of 50,000 jugera (Granius Lic., 9). The returns from this source must have been small till after 162. We may perhaps reckon them at about. . . . . .20,000,000 denarii.

b. The tithes from other public lands in Italy. The Picene and Gallic lands had been distributed by Flaminius and no longer brought in any returns. Much public land (trientabulum) had been assigned by way of mortgages for money loaned to the state during the Hannibalic war (Livy, 26, 36 and 31, 13). The rent on this was nominal and the Lex Agraria of 111 B. C. later turned over this territory to cancel the obligation.

c. The lands in the South taken over during the Punic war were rented for a mere tithe (App., *B. C.,* 1, 7). Beloch (*Bevölk.,* 320) reckons this land as amounting to about 10,000 sq. kil. (exclusive of the high mountains). Deducting a half for early colonization and rough land, we have remaining about 2,000,000 jugera. Or to approach the question differently, if we assume that 50,000 of the 74,000 mentioned in the increase of men in the Gracchan census had each received 30 jugera and that 1,000 landlords had each been left their legal amounts of 500 jugera, the same figure is reached. If a half of this territory could have been used for wheat, the annual returns to the state in tithes would have amounted to 4,000,000 modii the year. But of course the land was too far away from good markets to develop into very profitable cultivation. We may perhaps hazard 1,000,000 denarii per year from this source, or for 43 years, some......43,000,000 denarii.

5. *Provincial tithes.*

Sicily and Sardinia paid tithes in grain and these were carefully and honestly collected. (The second tithe, often collected in war times, was of course paid for.) During the Verrine days the Sicilian tithe amounted to about 3,000,000 modii of wheat plus some returns from other crops (Cic., *Verr.*, 2, 3, 163). The equivalent of 4,000,000 modii for both islands would be a liberal allowance for this period. This reckoned at 3 sesterces the modius for 43 years would bring about...130,000,000 den. The half-tithe of Spain, since only a small part of the country was as yet conquered and the wars there were almost continuous, hardly deserves consideration.

6. *Other vectigal.*

The salt monopoly was organized to provide a regular supply. Since salt was sold at the remarkably low price of 6 pounds for 1 *as* (Livy, 29, 37), we can hardly assume a profit to the state. There is evidence of a salt tax even in Sardinia at this time (*C. I. L.*, I^2, 2226).

The harbor dues (Livy, 32, 7, 3; 40, 51, 8) were 5% at the six Sicilian ports of collection and $2\frac{1}{2}$% at Italian harbors. The chief export of Sicily was the tithe of grain, which was exempt. Imports to Rome from the East came to be of some size after 188. To yield 1,000,000 denarii the goods in transit would have to amount to 40,000,000, and one may well doubt whether that figure was soon reached. In the year 60 B. C. the Italian harbor dues were abolished because they were not worth the annoyance they cost (Cic., *ad Quint.*, I, 1, 33). We may perhaps hazard an average of 1,000,000 denarii the year from 188 to 157. The other *vectigalia* mentioned by Polybius, 6, 17, such as returns from fishing rights and some public shops, could not have brought much over the cost of collection. For these various dues we shall allow for the period about 40,000,000 denarii. The 5% tax on the price of manumitted slaves went into a " sacred " treasury.

In 167 the Romans imposed on the Macedonians a tribute of 100 talents the year, which was less than half of what their royal tribute had been (Plutarch, *Paul.*, 28, 3). In ten years this amounted to 6,000,000 denarii.

These items of receipts, several of which are highly hypothetical, sum up as follows for 200-157:

Indemnities	152,100,000 den.
Booty (with mines till 178)	109,500,000 den.
Spanish mines after 178	50,000,000 den.
Citizen tax till 167	60,000,000 den.
Public land rents, in Italy	63,000,000 den.
Provincial tithes	130,000,000 den.
Other vectigalia	46,000,000 den.
	610,600,000 den.

Deduct:

Debt payment in 187	22,500,000 den.	
Surplus in 157	25,500,000 den.	
		48,000,000 den.
Receipts spent 200-157	c.	562,600,000 den.

B. Expenses.

1. *The army.* The chief expenses of the state during this period of severe warfare were for the army and navy. Common citizen soldiers received 120 denarii the year, out of which they paid for their rations, the sixty centurions of each legion received twice as much, and the cavalry three times as much. Soldiers of the allied contingents received about twelve bushels of wheat per year from the state treasury (Pol., 6, 39). At the beginning of this period each legion contained about 4,200 infantry and 300 horsemen. The number soon increased to 5,200 + 300, certainly before 182 (Livy, 40, 1, 5), probably in 192, when the allied contingents were enlarged. During the war with Perseus the legion had 6,000 infantry and 300 cavalry. The

allies provided at least 5,000 men for each legion at first, but in preparation for the war with Antiochus 7,500 infantry and 400 cavalry of the socii were usually assigned to each legion.

a. *The stipend for the legions.* The number of legions used rose from five in 199 to twelve in 190-188. Then for ten years the average seems to have been eight, after which ten were usually in the field until after the war with Perseus. Thereafter till 157 the average number was eight (see *Am. Jour. Phil.*, 1932, 10). Accordingly the average number of soldiers in service each year during the forty-three years was about 47,000 citizens and 60,000 allies. The state seems therefore to have paid out for stipends to the legions during this period about...300,000,000 den.

b. *Food for the allied troops.* Rome did not pay the allied troops but gave each man a bushel of wheat (4 modii) per month, and, as we shall see, wheat was normally worth about 3 sesterces the modius. However, in the Spanish and Gallic campaigns some wheat was brought in by foragers. In the campaigns in Greece and the East foraging was seldom possible (see under " agriculture " below for the source of supplies). If we assume that two-thirds of the wheat was procured by purchase or from the provincial tithes, the cost of supplying the allies would be about.....................64,000,000 den.

c. *Cost of army transport and materials.* Every legion needed at least 400 pack mules, a man to care for each, and food for both (Kromayer-Veith, *Heerwesen,* 394). The cost, as reckoned in the preceding chapter, would come to about 30,000,000 denarii. The cost for materials for the corps of engineers and makers of weapons, reckoned (as in chapter II) at about 6 denarii per man per year, would amount to about....................................... 20,000,000 den.
The two items would require about...............50,000,000 den.

2. *The cost of the navy.* This is difficult to estimate. At the end of the Second Punic War Rome had a good fleet of about 200 quinqueremes (Tarn, *Jour. Hell. Stud.,* 1907, 58). Many of these were old, but since Philip was not strong on the seas, while Rhodes and Attalus had respectable fleets, Rome needed only to fit out old vessels for the Macedonian war. Twenty ships were sent out at once (Livy, 31, 14, 3, and 22, 5). Later we hear of a fleet of about 70 ships, partly allied, at Gythium (Livy, 34, 26, 11). Probably not over 100

Roman quinqueremes were on the water between 200 and 191. The Greeks of South Italy, the *socii navales,* provided very few of these, not more than 12 of the quinqueremes, at times less (Livy, 26, 39; 36, 3, and 42; 42, 48).

In the war against Antiochus (192-188) Rome had a fleet of about 150 quinqueremes, some 50 of which were newly built (Livy, 35, 20, 12; 21, 1; 24, 8; 36, 2, 15). After this war most of the fleet was laid up, but in the years 181-178 we hear of 20 ships in service (Livy, 40, 18). In the war with Perseus a new fleet of about 100 quinqueremes had to be built, since many of the old ships were unserviceable (Livy, 42, 27, 1; 31, 7; 43, 12, 9). The whole fleet consisted apparently of about 150 ships. During this period it was customary to use Roman *liberti* and allied levies for the fleet (Livy, 36, 2, 15; 40, 18; 42, 27; 42, 31; 43, 12). Perhaps most of these received only food and equipment, not pay. But the number of men required was large if, as in the First Punic War, each ship required about 250 rowers and 100 marines.

We have no statement available for the cost of building new ships, but, as in chapter II, we shall use 15,000 denarii as our estimate for a Roman quinquereme (Busolt-Swoboda, *Griech. Staatskunde,* 1220; Robbins, in *Class. Phil.,* 1918, 363). The cost might therefore be estimated about as follows:

Cost of 150 new ships..........................	2,300,000 den.
Repairs of old................................	1,200,000 den.
Food for crews and marines.....................	30,000,000 den.
	33,500,000 den.

We have very little evidence regarding the expensive *transport service*. In the First Punic War, when Rome kept an active fleet of about 200 quinqueremes on the sea and had to carry provisions and men to the fleet and to the four legions operating in Sicily, there were at least 800 transports at one time (Pol., 1, 52, 6), that is, about four times as many vessels as in the navy. We do not know how large these boats were, but they had to be able to weather such storms as might arise on journeys between Rome and Lilybaeum. The smallest would certainly carry more than 300 amphorae (225 bushels, the upper limit of a senator's riverboat) while the larger might reach the standard size of merchant vessels—400 tons. (In the year 43 B. C. Dolabella's 100 transports were all over 50 tons, Cic., *Fam.*, 12, 14, 1; 12, 15, 2.) During the years 200 to 188, when transport service had to be kept for the armies and navies operating in and about Macedonia, Greece, Spain, Sicily, and Sardinia, we can hardly reckon on a smaller fleet of transports than that mentioned in Polybius for the First Punic War. Thereafter it was of course reduced in size, though hardly as much as the war fleet, since service to Spain, Sicily, and Sardinia continued. In 172-167 the transport arm was again called upon for very heavy work. We may venture to estimate the cost of the transport fleet serving both the armies and the navies (and remaining in more continuous service than the navy) at about three-fourths the cost of the navy, i. e. 25,000,000 den.

3. *Cost of public buildings.* A list of the public building operations is given below under " industry " and the cost is discussed under " semipublic finances." In the year 179 (Livy, 40, 46, 16) the censors received the whole vectigal of one year for use in the building operations of the next five years. Ten years later—when the vectigal was larger—the amount appropriated for five years was half of one year's vectigal (Livy, 44, 16). This is probably a normal appropriation for a lustrum. In Cato's censorship a lump sum of 6,000,000 denarii was apparently spent for a thorough repair and extension of the sewage system (Dionys., 3, 67). In the section dealing with " semipublic finances " we estimate these items as summing up to about 20,000,000 den.

4. *Other expenses.* The state did not pay its magistrates a salary, but each had a modest office force consisting of free people who were paid a small salary. It is probable that the aediles who served as commissioners of public works had by this time a force of public slaves to be used in the repairing of the water and sewage systems. There were also expenses for public games, the *ludi magni* (lasting ten days), the *ludi plebei* (four days), the *ludi Apollinares* (three days), and a few less expensive ones. In the empire, under Claudius, the state spent for the first two of these games 340,000 den. the year (Mommsen, *Röm. Forsch.*, II, 54), but in the Catonian day they could hardly have cost a third as much. For some slight data see Dionys., 7, 71, 2; Livy, 25, 12; 36, 2, 4; 39, 5, 7; 40, 44; Pol., 31, 28 (Loeb); Habel, " Ludi Publici " in *Realenc.*, Supp. V, 608 ff.

There were also expenses for the entertainment of *foreign envoys* and for the accounts of *Roman state commissions* sent abroad. Foreign envoys received rather small amounts, 4,000 or 5,000 *asses* and the cost of entertainment (Livy, 30, 17; 31, 9; 37, 3; 42, 6) with, occasionally, the gift of a horse. In the later period 2,000 *asses* was usual (42, 19; 43, 5 and 6 and 10, etc.). Such legations are mentioned some fifteen times, but not all are recorded. Roman commissions sent abroad are mentioned in Livy, 31, 2 and 11; 33, 24 and 35; 35, 31; 37, 55; 39, 33; and in several other places. One may doubt whether the sum of all these bills for envoys and legations came to more than 1,000,000 denarii during the period.

We do not know whether the custom had as yet arisen of charging against the treasury the cost of the general's cohort of friends and advisors used in the provinces. Probably something was subtracted from the booty for this item.

The sum total of these " other expenses " might readily fall below 1,000,000 denarii the year.

The treasury account for the period 200-157 seems, therefore, to have been somewhat as follows:

Receipts		Expenses	
Indemnities ...	152,100,000 den.	Army stipend..	300,000,000 den.
Booty (etc.)...	109,500,000 den.	Food for allies.	64,000,000 den.
Mines after 178	50,000,000 den.	Transport, etc..	50,000,000 den.
Tax till 167...	60,000,000 den.	Navy	58,500,000 den.
Land rents....	63,000,000 den.	Public buildings	20,000,000 den.
Tithes	130,000,000 den.	Supertaxes repaid	22,500,000 den.
Other vectigal..	46,000,000 den.	Other expenses...	40,000,000 den.
	610,600,000 den.		555,000,000 den.
		Balance in 157.	25,500,000 den.
			580,500,000 den.
	This leaves unaccounted for		30,100,000 den.

This attempt at estimates must, however, be taken as very decidedly conjectural at many points. It is offered simply as a very inadequate approximation, for the purpose of making use of the statistics that are available and of showing that reliance upon these statistics leads to reasonable results. It would not be surprising if full statistics, should

11

they ever come to light, would add 50% or subtract as much from these estimates. But it is something to know that in Cato's day, when Rome became master of the Mediterranean, the annual cost of the government was between $2,000,000 and $4,000,000.

It is also interesting to see that during this period military costs made up most of the expenses (77% of the income) and that nearly half the cost was paid from indemnities and booty. This is not true of any other epoch. After this period indemnities were seldom exacted and wars brought in relatively little booty except under Caesar and Pompey. During the latter part of the century mines provided a large part of the income and thereafter the state relied largely upon provincial tithes. During the Empire sales taxes, inheritance taxes, and the like grew in importance.

For sake of comparison we may note that in our budget of 1932, the military expenses (army, navy, interest and sinking fund on war debts, pensions to soldiers and care of veterans) came to 73% of our income.

IV. CIRCULATION AND COINAGE

Until 200 B. C. Rome was still deficient in silver coins, so that in the first triumphs from Spain and Gaul, the weight of the bronze taken was carefully reckoned. The new indemnities and the booty in silver and gold taken from 196 to 169 placed Rome on a firm silver basis. If we add up the silver and gold brought in from such sources and from the mines of Spain, we have bullion worth over 300,000,000 denarii. The gold was apparently not coined and, as we have noticed, there was a surplus in the treasury in 157. Perhaps some of the gold had been sold for silver that could be used by the mint; but it is probable that about 250,000,000 denarii in new silver were issued during some 43 years, at the end of which the citizen population was about 1,250,000 souls. This would mean an issue of about 200 denarii ($40) per person, which is very high, and prices may have risen somewhat in Italy. The gradual reduction of the bronze *as* from 1 ounce in 200 B. C. to ½ ounce about 100 B. C. may indicate a corresponding rise in the price of copper as against silver, and the apparent stability of the price of wheat, despite increased cultivation, points in the same direction. However, we must keep in mind that large banks with checking accounts were hardly known as yet, that Romans were apt to hoard their surplus in strong-boxes at home, that not a little left the country for imports and for soldiers' stipends abroad and that expanding business absorbed much of the surplus.

It has been argued that these indemnities drained off so much of the precious metals from the East that the nations there were forced to go off the silver standard. The Egyptian king, when attacked by Antiochus IV in 169, debased his silver drachmas and adopted a bronze coinage as standard for practical purposes. At the same time Perseus debased his silver in Macedonia when attacked by Rome. Very soon after the silver issues of the Achaean league were reduced, and in 171 the Parthian coinage suffered. The supply in the East did not suffice despite the fact that the Seleucids of the period resorted to the use of temple treasures (Heichelheim, *op. cit.*, 46-7, with citations of sources). However, it is questionable whether Rome's exactions were the chief cause of this abandonment of the standard. Alexander the Great had sent home some 180,000 talents in coins from Persia, while Rome's haul from Greece and Asia amounted to only some 30,000 talents. The reckless Ptolemies of this century were quite capable of wrecking a rich kingdom. Perseus spent far beyond his means, and so did Achaea. Rome's exactions had been severe, but they did not drain more than a sixth of the supply of gold and silver, and Roman investments in the East presently brought back some of this.

In estimating the silver that came to Rome we must add in the bonuses to soldiers and officers derived from the booty. Soldiers received only a few denarii at first, but in the three rich campaigns of the East in 191-188 a bonus of 50 denarii became more customary. In one instance, the troops that fought with Acilius in 191, then with Scipio in 190 and with Manlius in Galatia, accumulated three extra stipends and in addition donations amounting to 67 denarii each, that is, 427 denarii in three years, besides the ' regular stipend '. Livy (42, 32) says they came home rich. In fact they had made enough to buy a couple of acres of land. In the *American Journal of Philology,* 1932, 18 ff., I have estimated that nearly 20,000,000 denarii (some $4,000,000) came to the soldiers during the half century in this fashion.

Furthermore, officers also received a share of the booty (see " Manubiae " in *Realenc.* and in Daremb.-Saglio; also Mommsen, *Staatsrecht,* II, 516 ff.; Marquardt, *Staatsverw.*, II, 282 ff.). Generals were expected to devote their portion to religious dedications or to public games (Cic., *Lex Agr.*, II, 61), and during this period men like the Scipios, Flamininus, Paulus, and Cato did so. The profiting from this source, so customary in the next century, was not yet practiced to any extent. The temples erected by generals are usually recorded by Livy. He mentions Vejovis (31, 21, 12), Juno Sospita (32, 30, 10), Victoria (35, 9, 6), Vejovis on the Capitol (35, 41, 8), Venus (40, 34, 4), Pietas (40, 34), Lares Permarini (40, 52, 4), Diana (40, 52), Juno Regina (40, 52), and Fortuna Equestris (42, 10, 5); and Cicero, *pro Arch.*, 27, mentions Hercules Musarum. These temples, all told, probably did not cost a million dollars. Other officers gave games that cost from $1,000 to $20,000. It is not till about 170 B. C. that we hear of some private profit coming to generals from military operations. But we must reckon that some 20-30,000,000 denarii flowed to Rome by way of booty and bonuses that did not go to the treasury.

V. SEMIPUBLIC BUSINESS

Since each administration lasted only a year, it was difficult to erect and control bureaus for public work. The censors therefore adopted more and more the custom of letting public contracts, usually for five years, to corporations for the collection of taxes and the performance of public work. The corporations must consist of men of property (in Cicero's day the knight's census was 100,000 den.), and the corporations were permitted to form joint-stock companies of limited liability, which were not allowed in private business. These corporations had always performed some work for the state but were of little importance till the latter part of this period. The *locus classicus* for a description of their activity is a passage in Polybius written about 150 B. C. His words would not apply to any earlier period.

Polybius, 6, 17, 2-4:

πολλῶν γὰρ ἔργων ὄντων τῶν ἐκδιδομένων ὑπὸ τῶν τιμητῶν διὰ πάσης Ἰταλίας εἰς τὰς ἐπισκευὰς καὶ κατασκευὰς τῶν δημοσίων, ἅ τις οὐκ ἂν ἐξαριθμήσαιτο ῥᾳδίως, πολλῶν δὲ ποταμῶν, λιμένων, κηπίων, μετάλλων, χώρας, συλλήβδην ὅσα πέπτωκεν ὑπὸ τὴν Ῥωμαίων δυναστείαν, πάντα χειρίζεσθαι συμβαίνει τὰ προειρημένα διὰ τοῦ πλήθους, καὶ σχεδὸν ὡς ἔπος εἰπεῖν πάντας ἐνδεδέσθαι ταῖς ὠναῖς καὶ ταῖς ἐργασίαις ταῖς ἐκ τούτων· οἱ μὲν γὰρ ἀγοράζουσι παρὰ τῶν τιμητῶν αὐτοὶ τὰς ἐκδόσεις, οἱ δὲ κοινωνοῦσι τούτοις, οἱ δ' ἐγγυῶνται τοὺς ἠγορακότας, οἱ δὲ τὰς οὐσίας διδόασι περὶ τούτων εἰς τὸ δημόσιον.

" Through the whole of Italy a vast number of contracts, which it would not be easy to enumerate, are given out by the censors for the construction and repair of public buildings, and besides this there are many things which are farmed, such as navigable rivers, harbours, gardens, mines, lands, in fact everything that forms part of the Roman dominion. Now all these matters are undertaken by the people, and one may almost say that everyone is interested in these contracts and the work they involve. For certain people are the actual purchasers from the censors of the contracts, others are the partners of these first, others stand surety for them, others pledge their own fortunes to the state for this purpose."

If we take this passage as our starting point for a survey of the activities of the knights' corporations, it is first necessary to recall the fact that the conditions pictured in the passage had not existed long when it was written. For instance, most of the customs collections were instituted in the censorship of 179; not many contracts for public buildings were let out by censors before that year, and the letting of censorial building contracts outside of Rome seems to have been an innovation in 174 (see Livy, 41, 27, 11). It is also very doubtful whether the knights worked the Spanish mines before 179. A brief review of equestrian financial activities (omitting the earlier legendary references) will show that the knights very slowly developed the large organization mentioned by Polybius.

During the First Punic War the knights' companies were not used in the transport service: for this work the navy had some eight hundred vessels of its own. In 214, during the second war, the state once employed three companies of nineteen men to provide materials for the Spanish army, but with disastrous results. Some used rotten hulks that sank and collected state insurance on them (Livy, 23, 49; 25, 3). This may be the reason why in the subsequent wars in the East the state always seems to have bought its supplies through its own magistrates who provided for the transport (Livy, 36, 2, 12; 37, 2 and 50; 42, 31, 8). Even the small contract for horses and military garments in 167 seems to have been managed by the praetor and consul, though here possibly the knights may have been employed (Livy, 44, 16) as intermediaries.

In letting building contracts also there were periods of distrust. In 193 it was the aediles who undertook to build an emporium on the

Tiber and two porticos in the business section (Livy, 35, 10, 12). When in 184 Cato let his rather extensive contracts, he at once had trouble with the knights' companies (Livy, 39, 14; Plut., *Cato,* 19), and the quarrels between the knights and the censors came up in the Senate repeatedly. The contracts of 174 were not well executed, so that the censors of 169 excluded the operating companies from the privilege of bidding again (Livy, 43, 16; 44, 16, 8; 45, 15). The resulting distrust of them may be the chief reason why the draining of the Pontine marshes in 160 was intrusted directly to the Consul Cethegus (*cui ea provincia evenerat* [Livy, *Epit.* 46]). This is enough to show how hazardous it is to assume that Polybius' statement applies to any and every period of the century.

The collection of rentals, etc.

The knights did not collect the citizen tax at Rome (which ceased in 167); nor did they collect the tithes of Sicily and Sardinia or the half-tithes of Spain. They did collect the tithes and the *scriptura* on public lands in Italy, but here they had in general to deal with powerful citizen landlords from whom they would hardly be able to make large profits. If the legal allowance for collection was no larger than in Sicily (three-fifths of 1 per cent of the crop [Cic., *Verr.,* 2, 3, 116]), they presumably were left a very small margin of profit. We never hear of any complaints of profiteering in this particular field, for of course the *pecuarii* mentioned in Livy, 33, 42 and 35, 10 were grazers, not publicans. Beloch estimates the public land in Southern Italy at about 10,000 square kilometers (less than 4,000 square miles [*loc. cit.*]). Deducting a half for colonization and for rough land, we have about 2,000 square miles left. If—as is very unlikely—all of this were planted in wheat yielding 40 modii to the jugerum, Rome's tithe would be about 2,000,000 bushels, and the fee of the collectors would come to about 240,000 denarii the year, a sum that would have to cover all the operations in scores of townships before dividends were forthcoming. These contracts required some capital and a score of agents, but we need not let our fancy imagine returns of any great magnitude.

The *ager Campanus* was not treated like the rest of the *ager publicus,* because the original owners were left on the land as renters in so far as it was not sold (Livy, 28, 46; 32, 7) or colonized (Livy, 34, 45).

The fact that private possessors seized a large part of these lands (Livy, 42, 1, 6 and 19, 1 and Granius Licinianus, p. 9) for over forty years gives clear-enough proof that the rentals were not collected by business men. Finally, in 162 the urban praetor, Lentulus, was sent down to reclaim the state's equity in the occupied lands. He made a survey of the 50,000 jugera left, divided this into small lots, and rented these out at a fixed price (*ad pretium indictum* [Licin., p. 9; *Lex agraria* of 111 B. C., l. 21]). Probably the rental was a money equivalent of about one-third of the crop, usual for such public land. But there is never any indication that the knights' companies had any concern with Campanian lands.

The contract for the salt monopoly is not mentioned by Polybius. The censors of 204 had reorganized this so as to insure distributing stations in all towns, with fixed prices scaled according to the distance from the source of supply (Livy, 29, 37). Since the price was fixed at only one-sixth of an *as* per pound at Rome, Mommsen is probably right in saying that the organization was formed less with a view to profit than for the purpose of insuring a regular supply of salt. To manage this business some capital was required and a number of agents, but it probably yielded only a fair interest on the investment.

Port-dues.

There were some six harbor districts in Sicily, and a few in Spain. The 5 per cent port-dues at Sicilian harbors did not amount to much at a time when their main merchandise, grain, was used by the state and was therefore immune from port-dues. In Italy the censors of 199 (Livy, 32, 7) instituted tariff stations at Puteoli, Capua, and the southern colony which was being founded at Scolacium. The dues at Italian harbors were only $2\frac{1}{2}$ per cent. In 179 several new *portoria* were introduced (Livy, 40, 51, 8), presumably at the colonies founded after 199. Very few of these colonies developed important harbors. Rome and Puteoli were the only citizen-harbor towns of Italy that counted for much in this period (Rome could hardly have collected dues at Naples and Tarentum at that time). I think it would be very daring to suppose that the profit from the collection of these dues amounted to much before 150 B. C. But the work probably required a staff of several score of men and the capital had, of course, to be provided in advance.

Building contracts.

Polybius emphasizes particularly the building contracts and says that they extended all through Italy. It was not until 174, it seems, that censors began to direct building operations outside of Rome (Livy, 41, 27, 5-12), and then, of course, only in citizen colonies and municipalities, and with money supplied by the city in question. One censor of 174 questioned the propriety of doing this, and, though it was apparently still being done about 150—when Polybius wrote—there is little evidence that the procedure continued for long. We may assume that such contracts were profitable for some thirty years but probably not much more. As for the contracts in Rome, we have Livy's lists in Books xxx-xlv, and the lists seem to be fairly reliable. The censors of 199, 194, and 189 let very few contracts (Livy, 32, 7, 3; 34, 44; 37, 58). The censors of 184—Cato and Flaccus—were particularly interested in building streets and sewers (Livy, 39, 44, 5-7). Aemilius Lepidus and Fulvius, the censors of 179, built extensively, having a whole year's *vectigal* for the *lustrum* (40, 51, 2-7; cf. 40, 46, 16). It is to be noted that these two men were especially interested in providing harbor and retail facilities and that they also established several new customs stations. Their successors in 174, Fulvius and Postumius, also built vigorously in and out of Rome (41, 27, 5-12). The censors of 169, Claudius and Gracchus, had the use of half a year's *vectigal,* and part of this, apparently a half, was used in the purchase of Scipio's house and erecting the Sempronian Basilica there (Livy, 44, 16, 10). Thereafter there is, as we have seen, some indication that the Senate began to distrust the knights' companies. It is quite possible that the quarrels between censors, Senate, and knights over contracts—reported by Livy in 43, 16, 2; 44, 16, 8—resulted at times in the magistrates' taking direct charge of public improvements.

It is, of course, very difficult to get satisfactory estimates of what "a year's *vectigal*" (Livy, 40, 46, 16) amounted to or what it might have cost to build the harbors, sewers, porticos, and basilicas mentioned by Livy. The first mention of a definite sum for a year's *vectigal* is in 62 B. C. when it amounted to fifty million denarii (Plut., *Pomp.,* 45). But that was when Asia alone was producing ten million, when Spain, Africa, Narbonese Gaul, Macedonia, and Cilicia were all productive, when the port-dues had doubtless quadrupled, and the Campanian lands were bringing full rentals. If the *vectigal* was only fifty million in 62, it is difficult to see how it could have been a tenth of that amount in 179.

That may seem a small sum for the long list of buildings reported by Livy for that year, but we remember that the buildings were of modest proportions and that the cost of labor was amazingly cheap. Since good slaves cost only five hundred denarii, the daily wage (covering depreciation, interest, and upkeep) would be only about half a denarius the day (which is Cato's wage), and where free labor was used it would be only about one denarius: that is to say, the Roman contractor could use from twenty to forty laborers for the present wage of a single unskilled workman.

To be realistic, the early Basilica Aemilia, built in 179 of tufa blocks, 2 by 2 by about 3 feet, taken from the Grotta Oscura Quarry that belonged to the state, would require less than six thousand blocks. A slave, costing at most twelve *asses* per day, was expected to cut out eight blocks per day (Plaut., *Capt.,* 724). Six hundred denarii would therefore provide the stone. If we allow as much for barging and hauling, and double the amount for the laying of the stone by free labor, this all comes to only 2,400 denarii. Let us assume an equal amount for the columns of the same tufa and the stucco, and, to be generous, treble the amount for the timber ceiling and the roof tiling, we still arrive at only 12,000 denarii.

Even if we double this amount again in order to allow for decoration and for all possible underestimates, we are still within the sum of $5,000 for a building which today would cost more than $100,000. In 179 the complete list of buildings for which the year's *vectigal* was spent comprised a pier at Tarracina, a small theater—apparently only for the Apollo cult—the plastering of the Jupiter Temple, a dock, the piers for a bridge (completed in 142), the above-mentioned basilica, a market place outside the city, three porticos, and the reconstruction of the Apollo Temple. We know the approximate size and quality of most of these structures. The whole program ought not to have cost more than twenty times that of the basilica. At this rate it would be courageous to estimate the year's *vectigal* (land rentals, port-dues, etc.) as high as 2,000,000 denarii per year. But in order to be liberal we may take that figure, and in addition assume that in and after 174 the knights had—every fifth year—1,000,000 denarii to spend at the municipalities. This would mean at most a building program of about $600,000 the *lustrum* or $120,000 per year.

Mines.

We come next to the mines, which in Polybius' day were being exploited by the equestrian companies. The most important were the silver mines near New Carthage which, according to a later passage (Polybius, 34, 9), were at one time using forty thousand men. We do not know when these mines were turned over for exploitation by contract, but the most probable date seems to be 179, when the censors Fulvius and Lepidus, who in their building contracts did much to aid business, also instituted new *portoria* and *vectigalia* (Livy, 40, 51, 8). Scipio must have taken over these mines when he captured New Carthage in 209. He could hardly have closed them, since Rome then was in great need of money; and, since in 195 the governor of Spain had the control over them (Livy, 34, 21, 7), Scipio doubtless took over the Punic slaves who were in the mines and placed some of his own engineers in charge. The provincial governor seems then to have directed the operations. In 195 Cato, when governor of the province, reorganized the mines (Livy, 34, 21). Cato was not on friendly terms with the equites (Livy, 39, 44, 8 and Plut., *Cato*, 19), and there is no reason to suppose that he would surrender state supervision in favor of equestrian control, even if we dared assume that the companies had the capital to manage them. Furthermore, the sums of silver brought to the treasury by returning governors are so large up to 178 that we do best to accept the usual assumption that they included the produce of the mines.

The wars fought during this period were mostly on the rather barren plateau, and Schulten's recent excavations have proved that district exceedingly poor. I should assume that at least one-half of the amounts brought back by the governors came from the provincial administration of the mines. They average about $200,000 per year between 195 and 178.

The last general to report a large sum from Spain was Ti. Sempronius Gracchus, who was governor in 179, the very year that Fulvius and Lepidus instituted new *portoria* and *vectigalia* and did much also to encourage business (Livy, 40, 51, 8). To be sure, there was also less booty thereafter because there was less warfare, but after 179 we hear of several campaigns that resulted in no accretions to the treasury. It is likely that the knights' companies brought in the treasure of ore after 179. Twelve years later, according to Livy, 45, 18 and 29, 11, the state closed the newly acquired Macedonian mines on the assumption that exploitation by contract would work mischief. That was after the censors had quarreled with the companies in 174.

My conclusion, then, is that the knights' companies began to operate the Spanish mines about 178 when they were producing an average of about 1,000,000 denarii per year. At a later day Polybius (34, 9) informs us that these mines were producing 25,000 drachmas per day (about 9,000,000 denarii per year) for the state's account, and that 40,000 slaves were employed in them. This passage comes from Strabo, but probably belongs to the geographical excursus of Polybius which was written not long before the Gracchan period, probably about 140 B. C. Needless to say, silver mines worked so intensively could not have been as productive as there reported for very many years, but it is clear that the knights had succeeded in increasing production.

We may attempt an estimate of the financial operations that this statement of Polybius implies. Mining slaves in Spain—Diodorus (5, 38) says they were slaves—would cost less than slaves at Rome. Their upkeep would probably cost about the same as that of Cato's slaves, 40-50 denarii per year (see below). But a heavy allowance must be made for depreciation in the case of mine labor. The costs and profits would be somewhat as shown in Table I.

TABLE I

	Denarii
Investment, 40,000 slaves at 400 denarii.......	16,000,000
Smelters, quarters, tools, transport service.....	?10,000,000
	26,000,000
Annual outlay:	
Interest at 6 per cent.....................	1,560,000
Depreciation in mine slaves (10 per cent)....	1,600,000
Depreciation in plant (5 per cent)..........	500,000
Food and clothing for slaves..............	1,800,000
Total.............................	5,460,000

Since, when Polybius wrote, the state was receiving 9,000,000 denarii per year, the companies were presumably taking in an equal amount. This would leave about 3,500,000 denarii per year with which to pay salaries of managers and overseers and to cover dividends over and above the interest. The profits were apparently excellent so long as the good veins of ore lasted, but when mines give out the losses in liquidation are heavy.

In order to equip and operate mines requiring a capital outlay of 26,000,000 denarii, the knights must have counted on the participation of a rather large number of prosperous Romans. By way of illustration we might assume some such combination as shown in Table II.

TABLE II

	Denarii Each
20 members subscribing....................	500,000
500 partners subscribing....................	100,000
1,200 investors subscribing....................	5,000

In addition the state demanded that her returns be guaranteed by responsible persons. Finally, though most of the actual work was done by slaves, there would be need of no small number of managers, experts, overseers, and clerks. It is not surprising that Polybius was somewhat amazed at the number of people involved in the enterprise. But it is not likely that operations at these mines continued on such a scale for very many years.

Of the Macedonian mines we know very little. The royal gold and silver mines, from which Philip II had formerly drawn large sums, seem to have been fairly well exhausted by the time that Rome defeated Perseus. They were taken over in 167, but closed for the time being because, according to Livy, 45, 18, 4 (who sometimes reads his own convictions into writers of an earlier day), " neque sine publicano exerceri posse, et ubi publicanus esset, ibi aut ius publicum vanum aut libertatem sociis nullam esse." These mines were reopened in 158 and presumably placed under the control of the knights' companies. But we have no way of estimating their activities in Macedonia. There is reason to suppose that Philip and Alexander had fairly well exhausted them (Casson, *Macedonia, Thrace and Illyria,* 76).

To sum up, there is no doubt that Polybius is correct in saying that very many were interested in state contracts. But when historians assume from his words that many Romans were growing wealthy by means of these contracts, we may call for caution. Since Roman property values amounted to about $200,000,000 in the year 200 and probably to twice or thrice the sum when Polybius wrote, we do not find reason to suppose that over 2 per cent of that property was engaged in the equestrian contracts. Most of the money was still being invested in Italian lands, especially when the broad acres of Cispadane Gaul and of the districts devastated by the last war were being thrown open to settlers and public renters. We may suppose that during the most productive years of the Spanish mines some twenty-five men drew in as much as $8,000 per year, while some thousands drew in from $100 to $1,500; but such returns did not create great estates.

The fact still remains that during this whole century very few men climbed from equestrian rank into the senatorial aristocracy.

The knights' companies rose to considerable power in the Gracchan days, partly because the Asiatic contracts gave them opportunities to trade, to invest in mortgages, and to exact usurious rates of interest in the East; partly because by winning political recognition they could command the popular vote and secure favors from the state. The Senate took its revenge when Sulla came into power. He proscribed most of the wealthy knights (App., *B. C.*, 1, 95) and struck off the political privileges of the whole group. It is difficult to see how they could have operated their companies for several years thereafter. In fact, it is probable that Sulla took the Spanish silver mines away from the companies and sold them for ready money. Strabo (3, 2, 10) says that in his day they were in private hands, and Plutarch (*Crass.*, 2) assures us that Crassus had " numberless silver mines." Crassus, as we recall, was one of the most successful bidders at the auctions of Sulla. Since Sulla made free to sell for his own use public, sacred, and private property, he would hardly have hesitated to dispose of the mines. In Asia he removed the knights at least for a time from the collecting of state dues. It would seem probable, therefore, that it was during Sulla's dictatorship that the Spanish silver mines—such as were still productive—passed to private hands.

VI. AGRICULTURE

1. *Grain: External supplies needed for the army.*

At the end of the Second Punic War Scipio demanded from Carthage and secured for his army 500,000 modii (pecks) of wheat and 300,000 of barley, thereby diminishing the need for Sicilian wheat (Livy, 30, 16, 11). At the same time the wheat gathered in Spain for the war was released for Roman use, so that the aediles had a quantity of public grain which they distributed at the abnormally low rate of one denarius the bushel (four *asses* per modius; Livy, 30, 26, 5-6). Soon afterwards grain merchants bringing in grain from Sicily and Sardinia found the market so overstocked that they gave away their cargoes of wheat to the shipowners in payment for the freight charges (Livy, 30, 38, 5). In the year 200 the public grain was still so abundant that the aediles could again distribute it at one denarius the bushel (Livy, 31, 4, 6), and before the year was over (Livy, 31, 50, 1) the aediles were able to reduce the price at Rome on the stock brought back from Africa to half a denarius the bushel.

The Roman farmers, who had doubtless increased native production for war needs, must have been discouraged, but presently the demand increased again. When the Macedonian war broke out more grain was needed for the army than Rome could raise. Carthage, now an " ally," sent 200,000 modii to the army in Macedonia and a like amount to Rome (Livy, 31, 19, 2), and Massinissa sent 200,000 modii of wheat and a like amount of barley to Macedonia (Livy, 31, 19, 4; 32, 27, 2). These contributions would be about a fourth of what the army operating in Macedonia would use in one year. Livy, 32, 27, 2 adds that " large supplies also came from Sicily and Sardinia." When the Macedonian war was over the stock of public grain at Rome was so large that the aediles of 196 could distribute a million modii at one-half denarius the bushel (Livy, 33, 42, 8). It is to be noticed that these low prices are extraordinary and are for accumulated stores disposed of at the ends of wars. In the years 191 to 188 when two severe wars were on in the East with some eight legions and a large navy in operation (at least 100,000 men to feed), Rome was hard pressed for grain. In 191 she used the regular tithes of Sicily and Sardinia and bought an extra tithe in each island (Livy, 36, 2, 12). Then in Africa Rome bought an unknown quantity of wheat and 500,000 pecks of barley from

Carthage, and from Massinissa 800,000 modii of wheat and 550,000 of barley. Part was to go to Rome, whether for use in the western provinces, for home use, or as a reserve stock, we do not know (Livy, 36, 3 and 4). The barley was generally used for the cavalry. The text has a lacuna so that we do not know the amount of the Punic wheat, but it could hardly have been less than 800,000 modii. The Sicilian single tithe was 750,000 bushels of wheat in the Verrine days. We may estimate the double tithe of the two islands in 191 as at least 1,500,000 bushels. Rome therefore procured about 2,000,000 bushels of foreign wheat and about one-eighth as much barley in 191. The ten legions in the field would require about 1,200,000 bushels of wheat. The navy of over one hundred quinqueremes with over 400 men in each and probably some 400 transports would probably need most of the rest (at the usual rate of twelve bushels per man per year).

In 190 (Livy, 37, 2, 12) Sicily and Sardinia again supplied a purchased tithe in addition to the tithes due, and again the same amounts were provided for 189 (Livy, 37, 50, 9). In the winter of 188-7, after disastrous floods and during a pestilence, the price of grain rose so high at Rome that the aediles imposed fines on the grain merchants on the charge that they were hoarding it (*ob annonam compressam,* Livy, 38, 35, 5—cf. Plautus, *Trin.,* 484, *hac annona,* which is probably a reference to the hard times of 187). Thereafter we get little evidence about grain till the time of the next great war with Perseus. In 171 (Livy, 42, 31, 8) double tithes were again needed from Sicily and Sardinia, and this extra demand was probably continued throughout the war. But it did not suffice. Grain was also bought in Apulia and Calabria in the same year (Livy, 42, 27, 8). In 170 Athens provided 100,000 modii of wheat at the illegal demand of the Roman general (Livy, 43, 6, 2-3). In the same year Rome accepted for army use, apparently as a gift, 250,000 bushels of wheat and 125,000 of barley from Carthage, and a like amount from Massinissa (Livy, 43, 6, 11-14). Besides this we find that in the next year the general in Macedonia bought 20,000 modii of wheat in Epirus, presumably for the garrisons stationed in that region (Livy, 44, 16, 2).

In 169, while the war with Perseus was still on and Rome was buying grain in Epirus, the Rhodians asked the senate for permission to buy 150,000 bushels of wheat (100,000 medimni) in Sicily and it was granted (Polybius, 28, 2). This would be about one-third of

Sicily's tithe. (Presumably Rome exerted some supervision over the stocks of grain in the provinces during war times, both to secure her own supply and to prevent trade with those who might supply the enemy. There is no evidence—despite frequent generalizations from this one instance—that provincial trade was not free in times of peace. Indeed Livy, 30, 38, 5, implies that independent merchants handled some Sicilian grain. Cicero, *Verr.*, 5, 145 and 157 implies freedom of trade in Sicily and in *de Domo,* 11, Cicero says explicitly that Sicilian grain was sold in foreign lands).

To summarize: Grain was abnormally cheap when the victory at Zama released the stores of Spain, Sicily, and Africa. But as soon as the wars began again, there was scarcity. Whenever more than eight legions were in the field, the army used not only the regular island tithes but also a purchased tithe, and when ten or twelve legions were active, additional supplies had to be bought (or accepted as gifts) from Africa and elsewhere. In times of peace, when only five to six legions were used for garrisons or minor wars in Spain or Gaul, presumably the regular island tithes sufficed for the armies, while Italy was probably just about self-supporting. Six legions required approximately 720,000 bushels, which was nearly the normal island tithe. Presumably very little provincial grain was thrown on the open market at Rome between 196 and 150, and we may therefore infer that the cereal culture of Italy received encouragement, rather than disastrous competition, during the period of the great foreign wars: 218-146 B. C. The Ager Romanus had a population of over one million, which would require over 12,000,000 bushels of wheat per year; the whole of Italy would need some 60,000,000 bushels per year. It is apparent that the small fraction of the island tithe that might escape army use and reach Rome would seldom suffice during this period to endanger the market, since the whole tithe was little over 1% of Italy's needs. Competition at Rome's market from island districts situated any distance away would be excluded by the heavy cost of hauling wheat in wagons or on donkeys. We may conclude that Latian cereal culture received no severe setback between 196 and 146.

2. *Cato's book on Agriculture.*

Cato's *de Agricultura,* written probably about 175-150 B. C., is a brief monograph of about 20,000 words giving advice about farms and farming. Some of the information concerns gardening and cereal culture near Rome, much of it applies to olive and vine culture on estates near Monte Cassino and Venafrum, which are nearer Naples than Rome.

Cato's views on agriculture, Pref. 1-4:

Est interdum praestare mercaturis rem quaerere, nisi tam periculosum sit, et item fenerari, si tam honestum sit. maiores nostri sic habuerunt et ita in legibus posiverunt, furem dupli condemnari, feneratorem quadrupli. quanto peiorem civem existimarint feneratorem quam furem, hinc licet existimare. et virum bonum quom laudabant, ita laudabant, bonum agricolam bonumque colonum. amplissime laudari existimabatur qui ita laudabatur. mercatorem autem strenuum studiosumque rei quaerendae existimo, verum, ut supra dixi, periculosum et calamitosum. at ex agricolis et viri fortissimi et milites strenuissimi gignuntur, maximeque pius quaestus stabilissimusque consequitur minimeque invidiosus, minimeque male cogitantes sunt qui in eo studio occupati sunt.

" In preference to farming one might seek gain by commerce on the seas, were it not so perilous, and in money lending, if it were honorable. Our forefathers believed and enacted in their laws that, while thieves should be condemned for two-fold the amount taken, the receiver of usury should be held for fourfold, so that one may infer from this how much worse the usurer (money lender) was considered than the thief. When they praised a man as being good, they would call him a " good farmer " or a " good cultivator of the soil ": that they considered the highest praise. I consider the merchant on the seas an energetic man and well occupied at increasing his estate, but, as I said, his is a business that is full of dangers, and at times disastrous. From the farm come the bravest men and the most energetic soldiers; the gains of the farmers are the most respectable and most certain, and awaken least envy. Those who are occupied in farming are least given to unseemly thoughts."

Farming is preferred because of its respectability. Commerce on the sea is " perilous." Banking (lending money at interest) has not quite escaped the odium attached to it by the laws that were passed in the fourth century prohibiting the charging of interest; furthermore it had fallen into the hands of unrespected persons when interest-taking was illegal, and these same persons long continued to control the business. Plutarch (*Cato*, 21, 6) says that Cato did invest in mercantile loans on ships' cargoes. He probably did so secretly through an agent, and in

Campanian companies. In a political-military aristocracy agriculture naturally becomes the gentleman's occupation. Plutarch vouches for the fact that Cato was not averse to taking a share in the actual labor on the farm, but even in Cato's day few senators did that.

I, 7.   Cato's preference in crops:

praedium quod primum siet, si me rogabis, sic dicam: de omnibus agris optimoque loco iugera agri centum, vinea est prima, [vel] si vino ⟨bono et⟩ multo est, secundo loco hortus inriguus, tertio salictum, quarto oletum, quinto pratum, sexto campus frumentarius, septimo silva caedua, octavo arbustum, nono glandaria silva.

" If you ask me what kind of estate I should prefer if I had the choice of a hundred jugera (66 acres) in some excellent position, I may put my preferences in this order: the vineyard would come first if the place yielded good wine plentifully; second, the irrigated garden; third, a grove of willows; fourth, an olive orchard; fifth, a meadow; sixth, a field of grain; seventh, timber land; eighth, an orchard; ninth, an oak-wood yielding acorns (for hogs)."

Of course, the nature and the location of the land would determine the crop. This choice does not apply to a given farm. It seems to reveal the popularity in Cato's day of wine, vegetables, and olive culture over grain, timber, cattle, and hog raising. Or it may be merely a personal preference. Yet, in another passage (quoted by Cicero, de Offic., 2, 89), Cato seems to advocate grazing as the most profitable use of land. Irrigation was not feasible in a large part of Latium. Willows were used for baskets and wine props, and their bark was used for binding the vines. A vineyard of 25 acres needed the boughs of an acre of willows (Pliny, 17, 143).

X.   The olive-plantation:

Quo modo oletum agri iugera ccxl instruere oporteat. vilicum, vilicam, operarios quinque, bubulcos iii, asinarium i, subulcum i, opilionem i, summa homines xiii: boves trinos, asinos ornatos clitel-larios qui stercus vectent tris, asinum ⟨molarium⟩ i, oves c: vasa olearia instructa iuga v, ahenum quod capiat Q. xxx, etc. (a long list of implements follows):

" What is needed to equip an olive plantation of 240 jugera (160 acres): a slave overseer with his wife, five laborers (slaves), three ox-drivers, an ass-driver, a swineherd, a shepherd (13 in all); three ox-teams, three asses with pack saddles to bear the manure, an ass for the mill, a flock of 100 sheep, five complete presses, a bronze vat that holds thirty amphorae," etc. (the list includes three wagons, six plows, harrows, axes, sickles, pruning hooks, more than 150 large jars, mills, a loom, and much furniture, see the next section).

In giving a long list of implements needed, Cato reveals the fact that he is treating of capitalistic farming specializing on the one crop of olives, as when he requires the thirteen slaves to specialize on the care of the crop. However, he requires a flock of 100 sheep—presumably they are to graze under the trees—and a few plows and oxen to keep the orchard cultivated. The thirteen slaves do not suffice to gather and press the crop. This is done by contract and requires some fifty work people for a month: see ch. 144, 4. He has already specified (ch. 4) that land should be bought where operarii—free workmen—could be found. Some of the land was doubtless used for grain (cf. mills, sickles, 20 dolia for grain), some for vines (10 wine jars), and some for vegetables for the slaves (see ch. 143).

XI. The vineyard:

Quo modo vineae iugera c instruere oporteat. vilicum, vilicam, operarios x, bubulcum ɪ, asinarium ɪ, salictarium ɪ, subulcum ɪ, summa homines xvɪ: boves ɪɪ, asinos plostrarios ɪɪ, asinum molarium ɪ: vasa torcula instructa ɪɪɪ, dolia ubi quinque vindemiae esse possint culleum ᴅᴄᴄᴄ, dolia ubi vinaceos condat xx, . . .

" What is needed to equip a vineyard of 100 jugera (66 acres) in operation: the slave overseer with his wife, ten workmen (slaves, since the overseer is one), one ox-driver, one ass-driver, one to provide the willows, one swineherd, (16 in all); also two oxen, two dray asses, one ass for the mill; also three presses, jars enough for five vintages of 800 cullei each (i. e. 1600 amphorae), twenty jars to hold the grape-husks (and a long list of implements, including 2 wagons, 2 plows, harness, tools, and furniture).

If 100 jugera needed jars to hold 800 *cullei* for a year's pressing, one jugerum was meant to produce 8 *cullei* (= 1080 gallons) per year. Columella, 3, 3, reckons 7-10 cullei per jugerum as a possible yield, i. e. 950-1350 gallons per jugerum (1400-2000 gallons per acre) which is about three times a good yield of today. Today 10 workmen cannot care for more than 40 jugera, if the vines are to be staked and trimmed properly. However, Cato may have given less care than is usual today, and some of the vines may have been propped on trees (cf. Pol., 34, 11)—which would have saved some labor.

XIV.   Specifications for and cost of construction of farm house:

Villam aedificandam si locabis novam ab solo, faber haec faciat oportet. parietes omnes, uti iussitur, calce et caementis, pilas ex lapide angulari, tigna omnia, quae opus sunt, limina, postes, iugumenta, asseres, fulmentas, praesepis bubus hibernas aestivas Faliscas, equile, cellas familiae, carnaria ɪɪɪ, orbem, ahenea ɪɪ, haras x, focum, ianuam

maximam et alteram quam volet dominus, fenestras, clatros in fenestras
maiores bipedalis x, lumina⟨ria⟩ vi, scamna iii, sellas v, telas togalis
duas, [luminaria vi] paullulam pilam ubi triticum pinsat i, ful-
loniam i, antepagmenta, vasa torcula ii. hae rei materiem et quae
opus sunt dominus praebebit et ad opus dabit, serram i, lineam i
(materiem dumtaxat succidet, dolabit, secabit facietque conductor),
lapidem, calcem, harenam, aquam, paleas, terram unde lutum fiat . . .
huic operi pretium ab domino bono, qui bene praebeat quae opus sunt
et nummos fide bona solvat, in tegulas singulas ii S. . . .

Villa lapide calce. fundamenta supra terram pede, ceteros parietes
ex latere, iugumenta et antepagmenta quae opus erunt indito. cetera
lex uti villa⟨e⟩ ex calce caementis. pretium in tegulas singulas ii S.
loco salubri bono domino haec quae supra pretia posita sunt: ex signo
manipretium erit. loco pestilenti, ubi aestate fieri non potest, bono
domino pars quarta preti accedat.

" If you let a contract for a new farmhouse, the builder must make
all the walls as ordered from lime concrete, the pillars of squared stone,
all beams that may be needed, thresholds, door posts, crossbeams, supports, stalls for the cattle for winter and summer (of the Faliscan type),
a stable for horses, rooms for the slaves, three storerooms for meats, a
round table, two bronze containers, ten pig sties, a fireplace, a large
door, and a smaller one as the master may specify, windows, ten lattice
shutters two feet high for the larger windows, six light-vents, three
benches, five chairs, two looms for weaving togas, a small hand-mill for
grinding wheat, a laundry vat, the exterior adornments, two olive
presses.

The owner will supply the timber and everything else that may be
needed, and for the work he will supply a saw and a level (however,
the contractor will cut the trees, hew, saw, and fashion the timber).
The owner will also supply the stone, the lime, the sand, the water, the
straw and earth for the plaster. . . . For this work the price paid by
a good owner who provides the needed materials liberally and who pays
cash honorably shall be at the rate of two and a half (sesterces) per
roof-tile. . . .

A farmhouse of stone and lime. The foundation shall rise a foot
above ground, the rest of the walls shall be of sun-dried brick; place the
lintels and decorations that are necessary. Other specifications as in
the house made of lime concrete. The price of the work shall be at the

rate of two and a half (sesterces) per roof-tile as above, if the place is healthy and the owner reliable.   In an unhealthy place where the work cannot be done in the summer a fourth is added to the price by a reliable owner."

The foundation is of concrete or masonry, the walls of concrete or adobe. The proprietor furnishes the materials and some of the tools. The pay of the builder is reckoned at 2½ sesterces per roof-tile. (The Romans apparently estimated the price of houses by the tile for taxing purposes: see Dessau, *I. L. S.*, 6086, 28; Dio Cassius, 46, 31, 3; Cic., *Epist. ad Caes. Jun.*, I, frag. 5; also Hörle, *Catos Hausbücher*, 1929, 228; Frank, in *Mél. Glotz*, I, 377.) We do not know the size of the accepted standard tile, but it was probably about 1 square foot. Hence, if the farmhouse was 40 by 40 feet, it would use something over 1,600 tiles, and the cost of the work would be 4,000 + sesterces ($200).

The 2½ sesterces could not possibly be the cost of each tile, since one man could make at least 220 bricks per day (Dessau, 8675, cf. 8673-4), or about 70 for 1 sesterce. Tiles might cost twice as much. However, we must add that Cato's text in ch. 16 is somewhat uncertain. The reading is *ii id* which is generally restored to II S. It is just possible that *ii id* is a misreading of *vict* (= *victoriatus*, mentioned also in ch. 145, 3). This coin was still in circulation about 180 B. C. and was worth 3 sesterces, so that the cost would be about 4,800 sesterces instead of 4,000.

XXII, 3.   Cost of olive-crusher:

Trapetus emptus est in Suessano HS cccc et olei P. L. conposturae HS lx: vectura⟨m⟩ boum, operas vi, homines vi cum bubulcis HS lxxii: cupam ornatam HS lxxii; pro oleo HS xxv: S. S. HS dc[c]xxviiii.   Pompeis emptus ornatus HS cccxxciiii: vecturam HS ccxxc: domi melius concinnatur et accommodatur, eo sumpti opus est HS lx: S. S. HS dccxxiiii. . . . orbes emuntur ad Rufri macerias HS cxxc, temperantur HS xxx. tantidem Pompeis emitur.

" The olive-crusher was bought at Suessa for 400 sesterces and 50 pounds of oil; 60 sesterces for setting it up; the fetching of it required six men, with 6 boys to drive the oxen, six days = 72 sesterces; the vat cost 72 sesterces; the oil (50 pounds) was worth 25 sesterces. Complete cost 629 sesterces.   A crusher bought at Pompeii costs 384 sesterces, the hauling costs 280 sesterces; it is better to fit it up at home, this costs 60 sesterces.   Sum total 724 sesterces. . . .   New rollers for the mill may be bought at Rufrius' wall (at Nola) for 180 sesterces and fitted for 30 sesterces.   The price is the same at Pompeii."

Part of the price is paid for in 50 lbs. of olive oil, reckoned at ½ sesterce per lb. This fact is important. The haul—25 miles to Suessa and the return—takes an oxteam six days. Six slaves are used (a mill weighs about 4,000 lbs.) and the cost is 72 sesterces. Therefore, if the oxteam (that need not be hired) is counted as nil, the men count for 2 sesterces per day (cf. ch. 56). If the mill is bought at Pompeii—three times as far—the haul costs 280 sesterces. The mill from Suessa comes to $400 + 25 + 60 + 72 + 72 = 629$ sesterces. In this case a haul of 25 miles adds a sixth to the original cost of the mill. See Hörle, *Catos Hausbücher*, 193.

LVI–LX. Provision for slaves and cattle:

Familiae cibaria. qui opus facient per hiemem tritici modios IIII, per aestatem modios IIII S, vilico, vilicae, epistatae, opilioni modios III, etc. . . .

Vinum familiae. ubi vindemia facta erit, loram bibant menses tres: mense quarto heminas in dies, id est in mense congios II S: mense quinto, sexto, septimo, octavo in dies sextarios, id est in mense congios quinque: nono, decimo, un⟨decimo, duo⟩decimo in dies heminas ternas, id est ⟨in mense⟩ amphoram: hoc amplius Saturnalibus et Conpitalibus in singulos homines congios ⟨III S⟩: summa vini in homines singulos inter annum Q. VII. conpeditis, uti quidquid operis facient, pro portione addito: eos non est nimium in annos singulos vini Q. x ebibere.

Pulmentarium familiae. oleae caducae quam plurimum condito. postea oleas tempestivas, unde minimum olei fieri poterit, eas condito; parcito, uti quam diutissime durent. Ubi oleae comesae erunt, hallecem et acetum dato. oleum dato in menses uni cuique S. 1. salis uni cuique in anno modium satis est.

Vestimenta familiae. tunicam P. III S, saga alternis annis. quotiens cuique tunicam aut sagum dabis, prius veterem accipito, unde centones fiant, sculponias bonas alternis annis dare oportet.

Bubus cibaria annua in iuga singula lupini modios centum viginti aut glandis modios CCXL, faeni pondo DXX, ocini *, fabae M̊. xx, viciae M̊. xxx.

" Rations for the slaves: those who work during the winter should have 4 pecks of wheat per month; through the summer, 4½ pecks per month; the overseer, his wife, the foreman, and the shepherd, 3 pecks per month, etc. . . .

Wine for the slaves: when the grapes have been pressed, let the slaves be served after-wine for three months; in the fourth month half a pint of wine should be given per day, that is nearly 2 gallons the month; in the fifth, sixth, seventh, and eighth months, a pint of wine per day, that is 3¾ gallons per month; in the ninth, tenth, eleventh, and twelfth months a pint and a half per day, that is an amphora per month. On the Saturnalia and on the Compitalia give in addition 3½ congii (21 pints). Each man therefore is to have 7 amphorae of wine per year (in addition to the after-wine served for three months). To chained slaves add some in proportion to the work done. It is not too much if these receive 10 amphorae the year.

Relish for the slaves. Pickle down fallen olives for the slaves and the ripe olives that yield little oil; take care that they last as long as possible. When these have been consumed, give the slaves pickled fish and vinegar. Also allow to each slave a pint of oil per month. A peck of salt will do for each for a year.

Clothing for the slaves: a tunic 3½ feet long and a cloak every second year for each slave. When you give a new tunic or cloak, take back the old ones to make blankets of them. Every second year give the slave a pair of good wooden shoes.

To a yoke of oxen for one year 120 pecks of lupine or 240 pecks of acorns, 520 pounds of hay (*ocinum* is perhaps a lupine; the figure is lost), 20 pecks of beans, 30 pecks of vetches."

The slave's ration of wheat is about 4 modii (nearly one bushel) the month. He also receives 7-10 amphorae (48-68 gallons) of very cheap wine per year (the recipe, ch. 104, shows that only one-fifth is grape juice), some olives (amount not given, cf. ch. 144), a pint of oil per month, a peck of salt per year, and, to judge from ch. 66 and 143, the vilica provides vegetables, figs, and the like. The slave's clothing consist of a slave's blanket, a tunic and a pair of wooden shoes every second year. Without reckoning lodging, the keep of a slave would come to about 200 sesterces the year (reckoning the wheat at 2½ sesterces the modius). If he cost 2,000 sesterces at the age of 20 (see below) and gave twenty years of hard service before death, the total cost would be about 400-500 sesterces per year or about 1.5 sesterces per day. In chapter 22 his wage, reckoned at 2 sesterces the day, is therefore probably normal.

Work-oxen ate chiefly barley, acorns, and various kinds of beans. The ration of hay is small, but pasturing is also relied on (ch. 54). Instead of hay, foliage was often used (cf. *ibid.* and ch. 5).

CXXXVI–VII.   Shares due contractors for various kinds of farm-
     work:

Politionem quo pacto ⟨partiario⟩ dari oporteat. in agro Casinate et Venafro in loco bono parti octava corbi dividat, satis bono septima, tertio loco sexta; si granum modio dividet, parti quinta. in Venafro ager optimus nona parti corbi dividat. si communiter pisunt, qua ex parte politori pars est, eam partem in pistrinum politor. hordeum quinta modio, fabam quinta modio dividat.

Vineam curandam partiario. bene curet fundum, arbustum, agrum frumentarium. partiario faenum et pabulum, quod bubus satis siet, qui illic sient. cetera omnia pro indiviso.

"How field work (*politio*) ought to be let to the share-worker. In the districts of Casinum and Venafrum, if the soil is excellent, one pays the *politor* an eighth of the unthreshed grain; if the soil is but fair, one pays one seventh; on poor soil, a sixth; if one measures the grain (after threshing) with a peck measure, one gives a fifth. In the Venafran district one pays a ninth on the best land. If the owner and *politor* mill the grain in common, the *politor* pays for grinding at the rate at which he has been paid for his work i. e. he pays for his portion that goes to the mill. For barley and for beans the owner gives the *politor* a fifth at the threshing.

How vineyards are to be let out to a share-worker. He shall take care of the grounds, the orchard, and the grain plot. He shall have hay and fodder enough for the animals that he keeps there. All else shall be divided share and share alike (i. e. the owner gives him half the produce in return for all the work of vine-dressing, harvesting, and pressing)."

It has usually been assumed that the *politor* ("cleanser") was to weed the fields, and only that. (Even today in Italy gangs of men and women hoe grain-fields in the spring, not only to destroy weeds but to break the capillarity of the soil so as to conserve the moisture.) The mention of the *corbis* (the harvester's basket) shows that the *politor* also harvests before a division of shares is made, and the mention of the threshed grain (granum) measured by a peck-measure shows that he may be hired to do the threshing as well. In other words, the leisurely work of plowing, sowing, and harrowing is done by the owner with his villa slaves, whereas the work that has to be done with speed by the use of a larger force (the hoeing, the harvesting, and the threshing) is apt to go to a contractor who is called *politor* from the first of his tasks. The politor gets an eighth on good soil, a seventh or sixth on poorer soil. That is, since he has to work through a given acreage, his pay is kept constant (about 8 modii per jugerum whether the yield is 64, 56, or 48 modii per jugerum; cf. Varro, 1, 44 and Cic., *Verr.*, 3, 104; 112 for yields). If he also does the threshing, he gets a fifth of the grain.

These figures will give some indication of what a share-renter ought to get. If he receives 20% of the grain for weeding, harvesting, and threshing, he ought to receive nearly 50%, if in addition he also plowed, manured, provided the seed, sowed it and harrowed it in, for the seed required was about 5-6 modii per jugerum, the triple plowing would require three days' work with an ox-team (Pliny, 18, 178), and one man could probably harvest a jugerum per day (Varro, 1, 44). In other words, share-renting probably yielded the renter about a half of the crop on grain fields as in vineyards (cf. Cato, 137). This fact has apparently not been noticed (Cf. Frank, *Am. Jour. Phil.*, 1933).

We may add that, if the owner of the villa and its stock receives only a half of the crop and the crop averages about 60 modii the jugerum, his share would, at 3 sesterces the modius (a generous price), be only 180 sesterces per jugerum. Since allowance must be made for the cost of the farmhouse and implements, the land on a 100-jugera farm cannot be estimated as worth more than 1,000 sesterces the jugerum in Cato's day; and this is Columella's price for unimproved land two centuries later (Col., 3, 3, 8).

CXLIV. The contract for the olive harvest:

Oleam legendam hoc modo locare oportet. oleam cogito recte omnem arbitratu domini, aut quem custodem fecerit, aut cui olea venierit. oleam ne stringito neve verberato iniussu domini aut custodis. si adversus ea quis fecerit, quod ipse eo die delegerit, pro eo nemo solvet neque debebitur. qui oleam legerint, omnes iu⟨ra⟩nto ad dominum aut ad custodem sese oleam non subripuisse neque quemquam suo dolo malo ea oletate ex fundo L. Manli. qui eorum non ita iuraverit, quod is legerit omne, pro eo argentum nemo dabit neque debebitur. oleam cogi recte satis dato arbitratu L. Manli. scalae ita uti datae erunt, ita reddito, nisi quae vetustate fractae erunt. si non erunt reddet † eaeque arbitratu deducetur. siquid redemptoris opera domino damni datum erit, resolvito: id viri boni arbitratu deducetur. legulos, quot opus erunt, praebeto et s⟨tr⟩ictores. si non praebuerit, quanti conductum erit aut locatum erit, deducetur: tanto minus debebitur. de fundo ligna et oleam ne deportato. qui oleam legerit, qui deportarit, in singulas deportationes SS N. II deducentur neque id debebitur. omnem oleam puram metietur modio oleario. adsiduos homines L. praebeto, duas partes strictorum praebeto. .... accessiones: in M̊ ∞ cc accedit oleae salsae M̊ v, olei puri P. viiii, in tota oletate (SS v) aceti Q. v. quod oleae salsae non acceperint, dum oleam legent, in modios singulos SS S.S. ⟨ii⟩ dabuntur.

" One ought to let the contract for harvesting olives as follows: Gather all the olives carefully at the time appointed by the owner or the watchman appointed by him or by the buyer. Do not strip or beat the limbs unless permitted to do so by the owner or watchman. If any one disobeys, he shall have no pay for what he has gathered that day. The harvesters shall take oath before the owner or watchman that neither they nor any one else through their aid have stolen any oil during the harvest from the orchard of John Doe. If any one refuses to take this oath, he shall not be paid for what he has harvested. An oath is also required from each that he will gather the fruit to the satisfaction of John Doe. The ladders shall be returned in good order unless broken because of age. Unless they are returned, their cost shall be deducted. If the owner sustains any loss by some act of the contractor, he shall be indemnified, the cost being assessed by an arbitrator.

The contractor shall provide the pickers and strippers that may be needed; if he does not, the wage of the men shall be deducted from the contract price. No one shall carry away wood or olives from the estate. If a picker takes away any olives, 2 sesterces shall be deducted from his pay for each theft, and this shall not be credited to his account. The contractor shall measure out the olives clean (free from leaves) in an olive measure. He shall furnish 50 laborers, two-thirds of whom are to be hand-pickers. . . .

Gratuities: for every 1,200 pecks of olives gathered, 5 pecks of salted olives shall be added to the pay; 9 pounds of pure oil are added for the whole harvest season (or 5 sesterces) and 5 quartarii of vinegar. If the workmen do not receive the salted olives during the harvest, they shall receive the above-mentioned sum (2 sest.) per modius."

> The owner's staff of 13 slaves cannot gather or press the olives of so large an estate. A contractor with 50 laborers takes the job. Since the men take an oath and receive wages (145), Cato assumes that they are free men. " Manlius " is perhaps a former owner or a neighbor from whom Cato received the formula for the contract given here. The last four lines are difficult. The gratuity to the 50 pickers is 5 pecks of salted olives for each day's picking (of 1200 pecks), that is, almost a quart per day to each man. Each is also to have 9 pounds of oil (= c. 2.7 liters) for the season's picking, and 5 quartarii of vinegar (I have substituted the word *quartarius* for the usual reading *quadrantal* for obvious reasons). Finally, if the men do not receive the salted olives, they shall have money instead at the rate of 2 sesterces per modius. This gratuity comes to about ½ a sesterce per day per man (cf. T. Frank, in *Mélanges Glotz*, I, 377).

A rough calculation of returns on the olive plantation of 240 jugera (60 hectares) may be attempted, though there are many unknown items. I shall not count the cost of the 100 sheep which presumably are productive of some profit over costs. I shall count the land at 1,000 sesterces per jugerum as above, assuming that about 200 jugera are planted in trees, the cost of planting olives at half the cost given by Columella (3, 3) for planting vines, the thirteen slaves at Cato's rate of 2 sesterces per day. The cost of the crushing and pressing and picking can be approximated. Cato works four crushers and counts on pressing 1,200 modii the day (144, 5). Since Pliny (*N. H.*, 15, 23) requires four men to a machine per day and four per night to turn out 300 modii, it would require thirty-two men for thirty days to press Cato's crop. If the pay for free labor is about 3 sesterces, the crushing and pressing would cost about 2,800 sesterces. Cato specifies 50 pickers for the same period = c. 4,500 sesterces. The cost of the villa and equipment is more difficult to establish. The farmhouse (see comment on ch. 14) cost about 4,000 sesterces in labor alone. Perhaps the materials would cost an equal amount. The 6 oxen, the 4 asses, the 5 mills (629 sesterces each, ch. 22), the 2 bronze vats of 300 and 200 gallons capacity, the 3 wagons, 6 plows, and nearly 300 other implements mentioned in ch. 10 would readily bring the house and equipment up to 20,000 sesterces. The estimate of cost and profits would be something as follows:

Income:

200 jugera in trees set 30 feet apart (ch. 6)	=	6,000	trees
a tree produces about 15-20 lbs. of oil per year	=	100,000	lbs. oil
gross returns ($\frac{1}{2}$ sest. per lb.: ch. 22, 3)		50,000	sest.

Investment:

240 jugera land (see on ch. 136)...........	c. 240,000	sest.
cost of planting 200 jugera (see above)......	200,000	sest.
villa house and implements...............	20,000	sest.
	460,000	sest.

Annual expenses:

Interest on this sum at 6%........	27,600
Depreciation, 2% of orchard & villa.	4,400
13 slaves at 2 sest. per day.........	9,000
contract for picking..............	4,500
contract for pressing.............	2,900
	48,400

Profits, 50,000 — 48,400 =   1,600 sest. ($80)

The profits according to this estimate are very small, but if the farmer was assured 6% and a fair depreciation at a profession that was highly respectable, he was perhaps satisfied. Perhaps the land used for olives cost less than the wheat land on which our estimate of 1,000 sesterces per jugerum was based. But I have not included interest on the investment before the trees began to yield well (some ten years), assuming that grain and small crops raised between the trees might compensate in a measure, during that period.

At any rate, so far as we can discover from Cato's own figures, olive-raising in his day neither yielded great wealth nor entailed heavy losses.

Cato's book shows the beginnings of specialized farming with slave gangs on a relatively large scale. He specializes in olives or wine and he expects to go to the market for tools, implements and house-ware, even for some of the slaves' clothing, and the building is done by contract. However there is some home-weaving, the slaves do much repairing at home, and vegetables and grain for the slaves, and some fodder for the cattle (hardly the acorns), are found on the place.

But Cato does not expect to have slaves enough to take care of the heavy seasonal work. The olive picking and crushing are done by contract, unless the crop is sold on the trees (146). He also gives a form of contract for selling the wine crop on the vine and for the cultivation and harvesting of grain. And he speaks repeatedly of hired labor and the need of having the villa in a region where free labor is abundant (1, 3; 4, 4; 5, 4).

(Gummerus in Klio, Beiheft V; Heitland, *Agricola*, 164 ff.; Hörle, *Catos Hausbücher*, 149 ff. (1929); Curcio, *La Primitiva Civiltà Latina Agricola*, 1929; Guiraud, *La propr. fonc.* 566; Cavaignac, *Population et Capital*, 97; Drachmann, *Ancient Oil Mills and Presses.*)

3. *Putative Legislation in Favor of Italian Farm Products*

Cic., *de Rep.*, 3, 16 (written about 52 B. C.; dramatic date, 129 B. C.):

nos vero iustissimi homines, qui Transalpinas gentis oleam et vitem serere non sinimus, quo pluris sint nostra oliveta nostraeque vineae; quod cum faciamus, prudenter facere dicimur, iuste non dicimur, ut intellegatis discrepare ab aequitate sapientiam.

" We ourselves, indeed, the most just of men, who forbid the races beyond the Alps to plant the olive or the vine, so that our own olive groves and vineyards may be the more valuable, are said to act with prudence in doing so, but not with justice; so that you can easily understand that wisdom and equity do not agree."

This curious passage is the only one during the republican period that gives any basis for the theory that the Romans legislated in favor of Italian farm products. It is used as an argument for the assumption that Rome established a monopoly in favor of Roman wine and olive oil in the provinces. (See Mommsen, *R. Hist.*, 3, 415, and Rostovtzeff, *Soc. and Econ. Hist.*, 492, note 17 of Ch. I, who holds that Rome inherited the practices of Carthage. But Carthage had always sponsored monopolies, whereas Rome advocated free trade and open seas.)

The words of Cicero are surprising because Rome did not impose such restrictions elsewhere. Spain under Roman domination was raising wine in abundance about 150 B. C. (Pol., 34, 8) and continued to produce both wine and oil throughout the Republic (cf. Varro, 1, 8, 1; 1, 13, 6; App., *Iber.*, 64; Strabo, 3, 2, 6; 3, 4, 16) and the Empire (Pliny, *passim*). Proconsular Africa was too hot and dry to produce or use much wine (cf. App., *Pun.*, 71, " They use very little wine "), but the lex Agraria of 111 (l. 95) and Caesar's *Bell. Afr.* (43 and 67) prove that viticulture was not prohibited. Olive-culture was treated in Mago's book (Pliny, 17, 93), but it made progress slowly in Africa, not because of any prohibition, but because the best methods of raising olives on land that received less than fifteen inches of rain per year were not discovered till imperial times (see Frank, *Econ. Hist.*, 2nd ed., 455 ff.). Gaul also raised some wine (Varro, 1, 7, 8; Strabo, 4, 1, 2). Diodorus (5, 26) thought Gaul too cold to be favorable to wine, but he does not seem to know of any prohibition of it. Finally, since Marseilles was a successful producer of wine (Posidonius, in Strabo, 3, 4, 17), it is very doubtful whether—considering the high freights of the second century—the export wines of Campania could have competed with those of Marseilles, since the carriage from Puteoli to the Riviera would increase the price from 50 to 75%.

What then is the explanation of this solitary passage? In the first place the words are spoken by Furius, the *diaboli advocatus*, whose arguments were answered in the fourth book, now lost. Cicero probably had an answer for this charge as for the others made by Furius. He may well have given the facts in the case, that, though Rome had helped Marseilles subdue the peoples of Savoy in 154 and had in conjunction with her signed a treaty with the tribes, Rome was here acting merely as a supporter of Marseilles. Since *the hostages were given to Marseilles*, the treaty was probably drawn up by her and to her advantage (see Pol. 33, 10, 11, " Opimius delivered their territory at once to Marseilles and forced the Ligurians to give hostages at fixed intervals to the Marseillians "). The dramatic date of the *de Republica* is 129 so that the treaty referred to is probably that of 154, though one would hardly dare say that Cicero does not admit anachronisms in his dialogues and especially in this one which was for a time cast for speakers of his own day. We have no right, therefore, on the basis of this sole passage, quoted out of its context, to suppose either that the Romans were expecting to export wine to Gaul in 154 or that the Senate broke its custom this one time and imposed restrictions on subject peoples in favor of Roman agriculture or Roman trade (cf. Frank, *Rom. Imperialism,* 280). It may well be that the Romans later took advantage of this treaty for a while, but the fact is that no law or treaty *drawn up by Rome* during the Republic made any special provision for the marketing of Roman farm products.

Pliny, 13, 25, mentions the fact that the censors of 189 forbade the sale of *unguenta exotica* (imported perfumes). This, of course, was a sumptuary decree and not a protective measure. The perfume industry was in the hands of Capuans who were not yet Roman citizens, and the amount of oil used was too insignificant to cause any concern to the state.

4. *Inundations possibly due to deforestation.*

There are an unusual number of inundations of the Tiber noticed in this period. In 203, Livy, 30, 26; in 202, Livy, 30, 38 (the Tiber overflowed the Circus); in 193, Livy, 35, 9 (the lower parts of the city); in 192, Livy, 35, 21 (the Tiber swept away the two bridges below the island, some houses, and over villas in the country); in 189, Livy, 38, 28 (the Tiber overflowed twelve times, sweeping over the Campus Martius and other low parts of the city. The next year there was a pestilence, and grain also rose to such a high price that the aediles had to intervene, Livy, 38, 35 and 44).

These inundations were probably due to the deforestation of the regions north of Rome. The fact that inland towns like Perusia and Clusium offered timber for Scipio's ships in 205 (Livy, 28, 45) proves that deforestation around Rome and along the coast had gone far. Doubtless also the penetration of Roman landlords into Etruria, the building of new cities like Faleria Nova after 241, and of the new Volsinii after 264 had done something toward diminishing the area of the Ciminian forests. Some time during the second century Rome built a stone embankment (Grotta Oscura stone, cf. *Bull. Com.,* 1889, 169) to protect the city against floods, but this work was probably done after 169, for it is not mentioned in the extant part of Livy. Of course, the building operations at Rome during this period required very much heavy timber for roof beams. The fact that the consul of 160 was ordered to drain the Pontine marshes suggests that the Volscian mountains had already been stripped so bare that the alluvium from them had clogged the streams below.

VII. INDUSTRY, 200–150 B. C.

a. *Central Italy: arms, implements, terra cotta, etc.*:

Manufacturing of *arms* for Roman soldiers must have been extensive during this period when an average of nearly 40,000 soldiers went to the provinces every year fully equipped. Most of them (Pol., 6, 23) armed themselves with a sword, a spear, a lance, a bronze helmet, greaves, a breast-plate, and a shield (the well-to-do used a coat of chain-mail). Besides this an army of eight legions needed some 1600 skilled *fabri* (carpenters and smiths) to supply arms, machines, and equipment (Livy, 1, 43; Dionysius, 7, 59; Cic., *de Rep.* 2, 39). Presumably Rome and the municipalities between Rome and Capua supplied most of the weapons needed.

We have also to keep in mind the constant call for *implements and tools*—saws, hammers, chisels, axes, mallets, adzes, spades, and the like—which were needed for the building operations to be mentioned below, and for the private buildings of which we have little record. Furthermore the plain crockery, utensils, furniture, and clothing used at Rome and in Latium were of course made near by, since freighting was slow and costly (Cato, 22, counts that an ox-drawn wagon goes only 10-15 miles the day).

Again the making of wagons, plows, spades, sickles, pruning hooks, mattocks, buckets, etc. used on the farms must have supported a large industry. Here is Cato's equipment for his olive orchard of 160 acres (*de Agric.*, X):

Quo modo oletum agri iugera CCXL instruere oporteat. vilicum, vilicam, operarios quinque, bubulcos III, asinarium I, subulcum I, opilionem I, summa homines XIII: boves trinos, asinos ornatos clitellarios qui stercus vectent tris, asinum ⟨molarium⟩ I, oves C.

vasa olearia instructa iuga V, ahenum quod capiat Q. xxx, operculum aheni, uncos ferreos III, urceos aquarios III, infidibula II, ahenum quod capiat Q. v, ⟨operculum aheni,⟩ uncos III, labellum pollulum I, amphoras olearias II, urnam quinquagenariam unam, trullas tris, situlum aquarium I, pelvim I, matellionem, trullium, scutriscum, matellam, nassiternam, trullam, candelabrum, sextarium: plostra maiora, III, aratra cum vomeribus VI, iuga cum loris ornata III, ornamenta bubus VI.

irpicem I, crates stercerarias IIII, sirpeas stercerarias III, semuncias III, instrata asinis III.

ferramenta: ferreas VIII, sarcula VIII, palas IIII, rutra V, rastros quadridentes II, falces faenarias VIII, stramentarias V, arborarias V, securis III, cuneos III, fistulam farrariam I, forpicis II, rutabulum I, foculos II.

dolia olearia C, labra XII, dolia quo vinacios condat X, amurcaria X, vinaria X, frumentaria XX, ⟨labrum⟩ lupinarium I, serias X, labrum eluacrum I, solium I, labra aquaria II, opercula doliis seriis priva.

molas asinarias unas et trusatilis unas, Hispaniensis unas, molilia III, abacum I, orbes aheneos II, mensas II, scamna magna III, scamnum in cubiculo I, scabilla III, sellas IIII, solia II, lectum in cubiculo I, lectos loris subtentos IIII et lectos III: pilam ligneam I, fullonicam I, telam togalem I, pilas II, pilum fabarium I, farrearium I, seminarium I, qui nucleos succernat I, modium I, semodium I: culcitas VIII, instragula VIII, pulvinos XVI, operimenta X, mappas III, centones pueris VI.

" How one is to equip an olive farm of 240 jugera: a slave overseer with his wife, five slave laborers, three ox-drivers, an ass-driver, a swineherd, a shepherd; thirteen slaves in all.

Three ox-teams, three asses with pack saddles to bear out the manure, an ass for the mill, a hundred sheep.

Five complete olive crushers with presses, a bronze vat holding 30 amphorae (about 780 liters) with a cover and three iron hooks, three bronze water ewers, two funnels, a bronze vessel holding 5 amphorae (130 liters) with a cover and three iron hooks, a small basin, two amphorae for oil, a bronze vat holding 50 amphorae (1,300 liters), three ladles, a water bucket, a wash-bowl, a pot, a basin, a small platter, a vessel, a watering-pot, a ladle, a candle-holder, a pint-measure.

Three large wagons, six plows with iron points, three yokes with their harness, six sets of harness for oxen.

A harrow, four baskets to hold manure, three wagon boxes for manure, three half-size pack saddles, three saddles for asses.

Utensils of iron: eight rakes, eight hoes, four spades, five shovels, two four-toothed mattocks, eight hay-sickles, five grain sickles, five pruning hooks, three axes, three wedges, a pestle for spelt, two pairs of tongs, an oven-rake, two braziers.

A hundred large oil jars, twelve large basins, ten jars to hold grape-husks, ten to hold oil dregs, ten wine jars, twenty grain jars, a vat for beans, ten vats for liquids, a rinsing basin, a wash-basin, two water-basins, separate covers for these jars.

A mill drawn by asses, a hand-mill, a Spanish mill, three sets of mill-harness, a square table, two bronze platters, two tables for dining, three benches, a chair for the bedroom, three stools, four chairs, two armchairs, a bed, four cots tied with thongs, three ordinary cots, one wooden mortar, one tub for the laundry, one loom, two mortars (of stone), a pestle for beans, a pestle for spelt, one for seeds, and one to separate the seed, a peck measure, a half-peck measure, eight mattresses, eight bed-covers, sixteen pillows, ten tablecovers, three towels, blankets for six slaves."

The list includes the apparatus for the olive press room, the tools and implements of the farm and orchard, the jars of the store chamber, and the furniture of the workmen's quarters. The equipment for the owner's dwelling quarters is not mentioned. Besides the five ólive-mills and presses, the bronze vats of 300 and 200 gallons' capacity, the three wagons, a grain mill, and six plows, Cato mentions some twenty bronze implements, some sixty of iron and some three hundred other objects of wood, cloth, leather, etc. The industry of the towns that supplied numerous farms like that was far from insignificant. Chapter 11 gives a corresponding list almost as costly for the vineyard.

Plautus has Latin words for a large number of skilled workers: aurifices (workers in gold), arcularii (chest-makers), ampullarii (makers of leather bottles), calceolarii, sutores, solearii (shoe-makers), fabri, ferrarii (carpenters, iron workers), figularii (potters), lanarii, lintiones (dealers in wool, in linen), infectores (dyers), fullones (fullers), materiarii (wood workers), pelliones (workers in leather), pistores (millers and bakers), restiones (rope makers), scutiarii (shield makers), textores (weavers), etc. (see Lodge, *Lexicon Plautinum*). When, however, he speaks of fine clothing, he uses the Greek words of his originals. But his list of Latin words reveals a vigorous industry rather highly specialized.

The figured *pottery* of the Latin colony of Cales, made in the third century and down into the second, was sold throughout the center and south of Italy (*C. I. L.*, I², 405 ff., 2487 ff.) Samples have been found in Capua, Paestum, and as far south as Sicily, and northward to Rome, Caere, and Tarquinia. The so-called Megarian pottery made in southern Umbrian towns during the second century B. C. (*ibid.,* 418 ff.) was sold mostly near home and in southern Etruria. Much other cheap signed ware (pottery and clay lamps) has been found in the Esquiline graves of this period.

Much good *bronze ware,* especially mirrors and toilet boxes, pleasingly engraved, was made at Praeneste in the third century B. C. with fair samples belonging to the second. This industry was an inheritance from Etruscan and Campanian shops (*ibid.,* 545 ff.). One of the finest examples was the Ficoronian cista, found at Praeneste but made at Rome as the inscription shows: *Novios Plautios med Romai fecid.* This cista, however, was doubtless made before the second century.

Pacuvius is the only Roman painter known for this period, but there may have been others. Foreigners were usually imported to decorate temples. Wall painting at Pompeii begins about 150 B. C.

Pliny, *N. H.,* 35, 19:

Apud Romanos quoque honos mature huic arti contigit, siquidem cognomina ex ea Pictorum traxerunt Fabii clarissimae gentis, princepsque eius cognominis ipse aedem Salutis pinxit anno urbis conditae ccccl, quae pictura duravit ad nostram memoriam aede ea Claudi principatu exusta. proxime celebrata est in foro boario aede Herculis Pacuvi poetae pictura. Enni sorore genitus hic fuit clarioremque artem eam Romae fecit gloria scaenae. postea non est spectata honestis manibus, . . .

" Among the Romans, too, this art (of painting) very soon rose into esteem, for it was from it that the Fabii, a most illustrious family, derived their surname of " Pictor "; indeed the first of the family who bore it, himself painted the Temple of Salus, in the year of the City, 450; a work which lasted to our own times, but was destroyed when the temple was burnt, in the reign of Claudius. Next in celebrity were the paintings of the poet Pacuvius, in the Temple of Hercules, situate in the Cattle Market: he was a son of the sister of Ennius, and the fame of the art was enhanced at Rome by the success of the artist on the stage. After this period, the art was no longer practised by men of rank; " . . .

We do not yet know the date of the paintings of Juno's temple at Ardea mentioned by Pliny, 35, 115.

In the early part of the century the industries were still largely in the hands of free people, not of slaves as later, as we may infer from the names on some of the Praenestine, Umbrian, and Calenian ware. Cato's book also mentions a Tunnius, a Mennius, and other free folk who manufactured articles for the farms. Even Plautus worked for some time in a mill (Gell., 3, 3; Leo, *Pl. Forsch.,* 70, has no basis for his skepticism) and the father of the consul Varro (216 B. C.) sold meat. It must not be assumed, however, that Romans of good family often engaged in industry, even on a large scale. Cato does not mention it as a plausible source of income, and in that he exhibits the normal attitude of his day and his circle.

b. Etruscan Industry.

Etruscan industry was still in a flourishing condition in the third century, even if it was not producing the finest work (Livy, 28, 45, and Ducati, *Arte Etrusca,* 478 ff.). Of the cities which volunteered materials for Scipio's expedition in 205, Caere gave grain and supplies; Populonia, iron; Tarquinia, linen sail cloth; Volterra, wax for the ships, and grain; Arretium, 3,000 shields, 3,000 helmets, 50,000 javelins, the metal implements for 40 ships, and 30,000 bushels of wheat; Perusia, Clusium, and Rusellae gave fir timber for ships and much grain. Livy, 28, 45, 14-19:

Etruriae primum populi pro suis quisque facultatibus consulem adiuturos polliciti: Caerites frumentum sociis navalibus commeatumque omnis generis, Populonienses ferrum, Tarquinienses lintea in vela, Volaterrani interamenta navium et frumentum, Arretini tria milia scutorum, galeas totidem, pila gaesa hastas longas, milium quinquaginta summam pari cuiusque generis numero expleturos, secures rutra falces alveolos molas, quantum in quadraginta longas naves opus esset, tritici centum et viginti milia modium, et in viaticum decurionibus remigibusque conlaturos; Perusini Clusini Russellani abietem in fabricandas naves et frumenti magnum numerum; abiete ex publicis silvis est usus. (See chapter II, section 6 for translation).

It is to be noticed that Populonia, near the island of Elba, supplied iron, while the great manufacturing city seems to be the inland Arretium. The great slag-heaps of Populonia seem to belong to the last four centuries of the Republic (D'Achiardi, in *Studi Etruschi,* III, 1929, 398), and indicate an average of 10,000,000 tons of iron ore treated per year for that period. Diodorus, 5, 13, reveals the fact that the pig-iron smelted out at Populonia (after the timber of Elba had been used up) was largely sent to Puteoli, but Arretium must have taken some and many traces of forges have also been found at Populonia (Mancini, in *Miniera Italiana,* VI, 1922). Diod., 5, 13:

Τῆς γὰρ Τυρρηνίας κατὰ τὴν ὀνομαζομένην πόλιν Ποπλώνιον νῆσός ἐστιν, ἣν ὀνομάζουσιν Αἰθάλειαν. Αὕτη δὲ τῆς παραλίας ἀπέχουσα σταδίους ὡς ἑκατόν, τὴν μὲν προσηγορίαν εἴληφεν ἀπὸ τοῦ πλήθους τοῦ κατ' αὐτὴν αἰθάλου. Πέτραν γὰρ ἔχει πολλὴν σιδηρῖτιν, ἣν τέμνουσιν ἐπὶ τὴν χωνείαν καὶ κατασκευὴν τοῦ σιδήρου, πολλὴν ἔχοντες τοῦ μετάλλου δαψίλειαν. Οἱ γὰρ ταῖς ἐργασίαις προσεδρεύοντες κόπτουσι τὴν πέτραν καὶ τοὺς τμηθέντας λίθους κάουσιν ἔν τισι φιλοτέχνοις καμίνοις· ἐν δὲ ταύταις τῷ πλήθει τοῦ πυρὸς τήκοντες τοὺς λίθους καταμερίζουσιν εἰς μεγέθη σύμμετρα, παραπλήσια ταῖς ἰδέαις μεγάλοις σπόγγοις. Ταῦτα συναγοράζοντες ἔμποροι καὶ μεταβαλλόμενοι κομίζουσιν εἴς τε Δικαιάρχειαν καὶ εἰς τὰ ἄλλα ἐμπόρια. Ταῦτα δὲ τὰ φορτία τινὲς ὠνούμενοι καὶ τεχνιτῶν χαλκέων πλῆθος ἀθροίζοντες κατεργάζονται, καὶ ποιοῦσι σιδήρου πλάσματα παντοδαπά. Τούτων δὲ τὰ μὲν εἰς ὅπλων τύπους χαλκεύουσι, τὰ δὲ πρὸς δικελλῶν καὶ δρεπανῶν καὶ τῶν ἄλλων ἐργαλείων εὐθέτους τύπους φιλοτεχνοῦσιν· ὧν κομιζομένων ὑπὸ τῶν ἐμπόρων εἰς πάντα τόπον, πολλὰ μέρη τῆς οἰκουμένης μεταλαμβάνει τῆς ἐκ τούτων εὐχρηστίας. (The passage will be translated in Chapter IV, section 8).

Copper mines were still being worked between Populonia and Volterra, and, what is less generally known, tin, lead, and zinc were also mined there, so that the Etruscan bronze was to some extent a home product (D'Achiardi, *loc. cit.*). However, after Cato organized the newly acquired mines in Spain—which were far richer in metals— Etruscan mining and metal working began to decay. It is not improbable that the *Senatus consultum* which closed mining in Italy (Pl., *N. H.*, 33, 78: *vetere consulto patrum Italiae parci iubentium*) was imposed at the request of equestrian contractors who took over the Spanish mines. They would naturally look with disfavor upon the competition of private mining in Etruria. The Senate may also have wished to preserve the Italian supply in case Spain should ever be cut off. However this senatorial decree apparently did not apply to the iron mines at Elba—the product of which was of the highest importance to the army and to agriculturists. Many later references prove that these mines continued in operation. We do not know the date of the decree of the Senate, but, since Pliny calls it old, we may assume that it came out in the second century B. C.

There was little building in Etruria except in places like Luna, colonized by Rome. The Tuscan style with terra-cotta revetments and pedimental groups was still in vogue both in Etruscan towns and Roman colonies, but the moulding reveals less skill and artistry than during the preceding century. (See Ducati, *op. cit.*, 535 ff. on Luna, 538 on Bolsena, 539 on Civita Alba, 541 ff. on Arezzo.) No vases of real artistic merit have been found for this period in Etruria. The ordinary " Campanian ware " for household use was still made in abundance. Some fair bronze ware was still made there and occasionally even statuary of considerable merit (*e. g.* the *Arringatore* which probably is second century work, cf. Ducati, 546).

The Livian passage quoted (28, 45) indicates that an abundance of grain was being raised near Caere, Volterra, and Arretium, and that Tarquinii raised flax. The vine and olive had doubtless invaded Etruria also but would naturally not be mentioned in this connection. Polybius, 12, 4, 8, also remarks that " the droves of swine in Italy are exceedingly large, especially along the sea coast of Etruria and in Cisalpine Gaul " (where the oaks supplied an abundance of acorns).

The fact that Gracchus in passing through Etruria in 137 found the farms largely worked by slaves shows that the country had been passing into the slave-worked plantation system during the second century. Plut., *Ti. Gracchus*, 8, 7:

ὁ δ᾽ ἀδελφὸς αὐτοῦ Γάιος ἔν τινι βιβλίῳ γέγραφεν εἰς Νομαντίαν πορευόμενον διὰ τῆς Τυρρηνίας τὸν Τιβέριον, καὶ τὴν ἐρημίαν τῆς χώρας ὁρῶντα καὶ τοὺς γεωργοῦντας ἢ νέμοντας οἰκέτας ἐπεισάκτους καὶ βαρβάρους, τότε πρῶτον ἐπὶ νοῦν βαλέσθαι τὴν μυρίων κακῶν ἄρξασαν αὐτοῖς πολιτείαν.

" But his brother Gaius, in a certain pamphlet, has written that as Tiberius was passing through Tuscany on his way to Numantia, and observed the dearth of inhabitants in the country, and that those who tilled its soil or tended its flocks there were imported barbarian slaves, he then first conceived the public policy which was the cause of countless ills to the two brothers."

c. *Industry in the South.*

Cato's advice (135) on where to buy farm implements shows the Capuan industry was still flourishing.

Romae tunicas, togas, saga, centones, sculponeas: Calibus et Minturnis cuculliones, ferramenta, falces, palas, ligones, secures, ornamenta, murices, catellas: Venafro palas. Suessae et in Lucanis plostra, treblae: Albae, Romae dolia, labra: tegulae ex Venafro. aratra in terram validam Romanica bona erunt, in terram pull[e]am Campanica:

iuga Romanica optima erunt: vomeris indutilis optimus erit.   trapeti
Pompeis, Nolae ad Rufri maceriam: claves, clostra Romae: hamae,
urnae oleariae, urcei aquarii, urnae vinariae alia vasa ahenea Capuae,
Nolae: fiscinae Campanicae † eame utiles sunt.   funes subductarios,
spartum omne Capuae: fiscinas Romanicas Suessae, Casino* optimae
erunt Romae.

Funem torculum siquis faciet, Casini L. Tunnius.   Venafri C.
Mennius L. F.

"At Rome one buys tunics, togas, cloaks, patchwork cloth, and
wooden shoes; at Cales and Minturnae, capes, iron implements like
sickles, spades, hoes, axes; also furniture, bits and small chains; at
Venafrum, spades; at Suessa and in Lucania, wagons and threshing
sledges; at Alba and Rome, jars and bowls; at Venafrum, tiles; the
Roman plows are best for tough soil, the Capuan are best for black
loam; the yokes made at Rome are the best; the attachable iron plow-
point is best; presses may be bought at Pompeii or at Rufrius' wall at
Nola; locks and keys at Rome; bronze utensils like jars, oil urns, water
buckets, wine-urns, and the like at Capua and Nola; the Capuan
baskets . . . are useful.   Ropes for binding and all things made of
Alfa grass can be bought at Capua, the Roman type of basket at Suessa
and at Casinum . . . but the best are made at Rome.   L. Tunnius of
Casinum and C. Mennius the son of Lucius at Venafrum will make
strong ropes for the press."

Capua and Nola seem to make the best bronze utensils like buckets,
urns for wine, oil, and water, also plows for soft soil, ropes, and baskets.
The Roman colonies near Campania (Cales, Minturnae, Suessa) had
apparently learned something from Capuan industry, producing much
iron ware, sickles, spades, axes, chains, harnesses, and wagons.   It is
likely that the iron for such things was shipped down from Elba (Diod.,
5, 13).   Pompeii, Nola, and Suessa made the best mills and olive
crushers because they had a plentiful supply of leucitic lava.   Apparently Campania was still an industrial country noted especially for
its metal ware.

Except for Cato's list we have few explicit references to industry
till later.   Plautus once refers to fine Campanian tapestry (*Pseud.*,
146) and once (*Rud.*, 631) to the ointments that were very famous
afterwards.   Cato's book is evidence enough that wine and olive oil
are the chief products of the rich land.   The very fine bronze and silver

ware and the furniture of Capua that became so well known (Pliny, *N. H.*, 16, 225; 34, 95) may all belong to a later period.

The vigorous expansion of Pompeii apparently began at the end of this period, but definite evidence of it is hardly found till after 150 B. C. The southern cities had begun to recover from the disasters of the Hannibalic war as is proved by their expansion into Eastern commerce (see below).

d. *Building operations in Rome:*

196. Livy, 33, 27, 4. L. Stertinius, from booty, erected two arches in the Forum Boarium (see *Röm. Mitt.*, 1925, 334-8) and one in the Circus, and placed gilded statues on them.

195. Livy, 33, 42, 10. The aediles built a shrine to Faunus on the Island.

194. Livy, 34, 44, 5. The censors rebuilt and enlarged the Atrium Libertatis and the Villa Publica.

194. Livy, 31, 21, 12. The Temple of Vejovis erected by the general L. Furius.

194. Livy, 32, 30, 10. The Temple of Juno Sospita erected by the general C. Cornelius Cethegus (for this building see Frank, *Roman Buildings*, 128).

193. Livy, 35, 10, 12. The aediles built the Emporium on the Tiber, a porticus outside the Porta Trigemina and one outside the Porta Fontanalis.

193. Livy, 35, 9, 6. Cato, from booty, erected a shrine to Victoria Virgo.

193 (about). Festus, 258 L. The aediles rebuilt the " new shops " burnt in 210.

192. Livy, 35, 41, 8. The general Marcius Ralla built Vejovis inter lucos.

192. Livy, 35, 41, 10. The aediles built a porticus outside the emporium for wood-dealers.

191. Livy, 36, 36, 4. The temple of Magna Mater was dedicated; this was a censorial contract (much of the stone was hauled down from the Alban Hills).

191. Livy, 36, 36, 5. The temple of Juventas was dedicated; it had been vowed by a general.

190.   Livy, 37, 3, 7.   Scipio Africanus erected an Arch on the Capitoline with seven gilded statues and two *marble* basins; the next year he added *sejuges* (this is the first time marble is reported at Rome).

189.   Livy, 38, 28, 3.   Censors contracted for supporting walls for the east side of the Capitol and for a lava pavement from the Porta Capena to the temple of Mars.

189.   Livy, 38, 35, 4.   A statue of Hercules was erected by order of the priests.

187.   Cicero, *pro Arch.*, 27; Pliny, 35, 66.   M. Fulvius built a temple to Hercules Musarum and placed in it statues of Hercules and the Muses from Ambracia.

184.   Livy, 39, 44, 5-7.   The censors, Cato and Flaccus: opera deinde facienda ex decreta in eam rem pecunia, lacus sternendos lapide, detergendasque, qua opus esset, cloacas, in Aventino et in aliis partibus, qua nondum erant, faciendas locaverunt. et separatim Flaccus molem ad Neptunias aquas, ut iter populo esset, et viam per Formianum montem, Cato atria duo, Maenium et Titium, in lautumiis, et quattuor tabernas in publicum emit basilicamque ibi fecit, quae Porcia appellata est.

(The public water-basins were lined with stone, the sewers were cleaned wherever necessary, contracts were let for new ones on the Aventine and elsewhere.   Flaccus alone contracted for a pier at Neptunia and a road through the Formian mountain; Cato alone bought properties at the stone quarry and had the Basilica Porcia built there.) Dionysius, 3, 67, 5 quotes Acilius (c. 150 B. C.) on repairs of the sewage system made by the censors that cost 1,000 talents.   The reference is probably to this censorship of 184, since Acilius reports it. A thousand talents was one of the annual instalments received from Antiochus.   This was probably the heaviest expenditure made by any pair of censors during the century.   Cato was a typical Roman in insisting upon sanitation.

181.   Livy, 40, 34, 4.   L. Porcius, a general, built the temple of Venus Erycina.

181.   Livy, 40, 34, 5.   M'. Acilius Glabrio, a general, built the temple of Pietas.

179.   Livy, 40, 51, 2-7.   Censors Aemilius Lepidus and Fulvius were very active builders, spending a whole year's vectigal (cf. chap. 46):

Lepidus molem ad Tarracinam, ingratum opus, quod praedia habebat ibi privatamque publicae rei impensam inseruerat; theatrum et proscaenium ad Apollinis, aedem Iovis in Capitolio columnasque circa poliendas albo locavit; . . . M. Fulvius plura et maioris locavit usus: portum et pilas pontis in Tiberi, quibus pilis fornices post aliquot annos P. Scipio Africanus et L. Mummius censores locaverunt imponendos; basilicam post argentarias novas et forum piscatorium circumdatis tabernis quas vendidit in privatum; [et forum] et porticum extra portam Trigeminam, et aliam post navalia et ad fanum Herculis, et post Spei ad Tiberim aedem Apollinis medici. habuere et in promiscuo praeterea pecuniam: ex ea communiter locarunt aquam adducendam fornicesque faciendos.

(A pier at Terracina, a stage at the Apollo temple, stuccoing of the Jupiter temple, piers for a Tiber bridge, Basilica Aemilia and fish market, with shops, portico outside the porta Trigemina, another behind the navalia, rebuilding of Apollo temple, extension of some aqueduct on arches.)

179. Livy, 40, 52, 4. L. Aemilius Regillus, from booty, built the temple of Lares Permarini.

179. Livy, 40, 52, 1. M. Aemilius Lepidus erected from booty the temple of Diana and of Juno Regina.

174. Livy, 41, 27, 5-12. Censors Fulvius Flaccus and Postumius Albinus were also very active builders:

censores vias sternendas silice in urbe, glarea extra urbem substruendas marginandasque primi omnium locaverunt, pontesque multis locis faciendos; et scaenam aedilibus praetoribusque praebendam; et carceres in circo, et ova ad notas curriculis numerandis . . . dam, et metas trans . . . et caveas ferreas, per quas intromitterentur . . . feriis in monte Albano consulibus, et clivom Capitolinum silice sternendum curaverunt, et porticum ab aede Saturni in Capitolium ad senaculum, ac super id curiam. et extra portam Trigeminam emporium lapide straverunt stipitibusque saepserunt, et porticum Aemiliam reficiendam curarunt, gradibusque ascensum ab Tiberi in emporium fecerunt. et intra eandem portam in Aventinum porticum silice straverunt, et † eo publico ab aede Veneris fecerunt. iidem Calatiae et Auximi muros faciendos locaverunt; venditisque ibi publicis locis pecuniam, quae redacta erat, tabernis utrique foro circumdandis consumpserunt. et alter ex iis Fulvius Flaccus—nam Postumius nihil nisi senatus Romani populive iussu se locaturum *edixit* — ipsorum pecunia Iovis aedem Pisauri et Fundis et Potentiae etiam aquam adducendam, et Pisauri viam silice sternendam, et Sinuessae maga*lia addenda* aviariae, in his et clo*acas et muru*m circumducen*dum* . . . et forum porticibus tabernisque claudendum et Ianos tris faciendos. haec ab uno censore opera locata cum magna gratia colonorum.

(Lava pavements in city with sidewalks, rubble pavements outside, with several bridges, a stage for plays given by magistrates, repairs of the Circus with goal posts, counters, and iron cages for beasts, pavement of the Capitoline clivus, a portico below the Concord temple, pavement of the emporium, repairs of the porticos above it, a paved portico to the Aventine. Outside of Rome, with money provided by each city: walls for Calatia and Auximum and shops about their fora; temples of Jupiter at Pisaurum, Fundi, Potentia; water system, and stone pavements at Pisaurum; walls, sewers, and arches at Sinuessa.)

173. Livy, 42, 10, 5. Fulvius Flaccus built from booty the temple of Fortuna Equestris.

169. Livy, 44, 16, 9-11. Censor Ti. Sempronius built a basilica:

ad opera publica facienda cum eis dimidium ex vectigalibus eius anni attributum ex senatus consulto a quaestoribus esset, Ti. Sempronius ex ea pecunia, quae ipsi attributa erat, aedes P. Africani pone Veteres ad Vortumni signum lanienasque et tabernas coniunctas in publicum emit basilicamque faciendam curavit, quae postea Sempronia appellata est.

(When half the vectigal of a year was appropriated by the senate for public buildings, Sempronius with the money accorded him bought the house of Africanus and the shops near by and had built there the basilica later called the Sempronia.)

168 Festus, 188 L. Octavius, from booty, built Porticus Octavia, using bronze capitals (Pliny, 34, 13).

160. Livy, *Epit.* 46. The Pomptine marshes were drained by the consul Cornelius Cethegus, who was assigned the task by the Senate.

159. Velleius, 2, 1, 2 and 3, 1. A porticus around the Area Capitolina, by the censor Scipio Nasica.

Most of the public buildings at Rome after the Second Punic War were built in the Hellenistic style which the Romans had noticed in Sicily, South Italy, and Greece (Delbrück, *Hellenistische Bauten*, II, 124.).   In workmanship this meant that stone architraves with ornamental stucco friezes took the place of timber architraves covered in the Tuscan manner with terra-cotta revetments; though there were still a few instances of the Etruscan type erected at Rome (Ducati, *Arte Etrusca,* 543 ff. and figs. 649, 652).   The Hellenistic style became a possibility after the Romans had begun to avail themselves of the strong Alban tufa (about 250 B. C.) and later (about 150 B. C.) of Travertine limestone.   They soon developed great skill in making a durable white stucco that was moulded into decorative figures on the friezes.

The buildings of this period were not expensive.   The easily worked Grotta Oscura stone from state quarries was usually used for the walls. The Basilica Aemilia, for instance, would require about 6,000 blocks (averaging 2 by 2 by 3 feet) and since a slave costing only about 2 sesterces the day could cut out some 8 blocks per day (Plaut., *Capt.*, 724), the material for the walls need not cost over 1500 sesterces ($75.00).   The whole structure, which today might cost $100,000, probably came to about 5% of that sum, even though free labor was doubtless used for the more specialized work.

d. *Labor and wages: slaves.*

We cannot make any complete estimate of the number of slaves brought to Rome during this period, but the items given show that the slaves were very numerous.   In 198 Punic slaves conspired with those of the Punic hostages at Setia, Norba, and Praeneste to raise an insurrection, but failed.   They were apparently numerous (Livy, 32, 26). Scipio's captives were evidently sold at Rome.   In Macedonia 5,000 were taken prisoners in 197 (Livy, 33, 10).   How many were brought to Rome we are not told—possibly all.   Spanish captives—numerous in 195 (Livy, 34, 16 and 21) and in 184 (Livy, 39, 42)—were probably sent to the state mines in Spain.   In 189 the captives of Same were probably taken to Rome (Livy, 38, 29).   In 177 over 5,000 Illyrians were also taken (Livy, 42, 54 and 63).   The two largest hordes reported were from Sardinia and Epirus.   At Sardinia Sempronius boasted that the number slain and taken in 177 amounted to 80,000 (Livy, 41, 28). If a half were captives, sold at Rome, it would account for the glut of the market reflected in the saying *Sardi venales, alius alio nequior* (Festus, 428 L). Even more cruel was the enslavement of the 150,000 Epirotes in 167 (Livy, 45, 34) at the order of the Senate. This order might support an inference that the Senate was eager to provide cheap labor in Italy. It is soon after this importation of captives that census statistics decline. There must have been many Ligurian and Gallic captives also, but no lists are given. It would be reasonable to place the war captives of the period close to 250,000.

The slaves that rioted in Apulia in 185-180 were probably Tarentine and Locrian slaves who were persecuted because of their worship of Dionysus (*Class. Quart.,* 1927, 130).

There were also, of course, numerous slaves bought in Greece and Asia, though statistics are not available till a later period, and indeed the vigorous slave trade of Delos began after the Gracchan period. But the fact that there were 60,000 Syrians and Cilicians in Sicily to revolt in 135 indicates that the trade had progressed far before that day. Many of these may, of course, have been bought in Carthage when that city fell. Cf. Park, *Plebs in Cicero's Day,* 33-4.

Wages.

Cato (22, 3) sends 6 men (slaves) with an ox team and ox boys to fetch an olive mill. It takes 6 days and he estimates the cost at 18 denarii, apparently counting 2 sesterces per day for each man. We are not told what free labor cost, but it naturally could not rise much above the daily cost of slave labor. The soldier stipend, not a wage, was only $\frac{1}{3}$ a denarius per day.

At Delos (Heichelheim, *op. cit.,* 125-6) we note that the allowance for a slave's keep was considered about $\frac{1}{3}$ the wage of a laborer and at this rate the labor wage there in 170 B. C. would be about 1 denarius a day. (In Egypt, *op. cit.,* 123-4, and Westermann, in *Agric. History,* 1927, 43, the wage, like the cost of living, was only about $\frac{1}{4} - \frac{1}{3}$ as much as that of Delos.)

At Rome, where prices of food were not far from those of Delos, a drachma (den.) per day might be considered reasonable for a free man's wage. But we may attempt a closer reckoning on the supposition that it was about three times a slave's keep as at Delos. Now Cato (chapter 56) gives his slaves:

about 48 modii of home-grown wheat; at 2½ sest. = 30 den. the year

7 amphoras of mixed wine	= 7 den. the year ?
12 sextarii oil	= 2 den. the year ?
vegetables, figs, salt, etc.	
(in Greece reckoned = wheat)	= 30 den. the year
clothing and shoes	= 9 den. the year ?

about 78 den. the year

On this principle a labor wage would be $\frac{2}{3} - \frac{5}{6}$ of a denarius the day. We may test this calculation by estimating the annual cost of a slave who is worth about 500 denarii at the age of twenty and assuming that the life expectancy is about twenty years:

Amortization of 500 den. in 20 years	25 den.
Interest till written off	25 den.
Keep, cf. above	78 den.
	128 den.

It then appears that, if a slave can be hired out at 2 sesterces the day (180 denarii the year), he may bring a slight profit to his owner; and we may conclude that slave labor was worth that much, and that free labor may have earned about $\frac{2}{3} - \frac{5}{6}$ of a denarius per day.

The cost of living of a laboring man and wife on a wage of 300 denarii the year, which assumes that work is available almost the entire year, would be about as follows:

Wheat, 5 modii, each per month (the Gracchan amount at 3 sest.)	90 den.
Vegetables, oil, salt, etc.	90 den.
Dress	20 den.
	200 den.
This would allow for house-rent and extras, about	100 den.

In the labor household the wife probably is also a producer, but the presence of cheap slavery kept the wage from rising. There were no labor strikes for obvious reasons.

VIII. PRICES.

a. *Gold, Silver and Bronze.*

At the end of the Second Punic War Rome was issuing silver denarii weighing $3\frac{1}{3} - 3\frac{1}{2}$ scruples (they weigh $3.9 - 4.0$ grams), the bronze *as* of 1 ounce ($27 +$ grams) passing at 16 to the denarius, and there were probably still in circulation some gold coins issued in 3, 2 and 1 scruples tariffed at 60, 40, and 20 sestertii, respectively. (This gold was an emergency issue and, as gold had always up to this time been very scarce at Rome, this rate of about $17\frac{1}{2} : 1$ is not surprising, though in Greece the rate had varied from $12 : 1$ to $10 : 1$). The ratio between silver and bronze was about $112 - 108 : 1$.

From 200 to 150 no gold was issued at Rome because silver came to the treasury in very great abundance and was issued quite regularly at about 3.90 grams to the denarius. Gold in fact was not desired by the treasury; indemnities were regularly demanded in silver (by the talent), and when gold was offered in part payment Rome would not receive it except at the lowest Greek ratio of $10 : 1$ (Livy, 38, 11, 8, 189 B. C.). The treasury probably had to exchange such gold for silver at Rome and we may assume that the usual price of gold at Rome was very little if any above that price (Mommsen's calculation of $11.90 : 1$ in *Münzwesen*, 402, rests on an error). However, some time before 150 there was a temporary fall of one third in the price of gold because of the discovery of placer-gold by the Noricans not far north of Italy (Polybius in Strabo, 4, 6, 12). This influx of gold probably did not affect prices of commodities at Rome, since Roman coinage was then soundly based on a silver standard.

Copper on the other hand was apparently increasing in price during this period. The coins of about 200 show that 16 one-ounce ($27 +$ grams) *asses* passed for a denarius of 3.9-4 grams of silver, that is, a ratio of about $110 : 1$. But as silver coins became abundant and became standard in business, and as less effort was made to collect bronze for the treasury, bronze became gradually scarcer, and gradually rose in price. The bronze coins accordingly, which under official bimetallism had to conform somewhat reasonably to the market values of the metal, fell gradually in size from 27 grams to 23, 22, 20, 19; by 150 B. C. they had fallen to 18, and finally, in 89 B. C., to 13-14. About 150 B. C., therefore, the ratio seems to have been about $1 : 70$ whereas in

Egypt, then resting on a bronze basis, it was about 1 : 60. Plautus, *Cas.*, 10, seems to refer to these small coins.

It is doubtful, however, whether this rise of nearly 60% in copper prices can be taken as an index of a general rise in commodity prices from 200 to 150, because copper was far less sought after in this period by Rome than before, and the Etruscan hoards had largely been used up, while in the East it was employed more and more in coinage. Perhaps bronze had been drained off to some extent from Italy and was also going into the metal industry of Campania more rapidly than before.

If we reckon the denarius (3.9 grams) at the usual republican value of $\frac{1}{12}$th its weight in gold, it would be worth about 20 cents in present gold values, and a Roman pound of bronze would be worth about 15 cents in 200 and about 24 cents in 150 B. C.

b. *The price of wheat:*

We happen to have only abnormal prices quoted:

When in 211-210 Hannibal invaded Latium and destroyed the crops so that Rome had to buy wheat in Egypt, the famine price at Rome was 15 denarii for a Sicilian medimnus (Pol., 9, 44), that is, $2\frac{1}{2}$ denarii the modius ($2.00 the bushel) which was probably three or four times the normal price.

When the Punic war was over, releasing the military stores collected in Spain, Africa, and Sicily, the aediles at various times disposed of the surplus to the populace at low prices. In 203, Livy, 30, 26, 5, *annonae vilitate* . . . quod pace omnis Italia erat aperta, etiam quod magnam vim frumenti ex Hispania missam . . . aediles curules quaternis aeris vicatim populo discripserunt (= 1 sesterce the modius; Livy calls it an abnormally low price and gives the reason for it).

In 202, Livy, 30, 38, 5: per eos dies commeatus ex Sicilia Sardiniaque tantam vilitatem annonae effecerunt, ut pro vectura frumentum nautis mercator relinqueret. " The supplies coming from Sicily and Sardinia reduced prices (of grain) to such an extent that the merchant gave over the grain to the carriers for the freightage." (Freight charges from Athens to Delos, about 100 miles, were about $1\frac{1}{2}$ sesterces per modius—Heichelheim, *Wirtsch. Schwankungen*, 92.) Prices went as low as $\frac{1}{2}$ of a sesterce the modius after the Second Macedonian War, when the aediles sold off 1,000,000 modii of the military supply; Livy, 33, 42.

But these are very unusual prices.   In 123 Gracchus started a systematic corn-dole for the poor, selling it to them at 6⅓ *asses* the modius: Livy, *Epit.* 60, ut senis et triente frumentum plebi daretur; cf. Cicero, *pro Sest.*, 55, with Ascon., *ad Pison.*, 9.   This was regularly spoken of as a *largitio* that threw a heavy burden on the treasury (Cicero, *de Off.*, 2, 72; *Tusc.*, 3, 48; *Sest.*, 103; Diod., 35, 25; Vell., 2, 6, calls it a "gift"; Appian, *B. C.*, I, 21, "at the public expense."). We may then assume that it was at least a 50% reduction, and that the normal price may therefore have been about 3 sesterces the modius, which was the average price in Cicero's day (Cicero, *Verr.*, 3, 163).

We may draw an inference also from the military stipend of the knights.   According to Polybius (6, 39, 12), writing about 150 B. C., the knights received 30 denarii the month.   But the price of food and fodder—12 modii of wheat, and 42 of barley for two horses and two men—was deducted.   If wheat was reckoned at 3 sesterces the modius and barley at 2 (Pol., 34, 8, 7, quotes barley in Spain at ⅔ the price of wheat), the stipend would exactly cover the rations, a reasonable arrangement in the case of the well-to-do.   If barley sold at half the price of wheat, there would be a slight surplus.

Finally, since the soldier's stipend was sometimes calculated at 120 denarii the year, sometimes at 75 denarii plus wheat and clothing, we may reckon that the 45 denarii deducted means $3 \times 12 = 36$ denarii for wheat and 9 denarii for clothing (art. "Stipendium," in *Realenc.*). That is, the wheat is reckoned at 3 sesterces the modius.

We therefore think that 3 sesterces the modius (60 cents the bushel) was considered a normal price at Rome about the year 150 B. C.   The price seems high when compared with that of slaves, but the armies of the period required large quantities, from four to six million modii the year, which was more than the provincial tithe supplied, and the inflow of silver during this period kept commodity prices up.   The very low prices quoted by Polybius for Cisalpine Gaul will be noticed below.

At Delos barley sold at about 2⅖ sesterces the modius between 190 and 170 B. C. and there wheat was about twice the price of barley, that is 5 sesterces the modius, but it had to be imported (Heichelheim, *op. cit.*, 134).   The prices about 150 B. C. in the cornland of Egypt were lower, about 1¼ sesterces per modius (*ibid.*, 121), but there the king profited by collecting low-priced wheat in taxes and exporting it for higher prices; besides, the copper coinage was being tampered with by the state. See Corsetti, "Sul prezzo dei grani," *Stud. Stor.*, II, 72 ff.; Glotz, in *Jour. d. Sav.*, 1913, 16; Beloch, *Griech. Gesch.*, IV, 1, 313; Heichelheim, *op. cit.*; Rostovtzeff, "Frumentum" in *Realenc.*; for Egypt in third century, see Westermann, in *Agric. History*, 1927, 42 ff.

c. *Other Food stuffs:* Olive oil. Cato (22, 3) reckons one pound of oil (= ⅓ liter) at ½ sestertius. An amphora (26 liters) would then bring 39 sesterces, nearly 10 denarii. At Delos the price from 200 to 169 B. C. ranged through 16-18-12-15-20 drachmas the metretes (39 liters). The average, 15 drachmas, would give the same price as that cited by Cato. We may therefore consider Cato's price (7-8 cents the liter) about normal with, of course, a considerable range above and below according to the supply and the quality. Plautus (*Cat.*, 489) implies that the oil merchants of the Forum would at times " corner the market."

For ordinary *wine* we have no reliable Roman prices at this time. The low prices quoted by Polybius for the Po Valley and for Spain (2, 15, and 34, 8) are of little value, since high freight charges probably prevented transshipment. Egyptian prices are known, but Egypt was hardly a wine-producing country. Since at Delos ordinary wine sold at about ½ – ⅔ the price of ordinary oil, we may do best to assume the same for central Italy. If this is correct, the amphora of 26 liters would probably bring 5 denarii or 20 sesterces. This is somewhat above Columella's wholesale price of 15 sesterces the amphora for Nero's day (3, 3, 10).

The best grades (imported Chian and the finest native Falernian) were far more costly. Pliny, 14, 56, assumes that the price for Opimian Falernian (121 B. C.) was 100 sesterces the amphora. In 89 B. C. the censors set a maximum price for choice wines at 400 sesterces the amphora (Diod., 37, 3; Pliny, 14, 95; cf. *Am. Jour. Philol.*, 1931, 278). For Cato's period 3 – 5 cents the liter for ordinary wine seems to be a normal wholesale price.

For *meats* it is very difficult to find prices. The flesh of swine was much liked and, according to Polybius, 34, 8, it was imported from the Po Valley to Rome, and to the armies (doubtless only for the officers' mess). Beef, mutton, some veal and kid were in use in Plautus' day, though hardly eaten by the poor. Cato's slaves have no meat rations.

As for prices, those of Lusitania and Gaul given by Polybius (2, 15, and 34, 8) are explicitly called extraordinarily low. The hog of about 100 pounds that sells for 5 drachmas would provide pork at about 1⅓ *asses* the pound, since pork dresses at about ⅔ the weight of the animal. Similarly, if an ox (weighing perhaps 600 pounds, dressing down to

14

400 pounds) sold for 10 drachmas, the meat of an animal dressed for market would go for about $\frac{2}{5}$ of an *as* per pound. But freight charges to Rome would probably add $1-2$ *asses* per pound.

At Delos an ox for sacrifice sold at about $80-100$ drachmas in 180 B. C. (Beloch, *op. cit.*, 317). If this might be considered a grass-fed animal of about 600 pounds, weighing 400 pounds when dressed, we might suppose that beef could be sold at $4-5$ *asses* the pound. At Rome, if the ratio of the early fines (1 ox $=$ 10 sheep $=$ 100 Oscan pounds of copper) could be supposed to continue, we should assume that the ox would bring $62\frac{1}{2}$ denarii, somewhat below the Delian price. But with the inflow of metals prices would of course rise.

Finally, we have a curious item of questionable value in the sumptuary law of Licinius (end of the century, see Macrobius, 3, 17, 7-9, and Aul. Gell., 2, 24, 7). This law allowed 30 *asses* for the meat extras of a meal for certain days but, for certain other days of added restriction, 3 pounds of dried meat and a pound of salt fish. Presumably the 4 pounds mentioned cost no more than 20 *asses*.

These are very unsatisfactory items, but it is all that we have for this period at Rome. Perhaps when taken with the prices of Delos they should be interpreted to mean that beef could be sold at Rome for 5 or 6 cents a pound.

Luxuries in the way of imported food were beginning to come in. Cato once mentioned a young man who had imported a cask of pickled Pontic fish (tarichos) and paid 300 denarii for it, i. e. 7-8 denarii the quart (Diod., 31, 24; Pol., 31, 25).

d. *Clothing:* Cato (*de Agric.*, 59) assumes that a slave should have a pair of shoes, a tunic and a blanket every other year. Cato himself boasted (Plut., *Cato,* 4, 4) that his complete suit (toga, tunic, and shoes) never cost over 100 denarii; but by taxing women's wardrobes costing over 15,000 *asses* (nearly 1,000 denarii) with a 30% supertax (Livy, 39, 44), he leaves the inference that there were costly garments in use. In Plautus, Menaechmus (205) is represented as saying that he had given his wife a *pallium* costing 400 denarii, but I suspect that the audience took that as one of the jokes of the play. We may perhaps assume that a frugal Roman could dress respectably for 100 denarii.

e. *Price of slaves:* Normal prices are not available. The prices that occur in Plautus are usually meant to be humorous. The ransom price of the 1,200 Roman slaves found in Achaea in 195 was 500 drachmas (Plut., *Flam.*, 13, 4-5), while the manumission price in Greece was 300–500 drachmas (Foucart, *Main d'oeuvre*, 107). According to Polybius (31, 25; cf. Diod., 31, 24), Cato thought a plowman was worth 300 denarii or less, but Cato was frugal. As censor he taxed at luxury rates any slaves under twenty years of age who cost more than 625 denarii (Livy, 39, 44, 3). Plutarch (*Cato*, 4, 5) says that Cato never paid more than 1,500 denarii for a slave, but he would here have reference to skilled secretaries and the like. (Luxury slaves sometimes brought 24,000 denarii; Pol. 31, 25; Diod., 37, 3). It is perhaps best to adopt 500 denarii as a normal price for an able-bodied laborer, keeping in mind, however, that prices must have fallen considerably when Sempronius brought in thousands of Sardinian captives and when Aemilius Paullus raided Epirus for 150,000 captives. However, Roman plantations and ranches were expanding rapidly in this period and would quickly absorb any surplus of slaves. We have seen that in his *Agricultura* Cato estimates the daily wage of a slave at 2 sesterces. That would conform well with a price of 500 denarii. At Delos the " keep " in temple service was about ⅓ of a drachma per day.

A *cavalry horse* seems to have cost 1,000 one-pound *asses* in the fourth century, then 5,000 two-ounce *asses* or 500 denarii in the third (*Realenc., sub voc.* " Equites," 277). This seems to be a very high price if oxen sold at 60-80 denarii. Perhaps the allowance for horses was generous in view of the fact that only two were allowed and the knight had to pay for extra ones.

We add the passages cited regarding prices in the Po Valley, in Lusitania, and in the sumptuary laws of this period.

Polybius quotes prices for the Po Valley, which he says are extra-ordinarily low.

Polybius, 2, 15 (written about 150 B. C.) :

περί γε μὴν τῆς ἀρετῆς οὐδ' εἰπεῖν ῥᾴδιον. σίτου τε γὰρ τοσαύτην ἀφθονίαν ὑπάρχειν συμβαίνει κατὰ τοὺς τόπους, ὥστ' ἐν τοῖς καθ' ἡμᾶς καιροῖς πολλάκις τεττάρων ὀβολῶν εἶναι τῶν πυρῶν τὸν Σικελικὸν μέδιμνον, τῶν δὲ κριθῶν δυεῖν, τοῦ δ' οἴνου τὸν μετρητὴν ἰσόκριθον. ἐλύμου γε μὴν καὶ κέγχρου τελέως ὑπερβάλλουσα δαψίλεια γίνεται παρ' αὐτοῖς. τὸ δὲ τῶν βαλάνων πλῆθος τὸ γινόμενον ἐκ τῶν κατὰ διάστημα δρυμῶν ἐν τοῖς πεδίοις ἐκ τούτων ἄν τις μάλιστα τεκμήραιτο· πλείστων γὰρ ὑϊκῶν ἱερείων κοπτομένων ἐν Ἰταλίᾳ διά τε τὰς εἰς τοὺς ἰδίους βίους καὶ τὰς εἰς τὰ στρατόπεδα παραθέσεις, τὴν ὁλοσχερεστάτην χορηγίαν ἐκ τούτων συμβαίνει τῶν πεδίων αὐτοῖς ὑπάρχειν. περὶ δὲ τῆς κατὰ μέρος εὐωνίας καὶ δαψιλείας τῶν πρὸς τὴν τροφὴν ἀνηκόντων οὕτως ἄν τις ἀκριβέστατα κατανοήσειεν· ποιοῦνται γὰρ τὰς καταλύσεις οἱ διοδεύοντες τὴν χώραν ἐν τοῖς πανδοκείοις, οὐ συμφωνοῦντες περὶ τῶν κατὰ μέρος ἐπιτηδείων, ἀλλ' ἐρωτῶντες πόσου τὸν ἄνδρα δέχεται. ὡς μὲν οὖν ἐπὶ τὸ πολὺ παρίενται τοὺς καταλύτας οἱ πανδοκεῖς, ὡς ἱκανὰ πάντ' ἔχειν τὰ πρὸς τὴν χρείαν, ἡμιασσαρίου· τοῦτο δ' ἐστι τέταρτον μέρος ὀβολοῦ·

"Its fertility is not easy to describe. It produces such an abundance of corn that often in my time the price of wheat was four obols per Sicilian medimnus and that of barley two obols, a metretes of wine costing the same as the medimnus of barley. Panic and millet are produced in enormous quantities, while the amount of acorns grown in the woods dispersed over the plain can be estimated from the fact that, while the number of swine slaughtered in Italy for private consumption as well as to feed the army is very large, almost the whole of them are supplied by this plain. The cheapness and abundance of all articles of food will be most clearly understood from the following fact. Travellers in this country who put up in inns do not bargain for each separate article they require, but ask what is the charge per diem for one person. The innkeepers, as a rule, agree to receive guests, providing them with enough of all they require for half an *as* per diem, i. e. the fourth part of an obol."

The prices equate as follows (Polybius when dealing with small amounts equates *obol* = *sesterce*, otherwise 6 *obols* = 1 drachma = 1 denarius) :

wheat, ⅙ of a denarius per modius (⅐ the Roman price).
barley, at half the price of wheat.
wine, metretes (39 + liters = 1½ amphora) for about 1 *as*.

These prices seem preposterously low, but the Po Valley had no good market. The freight charge from the mouth of the Po (and there was as yet no port there for transferring goods from river barges to sea-faring ships) would be about an *as* per pound to Rome or Delos; a little less to Corinth or Tarentum. That is, the river barging and ship freight would alone equal the selling price of wheat and wine at these nearest markets. Swine and sheep could, of course, be exported to these markets, if they sold at about one-half the Roman price.

The fact that the Po Valley was so secluded from markets for heavy articles explains why little silver reached it, why bronze coins of old standards circulated there long after they fell out of use elsewhere, why slave labor was slow in developing there, and why the wool industry, with its relatively light products, prospered.

For a parallel case compare Polybius' list of prices for lower Lusitania in Spain, which was similarly excluded by distance from the markets for heavy goods.

Polybius, 34, 8, 7-10 : καὶ ὁ μὲν τῶν κριθῶν Σικελικὸς μέδιμνός ἐστι δραχμῆς, ὁ δὲ τῶν πυρῶν ἐννέα ὀβολῶν 'Αλεξανδρεινῶν· τοῦ δ' οἴνου δραχμῆς ὁ μετρητὴς καὶ ἔριφος ὁ μέτριος ὀβολοῦ καὶ λαγώς. τῶν δ' ἀρνῶν τριώβολον καὶ τετρώβολον ἡ τιμή. ὗς δὲ πίων ἑκατὸν μνᾶς ἄγων πέντε δραχμῶν καὶ πρόβατον δυεῖν. τάλαντον δὲ σύκων τριῶν ὀβολῶν, μόσχος δραχμῶν πέντε καὶ βοῦς ζύγιμος δέκα. τὰ δὲ τῶν ἀγρίων ζῴων κρέα σχεδὸν οὐδὲ κατηξιοῦτο τιμῆς, ἀλλ' ἐν ἐπιδόσει καὶ χάριτι τὴν ἀλλαγὴν ποιοῦνται τούτων.

"The Sicilian medimnus of barley costs one drachma and that of wheat nine Alexandrian obols, the metretes of wine costs a drachma, and a fair-sized kid or hare, one obol. Lambs are three or four obols apiece, a fat pig weighing a hundred minae costs five drachmae, and a sheep, two. A talent's weight of figs can be had for three obols, a calf for five drachmae and a ploughing ox for ten. The flesh of wild animals is scarcely thought worth pricing, but is given away for nothing or exchanged."

Here the prices are slightly higher than in the Po Valley. Spanish towns on the coast, from Gades to New Carthage, and the Roman mining camps near the latter, could probably take some of the products. But transshipment to Rome would hardly pay at this time except for articles of luxury. The comparative prices are:

wheat,	$\frac{1}{5}$ den. the modius (about one-fourth the Roman price)
barley,	$\frac{1}{6}$ den. the modius (probably = about one-half the Roman price)
wine,	$\frac{2}{3}$ den. the amphora (probably = about $\frac{1}{6}$-$\frac{1}{8}$ the Roman price)
plowing ox,	10 denarii
calf,	5 denarii
swine (100 lbs.,	5 denarii, about 1 cent the lb.)
sheep,	2 denarii
lambs,	$\frac{1}{2}$-$\frac{2}{3}$ denarius
kid,	$\frac{1}{6}$ denarius

It probably would have been profitable to transport the animals to Rome, if the supply had been large enough to invite a regular shipping service. An ox cost not much less than 70 denarii at Rome (see above), and the freight to Rome from Gades would probably have been about 40 denarii. In this case something besides the freight charge caused a difference of prices.

Prices in Sumptuary Laws: In 195 the Oppian law which was passed in 215, a war measure rather than an ordinary sumptuary law, was repealed. This law, passed when Rome was in very severe financial straits and in mourning for the defeat at Cannae, had forbidden women to have more than half an ounce of gold in their adornment or to wear dresses of several colors; Livy, 34, 1. Cato opposed the repeal but to no avail.

In 184 the censors, Cato and Valerius, taxed luxuries heavily; Livy, 39, 44, 1-3 (cf. Plut., *Cato*, 18, 2):

in censibus quoque accipiendis tristis et aspera in omnes ordines censura fuit. ornamenta et vestem muliebrem et vehicula, quae pluris quam quindecim milium aeris essent, ⟨deciens tanto pluris, quam quanti essent⟩, in censum referre iuratores iussi; item mancipia minora annis viginti, quae post proximum lustrum decem milibus aeris aut pluris eo venissent, uti ea quoque deciens tanto pluris, quam quanti essent, aestimarentur et his rebus omnibus terni in milia aeris attribuerentur.

"This censorship was also severe and rigid against all ranks in taking the census. Women's ornaments and dress and also vehicles which cost more than 15,000 *asses* the clerks under oath were ordered to record in the census at ten times their worth, furthermore slaves under 20 years bought after the last census for 10,000 *asses* or more should be recorded at ten times the price, and the tax on all these should be levied at 3 *asses* per thousand (of their raised valuation)."

Cato first specified certain articles bought above stated prices: women's ornaments or garments, table ware and vehicles priced at 15,000 *asses* or over (i. e. about 1,000 denarii), or slaves under twenty recently bought at 10,000 *asses* or more (625 denarii), and he ordered these taxed at ten times their value; then he placed three times the normal one-mill tax on this fictitious valuation. That is to say, such luxuries were taxed at 3%, whereas ordinary property was taxed at the usual $\frac{1}{10}$ of 1%. There is no proof that later censors continued this ruling. There were probably not many Roman articles of such value in 184. The ruling, therefore, was sumptuary in nature rather than of financial importance.

In 181 there was a lex Orchia that undertook to restrain the expenses of the table but, though it is mentioned frequently, its details are nowhere mentioned (see Cato, ed. Malc., 187; Schol. Bob. on *pro Sest.*, Stangl, 141; Macrob., 3, 17, 3 and 13: lex cibaria).

In 161 the consul C. Fannius Strabo passed a sumptuary law to which references are made in Macrobius, 3, 17, 3; Pliny, *N. H.*, 10, 139; and *Athen.*, 6, 108. An abstract of it appears in Aul. Gellius, 2, 24, 2-3:

senatus decretum vetus C. Fannio et M. Valerio Messalla consulibus factum, in quo iubentur principes civitatis, qui ludis Megalensibus antiquo ritu "mutitarent," id est mutua inter sese dominia agitarent, iurare apud consules verbis conceptis, non amplius in singulas cenas sumptus esse facturos quam centenos vicenosque aeris praeter olus et far et vinum, neque vino alienigena, sed patriae usuros, neque argenti in convivio plus pondo quam libras centum inlaturos.

Sed post id senatus consultum lex Fannia lata est, quae ludis Romanis, item ludis plebeis et Saturnalibus et aliis quibusdam diebus, in singulos dies centenos aeris insumi concessit decemque aliis diebus in singulis mensibus tricenos, ceteris autem diebus omnibus denos.

" an old decree of the Senate, passed in the consulship of Gaius Fannius and Marcus Valerius Messala (161 B. C.) provides that the leading citizens, who according to ancient usage ' interchanged ' at the Megalensian games (that is, acted as host to one another in rotation), should take oath before the consuls in set terms that they would not spend on each dinner more than one hundred and twenty *asses* in addition to vegetables, bread and wine; that they would not serve foreign, but only native, wine, nor use at table more than one hundred pounds' weight of silverware.

But subsequent to that decree of the Senate the law of Fannius was passed, which allowed the expenditure of one hundred *asses* a day at the Roman and the plebeian games, at the Saturnalia, and on certain other days; of thirty *asses* on ten additional days each month; but on all other days of only ten."

Here are both a *senatus consultum* and a *lex*. In the former, reference is certainly made to the expenses of a banquet for food, in addition to vegetables (and fruits), bread, and wine. The *lex* seems also to refer to meals for several persons and only to the extras over and above the standard Roman meal of bread, wine, and garden products. The list therefore refers chiefly to meats, fowl, and fish. The expenses permitted for these (presumably for the customary table for nine persons) are as follows:

on certain festivals	100 asses (25 sesterces)
ten other days each month	30 asses (7½ sesterces)
other days	10 asses (2½ sesterces)

Since up to the second century the Romans had not used much meat, this law was probably not a great hardship, though Polybius, 34, 8, implies that in his day pork was much used at Rome. But it shows that the luscious banquets mentioned in the comedies of Plautus were either taken from the Greek texts or were humorous inventions. The *senatus consultum* forbids serving foreign wine, but probably in order to limit expenses rather than to protect home industry, for certainly the limitation of meats was not devised to aid the rural voters.

Finally, it is significant of the scale of Roman living costs in 161 B. C. that it was possible to pass a law limiting the total cost of the meat bill of a festival banquet to one dollar, and equally significant that in serving the cheap meal a hundred pounds of silver plate could be used (apparently the plate taken as booty had been auctioned off by the treasury, and rather widely bought in the city).

We may now with due apologies for the nature of the evidence draw up a tentative list of what seem to be normal prices, remembering that we know nothing about the fluctuations; nor can we distinguish between wholesale and retail prices. We shall, as above, reckon the silver denarius of 4. – 3.9 grams at about 20 cents (1 den. = 4 sest. = 16 asses).

Gold: 12 - 10 times the price of silver

Copper-bronze: $1\frac{1}{3}$ pound coined $=1$ den. in 200 B. C.; twice as much in 150 B. C.

Wheat: 3 sest. the modius (60 cents the bushel)

Barley: $\frac{1}{2}$ - $\frac{2}{3}$ the price of wheat

Olive oil: amphora (26 + liters) for c. 10 den. (c. 7 - 8 cents the liter)

Wine, ordinary: about $\frac{1}{2}$ - $\frac{2}{3}$ the price of oil

Wine, finest imported: (50 years later) 1 - 4 den. the liter

Meat of cattle: 4 - 5 *asses* the Roman pound

Pork: possibly 6 - 7 *asses* the pound

Salt: $\frac{1}{6}$ of an *as* the pound from state monopoly

Clothing: Cato's suit of clothes, 100 den.

Clothing, women's expensive wardrobes: 1,000 den. (assumed by Cato)

Slaves, farm slaves: 300 - 500 den.

Slaves, luxury slaves: up to 24,000 den.; none of Cato's slaves cost over 1,500

Slaves: 625 den. is a luxury price in 184 B. C. for any slave under 20 years of age.

Wages: slave is reckoned as worth $\frac{1}{2}$ den. the day

Wages, free labor: probably $\frac{2}{3}$ - $\frac{4}{5}$ den. the day for working days

Houses: in Plautus, *Trin.*, 126, a fine house is bought for 4,000 den. (Plautus is not a safe guide, however)

Terence once received 2,000 den. from the aedile for a comedy (Suet., *Vita Terentii*)

For a cavalry horse the state apparently paid 500 denarii in the third century

Plow-oxen seem to have cost 60 - 80 den.

Sheep were early reckoned at $\frac{1}{10}$ the price of an ox; in Lombardy $\frac{1}{5}$.

IX. TRADE AND COMMERCE

Of trade in Italy at this time we hear little. Doubtless the small shop system, so well revealed in Pompeii at a later day, was in vogue. There the shop keeper generally made and sold his wares in the same small room. The various *fora* were also used, especially on market days (every eighth day) for the display and sale of goods. And the great festivals were usually days of profit for small tradesmen. Rome had a cattle market (forum Boarium) near the river from early days, a vegetable market (Forum Holitorium, the present Piazza Montanara), a fish market (Forum Piscarium), which burned down in 210 (Livy,

26, 27, 3). It was incorporated in the meat market (the Macellum), north of the Forum, by Fulvius in 179 (Livy, 40, 51, 5). The great market place for other articles was the Forum Romanum, which probably dates from the time of the kings.

The *fora* were of course open for trade every day, but were especially busy on the *nundinae*—every eighth day. It was customary for neighboring towns to arrange their series of market days in such a way as not to conflict with each other. In the Forum of each town, where the official calendar was posted, there was usually a list of the names of the neighboring cities engraved in stone and above each name a hole was cut for the insertion of a bronze nail indicating the market days of each town (*C. I. L.*, I², p. 218). Apparently traders were accustomed to follow the markets from town to town. Of the organization of the trades we shall speak in discussing the evidence found at Pompeii for the imperial period.

Land traffic was slow and relatively costly. We have seen (under *Agriculture*) that an ox team was not expected to cover more than some 18 kilometers the day and that 16% must be added to the cost of an olive mill for a haul of twenty-five miles. Pack mules are also mentioned for the transport of grain, wool, and the like (Pol., 9, 4, 3; Varro, *de R. R.*, 2, 6, 5, etc.; wagons, Pol., 21, 40, 11, Loeb.). Cato advises strongly having one's estate near a river in order to make use of the water-way. Roads were being built extensively during this period by the armies for the movement of troops, but of course they served the purposes of trade as well. The Flaminian way had already been built from Rome to Ariminum (in 220), and in 187 Lepidus extended the Via Aemilia from that point through Bologna to Piacenza, while his colleague ran a road from Arretium to Bologna. In his second consulship (175) Lepidus seems to have laid out the long road from Bologna through Padua to the recent colony of Aquileia. Later the via Postumia, over two hundred miles long, connected Aquileia, Verona, Cremona, and Placentia, where it joined a road to Genoa. All this construction is definite proof that the Po Valley was attracting a large number of settlers from central Italy. There can be little doubt that road-building and repairing went on in the older parts of Italy as well, but the evidence has escaped us.

Commerce between Rome and the East increased during this period, but apparently it was not to any great extent carried in Roman ships or under Roman auspices. Though Rome had formerly—when Carthage took the initiative—had commercial clauses in her treaties with Carthage, the new treaty of 202, drawn up by Rome, had no such clause so far as we know (Pol., 15, 18; the Punic vessel mentioned by Polybius, 31, 12, Loeb, at Rome's harbor was not a merchant vessel). Nor was such a clause included in the treaty with Philip in 196 (Pol., 18, 1; 18, 44; Livy, 33, 30), nor with Antiochus in 189, though the Rhodians were able to insert a clause safeguarding their own rights (Pol., 21, 45). And Rome made no trading treaty with Massinissa though he was a political ally (Fenestella, in *Hist. Rom. Frag.* p. 273). What is most strange is that, while Carthage had blocked the straits of Gibraltar for centuries and kept a monopoly of the rich metal trade of Western Spain and the British tin mines, Rome while opening the straits took no advantage of this great opportunity, so that the old Punic city of Gades grew rich on western commerce (Strabo, 3, 5, 3).

The only treaty on record containing special stipulations for a free port during this period is the one signed in 189 after the capture of Ambracia, situated on the Adriatic (Livy, 38, 44: portoria . . . dum immunes Romani ac socii nominis Latini essent—" provided the Romans and their Italian allies should be exempt from port dues.") The Italian traders of the south and east were therefore the ones who benefited by this treaty. Rome was so negligent of commercial interests that, in making terms with Nabis (197) and with the Cretans (189)— who conducted pirating expeditions—she did not attempt to clear them off the seas. Moreover she made no objection to Eumenes' blocking the Hellespont in 183-2, till the Rhodians raised the issue (Pol., 27, 7, 5).

Archaeological evidence points in the same direction. The numerous inscriptions of Delos—made a free port after the defeat of Perseus— show that the traders of Alexandria, Asia, Syria, Greece, and some South Italians took advantage of the new free port and that the names of Roman traders hardly appear there till some time after the Gracchan day (see Frank, in *Am. Hist. Rev.* (1913), 233 ff.; Hatzfeld, *Les Trafiquants* (1919); Holleaux, *Rome, La Grèce,* etc. (1921), 857 ff.; Durrbach, *Choix d'inscr. de Delos,* pp. 141-2; Rostovtzeff, in *Camb. Anc. Hist.,* VIII, 642 ff.).

Trade between Italy and Africa, 202-146: Fenestella (last decades, B. C.) is quoted by Suetonius (*Life of Terence*) as saying: nullo com-

mercio inter Italicos et Afros nisi post deletam Karthaginem coepto—
" no commerce was undertaken between the peoples of Africa and of
Italy till after Carthage was destroyed," i. e. 146 B. C. This means
that Rome had no commercial treaty with Massinissa, for in Fenestella's
day the word *Afri* had come to be limited to non-Punic Africans. What
trade there was with Carthage itself is not clear; Polybius, 15, 18 gives
the terms of the treaty of 202 rather fully, but mentions no commercial
clause. When Cato in 152 mentions *pavimenta punica* at Rome (Festus, 282 L), he refers of course to floor mosaics in the Punic *style,*
but the early mosaics of Rome do not seem to contain African materials. The African animals used in early games (Livy, 39, 22; 44,
18) may have been given by Massinissa, even if he had no trading
treaty. The only proof we have left is the one famous wine jar of
Trebius Loisius, a Silician or South Italian, who traded all the way
from Delos to Drepanum (*C. I. L.,* I², 425). The jar bearing his
name, that was found at Carthage, may indicate some trade with South
Italy or Sicily, or it may have contained beverage for the use of some
passing Greek ship. It is as well not to pack a vast amount of commerce into that amphora (for Punic trade of this period see Gsell, IV,
150-158, and Rostovtzeff, *Soc. Econ. Hist.,* p. 492; Ital. ed., p. 20:
where the same amphora is cited from *C. I. L.,* VIII, and X. Cato
and his figs (Pliny, 15, 74) have recently been forced to prove various
preposterous " policies.")

Rome's harbor facilities, however, were much improved during this
period, partly to take care of the large amount of material carried by
the hundreds of naval transports operated by the state, partly to provide facilities for foreign and native shippers. In 193 the aediles
built an emporium on the Tiber and a porticus above it (Livy, 35, 10,
12, see above on *Buildings*), presumably to aid the grain trade, and a
year later a porticus was erected for the timber dealers (Livy, 35, 41,
10). In 179 the censors built a dock on the Tiber, several porticos
nearby for traders and for retailers, the Basilica Aemilia, a fish market,
and some shops, besides a pier at Terracina (Livy, 40, 51, 2-7); and
the censors of 174 improved the emporium on the Tiber and the porticos above it (Livy, 41, 27, 5-12). This probably means that eastern
shipping to Rome was increasing rapidly after the war with Philip
and especially after the war with Antiochus.

Excavations have not revealed a rapid growth of the harbor town of

Ostia at this time. The new wall of the expanding port there belongs to the first century B. C. and seems to indicate a growth of the harbor during and after the Gracchan days (Calza, *Ostia*).

However, Puteoli was founded as a Roman tariff station in 199 B. C. and soon after received 300 citizen colonists to manage the town. Puteoli grew with some speed because shippers putting in there for Campanian articles had only to pay the Roman port dues ($2\frac{1}{2}\%$), whereas those shipping through Naples into Roman territory had to pay both the Neapolitan and the Roman dues. Puteoli came to be the popular port of embarkation for sea voyagers to the South and East (Livy, 36, 42, 191 B. C.; Livy, 45, 13, Masgaba; Livy, 45, 44, Prusias). Polybius, 3, 91, 4 calls it one of the remarkable towns of Italy, and Lucilius, writing in the Gracchan days, calls it a lesser Delos (*Luc.*, 3, 123; Dubois, *Pouzzoles Antique*, 64 ff.). It is possible that the iron industry (Diod., 5, 13) which did much to support Puteolan shipping had already begun, since Cato finds some of his iron implements in the Campanian region. The potteries, glass factories, etc. developed later.

Pompeii, which serves as something of an index of the prosperity that came to Central Italy because of eastern trade, began to expand rapidly before the Roman occupation in 80 B. C. But it is likely that none of the large palaces dates from before 150 B. C. The period of growth probably begins about the Gracchan times ("House of the Faun," "House of Pansa," of "Sallustius," etc.). The same is true of the farm villas outside of Pompeii (Carrington, *Jour. Rom. Stud.*, 1931, 110 ff.). Only two houses of the thirty-nine excavated in the rural district belong to the second century B. C. Of these, No. 22 (of Carrington's list) belonged to a resident farmer of modest means, while No. 29 was, at least in Roman times, owned by a Pompeian resident.

In the next chapter we shall discuss the recovery of trade in the southern cities of Italy.

Grain trade. The independent grain trade did not gain large profits through the wars, because so much of the grain used then was public property (tithes, a second tithe bought by the state, or gifts of allies). The naval transport service doubtless carried most of it. Even the Apulian and Calabrian grain bought for the army in 171 (Livy, 42, 27, 8) was procured by a state commission. After these wars, when the navy deteriorated, state contractors seem to have handled the grain. Grain merchants on the seas are mentioned in 202 (Livy, 30, 38, 5) when they found low prices at Rome. They may well have been South Italians. The Roman grain merchants who were fined for hoarding grain on a rising market in 188 (Livy, 38, 35) probably dealt mainly in the local market with the native supply. They might suffer badly when, as in 196, at the end of a war, the aediles disposed of superfluous public stock at low prices. However, no such procedure is mentioned between 196 and 150. We do not hear of the equestrian corporations handling grain on contract during this period.

The heavy cost of freightage from Rome to eastern harbors accounts somewhat for the slow growth of commerce on the seas and for the great difference in the cost of ordinary articles in the various countries. We have no data for freight rates for Rome, but there are some available for the Aegean. Heichelheim, *op. cit.*, 92 ff., shows that for about 250 (and the rates given there will suit the relative prices of wheat in Egypt and Delos from 200 to 150) it cost approximately 2 drachmas to transport (insured) a medimnus (6 modii) of wheat from Egypt to Delos, a distance of some 900 kilometers (less than 600 miles). A corresponding rate from Rome to Delos, or from Gades to Rome, or from the mouth of the Po to Rome (not far from 2,000 kilometers) would be about 2½ sesterces per modius, which is nearly the cost price of wheat at Rome. At this time it obviously did not pay to transship from Lusitania or Cisalpine Gaul to Rome any articles that did not bring at Rome at least an *as* per pound more than the purchase price at the place of origin. This would exclude such articles as grain, oil, ordinary wine, and figs from distant markets except when abnormally high prices prevailed, but it would not prohibit the shipment of hogs (cf. Pol., 2, 15), nor finer cloths, artistic furniture, and the like. This high cost of freightage may perhaps explain why the naval transport service continued to do duty during this period and why the low prices cited by Polybius for Gaul and Lusitania did not affect Roman prices; and it must be kept in mind in any attempts to compare the prices of Rome and of Delos. Since oil and wine cost about the same at Delos as at Rome it is hardly likely that Delian shipping which dealt in oil and wine at this time had anything to do with Latium or very much with Campania. Brundisium and Tarentum may possibly have sent such products to Delos before 150, but we have no evidence that they did.

X. ROMAN BANKING

We know little about Roman banking during this period. The numerous references to bankers in Plautus and Terence seem to be translations of Greek lines, though one, in the *Curculio* (480, sub veteribus ibi sunt qui dant quique accipiunt faenore), explicitly mentions the booths of the Forum, and indicates that Roman bankers not only lent money but paid interest on deposits. Since the state built and rented out money booths in the Forum (Livy, 9, 40, 16; 40, 51, 5), we may conclude that the business was considered necessary, as indeed it had been ever since Rome, by instituting the peregrine court in 242, had encouraged foreign traders to come to the city.

In discussing the financial difficulties of Scipio Aemilianus, Polybius (31, 27, quoted below) shows that bankers were trusted with large sums. Scipio, on the death of his mother, had to pay out the halves of the marriage portions for his two sisters which his mother had failed to pay. The total was 50 talents ($50,000) payable in three annual instalments, beginning ten months after date. Scipio deposited the whole sum with the banker, so that when the husbands came to draw the portions due they, much to their surprise, were given the total by the banker. In this case the creditors seem not to have received a check or draft, but the payee apparently deposited his sums with the banker, giving him the order to honor the claims of the creditors. This may have been the normal procedure at the time, even when the parties, as in this case, were friends and relatives.

The Greek name *Trapezita* is so frequently used that we may be sure that the business was largely in the hands of the Greeks, as it still was in Cicero's day (Herzog, *Bankwesen,* 16). This is also the implication in Livy, 35, 7, when he discusses the practice of the *socii* (193 B. C.) in lending money at rates which were not legal according to civil law. (What the legal rate was at this time we are not told. In the next year the aediles fined several money lenders, probably for exceeding it, Livy, 35, 41, 9). The passage in Livy, 35, 7, reads as follows:

Instabat enim cura alia, quod civitas faenore laborabat, et quod, cum multis faenebribus legibus constricta avaritia esset, via fraudis inita erat, ut in socios, qui non tenerentur iis legibus, nomina transcriberent;

ita libero faenore obruebantur debitores. cuius coercendi cum ratio
quaereretur, diem finiri placuit Feralia, quae proxime fuissent, ut, qui
post eam diem socii civibus Romanis credidissent pecunias, profiterentur, et ex ea die pecuniae creditae, quibus debitor vellet legibus, ius
creditori diceretur. deinde postquam professionibus detecta est magni-
tudo aeris alieni per hanc fraudem contracti, M. Sempronius tribunus
plebis ex auctoritate patrum plebem rogavit, plebesque scivit, ut cum
sociis ac nomine Latino creditae pecuniae ius idem quod cum civibus
Romanis esset.

" They were also disturbed by another concern, namely, that the
public was heavily distressed by usurious practices; and although avarice had been restricted by many laws respecting usury, yet a fraudulent
course had been adopted—that of transferring the securities to the subjects of some of the allied states, who were not bound by these laws, by
which means usurers overwhelmed their debtors by unlimited interest.
On considering the best method for putting a stop to this evil the senate
decreed that a certain day should be appointed for it, the next approach-
ing festival of the infernal deities, and that any of the allies who
should from that day on lend money to the Roman citizens should
register the transaction; and that all proceeding respecting such money,
lent after that day, should be regulated by the laws of whichever of the
two states the debtor should choose. Some time after, when the great
amount of debt, contracted through this kind of fraud, was discovered
by means of the registries, Marcus Sempronius, plebeian tribune, by
direction of the Senate, proposed to the people, and the people ordered,
that the laws relative to money lent between Roman citizens and the
subjects of any of the allied states, or of the Latin confederacy, should
be the same as those between Roman citizens." This law, the first to
extend the civil code over the affairs of the allies, was drastic, and
would probably not have been proposed unless much of the banking
business had been in the hands of non-citizens.

The remark of Cato in the preface of his *Agricultura* to the effect
that money lending was profitable but not respectable—with a reference
to the good old times (about 345 B. C.) when an interest charge was
recoverable at four times the amount paid—indicates the feeling of
Romans against money lenders long after the taking of interest was
legalized. The causes for this aversion are numerous: the memory
of the ancient illegality; the fact that the business was wholly in the

hands of foreigners and ex-slaves; the fact that it degenerated frequently into illegal lending to minors and the charging of usurious
rates; and finally the fact that in that agrarian society the landlords
often looked after their own financial affairs without employing the
services of middlemen. Had Romans engaged much in industry or
commerce, this feeling would have died out. The knight's corporations,
which entered into state contracts, borrowed much but apparently from
individuals against certificates. There is no indication that they dealt
with *argentarii*. In fact during the next period these companies and
not the bankers are the respectable investors of funds. Doubtless the
banking business was growing during the half century when more than
a thousand tons of silver were brought to Rome, but certainly not as
rapidly as it would have grown in an industrial state.

We should also notice the remark of Plutarch (*Cato,* 21, 6) that
Cato invested in marine loans (that is, in marine insurance). Since
shipping was very perilous, the rates on these loans were not restricted
and often rose to 20%. Cato had properties near Campania and may
have become interested in shipping risks in that region, though we may
suppose that the bankers of the Forum also concerned themselves with
this business. The fact that Cato drove the money lenders from Sardinia in 198 (Livy, 32, 27) does not mean that Roman bankers had
entered that province. Probably Punic usurers had remained in the
island after the Punic evacuation and Cato found their activities detri-
mental to the provincials.

XI. ESTATES, PRIVATE PROPERTY

A few large country estates are mentioned in casual references in
this period, though by no means as many as we might expect at a time
when much public land of the South was being exploited. Scipio Africanus acquired an estate at Liternum, a colony founded when he was
consul in 194 (Sen., *Epist.,* 86, 11; Val. Max., 2, 10). Perhaps he had
bought the property when the state sold land in that region in 205
(Livy, 28, 46). His friend Laelius had a villa at Puteoli, which was
also colonized in 194 (Suet., *Vita Terentii*), and his daughter Cornelia
had a villa at Misenum (Plut., *C. Gracch.,* 19). Aemilius Lepidus
owned a farm at Tarracina in 179 (Livy, 40, 51) and Aemilius Paulus
seems to have had a place at Velia, far in the South (Plut., *Paul.,* 39).

Cato's farms at Casinum and Venafrum have already been mentioned. These were apparently all productive properties.

The Scipios and Paulus had brought immense amounts of booty and indemnities to Rome (all told, some $50,000,000), and they may have retained an officer's portion. But the portion could hardly have been large, if we may accept Polybius' statements about the estates they owned. Paulus left at his death (Plut., *Paul.*, 39; Pol., 31, 28), a property of 370,000 denarii ($74,000). His sister Aemilia, the wife of Africanus, owned some property in her own right (Pol., 31, 26, see below), so that some of the money must have come by inheritance from her father, the consul of 216. Scipio Africanus may well have been worth 1,000,000 denarii ($200,000). He had promised a dowry of 300,000 denarii to each of his two daughters, but failed to pay more than half the sums promised (Pol. 31, 27). His adopted grandson, Aemilianus, refused to accept anything from Paulus' estate of 60 talents so that his brother might have as much as he. Presumably, therefore, the elder Scipio had left Aemilianus at least that much. These properties were therefore somewhat as follows:

The elder Scipio: at least $50 + 50 + 60 = 160$ talents ($160,000).
Paulus: 60 talents (Polybius), 370,000 drachmas (Plutarch).
His son Fabius received this whole amount.
Aemilianus had inherited at least as much from Scipio.
Scipio's two daughters brought in dowry 50 talents each to their husbands, Scipio Nasica and Sempronius Gracchus.

Presumably these were among the wealthiest families of the time.

It is probable that financial success during this period was largely due to investments in real estate. The city grew rapidly through the period, and land inside of a walled city with an increasing population mounts in value rapidly. Rural property was plentiful and cheap in 200. Those who invested then may well have prospered, since the military demands for wheat, barley, horses, mules, woolen clothing, and leather were heavy during the period; and the use of olive oil, wine, and all kinds of meat increased with the growth of the population and the influx of silver.

Finally, we should note that the increase of property in the hands of women led to the passage of the lex Voconia in 169 (Livy, *Epit.* 41). By this law a testator belonging to the *first class* could not in his will

15

leave to a woman as much as a half of his property. (In the case of intestacy the Twelve Tables protected the equal status of the children). The purpose of the law was, of course, to keep the bulk of the property in the hands of males who had to bear the unremunerated burdens of government. The force of the law was soon nullified, however, by the use of the *fidei commissum.* Hence in 40 B. C. the lex Falcidia, assigning a fourth of the property to the *heres,* was passed as a remedy. See Steinwenter, "Lex Voconia," in *Realenc.,* XII, 2, 2418, and Buckland, *A Textbook of Roman Law,* 287 and 337.

The passages to which we have referred above are as follows:

Polybius, 31, 26, 1-7 (The property of Aemilia, the wife of Scipio Africanus, and the generosity of Aemilianus):

Πρώτη μὲν γὰρ αὐτῷ μετήλλαξε τὸν βίον ἡ τοῦ κατὰ θέσιν πατρὸς μήτηρ, ἥτις ἦν ἀδελφὴ μὲν τοῦ κατὰ φύσιν πατρὸς αὐτοῦ Λευκίου, γυνὴ δὲ τοῦ κατὰ θέσιν πάππου Σκιπίωνος τοῦ μεγάλου προσαγορευθέντος. ταύτης ἀπολιπούσης οὐσίαν μεγάλην κληρονόμος ὢν πρῶτον ἐν τούτοις ἔμελλε πεῖραν δώσειν τῆς ἑαυτοῦ προαιρέσεως. συνέβαινε δὲ τὴν Αἰμιλίαν, τοῦτο γὰρ ἦν ὄνομα τῇ προειρημένῃ γυναικί, μεγαλομερῆ τὴν περίστασιν ἔχειν ἐν ταῖς γυναικείαις ἐξόδοις, ἅτε συνηκμακυῖαν τῷ βίῳ καὶ τῇ τύχῃ τῇ Σκιπίωνος· χωρὶς γὰρ τοῦ περὶ τὸ σῶμα καὶ τὴν ἀπήνην κόσμου καὶ τὰ κανᾶ καὶ τὰ ποτήρια καὶ τἄλλα τὰ πρὸς τὴν θυσίαν, ποτὲ μὲν ἀργυρᾶ, ποτὲ δὲ χρυσᾶ, πάντα συνεξηκολούθει κατὰ τὰς ἐπιφανεῖς ἐξόδους αὐτῇ, τό τε τῶν παιδισκῶν καὶ τὸ τῶν οἰκετῶν τῶν παρεπομένων πλῆθος ἀκόλουθον ἦν τούτοις. ταύτην δὴ τὴν περικοπὴν ἅπασαν εὐθέως μετὰ τὸν τῆς Αἰμιλίας τάφον ἐδωρήσατο τῇ μητρί, . . . ᾗ συνέβαινε κεχωρίσθαι μὲν ἀπὸ τοῦ Λευκίου πρότερον ἤδη χρόνοις πολλοῖς, τὴν δὲ τοῦ βίου χορηγίαν ἐλλιπεστέραν ἔχειν τῆς κατὰ τὴν εὐγένειαν φαντασίας.

"The first occasion (for generosity on the part of Aemilianus) was the death of the mother (Aemilia) of his adoptive father. She was the sister of his own father, Lucius Aemilius (Paulus), and wife of his adoptive grandfather, the great Scipio. He inherited from her a large fortune and, in his treatment of it, was to give the first proof of his high principle. This lady, whose name was Aemilia, used to display great magnificence whenever she left her house to take part in the ceremonies that women attend, having participated in the fortune of Scipio when he was at the height of his prosperity. For apart from the richness of her own dress and of the decorations of her carriage, all the baskets, cups, and other utensils for the sacrifice were either of gold or silver, and were borne in her train on all such solemn occasions, while the number of maids and men-servants in attendance was correspondingly large. Immediately after Aemilia's funeral (162 B. C.), all these splendid appointments were given by Scipio to his mother (Papiria), who had been for many years separated from her husband, and whose means were not sufficient to maintain a state suitable to her rank."

Polybius, 31, 27, 1-5 (The portions of Scipio's daughters):

Μετὰ δὲ ταῦτα ταῖς Σκιπίωνος μὲν τοῦ μεγάλου θυγατράσιν, ἀδελφαῖς δὲ τοῦ κατὰ ⟨θέσιν⟩ πατρός, . . . λαβόντος, αὐτὸν ἔδει τὴν ἡμίσειαν ἀποδοῦναι τῆς φερνῆς. ὁ γὰρ πατὴρ συνέθετο μὲν ἑκατέρᾳ τῶν θυγατέρων πεντήκοντα τάλαντα δώσειν, τούτων δὲ τὸ μὲν ἥμισυ παραχρῆμα τοῖς ἀνδράσιν ἔδωκεν ἡ μήτηρ, τὸ δ' ἥμισυ κατέλειπεν ἀποθνήσκουσα προσοφειλόμενον, ὅθεν ἔδει τὸν Σκιπίωνα διαλύειν τοῦ⟨το⟩ τὸ χρέος ταῖς τοῦ πατρὸς ἀδελφαῖς.

" In the next place he (Aemilianus) had to pay the daughters of the great Scipio, the sisters of his adoptive father, the half of their portion. Their father had agreed to give each of his daughters fifty talents, and their mother had paid the half of this to their husbands (Scipio Nasica and Ti. Sempronius Gracchus) at once on their marriage, but left the other half owing on her death (162 B. C.). Thus Scipio had to pay this debt to his father's sisters."

Polybius, 31, 27, 6-8 (Aemilianus pays the portions):

εὐθέως ὁ Σκιπίων συνέταξε τῷ τραπεζίτῃ τῶν εἴκοσι καὶ πέντε ταλάντων ἑκατέρᾳ ποιήσασθαι τὴν ἀνταπόδοσιν ἐν τοῖς δέκα μησί. τοῦ δὲ Τεβερίου ⟨καὶ⟩ τοῦ Νασικᾶ Σκιπίωνος, οὗτοι γὰρ ἦσαν ἄνδρες τῶν προειρημένων γυναικῶν, ἅμα τῷ διελθεῖν τοὺς δέκα μῆνας προσπορευομένων πρὸς τὸν τραπεζίτην καὶ πυνθανομένων, εἴ τι συνετέτακτο Σκιπίων αὐτῷ περὶ τῶν χρημάτων, κἀκείνου κελεύοντος αὐτοὺς κομίζεσθαι καὶ ποιοῦντος τὴν διαγραφὴν ἑκατέρῳ τῶν εἴκοσι καὶ πέντε ταλάντων, ἀγνοεῖν αὐτὸν ἔφασαν·

" But Scipio at once ordered his banker to pay each of them in ten months the whole twenty-five talents. When the ten months had elapsed, and Tiberius Gracchus and Scipio Nasica, who were the husbands of the ladies, applied to the banker and asked him if he had received any orders from Scipio about the money, and when the banker asked them to receive the sum and made out for each of them a transfer of twenty-five talents, they said he was mistaken; " . . .

Polybius, 31, 28, 1-8 & 11 (Aemilianus left his portion to his brother):

Μετὰ δ' ἔτη δύο μεταλλάξαντος τοῦ κατὰ φύσιν πατρὸς αὐτοῦ Λευκίου καὶ καταλιπόντος κληρονόμους τῆς οὐσίας αὐτόν τε καὶ τὸν ἀδελφὸν Φάβιον, καλόν τι καὶ μνήμης ἄξιον ἐποίησεν. ὁ γὰρ Λεύκιος ὑπάρχων ἄτεκνος διὰ τὸ τοὺς ⟨μὲν⟩ εἰς ἑτέρας οἰκίας ἐκδεδόσθαι, τοὺς δ' ἄλλους υἱούς, οὓς ἔτρεφε διαδόχους [καὶ] τοῦ γένους, πάντας μετηλλαχέναι, τούτοις ἀπέλιπε τὴν οὐσίαν. ὁ δὲ Σκιπίων θεωρῶν αὐτοῦ τὸν ἀδελφὸν καταδεέστερον ὄντα τοῖς ὑπάρχουσιν ἐξεχώρησε πάντων τῶν

ὑπαρχόντων, οὔσης τῆς ὅλης τιμήσεως ὑπὲρ ἑξήκοντα τάλαντα, διὰ τὸ μέλλειν
οὕτως ἴσον ὑπάρχειν αὐτῷ κατὰ τὴν οὐσίαν τὸν Φάβιον. γενομένου δὲ τούτου
περιβοήτου, προσέθηκεν ἕτερον τούτῳ δεῖγμα τῆς αὑτοῦ προαιρέσεως ἐμφανέστερον·
βουλομένου γὰρ τἀδελφοῦ μονομαχίας ἐπὶ τῷ πατρὶ ποιεῖν, οὐ δυναμένου δὲ δέξασθαι
τὴν δαπάνην διὰ τὸ πλῆθος τῶν ἀναλισκομένων χρημάτων, καὶ ταύτης τὴν ἡμίσειαν
εἰσήνεγκεν ὁ Σκιπίων ἐκ τῆς ἰδίας οὐσίας. ἔστι δ' οὐκ ἐλάττων ἡ σύμπασα τριάκοντα
ταλάντων, ἐάν τις μεγαλομερῶς ποιῇ . . . φήμης περὶ αὐτοῦ ⟨δια⟩ διδομένης, μετήλ-
λαξεν ἡ μήτηρ. ὁ δὲ τοσοῦτον ἀπέσχε τοῦ κομίσασθαι ⟨τι⟩ ὧν πρότερον ἐδωρήσατο,
περὶ ὧν ἀρτίως εἶπον, ὥστε καὶ ταῦτα καὶ τὴν λοιπὴν οὐσίαν τὴν τῆς μητρὸς ἅπασαν
ἀπέδωκε ταῖς ἀδελφαῖς, ἧς οὐδὲν αὐταῖς προσῆκε κατὰ τοὺς νόμους. . . . εἰς ἣν
ἴσως ἑξήκοντα τάλαντα δαπανήσας, τοσαῦτα γὰρ ἦν προειμένος τῶν ἰδίων, ὁμολογου-
μένην ἔσχε τὴν ἐπὶ καλοκἀγαθίᾳ φήμην . . .

"Two years later (160 B. C.), when his own father Aemilius died,
and left him and his brother Fabius heirs to his estate, he again acted
in a noble manner deserving of mention.   Aemilius was childless, as
he had given some of his sons to be adopted by other families and those
whom he had kept to succeed him were dead, and he therefore left his
property to Scipio and Fabius.   Scipio, knowing that his brother was
by no means well off, gave up the inheritance, the whole of which was
estimated at more than sixty talents, to him in order that Fabius might
thus possess a fortune equal to his own.   This became widely known,
and he now gave an even more conspicuous proof of his generosity.
His brother wished to give a gladiatorial show on the occasion of his
father's funeral, but was unable to meet the expense, which was very
considerable, and Scipio contributed the half of it out of his own fortune.   The total expense of such a show amounts to not less than thirty
talents if it is done on a generous scale.   While the report of this was
still fresh, his mother died, and Scipio, far from taking back any of
the gifts I mentioned above, gave them and the residue of his mother's
property to his sisters, who had no legal claim to it. . . . By the expenditure of perhaps sixty talents—for that was what he had bestowed
from his own property—his reputation for the second of these virtues
(nobility of character) was firmly established."

Plut., *Paulus,* 39, 1 and 5 (The estate of Paulus):

ἐπεὶ δὲ πεισθεὶς ὑπὸ τῶν ἰατρῶν ἔπλευσεν εἰς Ἐλέαν τῆς Ἰταλίας καὶ διέτριβεν
αὐτόθι πλείω χρόνον ἐν παραλίοις ἀγροῖς καὶ πολλὴν ἡσυχίαν ἔχουσιν, . . . Τὴν
δ' οὐσίαν αὐτοῦ μόλις ἑπτὰ καὶ τριάκοντα μυριάδων γενέσθαι λέγουσιν, ἧς αὐτὸς
μὲν ἀμφοτέρους τοὺς υἱοὺς ἀπέλιπε κληρονόμους, ὁ δὲ νεώτερος Σκηπίων τῷ ἀδελφῷ
πᾶσαν ἔχειν συνεχώρησεν αὐτὸς εἰς οἶκον εὐπορώτερον τὸν Ἀφρικανοῦ δεδομένος.

" Under the advice of his physicians he sailed to Velia in Italy, and there spent much time in country places lying by the sea and affording great quiet. . . . His estate, we are told, hardly amounted to three hundred and seventy thousand drachmas, to which he left both his sons heirs; but the younger, Scipio, who had been adopted into the wealthier family of Africanus, allowed his brother to have it all."

Polybius, 31, 25, 4-8 (Luxuries in Cato's day):

οἱ μὲν γὰρ εἰς ἐρωμένους τῶν νέων, οἱ δ' εἰς ἑταίρας ἐξεκέχυντο, πολλοὶ δ' εἰς ἀκροάματα καὶ πότους καὶ τὴν ἐν τούτοις πολυτέλειαν, ταχέως ἡρπακότες ἐν τῷ Περσικῷ πολέμῳ τὴν τῶν Ἑλλήνων εἰς τοῦτο τὸ μέρος εὐχέρειαν. καὶ τηλικαύτη τις ἐνεπεπτώκει περὶ τὰ τοιαῦτα τῶν ἔργων ἀκρασία τοῖς νέοις ὥστε πολλοὺς μὲν ἐρώμενον ἠγορακέναι ταλάντου, πολλοὺς δὲ ταρίχου Ποντικοῦ κεράμιον τριακοσίων δραχμῶν. ἐφ' οἷς καὶ Μάρκος ⟨ἀγανακτῶν⟩ εἶπέ ποτε πρὸς τὸν δῆμον ὅτι μάλιστ' ἂν κατίδοιεν τὴν ἐπὶ ⟨τὸ⟩ χεῖρον προκοπὴν τῆς πολιτείας ἐκ τούτων, ὅταν πωλούμενοι πλεῖον εὑρίσκωσιν οἱ μὲν εὐπρεπεῖς παῖδες τῶν ἀγρῶν, τὰ δὲ κεράμια τοῦ ταρίχου τῶν ζευγηλατῶν. συνέβη δὲ τὴν παροῦσαν αἵρεσιν οἷον ἐκλάμψαι κατὰ τοὺς νῦν λεγομένους καιροὺς πρῶτον μὲν διὰ τὸ καταλυθείσης τῆς ἐν Μακεδονίᾳ βασιλείας δοκεῖν ἀδήριτον αὐτοῖς ὑπάρχειν τὴν περὶ τῶν ὅλων ἐξουσίαν, ἔπειτα διὰ τὸ πολλὴν ἐπίφασιν γενέσθαι τῆς εὐδαιμονίας περί τε τοὺς κατ' ἰδίαν βίους καὶ περὶ τὰ κοινά, τῶν ἐκ Μακεδονίας μετακομισθέντων εἰς τὴν Ῥώμην χορηγίων.

" For some of the Roman youths had abandoned themselves to amours with boys and others to the society of courtesans, and many to musical entertainments and banquets and the extravagance they involve, having in the course of the war with Perseus been speedily infected by the Greek laxity in these respects. So great in fact was the incontinence that had broken out among the young men in such matters, that many paid a talent for a male favourite and many three hundred drachmas for a jar of caviar. This aroused the indignation of Cato, who said once in a public speech that it was the surest sign of deterioration in the republic when pretty boys fetch more than fields, and jars of caviar more than ploughmen. It was just at the period we are treating of that this present tendency to extravagance declared itself, first of all because they thought that now after the fall of the Macedonian kingdom their universal dominion was undisputed, and next because after the riches of Macedonia had been transported to Rome there was a great display of wealth both in public and in private."

A. Gell., 17, 6, 8 (Cato supports the lex Voconia):

Ipse etiam Cato mulierem demonstrare locupletem volens: " Mulier," inquit, " et magnam dotem dat et magnam pecuniam recipit," hoc est : et magnam dotem dat et magnam pecuniam retinet.   Ex ea igitur re familiari, quam sibi dote data retinuit, pecuniam viro mutuam dat. Eam pecuniam cum viro forte irata repetere instituit, adponit ei flagi- tatorem " servum recepticium ", hoc est proprium servum suum, quem cum pecunia reliqua receperat neque dederat doti, sed retinuerat;

" Cato himself too, wishing to describe the woman as rich, says : ' The woman brings a great dowry and holds back a large sum of money '; that is, she gives a great dowry and retains possession of a large sum of money.   From that property then which she kept for herself after giving her dowry, she lent money to her husband.   When she happened to be vexed with her husband and determined to demand the money back, she appointed to demand it from him a *servus recepticius,* that is, a slave of her very own, whom she had held back with the rest of the money and had not given as part of her dowry, but had retained."

CHAPTER IV

THE GRACCHAN PERIOD: 150–80 B. C.

I. CHRONOLOGY

149–8	Fourth Macedonian War
149–6	Third Punic War
147–139	Wars with Viriathus in Spain
146	Revolt of Achaeans
146	Destruction of Corinth and Carthage
143–33	Numantine War in Spain
136–32	Servile War in Sicily
133	Tribunate of Tiberius Gracchus
133	Kingdom of Pergamum willed to Rome
129	Province of Asia organized
123–2	Tribunate of Gaius Gracchus
121	Province of Narbonese Gaul organized
111–105	Jugurthine War
113–101	Wars with Cimbri and Teutones
103–100	Saturninus and Glaucia
91	Tribunate of Livius Drusus
90–88	Marsic or Social War
89–85	First Mithridatic War
87	Marian Revolt at Rome
83	Sulla's Return to Italy
82–79	Sulla dictator

II. LAND AND POPULATION

a. *Area of Ager Romanus.*

The Italian peninsula south of the Rubicon has about 130,000 square kilometers (about 50,200 square miles), while the part north of the Rubicon that belonged to Italy in Augustus' day had about 86,000 square kilometers (about 33,200 square miles), the sum total being about 83,400 square miles. By 150 B. C. the Roman ager is estimated by Beloch (*Röm. Gesch.,* 621) as having 37,000 square kilometers below the Rubicon and 18,000 above (together about 21,000 square miles) or about one-fourth of the whole of the peninsula.

215

Between 150 and 90 very little was added to this Ager Romanus, for
citizen colonies like Tarentum, Scolacium, and Dertona were apparently planted on public land already included. Eporedia on the other
hand was planted above the Po in 100 B. C. on land recently acquired.
However, after the Marsic War when the franchise was extended
throughout Italy to the Rubicon and to the Latin communities of the
Po Valley, the increase in area was very great. Below the Rubicon
the area of the Ager Romanus now rose from about 14,000 square miles
to about 50,200 (from 37,000 square kilometers to about 130,000
square kilometers). And above the Rubicon the *lex Julia* of 90 gave
the franchise as far as the Po (probably still excluding the Ligurians)
and also to Latin communities above the Po, certainly to Cremona, and
presumably to Aquileia. Since the Cispadane region east of Liguria
was already largely in the hands of citizens, the extension of Roman
ager north of the Rubicon probably did not exceed 5,000 square kilometers (1,930 square miles) at this time. But all the peoples of the
Po Valley not granted citizenship were grouped into Latin communities (called colonies), granted self government, and given the prospect
of early incorporation into the state. In fact, a large part of them
were Roman and Italian emigrants. We may therefore assume that
the *lex Julia* of 90 and the *lex Pompeia* of 89 together increased the
Roman ager from about 14,000 square miles to about 52,000 and in
addition created a new " Latin " region of about 24,000 square miles.

b. *Census Statistics* [1] (*free adult males*).

154 B. C.	324,000	(Livy, *Epit.* 48)
147	322,000	(Euseb. and Hier., Ol., 158)
142	328,442	(Livy, *Epit.* 54)
136	317,933 [2]	(Livy, *Epit.* 56)
131	318,823	(Livy, *Epit.* 59)

Comment on these statistics:

[1] See Beloch, *Bevölkerung*, and Klio, 1903, 471; E. Meyer, in *Handwörterbuch der
Staatsw.*[3], II, 906; Mommsen, *Staatsrecht*, II, 400, and III, 435; Herzog, in *Comment.
in honorem Th. Mommseni*, 124; Frank, in *Class. Phil.*, 1924, 329 ff.

[2] Between 154 and 136 the numbers fell off some 6,000, whereas one might have
expected an increase of some 30-50,000 in two decades. The Numantine War took
place during the most decided decrease, but this could hardly account for the serious
decline. Probably it was due to emigration to the Po Valley and to the negligence
of the censors after the tribute was no longer collected (after 167 B. C.).

125	394,736 [3]	(Livy, *Epit.* 60)
115	394,336	(Livy, *Epit.* 63)
86	463,000 [4]	(Hier., Ol., 173, 4)
70	910,000 [5]	(Phlegon, Ol., 177, 3; Livy, *Epit.* 98, gives 900,000)

c. *Colonies.*

The land distribution and colonization of the Gracchi were partly social-economic in purpose, i. e. to place on small lots the urban poor, partly military, i. e. to increase the number of property owners eligible for army service (a property qualification of 4,000 *asses* was still legal); and finally the colonization of Gaius Gracchus was planned for the development of certain harbor towns thought to be serviceable for commerce.

The colonies of Marius projected by Saturninus in 103-100, however, were planned for the settlement of the Marian veterans on lots given as a bonus for army service. The reason for this change in policy was the fact that Marius had opened the army to propertyless volunteers, perhaps with hints that substantial rewards would be forthcoming.

Sulla colonized some 23-27 legions on land expropriated in Italy

[3] The striking increase of 76,000 (24 per cent) during the lustrum after 131 is usually and plausibly explained as somehow connected with the Gracchan colonization. Since it had not been customary to employ the very poor in army service, there could have been no great incentive to enrolling them with great care in the census. But now, since Gracchus considered military needs in his distribution of lands, it is likely that the takers were scrupulously enrolled as potential soldiers, even though they did not at first have complete title to their plots. It may also be that the poor enrolled in the hope of getting lots.

[4] After the grant of the franchise to the Italians and the Cispadanes in 89 (provided they enrolled with a praetor) the census figures might well have trebled or quadrupled. However, it is apparent that the hatred evoked by the Senate's action in confining the new citizens to 8 of the 35 wards discouraged enrolment. At any rate the figure for the year 86 does not in any way represent the actual number of potential *cives*. In 225 there were about three times as many non-citizens as citizens in Italy. If the citizens numbered about 400,000 before the Marsic War and the non-citizens about three times as many, the total figure for Italy exclusive of Cispadane Gaul should have been about 1,600,000. The Cispadanes might well have brought the number to near 2,000,000. But some deduction must be allowed for the casualties of the Marsic War. See *Class. Phil.*, 1924, 332.

[5] Enrolment increased somewhat by the year 70, but since 82 Sulla had hindered the process by deleting the censorship, apparently to keep the Italians from voting (see Cic., *pro Milo*, 73). It is likely that the figure given for the year 70 is again a very low record of free adult males.

from his enemies. The five legions he had in the East had been refused pay by the state; he probably could keep them only by promises of future rewards. The other legions he had enticed away from the Marian armies in Italy or had levied in Italy by various inducements. Probably he also had to promise rewards in order to secure volunteers. As the usual looting, which soldiers expected in addition to their pay, would seldom be feasible in Italy, the promise of land was doubtless his remedy.

During this period all the colonies in Italy were for citizens. (Consult Mommsen's tentative list of Sullan colonies, in *Hermes,* 18, 163; Kornemann, " Coloniae," in *R-E.,* IV; Pais, in *Mem. Acc. Lincei.,* 1925, 345 ff.; the appropriate introductions of the *C. I. L.* volumes for Italy; Beloch, *Röm. Gesch.,* 488 ff.).

Colonies of the Gracchan Time

124 B. C.   *Fabrateria Nova,* to take the place of Fregellae, destroyed because of a revolt. Vell., 1, 15.

122   Scolacium, Tarentum, and Carthage. Vell., 1, 15. *Scolacium* was apparently at the " castra Hannibalis," first planted as a tariff station in 199. Livy, 32, 7.

Tarentum. The Greek Taras was subdued and remained an allied state, but was deprived of some land, on which the colony was planted by C. Gracchus. Strabo, 6, 3, 4; Pliny, *N. H.,* 3, 99.

Carthage in Africa. The status of colony was revoked, but the colonists were left in possession. See section on Gracchan legislation. Grumentum and Telesia may belong here, but may also belong to the foundations of Livius Drusus of 121. See below.

133-22   For the Gracchan settlements of individuals which must have been made in all parts of Italy, see below on the Gracchan boundary stones that have been found. The *libri Coloniarum* (or *regionum*), wholly distrusted by Mommsen, mention some forty places (mostly in the south) as settled by Gracchan commissions. The list is given by Pais, *loc. cit.,* 347 f. There is no way to check the list; it certainly omits some places and seems to be incorrect in others, but Pais is correct in holding that, though careless, the list is derived from good records. However a place-name on the list may only mean that a few individuals were settled there. The list shows little except that nine-tenths of the places mentioned were south of Rome. Livius Drusus was allowed by the Senate to outbid Gracchus in 122 by offering twelve colonies on the best of terms (see below). We are not told that the promise was fulfilled, but a few colonies may possibly be due to his efforts.

122 ? *Abellinum* in Samnium. Its official title was Veneria Livia (*C. I. L.,* X, p. 127) and Beloch, *Röm. Gesch.,* 493, plausibly assigns it to Livius Drusus (Mommsen and Kornemann assign it to Sulla).

122 ? *Allifae* and *Telesia* in Samnium and *Grumentum* in Lucania may belong to this period (see Beloch, *ibid.*), though they are commonly attributed to Sulla.

120 c. *Dertona* in Liguria is accepted for about the same period by Vell., 1, 15, but he is not very reliable.

118 *Narbo* in Gaul was founded in 118 by Licinius Crassus, who was then still a member of the Gracchan party. Planted outside of Italy as a trading post, it was drawn on Gracchan lines, despite the vigorous opposition of the Senate which intended to keep control of the provinces: Cic., *pro Cluent.,* 140: (Crassus) in dissuasione rogationis eius quae contra coloniam Narbonensem ferebatur, quantum potest de auctoritate senatus detrahit ("in speaking against the bill proposed to annul the colony of Narbo, Crassus belittled so far as he could the dignity of the Senate"). Cf. Cic., *Brut.,* 160; *pro Font.,* 13 and 34.

Marian Colonies.

103 ? Assignments of land to Marian veterans in the Bagradas valley in Africa, probably to some who had served in the Jugurthine war. (Auctor, *de Vir. Ill.,* 73: L. Apuleius Saturninus . . . ut gratiam Marianorum militum pararet legem tulit ut veteranis centena agri jugera in Africa dividerentur ("in order to gain the good will of the Marian soldiers Apuleius passed a law that 100 jugera should be given to each of the veterans"). *Thibaris* and *Uchi Maius* are later called Marian colonies (cf. *C. I. L.,* VIII, 26181, 15450, etc.). The legislation of this year (his first term as tribune) was *not* revoked, though that of 100 was. The Saltus region of Africa may well have received 5,000 settlers. For further evidence see Frank, in *Am. Jour. Phil.,* 1926, 170; Broughton, *Romanization of Africa,* 32. On the legislation of Saturninus see Von der Mühll, *Appuleius Sat.,* 76; F. W. Robinson, *Marius, Saturninus und Glaucia,* 64.

100   *Eporedia,* Vell., 1, 15, apparently on the battle ground where the Cimbri were defeated by Marius and Catulus.

The vast scheme proposed in 100 of colonizing Sicily, Greece, and Macedonia was rejected or voided (*de Vir. Ill.,* 73; Cic., *pro Balbo,* 48), though an oracle was found that permitted the commission to proceed for a while (Sibyllinis a populo Romano conditum jussis, Pliny, *N. H.,* 3, 123). We hear no more of the matter. A *Colonia Mariana* in Corsica is also attested by Seneca, *ad Helv.,* 7, 9, and inscriptions (*C. I. L.,* X, p. 838; cf. Pliny, *N. H.,* 3, 80). Presumably a part of the legislation of the year 100 was allowed to be carried out, to satisfy the Marian veterans.

Sullan Colonies.

81   Sulla confiscated vast areas in Italy and colonized some 120,000 veterans on them (Appian, *B. C.,* 1, 104), *i. e.,* 23 (Appian, *B. C.,* 1, 100) or 27 (Livy, *Epit.* 89) of his legions, but no historian gives a list of the towns, and the evidence is very defective. We may be fairly sure of the following:

Abella in Campania; see *C. I. L.,* X, 1210; Beloch, *op. cit.,* 511.

Arretium in Etruria; Cic., *ad Att.,* 1, 19, 4 (on a part of the town lands), *C. I. L.,* XI, 1849.

Florentia in Etruria with at least a part of the land of Faesulae; cf. Beloch, *op. cit.,* 611.

Hadria, Pliny, *N. H.,* 3, 110. The name Venerius, *C. I. L.,* IX, 5020, seems to point to Sulla. Cf. Mommsen's list in *Hermes, loc. cit.*

Interamnia Praetuttiorum in Picenum. Cf. Mommsen's list.

Nola in Campania. See Mommsen, *loc. cit.*

Paestum in upper Lucania. See Mommsen, *loc. cit.*

Pompeii in Campania. Cic. *pro Sulla,* 60.

Praeneste in Latium. Cic., *de lege agr.,* 2, 78.

Urbana in Campania. *Sullana:* Pliny, *N. H.,* 14, 62.

Aleria in Corsica. Pliny, *N. H.,* 3, 80.

There is no reason to suppose that the list is full.

Latin Colonies.

123   There were none of the old type; however, in 123, 3,000 Romans living in Spain (probably veterans) were colonized on the Balearic islands (Strabo, 3, 5, 1; Pliny, *N. H.,* 3. 77). Whether these were given Roman or Latin rights is not known.

89 The *lex Pompeia* of 89 gave Latin rights to Transpadanes (Caes., *B. C.,* 3, 87; Suet., *Jul.,* 8; Ascon. *in Pis.* Stangl, 3: Pompeius non novis colonis eas constituit, sed veteribus incolis manentibus jus dedit Latii: "He did not plant new colonies, but gave the Latin right to the inhabitants.") This was not an increase or change of landholders; however, since "Latins" gained citizenship by holding municipal office, the group of citizens increased until in 49 Caesar granted the franchise to all Latin communities above the Po.

Summary of Colonies.

During the Gracchan period down to the year 118 individual allotments of small plots were made to a large number of poor citizens (perhaps 50,000-75,000) largely urban proletariat. The land was taken from the illegal public holdings of Roman landlords and from Italian squatters. Several colonies (Tarentum, Scolacium, probably several others) were planted in Italy: the settlers here may have amounted to... 10,000

Two settlements of citizens were made outside of Italy (Carthage [122] and the colony of Narbo [118]): perhaps..... 10,000

About 100 B. C. settlements of Marian veterans were made at Eporedia north of the Po, *colonia Mariana* in Corsica, and probably in the region of Dougga in Africa: perhaps....... 10,000

The Sullan colonization of veterans in Italy extended to.... 120,000

In all probability the number of citizens colonized during the period was about... 225,000

The distributions of the Gracchi increased the number of small farms at the cost of landlords and Italian squatters. Since the plots were inalienable for several years, it is likely that many of the urban settlers learned to farm and remained, but our sources insist that after permission to sell was given the number of small plot-holders tended to diminish rapidly. The veterans of Sulla usually displaced better farmers of the municipalities, who became a danger to society. Since Sulla was a conservative, he probably did not confiscate many large holdings. Many of the veterans made poor farmers and left their lots. Nevertheless the colonization of the period doubtless increased the number of small holdings.

III A. PUBLIC FINANCES 150-90

I. EXPENSES

During this period our sources are so scant that it is impossible to prepare a full statement of income and expenses of the state. I shall merely put together what is known, taking the pre-Sullan period first.

The size of the Army.

The soldiers' stipend remained as before, 120 denarii per year, but a larger share of booty taken was now expected by the soldiers and, especially after the Marian introduction of the volunteer army, bonuses of land came to be promised and given. However these two items do not enter into the state accounts.

The army enrolment was about as follows:

Africa.

At Carthage in 149-6: 80,000 infantry and 4,000 cavalry (App., *Pun.,* 75). Probably 8 legions with their contingents were enrolled, for at this time (Pol., 6, 20) the legions had 5,000 citizen infantry and 300 cavalry, and 5,000 + 900 socii.

During the Jugurthine War we may assume 2 legions in 111 and 110 (Sall., *Jug.,* 28, 6), 3 in 109 and 108, and at least 4 during 107-105 (supplements, *ibid.,* 36, 1; 43, 3; 86, 4), that is, about 22 legions for a year. After the defeat of Jugurtha, the governor of Africa seems to have had merely a small garrison.

Spain.

The Lusitanian War lasted from 154 to 139, the Numantine War from 143 to 133. Appian, *Iberica,* 45-97, has given fairly full statistics of recruitments and losses and, at times, of the forces in the field, from which Schulten, *Numantia,* III, 38 ff. has skilfully reckoned the forces as follows:

In the Lusitanian War a praetor operated with one legion (average 5,300 citizens, 5,900 socii, with very few Spanish auxiliaries) from 154 to 146, while from 145 to 139 there were two legions, seldom full.

In the Numantine War, between 143 and 133, there were regularly two full legions with their socii, and in addition Spanish contingents that averaged about 5,000, but Scipio in his last year raised about

40,000 of these. For the rest of the time between 150 and 90 B. C. we may plausibly reckon that the Romans usually had one or two legions in each of the Spanish provinces. (After the year 90, of course, the Italian socii became citizens and served in the legions, but non-Italian socii and amici were henceforth called upon to send contingents in increasing numbers.) We may then estimate that in Spain between 150 and 90 B. C. about 150 full legions served for one year and in addition for a large part of the period, an annual average of some 5,000 Spanish auxiliaries.

Sicily.

Ordinarily Sicily had only a small guard with some Sicilian auxiliaries serving at call (Diod., 36, 4), but during the Servile War of 134-1, when the governors were consular (Fulvius, Piso, Rupilius), we may assume that at least two full legions served there for some four years. Again in the Second Servile War the praetor of 104 with only a small garrison force managed to collect 10,000 Italians and Sicilians (Diod., 36, 4, 3, and 4, 6). In 103 Lucullus was sent with 17,000 (*op. cit.*, 36, 8). The war lasted till 101. Probably a fair garrison was kept for a few years thereafter. For the years 150 to 90 we may assume that about 40 legions were in Sicily for a term of a year each.

Gallia Narbonensis.

125 to 122: operations against the Salluvii by Fulvius and Sextius probably involved 2 legions.
121: Domitius and Fabius conquered the province (with less than 30,000 men, Strabo, 4, 1, 11), probably 3 legions.

We may assume that a garrison force of one legion remained for a year.

108: the consul M. Junius Silenus defeated by Cimbri, 2 legions?
107: the consul L. Cassius defeated by Cimbri, 2 legions?
106: the consul Caepio at Tolosa   2 legions?
105: Caepio and Manlius were defeated at Orange; probably 6 or 8 legions with Gallic contingents: Livy, *Epit.* 67, 80,000 soldiers killed (probably an exaggeration).
104-101: Marius against Teutones, 3 legions (Plut., *Mar.,* 25: 32,000 soldiers).

Thereafter probably a garrison of one legion was kept there. Between 125 and 90 we may estimate for this region 55 legions for one year.

Gallia Cisalpina.

This was near enough to Rome so that consuls and proconsuls could generally meet invasions. We hear of their operations in 143 (vs. Salassi), 129 (Japudes), 118 (Stoeni), 117 (Dalmatians), 115 (Carni), 113 (Carbo vs. Cimbri), 102-101 (Catulus vs. Cimbri with 2 legions, Plut., *Mar.*, 25), 90 (Salluvii). Our records for this region are not full, but probably an average allowance of one legion per year would be fair. Between 150 and 90 B. C. we may estimate the use of about 60 legions for one year.

Macedonia and Greece.

Thalna probably had 1 legion in 149, Metellus probably 2 legions in 148 and 147, Mummius 23,000 soldiers, 3,500 equites and some Greek allies in 146-5-4 (Paus., 7, 16), probably 3 weak legions. The province thenceforth had a governor's garrison of at least one legion. Operations on the frontier (usually against Scordisci or Thraci) are reported in 134, 120, 116-108, 92-88, when there may at times have been two legions. Sulla took charge of Greece and the East in 87. For the 60 years from 149 to 90 we may estimate that 75 legions served for one year each in this field.

Asia.

While suppressing Aristonicus and establishing the province the Romans had at least two legions in Asia during 131-120 and large contingents from the neighboring kings and cities. Thereafter Rome kept a very small force there, depending upon the neighboring allies for military aid (Appian, *Mith.*, 11). Between 132 and 90 we may perhaps assume about 12 legions for one year.

Cilicia also had a small garrison after its subjugation in 100.

The items enumerated above amount to at least 470 legions serving for a year each, or an average of about 8 legions per year.

a. Cost of army upkeep.

Polybius gives a few welcome facts about the stipend and the allowance of corn for soldiers (6, 39, 12-15):

’Οψώνιον δ’ οἱ μὲν πεζοὶ λαμβάνουσι τῆς ἡμέρας δύ’ ὀβολούς, οἱ δὲ ταξίαρχοι διπλοῦν, οἱ δ’ ἱππεῖς δραχμήν. σιτομετροῦνται δ’ οἱ μὲν πεζοὶ πυρῶν ’Αττικοῦ

μεδίμνου δύο μέρη μάλιστά πως, οἱ δ' ἱππεῖς κριθῶν μὲν ἑπτὰ μεδίμνους εἰς τὸν
μῆνα, πυρῶν δὲ δύο, τῶν δὲ συμμάχων οἱ μὲν πεζοὶ τὸ ἴσον, οἱ δ' ἱππεῖς πυρῶν μὲν
μέδιμνον ἕνα καὶ τρίτον μέρος, κριθῶν δὲ πέντε. δόδοται δὲ τοῖς μὲν συμμάχοις
τοῦτ' ἐν δωρεᾷ· τοῖς δὲ Ῥωμαίοις τοῦ τε σίτου καὶ τῆς ἐσθῆτος, κἄν τινος ὅπλου
προσδεηθῶσι, πάντων τούτων ὁ ταμίας τὴν τεταγμένην τιμὴν ἐκ τῶν ὀψωνίων ὑπο-
λογίζεται.

" As pay the foot-soldier receives two obols ($\frac{1}{6}$ of a den.) a day, a
centurion twice as much, and a cavalry-soldier a drachma (a denarius).
The allowance of corn to a foot-soldier is about two-thirds of an Attic
medimnus a month ($= 4$ modii), a cavalry-soldier receives seven
medimni of barley and two of wheat. Of the allies the infantry
receives the same, the cavalry one and one-third medimnus of wheat
and five of barley, these rations being a free gift to the allies; but in
the case of the Romans the quaestor deducts from their pay the price
fixed for their corn and clothes and any additional arms they require."

The custom of having a praetorian guard and *comites* had also
grown up (Cic., *pro Arch.*, 11; *ad Fam.*, 5, 20, 7), so that we ought
to allow about 800,000 denarii the year for the stipend of a legion. In
addition the state gave the grain rations from 123 to 109, and these
would cost about 20,000,000 den. The sum total, based upon the army
figures given above, would therefore be nearly 420,000,000 denarii for
this period.

b. *Food for the army.*

C. Gracchus (Plut., 5) passed a bill in 123 that granted the legionaries as well as the allies their grain supply free of charge. The law
was repealed in 109. The grain-bill of the treasury should therefore
have increased considerably for 14 years. However, because of the
corn doles instituted in 123, the Sicilian tithe was no longer available
for the army. Hence generals were often expected to buy or ask
neighboring allies for food rations. The state voted the generals funds
for such supplies. Some generals paid for their materials, some
accepted the grain offered or demanded and returned the cost to the
treasury, some—and the number was increasing—accepted gifts of
grain and pocketed the money supplied by the treasury. There was also
growing the habit of letting soldiers foray and loot to make up to them
the cost of the grain reimposed in 109. The allies suffered much without a corresponding relief to the treasury. On the whole we may

16

assume that cost of food to the treasury bore about the same relation to
the number of legions as in the preceding period. (On supplies sent
from Rome see Sall., *Jug.*, 36, 1; 43, 3; on foraging Sall., *Jug.*, 54-56;
App., *Pun.*, 94; on requisitions from allies see Cic., *pro Font.*, 17.)

c. *The navy.*

The navy was not kept up after the war with Perseus ended. To
attack and blockade Carthage in 149 Rome had had only 50 quinqueremes and 100 smaller vessels (App., *Pun.*, 75). In the Spanish wars
a small fleet seems to have operated near Lisbon in 136 (Strabo, 3, 3,
1). To attack Jugurtha in 117 the legions had to march all the way to
Rhegium before embarking (Sall., *Jug.*, 28, 6); probably merchant
vessels were requisitioned for this transport. To attack the pirates of
Cilicia, Antonius managed to find a fleet (probably calling upon allies
for a part) which he drew over the isthmus of Corinth (Taylor and West
in *Am. Jour. Arch.*, 1928, 9; cf. *C. I.L.*, I², Supp., 2662). When the
Mithridatic war broke out in 88 Rome had a small fleet at the mouth
of the Black Sea that surrendered to the king without a struggle (App.,
Mith., 17 and 19). Sulla had to stay in Greece till his legate could
beg enough ships from Egypt, Syria, and Rhodes to open the sea (Plut.,.
Luc., 2, 3; App., *Mith.*, 33 and 56). Sulla probably had to pay in
order to get the ships speedily. The naval bill for this period would
hardly be more than half as much as during the preceding war.

For *arms* and *transport service* on land we may reckon that costs
had not diminished, since the state seems now to have adopted the
habit of having state armor factories (Cic., *in Pis.*, 87; *Rab. perd.*,
20). At Athens Sulla used 20,000 mules in his transport service (Plut.
Sulla, 12).

d. *Public Construction* (for list of buildings, see under *Industry*):

The most expensive public work of the period was the Marcian aqueduct built in 144-140 B. C. Nearly ten kilometers of it were above
ground on arches, the rest, some 80 kilometers, underground in a concrete channel. It cost the state about 180,000,000 sesterces (about
$9,000,000, Frontinus, *de Aq.*, 1, 7). Presumably the booty of Corinth
and Carthage was used for this work. At the same time the older
aqueducts, the Appia and the Anio Vetus, were repaired. Then, in
125, the aqua Tepula, some ten miles long and with a far smaller
channel, was built. Since these new aqueducts more than doubled the

water supply of Rome, we must assume a rapid expansion of the city
from 150 to 125. Very expensive roads were also built at this time in
Macedonia (via Egnatia, Pol., 34, 12), in Spain (via Herculea, Pol.,
3, 39), and in Italy (via Postumia, via Caecilia, via Popillia, etc.).
The provincial roads were probably built largely by military engineers
and by requisitioned provincial labor (Cic., *pro Font.*, 17, 18, of the
via Domitia in Gaul; cf. Plut., *Mar.,* 15; Livy, 39, 2, 6), but much
of the cost of tools and of material would fall on the treasury. The
extensive road-building by the Gracchans in Italy seems to have been
charged to the state (Plut., *Gracc.*, 7, 1, quoted below). The cost of
the drainage work near the Po, in 109 (Strabo, 5, 1, 11), doubtless
fell on the state, since it was a censorial contract.

The more important public buildings at Rome were the Aemilian
bridge (completed), the Mulvian bridge, the fort of the Janiculan, the
basilica Opimia, the temple of Magna Mater. The contract for Jupiter's temple was let; pavements were laid and warehouses built by
Gracchus, who also (to judge from the materials) supervised the repairs
and extension of the sewers. Probably the cost of the Aqua Marcia was
not more than a fifth of what was spent on public works during the
period.

The cost of games, of triumphs (funds for which were now voted
by the Senate, cf. Dio, Frag. 75), of legations and commissions, of public servants, and the like was constantly increasing, but there is no way
of estimating the amounts.

e. *Corn Dole.*

We cannot calculate the expense of the Gracchan dole, though the
ancients agree that it was a heavy burden (see section IV for the
sources). Since all adult males, whether very poor or not, had the
right to buy some 60 modii of wheat per year at about half price ($6\frac{1}{3}$
asses the modius), we may suppose that the Sicilian tithe—which had
usually gone to the soldiers at full price—now went to Rome at half
value. And, if that did not suffice, extra grain had to be bought to be
sold at a loss. The tithe of Sicily in 70 B. C. amounted to 3,000,000
modii, which would suffice for 50,000 takers and, if given at half price,
would involve a loss of about 1,000,000 denarii (at the price current in
70). Probably the number of claimants did not now exceed that number, though it rose to 320,000 in Cicero's day. The law of 118

attempted to restore the vectigal on public land in order to cover this expense, but that, too, was very soon revoked. Perhaps we may hazard an expense of 60,000,000 denarii for the corn dole between 123 and 90 B. C.

If one is to hazard a conjecture of the expenses for this period, one can do so only by comparing the army of this period with that of the preceding and then allotting the expenses for food, arms, and transport according to the ratio found. We recall that the treasury had some 25,000,000 denarii in 157, but this could not have lasted long in view of the expensive wars that ensued. The treasury statements that Pliny (*N. H.*, 33, 55) gave for the year 91 are unfortunately badly corrupted and cannot be used, but the fact that Livius Drusus resorted to silver-plating 12% of the denarii issued that year shows that the surplus was not large. My tentative estimate of expenses from 150 to 90 B. C. is largely based on conjectures and is merely designed to give my impression of the general region within which the budget may have operated.

Army stipend	ca. 420,000,000	den.
Food for allied troops	" 100,000,000	
Navy	" 30,000,000	
Arms and transport	" 100,000,000	
Public works	" 225,000,000	
Administration	" 200,000,000	
Corn doles	" 60,000,000	
	ca. 1,135,000,000	den.

The annual average from 150 to 90 would perhaps be about 20,000,000 denarii.

II. Income

a. *Tithes and other vectigalia.*

Our most definite piece of information is that about 63 B. C., before Pompey's new revenues began to flow in, the annual income of the treasury was about 50,000,000 denarii the year.

Plut., Pomp., 45 (citing the placards carried in Pompey's triumph):

ἔφραζε διὰ τῶν γραμμάτων ὅτι πεντακισχίλιαι μὲν μυριάδες ἐκ τῶν τελῶν ὑπῆρχον, ἐκ δὲ ὧν αὐτὸς προσεκτήσατο τῇ πόλει μυριάδας ὀκτακισχιλίας πεντακοσίας λαμβάνουσιν, ἀναφέρεται δὲ εἰς τὸ δημόσιον ταμιεῖον ἐν νομίσματι καὶ κατασκευαῖς ἀργυρίου καὶ χρυσίου δισμύρια τάλαντα, πάρεξ τῶν εἰς τοὺς στρατιώτας δεδομένων, ὧν ὁ τοὐλάχιστον αἴρων κατὰ λόγον δραχμὰς εἴληφε χιλίας πεντακοσίας.

" the inscriptions set forth that whereas the public revenues from taxes had been fifty million drachmas, they were receiving after the additions which Pompey had made to the city's power eighty-five million, and that he was bringing into the public treasury in coined money and vessels of gold and silver twenty thousand talents, apart from the money which had been given to his soldiers, of whom the one whose share was the smallest had received fifteen hundred drachmas."

It is difficult, however, to apportion this amount to the various sources. We shall leave the task for the next chapter, giving only the main items here. Macedonia paid 100 talents (600,000 denarii) after 167 B. C. The province was, however, very much enlarged in 146, and parts of Greece were added then and by Sulla (Delos, for instance, was paying taxes to Rome in 58; see the *lex Gabinia, C. I. L.,* I², 2500). We may reckon that from 150 to 63 the " Macedonian " tribute increased gradually from 100 talents to near 300. Asia fell to Rome in 133 by legacy. For ten years it was a very small province, but Gaius Gracchus added Phrygia, and after the Mithridatic wars, during which Rome lost her tribute, the taxes were increased again. Under Hadrian, after Caesar had reduced the taxes, the province yielded 7,000,000 denarii (Philostr., *Vita Soph.,* 2, p. 57 K). Probably 10 to 15 million would be a fair amount for 63. For present purposes I shall adopt the estimates of Böttcher (*Die Einnahmen der röm Rep.*), since we are concerned here with totals. He estimates (p. 69) the distribution of the 50 million denarii about as follows: Sicily 4, Sardinia and Corsica 1½, Macedonia 2, Asia and islands 15, Spain 6, Gallia Narbonensis 6, Africa and Cyrene 6, and all the other vectigalia 10.

Now these would be the tributes in 63, after many years of general peace. Perhaps half the amount would be a fair estimate for the year 90, and one-fifth for the year 150, before Africa, Asia, Gaul, Cyrene, Cilicia, and the larger part of Spain had been acquired.

We have very few facts about other *vectigal*. The mines yielded heavily at times, at others less. When the state sold the silver mines of Spain (apparently in the Sullan period), they had probably run to a low yield. There was no longer a citizen tribute; the Italian tithe-land was largely disposed of by the Gracchi. On the other hand we must assume a considerable increase in the returns on the Campanian public land, and especially on port dues, for, despite the growth of piracy, Italian commerce expanded much with the increase of wealth and the expansion of the empire. We hear of port collections at the Asiatic harbors, at Aquileia and in Narbonese Gaul, that is to say, the tariff bureau had been thoroughly equipped.

If the *vectigalia* mentioned above increased fairly steadily from about 10 million to about 25 million from 150 B. C. to 90 with, of course, some deductions during provincial wars, we may well estimate the sum total for the sixty years at about 1,000,000,000 denarii.

b. *Booty.*

We have fewer definite facts concerning booty than before. *Carthage* fell in 146 and was completely plundered, though only after the inhabitants had destroyed much. Pliny (33, 141) gives the amount of silver taken to Rome as 4,370 pounds. There must also have been much gold, but we are not told how much.

Corinth was also rich and was thoroughly sacked, but no figures have come down to us. Since the treasury of Rome, despite its strain, could pay out 45,000,000 denarii for a new water supply in 144, we may assume that at least that amount had come from these two cities.

Jugurtha surrendered 2,800 talents of silver to Metellus (nearly 17 million denarii, Sall., *Jug.,* 62, 5), and Marius later carried from Africa nearly a fourth as much in gold and silver (Plut., *Mar.,* 12, 4). The war, though expensive, probably paid for itself.

No sums are given for the Spanish, Gallic, Cimbric, and Asiatic campaigns, but these probably yielded the treasury little after the hungry generals and soldiers had had their shares. Perhaps the complete item of booty that went to the treasury might be estimated at about 100,000,000 denarii.

Quite apart from booty we must include in the reckoning the unspecified amounts that were derived from the auction of the personal possessions of the Pergamene king left by will to Rome in 133 (Pliny, 33, 149, auctionibus regiis), and of those left by the king of Cyrene in 97 (Livy, *Epit.* 70). These would amount to a few million denarii.

If we compare these estimates with those of the preceding period we note that in the Catonian period indemnities and booty paid a large part of expenses of the government, while in this period booty made up only about ten per cent of the income, and provincial tithes, mines, and tariff dues bore the burden of expense. The Romans of Italy now paid no direct taxes for the general government, and the 5 per cent tax on manumitted slaves (the sacred treasure) and the port tariff (2-5 per cent), the only indirect taxes chargeable in Italy, concerned only a portion of the citizens.

III B. PUBLIC FINANCES FOR 90-80 B. C.

We take this period separately, for here all semblance of regularity disappears. During the Social War the state confessed to complete bankruptcy, and in the Sullan Wars that followed Sulla deliberately adopted the Oriental theory of autocracy, compelled the Senate to give him absolute power over life and property, and confiscated sacred, public, and private property whenever he was in need. His purse served as state treasury for several years and he appropriated whatever he needed to keep it replenished. His pocket book was full when he resigned. We shall not attempt ledger accounts but merely mention the items known.

We have no lists of the legions for the Social War, though Appian (*B. C.,* 1, 40 ff.) gives an extended account of heavy casualties. Domaszewski (*Bellum Marsicum,* in *Sitz. Akad. Wien,* 1924, 32-3) estimates from the known strength of some of the armies that about 20 legions were in service for about two to three years. We know from the marked slingshots found at Asculum (*C. I. L.,* I², 867-74) that at least legions 9, 10, and 15 were active at that place (Livy, *Epit.* 74, says 75,000 men). Though the socii of central Italy had revolted, it was apparently possible to fill the legions to the standard numbers (Perpenna had 10,000 men; Appian, *B. C.,* 1, 41). The need was very great and doubtless Rome offered expensive inducements to foreign auxiliaries. The treasury ran dry. Silver plated coins, first suggested by Drusus for the expenses of his reforms, were struck throughout the war, as coin hoards show (see below), and when Sulla needed funds for the Mithridatic War in 88, some 9,000 pounds of gold had to be taken from the property of the temples for his equipment (Appian, *Mith.,* 22).

After Sulla's departure, when a new civil war broke out at Rome, the treasury took advantage of the Valerian law, meant for private

debtors, and cancelled three-fourths of its debts (Cic., *pro Font.*, 1).
Later, when Sulla threatened war, Cinna and Carbo raised about
200,000 troops (Appian, *B. C.*, 1, 82; Plut., *Sulla*, 27, 5: 450 cohorts)
and the gold and silver ornaments of the temples were melted down to
meet military expenses (Val. Max., 7, 6, 4, ne militibus stipendia
deessent).

Sulla, meanwhile, receiving no support from home and having 5
legions with large contingents to pay (Appian, *B. C.*, 1, 79; *Mith.*,
30), and having to gather a large fleet from the eastern states, exacted
whatever he needed. First he robbed the temples of Delphi, Olympia,
and Epidaurus (Plut., *Sulla*, 12), later indemnifying them in part by
land which he had expropriated from the Thebans (Plut., *Sulla*, 19,
11). Lucullus was set the task of coining gold for Sulla. The sale
of captives brought some funds; Mithridates was let off with a mild
indemnity of 2,000 talents (Plut., *Sulla*, 22, 8 and 23), but the
wretched Asiatics were condemned to pay 20,000 talents in " indemnities " and in delinquent tribute of five years (Appian, *Mith.*, 62; Plut.,
Sulla, 25, 4). Since Sulla needed money for the attack on Rome, he
pocketed most of this, depositing in the treasury only about a fifth of
it (15,000 pounds of gold and 115,000 pounds of silver, Pliny, 33, 16),
and even this part he drew upon whenever in need.

On his return with only about 5 legions (Appian, *B. C.*, 1, 79),
Sulla beat or bought over army after army of his opponents (they had
had 200,000 men). To pay expenses and to reward himself and his
friends, he instituted proscriptions (Livy, *Epit.* 89) and confiscations
on a vast scale, and he seems to have emptied the sacred treasury (see
next chapter). He died the richest man in Rome (Pliny, 33, 134).
What was left in the state treasury we are not told. Obviously it is
hardly feasible to attempt any reconstruction of the public finances for
the years 90-80 B. C.

IV. ECONOMIC LEGISLATION, 133-80

1. *Tiberius Gracchus.*   a. *Conditions in Italy.*

Appian, *Bell. Civ.*, 1, 7 (Appian is probably the most reliable source):

Ῥωμαῖοι τὴν Ἰταλίαν πολέμῳ κατὰ μέρη χειρούμενοι γῆς μέρος ἐλάμβανον καὶ
πόλεις ἐνῴκιζον ἢ ἐς τὰς προτέρον οὔσας κληρούχους ἀπὸ σφῶν κατέλεγον. καὶ
τάδε μὲν ἀντὶ φρουρίων ἐπενόουν, τῆς δὲ γῆς τῆς δορικτήτου σφίσιν ἑκάστοτε γιγ-

νομένης τὴν μὲν ἐξειργασμένην αὐτίκα τοῖς οἰκιζομένοις ἐπιδιῄρουν ἢ ἐπίπρασκον
ἢ ἐξεμίσθουν, τὴν δ' ἀργὸν ἐκ τοῦ πολέμου τότε οὖσαν, ἣ δὴ καὶ μάλιστα ἐπλήθυεν,
οὐκ ἄγοντές πω σχολὴν διαλαχεῖν ἐπεκήρυττον ἐν τοσῷδε τοῖς ἐθέλουσιν ἐκπονεῖν
ἐπὶ τέλει τῶν ἐτησίων καρπῶν, δεκάτῃ μὲν τῶν σπειρομένων, πέμπτῃ δὲ τῶν φυτευομένων. ὥριστο δὲ καὶ τοῖς προβατεύουσι τέλη μειζόνων τε καὶ ἐλαττόνων ζῴων. καὶ
τάδε ἔπραττον ἐς πολυανδρίαν τοῦ Ἰταλικοῦ γένους, φερεπονωτάτου σφίσιν ὀφθέντος,
ἵνα συμμάχους οἰκείους ἔχοιεν. ἐς δὲ τοὐναντίον αὐτοῖς περιῄει. οἱ γὰρ πλούσιοι
τῆσδε τῆς ἀνεμήτου γῆς τὴν πολλὴν καταλαβόντες καὶ χρόνῳ θαρροῦντες οὔ τινα
σφᾶς ἔτι ἀφαιρήσεσθαι τά τε ἀγχοῦ σφίσιν ὅσα τε ἦν ἄλλα βραχέα πενήτων, τὰ μὲν
ὠνούμενοι πειθοῖ, τὰ δὲ βίᾳ λαμβάνοντες, πεδία μακρὰ ἀντὶ χωρίων ἐγεώργουν,
ὠνητοῖς ἐς αὐτὰ γεωργοῖς καὶ ποιμέσι χρώμενοι τοῦ μὴ τοὺς ἐλευθέρους ἐς τὰς
στρατείας ἀπὸ τῆς γεωργίας περισπᾶν, φερούσης ἅμα καὶ τῆσδε τῆς κτήσεως αὐτοῖς
πολὺ κέρδος ἐκ πολυπαιδίας θεραπόντων ἀκινδύνως αὐξομένων διὰ τὰς ἀστρατείας.
ἀπὸ δὲ τούτων οἱ μὲν δυνατοὶ πάμπαν ἐπλούτουν, καὶ τὸ τῶν θεραπόντων γένος ἀνὰ
τὴν χώραν ἐπλήθυε, τοὺς δ' Ἰταλιώτας ὀλιγότης καὶ δυσανδρία κατελάμβανε,
τρυχομένους πενίᾳ τε καὶ ἐσφοραῖς καὶ στρατείαις. εἰ δὲ καὶ σχολάσειαν ἀπὸ
τούτων, ἐπὶ ἀργίας διετίθεντο, τῆς γῆς ὑπὸ τῶν πλουσίων ἐχομένης καὶ γεωργοῖς
χρωμένων θεράπουσιν ἀντὶ ἐλευθέρων.

" The Romans, as they subdued the Italian peoples successively in
war, used to seize a part of their lands and build towns there, or enroll
colonists of their own to occupy those already existing, and their idea
was to use these as outposts; but of the land acquired by war they
assigned the cultivated part forthwith to the colonists, or sold or leased
it.[1] Since they had no leisure as yet to allot the part which then lay
desolated by war (this was generally the greater part), they made
proclamation that in the meantime those who were willing to work it
might do so for a toll of the yearly crops, a tenth of the grain and a
fifth of the fruit.[2] From those who kept flocks was required a toll of
the animals, both oxen and small cattle. They did these things in
order to multiply the Italian race, which they considered the most
laborious of peoples, so that they might have plenty of allies at home.[3]
But the very opposite thing happened; for the rich, getting possession
of the greater part of the undistributed lands, and being emboldened
by the lapse of time to believe that they would never be dispossessed,
absorbing any adjacent strips and their poor neighbours' allotments,
partly by purchase under persuasion and partly by force, came to culti-

---

[1] This applies especially to the period 400-200 B. C.

[2] This is especially true of the lands acquired during the Hannibalic War. Appian
adds in the next chapter that the legal limit was 500 jugera.

[3] This correctly implies that Italians as well as Romans occupied such land, and
that one chief motive for a reform was a desire for more soldiers.

vate vast tracts instead of single estates, using slaves as labourers and herdsmen, lest free labourers should be drawn from agriculture into the army. At the same time the ownership of slaves brought them great gain from the multitude of their progeny,[4] who increased because they were exempt from military service. Thus certain powerful men became extremely rich and the race of slaves multiplied throughout the country, while the Italian people dwindled in numbers and strength, being oppressed by penury, taxes, and military service. If they had any respite from these evils they passed their time in idleness, because the land was held by the rich, who employed slaves instead of freemen as cultivators."

Plut., *Ti. Gracch.*, 8, 1-3:

Ῥωμαῖοι τῆς τῶν ἀστυγειτόνων χώρας ὅσην ἀπετέμοντο πολέμῳ, τὴν μὲν ἐπίπρασκον, τὴν δὲ ποιούμενοι δημοσίαν ἐδίδοσαν νέμεσθαι τοῖς ἀκτήμοσι καὶ ἀπόροις τῶν πολιτῶν, ἀποφορὰν οὐ πολλὴν εἰς τὸ δημόσιον τελοῦσιν. ἀρξαμένων δὲ τῶν πλουσίων ὑπερβάλλειν τὰς ἀποφορὰς καὶ τοὺς πένητας ἐξελαυνόντων, ἐγράφη νόμος οὐκ ἐῶν πλέθρα γῆς ἔχειν πλείονα τῶν πεντακοσίων. καὶ βραχὺν μὲν χρόνον ἐπέσχε τὴν πλεονεξίαν τὸ γράμμα τοῦτο, καὶ τοῖς πένησιν ἐβοήθησε κατὰ χώραν μένουσιν ἐπὶ τῶν μεμισθωμένων καὶ νεμομένοις ἣν ἕκαστος ἐξ ἀρχῆς εἶχε μοῖραν. ὕστερον δὲ τῶν γειτνιώντων πλουσίων ὑποβλήτοις προσώποις μεταφερόντων τὰς μισθώσεις εἰς ἑαυτούς, τέλος δὲ φανερῶς ἤδη δι᾽ ἑαυτῶν τὰ πλεῖστα κατεχόντων, ἐξωσθέντες οἱ πένητες οὔτε ταῖς στρατείαις ἔτι προθύμους παρεῖχον ἑαυτούς, ἠμέλουν τε παίδων ἀνατροφῆς, ὥστε ταχὺ τὴν Ἰταλίαν ἅπασαν ὀλιγανδρίας ἐλευθέρων αἰσθέσθαι, δεσμωτηρίων δὲ βαρβαρικῶν ἐμπεπλῆσθαι, δι᾽ ὧν ἐγεώργουν οἱ πλούσιοι τὰ χωρία, τοὺς πολίτας ἐξελάσαντες.

" Of the territory which the Romans won in war from their neighbours, a part they sold, and a part they made common land, and assigned it for occupation to the poor and indigent among the citizens, on payment of a small rent into the public treasury. And when the rich began to offer larger rents and drove out the poor, a law was enacted forbidding the holding by one person of more than five hundred acres of land. For a short time this enactment gave a check to the rapacity of the rich, and was of assistance to the poor who remained in their places on the land which they had rented and occupied the allot-

---

[4] Note that slaves married and had numerous children.

The important studies of the period are Mommsen's chapters in his *Roman History*; Greenidge, *A History of Rome*; E. Meyer, in *Kleine Schriften²*, I, 363; Cardinali, *Studi Graccani*, 1912; Fraccaro, *Studi sull'età dei Gracchi*, 1914; E. v. Stern in *Hermes*, 1921, 229-301; Carcopino, *Autour des Gracques*, 1928; Last, in *Cambridge Ancient History*, Vol. IX; Vancura, "Leges Agrariae." in *R-E.*, XII, 1150 ff.

ment which each had held from the outset. But later on the neighbouring rich men, by means of fictitious personages, transferred these rentals to themselves, and finally held most of the land openly in their own names. Then the poor, who had been ejected from their land, no longer showed themselves eager for military service, and neglected the bringing up of children, so that soon all Italy was conscious of a dearth of freemen, and was filled with gangs of foreign slaves, by whose aid the rich cultivated their estates, from which they had driven away the free citizens."

Plut., *Ti. Gracch.*, 8, 7:

ὁ δ' ἀδελφὸς αὐτοῦ Γάϊος ἔν τινι βιβλίῳ γέγραφεν εἰς Νομαντίαν πορευόμενον διὰ τῆς Τυρρηνίας τὸν Τιβέριον, καὶ τὴν ἐρημίαν τῆς χώρας ὁρῶντα καὶ τοὺς γεωργοῦντας ἢ νέμοντας οἰκέτας ἐπεισάκτους καὶ βαρβάρους, τότε πρῶτον ἐπὶ νοῦν βαλέσθαι τὴν μυρίων κακῶν ἄρξασαν αὐτοῖς πολιτείαν.

"But his brother Gaius, in a certain pamphlet, has written that as Tiberius was passing through Tuscany on his way to Numantia, and observed the dearth of inhabitants in the country, and that those who tilled its soil or tended its flocks there were imported barbarian slaves, he then first conceived the public policy which was the cause of countless ills to the two brothers."

It was in Tuscany that Tiberius saw the effects of slave economy, but the same conditions prevailed in Latium, parts of Campania, and in the South. Here again the military motive is stressed, though in 8, 5, Plutarch also mentions the philosophic doctrines of Tiberius' teacher and of his mother as incentives.

There are additional references to economic conditions in Livy, 34, 4, 9; Sall., *Jug.*, 41; and to the limits of holdings of public land imposed by the Licinian-Sextian law in Livy, 6, 35; Cato, *ap. Gell.*, 6, 3, 37; and Varro, *R. R.*, 1, 2, 9.

b. *The Law of Tiberius Gracchus.*

Appian, *B. C.*, 1, 9 and 10:

ἐπὶ δὲ τῷ δουλικῷ δυσχεράνας ὡς ἀστρατεύτῳ καὶ οὔποτε ἐς δεσπότας πιστῷ, τὸ ἔναγχος ἐπήνεγκεν ἐν Σικελίᾳ δεσποτῶν πάθος ὑπὸ θεραπόντων γενόμενον, ηὐξημένων κἀκείνων ἀπὸ γεωργίας, καὶ τὸν ἐπ' αὐτοὺς Ῥωμαίων πόλεμον οὐ ῥᾴδιον οὐδὲ βραχύν, ἀλλὰ ἔς τε μῆκος χρόνου καὶ τροπὰς κινδύνων ποικίλας ἐκτραπέντα. ταῦτα δὲ εἰπὼν ἀνεκαίνιζε τὸν νόμον μηδένα τῶν πεντακοσίων πλέθρων πλέον ἔχειν. παισὶ δ' αὐτῶν ὑπὲρ τὸν παλαιὸν νόμον προσετίθει τὰ ἡμίσεα τούτων· καὶ τὴν λοιπὴν τρεῖς αἱρετοὺς ἄνδρας, ἐναλλασσομένους κατ' ἔτος, διανέμειν τοῖς πένησι.

10. Τοῦτο δ' ἦν, ὃ μάλιστα ἠνώχλει τοὺς πλουσίους, οὐ δυναμένους ἔτι ὡς

πρότερον τοῦ νόμου καταφρονεῖν διὰ τοὺς διαιροῦντας οὐδὲ ὠνεῖσθαι παρὰ τῶν κληρου-
μένων· ὁ γάρ τοι Γράκχος καὶ τόδε προϊδόμενος ἀπηγόρευε μὴ πωλεῖν.

" He (Tiberius Gracchus) inveighed against the multitude of slaves
as useless in war and never faithful to their masters, and adduced the
recent calamity brought upon the masters by their slaves in Sicily,
where the demands of agriculture had greatly increased the number of
the latter; recalling also the war waged against them by the Romans,
which was neither easy nor short, but long-protracted and full of vicissitudes and dangers.   After speaking thus he again brought forward the
law providing that nobody should hold more than the 500 jugera of
the public domain.   But he added a provision to the former law, that
the sons of the occupiers might each hold one-half of that amount, and
that the remainder should be divided among the poor by three elected
commissioners, who should be changed annually.

10. This was extremely disturbing to the rich because, on account
of the triumvirs, they could no longer disregard the law as they had
done before; nor could they buy the allotments of others, because
Gracchus had provided against this by forbidding sales."

Livy, *Epit.* 58:

Ne quis ex publico agro plus quam mille jugera possideret.

" that no one should possess more than a thousand jugera of public
land."

Plut., *Ti. Gracch.*, 9. 2:

καὶ δοκεῖ νόμος εἰς ἀδικίαν καὶ πλεονεξίαν τοσαύτην μηδέποτε πραότερος γραφῆναι
καὶ μαλακώτερος. οὓς γὰρ ἔδει δίκην τῆς ἀπειθείας δοῦναι καὶ μετὰ ζημίας ἣν παρὰ
τοὺς νόμους ἐκαρποῦντο χώραν ἀφεῖναι, τούτους ἐκέλευσε τιμὴν προσλαμβάνοντας
ἐκβαίνειν ὧν ἀδίκως ἐκέκτηντο, καὶ παραδέχεσθαι τοὺς βοηθείας δεομένους τῶν
πολιτῶν.

" And it is thought that a law dealing with injustice and rapacity so
great was never drawn up in milder and gentler terms.   For men who
ought to have been punished for their disobedience and to have surrendered with payment of a fine the land which they were illegally
enjoying, these men it merely ordered to abandon their unjust acquisitions upon being paid their value, and to admit into ownership of
them such citizens as needed assistance."

Cic., *de Leg. Agr.*, 2, 81, mentions that the Campanian lands (which
were rented at much higher rates) were not touched by this law.   The

plots distributed by the Gracchan commission were apparently 30 jugera (at least not over 30) to judge from a reference to them in the law of 111 B. C. (line 14) :

(si quis . . .) agri jugera non amplius xxx possidebit habebitue.

" If anyone . . . shall not possess or hold more than 30 jugera."

c. *Arguments For and Against the Law.*

Appian, *B. C.*, 1, 10 :

συνιστάμενοι δὴ κατὰ μέρος ὠλοφύροντο καὶ προύφερον τοῖς πένησιν ἀρχαῖά τε ἔργα ἑαυτῶν καὶ φυτὰ καὶ οἰκοδομίας, καὶ τιμὴν ἔνιοι δεδομένην γείτοσιν, εἰ καὶ τήνδε μετὰ τῆς γῆς ἀπολέσουσι, τάφους τε ἔνιοι πατέρων ἐν τῇ γῇ καὶ διαιρέσεις ἐπὶ τοῖς κλήροις ὡς πατρῴοις, οἱ δὲ καὶ προῖκας γυναικῶν ἐς ταῦτα ἀνηλωμένας ἢ τὴν γῆν παισὶν ἐμπροίκιον δεδομένην, δανεισταί τε χρέα καὶ ταύτης ἐπεδείκνυον, καὶ ἄκοσμος ἦν ὅλως οἰμωγὴ καὶ ἀγανάκτησις. οἱ δ᾽ αὖ πένητες ἀντωδύροντο ἐξ εὐπορίας ἐς πενίαν ἐσχάτην καὶ ἀπ᾽ αὐτῆς ἐς ἀγονίαν, οὐ δυνάμενοι παιδοτροφεῖν, περιφέρεσθαι. στρατείας τε ὅσας στρατεύσαιντο τὴν γῆν τήνδε περιποιούμενοι, κατέλεγον καὶ ἠγανάκτουν, εἰ τῶν κοινῶν ἀποστερήσονται, ὠνείδιζόν τε ἅμα αὐτοῖς αἱρουμένοις ἀντὶ ἐλευθέρων καὶ πολιτῶν καὶ στρατιωτῶν θεράποντας, ἄπιστον ἔθνος καὶ δυσμενὲς αἰεὶ διὰ τοῦτο ἀστράτευτον. τοιαῦθ᾽ ἑκατέρων ὀδυρομένων τε καὶ ἀλλήλοις ἐπικαλούντων, πλῆθος ἄλλο, ὅσον ἐν ταῖς ἀποίκοις πόλεσιν ἢ ταῖς ἰσοπολίτισιν ἢ ἄλλως ἐκοινώνει τῆσδε τῆς γῆς, δεδιότες ὁμοίως ἐπῇεσαν καὶ ἐς ἑκατέρους αὐτῶν διεμερίζοντο.

" They (the opponents of Gracchus) collected together in groups, and made lamentation, and accused the poor of appropriating the results of their tillage, their vineyards, and their dwellings. Some said that they had paid the price of the land to their neighbours. Were they to lose the money with the land? Others said that the graves of their ancestors were in the ground, which had been allotted to them in the division of their fathers' estates. Others said that their wives' dowries had been expended on the estates, or that the land had been given to their own daughters as dowry. Moneylenders could show loans made on this security. All kinds of wailing and expressions of indignation were heard at once. On the other side were heard the lamentations of the poor—that they were being reduced from competence to extreme penury, and from that to childlessness, because they were unable to rear their offspring. They recounted the military services they had rendered, by which this very land had been acquired, and were angry that they should be robbed of their share of the common property. They reproached the rich for employing slaves, who were always faithless and ill-disposed and for that reason unserviceable in war, instead of

freemen, citizens, and soldiers. While these classes were thus lament-
ing and indulging in mutual accusations, a great number of others,
composed of men who lived in colonies or the free towns, or persons
otherwise interested in the lands and who were under like apprehen-
sions, flocked in and took sides with their respective factions."

Members of the Latin colonies and of Italian cities had to some extent
occupied public lands as members of the old federation. The new
law proposed to draw in illegal holdings of citizens and allies alike,
but to distribute new lots *only to citizens.* Hence the allies had a real
grievance as Cicero remarks in the *de Rep.*, 3, 41:

Ti. Gracchus . . . sociorum nominisque Latini jura neglexit ac
foedera.

" Tiberius Gracchus . . . violated the treaty rights of our allies and
the Latins."

It was to meet this charge that Gracchus promised later to do what he
could to gain the franchise for non-citizens.

The land commission of three men was elected by the people and had
full right to judge what was public land, to draw in illegal holdings,
and to distribute plots. It was called a commission of III viri agris
judicandis adsignandis (Livy, *Epit.* 58; *C. I. L.,* I, II², 582, 1. 7;
also 639-44). We have four surveyors' boundary stones of the year
132-1 bearing the names of the commissioners Gaius Gracchus, Appius
Claudius, and Licinius Crassus (the last named having been elected to
take the place of Tiberius Gracchus, murdered in 132), *C. I. L.,* I, II²,
639-642. We have also two similar stones of the next year bearing
the names of M. Fulvius, Gaius Gracchus, and Papirius Carbo (*Ibid.,*
643-4). Fulvius and Papirius had been elected in the place of Claudius
and Crassus, both dead. In their year of office the judicial powers were
taken away (Appian, *B. C.,* 1, 19). All of these stones were found in
southern Italy on land presumably acquired by Rome during the Hannibalic War (namely at Atina, near Capua, near Suessula, near Salerno,
and near Compsa). We have also a stone (*C. I. L.,* 719) from the year
82 B. C. which testifies that it is a later restoration—of one similar to
no. 639. This was found near Fanum in the Ager Gallicus, showing
that some of the Ager Gallicus was still public land as late as the Gracchan times. A stone has also survived (Dessau, 28) at Carthage bear-

ing the names of the III viri of 122. Finally we have the milestone of Popillius, the consul of 132, a bitter enemy of Gracchus: *C. I. L.*, I², 638:

⟨P. Popillius C. F. cos⟩ (cf. no. 637)
viam fecei ab Regio ad Capuam et
in ea via ponteis omneis, miliarios,
tabelariosque poseivei . . . .
. . . . eidemque
primus fecei ut de agro poplico
aratoribus cederent paastores.
Forum aedisque poplicas heic fecei.

" I, Publius Popillius, son of Gaius, consul, built the road from Rhegium to Capua and constructed all the bridges and placed the milestones and post stations . . . and I, too, first caused the grazers to give way to farmers on the public land. I built the forum and public buildings here (at Polla, *i. e.* Forum Popilli)."

This man was banished in 123 for his part in the persecution of Tiberius Gracchus. It is surprising that he took credit for aiding in the execution of the legislation he so firmly opposed.

There is no explicit evidence as to the number of men who received lots, but since the census rose (see above) some 75,000 by the year 125, we may surmise that actual and prospective recipients were about that number. If one assumes (it is merely an assumption) that some 50,000 men received 30 jugera each, the amount distributed would come to about 1,000,000 acres or about 7 per cent of the Ager Romanus.

If we can assume that the wealthy landlords had to surrender a million acres of tithe-paying land, we must be ready to consider that the law cut very severely into the profits of the wealthy. And many Italian landlords suffered as well as the Romans (Cic., *de Rep.*, I, 31: foederibus violatis; *ibid.* 3, 41: Ti. Gracchus neglexit foedera, cf. App., *B. C.*, I, 18). It was far from being a fair compensation to landholders that they were henceforth excused from paying tithes on the residue left them. This expropriation of public land may be one of the reasons why commercial investments became more attractive after the Gracchan days, why provincial governors devised new methods of recouping their losses in the provinces, and it doubtless had something to do with the Italian revolt in 91 (see Carcopino, in *Bull. Guillaume Budé*, 1921, 1-23).

2. *The Legacy of Attalus to Rome.*

Livy, *Epit.* 58:

Heredem autem populum Romanum reliquerat Attalus, rex Pergami.

" For Attalus, the king of Pergamum, had made the Roman commonwealth his heir."

Strabo, 13, 4, 2:

κατέλιπε δὲ κληρονόμους 'Ρωμαίους.

" He left the Romans as his heirs."

References to this testament occur also in Plut., *Ti. Gracchus,* 14;
Justinus, 36, 4, 5; App., *Mith.,* 62; Livy, *Epit.* 59; in the inscription
no. 249 of Fränkel, *Inschr. v. Perg.,* I; etc.

For details concerning the legacy see Broughton's section on Asia.
See also Rostovtzeff, *Economic Policy of the Pergamene Kings,* in
"Anatolian Studies presented to Sir William Ramsay," 375 f., regarding the Attalid properties and industries. Rome later reorganized the
province, but at this time took and sold the personal property of the
king, including many of the slaves and much of the furnishing of the
palaces of the king.

Pliny, *N. H.,* 33, 149:

Romae in auctionibus regiis verecundia exempta est.

"All moderation came to an end when the king's properties were
auctioned off at Rome."

See numerous references in *Thes. L. L.* to *Attalica aulaea, gaza, vellera,* etc.
(especially tapestries with designs in gold thread): Varro, fr. 68: ex hereditate
Attalica aulaea, clamides, pallae, plagae, vasa aurea; Prop., 2, 32, 12; Hor., *Carm.,*
1, 1, 11; Pliny, *N. H.,* 8, 196; etc.

The Gracchan proposals to use the Attalic inheritance:

Livy, *Epit.* 58:

deinde cum minus agri esset quam, quod dividi posset, sine offensa
etiam plebis, . . . legem se promulgaturum ostendit, ut his, qui Sempronia lege agrum accipere deberent, pecunia, quae regis Attali fuisset,
divideretur.

" Then when there proved to be less land than was needed for
division, if the plebs were to be satisfied . . . he let it out that he
would propose a bill to the effect that the moneys which had belonged
to Attalus should be divided among those who ought to receive land
under the Sempronian law."

Plut., *Ti. Gracch.* 14:

Ἐπεὶ δὲ τοῦ Φιλομήτορος Ἀττάλου τελευτήσαντος Εὔδημος ὁ Περγαμηνὸς ἀνήνεγκε
διαθήκην ἐν ᾗ κληρονόμος ἐγέγραπτο τοῦ βασιλέως ὁ Ῥωμαίων δῆμος, εὐθὺς ὁ

Τιβέριος δημαγωγῶν εἰσήνεγκε νόμον ὅπως τὰ βασιλικὰ χρήματα κομισθέντα τοῖς
τὴν χώραν διαλαγχάνουσι τῶν πολιτῶν ὑπάρχοι πρὸς κατασκευὴν καὶ γεωργίας
ἀφορμήν.

"And now Attalus Philometer died, and Eudemus of Pergamum
brought to Rome the king's last will and testament, by which the Roman
people was made his heir. At once Tiberius courted popular favour by
bringing in a bill which provided that the money of King Attalus, when
brought to Rome, should be given to the citizens who received a parcel
of the public land, to aid them in stocking and tilling their farms."

The administration of financial and of provincial matters by the assembly was
an innovation bitterly resented by the Senate. To what extent Plutarch is correct
about the use of the money in " stocking " the farms we cannot say. No other
authority supports him explicitly. Livy apparently thought the money was to be given
in lieu of lots. At any rate Gracchus passed a law disposing of the royal property,
and presumably the agrarian commission used the proceeds, but very much money
was needed to finance the commission with it large retinue of surveyors and agents.

3. The legislation of Gaius Gracchus.

Gaius Gracchus, elected tribune in 124, continued the social and economic reforms of his brother.

a. Cic., pro Rab. Perd. 12:

C. Gracchus legem tulit ne de capite C. R. injusso vestro judi-
caretur.

" Gaius Gracchus passed a law that no citizen should be condemned
to death except by your command."

Cf. Plut., C. Gracch., 4, etc. The law, which was a restatement of old laws, was
aimed at the procedure used by the Senate in 132, and Popillius, the consul of that
year, was accordingly banished. Cf. Cic., pro Domo, 82; Diod., 35, 25, etc.

Plutarch summarizes the other proposals of Gaius as follows:

Plut., C. Gracch. 5:

Τῶν δὲ νόμων οὓς εἰσέφερε τῷ δήμῳ χαριζόμενος καὶ καταλύων τὴν σύγκλητον,
ὁ μὲν ἦν κληρουχικὸς ἀνανέμων τοῖς πένησι τὴν δημοσίαν, ὁ δὲ στρατιωτικὸς ἐσθῆτά
τε κελεύων δημοσίᾳ χορηγεῖσθαι καὶ μηδὲν εἰς τοῦτο τῆς μισθοφορᾶς ὑφαιρεῖσθαι
τῶν στρατευομένων, καὶ νεώτερον ἐτῶν ἑπτακαίδεκα μὴ καταλέγεσθαι στρατιώτην·
ὁ δὲ συμμαχικὸς ἰσοψήφους ποιῶν τοῖς πολίτας τοὺς Ἰταλιώτας. ὁ δὲ σιτικὸς
ἐπευωνίζων τοῖς πένησι τὴν ἀγοράν. ὁ δὲ δικαστικός, ᾧ τὸ πλεῖστον ἀπέκοψε τῆς
τῶν συγκλητικῶν δυνάμεως. μόνοι γὰρ ἔκρινον τὰς δίκας, καὶ διὰ τοῦτο φοβεροὶ
τῷ τε δήμῳ καὶ τοῖς ἱππεῦσιν ἦσαν, . . .

" Of the laws which he proposed by way of gratifying the people and

17

overthrowing the senate, one was agrarian, and divided the public land among the poor citizens; another was military, and ordained that clothing should be furnished to the soldiers at the public cost, that nothing should be deducted from their pay to meet this charge, and that no one under seventeen should be enrolled as a soldier; another concerned the allies,[1] and gave the Italians equal suffrage rights with Roman citizens; another related to the supplies of grain, and lowered the market price to the poor; and another dealt with the appointment of judges. This last law most of all curtailed the power of the senators; for they alone could serve as judges in criminal cases, and this privilege made them formidable both to the common people and to the equestrian order."

b. *Lex frumentaria.* Livy, *Epit.* 60:

> frumentariam (legem) ut senis et triente frumentum plebi daretur.

"He passed a grain law that wheat should be given the plebs for $6\frac{1}{3}$ asses the modius."

This would be about 25-30 cents the bushel, probably about half the normal price.

Schol. Bob. Stangl, 135, 8, gives the same price. Appian, *B. C.*, 1, 21; Plut., *C. Gracch.*, 5, and Vell., 2, 6, erroneously call it a free gift of grain at the public expense. That the price was very much below the normal is proved by these references, and by the fact that Cicero calls it a *largitio* (*De Off.*, 2, 72, and *Tusc. Disp.*, 3, 48):

> cum largitiones maximas fecisset et effudisset aerarium.

"When he gave lavishly and emptied the treasury."

For storing the public grain for later disbursement he built public granaries. Cf. Plut., *C. Gracchus,* 6, and Festus, 370, L.:

> Sempronia horrea . . . ad custodiam frumenti publici.

The aristocratic view (Diod., 35, 25, from Posidonius) was that Gracchus used these largesses to buy votes. They certainly accomplished that, and the building of granaries would indicate that the institution was not meant for only one year, till projected colonization might remove the crowds. However, Gracchus had read deeply in the social philosophy of the Greek Stoics, who had long advocated state charities as a duty. See my *Economic History*[2], 134, and Last, in *Camb. Anc. Hist.*, IX, ch. iii.

---

[1] This bill did not become a law.

c. *Lex Agraria.*

Livy, *Epit.* 60:

Tulit . . . legem agrariam quam et frater ejus tulerat . . .

" He passed the agrarian law that his brother had passed " . . .

That is, he probably passed a law giving back full judicial powers to the agrarian commission so that it could operate effectively again. Plut., *C. Gracch.*, 6; Cic., *de Leg. Agr.* 1, 21 refer to it; also the lex agr. of 111 B. C., *C. I. L.*, I², no. 585, 1. 6, and Sic. Flacc., *de cond. agr.*, 136.

Since even Tiberius found a shortage of land for distribution, Gaius could not have discovered much for his purpose. Hence he later projected colonization partly outside of Italy (see below). However, the reference in the law of 111 B. C. to lands called viasii vicani (*loc. cit.*, 1. 11), lands given along public roads as payment for the obligation of keeping such roads in repair, probably points to a new clause now added to the law of Tiberius. The state doubtless had to buy such lands at convenient places, if they were not available, or trade in suitable plots for plots of public land situated elsewhere.

d. *The Lex Judiciaria.*

The jury panels were henceforth to be drawn from the body of knights and not from the Senate. This law, though not dealing with an economic subject, should be mentioned here because it gave a definite state-function of importance to the knights (the men of property) and thereby created a new political class of quasi-nobles that grew greatly in importance as a party often opposed to the Senate. The senators objected to the bill strenuously because after its passage they would no longer be tried in court by their peers, but by jurors of a class despised by them. Gracchus was conscious of the fact that his law would create a decided cleavage between men of property and the nobility (" he said he had thrown daggers into the Forum," Cic., *de Leg.*, 3, 20) and that the Senate's influence would be diminished by it.

Appian, *B. C.*, 1, 22:

φασὶ δὲ κυρωθέντος μὲν ἄρτι τοῦ νόμου τὸν Γράκχον εἰπεῖν, ὅτι ἀθρόως τὴν βουλὴν καθῃρήκοι, τοῦ δ' ἔργου προϊόντος ἐς πεῖραν μειζόνως ἔτι ἐκφανῆναι τὸ ἔπος τὸ Γράκχου. τό τε γὰρ δικάζειν αὐτοὺς Ῥωμαίοις καὶ Ἰταλιώταις ἅπασι καὶ αὐτοῖς βουλευταῖς, ἐπὶ παντὶ μέτρῳ, χρημάτων τε πέρι καὶ ἀτιμίας καὶ φυγῆς, τοὺς μὲν ἱππέας οἷά τινας ἄρχοντας αὐτῶν ὑπερεπῆρε, τοὺς δὲ βουλευτὰς ἴσα καὶ ὑπηκόους

ἐποίει. συνιστάμενοί τε τοῖς δημάρχοις οἱ ἱππεῖς ἐς τὰς χειροτονίας καὶ ἀντιλαμ-
βάνοντες παρ' αὐτῶν, ὅ τι θέλοιεν, ἐπὶ μέγα φόβου τοῖς βουλευταῖς ἐχώρουν· ταχύ
τε περιῆν ἀνεστράφθαι τὸ κράτος τῆς πολιτείας, τὴν μὲν ἀξίωσιν μόνην ἔτι τῆς
βουλῆς ἐχούσης, τὴν δὲ δύναμιν τῶν ἱππέων. προϊόντες γὰρ οὐκ ἐδυνάστευον μόνον·
ἀλλὰ καὶ σαφῶς ἐνύβριζον τοῖς βουλευταῖς παρὰ τὰς δίκας.

"It is said that soon after the passage of this law Gracchus
remarked that he had broken the power of the Senate once for all, and
the saying of Gracchus received a deeper and deeper significance by the
course of events. For this power of sitting in judgment on all Romans
and Italians, including the senators themselves, in all matters as to
property, civil rights, and banishment, exalted the knights to be rulers
over them, and put senators on the level of subjects. Moreover, as the
knights voted in the election to sustain the power of the tribunes, and
obtained from them whatever they wanted in return, they became more
and more formidable to the senators. So it shortly came about that the
political mastery was turned upside down, the power being in the hands
of the knights, and the honour only remaining with the Senate. The
knights indeed went so far that they not only held power over the
senators, but they openly flouted them beyond their right."

Probably neither Gracchus nor the senators foresaw at this time the full import
of the change in the jury panels, for this became apparent only after some years
when the knights, while gathering taxes in Asia, came into conflict with the senatorial proconsuls who tried to protect the tax-payers. References to this law are
found in Livy, *Epit.* 60 (apparently a reference to a first proposal, later amended);
Appian, *B. C.*, 1, 22; Cic., *Verr.*, 1, 38; Diod., 35, 25, and 37, 9, etc. A fragment
of a judiciary law called the *lex repetundarum*—which is plausibly identified with
the Gracchan law—is found in *C. I. L.*, I², 583. For commentary on this fragment
see Mommsen, *Ges. Schriften*, I, 1-64, and Hardy, *Six Roman Laws*, 1-34. The law
was superseded by a *lex Servilia* (of Glaucia) before or during 111 B. C.

e. *Lex de provincia Asia.*

Cic., *Verr.*, 3, 12: aut censoria locatio constituta est ut Asiae lege
Sempronia (Cicero, in speaking of the various methods of collecting
taxes in the provinces, says "or a contract is let by the censors as in
Asia, according to the Sempronian law."). Cf. Appian, *B. C.*, 5, 4;
Fronto (*Nab.*) 135; Schol. Bob. Stangl 157 (in *pro Planc.*, 31). For
the effects of the law on Asia see Broughton's section on *Asia.*

The contract-system of tax-gathering was already employed in Sicily, but there
the contracts were let to Sicilians, under a law carefully guarding the interest of
the natives. For Asia the contracts were let by the censors to Roman knights. A
collection of tithes rather than of specified sums might be beneficial to tax-payers
where crops were uncertain, but the system led to oppression except when the

governors were very vigilant in protecting the interests of the natives. Asia soon suffered much from undue exactions, and the knights profited greatly from opportunities to lend money and make investments in Asia. The expansion of Roman equestrian business in the East as revealed in the inscriptions of Delos dates from the passage of this law. There is no reason for assuming that Gracchus foresaw the later evils of this law, for there had as yet been little evidence of undue exploitation on the part of the equestrian companies in the numerous public contracts that they had executed in Rome.

f. *Colonies established.*

Livy, *Epit.* 60:

Effecit ut complures coloniae in Italia deducerentur et una in solo dirutae Carthaginis.

" He had many colonies planted in Italy and one on the site of Carthage which had been destroyed."

This refers to a Sempronian law and to the *lex Rubria,* Plut., *C. Gracch.,* 10, *Complures coloniae in Italia* may be an exaggeration, though the unreliable *Liber Coloniarum* mentions Gracchan foundations in several places. Velleius, 1, 15, mentions only Scolacium and Tarentum for Italy. Plut., *C. Gracchus,* 8, mentions Tarentum and Capua. Capua certainly was not disturbed (Cic., *de lege Agr.,* 2, 81), but some Campanian lands may have been used. The *lex Agraria* of 111 B. C. shows that in order to get lands for colonies Gracchus in some cases traded plots of public lands elsewhere for portions needed (*C. I. L.,* I², 585, ll. 4 and 27).

Plut., *C. Gracchus,* 9, 2, speaks of two colonies to consist of " the most respectable people." This is usually interpreted as meaning that, for his seaport colonies, Gracchus selected with care men capable of developing the commercial facilities of Tarentum and Scolacium.

The colonization of Carthage met with great opposition, probably because it struck another blow at senatorial administration of provinces and endangered senatorial investments there. The Senate spitefully insisted that citizens settling in Carthage must come all the way to Rome to enroll in the census (Vell., 2, 7).

The allotments at Carthage seem to have been unusually large (200 jugera, *lex agr.* of 111 B. C., l. 60) and to have gone to nearly 6,000 men " chosen from the whole of Italy," and were held by full quiritary rights like land in Italy (Appian, *Punica,* 136, and *B. C.,* 1, 24). The law colonizing Carthage (the *lex Rubria*) was repealed, to be sure (*lex Agr.* of 111 B. C., *C. I. L.,* I², 585, 59: lege Rubria, quae fuit, cf.

Plut., *C. Gracch.* 9), but the later law just mentioned (ll. 59-65) confirmed the allotments in full ownership to those who had settled there, provided the legal acreage and number were not exceeded. For the colonization in Africa see the forthcoming section on Africa, by R. M. Haywood.

g. *Other activities of Gracchus.*

a. *New revenues*: Vell., 2, 6, 3:

nova constituebat portoria " he established new harbor-tariff stations." Cf. Gell., 11, 10.

b. *Road-building.* Appian, *B. C.*, 1, 23: " he built long roads through Italy," doubtless not only to give work, but also to facilitate transportation for the new settlements. Plutarch also mentions the roadbuilding with enthusiasm but without telling where the roads were.

Plut., *G. Gracchus*, 6, 3-4:

ἔγραψε δὲ καὶ πόλεις ἀποικίδας ἐκπέμπεσθαι, καὶ τὰς ὁδοὺς ποιεῖσθαι, καὶ κατασ-κευάζεσθαι σιτοβόλια, τούτοις ἅπασι πραττομένοις αὐτὸν ἄρχοντα καὶ διοικητὴν ἐφιστάς, καὶ πρὸς οὐδὲν ἀποτρυόμενος τῶν τοσούτων καὶ τηλικούτων, ἀλλὰ καὶ θαυμαστῷ τινι τάχει καὶ πόνῳ τῶν γινομένων ὡς μόνον ἕκαστον ἐξεργαζόμενος, ὥστε καὶ τοὺς πάνυ μισοῦντας αὐτὸν καὶ δεδοικότας ἐκπλήττεσθάι τὸ διὰ πάντων ἀνύσιμον καὶ τελεσιουργόν. οἱ δὲ πολλοὶ καὶ τὴν ὄψιν αὐτὴν ἐθαύμαζον, ἐξηρτημένον ὁρῶντες αὐτοῦ πλῆθος ἐργολάβων τεχνιτῶν πρεσβευτῶν ἀρχόντων στρατιωτῶν φιλολόγων, . . .

" Besides all this, he proposed measures for the colonisation of several cities, *for making roads,* and for building public granaries; of all which works he himself undertook the management and superinten-dence, and was never wanting to give necessary orders for the despatch of all these different and great undertakings; and that with such wonderful expedition and diligence, as if he had been but engaged upon one of them; insomuch that all persons, even those who hated or feared him, stood amazed to see what a capacity he had for effecting and completing all he undertook. As for the people themselves, they were transported at the very sight, when they saw him surrounded with a crowd of contractors, artificers, public deputies, military officers, soldiers, and scholars."

This passage would imply that Gracchus not only employed the regular contractors, but at times took direct charge of public works. Appian, *B. C.*, 1, 23, also says that in his public works Gracchus " put a multitude of contractors and artisans (ἐργολάβων καὶ χειροτεχνῶν) under obligations to him."

c. He proposed, but could not carry, his *franchise bill* in favor of
the Italic allies. Apparently this bill was to offer full citizenship to
the Latins and Latin rights (or at least the restricted voting rights of
Latins) to the other allies. So Appian, *B. C.*, 1, 23. The title of the
speech of Fannius *de sociis et nomine Latino* (Cic., *Brut.*, 99) implies
that there were two parts. Vell., 2, 6, 2, and Plut., 5, 2, and 8, 3, are
inexact in mentioning only a franchise bill for the whole of Italy. The
failure of this bill because of the selfishness of the plebeian assembly
ultimately led to the Social War.

4. *The later revision of the Gracchan laws.*

Appian, *B. C.*, 1, 23 (so also Plut., 9):

Λίβιόν τε Δροῦσον, ἕτερον δήμαρχον, ἔπεισε κωλῦσαι τοὺς Γράκχου νόμους, οὐκ
ἐπιλέγοντα τῷ δήμῳ τὰς αἰτίας· δέδοται δὲ τῷ κωλύοντι μηδ' ἐπιλέγειν. ἔδωκαν
δ' αὐτῷ καὶ φιλανθρωπεύσασθαι τὸν δῆμον δώδεκα ἀποικίαις· ᾧ δὴ καὶ μάλιστα
ὁ δῆμος ἡσθεὶς τῶν Γράκχου νόμων κατεφρόνησεν.

"The Senate also persuaded Livius Drusus, another tribune, to
interpose his veto against the laws proposed by Gracchus, but not to
tell the people his reasons for doing so; for a tribune was not required
to give reasons for his veto. In order to conciliate the people the
senators gave Drusus the privilege of founding twelve colonies, and
the plebeians were so much pleased with this that they scoffed at the
laws proposed by Gracchus."

This extensive plan apparently was not carried out though a few small colonies
may have been planted, but it served to check the career of Gracchus.

Appian, *B. C.*, 1, 27:

Καὶ ἡ στάσις ἡ τοῦ δευτέρου Γράκχου ἐς τάδε ἔληγε· νόμος τε οὐ πολὺ ὕστερον
ἐκυρώθη τὴν γῆν, ὑπὲρ ἧς διεφέροντο, ἐξεῖναι πιπράσκειν τοῖς ἔχουσιν· ἀπείρητο
γὰρ ἐκ Γράκχου τοῦ προτέρου καὶ τόδε. καὶ εὐθὺς οἱ πλούσιοι παρὰ τῶν πενήτων
ἐωνοῦντο, ἢ ταῖσδε ταῖς προφάσεσιν ἐβιάζοντο. καὶ περιῆν ἐς χεῖρον ἔτι τοῖς πένησι,
μέχρι Σπούριος Θόριος δημαρχῶν εἰσηγήσατο νόμον, τὴν μὲν γῆν μηκέτι διανέμειν,
ἀλλ' εἶναι τῶν ἐχόντων, καὶ φόρους ὑπὲρ αὐτῆς τῷ δήμῳ κατατίθεσθαι καὶ τάδε τὰ
χρήματα χωρεῖν ἐς διανομάς. ὅπερ ἦν μέν τις τοῖς πένησι παρηγορία διὰ τὰς διανομάς,
ὄφελος δ' οὐδὲν ἐς πολυπληθίαν. ἅπαξ δὲ τοῖς σοφίσμασι τοῖσδε τοῦ Γρακχείου
νόμου παραλυθέντος, ἀρίστου καὶ ὠφελιμωτάτου, εἰ ἐδύνατο πραχθῆναι, γενομένου,
καὶ τοὺς φόρους οὐ πολὺ ὕστερον διέλυσε δήμαρχος ἕτερος, καὶ ὁ δῆμος ἀθρόως
ἁπάντων ἐξεπεπτώκει.

"Thus the sedition of the younger Gracchus came to an end. Not
long afterward a law was enacted to permit the holders to sell the land

about which they had quarrelled; for even this had been forbidden by
the law of the elder Gracchus.   At once the rich began to buy the
allotments of the poor, or found pretexts for seizing them by force.
So the condition of the poor became even worse than it was before,
until Spurius Thorius, a tribune of the people, brought in a law providing that the work of distributing the public domain should no longer
be continued, but that the land should belong to those in possession
of it, who should pay rent for it to the people, and that the money
so received should be distributed; and this distribution was a kind of
solace to the poor, but it did not help to increase the population.   By
these devices the law of Gracchus—a most excellent and useful one,
if it could have been carried out—was once for all frustrated, and a
little later the rent itself was abolished at the instance of another
tribune.   So the plebeians lost everything."

Here are three laws mentioned. The first (permitting the holders of allotments
to sell their lots) may belong to the legislation of Livius Drusus, referred to above.
The law of Thorius seems to be the law of 119-118 mentioned by Cicero, *Brut.*, 136:
Sp. Thorius . . . qui agrum publicum, vitiosa et inutili lege, vectigali levavit. (This
obscure passage is thus plausibly translated by Hardy, *Six Roman Laws*, 47: " He
relieved the public land from an irregular and useless law [the Gracchan] by impos-
ing a vectigal." That is to say, in order to save the possessors of the 500 jugera
lots from further molestation on the part of agitators, he reimposed a vectigal, but
granted the holders the right to hold possession in perpetuity.) According to Appian,
the vectigal was to be used for the plebs, apparently to help pay for the corn dole.
The third law mentioned—all too briefly—by Appian in connection with the abro-
gation of all returns (on the 500 as well as the 30 jugera lots) is apparently the
great law of 111 B. C. of which we have considerable fragments in *C. I. L.*, I², 585.
This law is well discussed by Hardy, *op. cit.* In view of the claims of some nobles
that all the Gracchan legislation was illegal, and of the uncertainties caused by
later revision, the great legislator who drew up this law selected in a spirit of
fair compromise the valid statutes of the recent years, put them into one code,
and had it passed by the Senate and assembly with all due observance of the laws.
Henceforth there was no more question of the legality of the clauses included. The
chief items regarding private land in this law are the following:

1. The estates of 500 jugera untouched by the Sempronian law shall be private
   property and freed from the vectigal imposed in 118.
2. Likewise all colonial assignments made by the Gracchan boards.
3. Likewise the lands assigned in small holdings by the Gracchan boards.
4. Likewise lands given in exchange for private land taken by the boards for state
   use or for colonization.

The first eight lines of the agrarian law of 111 B. C. (*C. L. L.*, I²,
p. 458) read as follows:

I   Quei ager poplicus populi Romanei in terram Italiam P.
      Muucio L. Calpur[nio ços. fuit, extra eum agrum, quei ager

ex lege plebeive sc(ito), quod C. Sempronius Ti. f. tr(ibunus)
pl(ebei) rogavit, exceptum cavitumve est nei divideretur . . .

II quem quisque de eo agro loco ex lege plebeive sc(ito) vetus
possessor sibei a]grum locum sumpsit reliquitve, quod non
modus maior siet, quam quantum unum hominem ex lege ple-

III beive sc(ito) sibei sumer[e relinquereve licuit; quei ager pupli-
cus populi Romanei in terra Italia P. Muucio L. Calpurnio
cos. fuit, extra eum agrum, quei ager ex lege plebeive sc(ito),
quod C. Sempronius Ti. f. tr. pl. rogavit, exceptum cavitumve
est nei divideretur . . . quem agrum locum] quoieique de eo
agro loco ex lege plebeive sc(ito) IIIvir sortito ceivi Romano
dedit adsignavit, quod non in eo agro loco est, quod ultr[a . . .

IV quei ager publicus populi Romanei in terra Italia P. Muucio
L. Calpurnia cos. fuit, extra eum agrum, quei ager ex lege
plebeive scito, quod C. Sempronius Ti. f. tr. pl. rogavit, exceptum cavitumve est nei divideretur, de eo agro loco quei ager
locus ei, quei agrum privatum in publicum commutavit, pro
eo agro loco a IIIviro datus commutatus re]dditus est; ⁓ quei
ager publicus populi Romanei in terra Italia P. Muucio L.
Calpurnio cos. fuit, ex[t]ra eum agrum, quei ager ex lege
[plebeive sc(ito), quod C. Sempronius Ti. f. tr. pl. rogavit,

V exceptum cavitumve est nei divideretur . . . quod eius quisq]ue
agri locei publicei in terra Italia, quod eius extra urbem
Roma⟨m⟩ est, quod eius in urbe oppido vico est, quod eius
IIIvir dedit adsignavit, quod [. . . tum cum haec lex rogabitur

VI habebit possidebitve; . . . quei ager publicus populi Romanei
in terra Italia P. Muucio L. Calpurnio cos. fuit, extra eum
agrum. quei ager ex] lege plebive scito, quod C. Sempronius
Ti. f. tr. pl. rog(avit), exceptum cavitumve est nei divideretur,
quod quoieique de eo agro loco agri locei aedific[iei . . .

VII q]uibu[s . . . i]n terra Italia IIIvir dedit adsignavit reliquit
inve formas tabulasve retulit referive iusit: ⁓ ager locus aedifi-
cium omnis quei supra scriptu[s est . . . extra eum agrum
locum de quo supra except]um cavitu[mve est, privatus esto

VIII . . . eiusque locei agri aedificii emptio venditi]o ita, utei
ceterorum locorum agrorum aedificiorum privatorum est, esto;
censorque queiquomque erit fa[c]ito, utei is ager locus aedifi-

cium, quei e[x hace lege privatus factus est, ita, utei ceteri agri loca aedificia privati, in censum referatur.

These are translated by Hardy (*Six Roman Laws,* 56 ff.) as follows:

I   " As respecting the public land belonging to the Roman people within Italy in the consulship of P. Mucius and L. Calpurnius (133 B. C.), excluding that land (Campanian) which by the law or plebiscite of G. Sempronius Gracchus, tribune of the plebs, was by special enactment excepted from division, whatso-

II   ever land or ground each several original possessor in accordance with the law or plebiscite took or retained for himself, provided that the measure of such land shall not exceed the amount (500 jugera) which by the said law an individual may take or retain.

As respecting the public land belonging to the Roman people within Italy in the consulship of P. Mucius and L. Calpurnius, excluding that land which by the law or plebiscite of G. Sempronius Gracchus, tribune of the plebs, was by special enactment excepted from division . . . whatever land or

III ground a triumvir, in accordance with the law or plebiscite, has given or assigned to any Roman citizen allotted to a colony,

IV   not lying beyond. . . .

As respecting the public land belonging to the Roman people within Italy in the consulship of P. Mucius and L. Calpurnius, excluding that land which by the law or plebiscite of G. Sempronius Gracchus, tribune of the plebs, was by special enactment excepted from division . . . whatever such land has been given, assigned, or rendered by a triumvir to an individual, in return for private land exchanged for public;

As respecting the public land belonging to the Roman people within Italy in the consulship of P. Mucius and L. Calpurnius, excluding that land which by the law or plebiscite of G. Sempronius Gracchus, tribune of the plebs, was by special enactment excepted from division . . . whatever portion of such

V   public land or ground, within Italy or outside the city of Rome, or in a city, or in a town or village (30 jugera lots), any individual shall hold or possess, at the time when this measure

VI   becomes law, such land having been given or assigned by a triumvir;

As respecting the public land belonging to the Roman people within Italy in the consulship of P. Mucius and L. Calpurnius, excluding that land or ground which by the law or plebiscite of G. Sempronius Gracchus was by special enactment excepted VII from division . . . whatever portions of such land or ground within Italy a triumvir has given or assigned or left to any individual, or has entered or caused to be entered in the land lists and schedules;

All such land, ground or building above mentioned, excluding that land or ground specially excepted, as aforesaid (*i. e.* Cam-VIII panian), shall be private land, and of all such land, ground or building there shall be the same right of purchase and sale as for other private lands, grounds or buildings; and the censor for the time being shall see that such land, ground or building, made private by this law, shall, like other lands, grounds or buildings, be entered in the census."

In addition to the items mentioned in these lines there were various classes of public land and land with state servitudes, the condition of which was fully defined by this law:

1. The *Ager Campanus* made public in 210 and held in small lots by holders paying normal rents to the censors remains untouched (by the exception found in part in ll. 2, 3, 4, and given explicitly by Cic., *de lege Agr.*, 2, 81).

2. The public lands (*viasii vicani*) given in return for pledges to repair roads are to remain as Gaius Gracchus had defined them (ll. 11, 12).

3. The so-called *trientabula* fields which the state, instead of repaying war contributions, had given in 200 B. C. to be held at a nominal fee until such time as the holders should demand the cash contributed. These fields were to continue under the same provision (l. 32). Since these lands were now more valuable than in 200, there was no probability that the holders would surrender them.

4. The *Ager Compascuus* should remain public property as before. There were two kinds: rough pasture-land that the state had assigned for the use of definite communities (ll. 14, 15); (b) similar tracts not definitely assigned (l. 25). On the first the individual citizens of the

given community could graze 10 cattle and 50 sheep free of charge, paying the regular *scriptura* for any larger numbers; on the second type, open to all grazers up to the legal limit of 100 and 500 animals respectively, the same rules held. In both cases, enclosure, cultivation, and restriction of rights were forbidden.

Finally, the regulation of public lands in Africa (ll. 45-96) and at Corinth (96-104) was defined (see sections on Africa and Greece). Here we need only state that the rights of the settlers in Africa under the Rubrian law were confirmed, though the law had been repealed in 122, and that the law also ordered surveys of the public land with a view to offering it for sale. Probably the stress of the Jugurthine and Cimbrian wars together with the cost of the corn dole had imperilled the state treasury, and probably also the Roman landlords who had lost much of their possessions in public land at home were thought to be ready to buy in Africa and Corinth. How much was sold under this provision we do not know.

The results of the agrarian legislation from 133 to 109 B. C. were somewhat as follows:

1. The landlords, Roman and Italic, who had specialized in occupying and farming arable public lands—especially in the South where such occupation was connived at after 200 B. C.—suffered a very severe economic setback, but they received their legal quotas free of tithe. It is not improbable that they lost an aggregate of 1,000,000 acres of arable land. Grazing on public land was similarly limited to the legal number of animals. This may account in part for the diminution of power of the Senate during the next decade, and also for the growing greed of exploiting magistrates who attempted to recoup their fallen fortunes in the provinces.

2. It is not unlikely that some 50 – 75,000 of the proletariat of Rome received plots of 30 jugera or under, at first inalienable and subject to a small vectigal, but after the death of G. Gracchus given outright as saleable and rent-free property. Though our sources insist that there was a widespread sale and abandonment of lots thereafter, we may assume that a fairly large proportion of these settlers remained after a compulsory stay of over ten years, and that there were accordingly more citizens available for the army.

3. There were probably no more arable public lands left in Italy for distribution except the Campanian lands that had been carefully left untouched by all the legislators. The old system of land distributions, therefore, came to an end.

5. *Economic measures after 104.*

In 104 the tribune L. Marcius Philippus, later a supporter of the Senate, attempted to pass some agrarian bill, but it was vetoed (Cic., *de Off.*, 2, 73). He supported his measure in a speech in which he made the statement that there were not 2,000 men in the state who owned property (qui rem haberent). The statement, often quoted by historians, is not worthy of the slightest credence since it was a wild exaggeration made by an excited agitator. Sulla found many thousand men rich enough to deserve proscription even after the severe times of the Social and Civil Wars.

In 103 Saturninus was tribune and passed an agrarian law for the settlement of some soldiers of Marius (*de Vir. Ill.*, 73). For this law, which was not repealed, see above. The second tribunate in 100, full of wild proposals for larger doles (grain at less than one *as* the modius) and land grants, need not concern us because all these bills were annulled (*Auctor ad Her.*, 1, 21; Livy, *Epit.* 69; Appian, *B. C.*, 1, 29; Cic., *pro Balbo*, 48, *de Leg.*, 2, 14; etc.). In 99 Titius, a tribune, again tried to pass an agrarian law, but without success (Obsequens, 106; Val. Max., 8, 1, 3; Cic., *pro Rab.*, 24). In 95 the consuls Crassus and Scaevola passed a law striking off the citizen rolls the names of Italians who had secured enrolment under censors who had been lenient. This brought to a crisis the contention for the franchise (Cic., *pro Cornel.*, 1, 20, and Asconius' comment).

In 92 the censors expelled all rhetors who taught in Latin (Suet., *de Rhet.*, 1; Cic., *de Or.*, 3, 93). The decree contended that the new slipshod method did not provide a thorough education. Some historians have assumed that the purpose of the decree was to abolish an inexpensive short-cut to the advocate's profession which enabled the populace to enter the Forum effectively against the nobility (cf. Münzer, "*Licinius*," in *R-E.*, XIII, 261). Whether this entered into their purpose one cannot say.

In the same year P. Rutilius Rufus, who as *legatus* of the proconsul of Asia had tried to protect the provincials against the abuses of the knights, was falsely accused for misrule and banished by the equestrian panel. Livy, *Epit.* 70: invisus equestri ordini, penes quem judicia erant, repetundarum damnatus. This notorious case reveals the knights at the zenith of their power (see also Cic., *Brut.*, 115; Dio Cass., frag. 95; Vell., 2, 13) and willingness to abuse it for profit.

In 91 M. Livius Drusus as tribune attempted at first to get the jury panels back to the Senate; in order to secure the support of all parties he proposed an omnibus bill, offering to elevate 300 knights to the Senate and to give the people doles and land (Appian, *B. C.*, 1, 35; 36; Diod., 37, 11; Cic., *pro Cluent.*, 153, and *de Or.*, 3, 1). Finally, to appease the Italians who feared injustice from new land laws, he agitated for their franchise. His laws, though passed, were declared void by the Senate on the ground that omnibus bills were illegal. The only law of his that seems to have survived was one that secured inflation (to pay the expenses of his social proposals) by the addition of plated coins to the regular silver coinage (see below). The agitation for the franchise led directly to the Social (Italian) War.

For the Social War see the political histories of Mommsen, Heitland, *Camb. Anc. Hist.*, IX, etc. We discussed above the heavy cost of the war and the financial measures taken to pay for it.

In 88 the tribune P. Sulpicius Rufus favored a just distribution of the enfranchised Italians among all the 35 wards, and, in order to secure votes for the measure, bargained with Marius, giving him the command of the Mithridatic war in the place of the legal appointee, Sulla, the consul. This led to the first civil war. Sulla marched on Rome. The Sulpician plebiscite was repealed, Sulla went to Asia, and the democrats under Cinna and Marius, and later under Carbo, ruled Rome till Sulla's return in 83.

Sulla's return led to a disastrous civil war, to his dictatorship with the proscription of his enemies, and to the construction of a new and ultra-conservative constitution. Appian, *B. C.*, 1, 95, reports 1600 knights and 40 senators slain, besides many others. The property was sold, usually at a very low price, and generally to Sulla's partisans. The purchase price went to the treasury, which Sulla used personally in the manner of an Oriental autocrat. A large number of cities were deprived of their land, which was given to the soldiers (about 120,000; see above). The laws of economic import passed by Sulla ended the corn dole for the time (Gran. Lic., 34; Sall. *Orat. Lep.*), deprived the tribunes of the right to initiate legislation (Livy, *Epit.* 89), and abolished the censorship (Cic., *div. in Caec.*, 8, and Schol. Gron. *ad loc. pro nobilitate*). By abolishing the censorship Sulla apparently wished to make it difficult for the new citizens (mostly of democratic sympathies) to register and vote. Sulla's laws also placed the jury panels in senatorial hands as before the Gracchan period (Vell., 2, 32; Cic., *Verr.*, 1, 37), and this, of course, made the courts more conservative.

V. SEMIPUBLIC FINANCES: THE KNIGHTS

1. *Tithes, grazing taxes, and port dues collected by the knights.*

The tithes and grazing taxes of Italy were gathered by the publicans as before (see preceding chapter for estimates). But by the Gracchan legislation most of the tithe-land and some of the grazing land were given to settlers, and there was little left for the publicans to do in such affairs. The rental of the Campanian land was not collected by them. The knights also profited somewhat by collecting state debts, as appears from the *lex agraria* of 111 B. C. (*C. I. L.*, I², 585, l. 70).

The 2 - 5 per cent port dues increased very much in amount. C. Gracchus instituted new harbor dues (nova constituebat portoria, Vell., 2, 6, 3), doubtless in Asia (Cic., *Pomp.*, 15, ex portu), and perhaps in the other provinces, if they had not already been instituted there. Aquileia had port dues in 70 (Cic., *pro Font.*, 2) and Rome would certainly continue port dues in Macedonia when making it a province in 148. "Free" and allied cities were, of course, immune and the elaborate tariff boundaries of the later day were not yet thought of. However dues were certainly collected at all citizen harbors of Italy, at Narbo in southern Gaul, at some six harbors of Sicily, and at several of Spain and Macedonia (Rostovtzeff, *Staatspacht*, 391, mistakes Gallic taxes for Roman ones mentioned in Caes., *Bell. Gall.* 1, 18, and 3, 1).

Besides, trade was rapidly increasing, especially after Asia became a province. Hence we should assume that by 100 B. C. Rome was probably receiving a few million denarii per year from this source, and that the companies were earning a similar amount in the collecting.

The tithe of Sicily was still collected by Sicilians and the tax of Spain was collected by the quaestors, but by the Gracchan law of 123 the Asiatic tithe and cattle tax (*scriptura*) were given to the equestrian corporations to collect on contract. The returns from Asia amounted,

with port dues, to about 10,000,000 denarii per year (see above). This
was, of course, the net proceeds as calculated by the societies after they
had paid themselves a tenth of the tithe for collection (Cic., *pro Rabir.
Post.*, 30), that is, about 1,000,000 denarii. We are not told how the
produce in kind was turned into cash (which the state demanded).
Presumably the publicans could either bargain at each city for cash
(in some cases lending the money at high interest), or they might collect
the produce and go into the market with it. The *lex de Termessensibus*
(Dessau, 38, line 35) shows that the state secured free ports in Asia
for the goods handled by the publicans. That their business led to
extensive enterprises is clear from the fact that in the year 88 there
were 80,000 Italians in Asia (Memnon, *F. H. G.*, III, 31; Appian,
Mith., 22). At a later day the tax contracts of Asia seem to have been
the mainstay of equestrian profits. The illegal and oppressive exactions
of the knights were disclosed by Scaevola and Rutilius (Diod., 37, 5, 1;
Livy, *Epit.* 70).

2. *Mines:*

The mines of Macedonia, closed in 167, were opened again in 158
(Cassiod., *Chron.* ad 158), but whether to native or Roman contractors
we do not know. Since the Macedonian republics began coinage that
year, it is quite possible that the industry was left in native hands.

In Italy Rome had gold mines at Victumulae—not far from Vercellae—for a while, which the publicans exploited under a provision
not to use over 5,000 laborers (Pliny, 33, 78; Strabo, 5, 1, 12).
Since the Salassi were washing placer gold as early as 143 (Strabo,
4, 6, 7), we may suppose that the order fell within this period. In
fact the two mines may possibly be the same, or at least belong to the
same lode.

The Spanish mines (discussed in the preceding chapter) seem to
have been very profitable during this period. Polybius, 34, 9 (quoted
by Strabo, 3, 2, 10) says:

(Πολύβιος δὲ) τῶν περὶ Καρχηδόνα Νέαν ἀργυρείων μνησθεὶς μέγιστα μὲν εἶναί
φησι, διέχειν δὲ τῆς πόλεως ὅσον εἴκοσι σταδίους, περιειληφότα κύκλον τετρακοσίων
σταδίων, ὅπου τέτταρας μυριάδας ἀνθρώπων μένειν τῶν ἐργαζομένων, ἀναφέροντας
τότε τῷ δήμῳ τῶν Ῥωμαίων καθ᾽ ἑκάστην ἡμέραν δισμυρίας καὶ πεντακισχιλίας
δραχμάς.

" Polybius, in speaking of the silver mines near New Carthage,
says they are very extensive and are distant about twenty stades from

the town, extending in a circle for four hundred stades. Here forty thousand miners lived who at that period produced for the Roman government a daily sum of twenty-five thousand drachmae."

This passage probably belongs to the period 145–135 B. C. While successful operations lasted, the Roman treasury drew some 9,000,000 denarii the year as we have said, and, since contract mining was conducted on a basis of fifty per cent of the treasure, the company presumably had an equal amount. In the third chapter we have calculated that while this mining lasted the profits that fell to the operating companies may well have been near 4,000,000 denarii the year.

Strabo (3, 2, 10) goes on to say that in his day the silver mines of Spain were no longer state property but had passed over to private ownership (οὐ μέντοι δημόσια.. ἀλλ' εἰς ἰδιωτικὰς μετέστασαν κτήσεις). The gold mines alone were then in state possession. We have no definite statement of why the silver mines became private property. Possibly many of the mines gave out under intensive exploitation so that the contractors abandoned them, and the state then disposed of them. New veins would presumably be discovered by private enterprise, and, though ores usually occur in unclaimed mountainous country, which naturally belonged to the sovereign, Rome may have been careless about asserting her claims against squatters, especially as there was as yet no official survey of Spain. As for the old silver mines that were still productive, the question is more difficult. We have suggested above that when Sulla was in great need he may have sold them for ready money. It is significant that Crassus, who grew rich by dealing in Sulla's auctions, became at this time the owner of " numberless silver mines " (Plut., Crass., 2, 5: ὄντων δ' αὐτῷ παμπόλλων ἀργυρείων). Crassus had been in Spain while his father was governor there (96–93 B. C.) and this governor wrote an official report to Rome about tin mines (Strabo, 3, 5, 11). Sulla made free to confiscate and sell public, private, or sacred property (temple properties in Greece: Plut., Sulla, 12; plots on the Capitoline hill and temple treasure: Oros., 5, 18, 27, App., Mith., 22; Rome's tribute to kings and allies: Plut., Comp. Lys. et Sull., 3). Furthermore, after Sulla had killed 1600 of the richest knights (Appian, B. C., 1, 95), it is difficult to see how the equestrian companies could have continued to function. Sulla deprived them for a time of the tithe contracts in Asia (App., Mith., 62; Cic., pro Flacc., 32; ad Quint., 1, 1, 33), partly because of hatred toward

18

them, and partly, perhaps, because they would not for some time to come be financially able to carry on as before. My suggestion, then, is that Sulla probably auctioned off the silver mines. Of the lead mines in Spain at this time we know little, but a lead bar found in Spain with a stamp from this period has been found (*C. I. L.*, 2, 1001). Later these mines were very productive.

3. *Participation in Building Contracts:*

The knights probably had no share in building the long provincial roads, since the military organization conducted the work (for military work see Plut., *Mar.*, 15: a canal; Cic., *pro Font.*, 17: a road; Frontin, *Strat.*, 4, 1, 15: ship building). The Janiculan fort (about 142, Richter, *Topogr.*, 51; 120) may also have been executed by military engineers. However, the repairs of the *via Caecilia* (see Dessau, 5799, probably in Sulla's day) were made by contractors, some of whom were freedmen, and it may be that the *via Postumia*, 148 B. C., and the *via Popillia*, c. 132 B. C., were built by private contractors.

The large censorial contracts of M. Aemilius Scaurus in 109 probably fell to the knights. These were the second *via Aemilia*, from near Volterra to Dertona, the Mulvian bridge (*Vir. ill.*, 72; Strabo, 5, 1, 11), and the system of drainage canals dug between Parma and the Po, barely mentioned by Strabo (5, 1, 11): "Scaurus drained the plains by running navigable canals from the Po as far as Parma." Presumably the canals were also to serve as waterways. Finally there is a single mention of new shipyards designed by Hermodorus of Salamis, probably a state contract (Cic., *de Or.*, 1, 62).

The most expensive public enterprise near the city was the building of the Marcian aqueduct in 144–140 together with the repairs of the Appia and Anio Vetus, by the praetor Q. Marcius Rex. Frontinus, *Aqueducts*, 1, 7:

. . . Ser. Sulpicio Galba Lucio Aurelio Cotta consulibus cum Appiae Anionisque ductus vetustate quassati privatorum etiam fraudibus interciperentur, datum est a senatu negotium Marcio, qui tum praetor inter cives ius dicebat, eorum ductuum reficiendorum ac vindicandorum. Et quoniam incrementum urbis exigere videbatur ampliorem modum aquae, eidem mandatum a senatu est, ut curaret, quatenus alias aquas posset in urbem perducere. . . . Priores ductus restituit et tertiam illis salubriorem . . . duxit, cui ab auctore Marciae nomen est. Legimus apud Fenestellam, in haec opera Marcio decretum sestertium milies octingenties, et quoniam ad consummandum negotium non sufficiebat spatium praeturae, in annum alterum est prorogatum. Eo tempore decemviri, dum aliis ex causis libros Sibyllinos inspiciunt, invenisse dicuntur, non esse fas aquam Marciam seu potius Anionem—de hoc enim constantius traditur—in Capitolium perduci, deque ea re in senatu M. Lepido pro collegio verba faciente actum Appio Claudio Q. Caecilio consulibus, eandemque post annum tertium a Lucio Lentulo retractatam C. Laelio Q. Servilio consulibus, sed utroque tempore vicisse gratiam Marci Regis; atque ita in Capitolium esse aquam perductam. Concipitur Marcia Via Valeria ad miliarium tricesimum sextum deverticulo euntibus ab urbe Roma dextrorsus milium passum trium. Sublacensi autem, quae sub Nerone principe primum strata est, ad miliarium tricesimum octavum sinistrorsus intra passus ducentos fontium . . . sub . . . bus petrei . . . stat immobilis stagni modo colore praeviridi. Ductus eius habet longitudinem a capite ad urbem passuum sexaginta milium et mille septingentorum decem et semis; rivo subterraneo passuum quinquaginta quattuor milium ducentorum quadraginta septem semis, opere supra terram passuum septem milium quadringentorum sexaginta trium: ex ea longius ab urbe pluribus locis per vallis opere arcuato passuum quadringentorum sexaginto trium, propius urbem a septimo miliario substructione passuum quingentorum viginti octo, reliquo opere arcuato passuum sex milium quadringentorum septuaginta duum.

" in the consulship of Servius Sulpicius Galba and Lucius Aurelius Cotta (= 144 B. C.), when the conduits of Appia and Old Anio had become leaky by reason of age, and water was also being diverted from them unlawfully by individuals, the Senate commissioned Marcius, who at that time administered the law as praetor between citizens, to reclaim and repair these conduits; and since the growth of the City was seen to demand a more bountiful supply of water, the same man was charged by the Senate to bring into the City other waters so far as he could. . . . He restored the old channels and brought in a third supply, more wholesome than these, . . . which is called Marcia after the man who introduced it. We read in Fenestella, that 180,000,000 sesterces were granted to Marcius for these works, and since the term of his praetorship was not sufficient for the completion of the enterprise, it was extended for a second year. At that time the Decemvirs on consulting the Sibylline Books for another purpose, are said to have discovered that it was not right for the Marcian water, or rather the Anio (for tradition more regularly mentions this) to be brought to the Capitol. The matter is said to have been debated in the Senate, in the consulship of Appius Claudius and Quintus Caecilius, Marcius Lepidus acting as spokesman for the Board of Decemvirs; and three years later the matter is said to have been brought up again by Lucius Lentulus, in the consulship of Gaius Laelius and Quintus Servilius, but on both occasions the influence of Marcius Rex carried the day; and thus the water was brought to the Capitol. The intake of Marcia is at the thirty-sixth milestone on the Valerian Way, on a cross-road, three miles to the right as you come from Rome. But on the Sublacensian Way, which was first paved under the Emperor Nero, at the thirty-eighth milestone, within 200 paces to the left [a view of its source may be seen]. Its waters stand like a tranquil pool, of deep green hue. Its conduit has a length, from the intake to the City, of 61,710½ paces; 54,247½ paces of underground conduit; 7,463 paces on structures above ground, of which, at some distance from the City, in several places where it crosses valleys, there are 463 paces on arches; nearer the City, beginning at the seventh milestone, 528 paces on substructures, and the remaining 6,472 paces on arches."

Since there were no censors in 144, public contracts would naturally be let by the consuls. Why the praetor was given the assignment we do not know, since there is no evidence that the consuls were away. Perhaps it was done because the Senate distrusted the consuls (Val. Max., 6, 4, 2). The enormous work, covering over 60 miles of conduits, nearly 7 of which rested on arches, was practically completed in 2 years. The water channel is nearly 1.7 by 2.5 meters and carried about 50,000,000 gallons of water per day. The work was magnificently done. The arches still to be seen near Porta Furba rest on piers of Anio stone (a haul of three miles at the nearest point). This seems to be the first use of this stone. The conduit rested on and was covered with Gabine stone slabs over six feet wide (the first use of this material, so far as is known). See Herschel, *The Water Supply of Rome*; Frank, *Roman Buildings*, 138; Platner and Ashby, *Top. Dict.*, 24. Presumably the praetor let out various contracts to a very large number of separate companies and individuals at Rome and in neighboring cities, for it is difficult to suppose that the enormous work could have been done by any one firm then in existence.

The Aqua Tepula was built under a censorial contract in 125. It was only a sixth as long as the Marcia and provided about one tenth the volume of water (Front., 1, 7). Cf. Platner and Ashby, op. cit., 27.

C. Gracchus also undertook a vast program of road-building and the construction of granaries, but no details concerning this work are given.

Festus, 370: Sempronia horrea . . . lege Gracchi ad custodiam frumenti publici. Cf. Plut., C. Gracc., 6, and Appian, B. C., 1, 21, quoted above.

The nature of the materials used proves that the second story of the prison (Tullianum) and at least the outlet of the Cloaca Maxima were constructed about this time (Frank, Roman Buildings, 42 and 142). Probably much sewer building and paving was carried out in the period, since the extensive building of aqueducts proves that the city was growing rapidly. This would all be censorial work let to contractors.

The rebuilding of the Concord temple in 121 (Appian, B. C., 1, 26) and of the Opimian Basilica were ordered by the Senate, and, though a consul supervised the work, it was probably done by equestrian companies. The same is true of the Metellan rebuilding of Magna Mater in 110 (Frank, op. cit., 96). Sulla seems also to have done some building and paving in Rome, but he doubtless let his contracts to independent contractors. All this work laid a heavy burden on the treasury, but the equestrian corporations had perhaps not much more than half of the work in their control.

The knights, however, had some other contracts. By Strabo's time the fishery rights in the western waters, especially about southern Spain, were well in the hands of societates, but we do not know whether they had begun to exploit them at this time.

4. Forests:

In 138 there was a famous inquiry at Rome regarding certain murders committed in the forests of Bruttium that were public property. In mentioning this, Cicero (Brut., 85) remarks that slaves of the publican companies that had the contract for producing pitch at Sila were involved in the charge. Later Strabo (6, 1, 9), Dionysius (20, 15), and Pliny (3, 74) still spoke of the woods of Sila as producing the best pitch. Since, according to Dionysius, the forests were excellent for ship and structural timber, it is likely that the companies also had contracts for timber cutting. What these contracts were worth we cannot say. Recently evidence has been found that the public forests behind Minturnae were in the hands of the publicans that extracted pitch.

It would be futile to attempt an estimate of all this contract work. Building and mining contracts certainly engaged much labor and money through most of the period; and after 123 the tithe contracts of Asia led to very lucrative business in the East. Many modest fortunes must have been made, and we should expect to find wealthy and influential knights making their way into the senatorial nobility in the period following. But very few did. P. Rupilius is a rare instance of a man who began as a humble tax collector and rose to the consulship (in 132; Val. Max., 6, 9, 8). The reason seems to be that Sulla's proscriptions quite wrecked the equestrian order and the large companies. It took a long time before the knights again reached the power they had exercised from 120 to 90.

VI. MONEY AND BANKING

1. *The supply of gold and silver.*

The volume of gold and silver kept increasing for Italy during the period, but precisely how much we cannot say. The mines of New Carthage (Strabo, 3, 2, 10) for a while brought 9,000,000 denarii annually to the state and as much to the knights who carried it to Rome. And these were not the only mines of Spain. Polybius (Strabo, 3, 2, 10), early reported silver at Castulo, Livy (28, 3) near Carteia, Cato (cf. Gell., 2, 22, 29) in the Pyrenees, and Posidonius, who travelled in Spain about 70 B. C., mentions the country of the Arotrebi in the northwest corner as productive of silver (Strabo, 3, 2, 9). Possibly some of the other places of Spain and of Gaul, mentioned later by Strabo (3, 2, 3; 3, 2, 8; 3, 4, 2, in Spain; 4, 1, 13; 4, 2, 1 in Gaul) had already begun to produce. It is quite probable that the Spanish mines alone yielded more silver and gold for Rome during the second part of the century than had come from the great indemnities and the booty during the first. Doubtless the gold mines above Vercellae, worked by some 5,000 men, also yielded good results for a few years (Strabo, 5, 1, 12; Pliny, 33, 78). The Macedonian mines, opened in 158, were not very productive, but for a while they were worth working. In Noricum,

Strabo (4, 6, 12; 5, 1, 8) quotes Polybius (before 120) as saying that rich placer-gold was discovered by the Celts and that when soon afterwards the Italians (presumably of Aquileia) joined in working the mine, the price of gold suddenly dropped a third throughout Italy. The Celts thereupon drove out the Italians. The passage shows, of course, that Italy became the chief market for the gold and, since Rome then had no gold coinage, the metal took its place in the market as any commodity, its price falling in relation to the silver denarius.

The passage reads as follows (Strabo, 4, 6, 12):

Ἔτι φησὶ Πολύβιος ἐφ᾽ ἑαυτοῦ κατ᾽ Ἀκυληΐαν μάλιστα ἐν τοῖς Ταυρίσκοις τοῖς Νωρικοῖς εὑρεθῆναι χρυσεῖον οὕτως εὐφυὲς ὥστ᾽ ἐπὶ δύο πόδας ἀποσύραντι τὴν ἐπιπολῆς γῆν εὐθὺς ὀρυκτὸν εὑρίσκεσθαι χρυσόν, τὸ δ᾽ ὄρυγμα μὴ πλειόνων ὑπάρχειν ἢ πεντεκαίδεκα ποδῶν, εἶναι δὲ τοῦ χρυσοῦ τὸν μὲν αὐτόθεν καθαρόν, κυάμου μέγεθος ἢ θέρμου, τοῦ ὀγδόου μέρους μόνον ἀφεψηθέντος, τὸν δὲ δεῖσθαι μὲν χωνείας πλείονος, σφόδρα δὲ λυσιτελοῦς· συνεργασαμένων δὲ τοῖς βαρβάροις τῶν Ἰταλιωτῶν ἐν διμήνῳ παραχρῆμα τὸ χρυσίον εὐωνότερον γενέσθαι τῷ τρίτῳ μέρει καθ᾽ ὅλην τὴν Ἰταλίαν, αἰσθομένους δὲ τοὺς Ταυρίσκους μονοπωλεῖν ἐκβαλόντας τοὺς συνεργαζομένους. ἀλλὰ νῦν ἅπαντα τὰ χρύσεια ὑπὸ Ῥωμαίοις ἐστί.

" Polybius further says that in his own time there was found, about opposite Aquileia in the country of the Noric Taurisci, a gold mine so well-suited for mining that, if one scraped away the surface-soil for a depth of only two feet, he found forthwith dug-gold, and that the diggings were never deeper than fifteen feet; and he goes on to say that part of the gold is immediately pure, in sizes of a bean or a lupine, when only the eighth part is boiled away, and that although the rest needs more smelting, the smelting is very profitable; and that two months after the Italiotes joined them in working the mine, the price of gold suddenly became a third less throughout the whole of Italy, but when the Taurisci learned this they cast out their fellow-workers and carried on a monopoly. Now, however, (in the Augustan day) all the gold mines are under the control of the Romans."

We have in Pliny three curious passages about mining in Italy. 3, 138: Metallorum omnium fertilitate nullis cedit terris, sed interdictum id vetere consulto patrum Italiae parci jubentium (Italy yields to no country in the richness of its ores, but mining was forbidden by an old decree of the Senate that ordered Italy to be spared). Also 33, 78 (after repeating the above): extat lex censoria Victimularum aurifodinae in Vercellensi agro qua cavebatur ne plus quinque milia hominum in opere publicani haberent (there is extant an old censorial order declaring that the gold mines of Victimulae should not employ over 5,000 men). Finally 37, 202: Metallis auri, argenti, aeris, ferri, quamdiu licuit exercere, nullis cessit terris (Italy was inferior to no country in veins of gold, silver, copper and iron so long as it was permissible to work them). Italy, of course, was never rich in ores.

Pais in *Dalle guerre Puniche,* II, 595 ff. comes to the conclusion that Rome was so concerned with agriculture that she forbade mining in Italy. That, of course, is an impossible explanation. Pliny seems to have some old *senatus consultum* in mind besides the censorial decree, but he does not give it. We cannot be certain of the facts till we know what the decree was. The *iron* mines of Elba, at least, were in operation through the last centuries of the Republic and well into the Empire. Perhaps at some time while at war with the Etruscans the Senate may have tried to have them closed. We know of no *silver* mines of any real productivity in Italy. If private enterprise started prospecting, it might be (say, after the Gracchan day) that the knights who bought the mining contracts in Spain might have objected to competition by private miners, but it is difficult to conjecture where such mines could have been. As for the gold mines of Victimulae, the state, having a sacred hoard in the treasury, might not care to see overproduction suddenly lower the price of its store, as happened when the Norican placer deposits were found. It could easily guard against this danger without ultimate loss to itself by limiting the number of miners, and 5,000 was not a low limit. Whatever the explanation of the restrictions, now lost, there are several reasonable hypotheses without assuming that the Senate was idiotic.

We have seen that the metals received by way of *booty* and *indemnities* were very much less in amount between 150 and 90 than before. Carthage had very little left when taken. The sums found in Corinth were probably large, though we are not told how large; most of the wars in Spain during this period were with the poorer tribes of the plateau, while the Jugurthine Wars brought in only some 3,000 talents. The Tolosan booty never reached the treasury; hence there was no record of it and exaggerated rumors about the amount spread abroad (Strabo, 4, 1, 13; Justinus, 32, 3, 10; Oros, 5, 15, 25). There had been large returns in captives, but here we are discussing metals. One should bear in mind that the officers and soldiers pocketed a much larger proportion of booty than before and that the sums reported to the treasury should probably be matched by such appropriations. (In the year 61, for instance, Pompey distributed over 50 per cent of his booty to his officers and soldiers; Pliny, 37, 16.).

In the Sullan decade there are reports of wild financing that we cannot control (see under *Public Finances*). Sulla took large amounts from Greek temples, ostensibly requiting them with land. The proceeds he coined in Greece for his army and presumably the soldiers spent most of it there (see Plut., *Luc.*, 2, 2; Grueber, *Coins of the Republic*, II, 459 ff.). Of the 20,000 talents taken from the Asiatics he carried to the treasury about one fifth (see above). But he had, of course, used much of it in Italy for stipends, gifts, and for his personal treasure. There was an unsuccessful attempt made later to recover some of it from his son (Cic., *pro Cluent.*, 94). Roman temple treasure was also put into circulation, since Sulla received 9,000 pounds of gold in 88 and the party of Cinna used great sums from the same source: cf. Val. Max., 7, 6, 4, and Pliny, 33, 16, who says that the younger Marius had 14,000 pounds of gold and 6,000 of silver, taken largely from the Capitoline temple when it burned in 83.

In general, then, we get the impression that the amount of new metals, due largely to productive mining, may well have kept up to the high level of 200-150 and that the metals that came to the knights, who conducted the mining, were more abundant than before. Officers and soldiers were also more liberally rewarded whenever booty was found. (Pliny, 33, 140-146: The younger Scipio had only 32 pounds of silverware at his death in 129, but his nephew, who conquered the Allobroges in 121, accumulated 1,000 pounds. Silver bed-frames and even cooking utensils of silver seem to come into frequent use during the Sullan period.) We therefore might expect a rise in the prices of commodities. However, we also notice that the use of silver plate and gold ornaments increased very much, removing precious metals permanently from circulation, that trade with the East expanded, and that the extension of the franchise through Italy and the inclusion in the Empire of Gaul and Asia greatly enlarged the field of commercial operations and investments. The increased production of the mines was probably absorbed fairly quickly as was the flow of gold from California in our railroad building and in the expenses of the Civil War of 1861-65.

2. *Coinage and Inflation.*

We have remarked that the treasury was in straits several times: in 150–146 (after which public land was offered for sale in Africa), after the lavish Gracchan laws were passed (when land was again offered for sale in Africa and at Corinth, see lex. agr. of 111), just before the Social War when Drusus proposed expensive laws, and repeatedly during the following wars in 90–80. Pliny reported the reserve in the treasury for the year 91 B. C. as he did for 157 and for 49, but in this case our manuscripts have lost an important line so that we do not know the amount of the gold and silver bullion, but only of the coined silver: Pliny, 33, 55: auri . . . ⟨argenti⟩ . . . ⟨numerati⟩ ⎡XVI⎤ XX DCCCXXXI. "gold . . . . . . ⟨coined silver⟩ 1,620,831 sesterces." At any rate the exceedingly small amount of coined silver shows that the sum total could not have been large. We shall here mention the attempts of the treasury to recoup by issuing " debased " coinage and by passing debtor laws.

Pliny, 33, 46: Livius Drusus in tribunatu plebei octavam partem aeris argento miscuit (Livius Drusus—tribune 91 B. C.—mixed the silver with an eighth of bronze). The coins that have survived are almost all pure silver (Grueber, *Coins of the Republic,* xlii), but a few silver-plated ones have been found despite the state's attempt to withdraw them later. Apparently the debasement was done by issuing one eighth of the coins in plated copper so that the inferior coins could be extracted later if need be. (See Grueber, I, no. 1292, p. 200, with note.) It would seem that the treasury was not well stocked with silver and that Drusus needed money for his proposed doles and colonization. The plating was not necessarily meant as a fraudulent coinage, for the plated coins lack ¼ in weight and were therefore easily recognized; the issue may in fact have been accompanied by a promise to redeem as soon as possible. It is a very interesting experiment, but since the coin was too small to carry a visible promise of redemption, since it would not pass in foreign trade, and since people were not used to token silver, there were many objections. The coinage seems to have continued for some five years till the popular outcry became too powerful and the praetors (of 85 or 84) decided to eliminate the cheap coins, establishing a state assay office for passing on coinage. See Cicero, *de Off.*, 3, 80 (and comment in *Realenc.*, " Marius Gratidianus "):

iactabatur enim temporibus illis nummus sic, ut nemo posset scire, quid haberet. Conscripserunt (praetores) communiter edictum cum poena atque iudicio constitueruntque, ut omnes simul in rostra post meridiem escenderent. Et ceteri quidem alius alio, Marius ab subselliis in rostra recta idque, quod communiter compositum fuerat, solus edixit. Et ea res, si quaeris, ei magno honori fuit; omnibus vicis statuae, ad eas tus, cerei; quid multa? nemo umquam multitudini fuit carior.

" Coins fluctuated so much in value in that period that no one could tell what he was worth. The praetors, acting in harmony, wrote out an edict defining penalties and legal action in case of infringement and decided that they should all mount the rostra together that afternoon; and while all the rest departed, some one way, some another, Marius Gratidianus went straight to the rostra, and by himself gave out what had been by common consent agreed upon by them. This act of his, I assure you, brought him great glory, for statues were erected to him on all the streets, and before these incense and tapers were burned. In a word, no one has been more loved by the multitude."

Pliny, 33, 132:

igitur ars facta denarios probare, tam jucunda plebei lege, ut Mario Gratidiano vicatim tota statuas dicaverit.

" Then the art of testing silver coins was established by a law so pleasing to the populace that they dedicated statues on all the streets to Gratidianus."

It is noteworthy that an aristocratic leader, Livius, introduced this coinage and that the partisans of the democratic leaders Cinna and Carbo abolished it and gained popularity by doing so. Furthermore, when Sulla returned, the statues of Gratidianus were thrown down (Pliny, 34, 27), and Sulla seems to have insisted that the state coinage must be accepted at face value; that is, he did not intend for the present to redeem any more light coins. (Paulus, *Sent.*, 5, 25, 1, which applies strictly to imperial coins, but refers back to a similar law of Sulla: lege Cornelia testamentaria tenetur, qui vultu principum signatam monetam, praeter adulterinam, reprobaverit, " he is held responsible under the Sullan law who refuses a coin stamped with the emperor's image ".) For this period, at least, it would seem that aristocratic leaders of the state were apt to entertain the idea of using in coinage the fiat of the state, while the populace and the business men wanted only sound money. Probably the base coins that remained were eliminated very soon after Sulla's fall, for relatively few plated coins have survived, and most of these are coins that were lost or buried between 91 and 88. Herzog, *Aus der Geschichte des Bankwesens*, has shown that the famous *tesserae*, made of bone (*C. I. L.*, I², 889-95) and bearing the letters *sp.* or *spect.* with a date, were probably used to seal bags of coins that had been inspected (spectavit). Such *tesserae* were especially in favor during and after the plated issues.

3. *Debtor laws.*

But this so-called "debasement" was not the only source of trouble to bankers and money-lenders. The sudden outbreak of the Social (Italian) War in 90 had frozen credits and endangered the property rights of Roman landlords who owned estates in the areas of the rebels. In 89 a praetor, A. Sempronius Asellio, had attempted to relieve the stringency and prevent foreclosures, apparently by trying to resuscitate an obsolete law against the taking of interest. Riots, incited by a tribune, ensued in which the money lenders of the Forum became violent, and the praetor was killed. Appian gives a brief account of the affair.

Appian, *B. C.*, 1, 54:

Τοῦ δ' αὐτοῦ χρόνου κατὰ τὸ ἄστυ οἱ χρῆσται πρὸς ἀλλήλους ἐστασίασαν, οἱ μὲν πράττοντες τὰ χρέα σὺν τόκοις, νόμου τινὸς παλαιοῦ διαγορεύοντος μὴ δανείζειν ἐπὶ τόκοις ἢ ζημίαν τὸν οὕτω δανείσαντα προσοφλεῖν. . . . ἔθους δὲ χρονίου τοὺς τόκους βεβαιοῦντος, οἱ μὲν κατὰ τὸ ἔθος ᾔτουν, οἱ δὲ οἷον ἐκ πολέμων τε καὶ στάσεων ἀνεβάλλοντο τὰς ἀποδόσεις· εἰσὶ δ' οἱ καὶ τὴν ζημίαν τοὺς δανείσαντας ἐκτίσειν ἐπηπείλουν.

Ὅ τε στρατηγὸς Ἀσελλίων, ᾧ ταῦτα προσέκειτο, ἐπεὶ διαλύων αὐτοὺς οὐκ ἔπειθεν, ἐδίδου κατ' ἀλλήλων αὐτοῖς δικαστήρια, τὴν ἐκ τοῦ νόμου καὶ ἔθους ἀπορίαν ἐς τοὺς δικαστὰς περιφέρων. οἱ δανεισταὶ δὲ χαλεπήναντες, ὅτι τὸν νόμον παλαιὸν ὄντα ἀνεκαίνιζε, κτείνουσιν αὐτὸν . . . καὶ ἡ σύγκλητος ἐκήρυσσεν, εἴ τίς τι περὶ τὸν Ἀσελλίωνος φόνον ἐλέγξειεν, ἐλευθέρῳ μὲν ἀργύριον, δούλῳ δὲ ἐλευθερίαν, συνεγνωκότι δὲ ἄδειαν· οὐ μὴν ἐμήνυσεν οὐδείς, τῶν δανειστῶν περικαλυψάντων.

"About the same time dissensions arose in the city between debtors and creditors, since the latter exacted the money due to them with interest, although an old law distinctly forbade lending on interest and imposed a penalty upon any one doing so. . . . . . But, since time had sanctioned the practice of taking interest, the creditors demanded it according to custom. The debtors, on the other hand, put off their payments on the plea of war and civil commotion. Some indeed threatened to exact the legal penalty from the interest-takers.

The praeter Asellio, who had charge of these matters, as he was not able to compose their differences by persuasion, allowed them to proceed against each other in the courts, thus bringing the deadlock due to the conflict of law and custom before the judges. The leaders, exasperated that the now obsolete law was being revived, killed the praetor . . . . . The Senate offered a reward of money to any free citizen, freedom to any slave, impunity to any accomplice, who should give testimony leading to the conviction of the murderers of Asellio, but nobody gave any information. The money-lenders covered up everything." (cf. Livy, *Epit.* 74; Val. Max., 9, 7, 4).

Since Valerius says that the creditors were stirred up by a tribune, L. Cassius (concitati a L. Cassio tribuno plebis), it is likely that Sempronius Asellio was not acting in the interest of the urban poor but in that of involved landlords who needed a moratorium until they could regain possession of their estates. It is not unlikely that the knights and small business men who had lent their surplus were here on the side of the money-lenders of the Forum. Asconius (Stangl, 69) says explicitly that the knights favored the democratic party. That the landlords were the men favored by the praetor would also appear from the proposal of the popular tribune, P. Sulpicius Rufus, in the next year, who passed a short-sighted plebiscite forbidding senators to incur debts of over 2,000 denarii; Plut., *Sulla*, 8: νόμον δὲ κυρώσας μηδένα συγκλητικὸν ὑπὲρ δισχιλίας δραχμὰς ὀφείλειν, " passing a law that no senator should incur debts of over 2,000 drachmas ". It seems to have been Sulpicius' idea that, if the nobility could be kept from going into debt, the Senate would not interfere with the business customs of the Forum. Of course, Sulla soon entered Rome (in 88) and all the Sulpician laws were revoked. Sulla seems actually to have passed a law in favor of debtors, though we have only a fragmentary reference to it; Festus, 516: Unciaria lex appellari coepta est quam L. Sulla et Q. Pom⟨peius Rufus⟩ tulerunt qua sanctum est ut debitores decimam partem . . . . . " the ' law of the twelfth part ' they began to call the law passed by Sulla and Pompeius (88 B. C.) by which it was permitted debtors . . . a tenth . . . . ".

Probably two clauses were in the law: (1) the words *debitores decimam partam* seem to imply an immediate reduction of a tenth of debts, and (2) the name *unciaria lex* (a later appellation) refers to a maximum rate of interest of an ounce to the pound per month, *i. e.* 12 per cent. Sulla, then, was not helping the poor with a Catilinarian program, but rather bringing some relief to the landlords who were in debt (Frank, " Financial legislation ", *Am. Jour. Phil.*, 1933).

By 87 the war had ended, Sulla went East, and the democrats took charge of the state. Many of the senators made the best of the situation and decided that it was wise to cooperate with the party in power. As the civil war continued and financial burdens increased, as the knights also suffered severely from the raid of Mithridates in Asia, all parties were now ready to admit that the problem of debts had to be faced again, and in 86 a drastic law was passed by the people, supported by all the propertied interests, remitting three-fourths of all debts. Sallust, *Cat.*, 33 : propter magnitudinem aeris alieni, *volentibus omnibus bonis*, argentum aere solutum est. " because of the magnitude of debts, silver (sesterces) was paid with bronze (asses) with the approval of all the conservatives ". Cf. Velleius (2, 23), who did not quite comprehend the conditions: Valerius Flaccus turpissimae legis auctor, qua creditoribus quadrantem solvi jusserat. " Valerius Flaccus—consul in 86—the proposer of a base law, whereby creditors were ordered to receive only a fourth ". This law remained in force for past debts, money-lenders suffered, and debts and mortgages were of course cleared off to a large extent.

We have two early references in Cicero to the operation of the law:

Cic., *pro Font.*, i :

defendo M. Fonteium, iudices, itaque contendo, post legem Valeriam latam . . . usque ad T. Crispinum quaestorem aliter neminem solvisse; hunc omnium superiorum, huius autem omnes, qui postea fuerint, auctoritatem dico secutos. . . . . . Laudas illum, quod dodrantarias tabulas instituerit; easdem Fonteius instituit et eodem genere pecuniae.

" For my defence, gentlemen of the jury, of Marcus Fonteius, my contention is that, since the enactment of the Valerian law, from his quaestorship until that of Titus Crispinus no one has ever paid otherwise; I assert that my client followed the example of all his predecessors, while all my client's successors have followed his. . . . . . You praise Hirtuleius for his method of making reductions of three-fourths in the accounts; Fonteius instituted the same method with regard to the same type of money."

Fonteius was quaestor of the treasury in 85 or 84 and repaid state debts according to the Valerian law, that is, he paid only 25 per cent. Hence the state also profited somewhat by the law; but since the Roman state could not diminish the pay of soldiers and, in fact, did not often accumulate debts, the public treasury probably lost more than it gained by the law.

Cic., *pro Quinctio*, 17 (81 B. C.):

Cum pecuniam C. Quinctius P. Scapulae debuisset, per te, C. Aquili, decidit P. Quinctius, quid liberis eius dissolveret. Hoc eo per te agebatur, quod propter aerariam rationem non satis erat in tabulis inspexisse, quantum deberetur, nisi ad Castoris quaesisses, quantum solveretur. Decidis statuisque tu propter necessitudinem, quae tibi cum Scapulis est, quid iis ad denarium solveretur.

"Since Gaius was indebted to Publius Scapula, his brother Publius, according to your decision, Aquilius, settled how much he had to pay to Scapula's children. The question had to be settled by you, because, owing to the rate of exchange, it was not enough to examine the account-books for the amount of the debt, but also you had to make inquiries near the temple of Castor how much he had to pay. You settled the question, and, in consideration of your intimate friendship with the Scapulae, decided how much ought to be paid to them, reckoning in *denarii*."

Publius Quinctius had inherited from his brother a debt to Scapula incurred before 86. He seems to have paid it about 83 B. C. (The speech was delivered in 81). In paying debts in 83 not only would he come under the benefit of the Valerian law (quid iis ad denarium) but also under the law of Gratidianus that insisted on eliminating plated coins. Hence he had to take his money to the Castor temple to have it tested and vouched for (ad Castoris).

4. *Banking.*

This, as we see, was a period of great uncertainty for money-lenders. In the first part much money flowed to Rome from mines, and money must have been plentiful. Since, according to Polybius, 6, 17, state-contracts involved large borrowed sums, we may assume that men who had ready money profited. Then, when Gracchus opened up Asia to tax-contractors and investors and the trade through Delos increased, we must assume large profits for Roman financiers in the East. But the period of 91–80 was disastrous. The Livian law of 91 introducing plated coins caused trouble and the Social War endangering property-holdings through Italy caused more difficulties. Sulla found it necessary to introduce a legal maximum on interest rates (12 per cent), as we have seen. Then came the Mithridatic devastation of Asia whereby the knights suffered severe losses and with them their sureties at Rome, and for five years the *equites* could do no business in Asia. Then came the Valerian law of 86 remitting three-fourths of all debts. From this, of course, money-lenders suffered most, and they had doubtless lost sympathy by their riots in 89 and the murder of the praetor so that they were unable to resist the Valerian law.

When Sulla imposed a fine of 20,000 talents on the Asiatic communities (App., *Mith.*, 62-3; Plut., *Sulla*, 25, *Luc.*, 7 and 20), the victims had to resort to money-lenders who charged high rates of interest. We shall discuss the results later. Suffice it here to say that some Roman money then went East, though—considering Sulla's hostility to the knights and bankers—we can hardly suppose that any large proportion came from Rome to aid Sulla's expropriations. Probably eastern money was largely involved in this venture and in the subsequent losses when Lucullus declared the interest charges exorbitant and cancelled most of them. But when Sulla returned to Rome in 83 and instituted against all his enemies his atrocious proscriptions, in which 1600 knights fell, it is difficult to see how the bankers of the Forum survived. Some poor scions of decaying families, men like Crassus and Catiline, seized the opportunity to get good bargains during Sulla's proscriptions, but we do not hear that bankers of obscure families found opportunities to profit in the same way.

The " tesserae consulares " or seals for money bags, mentioned above (see *C. I. L.*, I², 889-951, 2517, 2663a-c, discussed by Herzog, *Aus der Geschichte des Bankwesens*) might give us some needed information about banking, if we knew precisely what they were. We have over 60 of them, mostly from Rome (four from Capua, two from Pompeii, and a few others from Italian towns, but only one from outside of Italy). They date from 96 B. C. to Nero's age. The usual form of inscription on the four sides respectively may be illustrated by No. 907:

Philargyrus

Epilli

Sp(ectavit) Kal. Jan(uariis)

M Tul(lio) C Ant(onio consulibus)

That is, " Philargyrus (the slave and agent) of Epillius, inspected (and sealed this) on the first of January in the consulship of Cicero and Antonius " (i. e. 63 B. C.).

Cary (*Jour. Rom. Stud.*, 1923, 110) has pointed out that some sixteen of the firm names of the republican period also occur among business men of Delos, but he is careful to add that these names are not unusual. Furthermore none of these *tesserae* have as yet been found in Delos. It has been noticed that fifteen of the same period contain names that occur among the two hundred known names of knights, but again the names are common ones. If these marks had reference to the law of Gratidianus of 85 which ordered the inspection of coins and the withdrawal of plated ones, we should expect a state seal. If private firms of *argentarii* entered the business of testing for a fee, we should expect a few offices to do the business, but nearly every new *tessera* found provides a new name. Furthermore the firm names represented are almost all Roman, whereas the *argentarii* of the Republic seem to have been largely foreigners. Finally one has recently been found (*C. I. L.*, I², 2663 a) issued in 94 by an agent of a mining firm, which proves at least that some were not used by bankers. It reads as follows:

> Piloxen. Soc. Fer.
> C. Coil L. Dom.
> Spectavit
> N. Apr.

Perhaps the best hypothesis at present is that during a time when much foreign and some plated money circulated at Rome, business firms, merchants, bankers, knights and landlords who had frequent dealings in sums of a thousand sesterces (presumably), adopted the custom of testing and conveying in sealed bags the larger amounts. The seals then bore the name of the owner and his " financial secretary," with the date of sealing. If this should prove to be correct, only a fraction, though perhaps a considerable fraction, of the seals belonged to bankers. We have so little information about individual *argentarii* for this period that I shall leave further consideration of the subject of banking till I reach the next period.

19

VII. COMMERCE

1. *The prosperity of Delos.*

We have noticed that Romans were reluctant to trade on the seas, though their allies in the south of Italy took advantage of Rome's prestige and expanded their activities both east and west.   When Rome, after her victory over Perseus, declared Delos a free port, that sanctuary, which had always treated all traders with equal hospitality, soon became a meeting place of Aegean shippers.   When Corinth fell, Delos became the favorite market for traders that exchanged goods between the Aegean and the Adriatic, and when Carthage was destroyed, the Syrian traders who had resorted to North Africa preferred to exchange their goods at Delos.   Later, when Gaius Gracchus turned over the tithe-gathering of Asia to Roman publicans, Delos became the favorite way-station for these also.   The publicans, of course, had to gather a large staff of agents who could speak Greek, and they doubtless found their men at the ports of South Italy and at Delos.   The tithe-gathering in Asia quickly revealed extensive opportunities in lucrative business ventures, especially in placing mortgages and in lending money to the cities and to individuals who were delinquent in their taxes.   The *lex Antonia* of 72 B. C. (Dessau, 38, l. 35), by securing free ports for the goods of the publicans, seems to justify the inference that the tithe was sometimes taken in kind and marketed by the publicans for an added profit.   At any rate the publicans were apparently in trade.

Rhodes had formerly done much to police the eastern seas, but after Delos became a free port, the trade of Rhodes fell and she could no longer afford to maintain a strong fleet.   The result was that piracy, which had sprung up on the Cilician coast, became a menace to trade. Rome was now master of the Aegean, but took only half-hearted measures toward suppressing the nuisance.   This dilatory behavior is rather characteristic of the Senate, which, controlled by landlords, found it difficult to think in any but agrarian terms.   If Roman landlords had provided any large part of the wine and oil that had begun to flow eastward, it is difficult to see how they could have been so obtuse to the interests of trade.   It was during the democratic interlude of 103-100 that some vigorous steps were first taken against the pirates.   In 102 M. Antonius was sent out to take Cilicia, their stronghold, the principal motive being in this case to suppress the pirates who carried on kidnap-

ping expeditions on land and sea.   It was the complaint of the king of
Bithynia to Marius that spurred Rome to action.   The next year the
people, after listening to a Rhodian delegation, passed the famous law
found at Delphi (*Supp. Ep. Graec.*, III, 378, with bibl.) which called
upon all allied cities and nations to refuse the pirates admission to their
harbors, in order that " Roman citizens and Italian allies might in
safety carry on business on the seas."   This action also was taken by
the democratic assembly.   The citizens here mentioned may well be
largely people of the Campanian region, but the law would of course
be of aid to the publicans of Rome, who had a closer alliance with the
Marian party than with the Senate.   And yet even this law was passed
at the initiative of *Rhodes.*

Later the pirates were aided and abetted by Mithridates (Appian,
Mith., 63; 92) and Rome had to fit out expeditions against them as a
part of her campaign against the king; but apart from the exigencies
of this greater warfare little was accomplished, and as we shall see in
the next chapter nothing of importance was done till the knights, in
control of the assembly, disregarded the Senate and sent Pompey to
clear the seas (Ormerod, *Piracy in the Ancient World*; also Chapter
VIII of *Camb. Anc. Hist.*, IX, with bibl.).

2. *The Italian business men at Delos.*

The earlier inscriptions of free Delos show that the traders of
Alexandria, Syria, and Asia were quick to take advantage of the free
port.   But even before that time a banker of Syracuse is found there
(Durrbach, *Choix d'inscriptions de Délos*, no. 66) and by 157 B. C.
we find the name of a Tarentine banker as well (*ibid.*, p. 88).   After
the fall of Carthage and Corinth many south Italians appear there.
In the Greek inscriptions they are usually called ῾Ρωμαῖοι, so that our
archaeologists at first assumed that they were Roman citizens, but the
inscriptions written in Latin used the more correct designation *Italici*
(Frank, in *Classical Journal*, 1910, 99; Hatzfeld, in *Bull. Corr. Hell.*,
1912, 130).   None of the traders mentioned can be referred to the
city of Rome before the Gracchan day.   The provenience of these
traders is mentioned in relatively few cases.   The list as given by
Hatzfeld, *loc. cit.*, is as follows: Naples (several); Cumae; Velia (6);
Syracuse (4, and probably we should add Trebius Loisius); Petelia;
Heraclea (6); Locris; Tarentum (4); Azetium in Apulia (2);
Canusium; Lanuvium; Fregellae; Ancona.   Moreover a large number

of the names recorded are such as one finds only in Campania and the South. Incidentally, this is evidence that the South Italian towns were still rather more prosperous than one would gather from Ciaceri, *Storia della Magna Grecia*, III, 256 ff.

The *Italici* at Delos, whether traders or their agents (freedmen or slaves), usually formed themselves into clubs. The earliest known of these called itself the Mercuriales (in Greek, *Hermaistai*) and is mentioned in a dedication of about 140 B. C. The club at that time had six magistri (Durrbach, nos. 86, 96), partly free men, partly freedmen. Hatzfeld, *B. C. H.*, 1912, 155, records six other inscriptions of the kind extending down to about 50 B. C.

The collegium called the Apolloniastai (Durrbach, 97) and that of the Neptuniales or Poseidoniastai (*ibid.,* 98) are of the same general kind, the latter consisting in the main of shippers. Several times these three collegia act together in giving gifts or honors (*ibid.,* 116, dated 113 B. C.; of the 12 magistri 6 are ex-slaves). The Competaliastai (*ibid.,* 145) seem to consist entirely of slaves and freedmen, presumably of humble folk serving as agents and clerks. All of these clubs consist of Italians—some using the Greek language, others Latin—and, so far as can be determined, the traders come from a variety of places but almost always from towns south of Rome. Besides these groups, which took their names from their " patron-saints," there is in the Sullan period a club of Olearii (*ibid.,* 141), apparently composed of members who were all from Italy. The Italian wine dealers (*ibid.,* 142) and apparently the bankers (argentarii, *ibid.,* p. 213) also organized in a similar way.

These groups did not, as was formerly supposed, have anything to do with the government of Delos, nor does there seem to have been any general organization (*conventus*) of the Italians at Delos, any more than there is of the American or English " colony " in Rome or Paris today. Whenever the population of the island met to adopt resolutions, the Italians—though numerous enough to receive special mention—met with the Athenian residents and other traders in a wholly unofficial way. The usual formula in such dedications of the foreign group about 120 B. C. is: " The Athenians dwelling in Delos and the Italians sojourning there and the merchants and shippers."

Here are two representative inscriptions of Italians at Delos that are written in both Latin and Greek:

1. *C. I. L.*, I², 2236:

C. Heius T. f. Libo   L. Pompilius [L. F.]
Q. Saufeius P. f. Treb.   A. Cottius N. f.
L. Veturius P. f.   M. Umbricius M. f.
D. Ampius Q. l.   L. Aufidius L. C. l. Dorot. minor
L. Paconius L. l. Trup.   C. Seius Cn. l. Heracleo
Ti. Maecius L. l.   Cn. Tutorius P. l. Olumpiod.

magistreis de sua pecunia Iovei Sequndano.

The Greek version (omitted) shows that the dedication was made by the *magistri* of the three main clubs of Mercury, Apollo, and Neptune. It may be noticed that six of the men are ex-slaves. The date is about 110 B. C.

2. *C. I. L.*, I², 2235:

Μαάρκος Γράνιος Μαάρκου Ἡρᾶς, | Διόδοτος Σήιος Γαίου καὶ Γναίου, | Ἀπολ-
λώνιος Λαίλιος Κοίντου, | Πρέπων Ἄλλιος Μαάρκου, | Νίκανδρος Ῥασέννιος
Μαάρκο[υ], | Διὰ Ἐλευθέριον ἀνέθηκαν. |

M. Granius M. l. Her., | Diodotus Seius C. Cn. s., | Apollonius Laelius Q. s., | Prepon Alleius M. s., | Nicandrus Rasenni M. s., | Iovem Leiberum statuer.

Here there are four slaves and one ex-slave. The cognomina of the freedmen and slaves are quite regularly Greek, the nomina are usually those of Campanian and Lucanian Italians. For other inscriptions of the kind see *C. I. L.*, I², nos. 705, 714, 830, 831, 845, 2232-59, 2651, and Durrbach, *Choix d'inscriptions de Délos*.

3. *Roman and Italian traders in the provinces.*

During the same period we find Italians trading here and there in other parts of *Greece* and the islands, at Delphi, at Argos, in Boeotia, Euboea, on the islands of Tenos, Amorgos, Chios, and Cos, and at Athens, where there are not only inscriptions by many individuals but also mention of a Roman " colony " (see Hatzfeld, *Les Trafiquants*, 41, and the section on Greece). It is interesting to note that Roman business brought the Roman denarius into repute in Greece so that about 100 B. C. we find values given in denarii in Boeotia (*Inscr. Graec.*, 7, 4147).

Asia Minor shows the largest groups, especially after the Gracchan plan of tax-gathering was adopted in 123, but even before, the list of the 200 strangers staying in Pergamum in 133 contains at least seven Italic names. Even officials were not above making business deals. Roman staff officers lent the king of Bithynia money in 89 (Appian,

Mith. 11), and Verres, while quaestor of Dolabella, made investments in Asia (Cic., *Verr.*, 2, 1, 91). In 88 Mithridates, on invading the Roman province, gave orders to kill " all Romans and Italians including women, children, and freedmen of Italic stock " (App., *Mith.*, 22). It is reported that 80,000 were killed (Memnon, *F. H. gr.*, 31: μυριάδας ὀκτὼ ἐν μιᾷ καὶ τῇ αὐτῇ ἡμέρᾳ τὸν διὰ ξίφους ὄλεθρον ὑποστῆναι " on one day 80,000 fell by the sword "; Val. Max., 9, 1, 3: Una epistola L̄X̄X̄X̄ civium Romanorum in Asia per urbes negotiandi gratia dispersa interemit " by one order he destroyed 80,000 Roman citizens (?) scattered about the cities of Asia for the sake of business." A quotation of a contemporary, Posidonius, is given in Athenaeus, 5, 213, repeating a speech that was delivered at Athens just before the massacre: " Of all the other Romans some are prostrated before the images of the gods, while the rest have changed their dress to square cloaks (the Greek garb) and *once more* call themselves by the countries to which they originally belonged." This means that they were largely south Italians who had hastily assumed the Roman toga the year before when they heard of the grant of franchise to the whole of Italy, and that on the approach of Mithridates they doffed the new Roman dress, reassuming their Greek garb. Probably the freedmen of eastern origin did the same. This therefore implies that not very many actual citizens were in Asia, but that the publicans had non-citizen agents there and that the independent business men of the West who were also operating there—a very large number—were from the part of Italy where the toga had not been worn more than a year. However, the sources are not wholly incorrect in calling them *cives,* even if few of them had had time to register as such.

Later, when peace was restored by Lucullus, many Roman knights went to Asia in person to pick up the bargains in the wake of the havoc wrought there more by Sulla than by Mithridates (Cic., later, *lex Man.*, 17, 18, mentions not only the tax-gathering but also the investments; but the conditions disclosed by Cicero's letters must not be read into the period 125-88 when South Italians were in the majority among the negotiatores of Asia).

To *Sicily,* Italians of the South had resorted for business at an early day. In fact the Mamertines invaded and took possession of Messina before the First Punic War. During the second war, in 205, the Syracusans appealed to Scipio for aid against a lawless group *Italici generis* (Livy, 29, 1, 16) and a few years later a group of Italians at Halaesa raised an honorary inscription to the Roman governor of the island:

Italicei L. Cornelium Scipionem honoris caussa (*C. I. L.*, I², 612, apparently in 193 B. C.).

Since the equestrian *societates* of Rome were not permitted (though individual knights were) to accept tithe-gathering contracts in Sicily (Carcopino, *La loi de Hiéron*, 86), the knights did not spread over Sicily as quickly as they might have, but it is clear from the Verrine orations (see next period) that many Romans owned farms and ranches and did various kinds of business there. However, it is difficult to sift the evidence regarding the provenance of these men because by the year 70 many of the distinguished Sicilians bore Latin names, having been given citizenship, and all the South Italian men living in Sicily had won citizenship in 89 because of the Social War. Cicero even claims, for the sake of the effect, that the Italian pirates (who probably had not registered in 89) were Roman citizens. Diodorus in writing of the Servile War of 134 repeatedly speaks of the rich *Italici* who had large estates and ranches with hordes of slaves in Sicily.

Cf. 34, 2, 27: " The richest of the Sicilians emulated the *Italici.*"
Ibid., 32: " The *Italici,* who possessed the largest fields in Sicily."
Ibid., 34: " Damophilus of Enna . . . who had very wide fields and very large flocks emulated the *Italici* who dwelt in Sicily, etc."

The one passage (*ibid.*, 31) in which he refers to Roman knights apparently concerns a later day, when knights were on the jury panels (therefore, after 123). It probably comes not from his source but from a mistaken inference:

οἱ πλεῖστοι γὰρ τῶν κτητόρων ἱππεῖς ὄντες ἐντελεῖς τῶν Ῥωμαίων, καὶ κριταὶ τοῖς ἀπὸ τῶν ἐπαρχιῶν κατηγορουμένοις στρατηγοῖς γινομενοὶ, φοβεροὶ ταῖς ἀρχαῖς ὑπῆρχον.

" Most of the possessors being Roman knights, who were then *judices* of the courts that tried the governors after their term of office, were naturally feared by the governors."

It is clear then that South Italians invaded Sicily during the second century B. C., at the very time when the Romans were spreading over Italy. Indeed it is very likely that when Italians were driven off the public lands by Roman renters and by the Gracchan assignments, they moved into Sicily in large numbers, especially after the devastation of Sicily by the first Servile War, which gave immigrants a chance for a new start. However, the evidence is too scanty to complete the story. (For conditions in Sicily see the forthcoming section on Sicily).

The Romans and North Italians on the other hand seem to have spread northward into Cisalpine and Narbonese *Gaul,* and of course chiefly into farming and ranching. Precise evidence is here again lacking, but the very fact that in 89 all of Cispadane Gaul could be given full citizenship and Transpadane Gaul could be granted Latin rights is proof enough that Romanization had gone on rapidly. The Alpine passes were well protected by Rome during the period, and the continued road building and the draining of the marshes (by Scaurus in 109) show that the state approved of the movement. In Augustus' day the whole fertile valley was a garden. Aquileia had not yet become the great clearing house of the upper Adriatic that it was to be during the Empire, but the fact that Rome had a tariff-station there at least as early as 75 (Cic., *pro Font.*, 2) shows that it was already an important harbor.

Narbonese Gaul was soon overrun by Romans after the Domitian way was built to Spain and the citizen colony was planted at Narbo in 118 B. C. The Rhone canal built by Marius in 103 was made for the purpose of bringing up military supplies (Pliny, 3, 33; Strabo, 4, 1, 8). For our period we have few facts, but two speeches of Cicero, the *Pro Quinctio*, 81 B. C., and the *Pro Fonteio*, which gives hints of conditions in 74 B. C., reveal what had been going on. The *Pro Quinctio* deals with a partnership by two Romans (both apparently from the city), formed many years before 81 B. C. The men engaged on an extensive scale in farming and grazing north of Narbo (pecuaria res ampla et rustica sane bene culta et fructuosa, *ibid.,* 12). The *Pro Fonteio* has many exaggerations in emphasizing the fact that citizens, though numerous in Narbonese Gaul, had not been called in as witnesses by the prosecution. But even after proper deductions are made one gains the impression that Narbo had served as a wide channel in pouring Romans into Gaul.

Cic., *pro Font.,* 11-12:

Referta Gallia negotiatorum est, plena civium Romanorum. Nemo

Gallorum sine cive Romano quicquam negotii gerit, nummus in Gallia nullus sine civium Romanorum tabulis commovetur. Videte, quo descendam, iudices, quam longe videar ab consuetudine mea et cautione ac diligentia discedere. Unae tabulae proferantur, in quibus vestigium sit aliquod, quod significet pecuniam M. Fonteio datam, unum ex tanto negotiatorum, colonorum, publicanorum, aratorum, pecuariorum numero testem producant; vere accusatum esse concedam.

" Gaul is packed with traders, crammed with Roman citizens. No Gaul ever does business independently of a citizen of Rome; not a penny changes hands in Gaul without the transaction being recorded in the books of Roman citizens. Mark my condescension, gentlemen, and how far I am departing from my customary habits of caution and exactitude. Let one single account be produced in which there is a single hint indicating that money has been given to Fonteius; let them bring forward the evidence of one single trader, colonist, tax-farmer, agriculturist, or grazier out of all the inhabitants; and I will grant that the charge is a true one."

In chapter 46 of this speech the Romans in Gaul are designated in four groups: publicani, agricolae, pecuarii, ceteri negotiatores (publicans, farmers, grazers, and *other* business men). Since the contract system was not used in Gaul for the collection of the regular stipend, we may suppose that the publicans were there to gather the cattle-tax on public pastures and the harbor- and road-dues.

Of Roman business enterprises in *Spain* we know but little for this period except about the mining contracts spoken of above. But such activity must have disclosed the business opportunities available to knights who visited the peninsula. We must remember, however, that the richest part of Andalusia was already well occupied by Punic settlers (Strabo, 3, 2, 13) and that these were as shrewd business men as any Romans. The roads built by the Romans were military ones, and the light-house erected at the mouth of the Baetis by Servilius Caepio (Strabo, 3, 1, 9) and the dock at Lisbon (*ibid.*, 3, 3, 1) were probably meant to serve especially the needs of the military transports that carried supplies to the armies.

The great and rich Punic city of Gades that succeeded Carthage in the Atlantic trade (Strabo, 3, 1, 8; 3, 2, 1; 3, 2, 6; 3, 5, 3) was not

disturbed.   Her clearing house was Rome, and her merchants spent
their leisure in the wine shops and gardens of Rome (Strabo, 3, 5, 3).

Africa also was soon invaded by Italian *negotiatores,* in fact some
were in Carthage before it fell (Pol., 36, 7; App., *Pun.,* 92), but these
were apparently the southern type of Greco-Italic trader rather than
the northern land-hungry type.   After Carthage was destroyed, the
Punic towns like Utica and Hadrumetum doubtless captured some of
the trade with the Numidians, but Massinissa, who had developed agriculture in the interior brilliantly, had had many friendly contacts with
Rome and his successors continued these relations.   C. Gracchus sent
some 6,000 farmers to Africa, who doubtless needed to keep in touch
with Rome.   Gracchus probably meant to open a port there, but on
his death the Senate took no interest in the settlement.   It is therefore
not surprising that during the Jugurthine War we hear of Romans
and Italians at Utica and Vaga (Sall., *Jug.,* 64, 5: negotiatores, magna
multitudo, and 47, 1: Italici generis) and especially of a group at
Cirta that was strong enough to direct the defence of the town against
Jugurtha (Sall., *Jug.,* 21, 2: multitudo togatorum; 26: Italici, quorum virtute moenia defensabantur . . . negotiatores).   For details see
the section on Africa.   An Italian wine cask bearing the consular date
of 107 B. C. has been found at Lepcis (*C. I. L.,* I², 697).

Finally several dedications at Delos (Durrbach, 105-8, *C. I. L.,* I²,
845) show that Italian traders had also invaded Alexandria from
Delos as early as the Gracchan days.

The remarkable growth of *Pompeii* during the " tufa period " (especially from 150 to 80 B. C., see below) is of course significant.
It would seem that Pompeii preceded Rome by a decade or two in
raising large public buildings and splendid palaces.   Evidently the
pax Romana brought wealth more quickly to the industrial and commercial South Italians than to the agrarian-minded Latins.   It is
impossible to assume that agriculture alone accounted for the splendid
houses of this time.   Perhaps, even though the harbor of Pompeii was
not of the best, commerce throve there because the town was outside
the customs limits of Naples and Puteoli.

VIII. INDUSTRY

1. *Agriculture*.

This period marks several changes in Italy's chief industry, agriculture. Cato's book, probably written about 170 B. C., reveals an increase in horticulture and stock raising and an extensive use of slave labor on large farms. This tendency continued till Tiberius Gracchus attempted to halt it, not only for the sake of relieving unemployment in the city but also with a view to increasing the free stock of Italy and checking the growth of the hordes of slaves. It was the sight of the vast slave-worked estates in Etruria that inspired his reforms. We have seen how he and his brother succeeded in settling large numbers of urban poor on small farms. However we are also told that, when these small allotments were made saleable by law, the drift toward the cities set in again. The attempts of Saturninus and later of Drusus to revive the agrarian reforms of the Gracchi broke against the opposition of the Senate. Thereafter the distribution of some 24 legions by Sulla on confiscated land probably did not aid farming much. Sulla was a friend of the large land-holders, and confiscated land chiefly from Italian communities filled with farmers. His veterans were probably less skilful than the dispossessed. And, when in his proscriptions he struck especially at the knights, the estates of the proscribed were usually bought at auction by other wealthy men. It is likely that his work increased the large holdings of Roman nobles at the expense of Italians.

How the Gracchan dole and colonization affected the Roman market for wheat we hardly know. These efforts may have deprived the Roman market of 100,000 buyers (consumers of some 1,200,000 bushels). But since Rome was now rapidly growing—witness the doubling of the water supply by the aqueducts of 140-125—we cannot be sure that the loss distressed the farmers. At any rate Latium was no longer primarily a cereal land.

We have no prices of wheat cited during the period, but it is fair to assume that the prices given by Cicero for the year 70 ($2\frac{1}{2}$—5 HS the modius, an average normal of 3) would not be far wrong for this time. The wars in Spain called for public supplies in 150-133; those of Greece and Carthage from 150 to 145 likewise. Then till the Gracchan day there was a drop in army needs. But the Jugurthine and Cimbric Wars, from 110 to 100, again called repeatedly for *commeatus*

(Sall., *Jug.*, 36, 43). Peace followed, which probably lowered prices, but from 90 to 80, when large parts of Italy were devastated, prices must have risen very much. Cicero speaks gratefully of the supplies that came from Sicily and Campania during that period (*Verr.*, 2, 2, 5; *Leg. agr.*, 2, 80).

Wine and *olive* raising prospered. At Rome several wine casks from Campania have been found bearing consular dates around 100 B. C. (*C. I. L.*, I², 699-703). The price at which M. Seius sold oil to the people during his aedileship in 74 (10 pounds per *as,* Pliny, 15, 2) is no indication of market values, since he was trying to sell off a bad reputation (Cic., *de Off.*, 2, 58; he also gave grain at an *as* the modius). Pliny's statement (15, 2) that Italy did not export oil till 52 B. C. has been proved incorrect by Hatzfeld, *B. C. H.*, 1912, 140, who shows that a group of Italian oil merchants was selling oil at Delos in the Sullan period, and that a part at least came in jars that bore Latin trademarks.

The various grades and vintages of Italian wine now began to be differentiated. Pliny thinks that the date of the vintage was first marked on casks in 121 B. C. (14, 94). The Falernian of the Opimian year, 121, was long famous. In fact some was served at a banquet given to Caligula 160 years later according to Pliny, 14, 56. Pliny (14, 87) also says that Italian wine began to have some reputation abroad about 150 B. C. (auctoritatem post DC urbis annum coepisse), but imported wines were preferred till the Augustan period (diu transmarina in auctoritate fuerunt et ad avos usque nostros, 14, 95). Choice wines, domestic as well as foreign, began to bring good prices. Pliny, 14, 56, assumes that the Opimian served at Caligula's banquet had originally cost 100 HS the amphora (26 liters, *i. e.* nearly 20 cents the quart, about 5 times the price of *ordinaire;* see third chapter).

The censors of 89 set a maximum retail price on costly domestic and imported wines of 8 *asses* per *quartarius* (= quadrans; Pliny, 14, 95: nequis vinum Graecum Amineumque octonis aeris singulos quadrantes venderet [cf. *Am. Jour. Phil.*, 1931, 278 for the reading based upon Diod., 37, 3, 5]. This would make a price of about 60 cents the liter [nearly 100 denarii the amphora]). Diodorus, 37, 3, 5, refers to the same price for the time of the Social war:

" for a jar of wine (he refers to Falernian and Chian) would sell for a hundred denarii."

The passage in Pliny (14, 95-6) just referred to runs as follows:

P. Licinius Crassus L. Iulius Caesar censores anno urbis conditae DCLXV edixerunt, ne quis vinum Graecum Amineumque octonis aeris singulos quartarios (text gives *quadrantalia*) venderet. haec enim verba sunt. tanta vero Graeco vino gratia erat ut singulae potiones in convictu darentur.

Quibus vinis auctoritas fuerit sua inventa, M. Varro his verbis tradit: " L. Lucullus puer apud patrem numquam lautum convivium vidit in quo plus semel Graecum vinum daretur. ipse cum rediit ex Asia, milia cadum congiarium divisit amplius centum. C. Sentius, quem praetorem vidimus, Chium vinum suam domum inlatum dicebat tum primum, cum sibi cardiaco medicus dedisset. Hortensius super X̄ cadum heredi reliquit."

" P. Licinius Crassus, and L. Julius Caesar, who were Censors in the year from the Building of the City 665 (89 B. C.), issued an edict forbidding the sale of either Greek or Aminean wine at a higher price than eight asses the quartarius—for such, in fact, are the exact words of the edict. Indeed, the Greek wines were so highly valued, that not more than a single cup was served to a guest during the repast.

M. Varro gives us the following statement as to the wines that were held in the highest esteem at table in his day: L. Lucullus, when a boy, never saw an entertainment at his father's house, however sumptuous it might be, at which Greek wine was handed around more than once during the repast: whereas he himself, when he returned from Asia, distributed as a largess among the people more than a hundred thousand casks of the same wine. C. Sentius, whom we have seen Praetor, used to say that Chian wine never entered his house until his physician prescribed it to him for the cardiac disease. On the other hand, Hortensius left ten thousand casks of it to his heir."

In discussing the work of Varro in the next chapter we shall have fuller evidence about the state of farming and horticulture. It may be well to add that when the senators soon after 146 ordered a translation of the books on farming written by Mago the Carthaginian, their intention was, no doubt, to gain information about methods of dry-farming applicable to the recently acquired lands in Africa rather than, as Mommsen supposed, to serve Italian farmers at home. Climatic conditions in Latium are so different from those of Africa that very little of it would be of any use to Italians (see " Mago," in *R-E.*— in part misleading).

2. *Building.*

We have noticed above the great amount of construction work, in the making of roads, aqueducts, sewers, and public buildings. This must have been a period of development, not only for military engineers, public contractors, and skilled workmen, but for slaves who could be trained in all kinds of constructional work. It is the period in which the most important building materials of the future come into use: Greek marble was imported for the temples of Jupiter and Juno in 146; travertine from near Tibur began to displace tufa in architraves, thereby permitting a wider spacing of columns; a stronger cheap tufa (the Anio) was introduced for heavily burdened walls (in place of the fragile Grotta Oscura and the brittle Monte Verde tufas); and before 121 the art of making a strong concrete out of the abundant volcanic ash was discovered, which resulted in stronger foundations and walls at less expense and very soon in the construction of lasting vaults (cf. Frank, *Roman Buildings of the Republic*).

There were also a number of temples vowed and erected by generals and private citizens who could choose their contractors outside of the equestrian companies if they wished. Q. Caecilius Metellus, the conqueror of Macedonia, vowed and built of Greek marble the two great temples of Jupiter and Juno (146 B. C.) in the campus, enclosing them with porticos. He hired a Greek architect, Hermodorus of Salamis, for the work (Vell., 1, 2, 3; Vitr., 3, 2, 5). In front he placed Lysippus' fine equestrian statues of Alexander's generals and inside other works of art that he brought as booty. Brutus presently (138 B. C.) used the same Hermodorus to draw plans for his temple of Mars, paid for by Spanish booty (Nepos, fr. 13, p. 120, Halm). This was built to contain statues of Mars and Venus by Scopas (Pliny, 36, 26). Other shrines of lesser note were the temple of Hercules Victor (142, from the booty of Corinth), a Venus temple (114, Ovid., *Fasti,* 4, 159), a temple of Fortuna vowed by Catulus during the battle with the Cimbri in 101 (Cic., *de Leg.,* 2, 28), and one to Honos and Virtus vowed by Marius in the same war (Festus, 468). The architect of this temple was a Roman, C. Mucius, and was apparently very successful (Vitr., 3, 2, 5 and 7, praef. 17). That Romans were learning the art well is shown by the fact that two Romans (C. and M. Stallius) were placed in charge of the rebuilding of the Odeum at Athens by Ariobarzanes after the havoc wrought by Sulla (Vitr., 5, 9; *Ins. Gr.,* 3, 541), just as Cossutius, some time before, had been hired by Antiochus Epiphanes (c. 170) to complete the Olympeion at Athens. There was also a new temple to Felicitas (exact date unknown, built from Spanish booty, Strabo, 8, 6, 23), and the following temples were restored: Concord in 121; Castor in 117; Fides and Mens in 115; Magna Mater in 111; and two temples in the Forum Holitorium (Platner and Ashby, *Top. Dict., sub voc.*). The two northernmost temples recently excavated in the Area Argentina seem also to belong to about 100-80 B. C. Most of these temples are larger than those of the preceding epoch and, where remains are extant, show a decided advance in construction and artistry. This was, then, a period of extensive construction. Architects, contractors, stone cutters, workers in stucco ornamentation, and large gangs of slaves were busy most of the time. There was as yet little artistic marble carving, however. That did not come till the Augustan period.

There was also much private building with the expansion of the city, but of this we hear little. We learn (Val. Max., 8, 1, 7) that the censors of 125 had to enforce the law that limited houses to three storeys. The orator Crassus had a house on the Palatine costing 1,500,-000 denarii ($300,000) when he was censor in 92 B. C. The houses of Marius, Catulus, and Aquilius were said to be even more costly (Pliny, 17, 2-3; Val. Max., 9, 1, 4), and in 78 Lepidus the consul had the finest house in Rome (Pl., 36, 109) using some Numidian marble in it. This is the first mention of this marble. But all of these houses were soon to be surpassed by the palaces of Sulla and Lucullus. Yet a yearly rental of a house at 6,000 HS ($300) was frowned upon as a needless luxury by the censors of 125 (Vell., 2, 10, 1).

These houses were probably built of concrete covered with stucco. That of Crassus also had six columns of Hymettian marble (the first marble columns recorded for a private dwelling at Rome, but they were only 12 feet high). Private warm baths (*pensiles, i. e.* with floors raised over a space for hot air) were now being put into the larger houses. The enterprising oyster fancier and real estate agent, Sergius Orata, c. 95 B. C., would remodel houses by adding this new improvement and sell them at an increased price (Pliny, 9, 168). Most of the ordinary houses were built of sundried brick or stucco (Varro, *Sat.,* 524; Buech: Antiqui nostri in domibus latericiis . . . habitabant; cf. Augustus' statement: "I found the city built of sundried brick and left it marble "; Vitruvius, 2, 3, writing in the early Augustan period, still gives full directions for making adobe walls).

At Pompeii there was a remarkable activity in public and private construction from about 150 to 90 B. C. It is to this period that we must assign the splendid Basilica (about 180 by 80 feet) in Ionic style (Mau-Kelsey, 70), the temples of Jupiter and of Apollo in excellent Hellenistic workmanship, the large theatre, and the original Stabian baths. To this period also belong some of the finest private houses of Pompeii: those of "Pansa," the "Faun," "Sallustius," the "Labyrinth," "Epidius Rufus," the "Centaur," "the citharist," the "silver wedding," and several others. The last mentioned has a splendid tetrastyle atrium measuring more than forty feet square. Many houses have fine floor mosaics that were never again matched in Italy, made, it would seem, by Alexandrian craftsmen. The walls were decorated in the incrustation style, and their stucco decorations are in the best taste. A striking fact revealed by the excavations at Pompeii is that many of these larger houses (the house of the "Faun" measures about 315 by 110 feet) were built over the foundations of groups of older houses, which indicates that at this time wealth was rapidly increasing. The people of Pompeii, though not Romans, were apparently profiting decidedly by Rome's advance into the East. Pompeii may thus be taken as a kind of barometer of Italian prosperity from 150 to 90 B. C., and we may plausibly infer that Rome was itself growing somewhat in the same manner, though perhaps more tardily. Possibly the Roman palaces of the Sullan day mentioned above were no more splendid than than those that had arisen at Pompeii two or three decades before, though the ground was doubtless more expensive.

Outside Rome and Pompeii we happen to have little evidence of building, but the towns were doubtless growing. Alatrium put in an expensive water-system using a cement syphon (*C. I. L.*, I², 1529-30), and Cora built a very beautiful temple of Castor and Pollux (*ibid.*, 1506).

3. *Manufacturing.*

The iron industry must have flourished as before in order to provide the enormous amount of arms, tools, farm and household implements that were needed. We happen to know that the iron mines of the island of Elba continued to be exploited from the Etruscan times down to the late Empire, but, since the forests of the island and the mainland coast nearby were not very abundant, the factories of Puteoli (where there was timber, and a good harbor) had taken up the work of producing wares out of the ore:

Diod., 5, 13:

Τῆς γὰρ Τυρρηνίας κατὰ τὴν ὀνομαζομένην πόλιν Ποπλώνιον νῆσός ἐστιν, ἣν ὀνομάζουσιν Αἰθάλειαν. . . . πέτραν γὰρ ἔχει πολλὴν σιδηρῖτιν, ἣν τέμνουσιν ἐπὶ τὴν χωνείαν καὶ κατασκευὴν τοῦ σιδήρου, πολλὴν ἔχοντες τοῦ μετάλλου δαψίλειαν. οἱ γὰρ ταῖς ἐργασίαις προσεδρεύοντες κόπτουσι τὴν πέτραν καὶ τοὺς τμηθέντας λίθους κάουσιν ἔν τισι φιλοτέχνοις καμίνοις· ἐν δὲ ταύταις τῷ πλήθει τοῦ πυρὸς τήκοντες τοὺς λίθους καταμερίζουσιν εἰς μεγέθη σύμμετρα, παραπλήσια ταῖς ἰδέαις μεγάλοις σπόγγοις. ταῦτα συναγοράζοντες ἔμποροι καὶ μεταβαλλόμενοι κομίζουσιν εἴς τε Δικαιάρχειαν καὶ εἰς τἆλλα ἐμπόρια. ταῦτα δὲ τὰ φορτία τινὲς ὠνούμενοι καὶ τεχνιτῶν χαλκέων πλῆθος ἀθροίζοντες κατεργάζονται, καὶ ποιοῦσι σιδήρου πλάσματα παντοδαπά. τούτων δὲ τὰ μὲν εἰς ὅπλων τύπους χαλκεύουσι, τὰ δὲ πρὸς δικελλῶν καὶ δρεπάνων καὶ τῶν ἄλλων ἐργαλείων εὐθέτους τύπους φιλοτεχνοῦσιν· ὧν κομιζομένων ὑπὸ τῶν ἐμπόρων εἰς πάντα τόπον πολλὰ μέρη τῆς οἰκουμένης μεταλαμβάνει τῆς ἐκ τούτων εὐχρηστίας.

"Near the town of Etruria called Populonia lies Ilva . . . It abounds in siderite which they mine for smelting and making of iron, since it contains much of this metal. Those engaged in this work crush the rock and roast it in furnaces skilfully made for the purpose. When it has been melted in a strong fire, they cut the matter into parts that look like large sponges. Merchants buy these with money or an exchange of goods and carry them to Dicaearchaea (Puteoli) and other ports. Men who engage the labor of smiths buy these masses of ore and make all kinds of implements of them. Some parts they hammer into weapons, other into hoes, sickles, and other useful implements. Then merchants carry these everywhere and they are used in every part of the world."

In this part of Book V Diodorus usually copies Timaeus (3rd century B. C.), but the situation described probably continued to his own day (60-30 B. C.) for the slag-heaps at Populonia (from smelting rather than forges) seem to have grown up especially from about 200 B. C. to 300 A. D. (Minto, *Populonia*, 9). Varro (quoted by Servius, on *Aen.*, 10, 174) said that the smelting was no longer done in Ilva, and Strabo confirms this somewhat later, 5, 2, 6: "I saw—at Populonia— the men who worked the iron brought over from Ilva; for it cannot be thoroughly smelted in the furnaces on the island and the ore is sent at once to the mainland." It is, of course, possible that there were also some smiths at Populonia. Those at Puteoli were also famous in Pliny's day (35, 106). The state had armories of its own before 100 B. C. (Cic., *pro Rabir. Perd.*, 20; *In Pis.*, 87).

To the important Campanian industries in bronze and silver ware,
20

furniture, and the like there are no references in this period, though
we must assume that they continued to flourish vigorously.

There are some curious notices of an enterprising Roman, Sergius
Orata, who, when Baiae became a fashionable summer resort, undertook to raise oysters (Pliny, 9, 168) and trout (*ibid.*, 170) at the
Lucrine lake for the epicures. This is the first mention in Italy of the
kind of industry that became popular in Varro's day. When in 97
B. C. the censors claimed for the state the fishing rights in the lake,
Sergius seems to have sold some of his property without giving notice
of this new fact. Hence he found himself involved in lawsuits not
only with the contractor whom he tried to circumvent but also with the
purchaser of his villa. Sergius secured very eminent counsel, so that
the case is frequently mentioned (Cic., *de Or.*, 1, 178; *de Off.*, 3, 67;
Val. Max., 9, 1, 1; etc. Cf. Münzer, " C. Sergius Orata," in *Realenc*).

Of the state of Roman industry in general we hear little because
the sources are so inadequate, and excavations in Italy have revealed
very little of interest for the period. Tools, implements, clothing, and
household ware must have had a good market in the growing state, but,
when we hear of remarkable ware, it is generally imported. The
treasures of the kingdom of Pergamum, brought to Rome and sold at
auction, contained vast amounts of fine fabrics from the royal factories and palaces, tapestries, spreads, and hangings woven with gold
(Attalica), and fine textiles and clothing (*aulaea, clamides, pallae,
plagae,* Varro, fr. 68. Cf. Prop., 2, 32, 12; Pliny, 8, 196; 33, 63;
36, 115; 37, 12; and Rostovtzeff in *Anatolian Studies, in honor of
Ramsay,* 375 ff.). Such imports taught the Romans where to buy fine
textiles. Trade accordingly increased with the East, but we do not
hear that industry in Italy undertook to compete with the East with
respect to such fine articles. To be sure, generals brought many skilled
craftsmen to Rome among their captives, and private individuals would
buy and employ some of these in their households (Varro, *R. R.*, 1, 16,
4; Nepos, Att., 13), but we do not yet hear of larger establishments
formed to make use of such labor.

It is significant at least that the writers of Roman comedy in the
Sullan period liked to choose their characters from among the small
artisans: the pistor (baker), pictor (painter), fullo (fuller), cento-
narius (blanket-maker), restio (rope-maker), lignaria (cabinet-maker),
and the like (these are titles of the plays of Pomponius and Novius).

Doubtless Campanian factories that made furniture, bronze and silver ware, and ointments in large quantities in the Augustan day were even now busy and the woolen and timber trade that Strabo later mentions, especially for Cisalpine Gaul, engaged much labor at this time also. Since in Strabo's day Padua had the largest number of well-to-do men of any town in Italy outside of Rome, we may assume that her industries had been profitable for some time. However, Romans of any pretension did not go into industrial work. We hear of only one man during the period who gained wealth by manufacturing, and that was in public contracts for weapons during the Social War (Cic., *in Pis.,* 87: Videras . . . bello Italico repleri quaestu vestram domum cum pater armis faciendis tuus praefuisset. "In the Italic war (89) you saw your house filled with profit when your father had charge of the factories for making arms "). We learn no more about such factories at this time. Later they were common; Piso, in fact, had one in the province of Macedonia in 48, when he became a munition profiteer as his father had been in 89.

IX. LABOR

Italy suffered a considerable loss of young men in the warfare in Spain (150-133), in Gaul between 110 and 102, and especially during the Social and Civil Wars of 90-88 and 83-82 in Italy. Even if we assume that the heaviest losses in Spain fell on the Spanish auxiliaries, we should reckon from the lists of Appian, *Iber.,* 60-98, some 25,000 Italian casualties. The attack of the Cimbri and Teutones cost even more. The losses of the Social War are put by Appian at 100,000 on each side. After about 105 the recruits were no longer confined to the propertied classes so that the urban poor and the farm laborers now bore a large share of the sacrifice. In considering the loss of men to Italy one must also keep in mind the migrations going on to the new provinces, though we have no way of estimating the number of emigrants.

To compensate, Roman generals brought home numerous captives and traders brought slaves from the markets. The many Spanish captives may well have been sold to the mining societies of Spain. Marius took some captives at Aquae Sextiae and again about 60,000 Cimbri at Vercellae (Plut., *Mar.,* 27, 3). A large part of Spartacus' revolters later proved to be Germans and Celts (Sall., *Hist.,* 3, 96, M.). They had apparently been sold to farmers and ranchers around Campania and in the South. Appian reports some 60,000 captives from Carthage in 146 (*Pun.*, 126 and 130). Scipio's speech, reported by Val. Max., 6, 2, 3, and Vell., 2, 4, 4, implies that many of these were sold at Rome (see below). Sulla took a "large number of prisoners" when he defeated the Asiatic hordes of Mithridates at Chaeronea in 86 (App., *Mith.*, 45). Since the enemy had been 120,000 strong, we may estimate the captive horde at some tens of thousands, and he also seized and sold what slaves he found at Athens (App., *Mith.*, 38). The slave trade also brought a great number of Orientals. When Marius in 104 asked the king of Bithynia for auxiliaries, the king made the apt response (Diod., 36, 3) that "most of his people had been stolen by the publicans and were serving as slaves in the provinces" (presumably in Asia and Sicily). The reply was of course not precisely exact, but one can condone the exaggeration for a fact pointedly expressed. The pirates had doubtless done the kidnapping and sold the slaves at the Delian market; and Roman purchases encouraged the nefarious trade. If Bithynia suffered thus, we may assume that Cappadocia, Syria, and Egypt did also. Slaves who could speak Greek were in especial demand.

We see from these references that Italy was able to keep itself well supplied with labor, even if the new supply, taking the place of the old native one, was gradually changing the nature of the Italian people. Apparently the new people won freedom and citizenship with the same readiness as before, if there is any point in the remark made by Scipio Aemilianus in 130. When he was speaking to the voting assembly and the people hissed his remarks, he said (Vell., 2, 4, 4): qui possum vestro (clamore) moveri quorum noverca est Italia? (How can I be disturbed by the shouts of men like you, to whom Italy is only a step-mother?) (Val. Max., 6, 2, 3, has the version "whom I have brought as captives.")

We hear at this time of several sons of slaves who reached some prominence in the state. A. Gabinius, the tribune of 139 who introduced the secret ballot, was "Vernae nepos" (Livy, *Epit.*, Oxyr., line 193); P. Furius, a tribune in 99, was a son of a libertus (App., *B. C.*, 1, 33); a senator by the name of Popilius, a son of a libertus, was struck from the senatorial roll in 74 (Cic., *pro Cluent.*, 132). Caecilius Niger, Cicero's opponent in the Verrine case, an ex-quaestor, may also belong in this group. He was of Sicilian birth and had taken his name

from his benefactor—but it may well be that he was of free Greek
stock (Cic., *Div. in Caec.*, 4).

In the next period the slaves revolted in Italy under the leadership
of Spartacus.   Before that we hear of little trouble with slaves except
for two or three instances of small groups that revolt against their own
masters: at Nuceria some 30 slaves, and at Capua a group of 200
(Diod., 36, 2).   The rioting under the knight Vettius mentioned in
the same passage was not a revolt, but a neighborhood feud in which a
master used his slaves in an attack upon a neighbor.

For further notes on slavery and labor I shall refer to our survey of
the next period, but I wish to call attention here to a peculiar instance
of what might be called serfdom that was apparently suppressed.   In
Cicero's *Pro Cluentio*, 43, we hear of one sole instance of temple serfs
in Italy (like the *hieroduli* so numerous in Asia and Greece; see Haywood, in *Am. Jour. Phil.*, 1933).

Cic., *pro Cluent.*, 43:

Martiales quidam Larini appellabantur, ministri publici Martis
atque ei deo veteribus institutis religionibusque Larinatium consecrati:
quorum cum satis magnus numerus esset, cumque item, ut in Sicilia
permulti Venerii sunt, sic illi Larini in Martis familia numerarentur,
repente Oppianicus eos omnes liberos esse civesque Romanos coepit
defendere.

" There were at Larinum certain persons called Martiales, the official
priests of Mars, dedicated to the service of the god by local regulations
and religious ordinances of great antiquity.   Their number was considerable: moreover, as is the case with the numerous priests of Venus
in Sicily, these priests of Mars at Larinum were regarded as belonging
to the household of the god.   But despite this Oppianicus suddenly
began to maintain the plea that they were free men and Roman citizens."

The case was taken to court at Rome, but Cicero does not mention the
outcome.   Since Roman law had no place for what we call serfs, and
since the men in question could hardly be called slaves, the court which
had to make some category for these *hieroduli* under civil law, now that
all of Italy had the franchise, would probably have had to recognize
them as citizens.   Perhaps the court compromised by calling them
liberti of the temple.   The libertus numinis Aesculapi of Apulum
(*C. I. L.*, 3, 1079) might then be a parallel.   Strabo, 6, 2, 6, says of

the *hieroduli* of Eryx in Sicily mentioned by Cicero: " the multitude of temple slaves has disappeared," though the temple was " still held in exceptional honor." One wonders whether the same thing had happened with the serfs of Etruria whenever the Romans came there. We shall speak of the *coloni* of Domitius in the next chapter. On the question of the Cost of Living we can only give the references to the sumptuary laws of Licinius and Sulla provided by Aulus Gellius (cf. " *Sumptus,*" in *R-E.*) :

A. Gell., 2, 24, 7:

Lex deinde Licinia rogata est, quae cum certis diebus, sicuti Fannia, centenos aeris inpendi permisisset, nuptiis ducenos indulsit ceterisque diebus statuit aeris tricenos; cum et carnis aridae et salsamenti certa pondera in singulos dies constituisset, quidquid esset natum e terra, vite, arbore, promisce atque indefinite largita est.

" Next the Licinian law (between Gracchus and Sulla) was passed which, while allowing the outlay of one hundred asses on designated days, as did the law of Fannius, conceded two hundred asses for weddings and set a limit of thirty for other days; however, after naming a fixed weight of dried meat and salted provisions for each day, it granted the indiscriminate and unlimited use of the products of the earth, vine and orchard."

A. Gell., 2, 24, 11:

. . . (Sulla) legem ad populum tulit, qua cautum est ut Kalendis, Idibus, Nonis diebusque ludorum et feriis quibusdam sollemnibus sestertios trecenos in cenam insumere ius potestasque esset, ceteris autem diebus omnibus non amplius tricenos.

. . . " Lucius Sulla . . . proposed a law to the people, which provided that on the Kalends, Ides and Nones, on days of games, and on certain regular festivals, it should be proper and lawful to spend three hundred sesterces on a dinner, but on all other days no more than thirty."

A. Gell., 2, 24, 14:

Postrema lex Iulia ad populum pervenit Caesare Augusto imperante, qua profestis quidem diebus ducenti finiuntur, Kalendis, Idibus, Nonis et aliis quibusdam festis trecenti, nuptiis autem et repotiis sestertii mille.

" Lastly, the Julian law came before the people during the principate of Caesar Augustus, by which on working days two hundred sesterces is the limit, on the Kalends, Ides and Nones and some other holidays, three hundred, but at weddings and the banquets following them, a thousand."

X. ESTATES, SOURCES OF WEALTH

1. *Estates.*

The data that we have for the period generally refer to the unusual instances, mentioned because of law-suits or striking wrongdoing or strange circumstances. They must not be taken as giving the normal economic situation.

We have several references to suburban and seaside villas, which are seldom connected with productive estates. Cumae and Baiae, the Alban hills, Tibur, and the seacoast from Tarracina to Alsium were coming to be the favorite places for these. Marius had a villa at Baiae which was sold in the proscriptions of Sulla to a Cornelia (apparently a daughter of Sulla. See *R-E.* " Cornelia," 412) for 75,000 denarii and soon after was bought by L. Lucullus for 2,500,000 (Plut., *Mar.,* 34). Laelius, Rutilius Rufus, and Scipio Aemilianus had villas at Formiae (perhaps with vineyards; Cic., *de Rep.,* 1, 61; *de Nat. D.,* 3, 86; *de Fato, fr.,* 5). Marius' villa in Campania was sold in the Sullan proscriptions to Curio (*Schol. Bob.* Stangl., 89). Sulla had a villa at Puteoli to which he retired in 79 (App., *B. C.,* 1, 104). Aemilius Porcina was one of the first to have a house at Alsium and was censured in 125 for building higher than the legal limit (Val. Max., 5, 1, 7 D). M. Junius Brutus of the Gracchan period (Realenc., " *Junius,*" No. 49) had estates in the Alban hills, at Tibur, and at Privernum, but to judge from the character of the man they were probably all productive (Cic., *pro Cluent.,* 141). Inscriptions show that Galba had a villa at Tarracina (*C. I. L.,* I², 694), Metella had one at Tibur (*ibid.,* 733) and the Fulvian family had property in Samnium (*ibid.,* 825).

We do not happen to have many definite references to the productive farms and ranches owned by Italians and Romans all over Italy. The fact that hundreds of senators and knights lived at leisure in the city, drawing their income usually from landed investments, shows that the lack of information is merely due to chance. In reading such speeches of Cicero as the *pro Roscio Amerino,* the *pro Cluentio,* and the *pro Caecina,* that deal with municipal folk, one gains the impression that small Italian villages far from Rome still had wealthy landlords among the native population. Roscius owned thirteen farms near his native town of Ameria which were valued at 6,000,000 HS. Cluentius and Oppianicus, both Samnites of Larinum, and their like, had productive estates and ranches. The small hill-town of Atina had a large number of men who were wealthy enough to rank as knights, most of them doubtless making their profits from ranching and horticulture (Cic., *pro Planc.*, 32-3). Great wealth was probably not accumulated with speed in such places, but families that lived simply and dealt shrewdly could in a few generations become powerful in their communities. The twelve leaders of the Italian revolt in 90 were men of means and influence in their tribes; men like Pompey of Picenum, Cicero and Marius of Arpinum, and the Asinii of Teate had prospered on landed estates. The poet Lucilius of Suessa seems to have had good properties in Apulia, Bruttium, and Sicily, to judge from the fragments of his Satires. We hear of L. Helvius who lived in Apulia (Oros., 5, 15, 20), of Cicero's colleague, Antonius, who owned ranches (*Asc.* Stangl., p. 68), of a Lollius who had land on the slopes of Aetna (Cic., *Verr.*, 3, 61), of Octavius, the grandfather of Augustus, who had property at Velitrae (Suet., *Aug.*, 2, 2), of a knight, T. Vettius, who worked estates with 400 slaves in Campania (Diod., 36, 2), and of the three farms of Junius Brutus mentioned above.

2. *Sources of Wealth.*

The substantial incomes throughout Italy doubtless came from landed property, ranches, and fruit farms, a few instances of which we have mentioned above. The semi-public enterprises of the knights and the participation in commerce and trade of the *negotiatores,* already discussed, must have accounted for some. However, our casual references of this period happen to give the names of only four men of this class: two publicans, *i. e.* P. Rupilius (who became senator) and C. Curtius (mentioned in Cic., *pro Rab., Post* 3) and two knights in the banking business, S. Alfenus (Cic., *pro Quinct.,* 21) and Q. Caecilius (Nepos, *Att.,* 5). We may also assume that dealing in real-estate in the growing city was profitable at this time.

Another source of wealth was *conquest.* Consuls and praetors sought provinces where wars were in progress in order to profit from the booty, of which there was now less and less accounting. Pompey's method of withdrawing a fifth of the plunder for himself and his officers before giving any to his soldiers and to the treasury (Pliny, 37, 16) was not considered reprehensible. Others, like Marius and Sulla, were less liberal. Appian (*Iber.*, 51) says bluntly that Lucullus, when he was in Spain, created a war because he was poor and needed money, and that Sulpicius Galba looted freely in 144 (App., *Iber.*, 60). At least half the campaigns in Spain in the years 150-134 were unjustly begun and brutally carried out, though there was relatively little wealth to be had in the part then being subjugated. Sulla, who began as a poor man, became the richest man in Rome, according to Pliny, 33, 134; he therefore rated at more than Crassus, who was worth over 200,000,000 sesterces ($10,000,000). Sulla, however, adopted methods not available to others, since, following the theory of eastern autocrats, he claimed ownership of all he had conquered, not only abroad, but in Italy. No great amount actually came out of captured war-booty (he received only 2,000 talents from Mithridates). But he used the temple treasures of Greece, imposed an indemnity of 20,000 talents on the Asiatics, sold the goods of the proscribed ostensibly for the state treasury, and he used all the income of the treasury at pleasure and without accounting. He was the only Roman before Caesar who adopted the Oriental theory of kingship with respect to ownership (Frank, *Jour. R. Stud.*, 1927, 150). (Cic., *Leg. agr.*, 2, 56: L. Sulla cum bona indemnatorum civium . . . se praedam suam diceret vendere. "When Sulla sold the goods of uncondemned citizens saying that he was selling his own booty"; Asconius, Stangl., p. 58: Sulla per multos annos . . . sumpserat pecunias ex vectigalibus et ex aerario populi R. "For many years Sulla took money out of the Roman income and from the public treasury." Cicero adds that proposals had frequently been made to bring Sulla's heir to an accounting, but that Sulla's friends had at first prevented it, and later statutes of limitation prevented recovery.) Sulla therefore stands quite alone in his methods of profiteering.

Marius is a more normal example. He, too, began his career relatively poor and ended as a very rich man. He had estates at Baiae, Solonium, and elsewhere, in fact "enough for a kingdom" (Plut., *Mar.*, 34, 35, 45). He probably pocketed much of the booty taken from Jugurtha, the Teutones, and the Cimbri (from the last, Marius and Catulus took 60,000 captives [Plut., *Mar.*, 27] which would bring a goodly amount. We do not know how much the treasury received). It is likely that at least a dozen men gained considerable wealth during the period in this manner (I include Sulla, Marius, Sulpicius Galba [Spain], Junius Brutus Callaicus [Spain], Cn. Domitius Ahenobarbus, and Fabius Aemilianus [Gaul], M. Livius Drusus [Macedonia], Q. Servilius Caepio [Spain and Gaul], Caecilius Metellus Numidicus [Africa], Lutatius Catulus [Cimbri], and Licinius Murena [Mithridates]). In some of these cases the war was of course legitimate, and the officers' proportion of the booty normal, though it must be added that the theory fairly well adhered to till 150—that the general's share should be used for temples or the public service—was now often forgotten.

More irregular was the *extortion* that came to be practiced frequently during the period, despite the new court created by a law of Calpurnius Piso in 149 because of some charges that had been brought in 154 (Livy, *Epit.* 47). The Calpurnian law was buttressed by the *lex Junia,* the *lex Acilia* (about 123), and the *lex Servilia* (about 111 B. C.). Nevertheless generals who had received campaign expenses before departing from Rome would demand grain from the allies, thereby saving a part of the expense-money for themselves, or would exact superfluous supplies for the auxiliaries required. How far this form of graft could go we shall see later in the notorious instances of Verres and Piso. There were many trials on this charge in our period, not all fair, since, as in the case of Rutilius Rufus, the governor was sometimes brought to court (the panel was equestrian most of the time after 123) simply because he had done his duty to the provincials by restraining the publicans. At any rate, it is not likely that before the time of the Social War great wealth was in any case acquired in this fashion. There were also ugly charges of the acceptance of bribes, especially against the senators who favored Jugurtha (Sull., *Jug.,* 40; Cic., *Brut.,* 128; Livy, *Epit.* 64: multos pecunia in Senatu corrupisse dicebatur). But such charges, often made for campaign purposes, were seldom proved. M'. Aquilius was also charged with accepting bribes and Cicero (*pro Flacco,* 98) thought him guilty despite his acquittal by the court.

Finally some of the fortunes of Cicero's day were due to participation in the lucrative trading in the property of those *proscribed* by Marius and Sulla. Crassus had made much of his enormous wealth in this way:

Plut., *Crass.*, 2 :

Ὅτε γὰρ Σύλλας ἑλὼν τὴν πόλιν ἐπώλει τὰς οὐσίας τῶν ἀνῃρημένων ὑπ' αὐτοῦ, λάφυρα καὶ νομίζων καὶ ὀνομάζων, καὶ βουλόμενος ὅτι πλείστοις καὶ κρατίστοις προσομόρξασθαι τὸ ἄγος, οὔτε λαμβάνων οὔτ' ὠνούμενος ἀπεῖπε.

" For when Sulla took the city and sold the property of those whom he had put to death, considering it and calling it spoil of war, and wishing to defile with his crime as many and as influential men as he could, Crassus was never tired of accepting or of buying it."

We do not know the source of the wealth of P. Crassus, the father-in-law of Tiberius Gracchus. It was estimated at about 25,000,000 denarii (Cic., *de Rep.*, 3, 13). He was the son of Mucius, who was well-to-do, and adopted by a Licinius who had large properties.

The case of Chrysogonus was disclosed by Cicero (*pro Rosc. Amer.*, *passim*). In one instance he had bought property worth 600,000 HS for a fraction of one per cent of its value. Catiline had also had his share of such profits. Lepidus, who turned against Sulla in 79, when charged with profiting from the auctions of proscribed goods, answered that he had not dared to refrain for fear of incurring Sulla's enmity, but was ready to make restitution (Sall., *Or. Lepidi*). At least he rebuilt the Basilica Aemilia. M. Curio, a famous senator, bought a house of Marius at a low price (*Schol. Bob.* Stangl., 89), a Cornelia (probably Sulla's own daughter) bought another (Plut., *Mar.*, 34) on which she seems to have made an enormous profit, and P. Sulla, another relative, profited in the same manner (Cic., *de Off.*, 2, 29). Even petty folk could profit in this way, if Sulla proved favorable. A centurion, L. Luscius, made 10,000,000 HS on the auctions (in payment for using his dagger at the behest of Sulla). He was later condemned for murder (Ascon. Stangl., 70). Pliny tells us that the younger Aemilius Scaurus had inherited wealth from both parents, from his father (the princeps senatus) who got plunder by aiding Marius, and from his mother, Metella, who had married Sulla and had grown wealthy by bidding in property of the proscribed (Pliny, 36, 116: vitricus Sulla, Metella mater proscriptionum sectrix, Scaurus pater . . . Mariani sodalicii rapinarum provincialium sinus: The sources of his wealth were " his father-in-law Sulla, his mother Metella who bought in at the proscriptions, and his father Scaurus, the receptacle of the provincial booty of the Marian crew ").

CHAPTER V

FROM SULLA TO AUGUSTUS

I. CHRONOLOGY, 80-30 B. C.

Here we shall give a brief summary of the events of economic importance.

1. *The Revolt of 78.*

M. Aemilius Lepidus, in standing for the consulship for 78, promised to have Sulla's laws annulled (Sall., *Hist.*, 1, 55, 16 M, *Oratio Lepidi*). He entered office January 1, 78, and proposed at once to recall those exiled by Sulla, to rescind Sulla's laws, to restore to their former owners all lands confiscated by Sulla, and to revive the corn-doles (Gran. Licin., p. 34, F; App., *B. C.*, 1, 107; Sall., *Hist.*, 1, 55, 24, *Oratio Lepidi*; and 77, 14, *Oratio Philippi*, M). Failing of support because Rome feared another upheaval he recruited a volunteer army in order to carry his measures by force. In Etruria the response was immediate; the exiles of Faesulae at once recaptured their city from the Sullan veterans. However, in a battle near Rome Lepidus was defeated by the other consul, Catulus (Livy, *Epit.* 90; Florus, 2, 11).

2. *Piracy.*

Cic., *Lex Man.*, 32-3 (a plea made by Cicero in 66 to place Pompey in command of the Mithridatic War):

Sociis ego nostris mare per hos annos clausum fuisse dicam, cum exercitus vestri numquam a Brundisio nisi hieme summa transmiserint? Qui ad vos ab exteris nationibus venirent, captos querar, cum legati populi Romani redempti sint? Mercatoribus tutum mare non fuisse dicam, cum duodecim secures in praedonum potestatem pervenerint? Cnidum aut Colophonem aut Samum, nobilissimas urbes, innumera-bilesque alias captas esse commemorem, cum vestros portus atque eos portus, quibus vitam ac spiritum ducitis, in praedonum fuisse potestate sciatis? An vero ignoratis portum Caietae celeberrimum ac plenissi-mum navium inspectante praetore a praedonibus esse direptum, ex Miseno autem eius ipsius liberos, qui cum praedonibus antea ibi bellum gesserat, a praedonibus esse sublatos? Nam quid ego Ostiense incom-modum atque illam labem atque ignominiam rei publicae querar, cum prope inspectantibus vobis classis ea, cui consul populi Romani prae-positus esset, a praedonibus capta atque oppressa est?

"Need I mention that the sea during those wars was closed to our allies, when your own armies never made the crossing from Brundisium save in the depth of winter? Need I lament the capture of envoys on their way to Rome from foreign countries, when ransom has been paid for the ambassadors of Rome? Need I mention that the sea was unsafe for merchantmen, when twelve lictors have fallen into the hands of pirates? Need I record the capture of the noble cities of Cnidus and Colophon and Samos and of countless others, when you well know that your own harbours and those, too, through which you draw the very breath of your life, have been in the hands of the pirates? Are you indeed unaware that the famous port of Caieta, when crowded with shipping, was plundered by the pirates under the eyes of the praetor, and that from Misenum the children of the very man who had previously fought there against the pirates were kidnapped by the pirates? Why should I lament the reverse at Ostia, that shameful blot upon our commonwealth, when almost before your own eyes the very fleet which had been entrusted to the command of a Roman consul was captured and destroyed by the pirates?"

By 77 the Cilician pirates, who had been encouraged to attack Roman commerce by Mithridates (App., *Mith.,* 63), had gained control of a large part of the Mediterranean. The Sullan régime, hostile to the knights, had neglected to police the seas. But in 77 the Senate sent P. Servilius Vatia to attack the pirates at their strongholds in Cilicia. He punished them severely, but by taking their lands away from them south and north of the Taurus range he aggravated the evil for the future (Oros., 5, 23; Cic., *Verr.,* 1, 56; Cic., *lex Agr.,* 2, 50; Ormerod, *Piracy in the Ancient World,* 213 ff.). Hence, in 74, an expedition had to be sent against Crete where many of the pirates had made their new headquarters. The Senate chose one of its weakest men for the task, M. Antonius, giving him unlimited authority for the task (Pseudo-Asc., *in Verr.,* 2, Stangl., p. 259; App., *Sic.,* 6). He accomplished little. It was to cooperate with him that Verres, the governor of Sicily, was ordered to clear the harbors of his island, but his small fleet of ten Sicilian ships was captured and burned by the pirates. We may infer from the remarks of Verres (Cic., *Verr.,* 5, 91; 97; 158) that many Italians who had not accepted Roman citizenship in 89 had joined the Sertorian army in Spain, and on the defeat of Sertorius had taken to freebooting in conjunction with the Cilician and Cretan pirates. Such were the " citizens " whom Cicero charges that Verres executed without trial (*Verr.,* 5, 146-170).

After the death of Antonius, Q. Metellus was sent out to continue the work in 68, but wasted his time in subduing the towns of Crete. It is apparent that the Senate had now been forced by a disgraceful situation to take some slight interest in the commerce on the seas, but in choosing men like Antonius and Metellus, who feared the water and were concerned only in storming villages for plunder, it mismanaged the whole problem.

The stoppage of shipping and a general failure of crops in 75 led to a renewed demand for corn doles to which the Senate acceded in 73 by passing the lex Terentia Cassia (Cic., *Verr.*, 3, 163; 173; 5, 52). The Gracchan price of 6⅓ asses per modius was apparently adopted (Ascon., *in Pis.*, Stangl., 15: senis aeris ac trientibus. Cf. Ruggiero, *Diz. Epig.*, " Frumentatio," 232).

3. *Spartacus.*

In 73 Spartacus, a Thracian captive, who was being trained at Capua as a gladiator, escaped with some 70 others, and with amazing skill collected and equipped an army of slaves especially from the Cimbric, Teutonic, and Celtic captives (Caes., *B. G.*, 1, 40; Livy, *Epit.* 97) who were working on the farms and ranches of southern Italy. Since Rome kept no army in Italy, they reasoned that they could break through and make their way to their home countries. Their agents quickly gathered recruits from all of southern Italy, so that they were able to hold their own for two years, plundering a large part of the peninsula. The numbers they gathered are given variously between 60,000 and 120,000 (Vell., 2, 30, 6; Oros., 5, 24; Appian, *B. C.*, 1, 116-118). Crassus finally defeated the slaves in three successive battles in which most of them fell (Livy, *Epit.* 95-97; Plut., *Crass.*, 8-10; App., *B. C.*, 1, 116; Oros., 5, 24; see Münzer, " *Spartacus* " in Realenc. for all the references). The Romans seem to have learned from this experience that slave-economy might prove unprofitable. The custom of liberating good farm slaves and employing them as renters (coloni) won favor in the late Republic and early Empire.

4. *Pompey and Crassus.*

In 71 Pompey and Crassus (both ex-Sullans) were elected to the consulship for 70 on a promise to revise several of Sulla's laws. The jury panels were now divided evenly between the senators, the knights, and the *tribuni aerari* (Asc., *in Pis.*, Stangl., p. 21; Cic., *ad Att.*, 1, 16, 3). The censorship was also restored to please the popular party (Cic., *Div. in Caec.*, 8; Livy, *Epit.* 98). This enabled new citizens to register throughout Italy; the censors also struck off the names of 64 senators, mostly Sullan satellites. The tribunician powers, annulled by Sulla, were also restored (Livy, *Epit.* 97; Vell., 2, 30; Cic., *de Leg.*, 3, 22). This last measure practically destroyed senatorial control over legislation.

5. *The Gabinian law, 67 B. C.*

The knights and business men, who had to some extent recovered from the disasters of the Sullan day, and were more and more making investments in Asia, desired an effective clearing of the seas. Pompey, idle since his consulship, desired the task; the people, who had suffered from the crippling of traffic, were ready to support the knights. But the Senate, fearing Pompey, being little concerned with commerce, and wishing to keep the control of provincial affairs in its own hands, opposed the proposal. A tribune, Gabinius, was found to bring the bill before the assembly, despite the Senate's opposition. This measure gave Pompey (he was specifically named in a second bill) supreme command over all the seas for a period of three years with ships up to the number of 500 if needed, an army, and an immediate appropriation of 6,000 talents together with authorization to use any available revenues and also an order to draw on Roman allies for whatever might be needed (Plut., *Pomp.,* 25; Vell., 2, 31; App., *Mith.,* 94). Pompey cleared the seas in three months, destroyed the pirate fleets, and settled the bandits on public land in the provinces to keep them from further temptation. Roman seas did not again suffer from organized piracy for several hundred years.

6. *The Manilian Law.*

Cic., *Lex Man.,* 17-18 (Roman investments endangered by Mithridates):

quod ad multorum bona civium Romanorum pertinet; quorum vobis pro vestra sapientia, Quirites, habenda est ratio diligenter. Nam et publicani, homines honestissimi atque ornatissimi, suas rationes et copias in illam provinciam contulerunt, quorum ipsorum per se res et fortunae vobis curae esse debent.

" I mean the fact that there are many Roman citizens whose property is affected by this war (with Mithridates); and wise men like yourselves know that their interests demand your careful consideration. For in the first place the honourable and distinguished men who farm our revenues have transferred their business and their resources to that province (Asia), and their interests and fortunes ought, on personal grounds, to be your concern."

Deinde ex ceteris ordinibus homines gnavi atque industrii partim ipsi in Asia negotiantur, quibus vos absentibus consulere debetis, partim eorum in ea provincia pecunias magnas collocatas habent.

" Moreover, of those other classes there are men of energy and industry who are some of them personally engaged in business in Asia, and you ought to consult their interests in their absence; while others of them have vast sums invested in that province."

Cic., *Lex Man.*, 19:

Nam tum, cum in Asia res magnas permulti amiserant, scimus Romae solutione impedita fidem concidisse. Non enim possunt una in civitate multi rem ac fortunas amittere, ut non plures secum in eandem trahant calamitatem. A quo periculo prohibete rem publicam et mihi credite, id quod ipsi videtis, haec fides atque haec ratio pecuniarum, quae Romae, quae in foro versatur, implicata est cum illis pecuniis Asiaticis et cohaeret; ruere illa non possunt, ut haec non eodem labefacta motu concidant.

" For, coinciding with the loss by many people of large fortunes in Asia, we know that there was a collapse of credit at Rome owing to suspension of payment. It is, indeed, impossible for many individuals in a single state to lose their property and fortunes without involving still greater numbers in their own ruin. Do you defend the commonwealth from this danger; and believe me when I tell you—what you see for yourselves—that this system of credit and finance which operates at Rome, in the Forum, is bound up in, and depends on capital invested in Asia; the loss of the one inevitably undermines the other and causes its collapse."

In 66 the tribune, Manilius, in the same manner as Gabinius and working for the same interests, assigned to Pompey with unlimited resources and powers the war over Mithridates, which Lucullus had failed to bring to a successful close. Lucullus had incurred the enmity of the knights and money lenders by reducing by fiat the debts of the Asiatic communities that had grown from the Sullan exaction of 20,000 talents 17 years before. And it was also known that he was not as willing to establish new provinces as were the knights; he had in fact given Syria and a part of Cilicia back to the Seleucids. Pompey seemed more likely to favor expansion that would profit the knights. Pompey did his work speedily, added Pontus and Syria to the list of

21

provinces, and enlarged Cilicia and Bithynia, thereby extending Rome's income some 70 per cent. (Plut., *Pompey*, 45, see section III) and the field of operation of Roman capital very appreciably. He also enriched his officers and men and brought 50 million denarii into the treasury by way of booty. We shall revert to the economic results later.

While Pompey was in the East, party leaders fearing that he would return with his great army as the arbiter of Rome, as his master Sulla had done, attempted to forestall him by securing for themselves effective power and resources. Crassus, a rival of Pompey, and Julius Caesar, now showing signs of harboring large ambitions, first proposed to seize Egypt (Suet., *Jul.*, 11; Plut., *Crass.*, 13; Cic., *de leg. agr.*, 2, 41), but this plan was successfully stopped by the conservatives. These two men then proposed a lavish agrarian bill through a tribune, Servilius Rullus, the chief purpose of which was to use the new revenues acquired by Pompey in purchasing lands for the poor. The commission was also to have whatever forces might be needed to carry out the project. The widespread support of the radical proposals made by Catiline the year before had disclosed much poverty and suffering. It is likely that Crassus and Caesar planned to outbid Catiline and become the popular leaders in his place, and at the same time to manoeuvre themselves into a solid position of power against Pompey. Cicero, just entering on his office as consul, in a series of speeches disclosed the danger of a war with Pompey if the measure were carried, and so defeated it (cf. Cary, in *Camb. Anc. Hist.*, IX, chapter XI). We quote one paragraph from Cicero's second speech, referring to the proposal to sell the public land in the provinces.

Cic., *Leg. Agr.*, 2, 50-51:

Iubet venire, quae Attalensium, quae Phaselitum, quae Olympenorum fuerint, agrumque Agerensem et Oroandicum et Gedusanum. Haec P. Servili imperio et victoria, clarissimi viri, vestra facta sunt. Adiungit agros Bithyniae regios, quibus nunc publicani fruuntur; deinde Attalicos agros in Cherroneso; in Macedonia, qui regis Philippi sive Persae fuerunt, qui item a censoribus locati sunt et certissimum vectigal . . . Ascribit item auctioni Corinthios agros opimos et fertiles et Cyrenenses, qui Apionis fuerunt, et agros in Hispania propter Karthaginem novam et in Africa ipsam veterem Karthaginem vendit, . . . adiungit regios agros, Mithridatis qui in Paphlagonia, qui in Ponto, qui in Cappadocia fuerunt, ut eos decemviri vendant.

(Servilius Rullus) " orders everything to be sold which belonged to the inhabitants of Attalia, Phaselis, Olympus, and the land of Agera, Oroanda, and Gedusa. These territories became yours by the victorious campaigns of the illustrious Publius Servilius (77 B. C.). He adds the royal domains of Bithynia (inherited in 74 B. C.), of which the farmers of the revenue now have the enjoyment; next the lands of Attalus in the Chersonese (inherited in 133); those in Macedonia, which belonged to Philip or Perseus (taken in 168), and were also farmed out by the censors, and are a sure source of revenue. He also includes in the sale the rich and fertile lands of Corinth (taken in 146) and Cyrene (inherited in 74), which belonged to Apion; and sells the territories which you possess in Spain near New Carthage (taken by Scipio in 210) and in Africa old Carthage itself (taken in 146), . . . he adds the royal lands of Mithridates in Paphlagonia, Pontus, and Cappadocia (recently taken by Pompey), in order that the decemvirs may sell them."

These had generally been the private estates of former enemies, and the list makes up almost a complete account of the *ager publicus* of Rome at the time. Rome seems not to have expropriated as " public land " the stipendiary lands of her enemies (see Frank, " Dominium in Solo Prov.," *Jour. Rom. Stud.*, 1927, 141).

7. *The Catilinarian Conspiracy.*

Sallust, *Catiline,* 33, 1 and 4-5 (the letter of Manlius, a Catilinarian general) :

Deos hominesque testamur, imperator, nos arma neque contra patriam cepisse neque quo periculum aliis faceremus, sed uti corpora nostra ab iniuria tuta forent, qui miseri egentes violentia atque crudelitate faeneratorum plerique patriae sed omnes fama atque fortunis expertes sumus. neque cuiquam nostrum licuit more maiorum lege uti neque amisso patrimonio liberum corpus habere : tanta saevitia faeneratorum atque praetoris fuit. . . . libertatem (petimus) quam nemo bonus nisi cum anima simul amittit. te atque senatum obtestamur, consulatis miseris civibus, legis praesidium, quod iniquitas praetoris eripuit, restituatis, neve nobis eam necessitudinem inponatis, ut quaeramus, quonam modo maxume ulti sanguinem nostrum pereamus.

" We call gods and men to witness, general, that we have taken up arms neither to injure our country, nor to occasion peril to any one, but to defend our own persons from harm; who, wretched and in want, have been deprived, most of us, of our homes, and all of us of our character and property, by the oppression and cruelty of usurers; nor has any one of us been allowed, according to the usage of our ancestors, to have the benefit of the law, or, when our property was lost, to keep our persons free. Such has been the inhumanity of the usurers and of the praetor. . . . We desire only our liberty, which no honourable man relinquishes but with life. We therefore conjure you and the senate to befriend your unhappy fellow-citizens; to restore us the protection of the law, which the injustice of the praetor has taken from us, and not to lay on us the necessity of considering how we may perish, so as best to avenge our blood."

Sallust, *Catiline,* 37, 4-9 (Sallust's statement regarding the causes of the revolt):

sed urbana plebes, ea vero praeceps erat de multis causis. primum omnium, qui ubique probro atque petulantia maxume praestabant, item alii qui per dedecora patrimoniis amissis, postremo omnes, quos flagitium aut facinus domo expulerat, ei Roman sicut in sentinam con-fluxerant. deinde multi memores Sullanae victoriae, quod ex gregariis militibus alios senatores videbant, alios ita divites, ut regio victu atque cultu aetatem agerent, sibi quisque, si in armis foret, ex victoria talia sperabat. praeterea iuventus, quae in agris manuum mercede inopiam toleraverat, privatis atque publicis largitionibus excita urbanum otium ingrato labori praetulerat. eos atque alios omnis malum publicum alebat. quo minus mirandum est homines egentis, malis moribus maxuma spe, rei publicae iuxta ac sibi consuluisse. praeterea, quorum victoria Sullae parentes proscripti, bona erepta, ius libertatis inminu-tum erat, haud sane alio animo belli eventum exspectabant.

" As for the populace of the city, they had become disaffected from various causes. In the first place, such as everywhere took the lead in crime and profligacy, with others who had squandered their fortunes in dissipation, and, in a word, all whom vice and villany had driven from their homes, had flocked to Rome as a general receptacle of impurity. In the next place, many, who thought of the success of Sulla, when they had seen some raised from common soldiers into senators, and others so enriched as to live in regal luxury and pomp, hoped, each for himself, similar results from victory, if they should once take up arms. In addition to this, the youth, who, in the country, had earned a scanty livelihood by manual labour, tempted by public and private largesses, had preferred idleness in the city to unwelcome toil in the field. To these, and all others of similar character, public disorders would furnish subsistence. It is not at all surprising, therefore, that men in distress, of dissolute principles and extravagant expectations, should have consulted the interest of the state no further than as it was subservient to their own. Besides, those whose parents, by the victory of Sulla, had been proscribed, whose property had been confiscated, and whose civil rights had been curtailed, looked forward to the event of a war with precisely the same feelings."

The causes of the Catilinarian conspiracy are fairly well summarized in these passages. Manlius represents the point of view of the debtors. It is evident from his letter that the conservative praetors at times disregarded the old Papirian law to such an extent that peonage and imprisonment for debt were being permitted.

Sallust's own statement enumerates among the disaffected 1) bankrupt people and criminals, 2) the people who hoped for new opportunities as in the Sullan wars, 3) young farmers tired of hard toil, 4) those who had been deprived by Sulla of the right to hold office. Sallust goes on to say that ambitious men hoped by a revolution to reach power before the return of Pompey might impose a strong master (cf. Plut., *Cic.*, 10-14).

Catiline himself was not a reformer. He had been one of Sulla's satellites, had made some money by bidding in the goods of proscribed democrats, had lost his reputation by misruling Africa, and was ready to win the consulship on any program. General dissatisfaction with senatorial rule determined his program. He spoke in favor of agrarian laws and of debt cancellation, but lost the election to Cicero. He then gathered up a group of disaffected people and organized an army secretly among Sullan veterans who had failed at farming, the unfortunates who had been driven off their farms by Sulla, and other folk with real or fancied grievances. Toward the end of the year he was ready to strike with an army of 20,000 volunteers. Cicero, however, was able to arrest Catiline's chief lieutenants in the city and have them executed for treason. Catiline's army then took fright, and dwindling to 3,000, was easily defeated. The movement had the effect of severing the knights from the tribunician following, and for a period of at least three years united them with the aristocracy into a party of property holders (Sall. *Cat.*; Cic., *in Cat.*, I-IV; Appian, *B. C.*, 2, 2 ff.).

8. The "first triumvirate."

The Senate, led by Lucullus, refused to ratify Pompey's acts in the East and to give his soldiers a land grant, and under the leadership of Cato refused to make concessions to the knights, who had lost money on their Asiatic contracts. Hence Caesar, popular with the common folk, was able to form a secret alliance with Crassus, who held the votes of the business classes, and with Pompey, who controlled the soldier vote and was a hero to a large part of the electorate. This so-called first triumvirate, put in operation in 59, marks the end of republican rule at Rome, for it was formed by means of a pledge between these three men that legislation and elections should conform to their mutual agreements. Since their proposals were obstructed by the Senate, they acted wholly through the assembly. The army of Pompey got its land grants, the knights obtained the remission of funds they had asked for, and Caesar received the province of Gaul for a term of five years (Suet., *Jul.,* 20). Cicero was removed by banishment on a charge that he had illegally executed the Catilinarians, and Cato was removed by the unwelcome gift of a province.

9. The Civil War.

After the death of Crassus, when Caesar was becoming the dominating element in the coalition, Pompey veered toward the Senate. The Senate accordingly felt strong enough to refuse Caesar's requests for an irregular election. Civil war broke out between Caesar and Pompey in 49. Economic motives are usually traced with ease in the case of civil wars, but not in this one. To be sure, the land-holding aristocracy of the Senate felt that their political prestige and their property rights would receive the more favorable consideration from Pompey, and that the Senate might be stripped of power by Julius Caesar if he won. By contrast, debtors and those who would like to take their chances in a new deal leaned toward Caesar. But leanings meant little in either case. Neither side depended upon or called on citizen volunteers to any considerable extent. Caesar relied upon his loyal army of ten legions thoroughly trained in the Gallic War. Pompey relied upon his six veteran legions in Spain (which failed him) and upon his great prestige with the eastern armies, the eastern kings, and the client states. Recruiting in Italy was tried by both, but the citizens of Italy saw little advantage between the two; they were convinced that the deciding elements were the armies already organized, and tried to stay out of the fray. General economic causes did not determine this war. It was the military forces created by the necessities of empire that were now seized by two ambitious men bent on winning supreme power. All men expected Caesar, in case of victory, to make himself autocrat; if Pompey should win, they expected the republican forms to remain merely as forms: the determining power would be Pompey. Caesar won and imposed on Rome a Sullan dictatorship, a version of Oriental autocracy, the economic effects of which we shall discuss later.

In the summer of 50 B. C. Caelius expressed the belief (Cic., *Fam.*, 8, 13, 2) that the rich conservatives (*vos senes divites*) would suffer if Caesar should come into power; and a little later (*Fam.*, 8, 14, 3) he says that in case of war Pompey would have the support of the Senate and the jury panels (after 52 these panels consisted of the wealthier members of the eligible groups). Caesar would have the support, he says, of debtors and all who feared legal prosecution.

In December (Cic., *Att.*, 7, 3, 5; 7, 7, 6) Cicero assumes that Caesar will have the support of "debtors, criminals, the urban plebs, and many ambitious young men," but he soon admits (*ibid.*, 7, 5, 4) that the conservatives are divided, and again (*ibid.*, 7, 7, 5) that the knights are friendly to Caesar, that money lenders are indifferent, and that landowners only wished to avoid war and would not oppose a Caesarian monarchy. (Perhaps Caesar was giving secret assurances to the financial interests.) As soon as the war broke out, Caesar proved that he would protect life and property, and after January Cicero reveals a stronger fear of confiscation and tyranny in case Pompey should win (Cic., *Att.*, 8, 11, 2; 9, 7, 3; 9, 10, 6; 9, 11, 3; 10, 7, 1; 10, 14, 2; 11, 6, 2; the following passages have some slight bearing on the question of economic motives: Cic., *Fam.*, 6, 6, 6; 8, 17, 2; 11, 28, 2; *Att.*, 8, 12 b).

Pompey did not succeed well at recruiting, though he tried hard. He already had two legions, about 10,000 men, on January 1, and managed to get only 12,000 more recruits in two months' levying. Caesar, in his rapid march, caught up with and enlisted the cohorts that Pompey's recruiting officers had gathered in the North. Caesar's independent levies succeeded little better. Aside from the men that he captured and enrolled in the North and at Corfinium, he seems to have got only some three legions from his call for volunteers. It is not apparent that Italy was enthusiastic for either side.

Rostovtzeff's theory (*Soc. Econ. Hist.*, 31) that Pompey counted on using vast numbers of semi-servile renters from the putative latifundia is not convincing. Pompey's failure at recruiting is proof to the contrary; Caesar would hardly have used the Pompeian recruits that he captured if they had been of that class; and finally the instance on which he relies—that of Domitius—hardly applies. Domitius used these only in an unofficial venture, and his coloni were from Etruria where serfdom had formerly been in vogue. This case cannot be generalized for the rest of Italy (see Haywood, "Some Traces of Serfdom," in *Am. Jour. Phil.*, 1933, 145 ff.).

10. Caesar's Dictatorship.

Among the laws passed or edicts issued during Caesar's dictatorship, there are several that show his keen interest in economic conditions. I

have mentioned his grant of citizenship to the Transpadanes in 49.
In the same year he attempted to restore shattered credit by permitting the interest already paid on debts to be deducted from the principal, and by permitting debtors to go into bankruptcy on the basis of
pre-war evaluations of property. In view of the fact that many had
acted on the belief that Caesar would cancel debts by decree, this was
accepted as a fair compromise at a time of general financial terror
(Plut., *Caes.*, 37; Appian, *B. C.*, 2, 198; Suet., *Jul.*, 42; Dio, 41,
36-37; Cic., *Fam.*, 9, 16, 7). Later, from 46 to 44, he instituted a
large series of reforms, many of which had not been put into operation
at his death and hence failed of execution. Caesar's widespread
colonization was the most striking element of his reforms. He sent
ex-slaves of the city to Spain, Corinth, and as far as Sinope, frequently
to places that needed shipping ports; he planted colonies of veterans
in Spain and Gaul, giving both Latin and Roman colonial charters far
and wide (see section II). It is especially noteworthy that he followed
the Gracchan effort to extend "Italy," giving what later jurists called
the *jus Italicum* to colonies in all parts of the world; for, since the
Senate had tried to keep the provincial tithes intact by opposing Roman
colonies in the provinces and since veterans preferred to have allotments near home, the dangerous conception was being formulated that
ownership of land in Italy carried larger rights than elsewhere. There
is no sign that Caesar harbored any such idea. In his plan the civil law
could and should extend as rapidly as possible over the Roman provinces, and in conformity with this view he gave the rights of citizenship lavishly. All the people of Gades—Punic though they were—
received the grant, as well as all Greeks at Rome practicing professions
and a great many important Celts and Spaniards.

At the same time he reduced the number of those receiving doles from
320,000 to 150,000, proclaiming that the number should not be
increased; and, following out the warning of the Gracchi, he also
decreed that on the ranches not more than two-thirds of the laborers
could be slaves.

Suet., *Jul.*, 42 and 44, 3:

Octoginta autem civium milibus in transmarinas colonias distributis,
ut exhaustae quoque urbis frequentia suppeteret, sanxit, ne quis civis
maior annis viginti minorve quadraginta, qui sacramento non teneretur,
plus triennio continuo Italia abesset, neu qui senatoris filius nisi con-

tubernalis aut comes magistratus peregre proficisceretur; neve ii, qui pecuariam facerent, minus tertia parte puberum ingenuorum inter pastores haberent. Omnisque medicinam Romae professos et liberalium artium doctores, quo libentius et ipsi urbem incolerent et ceteri adpeterent, civitate donavit.

De pecuniis mutuis disiecta novarum tabularum expectatione, quae crebro movebatur, decrevit tandem ut debitores creditoribus satis facerent per aestimationem possessionum, quanti quasque ante civile bellum comparassent, deducto summae aeris alieni, si quid usurae nomine numeratum aut perscriptum fuisset; qua condicione quarta pars fere crediti deperibat. Cuncta collegia praeter antiquitus constituta distraxit. 44, 3: siccare Pomptinas paludes; emittere Fucinum lacum; viam munire a mari Supero per Appennini dorsum ad Tiberim usque; perfodere Isthmum . . .

" Moreover, to keep up the population of the city, depleted as it was by the assignment of eighty thousand citizens to colonies across the sea, he made a law that no citizen older than twenty or younger than forty, who was not detained by service in the army, should be absent from Italy for more than three successive years; that no senator's son should go abroad except as the companion of a magistrate or on his staff; and that those who made a business of grazing should have among their herdsmen at least one-third who were men of free birth. He conferred citizenship on all who practised medicine at Rome, and on all teachers of the liberal arts, to make them more desirous of living in the city and to induce others to resort to it.

As to debts, he disappointed those who looked for their cancellation, which was often agitated, but finally decreed that the debtors should satisfy their creditors according to a valuation of their possessions at the price which they had paid for them before the civil war, deducting from the principal whatever interest had been paid in cash or pledged through bankers; an arrangement which wiped out about a fourth part of their indebtedness. He dissolved all guilds, except those of ancient foundation. . . . (He planned) to drain the Pomptine marshes; to let out the water from Lake Fucinus; to make a highway from the Adriatic across the summit of the Apennines as far as the Tiber; to cut a canal through the Isthmus . . . "

The assassination of Caesar in 44 was in the main due to political and patriotic motives, though it is evident that the words "loss of liberty" had also meant, to some extent, loss of property and especially loss of lucrative senatorial privilege (Cic., *Att.,* 14, 6, 1; 14, 10, 2). The civil war that followed was, like that between Caesar and Pompey, chiefly a struggle between ambitious chieftains who had armies in their control. The soldiers usually fought for the man who promised the most money—if the promise seemed properly guaranteed by negotiable prospects.

The triumvirs, who won—Antony, Lepidus, and Octavian—had to confiscate and proscribe brutally in order to keep their promises to their soldiers (see below). From 42 to 40 the citizens of some 25 towns were bluntly dispossessed of land to make way for the victorious soldiers. Once more large and small farms were taken for military settlers—and this time almost wholly in Italy. Soldiers received allotments, and the large plantation system suffered another setback. But the soldiers were not invariably successful in retaining their lots.

In 31 the quarrel between Octavian and Antony led to the final war, and Octavian became the master of the Roman Empire.

II. AREA, CENSUS, COLONIES

1. *Area of Ager Romanus.*

In 49 Caesar had various laws passed—in March and November— granting citizenship to the Transpadanes (Dio, 41, 36; *C. I. L.,* I², pp. 481 and 497). Strabo some fifty years later calls this region very prosperous and thickly populated. The area given citizenship included not only the Transpadane region from Triest to Ivrea—extending northward to the upper limits of the territory of Verona and Comum— but also the western Ligurian part of Cispadane Gaul that was not enfranchised in 89 B. C. The territory incorporated by Caesar had an area of about 25,000 square miles.

2. *Census Statistics: Free Adult Males.*

115 B. C.	394,336	Livy, *Epit.* 63
85	463,000	Hieron, Ol., 173, 4
69	900,000	Livy, *Epit.* 98
28	4,063,000	Augustus, *Res Gestae,* 3, 2

The figures for 115 and for 28 belong to full and accurate censuses; the others do not. The figures for 85 and 69, after the enfranchisement of Italy and Cispadane

Gaul, should have been nearer two million, since, as we have seen, Italy outside of the Ager Romanus had about three times as many inhabitants as Rome, the Cispadane region was very thickly settled, and many citizens had migrated to the provinces. The fact is that after the Social War the *Socii* cared little to go all the way to Rome to register and the Romans did not encourage them to vote. Hence the census even of 69 was not more than about half full (see *Class. Phil.*, 1924, 329 ff.).

After 69 we have no census for 41 years, when the figure is over four million. That census of 28 B. C. was full and accurate. Augustus sent registrars everywhere to take the enrolment; it was not necessary for provincials to travel to Rome as before. The addition of the populous Transpadane region in 49, the extensive colonization of Caesar and Augustus (see next section), the accurate enumeration of citizens in the provinces, and the normal increase of population through forty years will readily account for the figure of 28. It is probable that the census statistics would have been about as follows, if they had been full:

Year		Free adult males	All citizens
85	(after Italy enfranchised)	1,500,000	4,500,000
50	(increase of 35 years)	2,000,000	6,000,000
49	(Transpadane incl.)	3,000,000	9,000,000
40	(colonization and increase)	3,500,000	10,500,000
28	(colonization and increase)	4,063,000	12,000,000

It is not improbable that 3,500,000 of these male citizens lived in Italy, which would make the complete population of Italy about 14,000,000, if we use Dionysius' (9, 25) method of calculating. His method was doubtless based on the census of 28. There would then have been nearly 4,000,000 slaves in Italy in 28.

3. *Colonization.*

During the Marian and Sullan periods the colonies planted were not of the social-economic type of the Gracchans, but were devised rather to reward soldiers who had been promised bonuses at the end of service. But in 63 Servilius Rullus, acting, it would seem, for Crassus and Caesar, proposed an agrarian law of the Gracchan type, promising to pay for a wide-spread settlement of the urban poor on land to be purchased by money taken from the new revenues and booty that Pompey was to bring and from the sale of provincial public land. Cicero spoke against the bill and defeated it (Cic., *de lege Agr.*, I-III). In 61, when Pompey desired land for his soldiers, Flavius proposed a similar measure, adding allotments for soldiers. The money was to come from the use for five years of the new revenues derived from Pompey's conquests (Cic., *Att.*, 1, 19, 4: ut ager hac pecunia emeretur quae ex novis vectigalibus per quinquennium reciperetur.). These revenues amounted to 35,000,000 denarii the year (Plut., *Pomp.*, 45). That is, nearly $50,000,000 would be available for the purpose. Cicero approved, with some obvious amendments, " for it will drain the dregs of the city and people the scantily populated parts of Italy." But the senators blocked

the bill—partly through dislike of Pompey, partly because they had
set themselves since the Gracchan days against the principle of charita-
ble grants.

Pompey's colonies in the East were of a wholly different type. He
simply planned urban centers for the scattered population of the plains
and hills of Asia, partly in order to establish orderly local governments
with which Rome could deal, partly in order to facilitate the task of
collecting tribute through local agencies. The city was in each case a
nucleus for a large rural district and was usually placed at some cross-
road or near the water, where trade might center. The later history of
these colonies proves that the sites were well chosen. Only one colony,
Nicopolis, consisted of Roman citizens, and they were veterans of Pompey's army who preferred to remain in the East (on Pompey's colonies
see Rice Holmes, *The Roman Republic*, I, 209; 434-5).

In 59 Caesar passed two agrarian laws in the face of strenuous senatorial opposition. They took into consideration the desire of Pompey to
have lots for his soldiers and the democratic demand for charity. The
first one proposed to buy lands offered for sale in Italy, using Pompey's
booty for the purpose (Cic., *Att.*, 2, 6; Dio, 38, 1, 4-5, and 7, 3). If
the clause came from the Flavian law, the sum appropriated may well
have reached 175,000,000 denarii, but we do not know the amount. It
would seem that an insufficient amount of land was offered for sale,
for in April a second bill appropriated the public land of Campania
for the purpose (Suet., *Jul.*, 20; Livy, *Epit.* 103; Cic., *Att.*, 2, 16
and 17). A part of this was given in 10 jugera lots to 20,000 citizens
who had three or more children. What became of the evicted renters
we are not told. The process of settling was slow and the plan apparently expanded, for the affair of the Campanian lands was being discussed in 56 and in 51 (Cic., *Quint. fr.*, 2, 1; 2, 5; *Fam.*, 8, 10, 4),
and again, when Caesar was dictator, he made use of the privileges of
the bill to settle some of his veterans in Campania. However, this
colonization of 59 did not add new citizens; it probably compelled
some Campanians to emigrate.

In his later years Caesar colonized very extensively throughout Italy
and the provinces. The people of Rome, whom he sent to foreign
colonies, Suetonius reckons at 80,000 (*Jul.*, 42: Octoginta civium
milibus in transmarinas colonias distributis). They were largely ex-
slaves. We cannot now trace all his colonies, but we can make a rather
extensive list.

Having confiscated the property of many of those who fell in battle against him and of some who remained at enmity, he began as early as 47 to survey such lands and to settle soldiers here and there (Cic., *Fam.*, 9, 17, and 13, 4-8, where Cicero speaks of the activity of surveyors). Some temple property, probably of obsolete cults, was also used (Dio, 43, 47; App., *B. C.*, 2, 140). The later Liber Coloniarum also has indefinite references to settlements *lege Julia*. At Caesar's death his seventh and eighth legions had recently been settled near Capua, presumably on land given in 59 to Pompey's veterans, some of whom had fallen at Pharsalia (Nicolaus Dam., *Vita Caes.*, 31; Cic., *Phil.*, 2, 102). To judge from the names of the colonies, the veterans of the sixth legion were planted at Arlate (Arles, France) on land that Marseilles lost in her revolt in 49, and the veterans of the tenth were given lots at Narbo (see Kromayer, in *Hermes,* 1896, 1 ff.).

In Spain Caesar founded many colonies, chiefly of loyal Spaniards, doubtless largely of Spanish auxiliaries who aided him. To most of these he seems to have given Roman citizenship, and some of the towns were lifted to colonial dignity without change of property, as, for example, Tarraco (the coins are evidence) and Ucubi (*Bell. Hisp.*, 27). Some old towns like Hispalis (Seville, Dio, 43, 39; *Bell. Hisp.*, 35) and Corduba (*ibid.*) were plundered and given to Caesar's partisans because they had supported Pompey. Urso was for the same reason taken and settled by ex-slaves from Rome. We still have the charter of this colony (*C. I. L.*, I², 594). There are in Spain many other colonies, mostly of Roman citizens, that received their charters at this time, *e. g.* Ulia, Iptuci, Hasta, Asido, Illiturgi, Olisipo, but whether the natives were simply granted citizenship or whether new settlers were sent in we do not know. But at any rate most of these towns contained " citizens " from 45 on. The great commercial city of Gades was made a Roman municipality outright. In other words, Caesar, in the eyes of later jurists, simply extended " Italy " over large areas of Spain. It was probably not till some time afterwards that the theory arose that provincial soil ought not to be bought and sold *ex jure Quiritium*. Caesar, at any rate, behaved as though he supposed that, just as he had extended Italy (with civil law) over the Po to the Alps, he and his successors would in time extend all the privileges of Italy over the rest of the Empire. In Gaul he gave Latin rights over most of the Narbonese province—and that was meant as a step to the complete citizen status (Strabo, 4, 1, 12; Pliny, 3, 36).

In Africa also, where many veterans preferred to remain and where
many of the natives, both Semitic and Berber, had supported Caesar,
several small towns were given citizenship, and plans—carried out by
Augustus—to colonize Carthage were carefully drawn (Strabo, 17, 3,
15; Dio, 43, 50, 3; see section on Africa).

In the East the most famous Julian colony was Corinth (Strabo, 8,
6, 23; Plut., *Caes.*, 57). For this Caesar sent from Rome Greek and
Oriental ex-slaves who could speak the language of Greece and build up
an active trading center. The colony grew rapidly, even though it had
an unsavory reputation at the time of St. Paul. Had Caesar lived to
dig the Isthmian canal that he projected, Corinth might well have
become the largest city of the East.

Asia also received several colonies, largely of Roman freedmen,
planted at sea ports in order to develop trade with Rome. The most
important of these are Sinope (Strabo, 12, 3, 11, and Pliny, 6, 6),
Apamea on the Propontis (Strabo, 12, 4, 3; Pliny, 5, 149), and
Heraclea (Strabo, 12, 3, 6). It will be seen that in all this activity
Caesar had in view the development of trade and agriculture, the relief
of the unemployed of Rome, the removal from Rome of some of the
foreign stock, and to no small extent the colonization of veterans.

Extracts from Caesar's Municipal Charters

a. From the "Lex Julia Municipalis," an unfinished fragment; trans.
by Hardy, *Roman Laws and Charters,* Clarendon Press (see text in
C. I. L., I², no. 593; Dessau, 6085), ll. 20-23; 89-90; 142-148:

20. "As regards the roads which are or shall be within the city of
Rome or within one mile of the city of Rome; from the point where
continuous habitation ends it shall be the duty of every person, before
whose tenement any such road shall run, to maintain that road at the
discretion of the aedile to whom in accordance with this law that portion of the city shall belong. And it shall be the duty of the said aedile
to see that every such person required by this law to maintain any such
road running before his tenement shall maintain the said road at his
discretion; and that no water shall stand in such places whereby the
convenient use of the road by the public may be impaired."

89. "No person who is or shall be less than thirty years of age,
shall, after the first day of January in the second year from this date,

stand for or accept or hold the office of iivir or iiiivir or any other magistracy in a municipium or colonia or praefectura, unless he shall have served three campaigns on horseback in a legion, or six campaigns on foot in a legion " . . .

142. " In all municipia, coloniae, or praefecturae of Roman citizens, such as are or shall be within Italy, those persons who shall hold the highest magistracy or competence within such communities shall, at the time when the censor or any other magistrate at Rome shall take a census of the people, and within the sixty days next following upon his knowledge of such census being taken at Rome, proceed to take a census of all those persons belonging to their respective municipia, coloniae, or praefecturae who shall be Roman citizens; from all such persons, duly sworn, they shall receive their gentile names, their praenomina, their fathers or patrons, their tribes, their cognomina, their age, and a state- ment of their property, in accordance with the schedule set forth by the magistrate about to take the census of the people at Rome " . . .

Since patrons are included it is evident that *liberti* were listed; the statement as to property would have to include *slaves*. Hence it is apparent that from Caesar's time it was possible to find in the census records not only the lists of all citizens, free-born and freed, but also the number of slaves.

b. From the " Lex Coloniae Genetivae " of Urso in Spain, trans. by Hardy, *Three Spanish Charters*, p. 23 (see text in *C. I. L.*, I², no. 594; Dessau, 6087), sections 62, 70, 75, 82, 93, 98, 132:

62. " . . . The following shall be the rate of (annual) pay for such persons as are servants to the duoviri: for each scribe 1,200 sesterces, for each body servant 700, for each lictor 600, for each messenger 400, for each copyist 300, for each soothsayer 500, for a herald 300, for persons serving the aediles the pay shall be, for each scribe 800 sesterces, for each soothsayer 500, for each flute-player 300, and each herald 300, and the aforesaid sums it shall be lawful for the said persons to receive without prejudice " (most of these servants probably were on duty only a part of the time).

70. " All duoviri, except those first appointed after this law, shall during their magistracy at the discretion of the decuriones celebrate a gladiatorial show or dramatic spectacles to Jupiter, Juno, and Minerva, and to the gods and goddesses, or such part of the said shows as shall be possible, during four days, for the greater part of each day, and on the

said spectacles and the said shows each of the said persons shall expend
of his own money not less than 2,000 sesterces, and out of the public
money it shall be lawful for each several duovir to expend a sum not
exceeding 2,000 sesterces " . . .

75. " No person shall unroof or demolish or dismantle any building
in the town of the colonia Julia, unless he shall have furnished sureties,
at the discretion of the duoviri, that he has the intention of rebuilding
the same, or unless the decuriones shall have allowed such act by decree."
(Since the town expended money on the walls, it kept the right to say
how the enclosed area should be used.)

82. " As respecting lands or woods or buildings given or assigned
to the colonists of the colonia Genetiva Julia, that they may have public
use thereof, no person shall sell the said lands or woods, or lease the
same for a longer period than five years."   (This concerns public land
set aside to help defray public expenses.)

93. " No duovir, appointed or created after the establishment of the
colony, and no praefectus, left in charge by a duovir in accordance with
the charter of the colony, shall, concerning public ground or for public
ground, receive or accept from a contractor or leaseholder or surety any
gift or present or remuneration or any other favour " . . .

98. " In the case of the carrying out of any public work having been
decreed by the decuriones of the said colony, a majority of the
decuriones being present when the said matter is discussed, it shall be
lawful for such work to be carried out, provided that in any one year
not more than five days' work be decreed for each adult male, nor more
than three days' work for each yoke of draught animals."

132. " No candidate seeking office shall knowingly and with wrongful intent give or make largess of any gift or present or any other thing
with a view to his candidature. Nor shall any person with a view to
the candidature of another, provide entertainments, or invite any person
to dinner, or hold a banquet, or, knowingly and with wrongful intent,
give or make largess of any gift or present or any other thing. Any
person acting in contravention of this shall be condemned to pay to the
colonists of the colonia Genetiva Julia 5,000 sesterces, and may be sued
or prosecuted in accordance with this law for that amount through
recuperatores before a duovir or praefectus by any person at will."

The colonization carried on by the victorious triumvirs after the battle of Philippi in 42-40 was wholly of the Sullan type. In 43 the triumvirs had already promised to expropriate eighteen cities of Italy for their eighteen legions (App., *B. C.*, 4, 3). These did not suffice. The communities that showed sympathy for the cause of Brutus or had for any reason offended any of the triumvirs were brutally deprived of a part or of all of their land, which was then allotted to the soldiers of the victors. Twenty-eight legions, some 170,000 men, were given land (App., *B. C.*, 5, 3), and Italy was wrecked, as in Sulla's day.

Appian, *B. C.*, 5, 12:

καταλέγοντι δ' αὐτῷ τὸν στρατὸν ἐς τὰς ἀποικίας καὶ τὴν γῆν ἐπινέμοντι δυσεργὲς ἦν. οἵ τε γὰρ στρατιῶται τὰς πόλεις ᾔτουν, αἳ αὐτοῖς ἀριστίνδην ἦσαν ἐπειλεγμέναι πρὸ τοῦ πολέμου, καὶ αἱ πόλεις ἠξίουν τὴν Ἰταλίαν ἅπασαν ἐπινείμασθαι τὸ ἔργον ἢ ἐν ἀλλήλαις διαλαχεῖν τῆς τε γῆς τὴν τιμὴν τοὺς δωρουμένους ᾔτουν, καὶ ἀργύριον οὐκ ἦν, ἀλλὰ συνιόντες ἀνὰ μέρος ἐς τὴν Ῥώμην οἵ τε νέοι καὶ γέροντες ἢ αἱ γυναῖκες ἅμα τοῖς παιδίοις, ἐς τὴν ἀγορὰν ἢ τὰ ἱερά, ἐθρήνουν, οὐδὲν μὲν ἀδικῆσαι λέγοντες, Ἰταλιῶται δὲ ὄντες ἀνίστασθαι γῆς τε καὶ ἑστίας οἷα δορίληπτοι.

" The task of assigning the soldiers to their colonies and dividing the land was one of exceeding difficulty. For the soldiers demanded the cities which had been selected for them before the war as prizes for their valour, and the cities demanded that the whole of Italy should share the burden, or that the cities should cast lots with the other cities, and that those who gave the land should be paid the value of it; and there was no money. They came to Rome in crowds, young and old, women and children, to the forum and the temples, uttering lamentations, saying that they had done no wrong for which they, Italians, should be driven from their fields and their hearthstones, like people conquered in war."

We have no complete list of the districts that suffered from this wholesale confiscation, but from casual references we know the names of some 26, a part of which may belong to the settlements made after 31 (see Kornemann's list in *Realenc.*, 4, 524, nos. 54-79). Among the more important were Ariminum, Beneventum, Cremona (for which Vergil's property was taken), Firmum, Hispellum, Luca, Luceria, Pisae, Suessa, Sutrium, Tergeste, Venusia (where Horace lost his property). Needless to say, the distribution must have broken up many large estates of senators who had supported Brutus and Cassius, and thus have resulted temporarily, at least, in the increase of small-plot

22

farming. But we can hardly suppose that all the soldiers' lots remained intact for long.

Again after Actium (31 B. C.), when Octavian defeated Antony and became master of Rome, the veterans of the victor had to have their land-bonus. This time Octavian claims that he bought land for 600,000,000 sesterces ($30,000,000) for his troops (*Res Gest.*, ch. 3, 16: Pecuniam pro agris quos in consulatu meo quarto [30 B. C.] . . . adsignavi militibus, solvi municipis, ea summa sestertium circiter sexiens milliens fuit). The soldiers this time numbered about 120,000. Dio (51, 4, 6), whose account does not entirely agree with the passage just quoted, observes that some of the Italians who had aided Antony were settled at Philippi or Dyrrachium and that their lands were used for veteran colonies. In this case, then, there was a show of observing property rights, but here also soldiers supplanted farmers, and the extension of small lots continued. Later Augustus made a practice of buying land in the provinces for his veterans.

Whatever else happened in this period, Caesar's colonization tended to bind the various parts of the Empire to Italy by a community of interest and of sentiment, while the colonization of the Triumvirs and of Augustus up to 30 B. C. created some 300,000 small farms in Italy for soldiers—not all of whom were skillful farmers—and compelled a large number of dispossessed Italians to migrate to the provinces and to the cities.

III A. THE PUBLIC INCOME AND EXPENSES, 80–50

I. Income

a. *Provincial Revenues.*

No itemized statement of income and expenses can be made for the period as a whole, for here again the civil wars (49-6 and 43-2) bankrupted Rome and in both instances confiscation was resorted to, the extent of which is not recorded. For the first part of the period—from 80 to 50—we may base our reckoning on the valuable statement of Plutarch that before Pompey's victory in the East (63-60 B. C.) the state had 50,000,000 denarii ($10,000,000) per year at its disposal, to which Pompey added 35,000,000 (*Pomp.*, 45):

. . . ἔφραζε διὰ τῶν γραμμάτων ὅτι πεντακισχίλιαι μὲν μυριάδες ἐκ τῶν τελῶν ὑπῆρχον, ἐκ δὲ ὧν αὐτὸς προσεκτήσατο τῇ πόλει μυριάδας ὀκτακισχιλίας πεντακοσίας λαμβάνουσιν, ἀναφέρεται δὲ εἰς τὸ δημόσιον ταμιεῖον ἐν νομίσματι καὶ κατασκευαῖς ἀργυρίου καὶ χρυσίου δισμύρια τάλαντα, πάρεξ τῶν εἰς τοὺς στρατιώτας δεδομένων, ὧν ὁ τοὐλάχιστον αἴρων κατὰ λόγον δραχμὰς εἴληφε χιλίας πεντακοσίας.

" the inscriptions set forth that whereas the public revenues from taxes had been fifty million drachmas, they were receiving after the additions which Pompey had made to the city's power eighty-five million, and that he was bringing into the public treasury in coined money and vessels of gold and silver twenty thousand talents, apart from the money which had been given to his soldiers, of whom the one whose share was the smallest had received fifteen hundred drachmas."

Since Bithynia and Cyrene were added as provinces in 74 (App., B. C., 1, 111) and port dues increased steadily after 80, it would be fair to assume that the normal income was about 40,000,000 in the year 80 B. C., if it was about 50,000,000 in 62 B. C. Any attempt to apportion the items that made up the 50,000,000 would have to depend largely on estimates of areas in the provinces. In the Empire, after Caesar had reduced the Asiatic tithes by a third (App., B. C., 5, 4: " Caesar remitted to you one-third of what you paid." So also Plut., Caes., 48) and after the boundaries had been narrowed, the province of Asia was paying about 7,000,000 denarii (Philos., Vita Soph., p. 57 K). Twice that amount might be a fair estimate for 62 B. C. (See Boettcher; Die Einnahmen der röm. Rep.).

Sicily paid tithes on grain, oil, wine, and fruit, and on public pasture land a grazing tax for each head of cattle. The tithe on wheat in 70 amounted to 3,000,000 modii (750,000 bushels) and at 3 sesterces the modius it was worth 9,000,000 sesterces or 2,250,000 denarii (Cic., Verr., 3, 163). Since wheat was the most important staple, the combined Sicilian tribute probably did not exceed 4,000,000 denarii. Sardinia and Corsica did not have more than about a third as much profitable land, and their returns might be estimated accordingly. The original tax imposed on Macedonia was one half the royal tax or 600,000 denarii (Plut., Paulus, 28; Livy, 45, 18 and 29). After the wars of 149-6, and of Sulla (when certain taxes were imposed on Greece as well) we may reckon that the increase of the province of Macedonia and Achaea permitted a tribute of at least 2,000,000 denarii (Achaea was tributary at least in 40: App., B. C., 5. 77; Delos was apparently freed from tribute in 58, cf. the Lex Gabinia of 58, C. I. L., I², 2500: vecteigalibus leiberari).

Since Caesar could impose a tribute of 10,000,000 denarii on the *Gaul* that he had conquered (Suet., *Jul.*, 25; cf. Eutrop., 6, 17), *Narbonese Gaul* probably paid as much as a half or more, and *Spain,* now well cultivated except in the center and north, probably paid 5,-8,000,000. *Bithynia* may well have produced a fifth of the yield of Asia. *Africa* might yield about 4,000,000, since that was what Caesar reckoned for the wheat and oil of the second African province (Plut., *Caes.,* 55). In sum, the provincial dues would amount to about 40,000,000 in 63 B. C. About 10,000,000 denarii would then come from customs dues at harbors, and other less important sources like the monopolies on public forests, and the fishing, river, and salt taxes. Recently found inscriptions prove that even the small town of Minturnae contained publicans who were engaged in farming the revenues of the neighboring salt-pans and pitch-producing forests. We have no data regarding the yields of such revenues.

There were a few changes of importance between 60 and 50. In the year 60 the customs dues were somewhat reduced because in that year those of Italy were struck off (Dio, 37, 51, 3). The Campanian lands were also given away rent-free in 59. On the other hand Pompey's new provinces brought in some 35,000,000 denarii after 60 (Plut., *Pompey,* 45, quoted above). Hence we may assume an income of about 80,000,000 denarii between 60 and 50 B. C.

b. *Booty.*

During this period of 50 years there were relatively few campaigns that yielded booty for the treasury. Lucullus gathered in wealth; he was one of the most lavish spenders in Cicero's day. He gave over a million denarii to his soldiers (Plut., *Luc.,* 37) and at his expensive triumph he poured out nearly four million liters of wine (milia cadum divisit amplius centum; Pliny, 14, 96). But the treasury received only 2,700,000 denarii (Plut., *Luc.,* 37; Athen., 6, 109; Eutrop., 6, 10).

Pompey's combined triumph in 61 over the pirates, Tigranes, and Mithridates brought in amazing sums for that day, but the state received not much over a third of them. The accounts are as follows:

Pliny, 37, 16: $\overline{|MM|}$ HS ($=$ 50,000,000 denarii) to the state.
              $\overline{|M|}$ HS   ($=$ 25,000,000 denarii) to his legati
                                       and quaestors.

Plut., *Pomp.,* 45: 1500 denarii to each common soldier.

Appian, *Mith.,* 116, gives the sum total to men and officers as 16,000 talents. Hence the men (including centurions and tribunes) received a bonus of 71,000,000 (96,000,000–25,000,000) denarii for some six years of service. Since the distribution offered by Tigranes to Pompey (App., *Mith.,* 104; Strabo, 11, 14, 10) gave centurions twenty times as much as privates, and the tribunes six times as much as centurions, a legion of 4,000 men, 60 centurions, and 6 tribunes required nearly 9,000,000 denarii. That is, about 8 legions probably received the final bonus (and asked for land in addition).

The twenty-five million denarii paid to the higher officers went to some eighteen legati and two quaestors, after Pompey had taken his share. Pompey paid for a very expensive triumph, a votive offering to Minerva of over 2,000,000 denarii (Diod., 40, 4), and later built a great theatre. There is reason to suppose that he lent some money to the king of Cappadocia to equip his bankrupt kingdom (Cic., *Att.,* 6, 1, 3; 6, 2, 7; 6, 3, 5). At any rate, even if Pompey subtracted for himself a fourth of the amount set aside for officers, there would be nearly 800,000 denarii ($160,000) for each of the higher officers who had served some six years. These officers were important men, most of whom might have expected the emoluments of a governorship if they had not enlisted. The sums, therefore, unprecedented though they were, doubtless passed as reasonable in the circumstances (see Drumann-Groebe, IV, 486 ff., for a discussion of the figures). Vell., 2, 40, 3, says Pompey brought in more than any triumphator except Paulus, but since his figures for Paulus are incorrect (1, 9, 6), the statement has little value.

Julius Caesar provided the ugliest example in Roman history of provincial looting for personal gain. He went to Spain heavily in debt in 61 (Appian, *B. C.,* 2, 8, says he owed 25,000,000 sesterces) and created wars that cleared him of debt. We are not told how much the treasury received. He gathered immense wealth in Gaul in 59-50. According to Velleius, 2, 47, he slew 400,000 and captured even more (this is the lowest figure given). That number of captives, if sold at 250 denarii each—a low figure—would bring 100,000,000 denarii. And in addition he sold so much captured gold that the price of it fell a sixth (Suet., *Jul.,* 54, 2). Yet he was actually in debt to Atticus in 49 (Cic., *Att.,* 6, 1, 25) and he turned nothing into the treasury. He had raised four legions without authorization and probably had to pay for these till the year 56 (Cic., *Prov. Cons.*, 28). His chief of staff, Labienus, and his chief engineer, Mamurra, grew very wealthy (Cic., *Att.,* 7, 7, 6; Catullus, 114). His legati and officers probably received as much as Pompey had given his men; even Trebatius expected wealth (Cic., *Fam.,* 7, 16, 3). Caesar bribed Paulus for political support with 9,000,000 denarii (Plut., *Caes.,* 29, 3), Curio with 500,000 (Vell., 2, 48), and many others (App., *B. C.,* 2, 17; 26), and in 50 he gave 250 denarii to each of the 8,000 legionaries recalled into service (App., *B. C.,* 2, 29). He contributed to a lavish loan to Ptolemy (Plut., *Caes.,* 48, 4) for political reasons, and poured out bribes at the elections (App., *B. C.,* 2, 17). Some 15,000,000 denarii went to Rome for building-sites and for construction in his Forum to give glamor to his name (Cic., *Att.,* 4, 16, 14; Suet., *Jul.,* 26; Pliny, *N. H.,* 36, 103.). And we have not the whole story. To be sure, in his triumph in 46 he brought in 150,000,000 denarii from the sale of booty after laying heavy requisitions on Spain, Egypt, Asia, and Italy, but the treasury was then only one of his own pockets.

There were of course some honest governors left—Cicero mentions a number—but these usually avoided the needless raids that brought booty. In general we may say that from 80 to 50 the treasury probably did not receive any considerable amount from booty except the 50,000,000 denarii brought by Pompey. The few sums deposited between 49 and 30 were residues after requisitions had been made upon the provinces for the costs of the civil wars and need not be classed here.

II. Expenses

a. *Army.* Again the army was the most expensive item of the budget. At ordinary times from 80 to 50 some twenty legions were needed for the provinces (the 16th and 17th were in Macedonia; the 18th and 19th in Cilicia). But times were not always normal. From 80 to 70 extra legions were needed for the Sertorian War in Spain, for the defence of Rome against Lepidus in 77, for the war against Spartacus in 73-71 (Crassus had about eight legions in 71: App., *B. C.,* 1, 118). Lucullus fought Mithridates in Asia from 74 to 66 with an army of several legions; Pompey was voted 6,000 talents (36,000,000 denarii) for the war against the pirates, though he probably did not use all of this sum; and from 66 to 61 he had an army of about eight legions in his last Mithridatic War.

During the first triumvirate the rivalry of factions led to very heavy increases in the forces. Piso, Caesar's father-in-law, received four and a half million denarii for his Macedonian equipment as payment for loyal services to his superiors. Probably he was to have four legions. Gabinius, his colleague, received Syria with an army that was probably as large.

Julius Caesar gradually raised his army in Gaul from four legions to ten (Drumann-Groebe, III, 709) and, though he paid a part of the expenses from booty during the first three years, and seems to have fed the army by local requisitions (*B. G.*, 1, 16; 2, 3; 3, 7), the state probably had to appropriate any sum that he asked for from 56 on (Cic., *Prov., Cons.*, 28; *Fam.*, 1, 7, 10). Pompey received Spain with her four legions in 55 and gradually doubled this force. In the year 50 there were six citizen legions and a quasi-legion of Spaniards in Spain, and Pompey had one legion in Italy. Crassus also on receiving Syria in 55, raised the number to about eight (that is, he had seven at the Euphrates in 53 [Plut., *Crass.*, 20; 31] and probably one in his province).

This sums up to an average of about 23 legions per year from 80 to 60 and an average of 25 per year from 60 to 50.

The cost of the maintenance of a legion was also increasing. The generals supported expensive cohorts and staffs that received good salaries besides a portion of the booty. When Pompey had about six legions in Spain, he received 1,000 talents for their pay and expense account (Plut., *Caes.*, 28; *Pomp.*, 55); that is to say, we should count the appropriation for each legion as about 1,000,000 denarii per year (we counted 800,000 for the preceding period and about 600,000 for 200-150). Similarly in 58 Piso received 4,500,000 denarii for Macedonia with its army presumably of four legions (Cic., *in Pis.*, 86). In 49 Domitius set out for Gaul with one legion (App., *B. C.*, 2, 32) and carried 1,500,000 denarii (Caes., *B. C.*, 1, 23). The senators made a practice of being liberal in the appropriations for army equipment, for most of them hoped some day to have the advantage of similar treatment. What was left over belonged to the treasury, but there was seldom any residue. Cicero, for instance, saved 540,000 denarii of his appropriation (Cic., *Fam.*, 5, 20, 9; *Ad Att.*, 5, 11, 5. Since he had two legions, he presumably had received about 2,000,000 denarii). And when he deposited this residue in Asia with the intention of giving

a draft to the treasury, his officers were surprised (Cic., *Fam.,* 5, 20).
The theory of the senators was that, since they served the state gratis
through many expensive years, the appropriations for the province at
the end ought to be liberal enough to leave something over by way of
reimbursement. If Cicero's residue of $100,000 was normal, that
would after all be but meager pay for twenty years of faithful service
to the state, during which time he had received nothing. And this
sum he turned over to Pompey before the battle of Pharsalia. It would
seem that the state was paying on the average about 25,000,000 denarii
the year between 60 and 50 B. C., for the army alone.

b. *Navy.*

We do not know the size of the navies used by Servilius against the
Cilician pirates in 78-4 or by Antonius against the Cretans in 73-2. In
67, Pompey, in his war with the pirates, had some 270 vessels of all sizes
(App., *Mith.,* 94). A number of these were probably quinqueremes;
but the trireme had become the standard war vessel (App., *B. C.,* 2, 56
and 87) since, after the destruction of the eastern navies, Rome needed
speed rather than bulk in pursuing pirates. There is no reason to suppose that Pompey built up to the 500 permitted him. After his victory
he added 90 captured vessels to the fleet (Plut., *Pomp.,* 28). During
the next few years we hear of efforts to keep the fleet in repairs. For
instance in 62 the Senate appropriated somewhat over 4,000,000
denarii for the purpose, and an additional amount the next year (Cic.,
pro Flacco, 30). But the navy gradually deteriorated so that in 49
Pompey had to call on the eastern states for ships (Cic., *Att.,* 9, 9, 2).
In general it would seem that from 78 till about 60 the state tried to
have a respectable navy, but that no large portion of it was in actual
service for more than three or four years. The costs cannot be
estimated.

c. *Corn doles.*

The references to the corn laws are so fragmentary and careless that
we must avoid hasty conclusions, but here and there some definite
inferences may be drawn.

(1) After Sulla's death, Lepidus seems to have passed a moderate
corn law (" he passed a corn law without opposition that five modii of
grain [per month] should be given to the people ": Granius Licin.,

34 F. This author is careless, and *populo* does not necessarily mean to *all the people* nor does *darentur* necessarily mean that the grain was a free gift).

(2) In 73, when grain was scarce because of the Spartacan revolt, a new law, the Terentia Cassia, was passed. The chief purpose of this measure was to give instructions to the praetor on how to requisition grain. Cicero (*Verr.*, 3, 72) implies that after this law was passed, a supply of 33,000 medimni (200,000 modii) was about enough to satisfy the public distribution for a month. That is, some 40,000 people apparently received grain, and Sallust (*Hist.*, 3, 48, 19 M) thought that it was a gift. But Sallust is notorious for his anachronisms. If it was a free gift (which I doubt), the cost to the state would have been about 2,000,000 denarii the year.

(3) In 63, since the populace was rioting because of the failure of Catiline's conspiracy, Cato offered them a bribe in the form of an enlarged dole: presumably the number of takers had been definitely restricted by the previous laws. (Plut., *Cato min.*, 26: " Cato . . . persuaded the senate to conciliate the poor and landless multitude by including them in the distribution of grain, the annual expenditure for which was 1250 talents." Plut., *Caes.*, 8, gives the same sum, *i. e.* 7,500,000 denarii). Since the next law strikes off the payment of 6⅓ *asses* per modius, it is probable that Cato's law required the payment of that price also, but very much widened the scope of the distribution. At any rate we have Plutarch's estimate of the annual cost: 7,500,000 denarii—about 14 per cent of the income—from 63 to 58; and, if Plutarch is giving the complete cost of the dole, and not simply the cost added by Cato's law, and if corn that cost the state four sesterces was sold at 1½, then the number of recipients under Cato's law was about 200,000. (When large amounts of wheat were requisitioned in Sicily, the state paid four instead of three denarii for the second tithe).

(4) In 58 Clodius passed a law to give the dole free of all charges (Dio, 38, 13: τόν τε σῖτον προῖκα εὐθὺς διένειμε; Ascon., *in Pis.*, Stangl., 15: frumentum quod antea 6⅓ in singulos modius debatur, gratis daretur). Cicero's comment on this bill was that, when the price of 6⅓ *asses* was remitted, about one-fifth of the state's income was used up (*pro Sest.*, 55: ut remissis senis et trientibus quinta prope pars vectigalium tolleretur). These words mean, of course, not that the Clodian law alone cost one-fifth of the revenues, but that, after this law was

passed, the dole cost one-fifth of the 80,000,000 denarii, *i. e.* about 16,000,000 denarii, which is reasonable. For if there were 200,000 recipients before, there would readily be 260,000 as soon as the law was passed, if only because it would attract outsiders and because the rich freed their aged slaves so that they could feed at the public crib (Dio, 39, 24). Caesar in fact found the number of takers about 320,000 some ten years later (Suet., *Jul.*, 41). With *frumentum imperatum* at 4 sesterces the modius and the allowance 60 modii the year, 16,000,-000 denarii would feed about 266,000 people, which corresponds fairly well with Cicero's statement.

(5) But this did not suffice. For some reason sufficient grain did not come into the city, or the dole took too large a portion of what came, so that grain prices rose at Rome in 57 (for those who must buy). The Senate therefore authorized Pompey to organize a committee to look after the grain supply for five years. In 56 he was voted a sum of 10,000,000 denarii for the purpose, presumably for five years (Cic., *Att.*, 4, 1; *Quint.*, 2, 5). Dio (39, 24) adds that many slaves were manumitted in anticipation of the event. At best, even making no allowances for Pompey's expenses, this addition to the regular cost of the annual dole would be only about 16% for a period of five years and that was doubtless soon wasted on the increased number of recipients. (A late scholium on Lucan, 1, 319—see Weber's edition—says that Rome needed nearly 30,000,000 modii per year. Some historians use this statement as a basis for calculating Rome's population in Pompey's day; but the scholium comes from a very unreliable and undatable source, and furthermore we do not know to what period it refers. So far as we know, it may concern fourth century Rome.)

(6) In 46 Caesar found the number of recipients 320,000 and after a careful census of the city he cut the number down to 150,000 (Suet., *Jul.*, 41); since he sent 80,000 colonists from the city to the provinces, more than half of those struck off were apparently taken care of. The 150,000 would still cost the treasury some 9,000,000 denarii per year.

To sum up, then, the corn dole cost not over 2,000,000 denarii from 78 to 63, about 7,500,000 denarii from 63 to 58, about 16,000,000 after 58 plus an extra sum of 2,000,000 per year from 56 to 51, and the numbers of recipients rose constantly till 46, when the cost was reduced to about 9,000,000 denarii per year. Caesar instituted a regular grain-buying service. In 43, Antony had Brutus and Cassius placed in charge in order to remove them from Rome (Cic., *Att.*, 15, 9).

d. *Grants of Land.*

We do not know what the land grants cost in 59, but if the clause that Pompey favored in the Flavian law of 61 was repeated in the law of Caesar and Pompey in 59, the cost would be all the new revenues (35,000,000 denarii per year) for five years, or 175,000,000 all told. Let us assume for the argument that unimproved land could be bought at 250 denarii ($50) the jugerum and that ten-jugera lots were desired; this sum would suffice to settle over 14,000 families per year for each of five years. In view of the cry for doles and in view of the fact that Campanian land was also used, it is hardly likely that land was bought on such a scale. When Caesar, Pompey, and Crassus began to enlarge their armies, they doubtless were willing to check the colonization with a view to saving money for themselves and for the prospective colonization of their own huge armies. By the second law of 59 some 20,000 men were settled on Campanian public land (Suet., *Jul.*, 20, 3; Vell., 2, 44, 4; App., *B. C.*, 2, 10). In 57-6 Cicero supported Pompey's proposal to carry on more distributions in Campania, but Caesar stopped the discussion (Cic., *Quint.*, 2, 1; 2, 5; *Fam.*, 8, 10, 4). Cary, *Jour. Rom. Stud.*, 1929, 113, may be right in holding that a Caesarean plan for wider surveys with a view to colonization was adopted in 55. What these measures cost we cannot say.

e. *Public Buildings.*

This period was marked by great activity in the construction of public works, but few of these had to be paid for by the treasury. The booty of Gaul and of Asia and the wealth of Agrippa were spent on the greatest undertakings. Indirectly, of course, the state therefore paid the expenses, since generals withheld from the treasury what they spent on public works.

The more important works paid for by the treasury were the following:

The Capitoline temple, which was burned in 83, was ordered restored by Sulla, but the rebuilding took many years and the expenses probably fell largely in the post-Sullan period. Catulus dedicated the building in 69, before it was complete (Tac., *Hist.*, 3, 72; Cic.,

Verr., 4, 69; Livy, *Epit.* 98). The state did not bear the entire cost, for the people of Italy were asked to contribute to the very expensive enterprise (Val. Max., 9, 3, 8).

The Tabularium, a fireproof hall for official records and state papers, was also constructed by Catulus, the consul of 78, by order of the Senate. The inscription reads (Dessau, 35):

> Q. Lutatius Q. F. Q. N. Catulus cos. substructionem et tabularium de sentus sententia faciundum coeravit eidemque probavit.

It is a magnificent building, honestly constructed, and it must have taken some years to build.

In 62, the year after Cicero's consulship, Fabricius the *curator viarum* built the bridge to the island, the two splendid arches of which are still in place (Dessau, 5892). The corresponding Pons Cestius was probably built soon after.

We have nineteen terminal stones erected by the censors Servilius and Messala in 54 B. C. by order of the Senate, from the Mulvian bridge down as far as the Almo. They probably indicate the construction of a stone embankment built at no mean expense. (*C. I. L.,* I², 766, a-t). The great inundation of 54 (Dio, 39, 61) was probably responsible for this work.

We shall list the other public buildings erected from private funds under " building industry." Those we have mentioned here would not have been a heavy burden on the treasury, since they extend over a period of some thirty years.

We have not attempted a comparison of the income with the expenses, but we have enough to see that from 80 to 50 the state was at least a going concern, despite constant complaints of poverty (Sall., *Hist.,* 2, 98; 2, 47: " our revenues do not suffice for half our expenses," cf. Cic., *Prov. Cons.,* 11). From 55 to 50 its income was probably about 80,000,000 denarii ($16,000,000), not a huge amount for a state that extended from the Atlantic to the Euphrates. Over a third was probably being spent on the army and navy, probably a fourth on doles and grain supplies for the city, and a considerable amount on colonization. We should perhaps assume three or four million dollars for administrative expenses, the civil service, roads, sewers, repairs of public buildings, and for games. When Caesar crossed the Rubicon in 49, he found about 12,000,000 denarii in the " sacred treasury," but apparently not anything worthy of mention in the regular *aerarium*.

III B. THE PUBLIC INCOME AND EXPENSES, 50–30

I. Expenses

During the long period of civil wars after 50 B. C. the treasury was usually bankrupt.   In fact very little money ever reached the treasury, for the generals in the various provinces laid hands on all tribute before it left for Rome, and they laid extra requisitions on the regions they controlled.   In 49-8 the Senate was in Greece and called in the tribute of the East (Caes., *B. C.*, 3, 3).   By the end of 48 Caesar got possession of the returns from all provinces except Africa and a part of Spain.   By 45 he had these also.   But in 43 the Senate lost almost all the revenues. Those of the East went to Brutus and Cassius for two years.   Lepidus and Plancus controlled the West.   Asinius Pollio, though in Spain, lost his revenues to a quaestor who apparently had orders to abscond with them to Antony.   After Philippi the world was temporarily divided into three parts.   Antony held all the East, Lepidus Africa, and Octavian the West, but his enemy, Sextus Pompey, controlled the revenues of Sicily and Sardinia till 36.   None of these generals could possibly live on the regular income.   Deficits were constantly made up from extra requisitions, confiscations, and extra taxes.   We cannot make any general estimates, but can at least set down some of the significant items.

a. *The armies.*

From 50 to 30 the number of legions rose to very high figures and soldiers now received not only the Caesarean salary of almost twice as much as before but were constantly offered cash bonuses and further promises.   They went to the highest bidder.

In 48 Caesar, after leaving garrisons in Spain, Gaul, and Italy, crossed to Greece with 12 legions (Caes., *B. C.,* 3, 2) while Pompey had 11.   After Pharsalia Caesar must have had nearly 40 legions, since the 37th is mentioned in " Caes.," *B. Alex.,* 9, 3, and recruiting was not yet complete.   In 48-4 some of the veterans were settled in colonies, but the garrisons still remained large.   At the time of Caesar's death there were still 37 legions in service after the loss and dismissal of

about 15 of his own (not to speak of those lost by his enemies: Domaszewski, in *Neue Heid. Jahrb.*, 1894, 178). Italy had been compelled
to provide some 200,000 men for a war in which Italy had but little
interest.

In 44-3 Antony, Octavian, and Lepidus all recruited vigorously with
larger promises of extra stipends and land-bonuses. When the triumvirate was formed, Octavian had 11 legions, while Antony and Lepidus
had 23. Meanwhile Cassius and Brutus had gathered in all those
stationed in eastern provinces and had also recruited several till they
had 19 legions. That is to say, over 50 legions were again in the field
(Domaszewski, *op. cit.*, 184-6). After the battle of Philippi, where
many legions were lost, the remnants of the opposition army were dismissed and many were placed in colonies, so that new recruiting was
necessary for the war with Sextus Pompey and later for the battle of
Actium. It is probable that the number supported by the state from
40 to 31 B. C. was seldom under 40 and at times far more. In 31
Octavian had 45 legions and Antony 30 (Appian, *B. C.*, 5, 127; Dio,
51, 5, 6).

When the armies of the various generals rose to 70 and more legions,
the expense involved would have used every penny of income even if
the stipend had been the normal one of 120 denarii. But not only had
Julius Caesar raised the pay to 225 denarii (Suet., *Jul.*, 26, 3), but
most of the soldiers were hired by high bidding. We have lost much
of the data, but what is left will show that irregular pay often doubled
the costs of an army again, even after the regular stipend had been
doubled. For instance, Caesar had made such lavish promises to his
soldiers that at his triumph in 46 he gave each legionary 5,000 denarii,
each centurion 10,000 and each tribune 20,000 (App., *B. C.*, 2, 102;
Dio, 43, 21). That alone would probably be equal to about twice the
yearly income of the treasury. When in 44 Octavian began to tamper
with the legionaries, Antony had to pay about 16,000 of them 100
denarii each for their loyalty (App., *B. C.*, 3, 44). At the same time
Octavian gathered in some 10,000 of Caesar's veterans at a cost of 500
denarii ($= \$1,000,000$) and promised in case of war ten times the
amount (App., *B. C.*, 3, 40 and 48). Antony soon after made secret
promises to the soldiers of Asinius (Cic., *Fam.*, 10, 32, 4), and Decimus Brutus was forced to meet similar offers till he wasted all his
property, worth more than 10,000,000 denarii (Cic., *Fam.*, 11, 10, 5).

In these cases private funds were used, but after the war the victors recouped as best they could from the state; the losers forfeited their property and usually lost their lives as well. At Philippi, Brutus and Cassius had some 80,000 men. Before the battle the soldiers received a gift of 1,500 denarii—that sums up to $24,000,000—and before the second battle, when the number was less, Brutus again gave 1,000 denarii to each man, or about $12,000,000 (App., 4, 88; 100; 118). Those sums had been requisitioned in the provinces, and the victors doubtless found and appropriated most of the money after the battle.

b. *Navy.*

When the Civil War broke out in 49 Pompey found the fleet wholly inadequate and called upon the seaport cities of the East to provide vessels (Cic., *Att.,* 9, 9, 2: "All this fleet from Alexandria, Colchis, Tyre, Sidon, Aradus, Cyprus, Pamphilia, Lycia, Rhodes, Chius, Byzantium, Lesbos, Smyrna, Miletus, Cos, is being got ready to cut off the supplies of Italy," cf. Caes., *B. C.,* 3, 3). We learn later that Pompey got fifty ships from Egypt (Caes., *B. C.,* 3, 5, 3, and 3, 111, 3), sixty from Syrian towns (App., *B. C.,* 2, 71), twenty from Rhodes (Caes., *B. C.,* 3, 27, 2), fifty from Greek cities (Caes., *B. C.,* 3, 23), and an unknown number from Asia (Caes., *B. C.,* 3, 5, 3). The usual type was now the trireme. Pompey probably commandeered these ships with a promise to pay for them, after his victory. Since he was defeated, the loss doubtless fell on the cities and states that had provided them. Since Pompey's whole fleet numbered about three hundred (App., *B. C.,* 2, 87), it would seem that Rome had less than a hundred seaworthy vessels in 50 B. C.

Since Pompey had taken the fleet, Caesar was compelled to build another during the summer of 49. Hortensius produced seventy-five ships and Dolabella forty (App., *B. C.,* 2, 41 and 49), while Decimus Brutus built twelve (Caes., *B. C.,* 1, 36, 5). All told, Caesar had about 150, and of course the expenses for these fell on the state. Furthermore Caesar had to pay shippers and fishers liberally to provide transports for his daring crossing of the Adriatic.

There is little clear evidence about the navy from 48 to 43. When Brutus and Cassius went east in 43, they followed Pompey's example and requisitioned ships in the East. The Senate authorized them to order whatever was needed on promises to pay after the war (Cic., *ad Brut.*, 2, 4, 4; *Fam.*, 12, 28), and since the Republic fell, the burden of those costs fell on the East as in 48. Cassius collected about eighty ships (App., *B. C.*, 4, 72); Brutus built " many " (Plut., *Brut.*, 28). Before the battle of Philippi the republican fleet amounted to about 200 (App., *B. C.*, 4, 133). Meanwhile Sextus Pompey had been authorized by the Senate to take command of the state fleet in the western waters (App., *B. C.*, 4, 84). Hence Antony and Octavian had to build a new fleet for the crossing of the Adriatic. We are not told how large this was, but it did not command the sea.

After Philippi Antony needed a fleet to rule the East. In 40 B. C. he had some 200 ships (App., *B. C.*, 5, 55), most of which he had doubtless built. Presently Domitius brought him eighty of the republican fleet (*ibid.*, 25). Meanwhile Sextus Pompey gathered in a large part of the republican fleet till he must have had about 300. Against this Octavian had to build a new fleet at Misenum and Ravenna in 39 and 38 (App., *B. C.*, 5, 77; 78; 80; Dio, 48, 45, 7). In the battle between Octavian and Sextus at Naulochus some 300 ships fought on each side (App., *B. C.*, 5, 118) and many were not engaged. Later when the fleets of Lepidus and Antony came to help, Octavian seems to have had an enormous fleet of some 600 ships. This fleet he kept in fair condition after 36, though hardly in active service until in 31 he met and defeated Antony and Cleopatra at Actium (see Kromayer, in *Philologus*, 1897, 426 ff., on the Roman fleet from 67 to 31; Fiebiger in *Leip. Stud.*, 15, 277 ff.; Chapot, *La flotte de Misène*).

The manning of these fleets was less expensive than it had been 200 years before. Legionaries of the regular army (about 80-100 per ship) were put on board to do the fighting, and for crews slaves and freedmen were commandeered, except that in the East the cities that gave the vessels usually had to provide the crews as well.

II. INCOME

There is no way of estimating the sums that fall under the items of looting, billeting, exactions, confiscations in and out of Italy on the part of the various factional generals during the civil wars. Caesar (*B. C.*, 3, 32) complained bitterly because Pompey had imposed extra taxes (poll and property taxes) in the East and had exacted grain, arms, ships, engines of war, soldiers, and rowers, and had forced the

Roman citizens to "lend" money. But Caesar did the same things throughout these years. Strabo (14, 1, 42) happens to tell how Caesar exacted the enormous sum of 2,000 talents from Pythodorus, the millionaire of Tralles who had aided Pompey (Cic., *pro Flacco, 52*). How many other rich men of Asia (Strabo, 12, 8, 16) suffered similarly we do not know. Caesar had already forced Spanish cities to give him money or to buy security or honors (Dio, 41, 24). In Asia he reduced the tithes for the future but demanded contributions for present needs (Dio, 42, 6, 3). In Egypt he took what he needed (Dio, 42, 34), after Zela he collected in Asia what had been promised to Pompey the year before (Dio, 42, 49), and he appropriated the temple treasure at Tyre. His final visit to Spain was especially costly in that he collected heavy indemnities from all who had shown sympathy with the Pompeians (see also Suet., *Jul.,* 54; *Bell. Afr.,* 90; 97; 98; Plut., *Caes.,* 55; Dio, 42, 6, 3; 43, 39; 49, 24).

Caesar, having used up most of his Gallic booty, finding the treasury empty and the lucrative provinces in the hands of the Pompeians, found it necessary to adopt the Sullan theory of property-rights. The dictator was the autocrat and could dispose of properties as he might see fit (App., *B. C.,* 3, 20-21). Caesar, to be sure, proscribed few, if any, for the sake of money; it sufficed to take over the properties of those slain in battle (and in most cases the dower of the wives was respected; Dio, 43, 50). When he sold confiscated property, he called it " Caesar's property " (Cic., *Fam.,* 9, 7, 2; 9, 16, 3). Such sales began at once (Cic., *Att.,* 9, 8). Later they became very extensive. Thus Pompey's estates were sold—at a low price—for some 50,000,000 denarii. Antony bought the Tusculan and Falernian estates; Dolabella bought the Formian and Alban, while Demetrius, a freedman of Caesar, bought the Lucanian estate (Cic., *Phil.,* 13, 11; App., *B. C.,* 3, 4; Dio, 45, 9). After Caesar's death the state promised Pompey's son, Sextus, 50,000,000 denarii as an indemnity for these properties. Antony had also bought the villa of Scipio at Tibur (Cic., *Fam.,* 12, 2, 1), and P. Sulla, who led Caesar's right wing at Pharsalus, was a notorious purchaser of confiscated goods (Cic., *Fam.,* 15, 17, 2-3; 9, 10, 3; *de Off.,* 2, 29). In the year 46 Cicero mentions that Caesar's surveyors were active in the townships about Rome, apparently taking possession of the estates of the fallen (*Fam.,* 9, 17, 2; for other references to confiscations see Cic., *Fam.,* 4, 7, 5; 4, 10, 2; 4, 13, 2,

23

direptiones bonorum; 13, 4 and 5; 13, 7; 13, 8; 13, 29, 4). Besides these exactions and confiscations Caesar also laid forced loans upon individuals and cities (Dio, 42, 50-51), and he used the " sacred treasure " that had been stored up from a five per cent manumission tax. This amounted to about 12,000,000 denarii—enough to pay his legions about six months at the new rate of pay (Plut., *Caes.*, 35; App., *B. C.*, 2, 41; Cic., *Att.*, 7, 21; Caes., *B. C.*, 1, 14; Dio, 41, 17).

Orosius (6, 15, 5) says the sacred treasury contained 4135 pounds of gold and *nongenta* pounds of silver. Pliny (33, 56) says 15,000 lateres (bars) of gold, 30,000 of silver *et in numerato* (i. e. sesterces) 30,000,000. If Orosius' *nongenta* is emended to *nonaginta* (90,000 pounds of silver), it will practically agree with Pliny's 30,000,000 sesterces. I should suggest that in Pliny *et* should be changed to *i. e.*, making the sum explicative of the amount in bars (each bar having the value of 1,000 sesterces, *i. e.* 3 pounds). The two passages would then agree. Since Orosius' 90,000 pounds would be equivalent to 30,000 bars of 3 pounds each = 30,000,000 sesterces, the gold bullion would then be in pieces of $3\frac{1}{3}$ ounces, each one of which would yield 10 aurei of the Pompeian type of 80 B. C. (36 to the pound). In other words the $3\frac{1}{3}$ ounce bars of gold would have the same value (1,000 sesterces) as the 3 pound bars of silver; and the whole would amount to about 12,000,000 denarii, or 48,000,000 sesterces (cf. *Am. Jour. Phil.*, 1932, 360).

Caesar, of course, used the state revenues, such as they were, whenever he needed them, but he would also deposit his booty temporarily in the treasury. Velleius, 2, 56, 2, states that Caesar carried in his five triumphs some 600,000,000 sesterces (= 150,000,000 denarii) realized from the sale of booty. This is less than half the sum Appian (*B. C.*, 2, 102) gives for the four triumphs of 46 B. C. (65,000 talents silver, besides over 20,000 pounds of coronary gold). Since, according to Appian, Caesar at the same time gave each soldier 5,000 denarii (so also Dio, 43, 21; Suet., *Jul.*, 38, says 6,000), each centurion 10,000, and each tribune 20,000, it may well be that Velleius' amount actually refers to the portion placed in the treasury after these deductions had been made (the dole-takers, probably 150,000, also received 100 denarii each). If twelve legions (the number is not given) received the 5,000 denarii per man, that would account for the difference in the estimates of Velleius and Appian. At Caesar's death the treasury contained about 175,000,000 denarii (700,000,000 sesterces), presumably the sum that had been deposited in 46 plus a slight increase (Vell., 2, 60, 4; Cic., *Phil.*, 2, 93; 5, 11; 8, 26; 12, 12). In addition Caesar's estate, acquired of course from booty during the Civil War, was very extensive. Plutarch (*Cic.*, 43, 6; *Ant.*, 15) gives it as

25,000,000 denarii (cf. Suet., *Jul.,* 83; App., *B. C.,* 2, 143; Dio, 44, 35). And Caesar had used enormous sums, acquired in the same way, for triumphal games and festivals, for the dole, the buildings, and gifts:

Suet., *Jul.,* 38-39:

Veteranis legionibus praedae nomine in pedites singulos super bina sestertia, quae initio civilis tumultus numeraverat, vicena quaterna milia nummum dedit. Adsignavit et agros, sed non continuos, ne quis possessorum expelleretur. Populo praeter frumenti denos modios ac totidem olei libras trecenos quoque nummos, quos pollicitus olim erat, viritim, divisit, et hoc amplius centenos pro mora. Annuam etiam habitationem Romae usque ad bina milia nummum, in Italia non ultra quingenos sestertios remisit. Adiecit epulum ac viscerationem, et post Hispaniensem victoriam duo prandia; nam cum prius parce neque pro liberalitate sua praebitum iudicaret, quinto post die aliud largissimum praebuit. 39. Edidit spectacula varii generis: munus gladiatorium, ludos etiam regionatim urbe tota et quidem per omnium linguarum histriones, item circenses, athletas, naumachiam.

" To each and every foot-soldier of his veteran legions he gave twenty-four thousand sesterces by way of booty, over and above the two thousand apiece which he had paid them at the beginning of the civil strife. He also assigned them lands, but not side by side, to avoid dispossessing any of the former owners. To every man of the people, besides ten pecks of grain and the same number of pounds of oil, he distributed the three hundred sesterces which he had promised at first, and one hundred apiece to boot because of the delay. He also remitted a year's rent in Rome to tenants who paid two thousand sesterces or less, and in Italy up to five hundred sesterces. He added a banquet and a dole of meat, and after his Spanish victory two dinners; for deeming that the former of these had not been served with a liberality creditable to his generosity, he gave another five days later on a most lavish scale.

39. He gave entertainments of divers kinds: a combat of gladiators and also stage-plays in every ward all over the city, performed too by actors of all languages, as well as races in the circus, athletic contests, and a sham sea-fight." In other words Caesar, like an Oriental mon-

arch, kept his own and his state accounts together. If the state budget
was about 80,000,000 denarii in Caesar's consulship, twice the amount
was probably used during his dictatorship.

Finances were even more confused after his death. Antony laid
hands on the 175,000,000 denarii of the treasury in 44 (Cic., *Phil.*,
2, 93; 12, 12; *Att.*, 14, 14, 5; *Vell.*, 2, 60, 4). Part of this sum he
used in paying the debt of 10,000,000 denarii accumulated in buying
confiscated estates (Cic., *Phil.*, 2, 93), the rest he used in establishing
his power and building up an army. For when Octavian tampered
with his troops (offering 500 denarii per man; Cic., *Att.*, 16, 8),
Antony had to offer them 500 denarii each to retain them (App., *B. C.*,
3, 40 and 44). Lepidus, Octavian, and Decimus Brutus lavished
bribes on the same scale. Decimus Brutus spent on his troops his whole
fortune of 10,000,000 denarii and much that he had borrowed (Cic.,
Fam., 11, 10, 5).

In 43 the triumvirs proscribed and took the property of about 300
senators and 2,000 knights (App., *B. C.*, 4, 5; Dio, 47, 6, 5; 47, 17).
Nevertheless they were 200,000,000 denarii ($40,000,000) short of
actual needs (App., *B. C.*, 4, 31). They proceeded to expropriate the
property of 400 rich women, and to lay a forced loan of one year's
income (Dio, 47, 14, says one year's rental on houses and one half on
land) and a two per cent capital tax on all who possessed property worth
over 100,000 denarii (App., *B. C.*, 4, 34).

The senatorial government in 44 received very little income because
the generals withheld the provincial tribute. It therefore tried to raise
money by a citizen tribute of four per cent with an additional tax of
ten *asses* per roof-tile on property in the city (Dio, 46, 31, 3; Cic.,
Epist. ad Caes. Jun., frag. 5: "by the tax on roof-tiles, 60,000,000
sest. can be collected," in fact very much less came in—Cic., *Brut.*, 1,
18, 5; the roof-tile tax would amount to about one half a denarius per
square foot of building area). This was far from adequate for needs
and all the generals friendly to the Senate were asked to levy forced
loans in their provinces with promises to repay them after the war
(Cic. *ad Brut.*, 2, 4, 4; *Fam.*, 12, 28, 2; *Phil.*, 10, 26).

Brutus and Cassius gathered funds very successfully in the East.
The provinces they held were responsible for some 50,000,000 denarii
of tribute per year (those conquered by Pompey were expected to produce 35,000,000). But this, of course, did not suffice for the support

and equipment of 19 legions, since extra bonuses had to be promised constantly to offset the lavish offers of the triumvirs. Since the Senate authorized them to raise forced loans, they demanded from the Asiatic communities in two years the tribute due in ten (App., *B. C.*, 4, 74; 5, 5). Some of the cities that refused to raise the sums demanded were seized and destroyed; the rest took the warning and complied. Rhodes was captured and plundered, yielding 800 talents (Plut., *Brut.*, 32); some cities on the mainland suffered similarly and Cassius got nearly 1,500 talents from Tarsus (see Hercher, *Epist. Graeci*, 178 ff., for Brutus' requisitions. These letters attributed to Brutus may well be genuine). Brutus secured some 16,000 talents, nearly 100,000,000 denarii, by such means (App., *B. C.*, 3, 63; 4, 75), besides a fleet. A half of this might have sufficed for the republican army at normal pay, but as we have seen they had to pay 1,500 denarii per man to some 70,000 soldiers and that alone required as much as these exactions had brought in (App., *B. C.*, 4, 88 and 100).

The triumvirs won, and to pay their troops they had to begin once more to impose every form of exaction. Antony went through the eastern provinces demanding money. His argument was in general this: " we have 28 legions, 170,000 men to pay; since Italy must give land for the troops, you must give us money; you gave Brutus and Cassius the tribute of ten years; we demand the same." After many protests he consented to take the tribute of nine years in two (App., *B. C.*, 5, 5). Asia was bankrupt for a generation.

In Italy Octavian took the land needed. Little of the necessary money came to him from Antony. He " borrowed " the treasures of the temples at Rome and of several towns of Latium (App., 5, 24). In 42 he imposed a tax of 25 denarii for every slave and, in 39, a slave tax of half the amount, and an inheritance tax as well (App., 5, 67). In 36 he exacted 1,600 talents from Sicily (App., 5, 129) and in 31, to pay for the war against Antony, he laid on a 25 per cent income tax and on all ex-slaves worth 50,000 denarii or over a $12\frac{1}{2}$ per cent capital levy (Dio, 50, 10). Rome paid dearly for twenty years of civil wars, and was quite reconciled to a benevolent autocracy that might prevent further disaster.

a. *Summary of citizen taxes imposed in 50-30.*

In 60 the law of Metellus Nepos had abolished the port-dues of Italy

(Dio, 37, 51; Cic., *Att.,* 2, 16). Caesar restored these *portoria,* but apparently only on imports from foreign countries (Suet., *Jul.,* 43). (Caesar also " borrowed " from cities and individuals in Italy [Dio, 42, 50-51]. Whether this was virtually a " forced loan " or whether the moneys were ever repaid we do not know).

In 43 the Senate levied a four per cent capital tax on citizens and on the upper classes (senators only?) a property tax of ½ denarius on each roof-tile (Dio, 46, 31, 3). Cities and individuals were asked to supply arms, and the armorers were induced to work without pay (*ibid.* and App., *B. C.,* 3, 66).

In 43 the chief income was, of course, from proscriptions and confiscations, but in addition certain general taxes were imposed (Dio, 47, 14, 2): a year's rent on leased houses; a 50 per cent tax on the income of real estate (App., 4, 34), a year's income on property and a 2 per cent capital tax. These seem to have been temporary taxes.

In 31 (Dio, 50, 10) Octavian levied 25 per cent of a year's income, and in addition a 12½% capital tax on liberti worth over 200,000 sesterces ($10,000, which, incidentally, indicates that there were a number of rich ex-slaves).

IV. SEMIPUBLIC FINANCES: THE PUBLICANS

The equestrian companies came out of the Sullan dictatorship a wreck: Sulla had proscribed 1,600 knights and confiscated their property. By the year 70 they recovered to some extent by the introduction of new blood, and they prospered from then till the Civil War of 49. Caesar removed them from the tithe-collecting of Asia. Thereafter their operations were small and carefully watched. The disgraceful record of a century was ended.

We must enter somewhat into the details of their work. In 84 Sulla had called for a cash payment from Asia amounting to the enormous sum of 20,000 talents. He said this included the tithe for five years (presumably 88-84, when Rome seems to have received nothing from Asia) and a heavy indemnity for supporting Mithridates. This sum was taken directly and pro rata from the 44 regions into which he divided Asia (Plut., *Luc.,* 4; App., *Mith.,* 62; Cassiod., *Chron.,* 670; Cic., *pro Flacco,* 32; Strabo, 13, 1, 27; 13, 1, 35; 14, 2, 3). In the collection of this sum the publicans had no share except in so far as they were invited by the suffering communities to lend them money and help organize the undertaking, but it is likely that the publicans continued to collect the regular tithe (Cic., *Quint. fr.,* 1, 1, 33: " the Asiatics should not despise the publicans, since they could not pay the Sullan exactions without their aid "; cf. Rice Holmes, *The Roman Republic,* I, 395). It is likely that rich natives, like Pythodorus, lent the cities much of the money needed at this time.

The debts which the cities contracted in order to pay Sulla increased rapidly because usurious rates were charged and the cities constantly defaulted. Roman knights gradually increased their holdings of mortgages. In 14 years Lucullus found that the debts had risen sixfold and in 70 he took drastic measures to reduce them.

Plutarch, *Lucullus,* 20, 3.

τοιαῦτα μὲν κακὰ Λεύκολλος εὑρὼν ἐν ταῖς πόλεσιν ὀλίγῳ χρόνῳ πάντων ἀπήλλαξε τοὺς ἀδικουμένους. πρῶτον μὲν γὰρ ἑκατοστὴν ἐκέλευσε καὶ μὴ πλέον εἰς τοὺς τόκους λογίζεσθαι· δεύτερον δὲ τοὺς μακροτέρους τοῦ ἀρχαίου τόκους ἀπέκοψε· τὸ δὲ τρίτον καὶ μέγιστον ἔταξε τῶν τοῦ χρεωφειλέτου προσόδων τὴν τετάρτην μερίδα καρποῦσθαι τὸν δανειστήν· ὁ δὲ τόκον κεφαλαίῳ συνάψας ἐστέρητο τοῦ παντός· ὥστ᾽ ἐν ἐλάττονι χρόνῳ τετραετίας διαλυθῆναι τὰ χρέα πάντα καὶ τὰς κτήσεις ἐλευθέρας ἀποδοθῆναι τοῖς δεσπόταις.

" Lucullus in a short time freed the cities from all these evils and oppressions; for, first of all, he ordered there should be no more interest taken than one per cent (per month). Secondly, where the interest exceeded the principal, he struck it off. The third and most considerable order was, that the creditor should receive the fourth part of the debtor's income (till the debts were paid); but if any lender had added the interest to the principal, it was utterly disallowed. Insomuch, that in the space of four years all debts were paid and lands returned to their rightful owners."

Appian (*Mith.,* 83) adds that in order to get the remainder paid rapidly Lucullus imposed a " twenty-five per cent tax on crops, and taxes on slaves and house property." Thus the cities had to aid the rural folk to get rid of the burden.

The knights were strong enough in 67 to secure a real effort at clearing off piracy, for the Gabinian law was largely forced through by their efforts. And again, in 66, the Manilian law which placed Pompey in command in the East was their measure. By this plebiscite Pompey was to rid Asia forever of the fear of raids, and he was also to organize the territory taken from Mithridates into provinces where presumably the *societates* would have a further field of operation. Pompey did his work very effectively and added provinces which brought in perhaps three times as much as Asia. However, he did not extend over these the Asiatic system of contract gathering in its worst form. The collection of the pasture-tax and the harbor-dues was to be let by contract to Romans as elsewhere, but in the new provinces— Syria, the enlarged Bithynia, and Cilicia—the communities were to be responsible for the collection of the definite amounts imposed. However, even here, since the communities were unused to the task, some of them fell into the habit of letting their own local contracts to Roman *societates* or individuals that had the organization adopted for such work.

Our sources are not clear regarding the methods of tax-gathering thereafter. In Asia the knights continued to take their regular contracts, but we also have references to door-taxes and poll-taxes (*exactionem capitum atque ostiorum*, Cic., *Fam.*, 3, 8, 5) which are not easy to explain. Furthermore the knights seem to be engaged upon tax contracts in Bithynia, Cilicia, and Syria (the provinces annexed by Pompey despite the fact that here definite amounts had been stipulated so that contracts might be avoided. It is very likely that this confusion is due to the fact that our sources have failed to separate the Roman dues from local taxes and from the extra requisitions imposed by some of the governors for military needs and personal gain. The door and poll taxes of Asia seem to belong partly to local taxes collected on commission by Roman publicans (cf. Cic., *pro Flacco*, 44; 45; 70; *ad Fam.*, 3, 7, 2; the commission seems to be 10%, Cic., *pro Rab. Post.*, 30 " an addition of a tenth, as our collectors do with their one-percent "), partly to extra-legal exactions made by unscrupulous governors like Appius Claudius (cf. *pro Flacco*, 32; 33; 91; *ad Att.*, 5, 16; Caes., *B. C.*, 3, 32, 2). We hear of both of these types in Cicero's province of Cilicia, but almost only in the three districts that normally belonged to "Asia," and only temporarily to Cilicia (Cic., *ad Fam.*, 3, 8, 5; *Att.*, 5, 16, 2; 6, 2). On the whole it would seem that the provincial cities borrowed the poll and house taxes from Lucullus' four-year plan—perhaps Lucullus had found them in vogue—and not only continued to use them for local city needs and for the payment of extra impositions by governors, but also relied upon Roman publicans to gather for them such taxes on commission. The publicans did not always come out with a profit (Cic., *Fam.*, 13, 10).

In Sicily, as is apparent from the speeches of Cicero against Verres, the tithes of the wheat were not in the hands of the *societates*. The contracts had to be let individually in Sicily for the separate towns. Several Romans came down to bid, but as individuals; there were also some Romans residing in Sicily who would bid, but also native Sicilians, communities, and even serfs of the temple of Venus. Since the the commission allowed here was 6% of the tithe, the work was not very lucrative under ordinary circumstances. In Cicero's day the grazing-tax and the port-tax were collected by small companies that constituted branches of a larger company of publicans (Cic., *Verr.*, 2, 171-3; Carcopino, *La loi de Hiéron*).

A combination of societates.

In the censorship of 61 B. C. the companies that bid for the Asiatic tithe apparently offered too much. They thought that the holder of the Asiatic contract that year might find lucrative opportunities in the new provinces. It would seem that competition for the enterprise was keen. The company which secured the collection presently found itself losing money and it appealed to the Senate for a remission of a third, as it had a right to do under the Sempronian law (*Schol. Bob.* on Cic., *Stangl*, 155; Cic., *pro Plancio*, 24); but despite the aid of Caesar, Cicero, and Crassus, its efforts were for some time successfully obstructed by Cato (Cic., *Att.*, 1, 17; 1, 18; *pro Planc.*, 34; 35; App., *B. C.*, 2, 13; Dio, 38, 7, 4; Suet., *Jul.*, 20, 3). The strange thing is that Plancius, not a Roman but a native of the small town of Atina, was at this time the head of the company. One may perhaps infer that after Sulla's proscriptions wealthy men from the Italian towns entered into this business. Plancius held that the remission was justified because of hostile incursions into Asia; but, as there were no serious raids at this time, one suspects that the real trouble was that the Senate had that year sent out Quintus Cicero to Asia, an honest man who would not permit any irregularities. The members of the company suffered losses for two years and their anger was one of the real factors in bringing Crassus into Caesar's coalition, called the " first triumvirate." The tax contracts of Syria were also involved in this combination (Cic., *Prov. Cons.*, 11-12). Caesar during his consulship secured the remission by a plebiscite, and Cicero charges that the tribune Vatinius, who brought in the bill, speculated in the company shares, making a good profit on a certainty and securing a bribe in addition (*in Vatin.*, 29).

Perhaps because of the disastrous competition in 61 (Laurent-Vibert, in *Mél. d'Arch. et d'Hist.*, 1908, 175), the various companies operating in the East (Bithynia, Asia, and Cilicia) combined even more closely than those that operated in Sicily in 72-70. At any rate it seems that in 51 the *societas* of Bithynia consisted of a union of all the other eastern companies (Cic., *Fam.*, 13, 9, 2), and the friends of Cicero, who operated in Cilicia during his governorship in 51, also had connections in Asia and Bithynia. It would seem then that for this lustrum there was something of a monopoly in the eastern tax-gathering. However, their success could not have lasted long. Pompey took direct charge of finances in the East in 49 and, after his defeat in 48, Caesar forever ended the tithe-contracts of the provinces of Asia, throwing the responsibility for a reduced amount on the communities themselves (Plut., *Caes.*, 48). Thereafter there were only the *scriptura* and the port dues for the companies to gather, and in the early Empire they lost these also. The period had not been a very lucrative one for the Roman publicans.

We have a few notices concerning the activities of publicans elsewhere also. Cicero (*Fam.*, 13, 6a and 6b) mentions them in Africa in 56. Here there were public lands and harbors in their charge. In Narbonese Gaul they collected port and boundary tariffs (Cic., *pro Font.*, 19). The harbor stations at Aquileia and at Tergeste are mentioned in inscriptions of Cicero's day (*C. I. L.*, I², 2193 and 2215). Varro refers to the public sheep ranges of Apulia (*R. R.*, 2, 1, 16-17; 2, 2, 9); Cicero happens to mention that his wife, as well as Atticus, held some public land, apparently in Italy (*Att.*, 2, 15); recent inscriptions, not yet published, show that the pitch-forests and saltbasins near Minturnae were managed by publicans; in the famous *lex agraria* of 111 (line 70) there is a reference to the fact that the knights were called upon to collect state debts; and, finally, the sunken ship that was discovered a few years ago off Mahdia, Africa, contained lead billets bearing Latin names (*C. I. L.*, I², 2394, cf. 2995). Since the ship had come from the East (about 80 B. C.) the Latin names probably indicate some mining operations of the knights.

It is a curious fact that at this time the knights contributed very few men to the ruling nobility, though it must have been Gracchus' idea in giving them a position in the courts that they might rise into the aristocracy. Even Sulla, who was so brutal in his treatment of them, lifted 300 into the Senate when he had to increase its number respectably, but it is likely that most of these 300 were in fact scions of old noble families who had themselves failed to rise into the Senate. Nevertheless the knights made little progress. Cicero was the first knight to reach the consulship for a generation. Between the Gracchan and the Sullan period there had been several, but, so far as we know, it was not through wealth that they gained influence but through distinguished service in the army or through effective work as advocates in the Forum. In this period also very many wealthy business men— classed as knights because of their wealth—seem to have had no dealings with the public corporations. Of these we shall speak presently. Those known to have engaged in public contracts (see P. Schmidt, *Die römischen Ritter*), are C. Antistius, *magister scripturae,* in Sicily (Cic., *Verr.,* 3, 167); Sex. Caesius, in Asia (Cic., *Flacc.,* 68); C. Cestius (*ibid.,* 31, and *Att.,* 5, 13); Q. Minucius, in Sicily (*Verr.,* 3, 148); C. Mustius (*ibid.,* 1, 137); M. Papirius (Ascon., *in Mil.,* Stangl, 40); L. Peducaeus (Cic., *Flacc.,* 68); Cn. Plancius, of Atina, who formed many *societates* and was manager of many (Cic., *pro Planc.,* 32-35); P. Servilius, administrator of companies in Sicily (*Verr.,* 3, 167); P. Vettius Chilo, a brother-in-law of Verres (*ibid.*); L. Vibius (*Verr.,* 2, 182).

V. MONEY AND BANKING

1. *Circulation.*

During this period we are at a loss to estimate the amount of currency in circulation. The quantity of metals produced by the mines is unknown, but after the publican exploitation of silver mines ceased, there was probably a decrease from this source. That gold mines were not producing much would appear from the restricted amount of the state income (50,000,000 denarii in 62), most of which is accounted for by other sources, and also from the fact that for a while the state forbade the export of gold as well as silver from Italy. This general prohibition was imposed by the Senate in 63 (Cic., *in Vat.,* 12; *pro Flacc.,* 67), and it is probable that scarcity was also the main motive for the passage of the Gabinian law (probably in 67 B. C.: Cic., *Att.,*

5, 21, 12; 6, 2, 7) which forbade provincials to borrow money at Rome. The booty brought in by Pompey must have relieved the situation, for the Senate granted an exception to the law in 56 when the Salaminians borrowed some 50 talents at Rome.

Pompey brought 50,000,000 denarii of new metal to the treasury and distributed nearly 100,000,000 to his officers and men. This should have added 10-12 denarii to the circulation for every inhabitant of Italy. Caesar in turn sent down so much gold from Gaul that the price of the metal fell temporarily from 3,600 sesterces (the price of Pompey's aurei of 80 B. C.) to 3,000 per pound (Suet., *Jul.*, 54, 2). Since there was as yet no regular coinage of gold, the metal of course followed the laws of supply and demand.

We can obtain some—though not much—evidence about the relative amount of coinage from the number of types found in the coin hoards. The issues of 81-80 were very numerous and large (Grueber, I, 365-84). Then the issues for about two years seem to have been moderate, though silver was coined every year. In 70 again the number of coin symbols is large (*ibid.*, 422-31), and again in 64 (*ibid.*, 450-68). Then the custom of placing symbols on the coins went out of fashion so that the evidence is inadequate, but the extra issues ordered by the Senate in 61, 58, 55-4 probably indicate the use of Pompey's booty for extraordinary needs.

In 49 B. C. Caesar struck several issues of silver—also reviving the sestertius and quinarius—and he furthermore introduced an issue of gold, which henceforth remained a definite part of Rome's coinage. Doubtless he used for this the 4135 pounds of gold that he found in the sacred treasury (Orosius, 6, 15, 5) besides some gold that he brought from Gaul. These *aurei,* worth 25 denarii, were at first slightly heavier than $\frac{1}{40}$ of a pound, but the standard of 40 to the pound was soon adopted. In 46, at Caesar's quadruple triumph, very large amounts of gold and silver were issued in order to use the accumulated booty for the payment of stipends, bonuses, games, and public feasts. Since Caesar displayed about 400,000,000 denarii at this triumph (Appian, *B. C.,* 2, 102), most of which came from abroad (Gaul, Asia Minor, Egypt, and Africa), and left almost half this amount in the treasury at his death, we may assume that the new metals coined and distributed at this time may have amounted to at least 200,000,000 denarii, or 15-20 denarii per inhabitant in Italy.

There are some 20 different types of gold issues (of 40 *aurei* to the pound) known for the years 46-44 and, since Caesar displayed over 20,000 pounds of gold in 46 (App., *B. C.,* 2, 102), each issue may well have been of 1,000 pounds, that is, in amounts of 1,000,000 denarii. There were well over a hundred types of silver denarii issued in the same period and many also of quinarii and sesterces.

How much provincial tribute went into the coinage we can hardly say. We have reckoned this at about 40,000,000 denarii in 79, and at over twice that amount in 44. Since, however, some tribute was paid in kind and since the armies were usually stationed abroad and a considerable part of the tribute was recoined by provincial governors for the payment of the troops abroad, we cannot assume that most of the tribute brought metals to Rome. Furthermore so many Roman investments were being placed in the provinces and there was so large a balance of trade against Rome that it is doubtful whether the flow of metals from normal tribute and trade was actually Rome-ward. Eventually, of course, these investments produced a balance in favor of Rome, but for our period it is likely that renewed placements of investments abroad used more Italian credit than the profits brought.

After Sulla's day a great deal of gold and silver was being used in personal adornment, in table plate and in furniture, which diminished the metals available for currency, but this metal often came back into circulation later. Cicero, for instance, when near bankruptcy, ordered his plate sent to the mint for coinage (*Att.,* 11, 25; 12, 6) and, during the confiscations of the civil wars, such plate and ornaments were often seized and melted down for coinage. They served in fact as a hoard in times of stringency.

All this evidence is very indefinite, but we gain the impression that Rome's acquisitions of metals sufficed to enlarge the currency sufficiently to take care of the expanding needs. The provinces certainly lost much of their metals, not only from their hoards, but also from the currency with which they bought back the captives and cattle that they lost in raids. The exactions of Pompey, Caesar, Brutus, Cassius, and Antony went so far as to draw on old temple stores. However, most of the provinces drew back in trade and Roman investments a large part of the currency they lost. The Roman denarius and gold aureus became the standard coins throughout the Empire, though in the Asiatic provinces the local silver cistophorus (worth ¾ of a denarius) remained the common currency.

2. Banking.

Before Caesar's death Rome was probably the financial center of the Roman world. Yet no dominating banking firm grew up; since Roman law persisted in discouraging joint stock companies with limited liability in business not directly serving the state, and firms dealing in state contracts were given business for only five-year terms. Partnerships based on the full liability of each member could hardly grow to great size. Certain bankers entered into a wide range of enterprises: conducting auctions, changing foreign money, accepting deposits and current accounts of a limited kind, lending money on security, placing loans for customers, buying and selling real estate—usually for customers on definite orders—, keeping skilled agents in the provinces to place investments or make collections for customers, and to a limited extent issuing foreign drafts, if they had personal relations with some banker abroad. Here we may note some typical instances of each of these transactions (see Früchtl, A., *Geldgeschäft bei Cicero*).

The *nummularii* specialized in changing foreign coins for Roman, charging a percentage (*collybus,* or *agio*) for the service. While alloyed coins were still in evidence (until about 70 B. C.) they also charged a percentage for testing (*spectatio:* Cic., *Verr.,* 3, 181). They also bought metal (plate and ornaments), paying in denarii (Cicero, when in financial difficulty abroad, wrote Atticus to get money for his plate from Caelius, the banker: *Att.,* 11, 25, 3; 12, 6, 1).

Auctions: The Pompeian wax tablets, the records of the banker Caecilius Jucundus, show that much of his profit came from conducting auctions and charging a percentage (usually 1%) on the transactions. It was because auctioneers took municipal contracts that Caesar in his colonial charters forbade their standing for municipal offices.

Deposits: Cicero gives Atticus an order to draw on his deposit at the bank of Egnatius (*Att.,* 11, 3, 3; cf. 13, 3; 14, 3; 15, 4). Caesennia bought a farm and paid for it with an order on her banker (Cic., *pro Caec.,* 17). In the East deposits were usually made in temples which often paid no interest. At Rome deposits were at times made with bankers for convenience and safety and without interest. Current accounts against which checks might be freely drawn were not in use. When Cicero gave Atticus a draft on his banker, he doubtless wrote to the banker at the same time to honor the draft.

Money lending: Cicero borrowed from bankers of the Forum when he bought two villas in 60 (*Att.,* 2, 1, 11); later he borrowed from Vestorius, a banker of Puteoli (*Att.,* 6, 8, 5; 10, 13, 2), and from the Oppii (*Att.,* 8, 7, 3; 10, 4, 12; 10, 7, 3); Caelius and Vettienus were others with whom he had financial relations (*Att.,* 7, 3, 11; 10, 15, 4). In some of these instances the money was probably lent by a private person, the bank acting only as the agent. The Oppii, for instance, acted as agents for Caesar (*Att.,* 5, 1, 2).

However many wealthy Romans who would hardly have liked to be called bankers lent money through their own secretaries or in personal dealings with friends. Cicero often obtained a loan from Atticus, who was wealthy and spent most of his time caring for his own business interests, and once expressed the wish to borrow from Atticus' rich uncle but was deterred by the fact that the man was close-fisted and liked to find customers willing to pay 12 per cent (*Att.,* 1, 12, 1). When in debt for his Palatine house in 61 he mentions Axius, a senator, and two knights, Considius and Selicius, as men who may lend him something.

Caesar was a daring borrower. Before he reached the propraetorship of Spain he had borrowed over a million dollars. His friend Crassus went security for him for nearly 5,000,000 denarii, according to Plutarch (*Caes.,* 11, 1; *Crass.,* 7, 6). Cicero also borrowed freely. He once owed Caesar 800,000 sesterces, and 20,000 in interest (*Att.,* 5, 1, 2; 5, 5, 2; 5, 9, 2); he owed Caerellia an amount not specified (*Att.,* 12, 51, 3), Ovia a hundred thousand sesterces (*Att.,* 12, 21, 4), and several others handsome amounts. Nevertheless he also lent freely when he had any money. Pompey borrowed 2,200,000 sesterces from him a little before Pharsalia which was never repaid (*Att.,* 11, 1, 3; *Fam.,* 5, 20, 9). Other debtors were C. Antonius, his colleague in the consulship (*Att.,* 1, 12, 1; 1, 14, 7), Q. Axius, a senator's son (*Att.,* 10, 11, 2), and several men of lesser note. In other words wealthy Romans very frequently managed their own finances and did their own lending, borrowing, and investing directly or through their financial secretaries. In such circumstances money-lending by bankers was not apt to develop rapidly in Italy.

Discounting of a debt is mentioned as among the operations of the banker Vettienus (Att., 12, 3, 2). Collections as well as purchases also come within the banker's sphere of work (*Att.,* 13, 45, 3, and 46, 3; *Att.,* 10, 5, 3).

Finally bankers might arrange for *foreign exchange,* since they usually had correspondents and friends in foreign banks. But no general letter of credit was known. Each transaction required a special letter based upon private agreements. In several of these instances the exchange was secured not by a banker, but by some rich man who had foreign correspondents in several cities. Cicero drew funds at Ephesus and at Laodicea from houses that recognized Atticus' draft (*Att.,* 5, 13; *Fam.,* 3, 5, 4), and Cicero's son drew the money he needed while at school in Athens on a similar letter (*Att.,* 12, 24; 27). While at

Brundisium Cicero would draw money from the bank there on a draft secured by Atticus (*Att.,* 11, 1; 11, 2; 11, 3; 11, 13, 4), and Pompey drew by means of a double exchange the money that Cicero had deposited in Asia.

The *rates of interest* varied greatly. The legal maximum in Italy was apparently 12 per cent after Sulla's *unciaria lex,* but 6 per cent was the customary rate at this time (semissibus magna copia est: *Fam.,* 5, 6, 2, in 62 B. C.). In 54 money was lending at 4 per cent but went to 8 per cent during a political campaign in which large sums were spent (*Quint fr.,* 2, 14, 4; *Att.,* 4, 15, 7). Some shrewd money-lenders specialized in risky loans at 12 per cent (*Att.,* 1, 12, 1). In the provinces the governors and the decrees of the Senate permitted 12 per cent. In Asia that seems to have been the normal rate among the natives (*Supp. Epig. Graec.,* II, p. 104), but it was often exceeded, especially at times when the border was unsafe or the borrower financially weak. We have already mentioned the notorious case of 48 per cent in which Brutus was involved. Cicero was shocked at the rate and reminded Brutus' agents that the legal rate was 12 per cent. We do not yet know whether Brutus was responsible for the rate. (In the state of Maryland today petty brokers are allowed to collect $3\frac{1}{2}$ per cent per month on delinquent notes, the purpose of the permission being, so it is alleged, to frighten the borrower into speedy settlement).

VI. COMMERCE

First we may quote some prices that happen to be recorded, because they give us some conception not only of the demand for certain luxury articles but also of the provenience of goods and the types of commerce involved.

Large works of art and smaller *objets d'art* were generally imported: both old, famous statues and paintings, and recent pieces, probably of small artistic value. Much came, of course, by way of booty, but in Cicero's day there was a great deal of buying. Scaurus, for instance, as aedile, displayed 3,000 statues in his theatre, some of which he doubtless borrowed but most of which he must have purchased overseas, since marble workers were very scarce at Rome before 40 B. C. For works bought we have these prices: Caesar paid 80 talents (nearly $100,000) for two paintings by an artist of Byzantium (Pliny, 7, 126; 35, 136).

Agrippa paid the city of Cyzicus 1,200,000 sesterces ($60,000) for two paintings (Pliny, 35, 26). L. Lucullus placed an order for a statue of Felicitas with Arkesilaos, paying 1,000,000 sesterces ($50,000; Pliny, 35, 156). He also paid two talents ($2,400) for a *copy* of Pausias' painting of the "Flower Girl" (35, 125). His brother bought a colossal statue of Apollo in Pontus for 500 talents ($600,000; Pliny, 34, 39). Hortensius paid 144,000 sesterces ($7,200) for a painting by the obscure Kydias (35, 130). The prices paid by Verres for works of art in Sicily are not worth repeating, since he took advantage of forced sales or used his official powers and prerogatives to induce sales (cf. Cic., *Verr.*, 4, 14).

There was also a vigorous trade in minor works. Cicero once paid 20,400 sesterces ($1,020) for some trifling statuary with which to adorn his Tusculan gardens (*Att.*, 1, 7 and 8; 3; 4; 10). A pair of ornamented silver cups done by Zopyrus was quoted at $60,000 (1,200,000 sest.) and a cup by Pytheas sold for $2,000 (Pliny, 33, 156). Arkesilaus made a plaster model for a Roman customer from which to cast a cup. His price was $1,200 (6,000 denarii; Pliny, 35, 156). Gegania paid 50,000 sesterces for a bronze Tarentine candelabrum—but the price included a cheap slave (Pliny, 34, 11; *C. I. L.,* I², 1004). The craze for archaic objects is illustrated by the fact that Caesar's colonists at Corinth dug up the old graves of the city to find ancient vases and bronzes to sell to the Roman dealers (Strabo, 8, 6, 23). Eastern jewelry of the most expensive kind was also sought after. Pearls, for instance, were shown in Pompey's triumph and a lively market soon opened (Pliny, 37, 12). Caesar hoped to find pearls in Britain and failed, but somewhere he got one for $300,000 (6,000,000 sesterces) as a present for Servilia—the mother of Brutus (Suet. *Jul.*, 50). Metella's pearl which Horace mentions (*Sat.*, 2, 3, 239) was reported to be worth $50,000 (1,000,000 sesterces).

A fair conception of the decorative articles that Roman customers called for is provided by the cargo of a wrecked ship found on the African coast (off Mahdia) in 1907 (*C. R. de l'Acad.*, 1909, 650; *Mon. Piot.*, XVII, 29; *Rev. Arch.*, 1911, II, 92). The ship contained some sixty marble columns, many marble and bronze statues, much furniture inlaid with metal, candelabra, vases, and even Greek inscriptions. The statues were partly copies of old works, partly pretty decorative pieces recently made. The cargo was doubtless meant for Roman customers

24

and came from Athens. It was not unlike the consignments that New York " art-dealers " used to buy in Florence and Naples in the nineties. Some articles—lead ingots and lamps—seem to date the cargo at about 80-60 B. C.

One-piece table-boards of citrus-wood from Mauritania were also fashionable. Cicero paid $25,000 (500,000 sesterces) for one; other prices quoted for these a few years later are 1,000,000; 1,200,000; 1,300,000 sesterces (Pliny, 13, 92-3). Tapestries woven with mythological and figured designs were also collected (apparently, like the one described in Catullus 64, the far-distant ancestors of Anatolian and Persian fabrics). Verres paid 200,000 sesterces for a set in Sicily (Verr., 4, 28); Scipio Metellus charged that the stoical Cato had paid 800,000 sesterces ($40,000) for some Babylonian table spreads (Pliny, 8, 196). The tapestries of the East woven with gold threads were still popular (Verg., *Culex,* 62; Cic., *Verr.,* 5, 27) and became even more so in the Augustan period (*Thes. Ling. Lat.* sub *Attalicus*). The Tyrian and Tarentine wools, dyed in the rarest " purple ", were coming into use. Nepos says that in his youth (80-70 B. C.) the violet-tinted wool cost $20 the pound (100 denarii). The Tyrian " double dyed " purple was first used at Rome in 63, the price being $200 the pound (1,000 denarii; Pliny, 9, 137). Ordinary wool sold at the time for a few cents the pound.

These prices give some idea of the commerce in articles of luxury.

Of general objects of trade we can speak in more detail in dealing with the fuller sources of the next period. For the end of the Republic we have scant information, except for the few details given above, though we might well assume that the articles mentioned by Strabo for Augustus' day were already on the market. We know that slaves were constantly being purchased at Rome. Wheat came mostly from the tithes of Africa, Sicily, Sardinia. Caesar also arranged to have the tribute-wheat of Judea brought to Sidon, probably to be used by the eastern fleet (Josephus, *Ant. Jud.,* 14, 206). Pontic wheat was not yet exported to Rome (Pliny, 18, 63). The Puteolan grain dealers (Cic., *de Fin.,* 2, 84) got large contracts from Pompey when prices were high at Rome in 56-5 (Cic., *Fam.,* 13, 75 of C. Avianius Flaccus), and Caesar while in Gaul doubtless dealt with such men. It is not true, as is frequently stated, that Sicily was compelled to sell its grain to Rome, for Cicero (*De Domo,* 11) says explicitly that the deal-

ers there were selling elsewhere (in alias terras miserant), and in 46
C. Avianius, a Puteolan grain dealer, was operating in Sicily (Cic.,
Fam., 13, 79). In Syria and in the other provinces there was the same
freedom (Cic., *Verr.,* 2, 176; the blame that fell upon Flaccus for
letting a native export grain from Asia " when there was famine at
home " only confirms this fact: Cic., *pro Flacc.,* 17).

Native Italian wine was largely displacing foreign imports (Pliny,
14, 95-7), though it never drove them off the market. In his first two
triumphs Caesar served Chian wine as well as Falernian; in his third
consulship, Chian, Lesbian, and Mamertine (Sicilian) besides Falernian (Pliny, 14, 97). Hortensius left his heir 10,000 casks (26 liters
each) of Greek wine (Pliny, 14, 96). The maximum price permitted
by censorial decrees in 89 B. C. for the choice imports was about 75-80
cents the liter (96 denarii the amphora; Pliny, 14, 95), but ordinary
wine is quoted in Egyptian papyri of this time at about 4-5 cents the
liter. Probably the censorial decree of 89 remained valid for some
time.

The inscribed handles on wine and oil casks are, of course, rare from
this period, but the few we have show that casks lettered in Latin went
far and wide. The name Apolonida (Greek, but in Latin letters) is
found at Brundisium, Panticapaion (Russia), and in Heliopolis
(Egypt: *C. I. L.,* I², 2336; IX, p. 612). The names P. Arpini and
Arunti, L. F. are also found in Egypt (*C. I. L.,* I², 2337; 2340). The
name of Post. Cur(tius) is found on amphorae at Tarentum and Syracuse (*C. I. L.,* I², 2340; he is the Rabirius of whom we shall speak
later: cf. Cic., *pro Rab. Post.*).

Pliny (15, 2) says that olive oil began to be exported from Italy at
this time, but since Italian *olearii* were in Delos before the Mithridatic
War, he is probably in error (Durrbach, *Choix,* p. 230). We know that
during the Empire Rome imported large quantities of oil from Spain.
In 46 Caesar laid a tribute of 3,000,000 pounds of oil per year on
Lepcis in Africa (*Bell. Afr.,* 97).

For building material marble began to be imported in large quantities. Lepidus brought a small amount from the Numidian quarries in
78 (Pliny, 36, 49). Lucullus, cos. in 74, got black marble from the
Greek islands (*ibid.*); Mamurra began the custom of veneering walls
with Carrara marble, using Euboean (Cipollino) for columns (Pliny,
36, 49; Strabo, 10, 1, 6); and Phrygian quarries (near Synnada) also

came into use (Strabo, 12, 8, 14). Caesar used much marble in his public buildings so that the experimental stage was quite complete before Augustus "rebuilt Rome in marble."

Many animals were imported from Africa. The first elephant hunt was given in the circus in 99 and soon after a lion hunt (Pliny, 8, 19; 53). Presently such spectacles became customary and were expected every year. Pompey and Caesar as well as minor officials imported wild animals in droves to amuse the public.

From Egypt came the special products of that country. When Rabirius was financial superintendent of the king of Egypt in 55, his ships (the commercial fleet of the king?) put in on a memorable occasion at Puteoli with cargoes of paper (papyrus), linen, glassware, and various "cheap and showy" articles—presumably oriental ornaments (Cic., *pro Rab. Post.*, 40):

subductae naves Postumi Puteolis sunt; auditae visaeque merces fallaces quidem et fucosae, chartis et linteis et vitro delatis: quibus cum multae naves refertae fuissent, una non patuit parva.

"ships belonging to him put in at Puteoli; merchandise of his was reported and seen there. It is true that the goods invoiced were only cheap showy articles of paper, linen, and glass; many ships were packed with these, but there was one small ship the cargo of which was not revealed."

We have few references to Roman ships. Cicero, when ordering statuary from Athens, asked his correspondent to employ a certain Lentulus as shipper if possible (Cic., *Att.*, 1, 8; 9) but when sailing to Asia in 51 he hired Rhodian boats (*Att.*, 5, 12); when a courier went from Rome to Q. Cicero in Gaul, he took a boat down the river to Ostia and sailed north (*Quint. fr.*, 3, 2). Presumably he used a Roman ship. Vitruvius (2, 9, 16) mentions the shipping (or barging) of larch wood down the Po River to Ravenna and the Adriatic cities. Probably native boats were used here also. Caesar could with his own staff build ships on the English channel in 55 (Caes., *B. G.*, 3, 9; 4, 1; 5, 1); and again in 49 he tried to build a fleet against Pompey but with little success because he did not have command of the seas. In point of fact the war ships and transports of the Civil War were generally bought or requisitioned in eastern ports (*Att.*, 10, 8, 4; 9, 9, 2: Alexandria, Tyre, Sidon, Aradus, Cyprus, Pamphylia, Lycia,

Rhodes, Chios, Lesbos, Smyrna, Miletus, Cos, Byzantium, Colchis; cf. *Fam.*, 12, 14; 15). One gains the impression that, though shipping had begun to fall into Roman—or rather Italian—hands while the knights were prosperous before the Sullan wars, the eastern traders had largely recaptured the commerce on the seas after Delos fell. Cicero, in fact, assumes in 59 that the *negotiatores* of Asia use Greek ships (*Att.*, 2, 16, 4). Be that as it may, the seas were safe after 67 B. C. and commerce prospered even if not in Roman vessels. At Utica alone 200 merchant vessels were found in 49 B. C. by the Caesarian invaders (Caes., *B. C.*, 2, 25). It is unfortunate that we do not hear of what nationality they were.

In Cicero's day there is no evidence that packet-boats with regular schedules and prescribed rates had come in, as they did in the early Empire. Probably the older system, known from Greek commerce, was still in vogue. In that system independent ship-owners " tramped " from port to port with whatever cargo seemed to promise best profits, also " renting space " at times to merchants who had consignments for customers on the route (Huvelin, " *Negotiator*," in Darem.-Saglio). The old methods of maritime insurance were still popular, but any man might insure his own goods. Cicero, for instance, when sending cash from Cilicia to Rome, insured it himself (*Fam.*, 2, 17, 4). Sailing vessels kept close to land of necessity before the compass was known and, since danger from storms was worse near land, storms were seldom braved. In the winter practically all merchant vessels were laid up, partly of course because of the continued cloudiness that hid the stars (*Fam.*, 10, 31). At times ships moved very slowly. Cicero took over two weeks to cross the Aegean in 51 (*Att.*, 5, 12) and three weeks to reach Brundisium from Patrae in 50 (*Fam.*, 16, 9), though when he had a favorable wind he crossed from Corfu to Italy in one night. Letter carriers might take six weeks from Athens to Rome (*Fam.*, 16, 21) and, when Cicero was in Cilicia, letters often took from six to twelve weeks to reach his home. Of course these are slow journeys. In favorable weather one could sail from Alexandria to Sicily in six to seven days and to Puteoli in eight, and one could reach Ostia from Cadiz in six and from Tarraco in four (Pliny, 19, 3-4). Marius sailed from Utica to Rome in less than four days (Plut., *Mar.*, 8, 5).

Rome followed her policy of keeping all ports open to all trade. There were no monopolies, closed seas, or forbidden goods. If ever wine-raising had been forbidden in Gaul, Varro does not know it. He knows (*De R. R.,* 1, 7, 8) that Caesar's soldiers did not find vineyards, olive trees, and fruit orchards near the Rhine, but he attributes this to climatic conditions. We also hear (Pliny, 13, 24) that the censors of 89 (the ones who set maximum prices on wine) forbade the importation of foreign ointments (unguenta exotica). That was while Rome was in the midst of the disastrous Social War and money was very scarce. It was doubtless a war-measure, a part of the sumptuary decree of that year, for the measure was not long in effect. It is just possible also that the censors wished to please the Campanian industrials until danger of revolt might pass, but we have no evidence of this. (For further items see section X, INVESTMENTS.)

VII. AGRICULTURE

We shall first quote a few typical passages from Varro's *de Re Rustica,* from which we derive most of our information on agriculture for this period.

a. *The agrarian wealth of Italy.*
Varro, *R. R.,* 1, 2, 3 (the translations are largely those of Storr-Best, Bell, London, 1912):

Vos, qui multas perambulastis terras, ecquam cultiorem Italia vidistis?

" You who have wandered over many lands, have you ever seen any which was better cultivated than Italy?"

R. R., 1, 2, 6:
contra quid in Italia utensile non modo non nascitur, sed etiam non egregium fit? quod far conferam Campano? quod triticum Apulo? quod vinum Falerno? quod oleum Venafro? non arboribus consita Italia, ut tota pomarium videatur?

" On the other hand, in Italy every useful product not merely grows, but grows to perfection. What spelt is comparable with that of Campania, what wheat with the Apulian, what wine with the Falernian, what oil with the Venafrian? Is not Italy so stocked with fruit-trees as to seem one great orchard?"

b. *Free versus slave labor.*

R. R., 1, 16, 4:

itaque in hoc genus coloni potius anniversarios habent vicinos, quibus imperent, medicos, fullones, fabros, quam in villa suos habeant, quorum non numquam unius artificis mors tollit fundi fructum. quam partem lati fundi divites domesticae copiae mandare solent. si enim a fundo longius absunt oppida aut vici, fabros parant, quos habeant in villa, sic ceteros necessarios artifices, ne de fundo familia ab opere discedat ac profestis diebus ambulet feriata potius, quam opere faciendo agrum fructuosiorem reddat.

" Hence farmers prefer to employ the doctors, fullers and carpenters in the neighborhood, to whom they can give work year by year, rather than have their own on the farm, for the death of a single one of these craftsmen is apt to do away with the farm's profit. Rich men, with large estates, look to the home resources for the supply of this branch of the staff. For where towns or villages are too far away they procure smiths and all the other skilled workmen they need, and keep them on the farm so that their gang of slaves may not have to quit work and walk about making holiday on work-days, instead of rendering the land more profitable by their labor."

R. R., 1, 17, 2:

omnes agri coluntur hominibus servis aut liberis aut utrisque: liberis, aut cum ipsi colunt, ut plerique pauperculi cum sua progenie, aut mercennariis, cum conducticiis liberorum operis res maiores, ut vindemias ac faenisicia, administrant, iique quos obaeratos nostri vocitarunt et etiam nunc sunt in Asia atque Aegypto et in Illyrico conplures. de quibus universis hoc dico, gravia loca utilius esse mercennariis colere quam servis, et in salubribus quoque locis opera rustica maiora, ut sunt in condendis fructibus vindemiae aut messis.

" In all agriculture human beings are used—either slaves, or freemen, or the two together. Freemen are employed either where the farmer himself, helped by his family, tills the soil, as is the case with most peasant proprietors, or where freemen are hired, as when the more important agricultural operations, such as the vintage or the hay-cutting, are conducted by gangs of hired laborers, and by those whom our countrymen called *obaerati* (debtors)—who still exist in great numbers in Asia, Egypt, and Illyricum (here he means *serfs*). About laborers as a class I have this to say: it pays better in an unhealthy district to use hired laborers than slaves, and in a healthy district, too, for the more important work of the farm, such as the vintage or the harvest."

R. R., 1, 17, 5:

praefectos alacriores faciendum praemiis, dandaque opera ut habeant peculium et coniunctas conservas, e quibus habeant filios. eo enim fiunt firmiores ac coniunctiores fundo.

" You should enliven the interest of the overseers in their work by means of rewards, and should see that they have something of their own, and women slaves to live with them and bear them children, for this makes them steadier and more attached to the estate."

R. R., 1, 18, 2:

Saserna scribit satis esse ad iugera VIII hominem unum: ea debere eum confodere diebus XLV, tametsi quaternis operis singula iugera possit; sed relinquere se operas XIII valetudini, tempestati, inertiae, indiligentiae.

" Saserna writes that one man is enough for eight iugera, and that he should dig them over in forty-five days, though four days' work should suffice for each iugerum. The thirteen days left over he allows for cases of illness, bad weather, unskilfulness, and idleness."

R. R., 1, 22, 1:

quae nasci in fundo ac fieri a domesticis poterunt, eorum nequid ematur, ut fere sunt quae ex viminibus et materia rustica fiunt, ut corbes, fiscinae, tribula, valli, rastelli; sic quae fiunt de cannabi, lino, iunco, palmo, scirpo, ut funes, restes, tegetes.

" Nothing should be bought which can be grown on the farm and made by the household. Under this head come mainly things made of osiers and the wood the country supplies: such as baskets, frails, threshing sleighs, stakes, and rakes, as well as things made of hemp, flax, reeds, palm and bull-rushes, such as wagon ropes, bands, and mats."

c. *Fertilizing with green manure.*

R. R., 1, 23, 3:

quaedam etiam serenda non tam propter praesentem fructum quam in annum prospicientem, quod ibi subsecta atque relicta terram faciunt meliorem. itaque lupinum, cum minus siliculam cepit, et non numquam fabalia, si ad siliquas non ita pervenit, ut fabam legere expediat, si ager macrior est, pro stercore inarare solent.

" Some things should be sown with a view not so much to present profit as to next year's crop, because when cut down and left on the ground they improve the soil. Thus lupins, before they produce many pods—and sometimes beanstalks, if the podding stage be not so far advanced that it is profitable to pull the beans—are usually ploughed into poor land for manure."

d. *Harvesting.*

R. R., 1, 50, 1-2:

frumenti tria genera sunt messionis, unum, ut in Vmbria, ubi falce secundum terram succidunt stramentum et manipulum, ut quemque subsicuerunt, ponunt in terra. ubi eos fecerunt multos, iterum eos percensent ac de singulis secant inter spicas et stramentum. spicas coiciunt in corbem atque in aream mittunt, stramenta relincunt in segete, unde tollantur in acervum. altero modo metunt, ut in Piceno, ubi ligneum habent incurvum bacillum, in quo sit extremo serrula ferrea. haec cum conprendit fascem spicarum, desecat et stramenta stantia in segete relinquit, ut postea subsecentur. tertio modo metitur, ut sub urbe Roma et locis plerisque, ut stramentum medium subsicent, quod manu sinistra summum prendunt.

" Wheat is harvested in three ways: The first method is used in Umbria, where they cut the straw close to the ground and lay the sheaves as they are cut, on the ground. When they have got a good number of sheaves, they go over them again, and sheaf by sheaf they cut off the ears from the straw. The ears are thrown into a basket and sent to the threshing floor, the straw is left on the field to be taken away and stacked. In the second method of reaping, used, for instance, in Picenum, they have a curved piece of wood with a small iron saw at the end. This grasps a bundle of ears, cuts them off, and leaves the stalks standing in the field to be subsequently cut close to the ground. The third method—adopted near Rome and in most other places—is to cut the stalk, the top of which is held by the left hand, mid-way . . . "

R. R., 1, 52, 1:

quae seges grandissima atque optima fuerit, seorsum in aream secerni
oportet spicas, ut semen optimum habeat . . .

" Ears of the finest and best crop of wheat should be taken to the
threshing-floor and kept separate from the rest, so that the farmer may
have the best possible seed."

e. *Grazing.*

R. R., 2, 1, 16:

itaque greges ovium longe abiguntur ex Apulia in Samnium aestiva-
tum atque ad publicanum profitentur, ne, si inscriptum pecus paverint,
lege censoria conmittant. muli e Rosea campestri aestate exiguntur in
Burbures altos montes.

" People drive flocks of sheep a considerable distance from Apulia,
to spend the summer in Samnium (they must register their names with
the tax-farmer, lest, by grazing an unregistered flock, they incur the
penalties of the censor's law). And mules are in summer driven from
the plain of Rosea (near Terni) to the high mountains of Burbur (?)."

f. *Poultry and fowls.*

R. R., 3, 2, 14-15:

Certe nosti, inquam, materterae meae fundum, in Sabinis qui est
ad quartum vicesimum lapidem via Salaria a Roma. . . . Atque in hac
villa qui est ornithon, ex eo uno quinque milia scio venisse turdorum
denariis ternis, ut sexaginta milia ea pars reddiderit eo anno villae,
bis tantum quam tuus fundus ducentum iugerum Reate reddit.

" Doubtless you know my maternal aunt's farm in the Sabine country, which is twenty-four miles from Rome on the Via Salaria. . . .
In this villa the aviary alone turned out to my knowledge five thousand
thrushes worth three denarii apiece, so that in that year that depart-
ment of the villa brought in 60,000 sesterces, which is twice as much
as your farm of 200 iugera (130 acres) makes."

R. R., 3, 7, 10:

Romae, si sunt formosi, bono colore, integri, boni seminis, paria
singula volgo veneunt ducenis nummis nec non eximia singulis milibus
nummum.

" At Rome if a pair (of pigeons) are handsome, of good color, without blemish, and of a good breed, they sell quite commonly for 200 sesterces, while an exceptional pair will bring 1,000 sesterces."

Though Varro's three books were written in 37 B. C., five years after Philippi and the widespread colonization of soldiers, they do not reflect the consequences of this wide colonization, but rather conditions as they were before the Civil War, that is, in the period between 67 (the dramatic date of Book 2) and 54 (the assumed date of Book 3). Varro, however, writes for men of his class—rich landlords who can invest in the most profitable products and who farm with slave labor. He leaves us rather ignorant regarding the small farmers.

The impression one gains from him is that the landlords of the time invested in farms of moderate size (100-200 acres) which they cultivated intensively, and that, though each farmer was apt to specialize in the products most suited to the soil, the climate, and the market of each farm, there was a rapidly growing diversification of production between farms, due to the growth of a large class of rich consumers demanding a wide range of luxuries. New fruits were being constantly introduced on Roman farms from foreign countries, native and foreign fish, animals and fowl were being raised on a large scale in carefully prepared preserves and parks, and ranching was carried on with skill and with careful attention to scientific breeding. And yet this specialization, in so far as it did not keep in touch with the needs and resources of local communities, had to yield to necessity here and there. Varro (1, 22) knows that there are farms that are not near the adequate market places. In such instances the farm should produce its own " baskets, threshing implements, rakes, ropes, mats, etc." and it should have some of the more essential skilled workmen like smiths (1, 16, 4). But if a town with adequate facilities is near, the farmer " prefers to employ neighboring doctors, fullers, carpenters, etc."

Varro (1, 2, 3) insists that no country was so completely cultivated as Italy. That statement probably was true for 54 B. C., and yet Cicero in 59 spoke of the need of colonizing the waste places of Italy (Ad Att., 1, 19, 4), Livy (6, 12, 5), writing soon after Varro, says that the Volscian country had few inhabitants but slaves, and Appian (B. C., 5, 18), writing of the famine of 41, when Sextus Pompey had blocked navigation, says that Italian agriculture was ruined. Appian refers, of course, to the temporary ruin caused by the wholesale shifting of

owners by the heartless triumvirs in 41. All of these statements are
probably accurate for their time. Appian refers to a particularly
disastrous year; Cicero and Livy to particular places where slave
culture on a large scale had caused the native communities to dwindle.

One gains the impression from Varro's first book that wheat raising
was general throughout Italy. Etruria was especially important in
this respect (1, 44; 1, 9, 6): the land was rich and yielded fifteenfold,
i. e., since 5 modii to the jugerum were sowed, the harvest was 75 modii
to the jugerum or about 27 bushels to the acre. Apulia had the best
quality of wheat, Campania of spelt (1, 2, 6). Sybaris (1, 44) is also
highly praised but when Varro speaks of a hundredfold yield of Sybaris,
he is of course referring to the fact that at times a single seed may
produce a plant that carries a hundred grains. We expect such futile
statements from Pliny, but hardly from Varro. Special customs of
harvesting are attributed to Umbria, Picenum, and Latium (1, 50).
The city of Rome was not largely fed by Italian grain, since the city
had come largely to depend upon tithe-grain easily carried by water.
When Varro speaks of Africa and Sardinia as supplying the city (2,
pref. 3), he has in mind the fact that Sextus Pompey held Sicily in his
power, but we know from others (cf. App., *B. C.,* 5, 18 and 72) that this
severance of Sicily threatened Rome with starvation. The rest of Italy
was certainly self-supporting, and the good grainlands of Etruria and
Umbria that were near the Tiber must also have found Rome a fairly
convenient market.

Slaves were probably used generally in cereal culture, and Varro
assumes throughout that the workmen were apt to be slaves; but it is
interesting to find that in the one outstanding instance of renting on a
large scale the estate was in Etruria, which was chiefly cereal country.
I refer to the estate of Domitius Ahenobarbus, who was able to man
seven ships with his "slaves, freedmen, and *renters (coloni)* " to aid
Marseilles against Caesar in 49 (Caes., *B. C.,* 1, 34). Shortly before,
when besieged at Corfinium by Caesar, Domitius had promised each of
his soldiers—some 15,000 men—four jugera of land out of his own
possessions, if they would remain faithful (Caes., *B. C.,* 1, 17; Dio, 41,
11, says that the land had been bought in the Sullan confiscations).
Unless Caesar is exaggerating, this means that Domitius owned more
than 60,000 jugera (40,000 acres, over 60 square miles!). In Varro
there is no reference to such vast estates, and they must have been rare.

Be that as it may, leasing became a practical necessity in the case of such properties. Varro seldom mentions a *colonus* in the newer sense of *renter,* but the word is found in 1, 2, 17, and 2, 3, 7, in citations from a standard form for leaseholds. A few times for the sake of complete- ness he mentions hired free labor.

We have no specific data regarding the profits from cereal culture. We do not even know the price of land. Indirectly we may arrive at some inferences. In the third chapter we noticed that Cato's figures implied that land was worth about 1000 sest. per jugerum. Since it was customary to give veterans a bonus of about 10 jugera (Cic., *Att.,* 2, 16) and Augustus substituted a cash payment of 12,000 sesterces for this (Dio, 55, 23), he probably reckoned unimproved land at about 1,200 sesterces the jugerum ($90 the *acre*). Columella, 70 years later, considers such land worth on the average 1,000 sesterces the jugerum, or $75 the acre (3, 3, 8). One of the farmers mentioned by Varro (3, 2, 15) draws 30,000 sesterces annually from 200 jugera of land used for the farming and breeding of fine stock. At 6 per cent on the invest- ment the farm with its stock, its slaves, and its villa property would be worth 2,500 sesterces per jugerum. It is possible, then, that the land itself would have cost about a half of that. We may perhaps assume that unimproved arable land was worth on the average about 1,000- 1,200 sesterces the jugerum. Slave labor was very cheap, but worked slowly with hand-implements, transport was slow, wheat prices kept up fairly well (because of the demands of a large army and an insatiate dole) probably to at least 3 sesterces the modius (60 cents the bushel). In Etruria, where the yield was fifteenfold (Varro, 1, 44), a jugerum would therefore bear wheat (minus the seed) worth 200 sesterces at the market ($10 +), in Leontini of Sicily nearly as much (Cic., *Verr.,* 3, 112). Land in Italy was ordinarily tax-free. Wheat raising was probably remunerative.

Erosion and overcropping. We have no direct references to the subject of the deterioration of the soil in Italy because of erosion and intensive cropping, and some historians are bold enough to use the argu- ment ex silentio to the point of denying that there was any deteriora- tion. However it is not quite correct to say that the authors are silent. Farmers who have to work as hard as the Romans did to keep their lands fertile enough to grow crops must have been struggling with an impoverished soil.   Varro holds that one of the chief reasons for keeping sheep and cattle on the farm is the need for manure (1, 19, 3; 2, *pref.* 5; 2, 2, 12); he gives careful directions for the protection of the manure heap and, like the Chinese today, advised saving the human night-soil for the land (1, 13, 4).   He advocates leaving the land fallow every other year (1, 44, 3) and also plowing in green lupins and beans to enrich the soil (1, 23, 3); indeed he goes so far as to insist that in renting out dovecotes and the aviaries for thrushes the owner should sacrifice a part of the rental price for the bird droppings that could be used on the farm!   That is rather explicit evidence that the soil had suffered impoverishment.

Manure is of course not a complete fertilizer, nor was there an adequate amount of manure available for the farm when the custom came into vogue of pasturing sheep, cattle, and horses on the public cattle runs of the Apennines.

It may be apposite to refer to the report of President Hoover's commission called *Recent Social Trends in the United States*, New York, 1932. Here (Vol. I, p. 90) experts report that in our relatively new land and despite much use of chemical fertilizers the soil has suffered serious depletion from agriculture. Already one third of the sulphur, one fourth of the nitrogen, and one fifth of the phosphorus of the soil is gone. And the report on the effects of erosion is perhaps even more startling: 17,500,000 acres of land have permanently been lost to agriculture by erosion in our states, and the estimate is made that after fifty more years a fourth of our agricultural land will be completely ruined for farming. Italy is even more hilly than the average farm land of America and has always suffered severely from this evil. There is abundant evidence that the thin soil of Latium had suffered both from erosion and overcropping as early as the fifth century B. C. (Frank, *Econ. Hist.*, first chapter) and the process was continuing through the centuries.

This was a period of profitable experimentation in fruit raising, which gave a respite to soil tired of cereals.   To Varro the whole of Italy looked like an orchard (*pomarium,* 1, 2, 6).   It would seem that Roman generals, who were usually practical managers of estates, were eager to find and introduce new fruits of every kind.   Pliny (15, 102) says that Lucullus introduced the cherry from Pontus (about 74 B. C.), and that from Rome it had already spread as far as Britain.   Varro mentions several new varieties of figs brought from Asia and Africa (1, 41, 6).   The " Livian " and " Pompeian " figs were named from those who introduced them, probably Roman generals (Pliny, 15, 70). Matius, a friend of Octavian, was responsible for the introduction of some foreign apple trees (Pliny, 12, 13).   It was the same with a score of new varieties of grapes and olives.   Flower gardens were also being cultivated for profit. Varro recommends especially raising roses and violets for the city (1, 16, 3) and gives directions for the planting of bulbs—especially lilies and crocuses (1, 35). Of vineyards Varro says little. He accepts Cato's figures for the yield, from 10 to 15 cullei per jugerum (1, 2, 7), but this must refer to extraordinary instances. Good vineyards today seldom yield a third as much.

Grazing. In the speeches of Cicero we have casual references to rich Italians of the interior, like Cluentius and Ceius of Larinum (Cic., *pro Cluent.*, 161, 162) and the Plancii of Atina (Cic., *pro Plancio*), who were prospering in the grazing region. In Varro's day the raising of horses, cattle, sheep, and asses was carried on with large capital. Wool was used in most of the clothing; horses were used in great numbers in the army, in travel, and in the circus; asses and mules were in demand for draft animals and for plowing (Varro, 2, 6, 5; 1, 20, 3); cattle were needed as draft animals and provided beef, cheese, and milk (Varro, 2, 11, 3). It was because of the steady demand for these products that Varro places a higher value on good meadow land than Cato had (Varro, 1, 7). Varro himself was particularly interested in horse breeding in the meadows of Reate, where one of his favorite villas was situated, and in his flocks of sheep that wintered in Apulia but were driven to the public pastures in the Samnite mountains in summer (Varro, 2, pref. 6; 2, 1, 16-17). At Reate the breeders were interested only in pedigreed stock. As much as 400,000 sesterces ($20,000) might be paid for a stallion of good stock (2, 8, 3) and 60,000 or more for an ass (2, 1, 14).

Fowl, fish, game, etc. Large sums were invested in game and fish preserves and in " aviaries " for the breeding of all kinds of edible birds and fowls, and the first comers in the new business found it very profitable. A few specific instances may be mentioned. Seius, at Ostia, specialized in raising peacocks, a single one of which would bring 50 denarii ($10) and each egg—used chiefly for breeding—5 denarii (one dollar). From a flock of 100 he expected to bring in 15,000 denarii the year from the chicks alone (Varro, 3, 6, 3). It was Hortensius who had introduced this luxury (Pliny, 10, 45). A pair of the best pigeons for breeding would bring 50 denarii and Varro speaks of 100,000 sesterces as the normal cost of a well-appointed pigeon-farm (3, 7, 10 and 11). Fircellia, Varro's aunt, specialized in breeding thrushes, producing some 5,000 per year, which sold at 3 denarii (60 cents) each (3, 2, 15). This also was a relatively new industry (3, 5, 8), but many engaged in it (3, 4, 2). The other birds mentioned by Varro as profitable to raise are ducks, geese, cranes, teal, blackbirds (the merle, of course), reed-birds, quails, and guinea-fowls (3, 3, etc.). In paddocks and game-preserves deer, hare, wild boars, and the like were also raised for the market (Varro, 3, 2, 14; 3, 3) as well as for the villa. Fulvius had 40 acres, Hortensius 50, enclosed for the breeding of wild game (3, 12; 3, 13), and T. Pompeius had an enormous enclosure of 9,000 acres in southern Gaul for the same purpose (3, 12, 2).

There was also much breeding of fish in private streams and ponds, especially the rarer salt-water fish, but Varro insists that the expenses devoured profits. The costly fish ponds of Licinius Murena, Lucullus, Hortensius, and Philippus, made with channels from the sea, were at least a standing joke (Varro, 3, 2, 18; 3, 3, 10; 3, 17, 3; Columella, 8, 16, 5). See the remarks of Pliny, *N. H.*, 9, 170.

Eadem aetate prior Licinius Murena reliquorum piscium vivaria invenit, cuius deinde exemplum nobilitas secuta est Philippi, Hortensi. Lucullus exciso etiam monte iuxta Neapolim maiore inpendio quam villam exaedificaverat euripum et maria admisit, qua de causa Magnus̄ Pompeius Xerxen togatum eum appellabat. ⌈XL⌉ HS. e piscina ea defuncto illo veniere pisces.

In the same age, also Licinius Murena was the first to form preserves for other fish; and his example was soon followed by the noble families of the Philippi and the Hortensii. Lucullus had a mountain pierced near Naples, at a greater outlay even, than that which had been expended on his villa; and here he formed a channel, and admitted the sea to his preserves; it was for this reason that Pompeius Magnus gave him the name of " Xerxes in a toga." After his death, the fish in his preserves was sold for the sum of four million sesterces.

Latifundia. How far large farms were absorbing small ones at this time it is difficult to say. Too much has perhaps been made of two or three instances. Cicero happens to say in 63 that the small lots given by Sulla at Praeneste eighteen years before had, despite legal prescription, fallen into the hands of a few men (*de leg. Agr.*, 2, 78). However, this was wine-country near Rome and would naturally attract capitalistic enterprise. The estate of Domitius Ahenobarbus in Etruria must have been very large if we can believe Caesar's (unfriendly) report that he promised 4 jugera to each of his soldiers (Caes., *B. C.*, 1, 17). Domitius then had 15,000 men, but perhaps it was only to his own army of 4,000 that he made the promise. Dio (41, 11) asserts that he had bought the estate from Sulla. If this is true (Domitius never was a Sullan partisan), it is a special case. As we have seen, Lucullus, Pompey, Valgius, and some others had large estates acquired usually from booty or in the conscriptions, but the extensive estates known are not numerous. De Pachtere (*La table hyp. de Veleia*) in his examination of the Veleian mortgage lists of Trajan's day has pointed out that, though Mommsen was correct in holding that the 90 original plots of Veleia had fallen into the hands of 50 owners by Trajan's time, the small plots in the good valley-land were hardly affected by the process. It was in the hilly country where grazing paid better than farming that capitalists extended their purchases. It is quite certain that the colonization of Sulla, Caesar, and the triumvirs tended to stem the trend towards latifundia.

VIII. INDUSTRY 80–50 B. C.

Building Operations.

This was a period of very extensive building at Rome. The structures erected at public expense we have mentioned above—the Capitoline temple, the hall of records (Tabularium), some bridges, walls, and the Tiber embankments. The structures erected by rich men or victorious generals for public use were far more extensive. The more important of these are the following. Lepidus restored rather simply the old Basilica of his family in 78 (Pliny, 35, 13); in 74 Aurelius Cotta erected a new tribunal and apparently paved the Forum (Festus, 416 L.). In 55 Pompey completed the first stone theatre at Rome, a magnificent structure of peperino, concrete, and marble which Pliny says seated 40,000 (Ascon. *in Pis.*, 1; Cic. *Att.*, 4, 1, 6; *Vell.*, 2, 48). He also built temples to Hercules and to Minerva. In the same year Paulus began to reconstruct the old basilica Aemilia, borrowing money from Caesar (Cic., *Att.*, 4, 16, 14; Plut., *Caes.*, 29), but it was not completed till 34 when his son was consul (Dio, 49, 42). This was one of the most beautiful structures of Rome. In 54 Caesar began to spend lavishly of his Gallic booty. The Basilica Julia was begun that year, and he sent to his agents at Rome 60,000,000 sesterces

25

($3,000,000) with which to acquire land north of the Forum for a new Forum which was to be called the Julian. This Forum (which is now being excavated) was begun about 51 B. C. and required several years in the building. It cost 100,000,000 sesterces (Pliny, 36, 103; Suet., *Jul.*, 26; App., *B. C.*, 2, 68; 102; Dio, 43, 22).

During his dictatorship Caesar paved the Forum, built the new Rostra, started the Saepta (the voting quarters), a new Senate-house, a new theatre, and a large number of other structures. In 42 Plancus employed Gallic booty in building the Temple of Saturn to serve as a state Treasury (Suet., *Aug.*, 29; *C. I. L.*, 6, 1316), and the triumvirs began the erection of the temple to the deified Caesar (Dio, 47, 18, and 51, 22). About 38 Domitius Ahenobarbus built a temple to Neptune, and in 36 Domitius Calvinus rebuilt the Regia entirely of marble and inscribed the walls with the Fasti (consular and triumphal lists) of Rome (Dio, 48, 42; Pliny, 34, 48). In 36 Octavian began to build the splendid temple of Apollo and the library on the Palatine (Dio, 49, 15; 53, 1; Suet., *Aug.*, 29). The temple was not dedicated till eight years later. In 33 Agrippa, then aedile, undertook at his own expense (*i. e.* from booty) to enlarge the water supply of Rome by repairing the Anio Vetus, the Aqua Marcia, the Aqua Tepula, and to build a new aqueduct called the Julia (Frontinus, *de Aquis*, 1, 7-9), besides the splendid baths and the Pantheon in the Campus (see Platner and Ashby, for the bibliography on these buildings).

Such are the chief structures, which probably required as much money as the city had spent in buildings in the four centuries preceding. The construction of the period shows very solid workmanship and increasing artistry. The foundations were usually of concrete, the heavier walls of very strong stone (peperino, travertine, Gabine stone) or of concrete with a veneering, in the later period usually of Carrara marble. From the time of Caesar's dictatorship the columns and architraves are usually of marble, and there is a rapid improvement in artistic carving toward the end of the period. Mamurra (Pliny, 36, 48), Caesar's chief engineer in the Gallic campaign, seems to have been the first to use the Carrara marbles (while in Cisalpine Gaul with Caesar he may well have noticed them), but this period also marks the first importation on a large scale of Cipollino from Euboea (Pliny, 36, 48; Strabo, 10, 1, 6), of Numidian marble (Giallo Antico) from Schemtou (Lepidus in 78; Pliny, 36, 49), of Phrygian marble

(Pavonazzetto) from near Synnada (Strabo, 12, 8, 14), and of the marble of Hymettus (imported by Crassus, Pliny, 17, 6; 36, 7). The famous black stone of the Forum may well be an importation of Lucullus, who was using "Lucullan marble" in 74, the very year that the Forum pavement of Cotta was laid (Pliny, 36, 49; Festus, 416 L.). In architecture, as in agriculture, it was the army officer who saw the world and introduced new experiments to Rome.

Private dwellings were also going up with increasing magnificence in the city, the suburbs, and upon the fashionable villa sites. Cicero, who was far from wealthy, had a town house on the Palatine for which he paid 3,500,000 sesterces ($175,000; *Fam.*, 5, 6, 2). The house was appraised at 2,000,000, the lot at 1,500,000 (*Att.*, 4, 2, 5). His Tusculan house, apart from the grounds, was appraised at 500,000 sesterces, that of Formiae at 250,000 (*ibid.*). Besides these he also had villas at Arpinum, Asturae, Puteoli, and Pompeii, and his wife had apartment houses in Rome that brought in a yearly rental of 100,000 sesterces (*Att.*, 15, 17, 1; 16, 1, 5). They must have been worth 1,300,000 sesterces. Scaurus' villa at Tusculum was estimated at 30,000,000 sesterces ($1,500,000; Pliny, 36, 115). Lucullus had a magnificent villa at Tusculum (Plut., 39, 4; Varro, *R. R.*, 3, 4, 3) with farms in the neighborhood extending over several miles (Frontinus, *de Aquis*, 1, 5-10). His villa on the Pincian was famous for its gardens (Plut., 39, 2); his property at Cumae cost him 10,000,000 sesterces (Plut., *Mar.*, 34, 4). Besides these he had a house at Naples famous for its fish pond (Varro, *R. R.*, 3, 17, 9), and another on the island of Nesis (Cic., *Att.*, 16, 1). Crassus, who was perhaps the wealthiest man of his day, owning land worth 50,000,000 denarii (Pliny, 33, 134), confined himself to one house—a very splendid one (Plut., 2, 6) — but that was very unusual. Pompey, Hortensius, Antony, Metellus, and their companions had many costly properties. It was a common saying that Lepidus' mansion, which was the most magnificent at Rome in 78, was surpassed by a hundred others within thirty-five years (Pliny, 36, 109). This was in fact a time of great prosperity for architects and contractors. The labor, however, fell almost entirely to slaves.

Pompeii also provides some data regarding the building activity of this epoch, though it was a not wholly normal period for that city. Sulla had captured Pompeii in 89, and "colonized" it in 80. Hence there was a serious interruption in its economic life. We get the impression, however, that Sulla spared the city and its inhabitants and to a large extent settled his colonists on land taken from Stabiae, leaving the Pompeian landlords largely undisturbed. It was not long before the city recovered and showed signs of prosperity, though not quite at the rate it had in the preceding period. A new bath — near the Forum—was built at public expense soon after 80 B. C. (*C. I. L.*, I², 1628) and the old one (the Stabian) was largely rebuilt and enlarged (*ibid.*, 1635: the magistrates spent for this their own money that they were expected "to use on games or some monument"). A splendid temple to the Capitoline Jupiter was built in the forum (37 x 17 meters). A roofed theatre, probably for music, was now constructed near the larger open one (1633) and an amphitheatre was laid out, though it required some decades to complete this (1632). Some private houses were also built on a large scale or rebuilt, though none to compare with the palaces of the pre-Sullan days. The house of Lucretius Fronto (Reg., V, 4) is among the best. Those of Popidius Priscus (VII, 2, 20) and of Gavius Rufus (VII, 2, 16) were rebuilt, as well as several smaller ones. In other words, though the city suffered from what might have proved a permanent disaster, it soon shared in the prosperity of Italy that was general before the Civil War of 49. It is not impossible that most of the cities colonized by Sulla fared in the same way.

From other cities of Italy the evidence that has happened to survive is too meager to permit of definite conclusions. At Ostia we judge from the remains that the extensive walls of the colony were built about 80 B. C. At Praeneste we have a few notices in the inscriptions of the period regarding public construction: an aerarium (*C. I. L.*, I², 1463), a temple with a portico (1464), a rebuilding of the public baths (1473), and some paving (1470). There are also extensive remains of the Temple of Fortune, built after 80 B. C. At Tibur inscriptions mention two long porticoes, some street paving, and some arches built at public expense (1492, 4, 8), and considerable ruins of the Sullan period are still extant. At Signia a man built a temple of Hercules at his own expense (1503). The walls of Ferentinum were largely rebuilt (1522-3), possibly during the Social War, though more probably a few years later. The remains of the market are still visible. Atina spent some 50,000 sesterces on paving (1533), Arpinum built cisterns and sewers (1537) and a public laundry (1539: Arpino lies high on a hill and far from any stream). Fundi and Formiae erected town walls (1557-60, 63: probably about 49 B. C.). Grumentum and Aceruntia erected public baths (1690, 1693) and Thurii a basilica (1694). At Aquilonia the citizens with their own hands raised the town walls, an interesting case of community work (1714). At Telesia the praetor built two towers instead of giving games (1747). Aeclanum and Assisi constructed their walls at public expense (1722, 2112); Arretium and Spoletium built bridges (2087, 2107). We know that in the Po Valley in particular cities were growing rapidly, but these very cities have been so constantly inhabited and rebuilt that few important records have come down to us from republican times. (For the cities of the Po Valley see Bendinelli, *Torino Romana*; Brusin, *Aquileia*; Calderini, *Aquileia Romana*; Ducati, *Storia di Bologna*; Baratta, "Il sito di Spina," *Athen.*, 1932, 217; Pais, "Sulla romanizzazione della valle d'Aosta," *Rend. Acc. Linc.*, 1916).

If we had the cost of a number of known structures, we might be able to reach some dependable impression of the probable cost of material and labor, but we have little that is of service. The Corpus, I², 698, gives the Puteolan inscription of 105 B. C. which fully describes a porch and some other work to be done for 1500 sesterces. A few years ago I was informed by an Italian architect that the work would cost at least five times as much now.

We have also a few statements about the cost of road paving and I shall give these, though they are of little service, since they concern repaving, the depth of which is not given.

a) *C. I. L.*, I², 808 (time of Sulla). Repaving the Caecilian road with gravel: 20 miles, for 150,000 sesterces (600,000 *asses*); 22 (?) miles in rough country for 600,000 + sesterces (2,400,000 *asses*). If the road was 10 feet wide, as is probable, this would give from $\frac{6}{10}$ of 1 *as* to 2.2 *asses* the square foot (Roman) or from 6 to 20 cents the square yard. Considering the substantial character of Roman roads, this might well be less than a fifth of modern Italian costs. It is very interesting to find that these contracts on a public road are taken by freedmen and not by knights.

b) *C. I. L.*, I², 2537, gives a statement about a stone pavement of a road near Verulae laid by the duumviri of a town. Here 414 passus (2070 feet) were paved at 5 denarii, 3 *asses* the foot. If the road was

8 feet wide (a village road), the pavement cost 2 + cents the square foot (Roman) or about 20 cents the square yard. This of course is exceedingly cheap for a stone pavement.

c) We may compare these prices with an Hadrianic contract for paving (Dessau, 5875) found near Beneventum, where the Emperor bore two-thirds of the cost while the abutting properties bore one-third. Here 15,750 passus (78,750 feet) of repaving cost 1,716,000 sesterces. If the road was 10 feet wide, the cost was about 9 *asses* the square foot (Roman), or about a dollar the square yard. But the road lay in very rough country, and may have required some grading.

d) *C. I. L.*, I², 809, is a fragment recording the cost of pavements laid in Rome, probably before Sulla. Unfortunately only one price has survived (line 10), *i. e.* 100 sesterces per foot for a stone stairway, and the price probably included much expensive grading and substructure. We do not know the width of the staircase.

The only conclusion that we can reach from these few items is that during the Republic materials and labor were far less expensive than in present-day Italy.

Of *other industries* we know but little. Mining had generally fallen into private hands, and Crassus owned many of the mines (Plut., *Crass.*, 2), but that is all we are told. The slag heaps of Populonia prove that the Italian iron industry continued, as of course it must, since farming was in a prosperous condition and wars continued. Lead was coming increasingly into use for water pipes. The chief source of lead seems to have been the Spanish mines (Diod., 5, 36, 3; Strabo, 3, 2, 10). We hear also of cinnabar mines (Cic., *Phil.*, 2, 48; Pliny, 33, 118) at Sisapo in Spain, where publicans operated, and near Sinope in Asia. The new (second) style of wall frescoes with paintings depended much on this for its red color. Vestorius, the banker of Puteoli seems to have had a factory for the making of pigments (Vitruvius, 7, 11; Pliny, 33, 57). Metal work in Italy must have flourished, but the custom of cutting an enduring trade-mark or maker's name on copper and silver ware had not yet arisen, hence information is lacking.

The great amount of sheep-raising also implies much weaving. Since, however, each household employed the spare time of its slave-women at weaving, the work left less of a record than if factories and labor guilds had grown up in connection with the craft. We have only casual notices like that of Asconius (*in Mil.*, Stangl., 38: "the mob that stormed the palace of Lepidus tore everything, even the garments that were being woven on the looms in the atrium" cf. Varro, *Men. Sat.*, 190 B; *R. R.*, 1, 2, 21). In many of the later houses of Pompeii there are markings on the plaster recording the amount of spinning and weaving of each of the maids. Hence we are somewhat surprised to find even rare references to some professionals like the *centonarii* (a gild, at Praeneste *C. I. L.*, I², 1457, also the title of a mime of Laberius). Apparently the making of quilts was beyond the skill of the home, or perhaps the industry depended upon rags and patches collected from a large number of houses. A casual statement of Varro (*L. L.*, 9, 39) deserves notice, that, though the woolen cloth of the Po Valley and of Apulia looked alike, one paid more for the latter because it was stronger. This could hardly be said unless there was some uniformity in weave in each place. This may, of course, be due to the customs prevailing in domestic weaving, but it would be more easily explained if we might assume large establishments that kept a uniform standard. Such existed later both at Tarentum and in the North. Probably a few "factories" had already come into existence, that is, larger establishments that specialized in spinning and weaving. Fine fabrics and tapestries were probably still imported from the East. Verres, while governor of Sicily, placed orders with several skilled weavers for tapestries of the eastern type (Cic., *Verr.*, 4, 103) and was roundly rebuked for mixing governmental and personal affairs (cf. art. "Lana" in *R-E*).

The red earthenware that later became very famous was just beginning to be made at Arretium. We have a few signed pieces from this period found at various places from Arrezzo to Rome, which show that it had established its market (*C. I. L.*, I², 2327-34). In the next period it spread all over the western provinces. Rough earthenware was of course made everywhere. Stamped brick begins to appear in the towns of Picenum and the Po Valley (*C. I. L.*, I², 2296 ff.), but not yet at Rome, which had tufa near at hand. Roof-tiles were of course made in great abundance at Rome and had been for centuries. The new signed glassware—very inexpensive and made with the blowpipe—was also just coming into Roman industry, introduced, it would seem, from Syria (*C. I. L.*, I², 2400, XV, 6962).

Pliny, *N. H.*, 19, 23, gives a hint of how new uses were found for linen:

Postea in theatris tantum umbram fecere, quod primus omnium

invenit Q. Catulus, cum Capitolium dedicaret. carbasina deinde vela primus in theatro duxisse traditur Lentulus Spinther Apollinaribus ludis. mox Caesar dictator totum forum Romanum intexit *viamque sacram ab domo sua et clivum usque in Capitolium*, quod munere ipso gladiatorio mirabilius visum tradunt.

" In more recent times linens alone have been employed for the purpose of affording shade in our theatres; Q. Catulus having the first who applied them to this use, on the occasion of the dedication by him of the Capitol (69 B. C.). At a later period, Lentulus Spinther, it is said, was the first to spread awnings of fine linen over the theatre, at the celebration of the games in honour of Apollo. After this, Caesar, when Dictator, covered with a linen awning the whole of the Roman Forum, as well as the Sacred Way, from his own house as far as the ascent to the Capitol, a sight, it is said, more wonderful even than the show of gladiators which he then exhibited."

Such are the meager references to industry. They are by no means representative of the great amount of work that was being done.

IX. LABORERS AND PROFESSIONAL MEN

Varro's book, which was written for well-to-do Romans who owned land, assumes throughout that the work on the farms was done by slaves under the direction of a slave-overseer, a villicus. This may be accepted as the normal system in Cicero's day. Varro also assumes (1. 18. 1) that the number of slaves needed for vineyards and olive orchards would be about that which Cato designated; hence he must also assume that the vintage and olive picking were cared for outside the regular staff by contractors who bought the hanging crop or by hired (free) labor from the neighborhood (cf. 1, 16, 4; 1, 17, 2).

On small farms, which must have been numerous after all the military assignments, the farmer did his own work with the aid of his children, but Varro's book is hardly concerned with these. He barely mentions them (pauperculus cum sua progenie, 1, 17, 2; two brothers who have only one acre each; 3, 16, 10). Cf. the petty farmers mentioned in Horace, *Sat.*, 2, 2, 115, Sallust once (*Cat.*, 37, 7) refers to young men who go to the city to avoid the hardships of the farm. Vergil, who knew small-farm conditions in the Po Valley and in Campania, pictures the life and occupation of working farmers throughout his *Georgics*, but of course the romance of agriculture can ill afford to obtrude the slave.

Renting is also mentioned very little, because of the nature of our sources. Varro refers to rental contracts only incidentally (2, 3, 7; 1, 2, 17). Cicero seems to have rented out his estate at Arpinum in small farms (praediola, *Att.*, 13, 9, 2) and, when in financial straits, he rented out the vegetable garden of his Tusculan villa for $50 and some produce for the table (*Fam.*, 16, 18, 2). The estate at Cumae (*Att.*, 14, 16) had both slave overseers and procurators, so that both systems were used as on Horace's farm. We have seen that the wealthy Domitius also used both systems since he had coloni and slaves enough to man several ships (Caes., *B. C.*, 1, 34 and 56).

We get little information as to the use of money-rental versus share-renting. Indeed it is frequently denied that the share-rental mentioned by the imperial jurists could have existed in the Republic, since it is not definitely mentioned. But such a denial is preposterous. In any nation where crops are at all uncertain, as they are over half of Italy, the share system is a necessity. Individual circumstances also lead constantly to the same system. In fact it must have been common in the earlier centuries, since Rome was very slow at beginning coinage. And in Sicily, her first province, Rome took her tithe in kind. Cato uses the word *partiarius*, but in a slightly different sense; not of a renter, but of a man who does a certain task for a percentage of the product. We have seen that in Cato's day a share-renter on wheat-lands would probably get one-half of the crop, and that the *partiarius* of Cato's vineyard worked for half of the total yield (see ch. III, agriculture).

Free labor was still used on large farms for special tasks. As we have seen, Varro's acceptance of Cato's slave force also implies the use of outsiders for vintage and harvest, and Varro mentions these in 1, 17, 2. He also mentions the free artisans who make the rounds of farms too small to have skilled slaves (1, 16, 4), and the temporary employment of free labor in districts that are too unhealthy for permanent residents (1, 17, 2). The extra free labor for seasonal tasks is mentioned by Suetonius (*Vesp.*, 1), who says that Vespasian's great grandfather (about 50 B. C.) hired laborers in Umbria and brought them down into the Sabine country for such work. (In our middle states and in California large gangs of men follow the harvesting in the same manner.) On cattle ranches Varro implies that all the herdsmen are slaves, despite the fact that Caesar decreed that a third must be free labor (Suet., *Jul.*, 42; see Heitland, *Agricola*; Gummerus in *Klio, Supp.*, 1906, and Park, *Plebs in Cicero's Day*).

In the city domestic servants, secretaries, and the like were at this time wholly of the slave class, though competent helpers at work requiring intelligence and special skill often won their freedom and were expected to remain in service for pay or suitable emoluments. The slaves and freedmen incidentally mentioned by Cicero as being in his or some friend's household are the *janitor, cubicularius,* cook, various attendants, litter-bearers, messengers and letter-carriers, a household doctor (a trained slave), business managers, a *nomenclator,* a secretary at accounts, various slaves about the library like readers, copyists, clerks, and librarians. Cicero does not mention any skilled artisans in the list nor does he happen to mention weaving and smithing or carpentry at home. However, the slave who managed the estate of Cicero's brother was trusted to take a contract for an addition to the house that would cost 16,000 sesterces (*Quint. fr.*, 3, 1, 5; see Park, *The Plebs in Cicero's Day*).

Several of the slaves who held places of some responsibility won their freedom as, for instance, Chrysippus, who attended Cicero's son at Athens; Laurea and Philotimus, his own secretaries; Tiro, his reliable private secretary and agent; and Dionysius, a tutor. Cicero had nine or ten of these *liberti*. A very large part of the financial business of Rome at this time was carried on by freedmen who had won the trust of their masters while slaves, and both Caesar and Pompey trusted their private business and secret correspondence to ex-slaves, thus inaugurating the baneful custom of using *liberti* in affairs of state, that had to be broken up after the reign of Claudius.

Labor in industries.

During the Empire the columbaria of the poor (burial chambers with " pigeon-holes " for the urns) were filled with burial urns that had brief inscriptions giving the name and occupation under the " pigeon-hole." For that period some idea of the status of industrial workers can be secured. But inscriptions of this kind are very rare for the Republic. It is only from makers' marks on table-ware—mostly from Arretium—that we get any information regarding a large group of workers. Park's study of these marks from 40 to 10 B. C. in

The Plebs of Cicero's Day, 79 ff. (based on Oxé, *Rhein. Mus.*, 1904, 252), gives this result:

> The 13 owners of factories are free-born citizens, except possibly 2 or 3 freedmen.
>
> Some 123 workmen signing articles are slaves; 8 or 9 are ex-slaves.
>
> There is no evidence that free labor was employed at all.

Since the making of this table-ware required some skill, patient interest, and intelligence, there is no reason to suppose that other industries could not also rely upon slave-labor. The industry continued to prosper for about a century and it is noticeable that slave-labor continued to be used through the period, though it is also observable that some slaves won their freedom and became directors of branch factories, and that some of the freedmen became owners.

Inscriptions, which give much information regarding labor during imperial times, are relatively scarce for this period. However, we get the impression that the small-shop system, in which one workman with a helper or two makes and sells his articles either for his own account or for a patron, is as usual at Rome as in imperial Pompeii (see Frank, *Econ. Hist.*², 219 ff.). These shopkeeping workmen are usually freedmen and frequently belong to gilds. In the first volume of the Corpus we find a gild of bronze-workers (977) officered by freedmen magistri; a gild of goldsmiths with a freedman as magister in 1307; a gild of ring-makers in 1225. Other workers in metal or jewelry without mention of an organization are a *margaritarius* (jeweller dealing in pearls), 1212; a *vascularius* (maker of bronze ware), 1209; *spinter* (maker of bracelets), 1274. These three are also freedmen. Such freedmen were frequently set up in business by the patron who had manumitted them, and they presumably worked for shares in the profits. Other gilds of shopkeepers are those of the lanii (butchers, liberti, 978, 979) and of various nursery-men (980).

A former slave of King Mithridates and a friend of his dealt in frankincense and ointments (1334); and nine ex-slaves of three Trebonii kept shops for the sale of incense (1398-9). Here we may assume that their patrons owned a rather large enterprise in the preparation of Arabian products.

The famous Eurysaces, whose tomb is so conspicuous near the Porta Maggiore, was apparently a freedman who had a large wholesale bakery.

He took contracts from the city presumably to supply bread for public slaves, the city guard, prisoners, and the like (we cannot assume that the city had at this time begun distributing bread in the dole).

A few individual liberti, presumably from shops, are a vestiarius (1268), a gardener (1369), a butcher (1411), and a purpuraria (1413). There is a vegetable huckster (holitor, 1314) who bears the dignified name L. Horatius L. F. Vot(uria). He at least betrays no connection with the slave class.

The oldest columbarium of Rome belongs to this period. Nearly three hundred names of poor people were found in it (1015-1201). The status of the interred is seldom specified, but only seven give filiation; twenty-eight admit being liberti, and the numerous Greek cognomina prove that many others may have been. The whole group belonged to poor folk engaged in simple trades who were but a step above unskilled laborers. Finally we should mention that the flute players that performed at religious ceremonies were well organized (988, the ten officers—magistri—are liberti), and that the numbers of the Greek choral singers (2519) were organized into a burial society officered by two freedmen.

At Praeneste, near Rome, the gilds were also strong and consisted largely of freedmen. The wagon makers (cisiarii, 1449) had an organization of which the two magistri were liberti, the two ministri, slaves. Four liberti were magistri of the gild of butchers (1449); the gild of cooks (of the temple ?) was officered by four slaves (1447). Broken fragments of other inscriptions mention seven unspecified gilds (1451-7). Praeneste was an old industrial town, and its gilds probably had endured from early times. Spoletium had a fullers' gild (2108) whose officers were three liberti and a slave. As early as about 200 B. C. Falerii had a gild of cooks whose officers were free folk (364). This is all the information of any significance yielded by Italian inscriptions of the Republic. The gilds, of course, were formed for social purposes and for the sake of reducing the costs of religious offerings and of burial expenses. In a society resting on slave labor they could hardly exert pressure to raise wages or prices.

The Professions. Slaves were also being used in the professions, except in law, which was a gentleman's introduction to politics and was practiced without fees. The *architects* of a simpler day had been

Roman builders who had acquired practice and experience. Now that Hellenistic principles were being adopted and marble introduced—a material that Roman builders knew nothing about—, Greek architects were needed, and they were apt to teach docile slaves the mathematics and the standard architectural principles needed in order to keep the profession in their own hands. The builder usually employed by the Ciceros was Cyrus, a freedman (*Att.*, 2, 3, 2; 4, 10, 2; *Quint. fr.*, 2, 2, 2). Chrysippus, a freedman of Cyrus, did some work for Cicero, and was also in the service of Caesar (*Att.*, 2, 4, 7; 13, 29, 2; 14, 9, 1; *Fam.*, 7, 14). The famous Vitruvius, apparently a citizen, also began his activity in this period. However, for the great buildings constructed at the end of his life Caesar employed an Athenian (*Att.*, 13, 35).

Doctors were now usually Greeks, since the simple home remedies advocated by Cato had lost their vogue. And these Greeks also trained apt slaves. Their lore was all in Greek and they could not only train Greek-speaking slaves more readily than Romans but they could sell their trained slaves with good profit to rich householders who needed them in constant attendance. After the profession once fell into the hands of foreigners and liberti, Romans did not care to enter into it. Caesar offered citizenship to foreign doctors as well as to other men of the learned professions (Suet., *Jul.*, 42) but this offer came too late to give the craft the respectability it deserved. The presence of many quacks did nothing to improve the situation. Metrodorus (*Fam.*, 16, 20) and Alexio (*Att.*, 15, 2, 4), who served Cicero at various times, were apparently freedmen. Cicero's *pro Cluentio* (40, 176-186) happens to mention two Greek quacks that toured the country seeking victims, one of them being a slave. *C. I. L.*, I², 1684 is a tombstone of an immigrant from Tralles who was proud of his cures by means of wine. Glyco, the physician of the consul Pansa, who was in danger of being blamed for the death of his master, was apparently a freedman. Brutus (Cic., *ad Brut.*, 1, 6, 2) intervened in his favor because he was the brother-in-law of one of Brutus' freedmen. During the Empire the medical profession continued to be in the hands of Greek immigrants and of freedmen, and some of these grew very wealthy.

Actors in the legitimate drama were apparently never slaves during the Republic (" The Status of Actors," *Class. Phil.*, 1930). Roscius, a friend of Cicero, was a citizen, and Aesopus was apparently a Greek immigrant, who had been granted citizenship. Both of these men received very high pay for any performance and could earn 300,000 sesterces at a festival of a few days (Cic., *pro. Rosc. Com.*, 23). Few Romans, however, entered the profession in Cicero's day, so that it became customary to train slaves as actors and set them free before their first public appearance. In the mimes and pantomimes slaves appeared, women as well as men, but they apparently were quickly manumitted if successful. Dionysia, a dancing girl, probably a freed-woman, could make as much as 200,000 sesterces a year ($10,000: Cic., *pro. Rosc.*, 23).

Teachers. Since the all-important subject to acquire in school was Greek (literature, rhetoric, philosophy, etc.), no teacher could succeed who was not a master of Greek. Some of the famous teachers were foreigners and to these Caesar extended citizenship. Several were war-captives taken by Lucullus, Murena, and Pompey in the fall of Asiatic cities and sold to Romans who needed tutors or literary secretaries, and usually were set free. Among the liberti of this type Suetonius (*de Gram.*, 3-10) mentions Daphnis (sold for 700,000 sesterces), Gnipho, Praetextatus, Epicadus, Eros, and Lenaeus. The hundreds of Greek teachers who tutored in private families or kept ordinary grammar schools were mostly slaves or freedmen trained for such work. The fees were very low. Horace paid only eight cents per month in the school of a country town. Hence his teacher would require some eighty pupils in a class to make a decent laborer's wage. On the other hand Verrius Flaccus, the imperial tutor, received $5,000 the year (*ibid.*, 17).

Literature as a profession brought no emoluments of value, since books could be copied by private secretaries as readily as by the copyists of publishers. Hence copyrights were not practicable. During the Repub-lic, therefore, men who devoted themselves to literature were either men of means or men who received patronage from wealthy men. Literary slaves or freedmen, however, were employed as collaborators, " ghost-writers," and researchers. Cicero had the aid at various times of Nicias, Thyillus the poet, Valerius Cato, a poor poet whom some called a freedman, Tyrannio a grammarian, Tiro, a very well educated slave secretary, and several others.

The supply of slave labor.

Slaves were still plentiful, though the three-year war of the Spartacan revolt had cost the lives of more than a hundred thousand (Livy, *Epit.* 96-7; App., *B. C.,* 1, 117). Caesar is said to have taken more than 400,000 captives in Gaul in ten years (Vell., 2, 47); a large part of these must have been brought to Italy. Lucullus, Murena, Servilius, and Pompey sent in large numbers from the East from 80 to 63 B. C. The slave traders at Delos—presumably while such wars were in progress—sometimes had 10,000 to dispose of in one day (Strabo, 14, 5, 2). Furthermore, since the war with Spartacus proved the danger of having too many war-captives about, a liking for home-bred slaves (*vernae*) had increased and the custom of encouraging the slaves to marry not only in urban households but also on the farms was increasing. Varro thought this conducive to good temper in slaves as well as to profit (2, 1, 26; 2, 10, 6), Appian speaks merely of the profit in the increase of the *familia* (App., *B. C.,* 1, 7). Nepos (*Att.,* 13, 4) says that Atticus had only *vernae* in his household, and the *columbaria* of the Augustan day with their " pigeon-holes " in pairs show that the slaves of the larger households quite regularly were married (*Am. Hist. Rev.,* 1916, 697).

But the decrease of slaves through manumission was also considerable. Cicero remarks that a good slave could save enough to buy his freedom in seven years (*Phil.,* 8, 32). When in 57-6 Pompey looked after the corn dole, many set free their older slaves in order to transfer the cost of their upkeep to the state (Dio, 39, 24)). In the *pro Flacco* Cicero says somewhat rhetorically that rioting in the Forum was always due to the Orientals of Rome; and of course he refers to the enfranchised Orientals. We are somewhat surprised to hear that Caesar could send some 80,000 poor folk—mostly freedmen—out of the city to external colonies in 46-4 B. C. (Suet., *Jul.,* 42). With their dependents this probably meant a diminution of twice that number in the city's population. It would appear that slave labor was so plentiful that free labor could no longer find employment. And after these were gone, Caesar still had to grant a dole to 150,000 men of the same type. These hordes were by no means only people who had drifted in from the country to live on the dole. Manumitted slaves were numerous among them. We have one surprising fact about the number of manumissions that helps us explain the situation. The manumission tax was 5% of the value

of the slave.   It can be shown that in about 32 years—81-49 B. C.—the
receipts from this source were about 12,000,000 denarii (*Am. Jour.
Phil.,* 1932, p. 360).   Hence, since the average price of a slave was
about 500 denarii, it follows that about half a million slaves had been
freed in this period, or about 16,000 per year (of course they were not
all urban slaves).   A large part of these would, of course, have been
old—especially after the dole was increased in 63—and the death rate
of these liberti would accordingly be very high.   But this fact does
explain how Caesar found so large a body of unwanted freedmen about,
and it explains how it was possible for the political bosses of the last
ten years of the Republic to keep the city in a turmoil by their gangs of
hired thugs.

The price of slaves and the slave labor.

In Cato's day the rural slave was reckoned at about 300-500 denarii
and his day's work as worth about 2-3 sesterces (see chapter III).   This
was when the manumission records of Delphi reveal an average price
of about 400 denarii (drachmas) in Greece.   We have very little evidence for the Ciceronian period and the early Empire.   Caesar's war-
captives must have been a glut on the market at times, though this was
a period of financial expansion.   The large number of manumissions
would rather imply a full market.   Cicero gives one definite price of a
rather clever young slave who was thought capable of becoming a good
actor.   He was bought for 1,000 denarii and given a course of training.
The price must, of course, have been higher than that for ordinary
rural laborers.   Cicero also says that this slave was not strong and
would hardly have brought 3 sesterces per day as a laborer (Cic., *pro.
Rosc. Com.,* 28).   Slave labor was usually reckoned at about 3 sesterces
when slaves sold at about 500 denarii.   Petronius later speaks of an
offer of a reward of 1,000 sesterces for a fugitive slave.   Such
rewards were usually 50% of the value.   This gives us 500 denarii
again.   Finally, in Diocletian's edict, where prices of standard articles
and services are in general a trifle above those known for Cicero's day,
the wage of unskilled labor is about 10-20 cents a day plus food.   This
is wretchedly inadequate evidence, but it points toward a price that
wavers up and down near an average of 500 denarii for an able-bodied
laborer and of 3 sesterces a day plus food for his work.

Free labor, when it found a place, could not demand much more and

meet the competition. A denarius (20 cents) the day may perhaps be
a fair assumption. It was the wage in the eastern vineyard (*Math.*, 20,
2) and of the scribe in Caesar's Spanish colony (Dessau, 6087, 62).
Caesar raised the soldiers' stipend from $\frac{1}{2}$ denarius the day (without
food) to about 225 denarii plus food the year (cf. "Exercitus," in
Realenc., 1670). But his soldiers expected some booty and a fair
bonus at the end of their service. Augustus designated the bonus at
3,000 denarii for twenty years, that is, 150 denarii for each year (Dio,
55, 23). Hence the soldier who survived twenty years of fighting had
earned a trifle over one denarius the day plus twelve bushels of wheat
the year. And volunteers were usually plentiful in Augustus' day.
The wage scale in Egypt, a land practically closed to the world, was of
course far lower (West, in *Class. Phil.*, 1916, p. 304, and Westermann,
in *Agric. History,* 1927).

The cost of living for free labor.

In view of the abundance and cheapness of slaves, free laborers, as
we have seen, could hardly expect to earn more than a denarius (20
cents) a day, and then usually at temporary or seasonal tasks or at work
where the master did not wish to risk the health of slaves that he owned.
In Cicero's day a free laborer in the city might expect 5 modii of free
grain per month from the state, that is, $\frac{1}{2}$ sesterce in grain per day;
and he was usually entertained on holidays by the state and the magistrates so that he need not spend much for that item. His expenses were
for a little cheap clothing—if he generally went with bare feet and a
tunic, 5-10 denarii might do for a year. He probably could not afford
beef, pork, or poultry, but vegetables were cheap and he could afford
cabbages, beets, turnips, chestnuts, figs, lentils, and cheese, and a little
very cheap wine and olive oil. If the state supplied the grain, his food
bill for two need not amount to more than 2-2$\frac{1}{2}$ sesterces per day. For
his room he would have to limit himself to 30 sesterces ($1.50) the
month. In other words he must live as did most Italian laborers
sixty years ago, when the usual wage was one lira per day.

The common statement that money was worth three times as much
as in 1900—or any other date—is of little value. It is more important
to remember that the laboring-man competing with slaves could not buy
certain comforts and foods that are necessary in the modern households
of working men, while the nobleman, to keep up appearances, had to

26

have an amount of household help that would seem superfluous today. Wheat cost more in gold or silver in 49 B. C. than in 1932, vegetables only about a sixth as much, cheap clothing about a sixth, and far less was needed by the laborer in that warm climate.   A senator on the other hand used less wheat and more meat and fowl than a laborer.   The choice foods such as imported fish, thrushes, and the like, were not cheaper than today.   Ordinary meats, however, cost less.   The best clothing was fully as expensive.   Labor cost perhaps only 5-10 per cent of what it does in 1932, but he must have clerks, couriers, and a horde of domestic servants, that he does not need now.   Cicero spent $4,000 a year on the education of his son, and his house and lot cost him far more than a public official has to pay today.   It is impossible to strike an average, but it is fair to say that the men in public life at Rome had to spend fully as much for what was necessary to them as is spent today, while the poor had to confine themselves to the very cheapest articles, which were the only ones they could afford to buy.

Cicero's friend Atticus was well-to-do, but since he did not enter public life he was not called upon to spend money on display.   He was married, had one child, did some entertaining, but was known to be frugal.   His friend Nepos (*Att.*, 13, 6) says that he had examined the account books of Atticus and found that his expenses did not run over 36,000 sesterces ($1800) per year.

Machinery.   Labor-saving machinery was not entirely wanting, though slave economy was so universal as to discourage inventiveness except in lines where human hands failed to meet needs.   Before Rome came into being, farmers had learned to employ oxen, asses, and horses to draw plows and wagons, and traders had used ships at least since the third millennium before our era (see ch. II for Athenaeus' description of king Hiero's ship).   Builders early developed the crane with multiple pulleys and either human or animal power was applied to the ropes, or the stepped wheel was used.   The water-wheel as well as the screw-pump were employed in irrigation and in draining mines, and the principle of the syphon was freely used in connection with concrete water mains.   The water-wheel was also used for flour mills, at least in the Augustan day (*Gr. Anthol.*, 9, 418).   On the farms the olive crushers and grain mills were drawn by donkeys; the oil and wine presses were worked by levers in Cato's time, but the screw press came into general use in the early Empire.   For making wearing apparel

most households had spinning wheels and looms, and the better households had bathrooms with hot water heaters of the type not displaced
till gas came into general use.   The penny-in-the-slot machine and the
taximeter are ancient inventions, but were not much used.   In the
potteries there were not only elaborate furnaces but such things as the
revolving mould which saved labor, standardized the articles, and
destroyed artistry.   (See " Machina," in Darem.-Saglio; Diels, H.,
Antike Technik; " Heron " and " Archimedes," in *R-E.*; Granger's
trans. of *Vitruvius* in the Loeb Classics; Blümner, *Technologie,* etc.,
1875-1912; Drachmann, *Ancient Oil Mills and Presses* ; Rickard, *Man
and Metals* ; Bailey, *Pliny's Chapters on Chemical Subjects* ; Heiberg,
Math. and Physical Sciences ; Allbutt, *Greek Medicine in Rome* ; Gest,
Engineering; Neuburger, *Die Technik des Altertums*).

It is obvious that this relatively small use of machinery accounts in
some measure for the temperate course of Roman economic life.   Lacking expensive factories that incite feverish production they were in no
great danger of seriously glutting the markets.   There are no signs of
periodic crises due to overproduction.   The only serious economic crises
that we hear of were due to wars.   In 90 when Italy revolted and the
Roman landowners were cut off from their profits, they raised a cry for
a moratorium on debts, but that crisis passed with the war.   In 88
when Mithridates invaded Asia and killed off the publicans, the financial classes of the Forum were seriously struck, according to Cicero, for
many people had taken shares in the tax-farming companies.   Again
when Caesar crossed the Rubicon and a civil war was imminent, money
was hoarded and sales fell off.   But the modern type of economic crisis,
due largely to the lack of reasonable coordination between supply and
demand, was not heard of in the Roman world.

X.   INVESTMENTS AND SOURCES OF WEALTH

Investments in the Provinces.

This was a period of wide though irregular expansion into provincial
investments.   The chapters on Asia, Greece, Gaul, Spain, and Africa
will give the details for the provinces.   We need to treat them here only
from the viewpoint of Roman economic expansion.   We have seen that
the Gracchan recapture of the public lands in Italy prompted Romans
to enter provincial investments and that the official activities of the

publicans in Asia opened up ways and means for doing so. The wholesale confiscations of Sulla in Italy and the colonization of twenty-four legions there reminded men again that landholding in Italy was precarious. The drift to provincial investments continued after the seas were cleared of pirates and the borders of the Empire established. In the sixties and fifties of the century Roman *negotiatores* were everywhere. As early as 66 Cicero could say that any serious disaster in Asia caused a panic in the Forum (Cic., *Leg. Man.*, 17-18). And specific references to. Romans who " are in business in Asia " or in given cities, *e. g.* Pergamum, Smyrna, Tralles, Lampsacus are numerous (*e. g.* Cic., *pro Deiot.*, 26; *pro Flacc.*, 71; *Verr.*, 1, 69-74, etc.). In Cilicia there were enough Romans to provide a respectable contingent in the army (*Att.*, 5, 18), in Cyprus enough to require a special term of court (*Att.*, 5, 21). Caesar speaks repeatedly of Roman merchants in Gaul, and even undertakes to clear an Alpine pass for them (*Bell. Gall.*, 3, 1). In Spain Varro found it possible to levy a war contribution of 28,000,000 sesterces on citizens alone (Caes., *B. C.*, 2, 18). Cicero gives much casual information regarding individuals abroad, for Cicero, once a knight, and always friendly to the group, was constantly called upon to write letters of introduction to provincial governors in favor of business men operating in the various provinces.

Among the Romans who lent money to cities and princes the more important are the following: *M. Cluvius*, a banker of Puteoli, had lent to the following communities in Asia Minor: Alabanda, Mylasa, Caunii, Bargylia, and Heraclea in Caria (Cic., *ad Fam.*, 13, 56, 1-3). The city of Nicaea in Bithynia owed *T. Pinnius* about 8,000,000 sesterces ($400,000; *Fam.,* 13, 61). *Castricius* had recently collected a debt from Tralles in Lydia in 60 B. C. (Cic., *pro Flacc.*, 54) and held a note on Smyrna (*ibid.*, 75). *M. Anneius*, though a military officer under Cicero in Cilicia, had financial dealings with the city of Sardis (*Fam.*, 13, 55 and 57). Cicero's best friend, *Atticus*, had difficulty collecting a debt from Sicyon in Greece (*Att.*, 1, 13; 1, 20, 4; 2, 13, 2) and from Ephesus (*Att.*, 5, 13, 2; 5, 20, 10).

Members of the nobility also entered this kind of business with cities and kings, though usually as " silent partners."

Marcus Brutus had lent to Ariobarzanes, king of Cappadocia, and to Salamis, a city of Cyprus. In 50, when he had reason to suppose that a civil war was imminent, he pressed very hard for payment. His agent attempted to collect interest from Salamis at the rate of 48 per cent. It is probable that this rate had been entered in the agreement after a default and a renewal of the note. Cicero, who was governor of Cilicia in 50, pointed out the illegality of the rate, insisting on a reduction to 12 per cent. We cannot be sure whether the agent had demanded this rate on his own responsibility, and letters between Rome and Cilicia required so much time that the correspondence regarding the affair closed before we learn what was Brutus' response to Cicero's protest. The abuse of Brutus in this matter by our historians is based upon inadequate evidence. We only know that the agent led Cicero to believe Brutus responsible (Cic., *Att.*, 5, 21, 10-12; 6, 1, 5-7; 6, 2, 7-9; 6, 3, 5; Sternkopf, *Der Zinswucher des Brutus*, 1900; Byrne, A., *T. Pomponius Atticus*).

The great *Pompey* had also lent Ariobarzanes large sums with which to equip the kingdom granted him by Pompey. The interest alone ran to 400 talents the year ($2,400,000 in 50 when the son of the same name was king, Cic., *Att.*, 6, 1, 3). If this was at the usual provincial rate of 12 per cent, the debt amounted to $20,000,000, presumably including much back interest unpaid since 62 B. C. The whole transaction is significant. Pompey must have used much of the Mithridatic booty for this loan in 62—which was contrary not to law but to regularly accepted official behavior. It was illegal for a governor to have private financial dealings in his province, but Pompey may well have been excused by the Romans for financing a client kingdom which was expected to serve as a buffer state on the frontier. The dead king had used some of the money at least in colonizing a devastated area (*Att.*, 6, 1, 3; 6, 3, 5).

It is also probable that Caesar and Pompey as well as others had lent moneys to King Ptolemy Auletes (Suet., *Jul.*, 54, 3; Plut., *Caes.*, 48, 4), since they permitted the Governor of Syria to conduct Ptolemy back to Egypt. Rabirius Postumus seems to have represented not only himself but other bond-holders when he went to Egypt as Ptolemy's business agent in order to collect the king's revenues. The King at that time owed 10,000 talents ($12,000,000) to Romans on debts and recent services (Cic., *pro Rab. Post.*, 21; cf. *Fam.*, 1, 1; *Quint. Fr.*, 2, 2, 3; *pro Rab. Post.*, 6; 38, 41).

Such were the transactions with cities and states. There are also a large number of private business affairs mentioned for the provinces:

In the *Pro Fonteio* (11; 74 B. C.) Cicero says that the *Narbonese
province* was already full of Roman *negotiatores* and his speech *Pro
Quinctio* deals with a partnership in cattle-raising and farming in that
province.

Sicily.   Cicero in his attack upon Verres mentions Rome's interest in
the province, of course with some exaggeration in order to emphasize
the crimes of Verres:

Cic., *Verr.*, 2, 5-6.

Nos vero experti sumus Italico maximo difficillimoque bello Siciliam
nobis non pro penaria cella, sed pro aerario illo maiorum vetere ac
referto fuisse; nam sine ullo sumptu nostro coriis tunicis frumentoque
suppeditando maximos exercitus nostros vestivit, aluit, armavit.   Quid?
illa quae forsitan ne sentimus quidem, iudices, quanta sunt! quod
multis locupletioribus civibus utimur, quod habent propinquam fidelem
fructuosamque provinciam, quo facile excurrant, ubi libenter negotium
gerant; quos illa partim mercibus suppeditandis cum quaestu com-
pendioque dimittit, partim retinet, ut arare, ut pascere, ut negotiari
libeat, ut denique sedes ac domicilium collocare; quod commodum non
mediocre rei publicae est, tantum civium numerum tam prope ab domo
tam bonis fructuosisque rebus detineri.   Et quoniam quasi quaedam
praedia populi Romani sunt vectigalia nostra atque provinciae, quem
ad modum vos propinquis vestris praediis maxime delectamini, sic
populo Romano iucunda suburbanitas est huiusce provinciae.

"Nay, we in our time have found, in the critical days of the great
Italian war (90–89 B. C.), how Sicily has been to us no mere store-
house, but like the ancient and well-filled state treasury of our fathers'
days, supplying us with hides and shirts and grain, free of cost to
ourselves, to clothe, feed and equip our great armies.   Yes, and she
does us services, great services, of which we, gentlemen, I daresay, are
not even aware.   Many of our citizens are the richer for having a
profitable field of enterprise in this loyal province close at hand, which
they can visit so easily, and where they can carry on their business so
freely.   To some of these Sicily supplies merchandise, and sends them
away enriched with profits: others she keeps with her, to become,
according to their preference, corn farmers or stock farmers or business
men, and in short, to settle and make a home there.   It is a national
advantage of no trifling kind that so large a number of Roman citizens

should be kept so near their own country, engaged in occupations so honest and profitable. Our tributes and our provinces constitute our nation's landed estates, as it were; and thus, just as you, gentlemen, gain most pleasure from such of your estates as are close to Rome, so to the nation there is something pleasant in the nearness of this province to the capital."

Sicily was of course the nearest and oldest of the provinces and many Romans owned property there. Cicero mentions among these two persons of the senatorial class: Annaeus Brocchus (*Verr.*, 3, 93) and the wife of the consul Cassius (3, 97). The knights who are mentioned as property holders or as in business in Sicily are M. Caelius (*Verr.*, 4, 37), Calidius (4, 42), M. Cossutius (3, 55), Q. Lollius (3, 61), C. Matrinius (3, 60), Q. Minucius (2, 69), L. Raecius (5, 161), Otacilius Naso (*Fam.*, 13, 33), Papinius (*Verr.*, 4, 46), Petilius (2, 71), Septicius (3, 36), and L. Suetius (2, 31). In addition, a number of publicans are mentioned who were engaged chiefly in collecting the port dues and *scriptura*, and, to some extent, in the *decuma*. Furthermore there are some *negotiatores* at Syracuse and Panormus (*Verr.*, 2, 73; 5, 161, and *C. I. L.*, I², 836, found at Terracina) and elsewhere. The first impression on reading the Verrines is that Romans own Sicily, but Cicero has stressed the exactions of Verres against citizens for effect. A closer reading reveals the fact that many of the citizens are South Italians who had migrated to Sicily before citizenship was extended in 89, or native Sicilians who had received the franchise from governors of the province. He mentions the names of more than 60 Sicilians of importance and, when he lists six large landholders who had had trouble with their slaves (*Verr.*, 5, 10-16), it turns out that only one is a Roman citizen. Roman citizens were exploiting Sicily as well as Asia, but they were very far from owning any large proportion of the farms or urban property there. Julius Caesar finally gave *Latinitas* to all Sicilians, and Antony promised them the full franchise (Cic., *Att.*, 14, 12, 1), but Augustus revoked these gifts. The subject will be treated in full in the section on Sicily.

As investors in *Africa*, Cicero mentions C. Anicius, Pinarius, Q. Turius, Aufidius, and Aelius Lamia (*Fam.*, 12, 21; 24; 26; 27; 29). Lamia may well have originated the large property called the Saltus Lamianus which was imperial property in Hadrian's day (in Carcopino, *Mélanges de Rome*, 1906). At Patrae in *Greece* a banker who befriended Cicero spends most of his time (*Fam.*, 13, 17; 50), Mindius is a banker in Elis (*Fam.*, 13, 26), T. Manlius at Thespiae (*Fam.*, 13, 22), Aemilius Avianius at Sicyon (*Fam.*, 13, 27). Caesar mentions Roman business men in Gaul repeatedly (*B. G.*, 7, 3; 7, 44; 55; 90; 8, 4, etc.).

But *Asia Minor* was the favorite country for investments: Caerellia, the rich old lady who seemed to like Cicero's philosophic essays, had estates and accounts there (*Fam.*, 13, 72). Malleolus had invested while serving there as quaestor (Cic., *Verr.*, 1, 91). Appuleius Decianus had lived thirty years at Pergamum before 60 B. C. (*pro. Flacc.*, 70). Curtius Mithres, a freedman of Rabirius, lived at Ephesus (*Fam.*, 13, 69). Genucilius had foreclosed a mortgage at Parium (*Fam.*, 13, 53). Laenius Flaccus of Brundisium had affairs in Bithynia as well as Cilicia (*Fam.*, 13, 63). Aulus Trebonius had several agents operating in various parts of Cilicia (*Fam.*, 1, 3). Others interested in Asiatic investments are Marcilius (*Fam.*, 13, 54), P. Messienus (*Fam.*, 13, 51), L. Nostius (*Fam.*, 13, 46), L. Oppius (*Fam.*, 13, 43), Q. Selicius (*Fam.*, 1, 5, 4). At Volsinii in Etruria an inscription has been found that was set up by men who traded in Synnada in Phrygia (*C. I. L.*, I², 2663). Apparently Etruscan traders and investors still continued business relations with Asia in the late Republic.

This provincial business is not easily classified. The publicans had at first extended their operations from tithe-gathering to lending money individually at high rates to delinquents, placing mortgages and consequently becoming property owners if mortgages were foreclosed; they had also gone into collecting the community taxes on commission, which led to similar results. They had engaged in trade when grain, textiles, and slaves were to be had at profitable prices; they offered themselves as agents to Romans who wished to make investments and place their surpluses. Even natives of Asia visited Rome and sold properties or borrowed money at Rome. Wealthy Romans sent their business secretaries (usually Greek freedmen) to the provinces to place funds or pick up bargains, and Roman bankers sent agents out to do the same for their clients. And, as we have seen, Roman officials and soldiers stationed in the provinces were not above giving spare time to bargain-hunting.

Estates.

We have a few casual statements about the size of individual estates that may be of some value in determining what was considered wealth. Crassus, generally supposed to be the wealthiest man of his day, had at one time real estate estimated at 50,000,000 denarii ($10,000,000; Pliny, 33, 134). His whole property in 55 he inventoried at 7,100 talents ($8,500,000, Plut., *Crass.*, 2). He made most of the fortune himself. Pompey seems to have surpassed this figure. His property when confiscated was sold for about 50,000,000 denarii, but his son was once offered 70,000,000 ($14,000,000) by way of indemnity for it by the Senate (Dio, 48, 36). This is the largest property reported for any Roman of the Republic. The house of Clodius was worth 14,800,000 sesterces ($740,000; Pliny, 36, 103), and the Tusculan villa of Scaurus 30,000,000 sesterces ($1,500,000; Pliny, 36, 115). The younger Cato lived frugally on his inheritance of 720,000 denarii ($180,000; Plut., *Cato,* 4). Demetrius, a Syrian from Gadara, who was probably taken prisoner by Pompey but was quickly made a citizen to become one of Pompey's most reliable financial agents, left a property of 4,000 talents ($4,800,000; Plut., *Pomp.,* 2, 4, and 40). Lucullus paid 10,000,000 sesterces ($500,000) for his estate at Baiae, one of a great many (Plut., *Mar.,* 34; Front., *de Aq.,* 1, 5; 8; 10). Cicero's noted palace on the Palatine was modest in comparison: it cost him 3,500,000 sesterces ($175,000; Cic., *Fam.,* 5, 6, 2). Some other properties mentioned with their prices are: the 1,000 jugera property of Albanius costing 11,500,000 sesterces ($575,000; *Att.,* 13, 31), the house of the consul Messala worth 3,300,000 sesterces ($165,000; *Att.,* 1, 13, 6), Quintus Cicero's house costing nearly 1,000,000 sesterces ($50,000; *Att.,* 1, 14, 7), the estates of Roscius, a wealthy farmer of Umbria, worth 6,000,000 sesterces ($300,000; Cic., *pro Rosc. Amer.,* 6).

Cicero once remarks that an income of $30,000 the year (600,000 sesterces; Cic., *Parad.,* 49) would enable one to live like a gentleman— and that was about Cicero's own income (*Phil.,* 2, 40); Crassus on the other hand held that a man was not wealthy unless he could support a legion on his income (nearly 4,000,000 sesterces, or $200,000, that is, a property of about 70,000,000 sesterces). Probably not more than six men reached that figure in Cicero's day. Indirectly one may infer something from the fact that Caesar in his youth, when he had

very little property, could induce friends to endorse notes amounting
to more than a million dollars (Plut., *Caes.*, 5 and 11) simply on the
promise of a successful military and political career, and that Antony
in his youth could borrow 1,500,000 den. ($300,000; Cic., *Phil.*, 2, 45),
and later, when buying in the confiscated properties of Pompey, could
get endorsements of his notes up to two million dollars (Cic., *Phil.*, 2,
45).   To conclude, we may say that two or three men had properties
worth about $10,000,000 each (200,000,000 sesterces) in the last
decades of the Republic, that men of the political aristocracy needed at
least $500,000 (10,000,000 sesterces) in productive property besides
two or three pleasure villas that might cost half that amount, in order to
draw $20,000 the year for a comfortable living and correct appear-
ance; that business men usually were considered very wealthy who
had that amount; that a mere 400,000 ($20,000, that is, an income—
above personal earnings—of about $1,200) was all that the law re-
quired for enrolment among the knights.

Sources of income and of estates.

Many of the younger men who made their way to fame at Rome on
a moderate competence were men like Cicero who sprang from small-
town landholders, but details about them are usually missing.   It is
also difficult to say how many men rose from the commercial classes of
the post-Gracchan trading days.   Seius seems to be a man of this class,
if he is connected with Seius the trader of Delos, but we cannot point
to many.   Provincial investment and money-lending were a partial
source of income in very many instances—we have mentioned Pompey,
Brutus, Atticus, and several others.   Many also who had inherited a
competence spent all their time in managing and enlarging their diver-
sified investments.   Atticus' rich uncle seems to have been a careful
money-lender.   Atticus himself lent to states and individuals, bought
and managed a large ranch in Illyria, breeding horses and sheep, and
his slave women ran a kind of weaving-factory so as to market the wool
profitably; he also trained young slaves in various skilled occupations
and sold them at a profit; he kept skilled copyists and published books;
and for a while he owned a troop of gladiators (Nepos, *Att.*, 5, 2,
and 14, 2).

With the rapid growth of Rome dealers in real estate doubtless had
a chance to profit.   Damasippus (who earlier was an art-dealer and
ended as philosopher) dealt in real estate during Caesar's dictatorship.

He bought land near the Tiber, cut it into lots, and sold them at a uniform price (Cic., *Att.*, 12, 33). Crassus was more clever. He organized a private fire-brigade, presumably to protect his own large holdings, but he made profit from it because, when some house was burning, he would offer to buy the neighbors out at a low figure and then set his brigade on to protect his new property (Plut., *Crass.*, 2, 3). Perhaps, however, this version came from a campaign speech of some conservative.

The profession of advocate at law was profitable, though an old war measure of the third century had once forbidden the acceptance of fees. The recognized method of payment was to include a clause in one's will in favor of the advocate. Cicero, the most successful lawyer of Rome, received in this manner without accepting fees about 20,000,000 sesterces (a million dollars) in a period of about thirty years; that is, his law practice indirectly yielded him about $30,000 the year (Cic., *Phil.*, 2, 40; Plut., *Cic.*, 7). Hortensius, who accepted fees in the form of presents, probably gained much of his great wealth in this fashion.

The profession of acting—which was not considered open to men of the knighthood—was productive to a very few. Roscius, the friend of Cicero, before he entered the knighthood and refused pay, received 16,000 sesterces for one performance and as much as 500,000 the year ($25,000; Pliny, 7, 128; Macrob., 3, 14, 13; Cic., *pro Rosc. Com.*, 23, says 300,000), and doubtless Aesopus earned as much for he left a large fortune to his son (Pliny, 9, 122; 10, 141). And a young actor just beginning—once a slave, bought for 4,000 sesterces—made 100,000 sesterces the year (*pro Rosc. Com.*, 28).

We are much better informed about the incomes of prominent politicians and governors, especially the irregular ones that created unfavorable comment at election time. We must, however, consider election charges more often exaggerated than not. How far Roman nobles could go in their overbearing behavior toward provincials appears from the career of Antonius, the ex-consul, who when exiled for misappropriations went to the island of Cephallenia and " ruled the whole island like a king " (Strabo, 10, 2, 13). We have noted above that governors were given a liberal allowance for expenses and that the custom had now arisen of not returning any residue to the treasury, though a few did. This allowance, of course, was not a source of great wealth. More profit came in a few cases from treating a large share of the booty as legitimately belonging to the general, his staff, and his soldiers. This practice was never legalized, but was rather openly condoned. Repeatedly suits were threatened against Sulla's son and heir for keeping property that Sulla had acquired as booty, but action was always stopped because Sulla's acts had been covered by a general senatorial bill of approval (Cic., *Cluent.*, 94; *leg. Agr.*, 1, 12; Ascon. *Cornel.*, Stangl., 58, 5), and the Rullan bill in 63 B. C. contained a clause calling for a commission to confiscate all moneys that had been taken by way of booty and all "crown-gold" not given to the treasury or used for public purposes (Cic., *leg. Agr.*, 1, 12-13). From this procedure Pompey was to be exempted because he had been given full power to make whatever dispositions he chose. The Rullan bill failed for various reasons, but the proposal to investigate and confiscate shows that explanations were still expected. During this period there were only three large amounts of booty made available and in all three instances—the wars of Lucullus, of Pompey in the East, and of Caesar in Gaul—the generals and their *legati* collected much wealth. Under Pompey we have seen that about twenty *legati* received nearly $200,000 each and Demetrius, Pompey's personal adviser and financial secretary, managed to come out with 4,000 talents (Plut., *Pomp.*, 2, 4). Under Caesar, Labienus, his chief lieutenant, and Mamurra, his chief engineer, made "great wealth" (Cic., *Att.*, 7, 7, 6; Catullus, 29; 57; 114; and Suet., *Jul.*, 73), but no amounts are given. Caesar's business agent, Cornelius Balbus, a Phoenician of Gades, also acquired very great wealth (Dio, 48, 32). Caesar's strict legislation permitted gifts to officers for "benefits," which in Caesar's army amounted to a few thousand dollars (*Fam.*, 5, 20, 7). In the wars of the triumvirate the military men who profited most were Agrippa, Statilius Taurus, Sulpicius Quirinius, and Tarius Rufus, all men of the middle classes.

Irregular requisitions were the disgrace of Roman provincial government during this period, and these continued to some extent after Caesar's legislation in 59 which, if enforced, might have put an end to them. Cicero's speeches against Verres reveal the worst form of such graft, which, according to the prosecutors, amounted in three years to $2,000,000. However, since the prosecution at the end demanded restitution of only a tenth of this amount (Plut., *Cic.*, 8), the general charge was probably exaggerated. The favorite method of grafting was to requisition grain from the provincials and pocket the money allowed by the senate, or, as Verres did, to exact the grain when prices were high and grain scarce so as to invite a settlement in cash; another method, practiced by Appius Claudius (Cic., *Att.,* 5, 16; 5, 21, 10), Piso, and others, was to billet troops on a city and pocket the state allowance (or to threaten billeting and accept a bribe from the city for immunity). Another ugly form of requisition was to collect—or accept from fearful provincials—money for triumphal games or for magistrates' games. Quintus Cicero refused to permit an aedile to collect $10,000 in his province (Cic., *Quint. Fr.,* 1, 1, 26), but Piso collected 100 talents ($120,000) in Macedonia in the form of *aurum coronarium* (Cic., *in Pis.,* 90). Similarly Gabinius was accused of robbing Syria (Dio, 39, 55, 7; Josephus, a native, gives him a very good name). An even worse form of graft practiced by some underlings was the acceptance of retainers' fees (bribes) from provincials to present their cases to good advantage before their generals or before the Roman authorities. Both Gabinius and Scaurus—two of Pompey's *legati*—accepted money, 300 and 400 talents respectively, from Aristobulus of Judea, who wished to displace his elder brother as high priest. Fortunately Pompey decided the case on its merits and Aristobulus was taken to Rome as a prisoner of war (Josephus, *Ant. Jud.,* 14, 3, 2). There was also a form of graft that was not new but that revealed large possibilities for the first time in this period. This is best illustrated by the activities of Clodius and Mark Antony. Clodius was relatively poor till he became tribune; soon after he appeared as a man of large estates. Cicero says that, while controlling the legislative assembly, Clodius sent his agents to collect money from client princes for promises of legislative favors (Cic., *Harus. Resp.,* 29; *De Domo,* 66; 129; *Quint. fr.,* 2, 9, 2). Antony also, when he came into possession of the seal of Caesar and when Caesar's unpublished acts were confirmed without examination, sold to client princes favors that were attributed to Caesar (Cic., *Phil.,* 2, 109). Furthermore, officials at Rome, like Paulus and Curio, took bribes from Caesar in payment for supporting his cause in 50 (Plut., *Caes.,* 29, 3: 1,500 talents to Paulus; Vell., 2, 48: $500,000, 10 million sesterces, to Curio). On the damage done to Rome's name by extortion, Cicero spoke with vehemence in his *Manilian Law.*

Cic., *Lex. Man.*, 65:

Difficile est dictu, Quirites, quanto in odio simus apud exteras nationes propter eorum, quos ad eas per hos annos cum imperio misimus, libidines et iniurias. Quod enim fanum putatis in illis terris nostris magistratibus religiosum, quam civitatem sanctam, quam domum satis clausam ac munitam fuisse? Urbes iam locupletes et copiosae requiruntur, quibus causa belli propter diripiendi cupiditatem inferatur.

" Words cannot express, gentlemen, how bitterly we are hated among foreign nations owing to the wanton and outrageous conduct of the men whom of late years we have sent to govern them. For in those countries what temple do you suppose has been held sacred by our officers, what state inviolable, what home sufficiently guarded by its closed doors? Why, they look about for rich and flourishing cities that they may find an occasion of a war against them to satisfy their lust for plunder."

Several of the great fortunes were made from bidding in confiscated property at low prices. This was legal, of course, but met with some social disapproval. In the Sullan period we have noticed the cases of Catiline, Verres (Cic., *Verr.*, 1, 38), Crassus (Plut., *Crass.*, 6), Chrysogonus, Valgius (Cic., *leg. Agr.*, 3, 3), Metella (Pliny, 36, 116), Domitius (Dio, 41, 11), Scaurus (Pliny, 36, 116), and P. Sulla. Crassus and Scaurus kept and increased their wealth. We do not know what men are meant by Cicero's term " the seven tyrants," but they were apparently men who had purchased land freely in the Sullan confiscations (Cic., *de Leg. Agr.*, 3, 3): Crassus, Faustus, and Scaurus certainly; possibly Hortensius, Metellus, Domitius, and Catulus would come into the list. Scaurus' father, Aemilius Scaurus, had made some money by cooperating with Marius; later the son had inherited much from his mother, Metella, who had married Sulla and profited by buying cheap properties (Pliny, 36, 116). The same situation arose when Caesar sold the goods of his enemies. Here we have few records, but P. Sulla (*Fam.*, 15, 19, 3), Mark Antony (App., *B. C.*, 5, 79), and Servilia (*Att.*, 14, 21, 3) are mentioned among the guilty besides many less well known (*Att.*, 14, 10, 2). The confiscations of the triumvirs were very extensive, but little is known about the favored buyers until the imperial period.

One should not draw hasty conclusions from the facts that happen to survive, since men in public life were precisely the ones against whom unsubstantiated charges were made in the political pamphlets of that day. But it would seem that the larger fortunes during the last fifty corrupt years of the Republic came, not from business, but from military returns, from dealing in confiscated goods, and from various abuses of official power. To these sources are traceable the wealth of Lucullus, Caesar, Pompey, and Crassus, who were the richest Romans of the period.

We add a few quotations regarding two of the more notorious nabobs of the time, Crassus the triumvir and Scaurus.

Plut., *Crassus*, 2, 1-6:

τεκμήρια δὲ τῆς φιλοπλουτίας αὐτοῦ μέγιστα ποιοῦνται τόν τε τρόπον τοῦ πορισμοῦ καὶ τῆς οὐσίας τὸ μέγεθος. τριακοσίων γὰρ οὐ πλείω κεκτημένος ἐν ἀρχῇ ταλάντων, εἶτα παρὰ τὴν ὑπατείαν ἀποθύσας μὲν τῷ Ἡρακλεῖ τὴν δεκάτην καὶ τὸν δῆμον ἐστιάσας, τρεῖς δὲ μῆνας ἑκάστῳ Ῥωμαίων σιτηρέσιον ἐκ τῶν αὐτοῦ παρασχών, ὅμως πρὸ τῆς ἐπὶ Πάρθους στρατείας αὐτὸς αὑτῷ θέμενος ἐκλογισμὸν τῆς οὐσίας εὗρεν ἑκατὸν ταλάντων τίμημα πρὸς ἑπτακισχιλίοις. τὰ δὲ πλεῖστα τούτων, εἰ δεῖ μετὰ βλασφημίας εἰπεῖν τὸ ἀληθές, ἐκ πυρὸς συνήγαγε καὶ πολέμου, ταῖς κοιναῖς ἀτυχίαις προσόδῳ τῇ μεγίστῃ χρησάμενος.

Ὅτε γὰρ Σύλλας ἑλὼν τὴν πόλιν ἐπώλει τὰς οὐσίας τῶν ἀνῃρημένων ὑπ' αὐτοῦ, λάφυρα καὶ νομίζων καὶ ὀνομάζων, καὶ βουλόμενος ὅτι πλείστοις καὶ κρατίστοις προσομόρξασθαι τὸ ἄγος, οὔτε λαμβάνων οὔτ' ὠνούμενος ἀπεῖπε. πρὸς δὲ τούτοις ὁρῶν τὰς συγγενεῖς καὶ συνοίκους τῆς Ῥώμης κῆρας ἐμπρησμοὺς καὶ συνιζήσεις διὰ βάρος καὶ πλῆθος οἰκοδομημάτων, ἐωνεῖτο δούλους ἀρχιτέκτονας καὶ οἰκοδόμους. εἶτ' ἔχων τούτους ὑπὲρ πεντακοσίους ὄντας, ἐξηγόραζε τὰ καιόμενα καὶ γειτνιῶντα τοῖς καιομένοις, διὰ φόβον καὶ ἀδηλότητα τῶν δεσποτῶν ἀπ' ὀλίγης τιμῆς προϊεμένων, ὥστε τῆς Ῥώμης τὸ πλεῖστον μέρος ὑπ' αὐτῷ γενέσθαι. . . . ὄντων δ' αὐτῷ παμπόλλων ἀργυρείων, πολυτιμήτου δὲ χώρας καὶ τῶν ἐργαζομένων ἐν αὐτῇ, ὅμως ἄν τις ἡγήσαιτο μηδὲν εἶναι ταῦτα πάντα πρὸς τὴν τῶν οἰκετῶν τιμήν· τοσούτους ἐκέκτητο καὶ τοιούτους, ἀναγνώστας, ὑπογραφεῖς, ἀργυρογνώμονας, διοικητάς, τραπεζοκόμους.

" The chief proofs of his avarice are found in the way he got his property and in the amount of it. For at the outset he was possessed of not more than three hundred talents; then during his consulship he sacrificed the tenth of his goods to Hercules, feasted the people, gave every Roman out of his own means enough to live on for three months, and still, when he made a private inventory of his property before his Parthian expedition, he found that it had a value of seventy-one hundred talents. The greatest part of this, if one must tell the scandalous truth, he got together out of fire and war, making the public calamities his greatest source of revenue.

For when Sulla took the city and sold the property of those whom he had put to death, considering it and calling it spoil of war, and wishing to defile with his crime as many and as influential men as he could, Crassus was never tired of accepting or of buying it. And besides this, observing how natural and familiar at Rome were such fatalities as the conflagration and collapse of buildings, owing to their being too massive and close together, he proceeded to buy slaves who were architects and builders. Then, when he had over five hundred of these, he would buy houses that were afire, and houses which adjoined those that were afire, and these their owners would let go at a trifling price owing to their fear and uncertainty. In this way the largest part of Rome came into his possession. . . . And though he owned numberless silver mines, and highly valuable tracts of land with the slaves upon them, nevertheless one might regard all this as nothing compared with the value of his slaves he possessed,—readers, amanuenses, silversmiths, stewards, table-servants."

Plut., *Crassus*, 6, 6:

ἐν δὲ ταῖς προγραφαῖς καὶ δημεύσεσι πάλιν κακῶς ἤκουσεν, ὠνούμενός τε τιμῆς βραχείας μεγάλα πράγματα καὶ δωρεὰς αἰτῶν. ἐν δὲ Βρεττίοις λέγεται καὶ προγράψαι τινὰ οὐ Σύλλας κελεύσαντος, ἀλλ’ ἐπὶ χρηματισμῷ.

"However, during the proscriptions and public confiscations which ensued, he got a bad name again, by purchasing great estates at a low price, and asking donations. It is said that in Bruttium he actually proscribed a man without Sulla's orders, merely to get his property."

Pliny, *N. H.*, 33, 134-5:

ex eadem gente M. Crassus negabat locupletem esse nisi qui reditu annuo legionem tueri posset. in agris HS ⌐MM⌐ possedit, Quiritium post Sullam divitissimus, . . . multos postea cognovimus servitute liberatos opulentiores, pariterque tres Claudii principatu paulo ante Callistum, Pallantem, Narcissum. atque ut hi omittantur, tamquam adhuc rerum potiantur, C. Asinio Gallo C. Marcio Censorino cos. a. d. VI Kal. Febr. C. Caecilius C. l. Isidorus testamento suo edixit quamvis multa bello civili perdidisset, tamen relinquere servorum IIII, CXVI, iuga boum III DC, reliqui pecoris CCLVII, in numerato HS ⌐DC⌐, funerari se iussit HS ⌐X⌐.

" M. Crassus, a member of the same family, used to say that no man was rich who could not maintain a legion upon his yearly income. He possessed in land two hundred millions of sesterces, being the richest Roman citizen next to Sulla. . . . we have known of many manumitted slaves, since his time, much more wealthy than he ever was; three for example, all at the same time in the reign of the Emperor Claudius, Pallas, Callistus, and Narcissus. But to omit all further mention of these men, as though they were still the rulers of the empire, let us turn to C. Caecilius, C. l. Isidorus, who, in the consulship of C. Asinius Gallus and C. Marcius Censorinus (8 A. D.), upon the sixth day before the calends of February, declared by his will, that though he had suffered great losses through the civil wars,[a] he was still able to leave behind him four thousand one hundred and sixteen slaves, three thousand six hundred pairs of oxen, and two hundred and fifty-seven thousand heads of other kind of cattle, besides, in ready money, sixty millions of sesterces; he ordered a million sesterces spent on his funeral."

a. Hence he had acquired most of his wealth before imperial times.

Plut., *Crassus*, 7, 6:

καὶ ποτε τῷ Καίσαρι μέλλοντι μὲν εἰς Ἰβηρίαν ἐξιέναι στρατηγῷ, χρήματα δ' οὐκ ἔχοντι τῶν δανειστῶν ἐπιπεσόντων καὶ τῆς παρασκευῆς ἐπιλαμβανομένων ὁ Κράσσος οὐ περιεῖδεν, ἀλλ' ἀπήλλαξεν ὑποθεὶς αὐτὸν ἔγγυον τριάκοντα καὶ ὀκτακοσίων ταλάντων.

. . . " when Caesar was on the point of setting out for Spain as praetor in 61 B. C., and had no money, and his creditors descended upon him and began to attach his outfit, Crassus did not leave him in the lurch, but freed him from embarrassment by making himself his surety for eight hundred and thirty talents." (= 5,000,000 denarii).

Pliny, *N. H.*, 36, 113; 115; 116:

. . . M. Scauri, cuius nescio an aedilitas maxime prostraverit mores maiusque sit Sullae malum tanta privigni potentia quam proscriptio tot milium. . . . incensa villa ab iratis servis concremaretur HS ⌈CCC⌉ . . . unde enim illi vitricus Sulla et Metella mater proscriptionum sectrix? unde M. Scaurus pater, potiens princeps civitatis et Mariani sodalicii rapinarum provincialium sinus?

. . . " I am by no means certain that it was not the aedileship of M. Scaurus that inflicted the first great blow upon the public manners,

27

and that Sulla was not guilty of a greater crime in giving such unlimited power to his step-son, than in the proscription of so many thousands. . . . The loss was no less than thirty million sesterces, when Scaurus' villa was burnt by his servants in a spirit of revenge. . . . Where, in fact, was to be found such a step-father as Sulla, and such a mother as Metella, that bidder at all auctions for the property of the proscribed? Where such a father as Marcus Aemilius Scaurus, so long the principal man in the city, and one who had acted, in his alliance with Marius, as a receptacle for the plunder of whole provinces?"

XI. PRICES

Wheat.

Cicero (*Verr.*, 3, 163) says that Verres was ordered to buy wheat and pay three sesterces the modius for the "second tithe" and three and a half sesterces for what he purchased thereafter. A little later (3, 189) he says that a letter from Verres at one time quoted the Sicilian price at two to three sesterces; at another time (3, 174) the state ordered its supply at $2\frac{1}{2}$ sesterces; at another Verres bought it for two and a half and charged his government three and a half (3, 179). For the wheat which Verres needed for his own staff the state allowed him four sesterces the modius and for barley two sesterces (3, 188). The price in Sicily in 73-70, therefore, averaged between two and four sesterces, or about three. (That is, wheat cost on the average sixty cents the bushel in the producing country, possibly sixty-five to seventy at Rome. Our Chicago market averaged about fifty cents in 1932; three years before it averaged about a dollar and a half). There was, of course, no little fluctuation in the price, due usually to piracy, wars, delinquency on the part of market officials, extraordinary needs, or at times to crop failure. In the year 75 there was scarcity in Italy (Sall., *Hist.*, 2, 45-7 M.). Cicero as quaestor was ordered to buy great quantities of wheat in Sicily that year; hence in the spring of 74 the province was almost bare of grain so that, when the new praetor needed grain for his staff, he was faced with the very high price of twenty sesterces the modius (*Verr.*, 3, 214). But that need not be taken as a normal pre-harvest price. At the siege of Laodicea in 43 the prices rose to eight sesterces the modius in the city (Cic., *Fam.*, 12, 13, 4). Josephus (*Ant. Jud.*, 16, 2, 2) tells of a famine in Judea when the modius sold for eleven denarii (nine dollars the bushel), but of course such prices cannot be considered in making an average. At the other extreme we have the price at which Seius gave grain in order to buy popularity in 74—one *as* the modius (Cic., *de Off.*, 2, 58). It is a price that cannot be used. Although during the civil wars that followed the prices fluctuated seriously, especially when Sextus Pompey controlled Sicily from time to time, it is probable that at normal times prices remained fairly close to the average. (Near the end of Augustus' reign wheat once rose to about five and a half denarii because of a crop failure [Euseb., *Chron.*, 2, 146, Armen. version]. In 64 A. D. some effort had to be exerted to keep the price down to three sesterces (Tac., *Ann.*, 15, 39). Pliny (18, 90) gives the price of flour in his day at forty *asses* which means a rather high price of five sesterces the modius for wheat). In Egypt at the end of the Republic wheat sold between two and a half and three and a half Egyptian drachmas per artaba, making an average price of less than two sesterces the modius, but Egyptian prices were abnormally low. Diocletian's edict gives as the maximum price fifty debased denarii the modius (twenty cents the peck).

The price of barley (raised largely for horses, hogs, and oxen) was reckoned at one-half the price of wheat (*Verr.*, 3, 188).

Wine.

The only price we have for Rome is the maximum price for choice imported wine in a sumptuary decree of the censors of 89. This, as we have seen, was at retail 100 denarii per amphora of about 26 liters, or 75 cents the liter (Diod., 37, 3, 3; Pliny, 14, 95). *Ordinaire* must have been very much cheaper. In Egypt, where little wine was made, the common wine sold for about five cents the liter at this time (Heichelheim, *Wirtschaftliche Schwankungen,* 112), and the price was probably less in Italy. Columella (3, 3, 10) in Nero's day says that the cheapest sold at wholesale on the farm at 300 sesterces for 40 urns (525 liters). Ordinary wine might then have retailed at about 400 sesterces for 40 urns or about four cents the liter. A tavern sign at Pompeii advertises a drink (probably a sextarius) for one, two, or four *asses* according to grade (*C. I. L.*, 4, 1679). This would be from two to seven cents the liter. Two inscriptions of the second century A. D. yield prices of about four cents the liter (Dessau, 7213; 7212). In Diocletian's edict (2, 10) rustic wine sold at about six cents the liter, though good Italian wines imported to the East brought over three times as much. Since viticulture was a fairly steady industry and, as the marks of the wine jars show, commerce in the product prospered throughout the Mediterranean, we may generalize from these figures to the extent of saying that *vin ordinaire* probably could be had at three to four cents the liter (4-5 denarii the amphora), whereas the better brands ran from fifty to seventy-five cents the liter.

Olive Oil.

In the Catonian period oil, as we have seen, sold wholesale at about one and a half sesterces the liter. At Delos during the same period oil sold at 15-22 drachmas the keramion or about 1½-2 sesterces the liter (Heichelheim, 135), which is a trifle higher. Olive oil was then about fifty per cent costlier per liter than ordinary wine. In Diocletian's day the price of oil had about doubled in the East. Ordinary oil was then about eighteen cents the liter, while the best grade sold at about 30 cents. For Cicero's day it probably would be fair to assume a price of 2-3 sesterces the liter.

For meats we have no prices at this period except for some rare fowl. The more important prices of Diocletian's edict are as follows (par. 4):

Beef	4½ cents the English pound
Mutton	same
Pork	7 cents the pound
Lamb	same
Ham	best, 11 cents the pound
Fowl	12 cents each
Pigeons	5 cents each
Thrushes	2½ cents each
Geese	41 cents each
Peacocks	$1.20 each

Various prices of Varro for some of the fowl that were then for the first time being raised, were very much higher, *e. g.*: thrushes were 3 denarii each (60 cents) and peacocks 50 denarii ($10.00). But both thrushes and peacocks had just been introduced and brought high prices for breeding purposes. At Delos, in Cato's day, geese used in sacrifices were about the same price as in the *edict* 500 years later (Heichelheim, 135).

Since wheat, wine, and labor were about the same in Diocletian's day as in Varro's, or a trifle higher, we may fairly assume that the cost of ordinary meats and fowl in Cicero's day was slightly lower than that of 300 A. D., if not about the same.

For want of **prices of fruits and vegetables** for this period I shall quote from Diocletian's edict a few prices for the more ordinary ones that were as freely cultivated in Cicero's day as later:

Common apples	40 for 1.7 cents
Common figs	same
Grapes	two pounds for 1 cent

Dates	dried, 25 for 1.7 cents
Chestnuts	100 for 1.7 cents
Ordinary cabbage	10 for 1.7 cents
Ordinary lettuce	same
Beets	same
Turnips	20 for 1.7 cents

Beans, lentils, and peas about the same as wheat

To these we may add the following:

| Eggs | 5 cents the dozen |
| Dry cheese | 5 cents the pound |

I see no reason for assuming that in these common articles prices should have varied more than in the case of wheat, wine, and oil. If these prices represent the market of Cicero's day with any accuracy, it is evident that fruit and vegetables were very cheap in comparison with grain and meat. What kept grain relatively high was probably the great and persistent needs of the large armies through the centuries, and this fact had doubtless led to overcropping in grain and consequently to a relatively low production per acre. And since much grain, especially barley, was also required by horses, cattle, and hogs, and since the cutting of oaks reduced the supply of acorns for hogs, we can comprehend why meats were relatively higher than vegetables. It is apparent that slaves and free laborers could hardly be supplied with meat. Wheat and lentils they must have had, but the cost was heavy. Articles like cabbage, turnips, beets, chestnuts, some cheese, apples, dried figs, occasionally an egg, might readily come within their means. We understand why the poor prized the cheap sales of meat from sacrificial offerings and why St. Paul found arguments against Peter for not prohibiting its use.

Clothing.

Here again we are at a loss for prices. After giving for the republican period exorbitant prices for wool dyed in the rarest colors, Pliny (9, 138) says that cheaply dyed wool could at the same time be had for from 2 to 4 *asses* the Roman pound. With spinning and weaving done in the household by cheap slaves working during their leisure hours and with very little labor needed for sewing the garments, clothing must have been very cheap. Since styles of wearing apparel changed before Diocletian's day, and the edict does not quote prices of Italian goods, it would be misleading to quote from that document here.

Houses, cost and rental.

In 125 the censors rebuked a nobleman, Lepidus the Augur, for paying 6,000 sesterces rental for a house ($25 the month; Vell., 2, 10). That house could hardly have cost over $4,000. Velleius adds that in his day no senator would dare to live at so low a rental. Less than fifty years later senators were building houses that cost a hundred times as much. We need not repeat the figures given above. Senators of any distinction expected to pay from 500,000 to 2,500,000 denarii ($100,-000 to $500,000) for their town houses in Cicero's day, and to have a country house or two besides. A property of $50,000 was required by law as a minimum qualification for a senator, because he must be able to live at leisure in Rome to the end of his life in order to attend the Senate meetings at call, unless he was sent abroad on affairs of state. We have few prices of land. Unimproved farm land, as we have seen, was reckoned to be worth about $60–$70 the acre (1,000+ sesterces the jugurum). A suburban place of 1,000 jugera sold for 11,500,000 sesterces while Caesar was dictator (Cic., *Att.,* 13, 31), or about $850 the acre. Pliny was amazed at the 100,000,000 sesterces ($5,000,000) that Caesar paid for the land in the center of Rome for his new Forum (he says " for the ground alone "). Lanciani (*Ancient Rome,* 83-4) estimates the space used at about 90,000 square feet, which would make the land worth $44.45 per square foot. (Knapp, *Class. Weekly,* XXIII, 8, quotes a modern sale in New York for $800 the square foot). However, we cannot be sure that Caesar did not buy more than the bare area later covered by his Forum, and in that location it is very likely that there were some buildings on the ground. Cicero's house on the Palatine had a lot that was estimated as worth 1,500,000 sesterces ($300,000). The area of the lot on the brow of the hill could hardly have been over 15,000 square feet (250 × 60), which would make it worth $20 the square foot—a high price for a city lot even now, but the situation was one of the finest in Rome. We have no means of telling what the poor paid for their shacks or garrets in the Subura or Trastevere.

Let me add a few miscellaneous items for what they may be worth.

Caesar when captured by pirates had to pay a ransom of $60,000 (Suet., *Jul.,* 4), which is slightly above the standard American or Chinese price. Cicero was ready to offer $60,000 for a property to be used for a tomb (*Att.*, 12, 25). He paid $1,500 for a place at which to stay over night (diversorium) on his travels south (*Att.*, 10, 5). Terentia's dowry to Cicero was $20,000 (*Att.*, 15, 17; 16, 1). At Cremona a gentleman of this time bought a burial place for himself extending over nine acres (*C. I. L.*, I², 2137). In one of his famous *mots* Cicero said that a jury expected three million sesterces ($150,000) to acquit a culprit of praetorian rank (*Verr.*, 1, 1, 38). In 89, we are told, epicures would pay as much as $20 for a jar (26 liters) of pickled Pontic fish (Diod., 37, 3, 5). Columns like those of the Castor temple (about 30 feet high, 3 feet 4 inches at base, made of Alban stone, but not monoliths) could be bought and erected at $1,000 each (Cic., *Verr.*, 2, 1, 147). A street advertisement at Pompeii (*C. I. L.*, I², 1680) promises a reward of 65 sesterces for the return of a bronze urn lost or stolen from the wine tavern. The urn —apparently of the standard two-gallon size—would probably be worth $6.50, since finders could demand a half of the value of articles found.

This volume ends with the year 30 B. C., the year that marks the end of civil confusion and the virtual beginning of the imperial period. There is evidence in the next period that to some extent large-scale centralized manufacturing with extensive and well organized methods of distribution had already been introduced in this period, but it will be best to postpone the consideration of the organization of industry and trade until we reach the period where the evidence is available.

In general the economic trends of the Republic up to Sulla's time had been determined by the instincts and desires of agrarian groups, whether landlords or small farmers. From Sulla's time the confusion wrought by ambitious nobles in control of armies and provinces precluded the normal growth of industry, commerce, and capitalism. Wealth in any form, whether in Italy or the provinces, was then in constant danger of being exploited by the man who had seized political control. Augustus brought peace again, respect for life and property returned, commerce was safeguarded throughout the empire, the provincials were encouraged and aided to develop their resources in their own way and to enter into the channels of a world-wide trade if they would.

BIBLIOGRAPHY

FOR INTRODUCTION

1. The Early Sources

Berger, "Tabulae duodecim," in *Real-Enc.* (Pauly-Wissowa-Kroll).

Cambridge Ancient History, VII, Chapters X-XVI, by H. Last and H. Stuart Jones, 1928.

Costa, G., *I fasti consolari romani*, Milan, 1910.

De Sanctis, G., *Storia dei Romani*, I-II, Turin, 1907.

Frank, T., "Early Historians," in *Life and Lit. of Rom. Rep.*, Berkeley, 1930.

Kornemann, E., *Der Priesterkodex in der Regia*, Tübingen, 1912.

Kubitschek, W., *Grundriss der antiken Zeitrechnung*, Munich, 1928.

Last, H. and H. Stuart Jones, Chapters X-XVI, in *Cambridge Ancient History*, VII, 1928.

Leuze, O., *Die römische Jahrzählung*, Tübingen, 1909.

Lugli, G., "Le mura di Servio Tullio," *Historia*, 1933.

Pais, E., *Fasti triumphales populi Romani*, Rome, 1920-3.

Schön, G., "Fasti," in *R-E.* (Pauly-Wissowa).

Scott, I., "Early Roman Traditions," in *Mem. Am. Acad. Rome*, 1929.

Stuart Jones, H., chapters in *Camb. Anc. Hist.*, VII, 1928.

Täubler, E., *Unters. z. Geschichte des Dezemvirats*, 1921.

2. Archaeology and Geography

Adams, L. E. W., *A Study in the Commerce of Latium*, Bryn Mawr Diss., 1921.

Antonielli, U., "Appunti di paletnologia laziale," in *Bull. Palet. Ital.*, 1924, 154 ff.

Atti e Mem., Società Magna Grecia, Rome, 1928—.

Carcopino, J., *La louve du Capitole*, Paris, 1925.

Ciaceri, E., *Storia della Magna Grecia*, Rome, 1927-32.

Curtis, D., in *Mem. Am. Acad. in Rome*, III (1919), V (1925), on Etruscan Tombs.

De La Blanchère, "Cuniculus," in *Darem.-Saglio*.

Della Seta, A., *Italia Antica*, Bergamo, 1928.

———, *Cat. Museo di Villa Giulia*, 1918.

Ducati, P., *Storia dell'arte etrusca*, Florence, 1927.

Duhn, F. von, *Italische Gräberkunde*, Heidelberg, 1924.

Frank, T., *Roman Buildings of the Republic*, Am. Acad. in Rome, 1924.

Gabrici, E., "Cuma," in *Mon. Antichi*, XXII (1913).

Graffunder, P., "Rom," in R-E. (Pauly-Wissowa).

Grenier, A., *Bologne villanovienne*, Paris, 1912.

Groh, V., "I primordi di Roma," in *Rend. Pont. Acc. Arch.*, III, 215.

Heichelheim, F., "Land tenure, Ancient" in *Enc. Soc. Sciences*.

Hennig, R., "Die west. und nörd. Kultureinflüsse," in *Klio*, 1932.

Homo, L., *Primitive Italy*, London, 1927.

Jordan, H., *Topographie der Stadt Rom*, Berlin, 1878-85 (especially vol. III, 1907, by Ch. Huelsen).

Kahrstedt, U., "Phoen. Handel," in *Klio*, 1912.

Lutz, H. F., "Price Fluctuations in Ancient Babylonia," in *Jour. Econ. Business Hist.*, 1932, 335.

Montelius, O., *La civilisation prim. en Italie*, Stockholm, 1904.

Nissen, H., *Italische Landeskunde*, Berlin, 1883-1902.

Nogara, B., *Gli Etruschi e la loro civiltà*, Milan, 1933.

Philippson, A., *Das Mittelmeergebiet*, Leipzig, 1922.

Pinza, G., "Monumenti primitivi di Roma e del Lazio antico," in *Mon. Antichi*, XV (1905).

————, *Materiale per l'etnologia Etr. Laziale*, Milan, 1915.

Platner and Ashby, *Topographical Dictionary of Ancient Rome*, Oxford, 1929.

Poulsen, F., *Etruscan Tomb Paintings*, Oxford, 1922.

Putortì, N., *L'Italia antichissima*, Reggio, 1929.

Randall-MacIver, D., *Villanovans and Early Etruscans*, Oxford, 1924.

————, *The Iron Age in Italy*, Oxford, 1927.

Reallexicon d. Vorgeschichte, "Caere," "Praeneste," "Satricum," "Veii."

Rellini, U., *Le origini della civiltà italica*, Rome, 1929.

Rose, J. Holland, *The Mediterranean in the Ancient World*, Cambridge, 1933.

Schachermeyr, F., *Etruskische Frühgesch.*, Berlin, 1929.

Semple, E. C., *Geography óf the Mediterranean Region*, New York, 1931.

Sigwart, G., "Die Fruchtbarkeit des Bodens," *Schmollers Jahrb.*, 1915, 113.

Stella, L. A., *Italia antica sul mare*, Milan, 1930.

Strong, Eugénie, "The Art of the Roman Republic," Ch. XX of *Camb. Anc. Hist.*, IX.

Studi Etruschi, Florence, 1927-.

Täubler, E., "Terremare und Rom," in *Heid. Sitz.*, 1932.

Tamborini, F., "La vita econ. nella Roma degli ultimi re," in *Athen.*, 1930, 299.

Van Buren, E. D., *Figurative Terracotta Revetments in Etruria and Latium*, London, 1921.

3. LAWS, TREATIES, AND CONSTITUTION

Beloch, K. J., *Römische Geschichte*, Berlin, 1926.

Botsford, G. W., *The Roman Assemblies*, New York, 1909.

Bruns, C. G., *Fontes juris Romani* (7th ed. by Gradenwitz), Tübingen, 1909.

Costanzi, V., "Sulla cronologia del primo trattato tra Roma e Cartagine," in *Riv. Fil.*, 1925, 381.

De Sanctis, G., *Storia dei Romani*, I and II, Turin, 1907.

Fowler, W. Warde, *The Religious Experience of the Roman People*, London, 1911.

Frank, T., *An Economic History of Rome*, 2nd ed., Baltimore, 1927.

————, *Social Behavior in Ancient Rome*, Ch. V, Harvard Press, 1932.

Gelzer, M., "Latium," in *R-E*.

Girard, P. F., *Textes de droit romain*, Paris, 1923.

Grenier, A., *Le génie romain*, Paris, 1925.

Huvelin, P., *Études du droit commercial romain*, Paris, 1929.

Jolowicz, H. F., *Hist. Introd. to the Study of Roman Law*, Cambridge, 1932.

Last, H. and H. Stuart Jones, chapters X-XVI of *Camb. Anc. Hist.*, VII, 1928.

Meyer, E., "Plebs," in Conrad, *Handwörterbuch der Staatswiss.*

————, "Der Ursprung des Tribunats," in *Kleine Schriften*, I, Halle, 1924, 333.

Mommsen, T., *Röm. Staatsrecht*, Leipzig, 1888.

Neumann, K. J., *Die Grundherrschaft der röm. Republik*, Strassburg, 1900.

Niccolini, G., *Il Tribunato della plebe*, Milan, 1932.

Nilsson, M. P., "The Introduction of Hoplite Tactics at Rome, in *Jour. Rom. Stud.*, 1929.

Olmstead, A. T., "Land Tenure in the Ancient Orient," in *Am. Hist. Rev.*, 1926.

Pöhlmann, R., *Geschichte der sozialen Frage* (3rd ed., F. Oertel), Munich, 1925.

Premerstein, A. von, "Clientes," in *R-E*.

Radin, M., "Secare partis," in *Am. Jour. Philol.*, 1922, 32.

Rosenberg, A., "Zur Geschichte des Latinerbundes," in *Hermes*, 1919, 113.

Schwarze, K., *Beiträge zur Gesch. altröm. Agrarprobleme*, Halle, 1912.

Täubler, E., *Imperium Romanum*, Leipzig, 1913, 254 ff.

Vogt, J., *Die röm. Republik*, Freiburg, 1932.

Voigt, M., "Ueber die bina jugera," in *Rh. Mus.*, 1869, 52.

Weber, M., *Die römische Agrargeschichte*, Stuttgart, 1891.

Weiss, E., "Kollektiveigentum," in *R-E.*

Wenger, L., "Hausgewalt u. Staatsgewalt im röm. Altertum," *Miscell. Ehrle*, II.

Wissowa, G., *Religion und Kultus der Römer*, Munich, 1912.

4. ENCYCLOPEDIAS AND COLLECTIONS

Daremberg-Saglio, *Dictionnaire des antiquités grecques et romaines*, Paris, 1875-1919.

Encyclopaedia of the Social Sciences, New York, 1930-.

Pauly-Wissowa-Kroll, *Real-Encyclopädie*, Stuttgart, 1894- (referred to as *R-E.*).

Platner, S. and T. Ashby, *Topographical Dictionary of Ancient Rome*, Oxford, 1929.

Reallexicon der Vorgeschichte, hrsg. von M. Ebert, Berlin, 1924-32.

Ruggiero, E., *Dizionario Epigraphico di antichità romane*, Roma, 1895-.

Bruns, C. G., *Fontes Juris rom. ant.* (7th ed.), Tübingen, 1909.

Cagnat, R., *Inscriptiones Graecae ad res Romanas pertinentes*, Paris, 1906-.

Corpus Inscriptionum Latinarum, Berlin.

Dessau, H., *Inscriptiones Latinae Selectae*, Berlin, 1892-1916.

Mau-v.Mercklin-Matz, *Katalog der Bibliothek des Arch. Inst. in Rom*, Berlin, 1914-32. (For bibliography on the cities of Italy see vol. I, and supplement of 1930.)

For the Greek and Latin texts see the Teubner texts (*Bibliotheca Teubneriana*, Berlin), the Oxford texts (*Bibliotheca Oxoniensis*, London), the Loeb Classical Library (Heinemann, London; G. P. Putnam's Sons, New York), and the series published by the *Association Guillaume Budé* (Paris). Italian scholars have undertaken an archaeological survey of Italy, to be called *Forma Italiae*, Rome, and a new publication of all Roman inscriptions in Italy, to be called *Inscriptiones Italiae*, Rome.

CHAPTERS I AND II

1. GENERAL HISTORIES

Beloch, K. J., *Römische Geschichte*, Berlin, 1926.

Cambridge Ancient History, VII (1928); VIII (1930).

Carcopino, J., *Histoire romaine*, Paris, 1930-.

De Sanctis, G., *Storia dei Romani*, II, 1907; III, 1916, Turin.

Frank, T., *Roman Imperialism*, New York, 1914.

Gsell, S., *Histoire anc. de l'Afrique du Nord*, Paris, 1913-28.

Heitland, W. E., *The Roman Republic*, 2nd ed., Cambridge, 1923.

Melzer, O. and U. Kahrstedt, *Geschichte der Karthager*, Berlin, 1896-1913.

Mommsen, Th., *Römische Geschichte*.

Pais, E., *Storia di Roma*, Rome, 1926-8.

Piganiol, A., *La conquête romaine*, Paris, 1927.

2. ARCHAEOLOGY

Baratta, M., "Il sito di Spina," in *Athen.*, 1932, 217.

Calza, G., *Ostia*, Rome, 1925.

Della Seta, A., *Italia Antica*, Bergamo, 1928.

Ducati, P., *Storia dell'arte etrusca*, Florence, 1927.

Ernout, A., " Le parler de Preneste," in *Mem. Soc. Ling.*, 1905.

Frank, T., *Roman Buildings of the Republic*, Rome, 1924.

Fowler, W. Warde, *Religious Experience of the Roman People*, London, 1911.

Herschel, C., *Frontinus and the Water Supply of Rome*, New York, 1913.

Huelsen, Ch., *Topographie der Stadt Rom* (vol. III of Jordan), Berlin, 1907.

Jacobone, N., *Canusium*, Lecce, 1925.

Kaschnitz-Weinberg, G., " Studien zur Etruskischen und Frührömischen Porträtkunst," in *Röm. Mitt.*, 1926, 133.

Kluge, K. und K. Lehmann-Hartleben, *Die antiken Grossbronzen*, Berlin, 1927.

Lehmann-Hartleben, K., " Städtebau Italiens," in *R-E.*

Matthies, G., *Die praenestinischen Spiegel*, Strassburg, 1912.

Pagenstecher, R., *Die Calenische Reliefkeramik*, Berlin, 1909.

Platner, S. and T. Ashby, *Topographical Dictionary of Rome*, Oxford, 1929.

Poulsen, F., *Etruscan Tomb Paintings*, Oxford, 1922.

Rizzo, G., *La pittura Ellenistico-Romana*, Milan, 1929.

Saeflund, G., *Le mura di Roma repubblicana*, Rome, 1932.

Strong, E., " The Art of the Roman Republic," in *Camb. Anc. Hist.*, IX (1932).

Swindler, M. H., *Ancient Painting*, New Haven, 1929.

Wissowa, G., *Religion und Kultus der Römer*, Munich, 1912.

3. POLITICAL, CONSTITUTIONAL, AND LEGAL HISTORY

Beloch, K. J., *Der italische Bund*, Leipzig, 1880.

———, *Die Bevölkerung der gr.-röm. Welt*, Leipzig, 1886.

Botsford, G. W., *The Roman Assemblies*, New York, 1909.

Cambridge Ancient History, VII (1930), chapters by H. Stuart Jones, H. Last, F. E. Adcock, M. Holleaux, T. Frank; VIII (1931), chapters by B. L. Hallward.

De Sanctis, G., *Storia dei Romani*, III, Turin, 1916.

Fraccaro, P., " Lex Flaminia de agro Gallico," in *Athen.*, 1919, 23.

———, " La Storia dell' ant. esercito romano," in *Atti Cong. Studi Rom.*, 1931.

Frank, T., Dominium in Solo Provinciali," in *J. R. S.*, 1927.

Gelzer, M., *Die Nobilität*, Leipzig, 1912.

Leuze, O., *Zur Geschichte der röm. Censur*, Halle, 1912.

Mommsen, Th., *Röm. Staatsrecht.*

Münzer, F., *Röm. Adelsparteien*, Stuttgart, 1920.

———, articles on " C. Flaminius," " Licinius Stolo," in *R-E.*

Oertel, F., " Der Ebrovertrag," in *Rhein. Mus.*, 1932, 224.

Pais, E., *Ricerche sulla storia e sul diritto pubblico*, Rome, 1915, 21.

Vančura, J., " Leges Agrariae," in *R-E.*

4. SPECIAL TREATISES ON THIRD CENTURY

Beversdorff, G., *Die Streitkräfte der Karthager und Römer*, Berlin, 1910.

Bruno, B., *La terza guerra sannitica*, Rome, 1906.

Cambridge Ancient History, vols. VII and VIII, 1928, 1930.

Cary, M., " A Forgotten Treaty between Rome and Carthage," in *J. R. S.*, 1919.

———, " The Origin of the Punic Wars," *History*, 1922.

Cross, G. N., *Epirus*, Cambridge, 1932.

De Sanctis, G., *Storia dei Romani*, III, Turin, 1916.

Drachmann, A. B., " Sagunt und die Ebro-Grenze," in *Danske, Vidensk. Med.*, 1920.

Frank, T., " Rome, Marseilles, and Carthage," in *Military Historian*, 1916.

Gsell, S., *Histoire anc. de l'Afrique du Nord*, Paris, 1913-20.

Holm, A., *Geschichte Siciliens*, Leipzig, 1870-98.

Holleaux, M., " La politique romaine en Grèce," in *Rev. de Phil.*, 1926.

Huvelin, P., *Une guerre d'usure*, Paris, 1917.

Judeich, W., " König Pyrrhos römische Politik," in *Klio*, 1926.

Kromayer, J. und G. Veith, *Heerwesen und Kriegführung*, Munich, 1928.

Meyer, E., " Untersuchungen z. Gesch. d. zweiten pun. Kriegs," *Kleine Schriften*, II, Halle, 1924.

Meyer, P., *Der Ausbruch des ersten pun. Krieges*, Berlin, 1908.

Pais, *Storia della Sardegna e della Corsica*, Rome, 1923.

Schachermeyr, F., " Die röm.-punischen Verträge," in *Rhein. Mus.*, 1930.

Schnabel, P., " Zur Vorgeschichte des zweit. pun. Kriegs," in *Klio*, 1926.

Schulten, A., " Hispania," in *R-E.*

Tarn, W. W., " The Fleets of the First Punic War," in *J. Hell. St.*, 1907, 48.

Vulič, N., " Illyricum," in *R-E.*

5. ECONOMIC AND FINANCIAL

Billeter, G., *Geschichte des Zinsfusses*, Leipzig, 1898.

Carcopino, J., *La loi de Hiéron et les Romains*, Paris, 1919.

Cardinali, G., " Frumentum," in *Diz. Epig.*, III.

Cavaignac, E., *Population et Capital*, Paris, 1923.

Ciccotti, E., *Lineamenti dell' evoluzione tributaria*, Milan, 1921.

Clark, F. W., *The Influence of Sea-Power in the Roman Republic*, Diss. Chicago, 1915.

Deloume, A., *Les Manieurs d'Argent en Rome*, 2nd ed., Paris, 1892.

De Sanctis, G., *Storia dei Romani*, III, 2, especially pp. 323-37.

Frank, T., *Economic History of Rome*, 2nd ed., Baltimore, 1927.

Gummerus, H., " Industrie und Handel," in *R-E.*

Heichelheim, F., *Wirtschaftliche Schwankungen*, Jena, 1930.

Holleaux, M., *Rome, la Grèce*, etc., Paris, 1921.

———, " La politique romaine en Grèce," in *Rev. de Philol.*, 1926.

Jardé, A., *Les céréales dans l'antiquité grecque*, Paris, 1925.

Kniep, F., *Societas Publicanorum*, Jena, 1896.

Kornemann, E., " Coloniae," in *R-E.*

Marquardt, J., *Röm. Staatsverwaltung.*

Pais, E., *Storia delle colonizzazione di Roma antica*, Rome, 1923.

———, " Delle colonie Romane e Latini," in *Mem. Acc. Lincei*, 1923.

Robbins, F. E., " Cost to Athens of Second Empire," in *Class. Phil.*, 1918, 363.

Rose, J. Holland, *The Mediterranean in the Ancient World*, Cambridge, 1933.

Rostovtzeff, M., " Ptolemaic Egypt," ch. IV, in *Camb. Anc. Hist.*, VII, 1928.

———, *Studien zur Geschichte d. röm. Kolonates*, Leipzig, 1911.

Scalais, R., arts. in *Mus. Belge*, 1923, 243; 1928, 187.

Segrè, A., *Metrologia e circ. monetaria*, Bologna, 1928.

———, " Circulaz. e inflaz. monet." in *Historia*, 1929.

Tarn, W. W., " The Fleets of the First Punic War," in *J. H. S.*, 1907.

6. COINAGE

Babelon, E., *Monnaies de la rép. romaine*, Paris, 1886.

Bahrfeldt, M. von, *Röm. Goldmünzenprägung*, Halle, 1923.

———, in *Rivista Ital.*, 1899, 405 (on Romano-Campanian coins).

Cesano, S. L., arts. on early coins in *Notiz. d. Scavi*, 1928, 83 and 369.

Giesecke, W., *Italia Numismatica*, Leipzig, 1928.

Grueber, H. A., *Coins of the Roman Republic*, London, 1910.

Haeberlin, E. J., *Aes Grave*, Frankfurt, 1910.

Haeberlin, E. J., *Systematik des ältesten röm. Münzwesens*, Berlin, 1905.

Head, B. V., *Historia Numorum*, Oxford, 1911.

Mattingly, H., "The Romano-Campanian Coinage," in *Num. Chronicle*, 1924, 189. and 1932, 236.

———, "The First Age of Roman Coinage," in *J. R. S.*, 1929, 19.

Mommsen, Th., *Röm. Münzwesen*, Berlin, 1860.

Samwer, K. und M. von Bahrfeldt, *Geschichte des älteren röm. Münzwesens*, Vienna, 1883.

Sydenham, E. A., *Aes Grave*, London, 1926.

———, "The Victoriate," in *Num. Chronicle*, 1932, 73.

Willers, H., "Die röm. Goldprägung," in *Corolla Numis.* (1906), 310.

CHAPTER III

1. GENERAL

See the general works, mentioned above, of Beloch, Botsford, Carcopino, De Sanctis, Frank, Gsell, Heitland, Holleaux, Kahrstedt, Marquardt, Mommsen, Münzer, Pais, Wissowa.

Beloch, K. J., *Römische Geschichte*, Berlin, 1926.

———, *Griechische Geschichte*, IV, Berlin, 1925-7.

———, *Campanien*, ed. 2, Breslau, 1897.

Busolt, G. and H. Swoboda, *Griechische Staatskunde*, Munich, 1926.

Cambridge Ancient History, VIII, chapters by Holleaux, Benecke, Schulten, Frank, Rostovtzeff.

Cary, M., *A History of the Greek World from 323 to 146 B. C.*, London, 1932.

Colin, G., *Rome et la Grèce*, Paris, 1905.

Cross, G. N., *Epirus*, Cambridge, 1932.

De Sanctis, G., *Storia dei Romani*, IV, Turin, 1923.

Ferguson, W. S., *Hellenistic Athens*, New York, 1911.

Fraccaro, P., "Le fonte per il consolato di M. Porcio Catone," in *Stud. Stor.*, 1910.

Holleaux, M., "La politique rom. en Grèce," in *Rev. Phil.*, 1926, 194.

———, chapters in *Camb. Anc. Hist.*, VIII.

Homo, L., "Flamininus et la politique rom. en Grèce," in *Rev. Hist.*, 1916.

Horn, H., *Foederati*, Diss., Frankfurt, 1930.

Klotz, A., "T. Livius," in *R-E*.

———, "Die Bezeichnung, der röm. Legionen," in *Rhein. Mus.*, 1932, 143.

Kromayer, J. and G. Veith, *Heerwesen und Kriegführung*, Munich, 1928.

Marsh, F. B., *The Founding of the Roman Empire*, 2nd ed., Oxford, 1927.

Miltner, F., "Seekrieg," and "Seewesen," in *R-E.*, Supp. V.

Mommsen, Th., "Die Scipionenprozesse," in *Röm. Forsch.*, II, 417.

Niese, B., *Grundriss der röm. Geschichte*, 5th ed. by E. Hohl, Munich, 1923.

Nissen, H., *Kritische Untersuchungen*, Berlin, 1863.

Oliverio, G., "Stele di Tolemeo Neoteros," in *Cirenaica*, Bergamo, 1932.

Pais, E., *Fasti Triumphales*, Rome, 1920.

Parker, H. M. D., *The Roman Legions*, Oxford, 1928.

Schulten, A., *Fontes Hispaniae Antiquae*, Barcelona,

———, *Numantia*, III, IV, Munich, 1927 and 1929.

Tarn, W. W., "The Greek Warship," in *Jour. Hell. Stud.*, 1905, 137.

Wilcken, U., "Das Testament des Ptolemaios von Kyrene," in *Sitz. Pr. Akad.*, 1932, 315.

2. Archaeological and Economic

Ashby, T., " Die antiken Wasserleitungen der Stadt Rom," in *Neue Jb.*, 1909.

Barbagallo, C., " Il prezzo del bestiame," etc., in *Riv. Stor. Ant.*, 1908, 3 and 306.

————, " La produzione media dei cereali," in *Riv. Stor. Ant.*, 1904, 477.

Barthel, W., " Zur Geschichte der röm. Städte in Africa," in *Bonn. Jb.*, 1911, 82 ff.

Besnier, M., " Le Commerce du plomb," in *Rev. Arch.*, XI, XIII, XIV.

Blümner, H., *Technologie und Terminologie der Gewerbe*, I, 2nd ed., 1912.

Bolin, S., *Fynden av Romerska Mynt i Germanien* [coin hoards in rep. Italy, on p. (180)], Lund, 1926.

Broughton, T. R. S., *The Romanization of Africa*, Baltimore, 1929.

Carrington, R. C., " Studies in the Campanian *Villae Rusticae*," in *Jour. Rom. St.*, 1931, 112.

Cary, M., " The Sources of Silver for the Greek World," in *Mélanges Glotz*, Paris, 1932.

Charlesworth, M. P., *Trade Routes*, 2nd ed., Cambridge, 1926.

Curcio, G., *La primitiva civiltà latina agricola*, Florence, 1929.

Deloume, A., *Les Manieurs d'argent à Rome*, 2nd ed., Paris, 1892.

Drachmann, A. G., *Ancient Oil Mills and Presses*, Copenhagen, 1932.

Dubois, C., *Pouzzoles Antique*, Paris, 1907.

Ducati, P., *Storia dell' arte etrusca*, Florence, 1927.

Durrbach, F., *Choix d'inscriptions de Délos*, Paris, 1921.

Frank, T., " Mercantilism and Rome's Foreign Policy," in *Am. Hist. Rev.*, 1912-13, 233.

————, chapters on " Rome " and " Italy," in *Camb. Anc. Hist.*, VIII.

Gaertringen, F. Hiller von, " Rhodos," in *R-E.*, Suppl. V.

Glotz, G., " L'Histoire de Délos d'après les prix d'une denrée," in *Rev. Ét. Gr.*, 1916.

————, " Les salaires à Délos," in *Jour. d. Sav.*, 1913.

Gummerus, H., " Industrie und Handel," in *R-E.*

————, " Der röm. Gutsbetrieb," in *Klio*, Beiheft V, 1906.

Habel, " Ludi Publici," in *R-E.*, Supp. V.

Hatzfeld, J., " Les Italiens résidant à Délos," in *Bull. Corr. Hell.*, 1912.

————, *Les trafiquants italiens dans l'Orient hellénique*, Paris, 1919.

Haywood, R. M., *Studies on Scipio Africanus*, Baltimore, 1933.

Heichelheim, F., *Wirtschaftliche Schwankungen*, Jena, 1930.

Heitland, W. E., *Agricola*, Cambridge, 1921.

Herschel, C., *Frontinus and the Water Supply of the City of Rome*, New York, 1913.

Hoerle, J., *Catos Hausbücher*, Paderborn, 1929.

Holleaux, M., " Inscriptions de Délos," in *Bull. Corr. Hell.*, 1907, 374.

————, chapters in *Camb. Anc. Hist.*, VII and VIII.

Homolle, Th. and others, *Exploration arch. de Délos*, Paris, 1909-.

Kniep, F., *Societas Publicanorum*, Jena, 1896.

Kompter, H. O., *Die Römer auf Delos*, Diss., Münster, 1913.

Kornemann, E., " Colonia " and " Conventus," in *R-E.*

Kromayer, J., " Die wirtsch. Entwicklung Italiens," in *Neue Jb.*, 1914, 145.

Kubitschek, W., " Studien zu Münzen der röm. Republik," in *Wien. Sitz.*, 1911, 167 ff.

Lehmann-Hartleben, K., " Die antiken Hafenanlagen," in *Klio*, Beiheft 14.

Mau, A., *Pompeii in Leben und Kunst*, 2nd ed., 1908.

Meyer, E., *Kleine Schriften*, 2nd ed., Halle, 1924.

Nilsson, M. P., " Timbres amphoriques de Lindos," in *Bull Acad. Den.*, 1909.

Paris, P., " Timbres amphoriques de Rhodes," in *Bull. Corr. Hell.*, 1914, 308.

Park, M., *The Plebs in Cicero's Day*, Diss., Bryn Mawr, 1918.

Pfeifer, G., *Agrargeschichtlicher Beitrag zur Reform des Ti. Gracchus*, Diss., Erlangen, 1914.

Platner, S. and T. Ashby, *Topographical Dictionary*, Oxford, 1929.

Rickard, T. A., *Man and Metals*, ch. 8, New York, 1932.

Robbins, F. E., "Cost to Athens of Second Empire," in *Class. Phil.*, 1918, 363.

Rostovtzeff, M., chapters XIX and XX in *Camb. Anc. Hist.*, VIII, 1930.

———, "Frumentum," in *R-E.*

———, *Geschichte der Staatspacht*, Leipzig, 1902.

———, *A Large Estate in Egypt*, in *Wisc. Stud.*, 1922.

Roussel, P., *Délos Colonie Athenienne*, Paris, 1916.

Saeflund, G., "Studier Kring Forum Boarium," in *Eranos*, 1930.

Scalais, R., "Les revenus de l'agriculture," in *Mus. Belge*, 1927, 93.

———, "La politique agraire," in *Mus. Belge*, 1930.

Strong, E., "The Art of the Roman Republic," in *Camb. Anc. Hist.*, IX, 1932.

Sydenham, E., "The Victoriate," in *Num. Chron.*, 1932, 73.

Westermann, W. L., *Upon Slavery in Ptolemaic Egypt*, New York, 1929.

———, "Trapezite Banking," in *J. Econ. and Business Hist.*, 1931.

———, "Egyptian Agricultural Labor," in *Agric. History*, 1927, 34.

——— and C. J. Kraemer, *Greek Papyri*, New York, 1926.

——— and C. W. Keyes, *Tax Lists and Transportation Receipts*, 1932.

Ziebarth, E., "Hellenistische Banken," in *Zeit. Num.*, 1924, 36.

CHAPTER IV

General

a. *The Gracchan Period*

See the works mentioned above of Beloch, Bloch, Botsford, Carcopino, De Sanctis, Frank, Gsell, Heitland, Marquardt, Meyer, Mommsen, Niese, Pais, Piganiol.

Barthel, W., "Röm. Limitation in der Prov. Africa," in *Bonn. Jahrb.*, 1911, 39.

Beloch, K. J., *Römische Geschichte*, Berlin, 1926.

Broughton, T. R. S., *The Romanization of Africa*, Baltimore, 1929.

Cambridge Ancient History, IX (1932).

Carcopino, J., *Autour des Gracques*, Paris, 1929.

Cardinali, G., "Il Regno di Pergamo," in *Stud. Stor. Ant.*, 1906.

———, *Studi Graccani*, Genoa, 1912.

Chapot, V., *La province romaine d'Asie*, Paris, 1904.

Cichorius, C., *Römische Studien*, Leipzig, 1922.

De Sanctis, G., "Der Hellenismus und Rom," in *Propyl. Welt-Gesch.*, I.

———, *Problemi di storia antica*, chapters VIII and IX, Bari, 1932.

Fowler, W. W., "Notes on Gaius Gracchus," in *Eng. Hist. Rev.*, 1905.

Fraccaro, P., "Studi sull' età dei Gracchi," in *Stud. Stor. Ant.*, 1912-13.

———, "Ricerche su Gaio Graccho," in *Athen.*, 1925.

Frank, T., "Dominium in solo provinciali," in *Jour. Rom. Stud.*, 1927, 150.

———, "Roman Census Statistics from 225," in *Class. Phil.*, 1924, 329.

Gelzer, M., *Die Nobilität*, Leipzig, 1912.

Greenidge, A. H. J., *A History of Rome*, London, 1904.

Greenidge and Clay, *Sources for Roman History*, 133-70, Oxford, 1903.

Homo, L., *Les institutions politiques romaines*, Paris, 1927.

Kornemann, E., "Colonia," "Conventus," in *R-E.*

Last, H., chapters on the Gracchi, in *Camb. Anc. Hist.*, IX (1932).

Levi, M. A., *La costituzione romana dai Gracchi*, Florence, 1928.

Meyer, E., *Kleine Schriften*, 2nd ed., Halle, 1924.

Münzer, F., " Sempronii Gracchi," " Norbanus," in *R-E*.

Schulten, A., *Numantia*, III, IV, Munich, 1927-29.

Stern, E. von, " Zur Beurteilung der pol. Wirksamkeit des Ti. und C. Gracchus," *Hermes*, 1921, 229.

Stevenson, G. H., " The Provinces, etc.," ch. X, in *Camb. Anc. Hist.*, IX (1932).

Taeger, F., *Tiberius Gracchus*, Stuttgart, 1918.

b. *From Saturninus to Sulla's Retirement*

Asbach, J., *Das Volkstribunat des jüngeren M. Livius*, Bonn, 1888.

Barthel, W., " Zur Gesch. der röm. Städte in Africa," in *Bonn. Jahrb.*, 1911.

Bennett, H., *Cinna and his Times*, Menasha, 1923.

Bloch, G., *M. Aemilius Scaurus*, Paris, 1909.

Carcopino, J., *Sylla*, Paris, 1931.

Clerc, M., *Massalia*, Marseilles, 1929.

Domaszewski, A. von, " Bellum Marsicum," in *Abh. Akad. Wien*, 1924.

Drumann, W. and P. Groebe, *Geschichte Roms*.

Frank, T., " The Inscriptions of the Imp. Estates of Africa," in *Am. Jour. Philol.*, 1926, 55.

Fröhlich, F., " L. Cornelius Sulla," in *R-E*.

Hardy, E. G., " The Number of the Sullan Senate," in *Jour. Rom. St.*, 1916.

Holmes, T. Rice, *The Roman Republic*, I, Oxford, 1923.

Holroyd, M., " Jugurthine War," in *Jour. Rom. St.*, 1928.

Last, H., chapters on Sulla, in *Camb. Anc. Hist.*, IX (1932).

Levi, M. A., *Silla*, Milan, 1924.

Mommsen, Th., " Die Bürgercolonien, etc.," in *Hermes*, 18, 161.

Münzer, F., " C. Servilius Glaucia," in *R-E*.

Oehler and Lenschau, " Karthago," in *R-E*.

Robinson, F. W., *Marius, Saturninus und Glaucia*, Bonn, 1912.

Schulten, A., " Zur Heeresreform des Marius," in *Hermes*, 1928.

Seymour, P. A., " The Policy of Livius Drusus," in *Eng. Hist. Rev.*, 1914.

Von der Muehl, F., *De L. Appuleio Saturnino*, Basel, 1906.

Wiehn, E., *Die illegalen Heereskommanden*, Leipzig, 1926.

ECONOMIC HISTORY

Bang, H., " Die Herkunft d. röm. Sklaven," in *Röm. Mitt.*, 1910, 1912.

Belot, E., *Histoire des chevaliers romains*, Paris, 1866-73.

Campbell, W., *Greek and Roman Plated Coins*, New York, 1933.

Carcopino, J., *La loi de Hiéron*, Paris, 1924.

Corsetti, R., " Sul prezzo dei grani nell' antichita," in *Stud. Stor. Ant.*, 1893.

Deloume, A., *Les manieurs d'argent*, Paris, 1892.

De Sanctis, G., " Sallustio e la guerra di Giugurta," in *Problemi di Storia Antica*, Bari, 1932.

Durrbach, F., *Choix d'inscriptions de Délos*, Paris, 1921.

Fraenkel, M., *Die Inschriften von Pergamon*, Berlin, 1890-95.

Francotte, H., " Le pain gratuit dans les cités grecques," in *Mél. Nicole*, 151.

Frank, T., " Mercantilism and Rome's Foreign Policy," in *Am. Hist. Rev.*, 1912-13.

———, " Financial Legislation of the Sullan Period," in *Am. Jour. Philol.*, 1933.

———, " Farmers or Peasants," in *Soc. Behavior in Anc. Rome*, Harvard Press, 1932.

Grueber, H. A., *Coins of the Republic*, London, 1910.

Hardy, E. G., *Roman Laws and Charters*, Oxford, 1912.

Hatzfeld, J., " Les Italiens résidant à Délos," in *Bull. Corr. Hell.*, 1912.

28

Hatzfeld, J., *Les trafiquants italiens*, Paris, 1919.

Heitland, W. E., *Agricola*, Cambridge, 1921.

Herzog, R., *Aus der Geschichte des Bankwesens*, Giessen, 1919.

Judeich, W., " Die Gesetze des Gracchus," in *Hist. Zcit.*, 1913, 473.

Kahrstedt, U., " Die Grundlagen und Voraussetzungen der röm. Revolution," in *Neue Wege*, IV, 1929.

Kiessling, H. von, " Giroverkehr," in *R-E.*, Supp. IV.

Klingmüller, " Fenus," in *R-E.*

Kontchalovsky, D., " Recherches sur l'hist. du mouvement agraire des Gracques," in *Rev. Hist.*, 1926, 161.

Kromayer, J., " Die wirtschaftliche Entwıcklung Italiens," in *Neue Jahrb.*, 1914, 145.

Lehmann-Hartleben, K., " Die antiken Hafenanlagen," in *Klio*, beih. 14, 1923.

Levi, M. A., " Una pagina di storia agraria," in *Atene e Roma*, 1922.

Mau, A., *Pompeii*, 2nd ed., 1908.

Ormerod, H. A., *Piracy in the Ancient World* (cf. ch. VIII of *Camb. Anc. Hist.*, IX).

Pais, E., *Dalle guerre puniche*, Rome, 1918.

Pringsheim, F., " Zum röm. Bankwesen," in *Viertel. Soz. Wirtsch.*, 1919.

Rostovtzeff, M., " Notes on the Econ. Policy of the Pergamene Kings," in *Anatolian Studies in honor of Ramsay*, 375.

———, chapters XVIII-XX, in *Camb. Anc. Hist.*, VIII (1930).

———, chapter V, in *Camb. Anc. Hist.*, IX (1932).

Roussel, P., *Délos colonie Athénienne*, Paris, 1916.

Scalais, R., " La prospérité agricole et pastorale de la Sicile," in *Mus. Belge*, 1924, 77.

Stuart Jones, H., " A Roman Law concerning Piracy," in *Jour. Rom. Stud.*, 1926, 155.

Weber, Max, " Agrarverhältnisse im Altertum," in *Ges. Aufsätze*, Tübingen, 1924.

Wenger, L., " Prätor und Formel," in *Bay. Sitz.-Ber.*, 1926.

Westermann, W. L., " Warehousing and Trapezite Banking," in *Jour. Ec. Business Hist.*, 1930, 31.

Ziebarth, E., " Hellenistische Banken," in *Zeit. Num.*, 1924, 36.

Zulueta, F. de, " The Development of Law," ch. XXI in *Camb. Anc. Hist.*, IX (1932).

CHAPTER V

GENERAL

Adcock, F. E., chapters XV-XVII, in *Camb. Anc. Hist.*, IX (1932).

Boak, A. E. R., " The Extraordinary Commands from 80 to 48 B. C.," in *Am. Hist. Rev.*, 1918.

Botsford, G. W., *The Roman Assemblies*, New York, 1909.

Broughton, T. R. S., *The Romanization of Africa*, Baltimore, 1929.

Cambridge Ancient History, IX (1932).

Carcopino, J., " L'Afrique au dernier siècle de la rép. rom.," in *Rev. Hist.*, 1929, vol. 162.

Cary, M., chapters XI, XII, *Camb. Anc. Hist.*, 1932.

———, " Notes on the Legislation of Julius Caesar," in *Jour. Rom. St.*, 1929.

Ciaceri, E., *Cicerone e suoi tempi*, Rome, 1930.

Clerc, M., *Massalia*, Marseilles, 1929.

Domaszewski, A. v., " Die Heere der Bürgerkriege, etc.," in *Neue Heid. Jb.*, 1894.

Drumann, W. and P. Groebe, *Geschichte Roms*.

Ferrero, G., *The Greatness and Decline of Rome*, London, 1907-8.

Frank, T., " Census Statistics from 225," in *Class. Phil.*, 1924.

Graindor, P., *La guerre d'Alexandrie*, Cairo, 1931.

Gsell, S., *Histoire anc. de l'Afrique du Nord*, VII, VIII, Paris, 1928.

———, " Les premiers temps de la Carthage rom.," in *Rev. Hist.* (156), 1927.

Hall, C. M., *Nicolaus of Damascus's Life of Augustus*, Northampton, 1923.

Hardy, E. G., *Some Problems in Rom. Hist.*, Oxford, 1924.

Heinze, R., " Ciceros ' Staat ' als pol. Tendenzschrift," in *Hermes*, 1924.

Heitland, W. E., *The Roman Republic*, Cambridge, 1923.

Hignett, C., chapter XIII, in *Camb. Anc. Hist.*, IX (1932).

Holmes, T. Rice, *Caesar's Conquest of Gaul*, Oxford, 1911.

———, *The Roman Republic*, Oxford, 1923.

———, *The Architect of the Rom. Emp.*, Oxford, 1928.

Judeich, W., *Caesar im Orient*, Leipzig, 1884.

Jullian, C., *Histoire de la Gaule*, vols. II-IV, Paris.

Klotz, A., *Kommentar zum Bell. Hisp.*, Leipzig, 1927.

Kromayer, J., " Die Entwicklung der röm. Flotte, etc.," in *Philol.*, 1897.

———, " Die Militärcolonien Octavians und Caesars in Gallia," in *Hermes*, 1896.

——— and G. Veith, *Heerwesen*, etc., Munich, 1928.

Last, Hugh, chapter VII, in *Camb. Anc. Hist.*, 1932.

Levi, M. A., " La caduta della rep. Rom.," *Riv. Stud. It.*, 1924, 253.

Marsh, F. B., *The Founding of the Rom. Empire*, Oxford, 1926.

Meyer, E., *Caesars Monarchie*, etc., 2nd ed., Berlin, 1919.

Mommsen, Th., *Roman History; Röm. Staatsrecht; Ges. Schriften.*

———, " Die Provinzen Caesars Zeit," in *Ges. Schr.*, IV, 169.

Münzer, F., *Röm. Adelsparteien*, Stuttgart, 1920.

———, " Brutus Damasippus," " M. Licinius Lucullus," " C. Marius," in *R-E.*

Pocock, L. G., " P. Clodius and the Acts of Caesar," in *Cl. Quart.*, 1924, 59.

Premerstein, A. von, " Die Tafel von Heraclea," in *Zeit. Sav. St., Rom. Abt.*, 1922.

Rostovtzeff, M., chapter V, on Pontus, in *Camb. Anc. Hist.*, IX (1932).

Sternkopf, W., " Die Verteilung der röm. Prov. vor dem Mut. Kriege," in *Hermes*, 1912, 231.

Tarn, W. W., " Antony's Legions," in *Class. Quart.*, 1932.

Taylor, L. R., *The Divinity of the Rom. Emperor*, Middletown, 1931.

Tyrrell and Purser, Introductions to *The Correspondence of Cicero*, Dublin.

Wissowa, G., *Religion und Kultus*, Munich, 1912.

ECONOMICS AND ARCHAEOLOGY

Barbagallo, C., " Produzione media dei cereali e della vite," in *Riv. St. Ant.*, 1904, 477.

Barrow, R. H., *Slavery in the Roman Empire*, London, 1928.

Beigel, R., *Rechnungswesen und Buchführung*, Karlsruhe, 1904.

Bendinelli, G., *Torino Romana*, Turin, 1928.

Besnier, M., " L'interdiction du travail des mines," in *Rev. Arch.*, 1919, 51.

Billiard, R., *L'agriculture d'après les Georgiques de Virgile*, Paris, 1928.

Blümner, H., *Technologie und Terminologie*, Leipzig, 1875-1912.

———, *Die gewerbliche Tätigkeit*, Leipzig, 1869.

———, *Röm. Privat-Altertümer*, Munich, 1911.

Boethius, A., " Warenhäuser in Ferentino und Tivoli," in *Acta Arch.*, 1932.

Boettcher, K., *Die Einnahmen der röm. Republik*, Diss. Leipzig, 1915.

Brusin, G., *Aquileia*, Udine, 1929.

Büchsenschütz, B., *Die Hauptstätten des Gewerbfleisses*, Leipzig, 1869.

Byrne, A., *T. Pomponius Atticus*, Diss. Bryn Mawr, 1920.

Cagnat, R., *Études hist. sur les impôts indirects*, Paris, 1882.

———, " L'Annone d'Afrique," in *Mem. Acad. Inscr.*, 1916, 260.

——— and M. Besnier, " Mercatura," in *Darem-Saglio*, VI.

Calderini, A., *Aquileia Romana*, Milan, 1930.

Calza, G., *Ostia*, Rome, 1925.

————, " Il piazzale delle corporazioni," in *Bull. Com.*, 1916, 187.

Carcopino, J., " La Sicile agricole," in *Viertel. Soc. Wirtsch.*, 1906.

Cartellieri, W., " Die röm. Alpenstrassen," in *Philol.*, Supp., 1926.

Cáry, M., " The Land Legislation of Caesar's First Consulship," in *Jour. Phil.*, 1920, 174.

Cavaignac, E., " L'échelle des fortunes dans la Rome rép.," in *Ann. d'hist. écon.*, I, 481.

Chapot, V., *Le monde romain*, Paris, 1927.

Charlesworth, M. P., *Trade Routes*, Cambridge, 1926.

Ciccotti, C., " Il problema econ. del mondo antico," in *Nuova Riv. Stor.*, 1932.

De Pachtere, F., *La table hypoth. de Veleia*, Paris, 1920.

Dessau, H., " Gaius Rabirius Postumus," in *Hermes*, 1911, 613.

Dubois, C., *Pouzzoles Antique*, Paris, 1907.

Ducati, P., *Storia di Bologna*, Bol., 1928.

Duff, A. M., *Freedmen in the Early Rom. Empire*, Oxford, 1928.

Dureau de la Malle, A., *Économie politique des romains*, Paris, 1840.

Fowler, W. Warde, *Social Life in Rome*, London, 1909.

Frank, T., *Economic History of Rome*, 2nd ed., Baltimore, 1927.

————, " The Sacred Treasure, etc.," in *Am. Jour. Philol.*, 1932.

————, " Dominium in Solo Provinciali," in *Jour. Rom. Stud.*, 1927.

Früchtl, A., *Die Geldgeschäft bei Cicero*, Erlangen, 1912.

Gelzer, M., " Die röm. Gesellschaft zur Zeit Ciceros," in *Neue Jb.*, 1920.

Gest, A. P., *Engineering*, New York, 1930.

Grenier, A., *Archéologie gallo-romaine*, Paris, 1931.

Groener, F., *Fremdenverkehr zur Zeit Ciceros*, Bonn, 1926.

Grueber, H. A., *Coins of the Roman Republic*, London, 1910.

Gsell, S., " L'huile de Leptis," in *Rivista Trip.*, I, 41.

Gummerus, H., " Industrie und Handel," in *R-E.*

————, " Die Bauspekulation des Crassus," in *Klio*, XV.

————, " Der röm. Gutsbetrieb," in *Klio*, beih. 5, 1906.

Hahn, G., *Der Villenbesitz . . . zur Zeit der Republik*, Diss. Bonn, 1922 (only concluding ch. printed).

Hardy, E. G., *Roman Laws and Charters*, Oxford, 1912.

Hauger, A., *Zur röm. Landwirtschaft*, Hannover, 1922.

Haywood, R. M., " Some Traces of Serfdom in Cicero's Day," in *Am. Jour. Philol.*, 1933, 145.

Hehn, V., *Kulturpflanzen und Hausthiere*, Berlin, 8th ed., 1911.

Heitland, W. E., *Agricola*, Cambridge, 1921.

Herzog, R., *Aus der Gesch. des Bankwesens*, Giessen, 1919.

Huvelin, P. and R. Cagnat, " Negotiator," in *Darem.-Saglio.*

Jolliffe, R. O., *Corruption in Rom. Administration*, Diss. Chicago, 1919.

Juglar, L., *Quomodo per servos libertosque negotiarentur Romani*, Paris, 1902.

Keller, O., *Die Antike Tierwelt*, Leipzig, 1909.

Kornemann, E., " Collegium," " Colonia," " Conventus," " Fabri," " Bauernstand," and " Domänen," in *R-E.* (last two in Supp. IV).

Kroll, W., " Die röm. Gesellschaft in der Zeit Ciceros," in *Neue Jb.*, 1928, cf. *ibid.*, 1929.

————, *Die Kultur der Ciceronischen Zeit*, Leipzig, 1933.

Kühn, G., *De opificum Rom. condicione*, Halle, 1910.

Laum, B., " Banken," in *R-E.*, Supp. IV.

Levi, M., " La Sicilia ed il *dom. in solo prov.*," in *Athen.*, 1929, 514.

Marquardt, J., *Das Privatleben der Römer.*

Meyer, E., *Kleine Schriften*, II, Halle, 1924.

——, *Caesars Monarchie*, etc.

Oehler, J., " Argentarii," in *R-E.*

Olck, " Ackerbau," " Arbustum," " Flacks," in *R-E.*

Orth, F., " Bergbau," in *R-E.*, Supp. IV; " Lana " and " Landwirtschaft," in *R-E.*, XII.

Paribeni, R., " Cantores graeci," in *Mél. Lombroso*, Rome.

Park, M. E., *The Plebs in Cicero's Day*, Diss. Bryn Mawr, 1918.

Pârvan, V., *Die Nationalität der Kaufleute*, Breslau, 1909.

Pernice, E., *Die Hellenistische Kunst in Pompeji*, Berlin.

Platner and Ashby, *Topographical Dictionary*, Oxford, 1929.

Preisigke, F., *Girowesen im Griech. Aegypten*, Strassburg, 1910.

Rathke, G., *De Romanorum bellis servilibus*, Berlin, 1904.

Richter, G. M. A., *Ancient Furniture*, Oxford, 1926.

Rizzo, G. E., *La pittura Ellenistico-Romana*, Milan, 1929.

Robertson, D. S., *Handbook of Greek and Rom. Architecture*, Cambridge, 1929.

Rostovtzeff, M., *Social and Ec. Hist.*, Oxford, 1926; Germ. trans. with revised notes, 1931; Italian ed. (with revisions), Florence, 1933.

——, *Gesch. der Staatspacht*, supp. of *Philologus*, 1904.

——, " Caesar and the South of Russia," in *Jour. Rom. St.*, 1917.

——, " Frumentum," in *R-E.*

——, *Caravan Cities*, Oxford, 1932.

Salvioli, G., *Il capitalismo antico*, Bari, 1929.

——, " La produz. agric. in Italia romana," *Atti. Cong. St. rom.*, 1929.

Schmidt, P., *Die röm. Ritter*, Breslau, 1912.

Schnebel, M., *Landwirtschaft im Aegypten*, Munich, 1925.

Schultz, H., " Der Geldwert in Cic. Zeit," in *Socrates*, 1914.

Seel, O., *Sallust von den Briefen ad Caesarem*, etc., Leipzig, 1930.

Shipley, F. W., " Building Operations in Rome from the death of Caesar," in *Mem. Am. Acad.*, IX.

Stein, A., *Der röm. Ritterstand*, Munich, 1927.

Sternkopf, W., " Der Zinswucher des Brutus," in *Dortmund Progr.*, 1900.

Strong, E., " The Art of the Romans," ch. XX, in *Camb. Anc. Hist.*, IX, 1932.

Tambroni, F., " Il commercio delle opere d'arte," in *Atti Cong. di st. rom.*, I, 1929, 278.

Toutain, J., *L'économie antique*, Paris, 1927.

Waltzing, J. P., *Étude hist. sur les corporations* etc., Louvain, 1895-1900 (cf. *Mus. Belge*, 1901).

Warmington, E. H., *Commerce between the Roman Empire and India*, Cambridge, 1928.

West, L., " The Cost of Living in Roman Egypt," in *Class. Phil.*, 1916, 293.

——, *Imperial Roman Spain*, Oxford, 1929.

Wymer, J. E., *Marktplatz-Anlagen*, Munich, 1916.

WEIGHTS AND MEASURES

SURFACE

pes (foot) = 16 digits	=	.296 meters	=	about 11 inches
mille passuum (mile)	=	1480 meters	=	about 4856 feet
jugerum	=	.252 hectare	=	about .62 acre

MEASURES

quartarius (or quadrans) = $\frac{1}{4}$ sextarius

sextarius = .546 liter = 1.1 pint

amphora (quadrantal) = 48 sextarii = 26.2 liters = 27.67 qts.

culleus = 20 amphorae = 524 liters = 138 gallons (U. S.)

modius (dry measure) = 8.733 liters = 1.1 pecks (U. S.)

(hectoliter = 2.8 bushels or 26.4 gal. liquid, peck = 8.8 liters. I have generally called a *modius*, a peck, i. e. $\frac{1}{4}$ bushel. The Greek medimnus held about 6 modii.)

WEIGHTS

libra (pound) = 12 unciae = 288 scripulae = 327.4 grams = c. 9/10 lb. Troy

Oscan pound (4th century, B. C) = 273 grams

COINS AFTER 217 B. C.

denarius (4.-3.8 grams silver) = 4 sestertii = 16 one-oz. copper *asses* (from 268 to 217: 4.55 grams [= 2½ sestertii = 10 *asses*]), gold : silver :: 12 : 1 was usual ratio after 200 B. C.; hence we equate: *denarius* = 20 cents; *sestertius* = 5 cents; *as* = 1¼ cents (in values of 1932).

silver talent = 60 minas = 6000 drachmas. The drachma usually exchanged at par with the denarius, though slightly heavier at this time.

about 200 B. C. quadrigatus = 1½ denarius

"   "   "   victoriatus = ¾ denarius

INDEX